Third Edition

Successful Nonverbal Communication

Principles and Applications

Dale G. Leathers
University of Georgia

Allyn and Bacon
Boston • London • Toronto • Sydney • Tokyo • Singapore

Executive Editor: Carla F. Daves
Editorial Assistant: Andrea Geanacopoulos
Marketing Manager: Karon Bowers
Editorial-Production Administrator: Rob Lawson
Editorial-Production Service: Ruttle, Shaw and Wetherill, Inc.
Composition Buyer: Linda Cox
Manufacturing Buyer: Suzanne Lareau
Cover Administrator: Suzanne Harbison

Copyright © 1997 by Allyn & Bacon
A Viacom Company
Needham Heights, MA 02194
Internet: www.abacon.com
America Online: keyword: College Online

Library of Congress Cataloging-in-Publication Data
Leathers, Dale G., 1938–
    Successful nonverbal communication : principles and applications /
Dale G. Leathers. — 3e [ed.]
      p. cm.
    Includes bibliographical references and index.
    ISBN 0-205-26230-9
    1. Nonverbal communication (Psychology)   I. Title.
BF637.C45L435   1997
153.6'9—dc20   96-33007
                                                  CIP

Printed in the United States of America
10 9 8 7 6 5 4 3   01 00 99

Contents

Preface

The third edition of *Successful Nonverbal Communication: Principles and Applications* is specifically written for the instructors who teach and the students who enroll in the introductory course in nonverbal communication. I have taught such a course for many years. The book results from conversations I have had with students and from instructors who have described to me in detail the kind of book they would like to see written for introductory nonverbal communication. The success of the first two editions reinforced my conviction that there is a need for a book that is directly responsive to their concern.

Serious students of nonverbal communication have long recognized that knowledge of the subject gives the the potential to become more effective communicators. A source of frustration has remained, however. Most existing books on the topic focus exclusively on the *nature* of nonverbal communication. They describe and classify different types of nonverbal messages. They do not address the pressing need to demonstrate how knowledge of the informational potential of nonverbal cues can be used to communicate successfully in the real world. Continuing in the tradition of the first two editions, this third edition is designed specifically to meet that central need.

As with the earlier editions, I have endeavored to present the current research, theory, and terms of nonverbal communication in a style that introductory students can easily understand and even enjoy. I have been particularly pleased with many reports from students and their professors that they consider *Successful Nonverbal Communication* to be a "user-friendly" book. Again I have used stories, quips, personal experiences, and quotes that both balance the technical material and translate it into simple and direct language.

This third edition contains much new material that students should find particularly useful. The fact that the number of new and current references used in this edition is in the hundreds does not strike me as the most important. I have made a special effort to expand upon subjects that readers of the second edition found particularly interesting and useful. For example, Chapter 6, "Tactile Communication," contains expanded coverage of the functions of touch in the development of both romantic and sexual relationships. Similarly, Chapter 7, "Personal Appearance," has been substantially expanded to include new material on the impact of physical attractiveness on the self-concept of adolescents, a new treatment of contrasting views of physical attractiveness and its psychological consequences, and a completely new section on cosmetics as a medium of communication. Finally, Chapter 11, "Selling Yourself Nonverbally," contains a detailed new analysis of the impact of nonverbal communication on the credibility of presidential candidate Robert Dole as contrasted with President Clinton.

In addition, many other important subjects are treated in more detail. Thus, Chapter 5, "Proxemic Communication," has greatly expanded coverage of the concept of crowding and its communicative implications. Chapter 14, "Nonverbal Determinants of Successful Interviews," covers for the first time the interrelationship of pre-interview impressions and first impressions on success in the job interview. Chapter 16, "Successful Intercultural Communication," addresses the subtle question of how individuals fine-tune their nonverbal communication style in order to be as effective as possible in intercultural contexts.

This third edition contains two completely new chapters: Chapter 17 is titled "Physician–Patient Interaction" and Chapter 18 is "Courtroom Interaction." Chapter 17 provides the most comprehensive treatment to date of the specific functions of nonverbal communication in physician–patient interaction. The chapter features detailed profiles that compare the actual and desired features of physician–patient nonverbal communication. Finally, this chapter provides the reader with an original set of guidelines that can be used to facilitate effective physician–patient interaction via the effective use of nonverbal communication.

Chapter 18 examines in detail the importance and functions of nonverbal communication in the courtroom. The chapter draws on the latest research on the subject and is filled with anecdotes and interviews with leading attorneys as well and jury and trial consultants. For anyone interested in this subject, the section on the logistics of measuring impressions in the courtroom should prove to be particularly useful. This chapter includes original analyses done by the author and colleagues. The final section focuses on the impression management functions of nonverbal communication in the Anita Hill–Clarence Thomas Senate hearings, the William Kennedy Smith rape trial, and the O.J. Simpson murder trial.

The subtitle of this book, *Principles and Applications,* reflects my conviction that knowledge *about* nonverbal communication is not enough. We must also know *how to use* that knowledge to communicate successfully in applied settings. Thus, Part 3, "Successful Communication in Applied Settings," treats the subject of how to communicate nonverbally in important, real-world contexts in unprecedented depth and detail. Each of the six chapters in this part—"Nonverbal Determinants of Successful Interviews," "Female–Male Interaction," "Successful Intercultural Communication," "Physician–Patient Interaction," "Courtroom Interaction," and "The Communicative Impact of Microenvironmental Variables"—focuses on how to apply knowledge of nonverbal communication.

Readers of this book can assess the appropriateness of their own nonverbal communication by applying detailed sets of behavioral guidelines. The guidelines pinpoint the nonverbal communicative behaviors that are associated with success in detecting deception, formulating consistent messages, forming impressions, making a favorable first impression and a more enduring impression, interacting with members of the opposite sex, communicating with members of another culture, and interacting with one's physician. In short, the guidelines specify how knowledge of nonverbal communication should be used. They also represent an operational definition of successful nonverbal communication.

The third edition fully explores the central role nonverbal cues frequently play in areas such as relational communication, shaping interpersonal perceptions, personal selling, and the development of a positive self-concept. Because of its focus, the book can be particularly valuable as one of the required textbooks in introductory courses on subjects such as interpersonal communication, personal selling, and business communication. The first two editions were widely adopted by every type of educational institution: public and private research universities, four-year colleges, junior colleges, and community colleges. The third edition was designed to appeal to the same broad spectrum.

I would like to thank the following reviewers who have made many useful comments and suggestions: Dr. Donald B. Egolf, University of Pittsburgh; Nina Jo Moore, Appalachian State University; and Doris Werkman, Portland Community College.

The *Instructor's Manual* that accompanies this textbook has been designed to maximize its value to instructors and their students. It features detailed directions for using the textbook for both semester and quarter courses. Its in-class and out-of-class exercises can be used to explore the theoretical and practical implications of concepts discussed in the book.

The *Instructors Manual* further includes detailed sets of objective test items on each chapter that have been pretested on students taking the course. It also presents both long- and short-answer essay questions as well as chapter summaries with sets of key terms that are useful in reviewing for examinations.

Ashey Nodar made a major contribution as author of the *Instructor's Manual.* Her detailed summaries of the content of each chapter make it easy to study for exams. Her creative and realistic experiential exercises promote involvement.

In three earlier books on nonverbal communication, I referred to the helpful presence of Cat2. Cat2 was a dark brown Burmese cat with wonderful qualities. We spent nearly 20 years together. In the early years, I remember him draping himself around my neck or violently shaking a paw when he experienced the ultimate indignity of coming into contact with a drop of water. He spent countless hours sitting on my desk as I worked on my nonverbal communication books and other publications. In his last year or two, he sometimes fell off my computer hutch and began an inadvertent dance on my computer keyboard. His love for the family was unconditional as was ours for him. I regret to report that Cat2 died about a year after the publication of the second edition of *Successful Nonverbal Communication.* He has been succeeded by another Burmese cat of almost identical color and similar appearance. Although Cat2 will never truly be replaced, Cat3 frequently stalks into my study and joins me for a few hours of writing. Our affection for Cat3 is growing rapidly.

D G L

Nonverbal Communication

Chapter *1*

The Nature of Nonverbal Communication

Human interaction is a quest for meaning. We look anxiously to others to determine whether we have communicated our intended meaning. We are concerned that we may have communicated unintended meanings that will negatively affect the image we wish to project. If we are skilled in the art of impression management, we may cultivate a certain look or sound that is designed to control the judgments that people make about us. President Richard Nixon made repeated attempts to eliminate the shifty eye behaviors and nonfluencies that reinforced the widespread public perception that he was "Tricky Dick." Prime Minister Margaret Thatcher spent hours with a voice tutor doing "humming" exercises in order to lower the unpleasantly high pitch of her speaking voice. O. J. Simpson prosecutor Marcia Clark changed both her hairstyle and her wardrobe in order to appear more likable. Republican presidential candidate Robert Dole consciously tried to smile to dissociate himself from his persisting image of "Nasty Bob."

The individuals with whom we communicate are also on guard. They look apprehensively at us to judge whether they have accurately perceived our intentions. Do our communicative behaviors accurately reflect our inner feelings, or do they represent a carefully controlled presentation of self? The quest for meaning often produces, or results in, anxiety, apprehension, and uncertainty. This is because interpersonal communication is so complex.

The ways we communicate meanings are varied, and the sources of error in interpersonal communication are multiple. A single error may make us uncomfortable in an important situation. Multiple errors may be catastrophic.

Consider the following situations. You and your partner are at a fraternity party on your first date. As the evening progresses and the second keg of beer is tapped, you notice that your date's hand is resting lightly on your arm; you can detect a strong and rather rapid pulse. You make your judgments as to what your date is communicating to you. Later, you fidget on the doorsteps of the sorority house. Suddenly, you lean forward to kiss your date, but she turns her face away from you, recoils, and walks briskly into the sorority house. You are left alone, to ponder the complexities of the evening's communication situation.

Four years later, you are about to be interviewed by the head of a major advertising firm. The job interview is vitally important to you. You realize that you must communicate very effectively if you are to get the job offer. As you enter the interview room, you introduce yourself to the advertising executive and she offers you a seat on the other side of a small table. You feel that it is important to sustain eye contact, and you attempt to do so. The executive often looks away from you as she speaks, however. She frequently leans far back in her chair. You think you are doing well. As the interview concludes, you cannot help but notice that the advertising executive has her chin tilted up into the air and is looking down at you over her glasses. While looking at you, she remarks that she has found your résumé to be most unusual. You are then left alone to ponder the complexities of the afternoon's communication situation.

You could interpret these two situations in a number of different ways. Your goal is to determine what meanings you communicated and what meanings were communicated to you. To achieve such a goal you must recognize at least two facts. First, great differences often exist between what you think you communicated and what the other person actually perceived. Second, meanings may be communicated through a great variety of channels.

You may have interpreted your date's hand on your arm as an invitation to more intimate behavior later in the evening; the quickened pulse may have suggested a certain amount of arousal. Your date's perception of the situation may have been quite different. The hand on your arm could have been a sympathetic response to your nervous mannerisms. The quickened pulse may have been triggered by your date's apprehension as to what actions you would take on the dormitory steps. You need more information and more time before attempting a thorough analysis of this situation.

The job interview is also difficult to interpret. You have more facts at your disposal, however. You wisely focused on important factors in this situation. You should not be disturbed by the fact that the interviewer looked away from you as she spoke; this is characteristic eye behavior in an interview situation. You should be concerned about the interviewer's tendency to lean far back in the chair. Body lean is the best indicator of an individual's involvement in the situation. Your biggest problem is the ambiguous message your interviewer conveyed to you (her chin was perceptibly tilted in the air as she said, "I find your résumé to be most unusual"). The verbal and nonverbal cues convey conflicting meanings. Unhappily for you, the nonverbal cue—the upraised chin, in this case—is apt to be a much more accurate indicator of your interviewer's true feelings than the verbal cue.

Both situations emphasize what society has been slow to recognize: human beings do not communicate by words alone. Individuals have many sensory mechanisms that play a vital role in interpersonal communication. Undeniably, we speak and hear, but we also move, touch, and feel. As a communicator, we have a multidimensional capacity.

Some publications have drawn attention to nonverbal communication. Books such as *New Dress for Success,* by John T. Molloy (1988), *Here Comes Everybody,* by William Schutz (1971), and *Body Language,* by Julius Fast (1970) have served a useful purpose. Some of them may have had some undesirable side effects, however. They may have helped to create the misleading notion that knowledge of nonverbal communication is chiefly useful to investigate and invigorate a communicator's sex life.

The functional importance of nonverbal communication is hardly limited to the semantics of sex, however. LaFrance and Mayo (1978) documented that nonverbal cues serve a wide variety of valuable functions in the development of social relationships. The determinants of successful communication in real-world contexts are frequently nonverbal. To disregard the functions served by nonverbal cues is to invite unflattering characterization as an insensitive and inept communicator.

Most of us spend a great deal of time attempting to persuade others, to be liked or loved by others, to control others, and to enhance our own self-image. Whatever our communicative goal, the nonverbal channels of communication frequently function very effectively to help us attain it. To persuade others, for example, you must usually convince them of your honesty, sincerity, and trustworthiness. Think back to the last congressional hearing you observed on television. Did you think the witness was honest, sincere, and trustworthy on the basis of what the person said, or on the basis of the witness's nonverbal behavior?

Consider your attempts to develop an intimate relationship with another person. Did you assess the level of intimacy of the relationship primarily on the basis of the words that were spoken, or on the basis of the implicit messages communicated by nonverbal cues? Did you attempt to communicate your own feelings primarily by words or by nonverbal cues?

Consider also those instances of face-to-face interaction when you have tried to control the communicative behavior of another person. Among the primary means of control at your disposal were your gestures, your posture, and the way you used the small space that separated you.

Consider, finally, the great amount of time you spend trying to attain or to retain a positive self-image. To a very large degree, your self-image and social identity are shaped by your personal appearance. This image is controlled to a striking extent by nonverbal factors unrelated to the content of your speech.

The Functional Importance of Nonverbal Communication

[handwritten: purpose accuracy efficiency]

When we write of the functional significance of nonverbal communication, the obvious question is what do we mean by *functional*? The answer is complex. Most basically, the function of communication is the creation of meaning. The functional significance of nonverbal communication, therefore, is related to: (a) the *purposes* for which meanings are communicated (information, persuasion, and so on); (b) the *accuracy* with which meanings are communicated (facial communication has more potential than tactile communication, for example); and (c) the *efficiency* with which meanings are communicated (the time and effort required for the communication of meanings). In the next section of this chapter we will address the complex task of defining nonverbal communication.

Viewed from any of these perspectives, nonverbal communication has great functional significance in our society. In a great variety of situations, communicators can more easily achieve their communicative purpose by improving the accuracy and efficiency of their nonverbal communication.

More specifically, nonverbal communication has great functional significance, for six major reasons. First, nonverbal, not verbal, factors are the major determinants of meaning in the interpersonal context. Birdwhistell (1970) asserted that "probably no more than 30 to 35 percent of the social meaning of a conversation or an interaction is carried by the words" (p. 158). Mehrabian (1968) went even further, estimating that 93 percent of the total impact of a message is the result of nonverbal factors. Although Mehrabian's estimate has been criticized not only on methodological grounds but also because of the obvious implausibility of the estimate, Birdwhistell's estimate has been supported by other nonverbal researchers. Thus, Philpott (1983) concluded, after doing a statistical analysis of 23 studies, that slightly over two-thirds of communicated meaning can be attributed to nonverbal messages.

Children, army recruits, and dating couples often find themselves in communication situations that are similar in one respect: They must quickly and accurately determine the meanings of messages being transmitted to them. They typically rely on tone of voice, facial expression, and bodily movement to accomplish this purpose. Children soon learn that the tone and intensity of a parent's voice are their best guide to action. Army recruits do not determine the priority of directives from their drill sergeant by analyzing the manifest verbal content of those directives. They focus on the sense of physical involvement the sergeant conveys to them nonverbally through the notoriously rough and tough voice. When your boyfriend or girlfriend says no to your most artful advances, you do not stop and apply the semantic differential to the verbal response in order to measure his or her meaning. You rely on facial and bodily expressions as the primary determinants of intent.

Second, feelings and emotions are more accurately revealed by nonverbal than verbal means. Davitz (1969) has conducted an impressively detailed set of studies on emotional expression. He concludes that "it is the nonverbal, of the formal characteristics of one's environment . . . that primarily determine the emotional meaning of one's world" (p. 201). Expressions like "keep your chin up," "down in the mouth," and "walking on air" are much more than empty figures of speech. They have emotional referents that are rich in meaning and communicative significance.

The rapid development of sensitivity training, encounter sessions, psychiatric services, and, more recently, sexual therapy clinics is eloquent testimony to society's need to understand which emotions are communicated, how they are communicated, and how they are received. Because there are very few emotion-laden behaviors that universally take the same form, our need to understand variability in emotional expression is evident.

Significantly, we now know not only that nonverbal communication is our richest source of knowledge about emotional states but also that nonverbal cues are reliable and stable indicators of the emotion that is being conveyed or received. Specifically, we now know that nonverbal communication can provide us with the following information about emotions: (a) how sensitive communicators are to emotional expressions, measured in terms of accuracy of identification; (b) the kinds of emotional expressions that can be correctly identified; (c) the specific nature of incorrect identification of emotions; and (d) the degree to which communicators attend to the emotional meaning of a total communication (Leathers & Emigh, 1980).

We know too that our "emotional memories" are largely nonverbal in nature. Researchers (Westman & Wautier, 1994; Westman & Westman, 1993) have found that 74 percent of our first memories are nonverbal while only 45 percent have been talked about; 92 percent of these first memories in turn involve an emotional event. Furthermore, results from this recent research challenge the popular misconception that individuals must verbalize their memories in order to retrieve them.

Third, the nonverbal portion of communication conveys meanings and intentions that are relatively free of deception and distortion. Although verbal messages are frequently used with a high level of consciousness and intent (Newton & Burgoon, 1990), nonverbal cues such as gestures are rarely under the sustained, conscious control of the communicator. For this reason communicators can rarely use nonverbal communication effectively for the purpose of dissembling. In contrast, the verbal dimension of communication seems to obfuscate the communicator's true intentions much more frequently.

In an age that places a very high priority on trust, honesty, and candor in interpersonal relationships, nonverbal communication takes on added importance. Interpersonal relationships are built by using the most effective kinds of communication at our disposal. These are primarily nonverbal. Not only do nonverbal cues usually convey a communicator's real meaning and intent, but they also suggest, rather precisely, what the communicator thinks of us.

Even such nonverbal cues as gesture, posture, and facial expression may, of course, be under the conscious control of the communicator. For all but the consummate actor—and possibly the notorious used-car salesperson—such conscious control is a temporary phenomenon. In most cases, nonverbal cues are not consciously controlled for so long a period of time as verbal cues, nor do they serve as frequently to transmit deception, distortion, and confusion. Although nonverbal cues may be used to deceive, they are more likely to reveal deception than to conceal it.

Fourth, nonverbal cues serve a metacommunicative function that is indispensable in attaining high-quality communication. Often the communicator provides additional cues that clarify the intent and meaning of his or her message. Verbal expressions such as "now, seriously speaking" and "I'm only kidding" are metacommunicative. A comforting hand on the shoulder or a radiant smile may represent nonverbal ways of performing the same function. Although both verbal and nonverbal cues can function metacommunicatively, nonverbal cues seem to take precedence in the mind of the person receiving the message (Capella & Palmer, 1989).

But what does this mean? How do we know that nonverbal cues are so important metacommunicatively? I designed an experiment to answer those specific questions. One hundred subjects were exposed to a set of messages in which the words conveyed one meaning and the facial expressions of the "planted" communicators conveyed a conflicting meaning.

Imagine yourself in a small group and faced with the following situation: One of the discussants responds to a remark you have just made. As he responds, he scratches his head vigorously and gets a very confused expression on his face. Looking utterly confused, he says to you, "Yes, I understand. What you just said seems completely clear to me."

You are faced with a decision. To resolve the seeming contradiction in meaning, you must rely on either the verbal cues (words) or the nonverbal cues (facial expression). In the laboratory situation, the subject almost invariably relied on the facial expression as the true indicator of the communicator's meaning (Leathers, 1979a).

When the verbal and nonverbal portions of a message reinforce each other by conveying the same basic meaning, the metacommunicative value of the two types of cues is relatively unimportant. In contrast, when the verbal and nonverbal cues in a message convey conflicting meanings, the metacommunicative value of these cues becomes of primary importance. At that point the communicator, much like the subjects in the experiment, is faced with a serious problem. Should verbal or nonverbal cues be used to determine the meaning and intent of the message? In effect, the communicator must decide which type of cue has greatest metacommunicative value. Typically, people who face such a decision rely on nonverbal rather than verbal cues.

Mehrabian (1981) indicated that individuals employ a systematic and consistent approach to determine the meaning of conflicting cues. The impact of facial expression is of primary importance, tone of voice (or vocal expression) is next in importance, and words are the least important. In short, facial expressions have the greatest metacommunicative value. Words have the least value.

We can safely conclude, therefore, that nonverbal cues serve the primary metacommunicative function in interpersonal communication. Because the metacommunicative function is a crucial determinant of high quality communication, the proper decoding of nonverbal cues is one of the most important factors in attaining high-quality communication (Leathers, 1972).

Fifth, nonverbal cues represent a much more efficient means of communicating than verbal cues. Time is a vital commodity in many communication situations. Corporations willingly pay communication consultants handsome fees to improve the communicative efficiency of their executives. These executives want to know how to communicate more—in less time.

This goal is not easily achieved in our highly verbal culture. Verbal discourse is by its very nature a highly inefficient means of communication. Redundancy, repetition, ambiguity, and abstraction have become standard qualities of verbal discourse in the United States. Although their use is sometimes necessary, these qualities help to make communication inefficient.

Do qualities such as repetition and ambiguity represent inherent liabilities of verbal discourse, or do they simply reflect the ineptitude of the individual communicator? That question is probably debatable, but there is solid evidence to indicate that verbal communication is intrinsically more inefficient than nonverbal communication. Reusch and Kees (1956) wrote that

> in practice, nonverbal communication must necessarily be dealt with analogically and this without delay. Although verbal communication permits a long interval between statements, certain action sequences and gestures necessitate an immediate reply. Then the reaction must be quick and reflexlike, with no time to ponder or to talk. And whenever such a situation occurs, the slower and exhaustive verbal codifications are out of the question for practical reasons and are clearly more time-consuming and inefficient than nonverbal reactions. (p. 14)

These authors went on to point out that the nature of our language is such that words typically deal with the time dimension in a very inefficient manner. In a limited time frame there are few, if any, sequences of events that cannot be described more quickly with gestures than with words.

The old axiom that a picture is worth a thousand words may lack precision, universal applicability, and empirical verification. The axiom, however, suggests an idea of great importance in interpersonal communication.

Sixth, nonverbal cues represent the most suitable vehicle for suggestion. The nature of a communication situation often dictates that ideas and emotions can be more effectively expressed indirectly than directly. Suggestion is an important means of indirect expression in our society. When it is employed, either the verbal or the nonverbal channels may be used. For tangible reasons, however, suggestion is more closely associated with nonverbal than verbal communication.

In spite of the immense personal satisfaction and control potential associated with interpersonal communication, it is a high-risk endeavor. One's ego, self-image, and even psychological equilibrium are intimately bound up in the communicative interaction with other people. Most of us are so acutely sensitive about our own image that we devote a significant proportion of our efforts to preserving or enhancing that image. Hence, the integrative function of communication is becoming increasingly important.

Because many of us are so concerned about our own image, we prefer to use communication that has a maximum potential for enhancing our image with a minimum risk of deflating it. Nonverbal suggestion is a particularly suitable vehicle for attaining these ends. Because the seeming intent of nonverbal cues can always be denied, many of the negative psychological consequences that may result from nonverbal suggestions can probably be avoided. After all, the man across the room can never be sure that a woman's sustained and seemingly suggestive eye contact is not an idiosyncrasy rather than an open invitation to sexual intimacy. In contrast, as any frustrated lover knows, the most subtle suggestions couched in verbal terms do not provide the same psychological safeguards. Hence, although nonverbal suggestion does not entail the same risks as verbal suggestion, it may be used for the same purpose. For that reason, nonverbal communication is increasingly associated with suggestion.

In review, the intent of this part of the chapter has been to emphasize the compelling need to examine and expand our knowledge of nonverbal communication. To satisfy that need, we must understand the specific functions served by nonverbal communication. However, nonverbal communication and verbal communication are not separate, or completely separable, entities. Indeed, the enlightened student of communication would be well advised not to study one to the exclusion of the other.

Definitional Perspective: Nonverbal and Verbal Communication

Definitional Issues

Defining nonverbal communication is not a simple matter. On the one hand, some students of nonverbal communication seek to exclude the important area(s) of the subconscious encoding and decoding of nonverbal cues by placing the emphasis on conscious encoding and decoding. Thus, Ekman and Friesen (1969) argued in their early, influential article that nonverbal communication is limited to those nonverbal behaviors that are *intended* to be communicative. On the other hand, there seems to be a natural tendency to make the definition so inclusive that virtually everything is defined as nonverbal communication, including bodily smells, flags, and music.

The second definitional perspective has been strongly affected by the influential book, *Pragmatics of Human Communication* (1967) by Watzlawick, Beavin, and Jackson. They argued that the intent criterion for defining nonverbal communication is irrelevant. Any nonverbal behavior or cue is communicative if it is informative. In his insightful critique of various attempts to define nonverbal communication, Peter Bull (1987) wrote:

> *According to this view non-verbal cues are significant not because they constitute a generalized system of communication, but as a source of valuable information which only a skilled perceiver can learn to understand through careful observation. The same kind of assumption can also be seen to underlie the popular literature on body language (e.g., 1970), which seeks to instruct people on the tell-tale signs, for example, of sexual availability.* (p. 6)

The question of intent represents a central and persisting issue for those who seek to define nonverbal communication. If all nonverbal behaviors must both be encoded and decoded consciously and with intent, many nonverbal behaviors and cues that have traditionally been treated as communicative must be eliminated. In the 1988 presidential campaign more than one observer noted that Michael Dukakis's gestures were so restricted in scope that they would easily fit into a cigar box. Consciously encoded nonverbal behaviors and cues may not be limited enough to fit into a cigar box, but many vitally important kinds of nonverbal behaviors would be excluded if the first definitional perspective is accepted. What of gestural adaptors, for example? Gestural adaptors consist of those nonverbal behaviors of the encoder that operate out of awareness and are unintentional. Gestural adaptors such as the hand-to-face gesture and the hand over the mouth are known to tell us that a person's confidence is dissipating rapidly, or even that the person is engaging in deception.

The definition that focuses on intent is too restrictive not only because it eliminates many important kinds of nonverbal behaviors and cues that are generally recognized as part of nonverbal communication. Burgoon (1985) recognized further problems when she wrote:

> *One difficulty with this perspective is that it is very easy to deny intentionality for much of what goes on nonverbally. For example, a person who frowns when hearing something she doesn't like may later deny that she intended to frown. The question then become one of who arbitrates what was intentional and what was not—the source, an 'objective' observer, or who. If all behaviors that the source is unaware of or declaims responsibility for are ruled out as communication, then the nonverbal domain may become overly narrow.* (p. 349)

The second definitional perspective—that stresses that all nonverbal behaviors/cues that are informative are part of nonverbal communication—is also problematic. If we define nonverbal communication only from a decoder perspective, we place too much pressure on the decoder. We know, for example, that there are many cues that human lie detectors (decoders) perceive to be nonverbal behavioral indicators of deception that are not in fact reliable indicators (see Chapter 12). Thus, Bull (1987) wrote that a

> *second possibility is that non-verbal cues are commonly perceived as conveying a meaning which they do not in fact possess (decoding errors). . . so that the extent to which non-verbal cues operate as a communication system will vary substantially according to the perceptiveness of the decoder.* (p. 6)

A third definitional perspective used to define nonverbal communication was developed by Wiener, Devoe, Robinson, and Geller (1972). They emphasized that nonverbal communication must involve encoders and decoders using a socially shared signal system or code with intent. *Nonverbal behaviors that do not include intentional actions by the encoders and decoders may inform but they do not communicate.*

In spite of the sophistication and intuitive appeal of this third definitional perspective, it is susceptible to at least three criticisms. First,

> *this definition excludes from the domain of nonverbal communication any behavior that bears a direct, nonarbitrary relationship to that which it signifies. Potential candidates for exclusion are the facial, vocal, and bodily correlates of affective experiences, the various hesitation phenomena that appear to signify cognitive processing and at least certain aspects of proxemics.* (Siegman & Feldstein, 1987, p. 3)

In short, nonverbal communication must include both symbols and signs.

Many signs do not bear an arbitrary relationship to their referents. They actually resemble that to which they refer. They are iconic in nature. For example, if anyone has ever thrust an upraised middle finger in your face, you knew that you were observing an iconic sign that bore an uncomfortable resemblance to the physiological activity to which it refers. Secondly, as we shall see in the next chapter, some theorists of facial expressions argue that a facial expression of anger, for example, *is* anger. Finally, when a person turns red in the face and shakes a finger at you, it can be argued that these nonverbal behaviors are not symbols representing anger but iconic signs that *are* anger.

This third definitional perspective can be subjected to two other criticisms. First, the requirement that both nonverbal encoding and decoding behaviors be both intentional and systematic excludes those unintentional nonverbal behaviors that many people believe are most informative in interpersonal interaction. Second, this third definitional perspective says nothing about the importance of *context*. Indeed, some communication theorists argue that context is communication (Eaves & Leathers, 1991).

The preceding criticisms of existing definitional perspectives and the following discussion of the nature of the systems and subsystems of nonverbal communication support the following definition of *nonverbal communication:* the use of interacting sets of visual, vocal, and invisible communication systems and subsystems by communicators with the systematic encoding and decoding of nonverbal symbols and signs for the purpose(s) of exchanging consensual meanings in specific communicative contexts. This leads us to the question of what are the systems and subsystems that make up nonverbal communication?

Nonverbal Communication Systems and Subsystems

In 1976 I was the author of the first book that treated nonverbal communication as a set of interacting systems and subsystems that in turn interact with the verbal communication system, *Nonverbal Communication Systems* (Leathers, 1976). Although I do not treat the various kinds of nonverbal communication as systems throughout this book, I believe the systems approach to classification remains particularly useful. My current representation of interacting communication systems is presented in Figure 1.1.

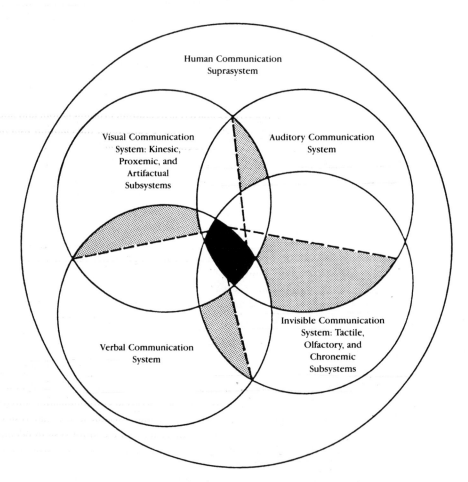

FIGURE 1.1   Verbal and Nonverbal Communication Systems Interacting in a Congruent State. (The dark gray color in the center suggests congruent interaction. When any part of the dark gray area becomes light gray, it suggests incongruent interaction between two or more of the systems. The areas colored light gray suggest the potential of each of the systems to interact with another system incongruently.)

Nonverbal communication comprises three major interacting systems: the *visual communication system,* the *auditory communication system,* and the *invisible communication system.* As subsequent chapters in this book will establish, the visual communication system is the most important nonverbal communication system for at least two reasons. Visual communication is the major source of nonverbal meaning, and the visual communication system in turn is made up of extremely important subsystems: *kinesic, proxemic,* and *artifactual* communication.

Kinesic communication is defined by its own subsystems of facial expressions, eye behaviors, gestures, and posture. Proxemic communication is defined by the use of space, distance, and territory for purposes of communication. Artifactual communication starts with the appearance of our face and body and includes all of the options communicators may use to modify their appearance.

The auditory communication system is an important communication system in its own right. As we shall discover, nine different sound attributes, which are susceptible to our conscious control, combine to give communicators' vocal cues their distinctive quality: loudness, pitch, rate, duration, quality, regularity, articulation, pronunciation, and silence. Vocal cues in turn serve three important communicative functions: the *emotion function,* the *impression management function,* and the *regulatory function.*

The invisible communication system is different from the visual and auditory communication systems in several respects. First, the subsystems of tactile, olfactory, and chronemic communication are defined by their dissimilarity rather than by their similarity. Second, whereas we recognize that olfactory and chronemic communication (see Chapter 16) are defined by messages that are invisible, tactile messages can obviously be seen. Note, however, that tactile messages can, and often do, communicate powerful meanings in the absence of any illumination and that the decoder of tactile messages relies on cutaneous receptors rather than eyesight to decode them.

Several qualifying comments about the invisible communication system are in order. First, a fairly convincing case can be made for the claims not only that individuals can communicate telepathically by extrasensory means but also that telepathic communication is an important subsystem that is part of the invisible communication system; this is a subject that I have addressed elsewhere (Leathers, 1976). Second, although olfaction is frequently cited as a specific kind of nonverbal communication, it is such a limited and inflexible type of communication that I do not give it separate treatment in this book. Burgoon (1985) recognized the serious limitations of olfaction as a nonverbal communication subsystem when she wrote that "natural body odors, although potentially usable as a signal system (much as nonhuman species use them), do not meet the criteria of a coding system because they are not intentional, voluntarily, encoded signals, nor do they evoke a consistent interpretation from receivers" (p. 349).

Whereas some authorities assess the potential of given kinds of nonverbal communication by describing the properties of their "codes" (Burgoon, Buller, & Woodall, 1989), I compare and contrast the potential of nonverbal communication systems and their subsystems by rating the potential of the "channels" that are used to communicate messages. Nonverbal communication channels differ with regard to

1. the speed with which they can transmit signals
2. the ability of the channel to separate its own signals from those of other channels

3. how accurately meanings are communicated through the channel
4. the effectiveness with which the channel communicates emotional information
5. the effectiveness with which the channel communicates factual information

The channel capacities of the nonverbal communication systems (and subsystems) differ substantially with regard to the five important attributes just identified. To attempt to highlight these differences, I previously rated the channel capacity for all of the nonverbal communication channels by using a five-point scale in which 5 = very good, 4 = good, 3 = average, 2 = poor, and 1 = very poor (Leathers, 1976). Although we need additional information for some channels to verify the accuracy of these ratings, they provide a useful profile for comparing the communicative potential of one nonverbal communicative channel with one or more others.

Let us take two examples to show how the ratings of the channel capacity of nonverbal communication systems and subsystems work. At present, I would rate channel capacity of facial expressions this way: speed = 5, channel separation = 5, accuracy = 4, emotional information = 5, and factual information = 2. The rated channel capacity of tactile communication is: speed = 1, channel separation = 2, accuracy = 3, emotional information = 4, and factual information = 1.

No other nonverbal communication system rivals facial expressions for either speed of transmitting meanings or for the communication of emotional information. Therefore, the face received ratings of 5 on the channel characteristics of speed and the communication of emotional information. Although tactile communication serves important functions, touching others to communicate meanings is a slow means of communication. Furthermore, we cannot touch other people unless we are close enough to them. Finally, the close relationship between touch and hand gestures is obvious. Hence, the channel separation of touch is rated less than average because tactile messages are often not clearly separated from proxemic and gestural messages.

Interaction with Verbal Systems

We should recognize that nonverbal communication rarely occurs in the absence of verbal communication (see Figure 1.1). Indeed, the major nonverbal communication systems typically interact with the verbal communication system to determine the type and intensity of meaning(s) that are being communicated. Our perspective on the interaction of the nonverbal and verbal communication systems is grounded in several central assumptions that are rarely made explicit in books such as this. First, there are a number of situations in which the nonverbal communication systems serve important functions but verbal communication simply does not occur. Second, there are situations in which the nonverbal communication systems assume the dominant and central role while the verbal communication system necessarily assumes the secondary role.

American Signing Language (ASL) helps illustrate the complex interrelationships between nonverbal and verbal communication. Ironically, the hearing-impaired have developed a complex "nonverbal language" that uses the interacting nonverbal communication systems to serve functions ordinarily reserved for verbal communication, that is, the formulation and transmission of thoughts and ideas via appropriate grammatical structures.

One of the students in my undergraduate course in nonverbal communication, Lisa Wernick, wrote an insightful paper on sign language as a complex type of nonverbal communication. Wernick emphasized that ASL is a fascinating example of the use of nonverbal communication, particularly facial and bodily cues, to understand, represent, and transmit the meanings of complex sentences.

More specifically, ASL has been developed in such a way that it illustrates how nonverbal communication can be used effectively not only to communicate complex ideas but also to demarcate the syntactic structure of a text. For example, when facial expressions serve as grammatical markers, they have three basic functions: (a) marking specific syntactic structures, (b) representing adverbs that are used with various predicates, and (c) accompanying particular lexical items (Wernick, 1991).

Hemispheric Processing

The hemispheres of the brain serve decidedly different communicative functions although the hemispheres do interact. Thus, neuropsychological research has clearly established that the right hemisphere of the brain (in right-handed persons) is primarily concerned with nonverbal functions of communication, whereas the left hemisphere focuses on verbal functions of communication. The recent research of Bowers, Bauer, & Heilman (1993) significantly expands our knowledge of the nonverbal communicative functions of the right hemisphere of the human brain. They found that the right hemisphere contains a "nonverbal affect lexicon" that uses separate sets of signals for facial expressions, vocal cues, and gestures. Moreover, the affect lexicon controlled by the right hemisphere of the brain is used to process and decode nonverbal messages of social importance that are exhibited by other individuals with whom we interact.

The intricate interrelationships between nonverbal and verbal communication is illustrated by the specialized role of the brain during communication. Don Stacks and Peter Andersen have been doing innovative research on *intrapersonal communication,* or the communication of the left and right hemispheres of the brain, for some time. In their provocatively titled article, "The Modular Mind," in *The Southern Communication Journal* (1989), they wrote that the idea that the left hemisphere controls verbal communication and the right hemisphere nonverbal communication is both outmoded and overly simplistic.

For effective communication to occur, a communicator's left and right hemisphere must frequently "communicate" with each other through the connecting link of the corpus callosum—"interhemispheric cooperation" is vitally important. For example, Stacks and Andersen write that "research on split-brain indicates that when the left hemisphere must interpret a message without right hemisphere input (through a severing of the corpus callosum), that message is interpreted *literally* without an analysis of the underlying emotional content of imagery required for a total understanding of the message" (p. 282).

Jaffe (1987) demonstrated further how complex the interrelationships of verbal and nonverbal communication are as reflected in the activities of the hemispheres of the brain. If you have a small brain or none at all, what goes in one ear may come out the other. For the average person, however, what goes in your right ear is processed by the left hemisphere of your brain, and what goes in your left ear is processed by the right hemisphere of your brain.

In general, information obtained from the right ear is used by the left hemisphere of the brain to decode and encode ideational information, whereas left ear information is used by the right hemisphere of the brain to decode and encode nonverbal messages. Furthermore, it is not surprising that

> *The speaker's right ear is primarily engaged in monitoring his own on-going speech; it would seem an efficient scheme to have the left ear turned to the procedural, paralinguistic interjections of the listener. The listener's right ear is engaged in selecting the proper linguistic syllables of the speaker for decoding; it would seem an efficient scheme to have his left ear turned to the intonational aspects of the message.* (p. 30)

Interrelationships between Nonverbal and Verbal Communication

When communication systems are functioning in the congruent state (communicating essentially the same or supplemental meanings), communication is apt to be of high quality. It is when the systems begin to function incongruently that trouble begins. Communication systems in incongruent or inconsistent states are grist for the analyst's mill. Few phenomena have greater diagnostic significance for the communication consultant than verbal and nonverbal communication systems functioning in an incongruent state (the interrelationships between nonverbal and verbal communication systems in both congruent and incongruent states is treated in detail in Chapter 13).

In this book we will document a number of conclusions or generalizations about the relationship(s) between verbal and nonverbal communication. The following generalizations are representative of the ones we shall make: The most accurate communication occurs when the verbal and nonverbal systems transmit consistent meanings; the visual communication system conveys substantially more affective information than the verbal communication system or any of the other nonverbal communication systems; when different communication systems interact in the congruent state, nonverbal communication frequently represents the dominant source of meaning; the nonverbal systems of communication seem to be far more effective than the verbal in building empathy, respect, and a sense that the communicator is genuine; and when communication cues are transmitted simultaneously, the different channels acting together have a compensatory and additive effect.

Burgoon (1985) wrote that "verbal and nonverbal channels are inextricably intertwined in the communication of the total meaning of an interpersonal exchange" (p. 347). She documented the complex nature of the interrelationships between nonverbal and verbal communication by providing the following five propositions:

1. In general adults rely more heavily on nonverbal than verbal cues in determining "social meaning."
2. Conversely, children attach greater importance to verbal than nonverbal cues before they reach puberty.
3. Adults rely most heavily on nonverbal cues when the meanings communicated by the verbal and nonverbal communication systems are inconsistent or in conflict.

4. The function(s) of a given attempt to communicate tends to determine whether the communicator will rely on one or more kinds of nonverbal communication or on verbal communication.

5. Individual communicators consistently exhibit a preference for either verbal or nonverbal communication as a source of information although the situation or context determines the preference of some communicators.

The Functions of Nonverbal Cues

Nonverbal cues serve a number of communicatively significant functions (Burgoon, 1985; Harper, Wiens, & Matarazzo, 1978; Patterson, 1994). They not only function as powerful determinants of interpersonal perception but they have a major impact on interpersonal relationships. Although nonverbal cues frequently reinforce or supplement information provided by the spoken word, they also provide specific kinds of information that cannot be obtained from speech communication.

A moment of reflection may help to confirm the central role nonverbal cues play in shaping interpersonal perceptions and behaviors. For example, the airplane passenger who conforms in appearance and mannerism to the highjacker profile is apt to be interrogated, at minimum; the highjacker profile is essentially nonverbal in nature. A prospective juror may be stricken if he or she does not conform to the profile the defense attorney or prosecutor wants or needs on the jury. The strike usually is based on information provided by nonverbal rather than verbal cues. Telephone callers seeking a first date run a high risk of rejection if their vocal cues suggest an undesirable personality profile.

To be more specific, what communicative functions are most directly associated with nonverbal cues? Authorities provide somewhat different answers to this question. Burgoon (1980) identified the six functions as symbolic representation, expressive communication, structuring interaction, impression formation and management, metacommunication, and social influence. In her distinctive treatment of the symbolic functions of nonverbal cues, Burgoon noted that the predisposition to attack, to escape, and to form affiliative bonds may be communicated in the most socially acceptable ways by nonverbal means. In addition, she emphasized the symbolic importance of such nonverbal cues as flags, black arm bands, picketing, marching, and music.

The most detailed classification of the functions of nonverbal cues, which is grounded in numerous empirical studies of those functions, was developed by Patterson (1982); he has subsequently refined and amplified his classification (1987; Patterson, 1994). He concludes that the major communicative functions of nonverbal cues are providing information, regulating interaction, expressing intimacy, exercising social control, and facilitating service or task goals. Our own classification of the functions of nonverbal cues is based on this model, with three modifications. Although the expression of intimacy focuses on the communication of emotions, the communication of emotions does not necessarily involve the expression of intimacy. Second, nonverbal cues clearly serve one other important function not identified by Patterson—metacommunication. Finally, the impression management formation and management function is so important that it is treated separately rather than as part of the social control function.

Nonverbal cues can, therefore, be used to serve six major communicative functions:

1. providing information
2. regulating interaction
3. expressing emotions
4. allowing metacommunication
5. controlling social situations
6. forming and managing impressions

These communicative functions of nonverbal cues are not mutually exclusive because any single attempt to communicate nonverbally may serve a number of functions.

The informative function of nonverbal cues is the most basic because all nonverbal cues in any communicative situation are potentially informative to both the encoder and the decoder. Nonverbal cues are a potentially rich source of information because encoders frequently are unaware of their own nonverbal cues. When this is the case, they may inadvertently communicate a constellation of meanings that reveal much about their self-image, social identity, attitudes, and behavioral propensities. Note that in the past section the distinction was made between behaviors that inform but are not communicative and communicative behaviors that inform; informative behaviors do not constitute communication but communicative behaviors clearly can inform.

In fact, I (Leathers, 1979b) suggest that nonverbal cues can provide certain distinctive kinds of information that cannot usually be obtained from the spoken word. The nonverbal behaviors of individuals reveal not only how they feel about themselves but how they feel about the individual with whom they are communicating. More specifically, nonverbal cues can be used to determine an individual's levels of *self-assurance* and *responsiveness*. The ability to determine those qualities at different points in time is indispensable to successful communication.

When the encoder's nonverbal cues are not consciously controlled and monitored by the encoder, the decoder derives from such cues the most valuable information. When the encoders nonverbal cues are consciously controlled and monitored, the informational value of such cues is minimized for the decoder. This is so because the conscious control and monitoring of nonverbal cues frequently takes the form of impression formation and management. In this case, impression managers strive to provide only those kinds of information that will help them attain their own objectives.

The second function of nonverbal cues, regulating interaction, is an important one. We know, for example, that managing accessibility to "the floor" and managing "floor time" can have an immediate and significant impact on the development of interpersonal relationships (Palmer, 1989). Although they are frequently nonreflective, nonverbal cues represent the most efficient and least offensive means of regulating interaction in interpersonal situations. To say "shut up, John" may trigger a hostile and defensive reaction; to communicate the same message by eye behavior or hand movement is a more socially acceptable way of achieving the objective. The sensitive communicator will recognize that the turntaking rules of a given culture are usually communicated nonverbally, and the cultural expectation is that such rules will not be violated.

The third function of nonverbal cues is to express emotions. As indicated previously, nonverbal communication represents the primary medium for the expression of emotions.

If we believe that successful communication requires a sensitive reading of, and response to, the feelings, moods, and emotions of those with whom we communicate, the expressive potential of nonverbal communication becomes particularly important. In subsequent chapters, we will demonstrate that more detailed and precise information about the emotions of communicators can be obtained from their nonverbal cues than from any other source. We will also caution that some of that information may be counterfeit, because certain kinds of nonverbal cues can be consciously controlled for purposes of deception.

The fourth function of nonverbal cues, metacommunication, is a particularly distinctive one. In effect, metamessages, in the form of nonverbal cues, aid the communicator both in assessing the intent and motivation of the message sender and in determining the precise meaning(s) of verbal messages. Burgoon (1980) defines metacommunication as the use of nonverbal messages to qualify, complement, contradict, or expand verbal or other nonverbal messages. The importance of the metacommunicative function of nonverbal cues is particularly apparent when an individual is confronted with the task of decoding a multichannel message that seems to be communicating inconsistent meanings.

Social control is the fifth function of nonverbal cues. It is perhaps the most important function, in view of its relevance to a wide variety of socially significant communication contexts in the real world. *Social control* means that one individual attempts to influence or change the behavior of another individual.

Efforts to exercise social control frequently take the form of persuasion. Edinger and Patterson (1983) have convincingly demonstrated that the social-control function of nonverbal communication is also centrally involved in carefully calculated efforts to enhance one's status, power, and dominance; to provide selective feedback and reinforcement; and to deceive. They maintain that impression management is a social-control function so broad in scope as to embrace the more specific control functions. They have written that, in a way, "all of the topics considered so far involve impression management. That is, in attempting to exert power, persuade others, provide feedback, or deceive, individuals are at least indirectly managing impressions" (p. 43)

Thus, impression formation and management constitute the sixth function of nonverbal behaviors and cues. We will emphasize that this function is vitally important to a great range of people in an almost unlimited number of real-world situations. In the modern world it is almost imperative that the attorney, the physician, the politician, the teacher and many other professionals have detailed knowledge of impression formation and management if they are to succeed. Because of the obvious importance of this function, separate chapters in this book are devoted to impression formation and to impression management.

In short, nonverbal cues serve a number of communicative functions that are vitally important to successful outcomes in the real world. The time is past when nonverbal communication can be treated as a support system of secondary importance whose chief use is to help clarify the meaning of the spoken word.

Communicating Nonverbally in Specific Contexts

Although the different kinds of nonverbal communication have been treated in detailed and enlightening textbooks by several authors, those texts, like their predecessors, are designed to tell us *about* nonverbal communication. For example, they define, identify, and describe different classes of visual cues, such as facial expressions, gestures, and posture. What these books do not do, however, is demonstrate *how* we can successfully communicate in a nonverbal way.

This book, *Successful Nonverbal Communication,* is designed to *demonstrate* how knowledge of nonverbal cues can be used to communicate more successfully in contexts of particular importance to the reader. As this chapter suggests, *detailed knowledge of nonverbal cues and their communicative functions can be used to communicate more successfully in a variety of real-world contexts.* Succeeding chapters provide concrete guidelines that indicate how knowledge of nonverbal cues should be used if we are to communicate successfully.

From a conceptual perspective, this book is a successor to my earlier book, *Nonverbal Communication Systems* (Leathers, 1976). Part 1 describes the different classes of nonverbal cues, illustrating the various kinds of information they can provide and comparing and contrasting their communicative functions. Particular attention is given to the specific kinds of nonverbal cues that are desirable and undesirable in different communicative contexts.

This book departs most sharply from conventional practice in the content of Parts 2 and 3. These sections are designed to demonstrate how the knowledge presented in Part 1 can be used by individuals to manage the impressions they make, and to communicate more successfully in particular settings. The value of this emphasis on application should be apparent to any person who has contemplated the communicative intricacies of an upcoming job interview, considered the formidable barriers to effective intercultural communication, or pondered the complexities of communicating in a sensitive way with a member of the opposite sex.

Do you create a favorable first impression? Do others judge you to be less credible in certain situations than you would like to be? Are you easily manipulated and deceived? Are you usually seen as an insincere and untrustworthy individual? If your answers to these questions give you cause for concern, the contents of Part 2 should prove to be valuable. You may not know how to sell yourself nonverbally, to detect deception, and to communicate consistently; you may not know how impressions are formed and managed. Each of these subjects is addressed in separate chapters in Part 2.

Chapters in Part 3 of this book focus on specific guidelines for using nonverbal cues to communicate successfully in applied contexts. The contexts range from the selection interview to the classroom to the conference room to the office. Special attention is given to the distinctive contextual features of female–male interaction and to intercultural communication, as well as to the distinctive requirements for successful nonverbal communication in each of these contexts.

The central importance of nonverbal skills development to effective interpersonal communication has been clearly documented (Rosenthal, 1979). This book not only emphasizes the importance of developing both general and specific kinds of nonverbal skills but also provides specific empirically based guidelines for developing these skills.

Many measures have been developed to assess the current level of a person's nonverbal skills development. With several exceptions, however, such measures are too expensive, too complicated, and too time-consuming to be of much value to the reader of a book such as this. The PONS Test, which provides a profile of nonverbal sensitivity, is a good example of a test that is so expensive and complicated that it will infrequently be used outside of the experimental laboratory (Rosenthal, Hall, DiMatteo, Rogers, & Archer, 1979).

Dane Archer was one of the developers of the PONS Test. He recognized the need for a straightforward and interesting measure of nonverbal skills. Archer along with Mark Costanzo has devised a highly creative test of nonverbal skills that can be used both to measure and develop such skills. The Interpersonal Perception Task (IPT) (1986) consists of 30 scenes of people interacting on videotape. The IPT is a measure of social intelligence that requires the "viewer" to test her or his skill in making five common types of social judgments: *intimacy, competition, deception, kinship,* and *status.* Social intelligence in turn is a concept developed by Archer that is defined as the ability to make accurate interpretations about people including their experiences, their individual characteristics, the nature of their relationships with others, and their emotions (Archer, 1980).

The profile of nonverbal decoding skills associated with social intelligence is now beginning to emerge. Interestingly, one's early family experiences seem to have a marked impact on social intelligence. Thus, an easy child temperament, harmonious parental relationships, and moderate paternal strictness are associated with good adult nonverbal decoding skills (Hodgins & Koestner, 1993). Conversely, inefficient nonverbal decoders when compared with efficient nonverbal decoders use a more restricted repertoire as a source of information and are less sensitive to the meanings of the nonverbal cues they seek to decode.

Finally, particular contexts are emphasized in this book because of their social significance and because of the importance of nonverbal cues in these contexts. The job interview is a good case in point. Existing knowledge suggests that the interviewee's verbal communication may contribute less to the relative success or failure of a job interview than his or her nonverbal communication. To undertake a job interview with no knowledge of the potentially powerful communicative effects of one's nonverbal cues may be ill advised, at best, and masochistic, at worst.

In short, this book is designed for the reader who wishes to use knowledge of nonverbal cues to communicate more successfully. Such knowledge is neither simple nor easy to apply. The judicious use of nonverbal cues should help one to communicate more successfully, but it does not guarantee success.

Summary

Nonverbal communication functions in vitally important ways in our society. Frequently, communicators can achieve their purpose by using accurate and efficient nonverbal communication. They must begin, of course, with a clear understanding of what nonverbal communication is and is not.

The functional importance of nonverbal communication is obvious when we realize that (a) nonverbal communication is usually the dominant force in the exchange of meaning in the interpersonal context; (b) feelings and emotions are exchanged more accurately by nonverbal than by verbal means; (c) meanings exchanged nonverbally are relatively free of deception and distortion; (d) nonverbal cues serve a metacommunicative function, which is indispensable in attaining high-quality communication; (e) nonverbal cues represent a much more efficient means of communicating than verbal cues; and (f) nonverbal communication is a particularly suitable vehicle for using suggestion.

Major functions served by nonverbal cues include providing information, regulating interaction, expressing emotions, allowing metacommunication, exercising social control, and impression forming and managing impressions. Of these six functions, the impression formation and management function is perhaps the most important in terms of its relevance to a wide variety of socially significant communicative contexts in the real world.

This book is designed for the reader who wishes to use knowledge of nonverbal cues to communicate more successfully in real-world contexts. This knowledge can be particularly valuable because the determinants of successful communication are frequently nonverbal.

References

Archer, D. (1980). *How to expand your social intelligence quotient.* New York: Evans.

Birdwhistell, R. L. (1970). *Kinesics and context.* Philadelphia: University of Pennsylvania Press.

Bowers, D., Bauer, R. M., & Heilman, K. M. (1993). The nonverbal affect lexicon: Theoretical perspectives from neuropsychological studies of affect perception. Special Section: Neuropsychological perspectives on components of emotional processing. *Neuropsychology, 7,* 433–444.

Bull, P. E. (1987). *Postures and gesture.* Oxford, England: Pergamon Press.

Burgoon, J. (1980). Nonverbal communication research in the 1970's: An overview. In D. Nimmo (Ed.), *ICA communication yearbook 4.* New Brunswick: Transaction Books.

Burgoon, J. K. (1985). Nonverbal signals. In M. L. Knapp & G. R. Miller (Eds.), *Handbook of interpersonal communication* (pp. 344–390). Beverly Hills, CA: Sage.

Burgoon, J. K., Buller, D. B., & W. G. Woodall (1989). *Nonverbal communication: The unspoken dialogue.* New York: Harper & Row.

Capella, J. N., & Palmer, M. T. (1989). The structure and organization of verbal and nonverbal behavior: Data for models of reception. *Journal of Language and Social Psychology, 8,* 167–191.

Davitz, J. R. (1969). *The communication of emotional meaning.* New York: McGraw-Hill.

Eaves, M. H., & Leathers, D. G. (1991). Context as communication: McDonald's vs. Burger King. *Journal of Applied Communication Research, 19,* 263–289.

Edinger, J. A., & Patterson, M. L. (1983). Nonverbal involvement and social control. *Psychological Bulletin, 93,* 30–56.

Ekman, P., & Friesen, W. V. (1969). The repertoire of nonverbal behavior: Categories, origins, usage, and coding. *Semiotica, 1,* 49–98.

Fast, J. (1970). *Body language.* New York: Evans.

Harper, R. G., Wiens, A. N., & Matarazzo, J. D. (1978). *Nonverbal communication: The state of the art.* New York: Wiley.

Hodgins, H. S., & Koestner, R. (1993). The origins of nonverbal sensitivity. *Personality and Social Psychology Bulletin, 19,* 466–473.

Jaffe, J. (1987). Parliamentary procedure and the brain. In A. W. Siegman & S. Feldstein (Eds.), *Nonverbal behavior and communication* (2nd ed., pp. 21–33). Hillsdale, NJ: Erlbaum.

LaFrance, M., & Mayo, C. (1978). *Moving bodies: Nonverbal communication in social relationships.* Monterey, CA: Brooks/Cole.

Leathers, D. G. (1972). Quality of group communication as a determinant of group product. *Speech Monographs, 38,* 166–173.

Leathers, D. G. (1976). *Nonverbal communication systems.* Newton, MA: Allyn.

Leathers, D. G. (1979a). The impact of multichannel message inconsistency on verbal and nonverbal decoding behaviors. *Communication Monographs, 46,* 88–100.

Leathers, D. G. (1979b). The informational potential of the nonverbal and verbal components of feedback responses. *Southern Speech Communication Journal, 44,* 331–354.

Leathers, D. G., & Emigh, T. H. (1980). Decoding facial expressions: A new test with decoding norms. *Quarterly Journal of Speech, 66,* 418–436.

Mehrabian, A. (1968). Communication without words. *Psychology Today, 2,* 51–52.

Mehrabian, A. (1981). *Silent messages.* (2nd ed.). Belmont, CA: Wadsworth.

Molloy, J. T. (1988). *New dress for success.* New York: Warner.

Newton, D. A., & Burgoon, J. K. (1990). The use and consequences of verbal influence strategies during interpersonal disagreements. *Human Communication Research, 16,* 477–518.

Palmer, M. T. (1989). Controlling conversations, turns, topics and interpersonal control. *Communication Monographs, 56,* 1–18.

Patterson, M. L. (1982). A sequential functional model of nonverbal exchange. *Psychological Bulletin, 89,* 231–249.

Patterson, M. L. (1994). Interaction behavior and person perceptions: An integrative approach. *Small Group Research, 25,* 172–188.

Patterson, M. L. (1987). Presentational and affect-management functions of nonverbal involvement. *Journal of Nonverbal Behavior, 11,* 110–122.

Philpott, J. S. (1983). The relative contribution to meaning of verbal and nonverbal channels of communication . . . a metaanalysis. Unpublished master's thesis, University of Nebraska.

Reusch, J., & Kees, W. (1956). *Nonverbal communication.* Berkeley: University of California Press.

Rosenthal, R. (Ed.). (1979). *Skill in nonverbal communication: Individual differences.* Cambridge, MA: Oelgeschlager, Gunn & Hain.

Rosenthal, R., Hall, J. A., DiMatteo, M. R., Rogers, P. L., & Archer, D. (1979). *Sensitivity to nonverbal communication: The PONS test.* Baltimore: Johns Hopkins University Press.

Schutz, W. C. (1971). *Here comes everybody.* New York: Harper.

Siegman, A. W., & Feldstein, S. (Eds.). (1987). *Nonverbal behaviors and communication.* (2nd ed.). Hillsdale, NJ: Erlbaum.

Stacks, D. W., & Andersen, P. A. (1989). The modular mind: Implications for intrapersonal communication. *The Southern Communication Journal, 44,* 273–293.

Watzlawick, P., Beavin, J. H., & Jackson, D. D. (1967). *Pragmatics of human communication: A study of interactional patterns, pathologies, and paradoxes.* New York: W. W. Norton.

Wernick, L. (1991, March). *The nonverbal communication of sign language.* Unpublished paper.

Westman, A. S., & Wautier, G. (1994). Early and autobiographical memories are mostly nonverbal and their development is more likely continuous than discrete. *Psychological Reports, 74,* 656–666.

Westman, A. S., & Westman, R. S. (1993). First memories are nonverbal and emotional, not necessarily talked about or part of a recurring pattern. *Psychological Reports, 73,* 328–330.

Wiener, M., Devoe, S., Robinson, S., & Geller, J. (1972). Nonverbal behaviors and nonverbal communication. *Psychological Review, 79,* 185–214.

Chapter *2*

Facial Expressions

> *The human face—in repose and in movement, at the moment of death as in life, in silence and in speech, when alone and with others, when seen or sensed from within, in actuality or as represented in art or recorded by the camera—is a commanding, complicated, and at times confusing source of information. The face is commanding because of its very visibility and omnipresence.*
> —EKMAN, FRIESEN, & ELLSWORTH, 1982, p. 1

The face has long been a primary source of information in interpersonal communication. It is an instrument of great importance in the transmission of meaning. Within a matter of seconds, facial expressions can move us to the heights of ecstasy or the depths of despair. We study the faces of friends and associates for subtle changes and nuances in meaning, and they in turn study our faces.

In a very real sense, our quest for meaning in this world begins and ends with facial expression. We study the faces of infants to determine their immediate needs, and they reciprocate by communicating many of their needs and emotional states through facial expressions. The elderly hospital patient studies the face of the surgeon to determine the chances of surviving the next operation, and the surgeon's facial expression often provides the definitive answer.

We know that the face may be used to complement or qualify the meaning of spoken messages and to replace spoken messages. We may also speculate that such facial features as a low forehead, thick lips, or oversized ears are all associated with undesirable personality characteristics, but such conclusions are speculative (Knapp, 1978). This speculation might of course be somewhat amusing for individuals who do not have low foreheads, thick lips, and oversized ears. Even if a connection between specific facial features and personality traits were firmly established, however, such a finding would tend to divert attention from the important communicative functions served by the human face.

We know too that facial expressions can serve many functions in their own right. The appearance of the face exerts a central and sometimes controlling impact on judgments of

24

physical attractiveness (Alicke, Smith, & Klotz, 1986). The appearance of a person's face in turn strongly affects how dominant the person is judged to be (Berry, 1990; Keating, 1985). "Babyfacedness" defines faces with distinctive physical features and babyfaced males are perceived to be naive, honest, kind, and warm (Berry & McArthur, 1985).

Smiling is another important part of facial expression. Nonsmiling communicators with lowered brows, for example, appear more dominant than their smiling counterparts who raise their brows (Keating & Bal, 1986). We know too that the types of smiles (Ekman, Davidson, & Friesen, 1990) and onset and offset times for smiles, can strongly affect the impressions a person makes. Appropriate smiles enhance credibility while inappropriate smiles are often viewed as part of an ingratiating self-presentation strategy (Bugental, 1986).

The communicative functions of facial expressions already identified are important. Their potential to affect the impressions people make and the relationships they develop is undeniable. These are not the central communicative functions served by the face, however, because other kinds of nonverbal messages serve the same functions and serve them more effectively. Vocal cues, for example, are the most powerful encoders of dominance.

The two most important functions of the human face are the communication of emotions and the identification of previously unidentified people. The preponderance of research has focused on the face as a medium of emotional communication, the function of overriding importance, to which we turn first.

The Face as the Most Important Source of Emotional Information

Successful communication places a premium not only on the ability to identify general emotional states of individuals with whom we communicate but also on the ability to differentiate among subtle emotional meanings that are constituents of the more general emotional states. The ability to identify fear is undeniably useful. However, the ability to distinguish special kinds of fear such as terror, anxiety, and apprehension is much more useful.

To obtain both general and specific emotional information, the communicator must develop the ability to decode facial expressions accurately because the human face is the most important source of emotional information. The face is the primary site for the communication of emotional states (Knapp, 1978) and, as such, is the primary signal system for communicating emotions. One prominent researcher has gone so far as to assert not only that facial expressions accurately communicate an individual's emotional states but also that facial expressions *are* emotions (Tomkins, 1962).

If the human face is unmatched in its ability to communicate emotions, we must begin with a fundamental question: What is emotion? Collier (1985) maintains that *emotion* is a complex but temporary psychological state involving physiological, experiential, and behavioral changes. Emotion theorists do not agree, however, on the precise nature of these changes or on the nature of the internal, neural phenomena that trigger them.

Levenson (1988) provided a particularly illuminating theoretical treatment of emotion and the vitally important role of the autonomic nervous system in controlling the emotion(s) that is experienced and displayed. He addresses such central questions as whether the categoric or dimensional models of emotion are most convincing, how many emotions there are, whether a baseline condition in a given person should be determined before studying autonomic nervous system (ANS) activity, how ANS activity is affected as the intensity of an emotion changes, how long an emotion lasts, and how verification procedures can be developed to establish what emotions individuals are feeling and when they are feeling them.

The theoretical study of emotion can be immensely helpful to the person who wants to make most effective use of the human face as a medium of emotional communication. In order to derive practical dividends from theories of emotion, Collier (1985) maintained that the researcher must answer three questions satisfactorily:

1. How much *control* do communicators have over their own expressive behavior?
2. How *aware* are communicators of the internal changes taking place within them and of the emotions being displayed facially?
3. What is the *relationship* between the actual display of emotional expressions via facial expressions and the physiological and experiential aspects of emotion?

These questions in turn highlight issues that are of critical importance in understanding and developing skill in both the encoding and decoding of facial expressions. Encoders who are not aware of the kind of emotion they are displaying on their face, for example, do not have the capacity to modify that facial expression in desired ways. Similarly, decoders who may be subliminally aware of but are not attending to a given facial expression may have little chance of decoding it accurately.

The nature of human emotions and the precise role of the face in expressing such emotions has not yet been determined. The importance of facial expression in human communication remains beyond dispute, however. There is agreement that the human face has great communicative potential. This is so in large part because the complex and flexible set of muscles in the human face may be used to communicate a great variety of facial meanings. The Facial Action Coding System (FACS), for example, was developed for the purpose of classifying the units of facial expression that are anatomically separate and visually distinguishable. FACS distinguishes 44 "action units" (Ekman & Friesen, 1978; Ekman et al., 1982). (The reader who is offended by jargon may be amused to discover that in this system the human smile is identified as Action Unit 12.)

Theorists and researchers disagree as to how the human face functions communicatively (Oster, Daily, & Goldenthal, 1989). Two major approaches—the categoric and the dimensional perspectives—have been used by researchers in an attempt to describe or identify with some degree of precision the meanings communicated by facial expressions.

The Categoric Perspective

Proponents of the categoric perspective maintain that the human face, at any given moment, transmits one dominant type of meaning, often associated with such affective states as happiness or anger. The meaning transmitted facially is believed to have a single referent that will stand out in the mind of the decoder. Although any given facial expression may combine two or more classes of meaning in the form of a facial blend (Ekman et al., 1982), the decoder will use a single categoric label to describe the dominant facial meaning that is displayed.

Classes of Facial Meaning

Not surprisingly, researchers who believe that the face functions categorically have attempted to identify and label all classes of meaning that they believe can be communicated accurately by facial expressions. Some of the earliest and most insightful research on the denotative functions of facial expression was conducted by J. Frois-Wittmann (1930). Using himself as the photographic subject, Frois-Wittmann made a series of 72 facial photographs. These photographs were designed to represent all the classes and subclasses of facial meanings that human beings were believed capable of communicating.

This early study suggested that facial expressions are most accurately described by means of classification. Pain, pleasure, superiority, determination, surprise, attention, and bewilderment were among the facial meanings most consistently and accurately classified by the subjects. At the same time, it became apparent that the denotative meaning of some facial expressions was unclear. For example, subjects often had difficulty distinguishing between hate and anger, disappointment and sadness, disgust and contempt, and horror and fear.

Frois-Wittmann may be faulted for failure to standardize the labels used to describe facial expressions, but he was ahead of his time in a number of ways. His detailed description of the facial muscles used to communicate certain emotions bears a striking resemblance to more recent efforts to develop "facial blueprints." Facial blueprints provide detailed information as to the types of facial MI (muscle involvements) that are used to express a given emotion. Furthermore, his use of a large number of descriptive labels suggests that he recognized that the face communicates not only broad classes of facial meaning but also subtle kinds of facial meaning that are constituents of the broader classes.

More recent attempts to describe the denotative meanings of facial expressions have focused on the attempt to use a limited number of descriptive labels that identify *only* the broader classes of meaning that are communicated by facial expression. Thus, Woodworth (1938) concluded that the six basic classes of meaning communicated facially are happiness, suffering, surprise, determination, disgust, and contempt. Of 390 subjects using six categoric labels, 366 correctly identified happiness. Accuracy of identification for the other expressions was suffering, 325; determination, 310; surprise, 304; disgust, 294; and contempt, 190.

Tomkins (1962) attempted to increase the precision with which facial expressions may be classified. He uses the following *sets* of labels to identify the eight classes of affective information that he contends can be communicated by facial expressions: (a) interest–excitement; (b) enjoyment–joy; (c) surprise–startle; (d) distress–anguish; (e) fear–terror; (f) shame–humiliation; (g) contempt–disgust; and (h) anger–rage. The first label in each pair represents a low-intensity manifestation of the given class of facial meaning, and the second represents a high-intensity counterpart.

In his influential book, *The Face of Emotion* (1971), Izard used the same set of labels to develop a decoding test that measured the ability of nine different national–cultural groups to identify facial expressions. Surprisingly, decoders were not forced to differentiate between facial interest and excitement or facial distress and anguish. They were simply asked to determine the meaning of a given facial expression by placing it in one of the eight categories.

Ekman and his associates (*Emotion in the Human Face,* 1982) completed an exhaustive review, summary, and analysis of many of the major studies that treat the face as if it functions categorically. They concluded that the face is capable of communicating seven basic classes of meaning: (a) happiness, (b) surprise, (c) fear, (d) anger, (e) sadness, (f) disgust/contempt; and (g) interest. Ekman continues to cite new findings that suggest that these basic classes of meaning are universal. They are universal, he claims, in that they are encoded and decoded at approximately the same levels of accuracy in a great variety of nations and cultures (Ekman, 1994).

In fact, Ekman maintained for at least 15 years that the facial displays of disgust and contempt represented categoric expressions that could not be reliably distinguished by American decoders; hence, he persisted in treating disgust/contempt as a hyphenated category. Recently, Ekman and Friesen (1986) modified their position by maintaining that they had discovered a pancultural facial expression unique to contempt. Although Ekman and Friesen seem to be quite impressed with what they claim is a new finding, other students of the human face seem less impressed and find their claimed "discovery" to be no discovery at all. In fact, a decade ago Leathers and Emigh (1980) provided substantial support for their claim that contempt is a separate category of facial emotion that can be decoded at levels of accuracy that meet or exceed most of the other basic emotions.

Not surprisingly, a debate currently rages in the pages of academic journals with Ekman and Friesen on one side and Izard on the other. The debate focuses on whether Ekman and Friesen have really discovered anything new and whether their facial blueprint for contempt is accurate (Ekman & Friesen, 1988; Ekman & Heider, 1988; Ekman, O'Sullivan, & Matsumoto, 1991; Izard & Haynes, 1988). Indeed, Izard and Haynes (1988) sharply challenge Ekman and Friesen's claim to have found the first empirical support for the existence of a pancultural expression of contempt on the grounds that (a) researchers since the time of Darwin (1872) have identified contempt as a separate category of facial expression, (b) Ekman and Friesen's representations of facial contempt are ambiguous, and (c) earlier data clearly established contempt as a separate category of facial expression and suggest that contempt may be a learned modification of a prototypical expression evolved from the infrahuman snarl.

Areas of the Face: Meaning Cues

The categoric perspective is particularly useful for individuals who wish to determine how accurately they can distinguish among the basic classes of emotion that can be communicated by facial expressions. In fact, there is now evidence to indicate that certain areas of the face provide meaning cues that are particularly useful in identifying specific kinds of emotions.

Although controversy still surrounds the defining features of facial contempt, the facial blueprint for disgust is rapidly being refined (Rozin, Lowery, & Ebert, 1994). The nose wrinkle characteristic of disgust, for example, is associated with irritating or offensive smells, and to a degree with bad tastes. Food that we find distasteful, as well as oral irritation, tends to elicit the gape and tongue extrusion form of facial disgust. Finally, the raised upper lip is most apt to be triggered by a wide variety of disgust elicitors, such as body boundary violations, inappropriate sex, poor hygiene, aversive interpersonal contacts, and certain types of moral offenses. In short, results from this research suggest support for a theory of disgust that focuses on bad tastes as elicitors of this category of facial emotion with the suggestion that disgust has evolved into a moral emotion.

The Facial Affect Scoring Technique (FAST) breaks down the face into three areas: the brows and forehead; the eyes, lids, and bridge of the nose; and the lower face (Ekman,

Friesen, & Tomkins, 1971). The upper portion of the face is apt to provide more useful cues for identifying anger than the lower part of the face, for example. Thus, when someone displays anger facially the brows are lowered and drawn together, vertical lines appear between the brows, and both the upper and lower lids exhibit tension.

In most cases the categoric approach features the use of posed facial expressions. You may find the use of spontaneous facial expressions more appealing. Intuitively spontaneous facial expressions seem more realistic because they more closely approximate the way people display facial expressions in real-world contexts; facial expressions are rarely "frozen" as they are in still photographs. In point of fact, spontaneous facial expressions have proved to have limited value in actual tests of facial decoding skills, however, because the levels of accuracy for decoders is extremely low. Thus, Wagner, MacDonald, and Manstead (1986) found that decoders were able to distinguish only three of seven types or categories of facial expressions at above chance levels: happiness, anger, and disgust. Even for these three emotions, decoders were 30 to 70 percent less accurate than decoders who identified posed facial expressions.

The Dimensional Perspective

Few would deny that the face is capable of functioning to communicate given types or categories of emotional meaning in a given context or situation. Many students of facial communication believe, however, that the face usually functions to communicate a limited number of dimensions of meaning. That is, at any particular time, the face conveys not one dominant meaning but a number of dimensions of meaning. Those who see the face as functioning as a multidimensional source of meaning have generally accepted the conceptual model developed by Osgood (1966) when he was attempting to identify and measure the dimensions of meaning that are conveyed by verbal means.

Dimensions of Facial Meaning

Until fairly recently, the multidimensional framework and the concept of semantic space had not been applied to the study of meanings transmitted by nonverbal means. In the 1950s, Schlosberg began research to determine *how* and *how many* meanings are communicated by facial expression. He concluded that facial communication is multidimensional and connotative because the face typically communicates not a single meaning but some combination of meanings. Specifically, Schlosberg (1954) found that meanings communicated by the face are adequately represented by three dimensions: (a) pleasant–unpleasant; (b) attention–rejection; and (c) sleep–tension.

Since then, Engen, Levy, and Schlosberg (1957) have done follow-up studies that tend to confirm the presence and stability of the same three dimensions in facial communication. The findings of Levy, Orr, and Rosenzweig (1960) and of Abelson and Sermat (1962) also support the existence of the same three dimensions of facial expression. Using *pictomorphs* (schematic faces) consisting of head shape and eyebrow, eyes, and mouth in various positions, rather than photographs, as his data base, Harrison (1967) also found that facial communication is represented by three dimensions: (a) approval, (b) social potency, and (c) interest. Similarly, in an impressively detailed study, Williams and Tolch (1965) found that facial expression includes the two dimensions of *general evaluation* and *dynamism* (they did not find the usual third factor).

Charles Osgood (1966) turned his attention from the study of verbal to nonverbal meaning two decades ago. Both his objective and his conceptual framework were as praiseworthy as they were in his earlier research on verbal meaning, which led to the development of the *semantic differential.* He wanted to determine how many dimensions of meaning accurately and adequately characterize facial communication. In pursuit of this objective, he treated facial communication as if it took place in "semantic space," a multidimensional space composed of an unknown number of dimensions of meaning. Osgood's factor-analytic research suggests that facial communication includes the following factors: (a) pleasantness, (b) control (represented by such specific expressions as annoyance and disgust versus amazement and excitement), and (c) intensity (rage, scorn, and loathing versus boredom, quiet, and complacency). A fourth, though weaker, factor is labeled "interest."

Osgood's research is supported by Mehrabian, who has adopted Osgood's concept of semantic space as well as his multidimensional approach to facial communication. As with Osgood, Mehrabian (1970) contends that facial communication consists of three dimensions of meaning, which he labels (a) evaluation, (b) potency or status, and (c) responsiveness.

Because so many researchers have found three dimensions of facial meaning, one might conclude that they have all found the same dimensions. Such a conclusion is not necessarily warranted. Often investigators apply their own, idiosyncratic labels to dimensions of meaning, making direct comparisons very difficult. Also, there has probably been a natural tendency to conclude that facial meaning comprises the same three dimensions as those of verbal meaning.

Indeed, some of our most impressive research suggests that facial communication includes not three but at least six dimensions of meaning. In an early study, Frijda and Philipszoon (1963) found four dimensions of facial meaning, which they identified as (a) pleasant/unpleasant; (b) naturalness/submission; (c) intensity of expression/control of expression; and (d) attention/disinterest. The second expression, naturalness/submission, was considered to be new, not previously found by the "three dimensional" students of facial communication. In a follow-up study, Frijda (1969) identified the four original dimensions as well as two others. Dimension 5 is now labeled "understanding/amazed," and dimension 6 is "simple/complicated." Frijda concludes that "the two studies both suggest the importance of not less than five dependent aspects of dimension, at least two or three more than in the usual analysis" (pp. 178–179).

In their exhaustive review and evaluation of the dimensional approach, Oster and coworkers (1989) concluded that recent models designed to identify and illustrate the interrelated dimensions of facial meaning have serious flaws. They conclude that whether "identification of (and appropriate responses to) emotional expressions on the basis of abstract dimensions could be as rapid or as accurate as identification in terms of categories—discrete—or fuzzy—is a question that has not been empirically addressed" (p. 131).

Controversy also remains with regard to how many dimensions of meaning can be communicated by facial means. From a review of research to date, we can, however, reach the following conclusions:

1. The face communicates evaluative judgments through either pleasant or unpleasant expressions that indicate whether the communicator sees the current object of his or her attentions as good or bad.

2. The face communicates interest or disinterest in other people or in the surrounding environment.
3. The face communicates intensity and, hence, the degree of involvement in a situation.
4. The face communicates the amount of control individuals have over their own expressions.
5. The face probably communicates the intellectual factor of understanding, or lack of it.

Each of the foregoing five dimensions of facial meaning has both positive and negative qualities. For example, although the face may communicate pleasantness in one situation, it may communicate unpleasantness in the next. Similarly, the face may communicate interest or disinterest, involvement or uninvolvement, control of emotions or lack of control. (Whether the quality of facial meaning is considered positive or negative will probably depend on the situation and numerous other factors.)

Clearly, the face has the potential to produce communication of very high quality in which the meanings transmitted and received are virtually identical. The preceding dimensional analysis of meaning in facial expressions establishes that the face is capable of conveying positive reinforcement, interest, involvement, a sense of control over oneself and the immediate environment, and an image of a thoughtful person deliberating on the facts. All of these meanings are of great importance in interpersonal communication and are necessary— singly and in various combinations—to produce high-quality communication.

At the same time, it is now obvious that the face is capable of communicating negative reinforcement, disinterest, withdrawal, lack of control, and a visceral rather than a thoughtful reaction to various messages. The potentially disruptive effects of such meanings are often dependent on matters such as context.

Side of the Face: Meaning Cues

If you subscribe to the categoric approach to facial expression, you will study the human face to try to determine which basic class of emotion is being communicated. You might be able to make more accurate judgments by concentrating on certain areas of the face. If you believe that the face functions to communicate *dimensions of meaning,* you will be particularly concerned with determining the *intensity* of the emotion being communicated facially. You may be able to *more accurately* assess intensity of emotion by concentrating on the left side of the communicator's face.

There is increasing evidence that the intensity of emotions is more accurately communicated on one side of the face than the other. Two sets of researchers (Mandal, Asthana, Madan, & Pandey, R., 1992; Sackeim, Gur, & Saucy, 1978) have found that emotions are expressed more intensely on the left side of the face. This phenomenon of the primacy of the left side of the face—in terms of the intensity of emotions expressed—may well be an inherited phenomenon. Thus, we know that the left side of the face is dominant in emotional expression for rhesus monkeys as it is for humans (Hauser, 1993). Although the results are typically complex and difficult to interpret, studies of individuals with brain damage also suggest that the right side of the brain and, consequently, the left side of the face provide the best cues to intensity of emotion (Borod, Koff, Lorch, & Nicholas, 1986). Although the evidence is far from conclusive at present, research done to date suggests that the *left side of the face provides more accurate intensity cues than the right side.* If true, this finding may be attributed to the fact that *facial displays of emotion,* as well as other kinds of nonverbal cues, *are controlled by the right side of the brain.*

As you look at the two photographs of the right and left sides of the face in Figure 2.1A and B, can you determine which emotion is being communicated and with what degree of intensity? Consider the face on the left side of the page first. Does the left side of the face communicate disgust and the right side happiness? Now consider the face on the right side of the page. Does the left side of the face communicate happiness and the right side disgust? Did the right or left side of the faces provide the most useful intensity cues?

The categoric and dimensional perspectives that are used to describe facial expressions should not be thought of as mutually exclusive, however. There is some evidence that the meaning communicated by a given facial expression can be determined most accurately by first placing that facial expression in a descriptive category, and then rating it for intensity. Ekman, perhaps the foremost proponent of the categoric perspective, conducted research (Ekman, Friesen, & Ancoli, 1980) to determine whether facial expressions provide reliable information both with regard to both the *kind* of emotion the encoder is experiencing and the *intensity* with which the emotion is experienced. The study seemed to confirm that *facial expressions are most accurately described by first classifying them and then rating them.*

(A)   **(B)**

FIGURE 2.1

The Face as a Means of Identifying Individuals

A second important function of the human face has received almost no attention by communication scholars. Have you or a friend ever been in a police lineup? Have you ever been asked to describe a person who assaulted you or robbed you? Have you ever wondered how your infant is able to identify his or her parents?

If these questions interest you, then it may be important for you to know that the appearance of the human face is the most reliable nonverbal source of information used to identify previously unidentified persons. Indeed, Ellis and Young (1989) treated this function of facial communication in detail. They concluded that the face is the most important source of visual information that people use to identify other human beings. They also contended that the ability of the average person to discriminate between hundreds of faces represents the ultimate in perceptual classification skills.

Forensic applications of face memory skills to identify missing persons or criminal suspects represent the most important use of this function. Interestingly, forensics experts are now using computer programs such as CAPSTAR and FRAME to store large quantities of facial information about a criminal suspect. "By using the power of the computer to store large quantities of facial information which can then be analyzed and evaluated on the basis of information obtained from a witness, some of the problems of using large mugfiles effectively are addressed" (Laughery & Wogalter, 1989, p. 545). Often a witness's memory of the suspect's face is so strong that the size of the mugfile can quickly be reduced and the probability of correct identification increases markedly. The face functions so effectively for purposes of personal identification that experts now are concentrating on developing the best means of describing the structure of the human face (Bruce, 1989).

The Deceptive Face: How to Recognize It and Guard Against It

Facial expressions are usually a reliable source of meaning, but in some situations they may be unreliable. In those situations, the enlightened communicator must know for which signs of facial deception to watch. It is when facial expressions are consciously controlled that they are most apt to be deceptive; the individual will make his or her facial expression conform to certain norms or *display rules.*

Facial display rules may be classified as *personal, situational,* and *cultural.* Personal display rules may dictate that we inhibit the harshest displays of facial expression when communicating with children or physically handicapped individuals, for example. Situational display rules may dictate that in certain business situations, for example, we modify or modulate genuine expressions of facial emotions, such as disgust, so as not to offend a client or colleague. Finally, cultural display rules may vary because cultural groups differ, not only in the intensity of their facial expressions but in the specific kinds of facial expressions they are likely to exhibit in public. We do know that Anglo-Saxons are more likely than Latins to consciously control their facial expressions. We also know that the Asian's repertoire of publicly displayed emotions is quite limited; and that certain kinds of specialized facial expressions are confined to certain parts of the world and even to certain regions of a given country.

The impact of display rules or the desire to deceive may make facial expressions misleading sources of information in some cases. Thus, LaFrance and Mayo (1978) distinguished between facial expressions that might be classified as *representational* and those that might be classified as *presentational*. Representational expression is associated with genuine facial expressions that accurately reflect the actual emotion that the communicator is experiencing. Presentation, in contrast, is the consciously controlled use of the face for purposes of public consumption. One type of facial presentation is the "emotional put-on," in which there may be a marked disparity between the facial emotion displayed and the emotion actually experienced. LaFrance and Mayo (1978) captured the difference between truthful and deceptive facial communication when they wrote that the "distinction has been characterized as one between *presentation* and *representation*. The presentation is a performance, an arrangement and appearance designed to be seen. Its connection is less to inner feelings than to outer effect. In contrast, the representation refers to the expression of inner feelings" (p. 32).

Whatever the reason for controlling facial expression, or, in some cases, "putting on a false face," the receiver should recognize that the sender is apt to use one of three techniques (Ekman & Friesen, 1984): (a) *qualifying,* (b) *modulating,* or (c) *falsifying.* The basic classes of facial meaning that might be communicated are qualified when you add another facial expression to the original in order to modify the impact. For example, the boss who gives the subordinate a look of anger, immediately followed by a look of bewilderment, may be trying to communicate to the subordinate that he or she is very upset by what the subordinate did, but does not want to believe that the subordinate really did it. Facial meaning is modulated when the intensity of the facial expression is changed to communicate stronger or weaker feelings than those actually being experienced. For example, you may communicate slight sadness, facially, when you feel abject grief.

Finally, facial falsification may take one of three forms. A person may: (a) *simulate,* by showing facial emotion when no emotion is felt; (b) *neutralize,* by showing no facial emotion although some emotion is felt; or (c) *mask,* by covering a felt emotion while displaying a facial emotion that is not really felt.

Whether facial deception is intentional or involuntary, deception complicates the task of the decoder and reduces the potential value of the face as a reliable source of emotional information. When facial deception is used, the question becomes how the receiver guards against being deceived by such facial expressions.

The best method of guarding against such deception is training to develop decoding skills. If the facial expression seems to lack spontaneity, to be poorly synchronized with the content of the words being uttered, or to involve seemingly calculated movement in the lower part of the face, beware. Finally, the receiver should be alert for involuntary micro-momentary facial expressions. These facial expressions usually last for only a fraction of a second. When these fleeting facial expressions contradict the meaning of more sustained facial expressions, facial deception may be occurring.

Measuring Sensitivity to Facial Expressions

The face may be used to deceive; nevertheless, it has unsurpassed potential for the communication of emotional information. We know now that individuals vary markedly in their ability to use the informational potential of the human face. Until quite recently, however, attempts to measure an individual's ability to decode meanings from facial expressions lacked specificity and precision. This was so because decoding tests did not require that decoders make fine distinctions between facial expressions that were closely related in meaning (Leathers & Emigh, 1980). Decoders were usually asked to view facial expressions and place them in one of seven or eight categories; each category represented one of the primary emotions.

The Facial Meaning Sensitivity Test

The Facial Meaning Sensitivity Test (FMST) represents the most detailed and precise measure of the ability to decode facial expressions that has been developed to date. In 1982, O'Sullivan evaluated eight measures of the ability to recognize facial expressions, including the Brief Affect Recognition Task (BART), Communication of Affect Receiving Ability (CARAT), and the Profile of Nonverbal Sensitivity (PONS). Until the introduction of the FMST, eight emotions, at most, were used for any test in which posed facial expressions were the stimuli. However, none of these eight tests included the detailed and difficult discriminatory tasks which are part of the FMST.

The accuracy in meaning of the FMST's facial photographs has been established through application of the test to a national sample of decoders. The validation procedure established not only that decoders using the FMST accurately distinguish among 10 basic classes of emotion communicated by facial expressions, but that they accurately label the subtle and closely related facial meanings that are constituents of each of the 10 broad classes of facial meaning.

The FMST is composed of a set of photographs of different facial expressions; it is a three-part test. The photographs in the test are all of the same person, Loren Lewis, who was chosen because she has an expressive and photogenic face. In recognition of her dedication, determination, and sensitivity, this series of photographs was called the Loren Lewis Series. The facial photographs that make up the FMST were chosen from more than 700 photographs of Loren Lewis from the many sessions held to develop the Loren Lewis Series.

Part I of the FMST (see Figure 2.2 on page 36) contains ten photographs that represent the 10 basic classes of facial meaning. Study them and place the photograph numbers in the appropriate blanks of the chart in Step 1.

STEP 1   Facial Meaning Sensitivity Test

Classes of Facial Meaning	Expression Number (From Figure 2.2)
Disgust	_____
Happiness	_____
Interest	_____
Sadness	_____
Bewilderment	_____
Contempt	_____
Surprise	_____
Anger	_____
Determination	_____
Fear	_____

FIGURE 2.2 Facial Meaning Sensitivity Test, Part I

The correct answers for Step 1 of the FMST are

disgust	= I	contempt	= IX
happiness	= III	surprise	= VII
interest	= VIII	anger	= VI
sadness	= X	determination	= IV
bewilderment	= II	fear	= V

On the following pages you will see 30 more photographs of facial expressions (Figure 2.3 on pages 38–39). Your task in Step 2 of the FMST is to group these facial expressions by class of meaning. Three of the photographs, for example, are intended to convey meanings that express a specific kind of disgust and, hence, should be perceived as part of that class of facial meaning. Among the 30 photos are three expressions that may be classified as specific kinds of happiness. Your task, then, is to select the three that you most closely associate with each of the 10 classes of facial meaning, using each photograph only once, and to place the photograph numbers in the appropriate blanks of the chart in Step 2.

STEP 2   Facial Meaning Sensitivity Test

Classes of Facial Meaning	Expressions That Are Part of Each Class (Expression Number From Figure 2.3)		
Disgust	_____	_____	_____
Happiness	_____	_____	_____
Interest	_____	_____	_____
Sadness	_____	_____	_____
Bewilderment	_____	_____	_____
Contempt	_____	_____	_____
Surprise	_____	_____	_____
Anger	_____	_____	_____
Determination	_____	_____	_____
Fear	_____	_____	_____

The correct choices for Step 2 of the FMST are

disgust	= 8, 12, 30	contempt	= 13, 24, 29
happiness	= 2, 9, 26	surprise	= 3, 16, 19
interest	= 6, 15, 23	anger	= 1, 20, 28
sadness	= 5, 7, 14	determination	= 11, 22, 25
bewilderment	= 4, 17, 18	fear	= 10, 21, 27

FIGURE 2.3   Facial Meaning Sensitivity Test, Part II

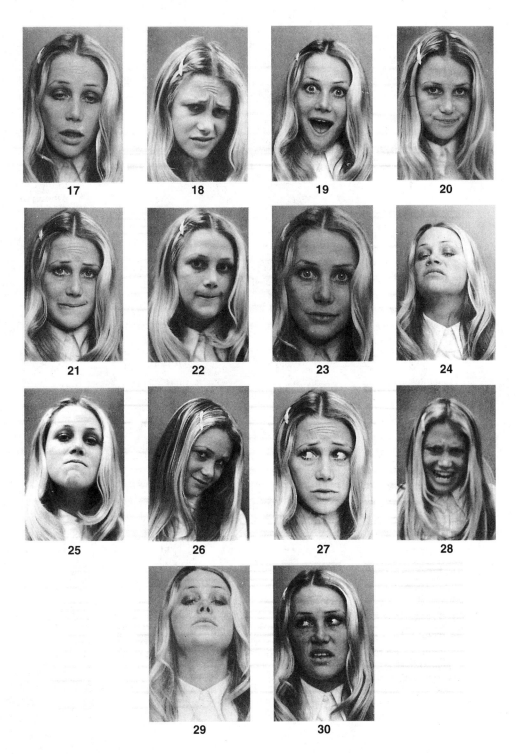

FIGURE 2.3   (Continued)

In Step 3 of the FMST you have a discriminatory task of correctly identifying very specific kinds of meaning. Consider the 30 photographs three at a time, and place the photograph number in the blank provided in the chart in Step 3. For example, you must decide whether picture 8, 12, or 30 communicates aversion. You must also identify repugnance and distaste in this series of three photographs.

STEP 3   Facial Meaning Sensitivity Test

Specific Kind of Facial Meaning			Photo Number: Choose From Among the Following Expressions (Use Figure 2.3)
Aversion _____	Repugnance _____	Distaste _____	8, 12, 30
Amazement _____	Flabbergasted _____	Astonished _____	3, 16, 19
Rage _____	Hate _____	Annoyance _____	1, 20, 28
Confusion _____	Doubt _____	Stupidity _____	4, 17, 18
Terror _____	Anxiety _____	Apprehension _____	10, 21, 27
Disdain _____	Arrogance _____	Superiority _____	13, 24, 29
Laughter _____	Love _____	Amusement _____	2, 9, 26
Disappointment _____	Distress _____	Pensiveness _____	5, 7, 14
Attention _____	Anticipation _____	Excitement _____	6, 15, 23
Stubborn _____	Resolute _____	Belligerent _____	11, 22, 25

The correct choices for Step 3 of the FMST are:

30, 12, 8	24, 13, 29
16, 19, 3	9, 26, 2
28, 1, 20	14, 5, 7
18, 4, 17	23, 6, 15
10, 21, 27	11, 22, 25

National Decoding Norms

Results in Tables 2.1 to 2.3 provide decoding norms for each step of the FMST. The sample of decoders who produced these decoding norms were 118 engineers and corporate executives, 82 university students, and 68 members of fraternal and civic organizations; 201 decoders were males and 67 were females. To determine whether the level of skill reflected in your own attempts to decode the FMST's facial expressions was good, average, or poor, you need to follow a simple procedure.

Results for each step of the FMST are scored separately because a weighted scoring system is used, with greater weight assigned to decoding decisions or answers that exhibited the highest degree of consensus. For Step 1, each correct answer (see Table 2.1) is worth 10 points, with a possible total of 100 points. The average score for the sample of decoders ($n = 268$) for Step 1 was 90.9, with a standard deviation of 13.13.

Scoring weights for Step 2 are given in Table 2.4. Thus, an individual classifying photographs 2, 9, and 15 as kinds of facial happiness is given 4 points for each choice, for a total of 12 points. If the individual placed only photograph 9 in the "happiness" category, the point total for that class of facial meaning is, of course, only 4. The possible scores for Step 2 range from 0 to 100. The average score was 72.4, with a standard deviation of 11.0. The same principle is used to compute your score for Step 3 of the FMST (see Table 2.5). For example, an individual who identified photographs 28, 1, and 20, respectively, as rage, hate, and annoyance is given 15 points. For Step 3, the possible range of scores is 0 to 101, the average score is 80.0, and the standard deviation is 9.8.

TABLE 2.1   Accuracy of Identification for Basic Classes of Meaning Communicated by Facial Expression: Step 1 of the FMST

Class of Meaning	Photograph Number	Percentage of Correct Identification by Decoders	Type of Decoding Error	z-Value
Happiness	III	98.88	Surprise (0.75%) Interest (0.37%)	42.84
Sadness	X	96.64	Bewilderment (2.24%) Interest (0.37%)	48.47
Surprise	VII	95.90	Fear (2.99%) Interest (0.37%)	48.08
Anger	VI	92.91	Determination (6.34%) Disgust (0.37%)	45.91
Fear	V	91.41	Bewilderment (5.22%) Interest (1.40%)	37.83
Contempt	IX	89.18	Disgust (5.60%) Determination (2.61%)	43.93
Disgust	I	88.01	Contempt (4.49%)	42.84
Interest	VIII	87.31	Bewilderment (4.85%) Surprise (2.24%)	42.95
Determination	IV	86.94	Anger (5.97%) Contempt (4.48%)	43.54
Bewilderment	II	82.46	Fear (7.37%) Interest (3.86%)	39.29

All z-values are significant beyond the 0.0001 level. The two types of decoding errors that occurred most frequently for each class of meaning are reported in the Type of Decoding Error column.

TABLE 2.2 Accuracy of Classification of Facial Photographs Into Classes of Meaning: Step 2 of the FMST

Class of Meaning	Photograph Number	Percentage of Decoders Correctly Classifying Each Photograph	Type of Decoding Error
Happiness	9	97.22	
	2	91.54	Interest (5.93)
	26	34.00	Interest (53.06)
	15	65.59	Happiness
Sadness	5	82.28	Fear (10.55)
	7	79.57	Bewilderment (7.18)
	14	70.17	Bewilderment (27.27)
Surprise	19	91.96	
	3	86.12	
	16	66.25	Fear (11.58); interest (12.36)
Anger	28	85.59	Fear (11.52)
	1	65.56	Determination (25.31); contempt (5.39)
	20	20.67	Disgust (48.56); contempt (11.54)
Fear	10	87.87	Determination (12.02)
	21	56.17	Bewilderment (21.70); sadness (16.60)
	27	62.98	Bewilderment (27.23); sadness (7.80)
Contempt	13	73.30	Determination (21.26)
	24	85.20	Disgust (5.00)
	29	75.57	Determination (14.47)
Disgust	8	72.93	Bewilderment (7.42); anger (6.11); contempt (5.48)
	30	56.67	Bewilderment (12.86); contempt (10.95); fear (10.00); anger (5.71)
Interest	6	91.95	
	23	81.86	Surprise (5.30)
	15	26.72	Happiness (65.59); surprise (6.48)
	26	53.06	Interest
Determination	11	71.49	Anger (27.00)
	25	69.70	Anger (17.31); contempt (8.66)
	22	51.91	Anger (29.36); interest (6.80); fear (5.10)
Bewilderment	18	77.12	Fear (6.78); sadness (6.36); disgust (5.93)
	17	56.52	Sadness (28.50); fear (5.80)
	4	18.69	Disgust (40.19); contempt (14.02); Anger (8.88); determination (7.94); interest (5.60)

TABLE 2.3   Accuracy of Identification of Specific Facial Expressions Within Each Class of Meaning

Class of Meaning	Photograph Number (From Figure 2.3)	Percentage of Correct Identification	Type of Decoding Error	Percentage of Decoders Correctly Identifying All Facial Expressions Within a Class
Anger	28	Rage (95.74)	Hate (3.49) Annoyance (0)	
	1	Hate (94.92)	Rage (3.49) Annoyance (1.94)	94.53
	20	Annoyance (98.96)	Rage (0.39) Hate (1.16)	
Happiness	9	Laughter (98.45)	Amusement (1.66) Love (0)	
	26	Love (91.09)	Amusement (8.53) Laughter (0)	90.27
	2	Amusement (90.31)	Love (8.14) Laughter (1.16)	
Bewilderment	18	Confusion (86.38)	Doubt (7.39) Stupidity (5.84)	
	4	Doubt (88.72)	Confusion (10.51) Stupidity (0.39)	85.66
	17	Stupidity (93.39)	Doubt (3.50) Confusion (2.72)	
Fear	10	Terror (98.44)	Anxiety (9.78) Apprehension (0.30)	
	21	Anxiety (77.43)	Apprehension (21.40) Terror (0.78)	76.74
	27	Apprehension (77.82)	Anxiety (21.40) Terror (0.39)	
Interest	23	Attention (89.92)	Anticipation (6.98) Excitement (2.33)	
	6	Anticipation (67.05)	Excitement (25.97) Attention (6.20)	66.16
	15	Excitement (71.32)	Anticipation (25.97) Attention (2.33)	
Sadness	14	Disappointment (56.59)	Pensiveness (25.19) Distress (17.44)	
	5	Distress (72.48)	Disappointment (21.71) Pensiveness (5.04)	53.91
	7	Pensiveness (86.61)	Disappointment (21.32) Distress (8.92)	
Contempt	24	Disdain (55.25)	Arrogance (33.07) Superiority (11.28)	
	13	Arrogance (47.47)	Disdain (35.41)	43.80

(continued)

TABLE 2.3   (Continued)

Class of Meaning	Photograph Number (From Figure 2.3)	Percentage of Correct Identification	Type of Decoding Error	Percentage of Decoders Correctly Identifying All Facial Expressions Within a Class
	29	Superiority (71.98)	Superiority (11.28) Arrogance (19.07) Disdain (8.56)	
Disgust	30	Aversion (78.68)	Repugnance (9.69) Distaste (11.24)	42.25
	12	Repugnance (49.61)	Distaste (43.02) Aversion (7.36)	
	8	Distaste (43.35)	Repugnance (40.70) Aversion (13.95)	
Determination	11	Stubborn (51.55)	Belligerent (32.95) Resolute (14.73)	37.98
	22	Resolute (67.05)	Belligerent (22.09) Stubborn (10.47)	
	25	Belligerent (44.19)	Stubborn (37.60) Resolute (17.83)	
Surprise	16	Amazement (45.74)	Astonishment (32.95) Flabbergasted (20.93)	20.62
	19	Flabbergasted (35.66)	Astonishment (34.11) Amazement (29.35)	
	3	Astonishment (32.17)	Flabbergasted (42.25) Amazement (24.03)	

TABLE 2.4   Weighted Sources for Step 2 of FMST

Class of Meaning	1	2	3	4	5	6	7	8	9	10	11	12	13	14	15	16	17	18	19	20	21	22	23	24	25	26	27	28	29	30	Class of Meaning
Happiness		4					4							4																	Happiness
Sadness				4	4								4																		Sadness
Surprise			4												4			4													Surprise
Anger	4																											4			Anger
Fear									3										3					3							Fear
Contempt											4										4						4				Contempt
Disgust						3		3																						3	Disgust
Interest					4															4			4								Interest
Determination										3												3			3						Determination
Bewilderment																3	3														Bewilderment

1	2	3	4	5	6	7	8	9	10	11	12	13	14	15	16	17	18	19	20	21	22	23	24	25	26	27	28	29	30

TABLE 2.5   Weighted Scores for Step 3 of FMST

Individual Facial Expressions Identified by Photograph Numbers

Anger				Happiness				Bewilderment		
1	20	28		2	9	26		4	17	18
Rage		5	Laughter		5		Confusion			5
Hate (5)			Love			5	Doubt	5		
Annoyance	5		Amusement	5			Stupidity		5	

Fear				Interest				Sadness		
10	21	27		6	15	23		5	7	14
Terror (4)			Attention			4	Disappointment			3
Anxiety	4		Anticipation	4			Distress	3		
Apprehension		4	Excitement		4		Pensiveness		3	

Contempt				Disgust				Determination		
13	24	29		8	12	30		11	22	25
Disdain	2		Aversion			2	Stubborn	2		
Arrogance (2)			Repugnance		2		Resolute		2	
Superiority		2	Distaste	2			Belligerent			2

	Surprise		
	3	16	19
Amazement		1	
Flabbergasted			1
Astonishment	1		

Compute your decoding scores for each step of the FMST and compare your decoding performance with the decoding norms of the sample of decoders. For Step 1, scores of 100 to 91 constitute good decoding, scores from 90 to 71 are average, and scores of 70 and below show poor performance. For Step 2, good, average, and poor decoding are determined, respectively, by the following range of scores: 100 to 83, 82 to 61, and 60 or below. For Step 3, 100 to 90 is good, 89 to 70 is average, and 60 and below is poor.

The Judgmental Process

You might profitably explore the judgmental processes that affect the encoding and decoding of facial expressions at this point. Intuitively you would probably assume that there would be a high correlation between the ability to encode and decode facial expressions. If you made this assumption, your intuition failed you in this case. Correlations between measured levels of skill in encoding and decoding facial expressions have repeatedly been found to be low (Oster, Daily, & Goldenthal, 1989). Why?

No obvious or generally accepted explanation exists. Momentary thought might suggest, however, that the encoding of facial expressions is often preceded by careful contemplation. We recognize that the nature of the situation; our own age, ethnicity, gender, and social standing; the age, ethnicity, gender, and social standing of the person with whom we are communicating; the degree to which a facial emotion expressed is actually felt; and whether we work in a people-oriented job may all affect the type and intensity of the emotion(s) we choose to display on our face; these same factors may affect the decoder's judgment as to the type of emotion she or he sees displayed (Gosselin, Kirouac, & Dore, 1995; Morgado, Cangemi, Miller, & O'Connor, 1993; Nelson & Nugent, 1990). Have I missed some factors that affect the facial expressions you choose to encode in given situations with given individuals?

The encoding of facial expression is clearly a skill that can be developed. We know that as you develop your ability to be emotionally expressive and your role-playing skills in a general sense, your ability to encode facial emotions is apt to increase (Tucker & Riggio, 1988). We know too that individuals who study the muscle involvements characteristic of certain facial emotions, and who practice expressing these emotions, will probably increase encoding skill (Leathers & Emigh, 1980).

At the same time, the facial expressions you choose to encode in public will probably be strongly affected by a variety of factors that have contributed to the distinctive social conditioning you have experienced within your own culture. Display rules, for example, dictate that certain emotions should and should not be expressed in certain cultures. The result frequently is that socially taboo emotions, when displayed facially within a given culture, are encoded at lower levels of accuracy.

The decoding of facial expressions is fundamentally different from encoding in a number of respects. We recognize immediately that by encoding facial expressions we run the risk of being labeled manipulative; the attempt to develop our decoding skills may, by contrast, be viewed as a sign of industriousness. In addition, the factors that affect decoding accuracy are frequently outside of one's awareness and not consciously controlled by the decoder.

We know that generally decoding accuracy is lower for men than it is for women; for the very young and old than for the middle-aged; for persons decoding spontaneous as opposed to posed facial expressions; for individuals who have no situational or contextual cues; for persons decoding the facial expressions of strangers; and for learning disabled children, adolescents, emotionally disturbed children, juvenile delinquents, and psychiatric patients (Gepp & Hess, 1986; Oster, Daily, & Goldenthal, 1989; Rotter & Rotter, 1988; Tucker & Riggio, 1988). In most cases, we are not sure why the groups identified experience deficits in decoding accuracy. You may want to give this subject additional thought.

Developing Sensitivity to Facial Expressions: Training Program

The fact that the decoding of facial expressions often takes place outside the decoder's conscious level of awareness does not mean that the decoder cannot become consciously aware of this activity. In fact, this is the first step in more accurately decoding facial expressions.

There can be little doubt that the ability to decode accurately the facial expressions of interactants in a variety of real-world situations is a vitally important communicative competency. *Such a competency, when fully developed, not only provides the interpreter of fa-*

cial messages with a reliable means of detecting facial deceit, but it also provides a sound basis for identifying the emotions, moods, and feelings actually being experienced by the interactants. That such information may be used to help achieve individual or organizational goals in given situations seems clear.

In particular, training programs should be designed for the express purpose of developing skill in decoding facial expressions. A detailed description of such a training program is the subject of another book. However, the following are some of the essential features and components of the training programs I have used for business groups.

One of the most useful training tools is videotape. Whenever possible, the facial expressions of interactants in communication situations should be videotaped and subjected to subsequent analysis. With the aid of the trainer, the interactants should study videotaped facial expressions in order to identify the use of display rules and techniques of facial management, to identify inconsistency in meaning between facial expression and words, and to identify the subtle nuances of emotional meaning that are being communicated by facial expression.

In addition to videotape, a training program should feature muscle-profile charts and facial blueprints. We now know which facial muscles are used to communicate such emotions as contempt and disgust, although this is a difficult distinction to make. Anyone who is fully familiar with the various facial muscles used to communicate facial disgust and contempt is not likely to make a decoding error when observing such facial expressions. In fact, decoding accuracy should be facilitated by familiarizing oneself with "families of facial expressions." Barrett (1993) argued incisively that emotions may properly be viewed as members of families of emotions. Thus, she claimed that "there are *intrinsic* but *not invariant* links between specific emotion families (e.g., fear, anger, shame/embarrassment)" (p. 154).

Finally, sets of facial blueprints should be used, in combination with model photographs of particular facial emotions. The facial blueprints developed by Ekman and Friesen (1984) are especially useful because they break down the face into three areas. The trainee would learn that different emotions are more easily recognized by concentrating on certain areas of the face. For example, in facial sadness, the inner corners of the eyebrows are raised, the inner corners of the upper eyelids are drawn up, and the corners of the lips are drawn down.

In short, measuring and developing the ability to use facial expression as a reliable source of emotional information should be a central concern to any individual who wishes to be a socially sensitive communicator. With awareness, that concern could be reflected in widespread efforts to use the full communicative potential of the human face.

Summary

Facial expressions serve many functions. The impressions a communicator makes are often strongly affected by the appearance of the person's face or by the muscle involvements that define a given facial expression. Facial appearance often exerts a disproportionate influence in judgments of overall physical attractiveness, for example. The position of facial features such as eyebrows may shape judgments of dominance. To smile or not to smile is an important decision because different image qualities are attributed to the smiling and nonsmiling communicator.

The two most important functions of the human face are the communication of emotions and the identification of previously unidentified people. Because of its universal importance in human interaction, the communication of emotions is the primary function of facial expression.

A theoretical understanding of the nature of emotion, in turn, is a prerequisite to a complete understanding of the potential of the human face as a medium of emotional communication. Emotion is a complex but temporary psychological state involving physiological, experiential, and behavioral changes. The communicator's primary concerns should be the degree to which he or she is aware of facial emotions being communicated, the degree of control that the individual can exercise over such emotions, and the relationship between internal states of the body and the emotion being displayed on the face.

The two major approaches used to explain how the face functions communicatively are the categoric and the dimensional perspectives. Researchers who embrace the categoric perspective believe that the face functions to communicate a given type or category of meaning at any given point in time. Results from categoric research have established that the face is capable of communicating at least eight basic classes of meaning: happiness, surprise, fear, anger, sadness, disgust, contempt, and interest. By concentrating on the facial muscles used in different areas of the face, decoders can increase their ability to differentiate accurately among these eight general classes of facial meaning.

The dimensional perspective is based on the assumption that facial expressions are dimensional in nature. Consequently, they are best described by the dimensions of meaning that define them. Most dimensional researchers have found that facial expressions vary with regard to how pleasant and interested the communicator seems to be, and there is some evidence to suggest that facial expressions reflect the communicator's degree of understanding. Recent research also suggests that emotions are displayed more intensely on the left as opposed to the right side of the face.

With the advent of computerized storage of information on the facial features of missing persons and criminal suspects, the face now also serves an important function as a means of identifying individuals. Forensic applications of face memory skills to identify missing persons or criminal suspects represent the most important use of this function.

Although facial expressions often accurately reflect the communicator's feelings, they may also be used to deceive. Genuine facial expressions are identified as representational, and deceptive facial expressions are known as presentational. In putting on a false face, communicators may use the techniques of qualifying, modulating, or falsifying.

Previous attempts to measure an individual's ability to decode meanings from facial expressions lacked specificity and precision. Most decoding tests lack precision because they do not require that decoders make the difficult discriminations between facial expressions that are closely related in meaning. Decoders can use the Facial Meaning Sensitivity Test (FMST) to measure their ability to make such difficult discriminations and compare their decoding accuracy against a set of decoding norms developed for the FMST. Readers who find their decoding skill to be deficient may wish to consider a training program designed to develop this important communicative skill.

References

Abelson, R. P., & Sermat, V. (1962). Multidimensional scaling of facial expressions. *Journal of Experimental Psychology, 63,* 546–554.

Alicke, M. D., Smith, R. H., & Klotz, M. L. (1986). Judgments of physical attractiveness: The role of faces and bodies. *Personality and Social Psychology Bulletin, 12,* 381–389.

Barrett, K. C. (1993). The development of nonverbal communication of emotion: A functionalist perspective. *Journal of Nonverbal Behavior, 17,* 145–169.

Berry, D. S, (1990). What can a moving face tell us? *Journal of Personality and Social Psychology, 58,* 1004–1014.

Berry, D. S., & McArthur, L. Z. (1985). Some components and consequences of a babyface. *Journal of Personality and Social Psychology, 48,* 312–323.

Borod, J. C., Koff, E., Lorch, M. P., & Nicholas, M. (1986). Deficits in facial expression and movement as a function of brain damage. In J. Nespoulous, P. Perron, & A. R. Lecours (Eds.), *The biological foundations of gestures* (pp. 271–293). Hillsdale, NJ: Erlbaum.

Bruce, V. (1989). The structure of faces. In A. W. Young & W. D. Ellis (Eds.), *Handbook on research face processing* (pp. 101–104). Amsterdam: North-Holland.

Bugental, D. W. (1986). Unmasking the 'polite smile': Situational and personal determinants of managed affect in adult-child interaction. *Personality and Social Psychology Bulletin, 12,* 7–16.

Collier, G. (1985). *Emotional expression.* Hillsdale, NJ: Erlbaum.

Ekman, P. (1994). Strong evidence for universals in facial expressions: A reply to Russell's mistaken critique. *Psychological Bulletin, 115,* 268–287.

Ekman, P., Davidson, R. J., & Friesen, W. V. (1990). The Duchenne smile: Emotional expression and brain physiology. II. *Journal of Personality and Social Psychology, 58,* 342–353.

Ekman, P., & Friesen, W. V. (1978). *Manual for the facial action coding system.* Palo Alto, CA: Consulting Psychologists Press.

Ekman, P., & Friesen, W. V. (1984). *Unmasking the face: A guide to recognizing emotions from facial expressions.* Englewood Cliffs, NJ: Prentice-Hall.

Ekman, P., & Friesen, W. V. (1986). A new pan-cultural facial expression of emotion. *Motivation and Emotion, 10,* 159–168.

Ekman, P., & Friesen, W. V. (1988). Who knows what about contempt: A reply to Izard and Haynes. *Motivation and Emotion, 12,* 17–22.

Ekman, P., Friesen, W. V., & Ancoli, S. (1980). Facial signs of emotional experience. *Journal of Personality and Social Psychology, 39,* 1125–1134.

Ekman, P., Friesen, W. V., & Ellsworth, P. (1982). Research foundations. In P. Ekman (Ed.). *Emotion in the human face* (2nd ed., pp. 1–6). Cambridge: Cambridge UP.

Ekman, P., Friesen, W. V., & Tomkins, S. S. (1971). Facial affect scoring technique: A first validity study. *Semiotica, 3,* 37–58.

Ekman, P., & Heider, K. G. (1988). The universality of a contempt expressions: A replication. *Motivation and Emotion, 12,* 37–58.

Ekman, P., O'Sullivan, M., & Matsumoto, D. (1991). Contradictions in the study of contempt: What's it all about? Reply to Russell. *Motivation and Emotion, 15,* 293–296.

Ellis, H. D., & Young, A. W. (1989). Are faces special? In A. W. Young & H. D. Ellis (Eds.), *Handbook of research on face processing* (pp. 1–26). Amsterdam: North-Holland.

Engen, T., Levy, N., & Schlosberg, H. (1957). A new series of facial expressions. *American Psychologist, 12,* 264–266.

Frijda, N. H., & Philipszoon, E. (1963). Dimensions of recognition of expression. *Journal of Abnormal and Social Psychology, 66,* 45–51.

Frijda, N. H. (1969). Recognition of emotions. In L. Berkowitz (Ed.), *Advances in experimental and social psychology.* New York: Academic.

Frois-Wittmann, J. (1930). The judgment of facial expression. *Journal of Experimental Psychology, 13,* 113–151.

Gepp, J., & Hess, D. L. (1986). Children's understanding of verbal and facial display rules. *Developmental Psychology, 22,* 103–108.

Gosselin, P., Kirouac, G., & Dore, F. Y. (1995). Components and recognition of facial expression in the communication of emotion by actors. *Journal of Personality and Social Psychology, 68,* 83–96.

Harrison, R. P. (1967). Picture analysis: Toward a vocabulary and syntax for the pictorial code: With research on facial communication. Unpublished paper.

Hauser, M. D. (1993). Right hemisphere dominance for the production of facial expression in monkeys. *Science, 26,* 475–477.

Izard, C. E. (1971). *The face of emotion.* New York: Appleton.

Izard, C. E., & Haynes, O. M. (1988). On the form and universality of the contempt expression: A challenge to Ekman and Friesen's claim to discovery. *Motivation and Emotion, 12,* 1–16.

Keating, C. F. (1985). Gender and physiognomy of dominance and attractiveness. *Social Psychology Quarterly, 48,* 61–70.

Keating, C. F., & Bal, D. L. (1986). Children's attributions of social dominance from facial cues. *Child Development, 57,* 1269–1276.

Knapp, M. L. (1978) *Nonverbal communication in human interaction* (2nd ed.). New York: Holt.

LaFrance, M., & Mayo, C. (1978). *Moving bodies: Nonverbal communication in social relationships.* Monterey, CA: Brooks/Cole.

Laughery, K. R., & Wogalter, S. (1989). Forensic applications of facial memory research. In A. W. Young and H. D. Ellis (Eds.), *Handbook of research on face processing* (pp. 519–547). Amsterdam: North-Holland.

Leathers, D. G., & Emigh, T. H. (1980). Decoding facial expressions: A new test with decoding norms. *Quarterly Journal of Speech, 66,* 418–436.

Levenson, R. W. (1988). Emotions and the autonomic nervous system: A prospectus for research on autonomic specificity. In H. Wager (Ed.), *Social psychophysiology and emotion: Theory and clinical applications* (pp. 17–41). Chichester: Wiley.

Levy, L. H., Orr, T. B., & Rosenzweig, S. (1960). Judgments of emotion from facial expression by college students, mental retardates, and mental hospital patients. *Journal of Personality, 28,* 341–349.

Mandal, M. K., Asthana, H. S., Madan, S. K., & Pandey, R. (1992). Hemifacial display of emotion in the resting state. *Behavioural Neurology, 5,* 169–171.

Mehrabian, A. (1970). A semantic space for nonverbal behavior. *Journal of Consulting and Clinical Psychology, 35,* 248–249.

Morgado, I. A., Cangemi, J. P., Miller, R., & O'Connor, J. (1993). Accuracy of decoding facial expressions in those engaged in people oriented activities vs. those engaged in nonpeople oriented activities. *Studia Psychologica, 35,* 73–80.

Nelson, C. A., & Nugent, K. M. (1990). Recognition memory and resource allocation as revealed by children's event-related potential responses to happy and angry faces. *Developmental Psychology, 26,* 171–179.

Osgood, C. E. (1966). Dimensionality of the semantic space for communication via facial expressions. *Scandinavian Journal of Psychology, 7,* 1–30.

Oster, H., Daily, L., & Goldenthal, P. (1989). Processing facial affect. In W. W. Young and H. D. Ellis (Eds.), *Handbook of research on face processing* (pp. 107–161). Amsterdam: North-Holland.

O'Sullivan, M. (1982). Measuring the ability to recognize facial expressions. In P. Ekman (Ed.), *Emotion in the human face* (2nd ed. pp. 281–317). Cambridge: Cambridge UP.

Rotter, N. G., & Rotter, G. S. (1988). Sex differences in the encoding and decoding of negative facial emotions. *Journal of Nonverbal Behavior, 12,* 139–148.

Rozin, P., Lowery, L., & Ebert, R. ((1994). Varieties of disgust faces and the structure of disgust. *Journal of Personality and Social Psychology, 66,* 870–881.

Sackeim, H. A., Gur, R. C., & Saucy, M. C. (1978). Emotions are expressed more intensely on the left side of the face. *Science, 202,* 434–436.

Schlosberg, H. (1954). Three dimensions of emotion. *Psychology Review, 61,* 81–88.

Tomkins, S. S. (1962). *Affect, imagery, consciousness, I.* New York: Springer-Verlag.

Tucker, J. S., & Riggio, R. E. (1988). The role of social skills in encoding posed and spontaneous facial expressions. *Journal of Nonverbal Behavior, 12,* 87–97.

Wagner, H. L., MacDonald, C. J., & Manstead, A. S. R. (1986). Communication of individual emotions by spontaneous facial expressions. *Journal of Personality and Social Psychology, 50,* 737–743.

Williams, F., & Tolch, J. (1965). Communication by facial expression. *Journal of Communication, 15,* 20.

Woodworth, R. S. (1938). *Experimental psychology.* New York: Holt

Chapter 3

Eye Behaviors

The eyes have been an object of fascination for centuries. "Writers, actors, visual artists, and advertisers have used eye expression and eye images throughout history as a primary mode of communication and representation because of our beliefs in the eyes as windows of the soul" (Webbink, 1986, p. 6). In fact a sociocultural preoccupation with the symbolism of the human eye goes back thousands of years to the beginning of recorded history.

Symbolically, "the divine eye" and "the evil eye" have assumed central significance in cultures as diverse as the ancient Egyptian, Mexican, and Greek cultures. The human eye has long had a special symbolic significance as a result of not only a belief in its all-seeing and omniscient capacity to observe every human action but also a belief in the omnipotent power of the eye.

In many cultures "the divine eye" has taken the form of a highly visible and powerful eye that keeps watch over every little thing with a relentless gaze. Not only was the cat goddess Bastet the dominant deity in Egypt for 2,000 years but her power was thought to derive from the magical properties associated with cats' eyes. In Mexico the eyes of the rain god Tlaloc were preserved for centuries as onyx inlaid in pyramids constructed for him; modern Catholicism in Mexico has preserved the importance of the divine eye by its placement in a triangle representing the Holy Trinity. Finally, the belief that "the divine eye" is representative of divinity and, hence, of supernatural powers was so strong in Greek mythology that Zeus, the far-seeing king of the Gods, could allegedly generate lighting with his glance (Webbink, 1986).

"The evil eye" is also reflective of the fact that members of many cultures have attributed great symbolic importance and power to the human eye. People have believed in "the evil eye" since at least the seventh century B.C. Argyle and Cook (1976) wrote that belief in "the evil eye"

> is still held in Morocco, and to a lesser extent in remote country areas of European countries. The belief was connected with the idea that vision was due to rays emanating from the eye, together with the belief that most deaths and accidents are caused by witches; it was supposed that a witch looking in a mirror would actually

leave a thin poisonous film on it. If a person possessed the evil eye, it was believed that he placed a curse on anyone he looked at. (p. 30)

In modern society we no longer believe that deities derive their powers from their eyes. We continue to have many beliefs about the symbolic significance of eye behaviors, however. These beliefs frequently take the form of stereotypes. The deceiver stereotype, for example, is based to a considerable extent on societal beliefs about the eye behaviors that deceivers characteristically exhibit. This stereotype suggests that honest and trustworthy individuals exhibit one type of eye behavior and devious and untrustworthy individuals exhibit another. A colleague and I (Leathers & Hocking, 1982) have done in-depth examinations of police interviewers' beliefs as to which nonverbal cues are the most useful indicators of the deception of a lying criminal suspect. The police interviewers are convinced that eye behaviors are the most reliable indicators of deception. In fact, one police interviewer for the Georgia Bureau of Investigation told me that he had never observed a lying criminal suspect whose pupils did not dilate at the time of deception.

The adjectives we use to describe the eyes suggest that we believe that human eyes serve an almost endless number of communicative functions and provide many different kinds of information. Have you ever encountered an individual whose eyes were hard, beady, sly, shifty, radiant, shining, dull, or sparkling? If so, you will probably admit that such eyes affected not only your perception of the person and your desire to interact with that person, but also your own behavior. In addition, human eyes have great communicative significance, as suggested by the numerous expressions used to describe eye behaviors; for example, the person is "shifty eyed" or "bug-eyed"; the person "gave me the eye" or "gave me the fish eye"; "see eye to eye," "have an eye to," "an eyesore," and "an eye-opener."

This chapter is designed to help you make most effective use of the great communicative potential of your eye behaviors. To do so you must understand the types of eye behaviors that you may exhibit. You must be familiar with the major communicative functions of eye behaviors and know which particular type(s) of eye behaviors serve each function most effectively and why they do so. Finally, you must know what modifications you should make if you are to overcome problems associated with your own dysfunctional eye behaviors. Each section of this chapter is devoted to one of these topics.

The Language of the Eyes

There may well be a language of the eyes with its own syntax and grammar (Webbink, 1986). If so, we are years if not decades away from understanding that language in a structural sense. There is, however, already a language of the eyes in a different sense—the language that consists of the set or lexicon of words that describe the types of eye behaviors exhibited individually or in interactions with other individuals.

Exhibited Eye Behaviors

Labels with definitions have been developed to describe the types of eye behaviors you can exhibit. Many but not all of the following eye behavior labels were suggested first by von

Cranach (1971). The labels were outlined by Harper, Wiens, and Matarazzo (1978) and clarified by Kleinke (1986). I have amplified them by drawing on my own research on eye behaviors as indicators of deception.

Eye contact simply suggests that two people are looking at each other but does not specify to what part(s) of the body/face the eye contact is directed. When you *face-gaze* you are looking at another person's face; *looking* and *gazing* are defined in general terms as a gaze in the direction of another person's face, unless otherwise specified. More specifically, *eye-gaze* means that your gaze is focused directly upon the other person's eyes.

When the eye behaviors of two communicators, as opposed to one, are being described, the word "mutual" is added. *Mutual gaze* is defined as two people gazing at each other's faces whereas *mutual eye contact* means two people are directing their gazes at each other's eyes.

Most but not all types of eye behaviors involve the direction of the gaze as part of the definition. For example, *gaze avoidance* is intentional avoidance of eye contact, whereas *gaze omission* is unintentional failure to make eye contact with another person. *Gaze aversion* is defined as a movement of your eyes away from your interaction partner's eyes. *Eye shifts* are defined by the movement of your eyes from a position of eye contact to non-contact.

Finally, some types of eye behaviors are defined not by directionality but by intensity or appearance cues. Thus, *staring* is a gaze or look that persists regardless of the eye behavior(s) of the other person. *Eye blinking* refers to the number of times your eyelids close per unit of time. *Eye-flutter* refers to the number of times your eyeballs exhibit slight but discernible horizontal or vertical movements per unit of time. Finally, *pupil size* is defined by the average size of the pupil diameter(s) of a person's eyes.

Measured Eye Behaviors

The language of the eyes is defined not only by the types of eye behaviors that you and one or more interaction partners exhibit but also by the types of eye behaviors that can be reliably measured. In their comprehensive description and evaluation of conceptual and measurement issues in eye behavior research, Exline and Fehr (1982) maintained that five types of gaze variables have been most frequently measured:

1. *Frequency:* the number of times that an individual looks at a conversational partner
2. *Total duration:* the number of seconds a communicator looks at a particular interaction partner
3. *Proportion of time:* the percentage of total interaction time that a communicator spends looking at or away from an interaction partner when engaging in a particular kind of communication, that is, speaking or listening
4. *Average duration:* mean or average duration of glances directed at an interaction partner
5. *Standard deviation of glances:* average duration of glances that provides information regarding variability in length of single glances

Although these eye behavior variables have been repeatedly and reliably measured, two measurement questions remain unanswered. Can glances directed at the interaction partner's eyes and face be reliably distinguished? Can we determine the degree to which individuals are consciously aware of different kinds of eye contact directed toward them?

The Functions of Eye Behaviors

The voluminous body of research on eye behaviors has clearly established what members of many cultures have believed through the ages: *Eye behaviors serve many vitally important communicative functions.* If for no other reason, eye behaviors would be functionally important because they are the primary center of visual attention. Research by Janik, Wellens, Goldberg, and DeLosse (1978) established that more visual inspection time is spent looking in the region of the eyes than at any other part of the body. Attention is focused on the eyes 43.4 percent of the time; the second most important area of visual attention is the mouth, where attention is focused 12.6 percent of the time.

Because people do concentrate their attention on the eye region it is reasonable to ask, why the eyes receive so much attention? The answer seems to be that people attend to the eyes because they serve a variety of important communicative functions. The eyes

1. indicate degrees of attentiveness, interest, and arousal
2. help initiate and sustain intimate relationships
3. influence attitude change and persuasion
4. regulate interaction
5. communicate emotions
6. define power and status relationships
7. assume a central role in impression management

The Attention Function

Eyes play an important role in the initiation of interpersonal communication because they signal a readiness to communicate. Argyle and Cook (1976) emphasized that mutual gaze "has the special meaning that two people are attending to each other. This is usually necessary for social interaction to begin or be sustained" (p. 170). Eye behaviors not only signal whether two people are attending to each other, however, but they also reflect the *degree* of mutual interest.

The importance of our eyes in gaining attention is apparent if you reflect for a moment. Have you ever given a member of the opposite sex "the eye"? Have you tried to gain the attention of a passing motorist with your eyes while hitchhiking? Have you tried to catch the eye of a waiter or a waitress in a restaurant while he or she in turn signaled readiness to serve or not to serve you by eye contact or avoidance?

Our eyes function effectively both to gain attention and to indicate our level of interest. Hess's research (1975) suggests that pupil size accurately reflects a person's level of interest. Pupils dilate as interest increases; they constrict when interest decreases. Hess stresses that pupils of the eyes are a potentially rich source of information because "the pupil of the eye is intimately connected to all parts of the brain, and as a result, we have the anomalous situation of having a piece of the brain sticking out of the human body for all the world to

CARTOON 3.1

see and to evaluate" (pp. 4–5). Metalis and Hess (1982a) have found that a person's pupil size reliably communicates two types of information about a communication: the attentiveness and interest of the listener and the pleasantness of the communicator's current object of attention.

In a general sense, Hess (1975) has established that pupil size accurately reflects the degree of a person's sexual arousal (the pupils of heterosexual individuals dilate when they watch nude members of the opposite sex), whether a person is responding positively or negatively to the attitudes and values of another person, and the intensity of a person's feelings about another.

Recent research suggests that pupil size can provide even more specialized information. Pupil size increases as the cognitive difficulty of a reading task increases (Metalis & Hess, 1986), and subjects' pupils dilate (their interest level goes up) when observing pictures of main course meals but not snacks (Metalis & Hess, 1982b).

Pupillometrics defines that area of scientific research that focuses on the measurement of psychopupil response. *Pupillography* in turn consists of the actual photographing of the pupils of the eyes at different points in time. Because pupil size can be used to measure level of interest, attitude change, and cognitive processes, pupillometrics has potentially great value in the areas of marketing and advertising.

The Persuasive Function

Eye behavior can also serve an important function in the modification of attitudes that are changed by persuasive communication (Harper et al., 1978). The persuader who wishes to be perceived as credible must sustain eye contact while speaking and being spoken to by the persuadee. To avoid a marked decline in their credibility, persuasive communicators must not be shifty eyed, look down or away from the persuadee frequently, blink excessively, or exhibit eye-flutter.

In his exhaustive review of eye behavior research, Kleinke (1986) documented the potentially powerful impact of eye behaviors on credibility and, ultimately, on persuasive effectiveness. He emphasized that a number of empirical studies support the stereotypic conviction that we tend to believe those individuals who look us directly in the eye, and individuals who do not are seen as deceitful. Thus, witnesses in courtroom trials have been judged as more credible when they did not avert their gaze from the attorney who was questioning them. Similarly, airline travelers who avoided eye contact were judged as more suspicious and suitable for search by airport inspectors than airline travelers who maintained eye contact. Results from a recent study suggest once again that the persuasive effectiveness of persons who maintain eye contact with potential persuadees is greater than those who do not (Hornik, 1987).

There can be little doubt that eye behaviors are important determinants of credibility. Researchers (Burgoon, Coker, & Coker, 1986; Burgoon & Saine, 1978) have provided convincing documentation for their claim that direct eye contact in our society is interpreted as a sign of credibility. Direct eye contact is apt to have a beneficial impact on both the communicator's perceived competence and trustworthiness. We generally assume that individuals who look directly at us know what they are talking about and are being honest with us. Conversely, when people avert their eyes before speaking to us or answering a question, we are likely to make inferences about them which will limit their ability to be effective persuaders. The averted eyes may be interpreted as an effort to keep something from us, in which case we find them less trustworthy, or we may infer that the individual is having difficulty formulating a coherent message, in which case we find the individual less credible in terms of competence.

Burgoon, Manusov, Mineo, and Hale (1985) found that gaze aversion significantly reduces one's chance of being hired in a job interview. Such a finding may be attributed in large part to the strong and decidedly negative impact of gaze aversion on the job interviewee's credibility. Burgoon and coworkers also found that individuals who maintain normal to high eye contact are judged to be much more credible than those who have eye contact of limited duration. More specifically, job interviewees with limited eye contact and gaze aversion were viewed as incompetent, lacking composure, unsociable, and passive. Secondly, they were judged to be unattractive—socially and physically—as task partners. Finally, the averted eyes were interpreted by the job interviewers as expressing dislike, detachment, disinterest, and tension.

Burgoon and associates (1985) concluded that individuals who have limited eye contact and who avert their gaze in an interview situation pay a stiff price in terms of their personal credibility. The researchers emphasized that "by virtue of negative meanings assigned to it as well as the detrimental evaluative and behavioral consequences, gaze aversion clearly qualifies as a negative type of violation" (p. 142).

The Intimacy Function

Eye behaviors play a central role in establishing, maintaining, and terminating interpersonal relationships. Thus, Malandro, Barker, and Barker (1989) wrote that

> *Eye contact determines the type of interaction that will take place and how the interaction will develop. Merely looking at another person is an indication of interest. Eye contact shows a willingness on your part to admit interest in others and allows others to gain information about you.* (p. 134)

Eye behaviors serve a more central role in the development of intimate relationships than any other type of nonverbal communication. Significantly, Webbink (1986) wrote:

> *The eyes, more than other parts of the body, signal a courageous openness between people through mutual gaze. Generally, the more prolonged the gaze, the more intensely the intimacy is experienced. . . . Mutual gazing plays a primary role throughout most interactions and is a reciprocal process particularly suited for enhancing a sense of sharing and thus, intimacy.* (p. 84)

The importance of eye behaviors in establishing intimate relationships becomes apparent when we consider some salient facts. Eye contact intensifies expressions of empathy and warmth, we typically "size up" other people and get a strong sense of who they are by looking at their eyes, and the willingness to engage in a mutual glance is a signal that some interaction is desired at minimum and sexual intimacy may be desired at the maximum. These facts in turn all bear upon the more general findings that honesty, empathy, and ultimately love are psychological states or conditions that are strongly affected by interactants' eye behaviors (Webbink, 1986).

Predictably, dating couples spend more time gazing at one another than do pairs of unacquainted individuals (Iizuka, 1992c). Relatedly, we know that romantic attraction for a potential partner increases as the degree of mutual gazing between the potential partners increases. Even among previously unacquainted individuals under experimental conditions, pairs of individuals who were asked to exhibit a high degree of mutual gazing expressed a greater desire to be paired with the same partner in the future (Williams & Kleinke, 1993).

We should not be surprised to learn, therefore, that eye behaviors assume a central role in the development of the most intimate type of human relationship, love. Kellerman, Lewis, and Laird (1989) focused their research efforts specifically on this subject. They found that individuals who gazed at their partner's eyes and whose partner in turn gazed back at their eyes reported significantly higher feelings of affection than individuals experiencing any other kind of eye contact. They found too that individuals who engaged in sustained mutual eye gaze experienced a significant increase in their liking for each other as well as significant increases in their feelings of passionate and dispositional love for their partner.

The Regulatory Function

The regulatory function of the eyes is an important one. In particular, eye behaviors serve the regulatory function by alerting the decoder that encoding is occurring and continuing, by signaling the encoder whether listening and decoding are occurring, and by indicating when the listener is to speak (Ellsworth & Ludwig, 1971; Kalma, 1992).

There is growing evidence that the eyes in combination with gestures serve effectively to communicate the turn-maintaining, turn-yielding, turn-requesting, and turn-taking cues which are central to conversational management. Eyes can regulate communicative interaction effectively in part because eye behaviors represent a much more subtle and socially acceptable way of revealing one's turn predispositions than such verbal expressions as "Damn it, Bob, don't interrupt me again" or "Shut up, Becky, I want to talk."

We cannot always predict how effective eye behaviors will be as conversational or behavioral regulators until we know more about the importance of factors such as race and culture, however (Kleinke, 1986). If you had been standing in line with me recently while waiting for a taxicab at an airport in Rome, you might have concluded—as I did—that neither your most assertive eye behaviors nor compelling gestures would be sufficient to make some individuals stay in line or take their turn.

Abele (1986) acknowledged the important regulatory function of the human eyes in social interaction in general. He maintained that eye behavior becomes even more important in regulating the interaction of intimates. If you believe that an equilibrium between approach and avoidance is important in intimate relationships, then gaze should function as an intimacy-regulating factor. For example, when the intimacy of a topic being discussed increases, there must be a compensatory decrease in gaze if equilibrium between intimates is to be maintained.

Finally, Kendon's classic study (1967) helped illuminate the regulatory function of eye behaviors through the extensive film recording of two-person conversations. The person attempting to communicate a message was identified as P, and the person to whom the message was directed was identified as Q. The time P spent looking at Q varied from 28 to 70 percent, depending on the individuals who were communicating. When P began addressing Q, 70 percent of the time P began by looking away from Q. Usually, P looked away from Q when P began talking; P typically looked at Q *when* P finished talking. In short, individuals usually look away from a person when they begin to talk, and while they are talking; and they are apt to look at you and pause if they wish you to respond.

The Affective Function

The eyes combine with the face to function as a powerful medium of emotional communication. Consider your reaction when you encountered persons whose eyes were cold, warm, hateful, passionate, or loving. You probably recognized that the language of the eyes is the language of emotion. As Schlenker (1980) so graphically put it, "The eyes universally symbolize affect. The look in another's eyes can signal the start of a romance or the end of one. As the poet's mirror to the soul, the eyes express and intensify the affect present in a relationship" (p. 258).

When one individual wishes to determine whether another is experiencing a positive or negative emotion, and the intensity of the felt emotion, he or she can observe the pupils of the other's eyes. Pupils enlarge when individuals experience positive emotions such as happiness or joy, and contract when negative emotions such as sadness or sorrow are being experienced.

In short, the eyes can accurately reflect *whether* a person is experiencing a positive or negative emotion and reveal the *intensity* of the emotion. Thus, the individual who wishes to make an accurate judgment about the moods and emotions of another individual should rely on the information revealed in both the face and eyes. *We display the kind of emotion we are experiencing in our face and the intensity of the emotion in our eyes.*

The Power Function

Are you reluctant to be hypnotized? Have you ever actively resisted the efforts of a friend or even a professional hypnotist to put you into a hypnotic trance? If so, you probably were fearful or at least apprehensive about the prospect of someone's exerting so much domination over you with his or her eyes that you would be forced to surrender conscious control of your actions to that person. Subconsciously, you may have dreaded the prospect of being "mesmerized" by the penetrating eyes of another person.

Interestingly, Franz Mesmer was an Austrian physician who developed a procedure for using his own eyes to cure the afflictions of his patients; Mesmer could induce trances by gazing into the eyes of his patients. Modern hypnosis relies on mesmerizing power to gain control over others and dominate them. Consequently, the "fear of being enveloped or devoured by someone's eyes, and a concomitant fear of having one's control surrendered to another, probably accounts for the reluctance of many people to be hypnotized" (Webbink, 1986, p. 40).

We have learned much about the central role of the eyes in establishing dominance and submissiveness among nonhuman primates. Monkeys and apes rely heavily on the stare to establish dominance; subordinate monkeys and apes respond with averted eyes. Many otherwise peaceful animals become so threatened by a stare from humans that they may attack. Animals also establish their place in a power hierarchy by their degree of visual attentiveness—the more visually attentive an animal is, the lower its place in the power hierarchy (Mitchell & Maple, 1985).

The eye behaviors of human beings also function as an effective and reliable index of the amount of power one individual possesses vis-à-vis another. People perceived as powerful usually *look* powerful. The license to stare at others for the purpose of domination is the exclusive prerogative of powerful people. In contrast, the averted and downward glance is universally recognized as a sign of weakness and submission. Individuals who are presumed to be afraid to look at others are judged to have minimal leadership capacity and are usually relegated to the perceptual category of low status.

Rasputin is a good case in point. Rasputin was born to modest circumstances in the nineteenth century in imperial Russia. He affected the image of a religious clairvoyant with a miraculous healing capacity. Finally, Rasputin rose to become the chief advisor to Tsar Nicholas and Empress Alexandra. Many high-level Russians who interacted directly with Rasputin attributed his great power to his remarkable eyes:

The full expression of his [Rasputin's] personality, however, seemed concentrated in his eyes. They were pale blue, of exceptional brilliance, depth and attraction. His gaze was at once piercing and caressing, naive and cunning, far-off and intent. When he was in earnest conversation, his pupils seemed to radiate magnetism. . . .

It was difficult to resist the power of Rasputin's steady gaze. (Massie, 1967, pp. 191–192)

Power, status, and personal dominance are all related to visual dominance behavior (Henley, 1977; Henley & Harmon, 1985). A fascinating study of the eye behaviors of ROTC cadet officers (Exline, Ellyson, & Long, 1975) illuminated the nature of this relationship. The study confirmed not only that low-power cadets were much more visually attentive than high-power cadets, but it also revealed that the low-power cadets who were most visually attentive were given the lowest leadership ratings by their commanding officers.

The visual dominance ratio is now perhaps the best measure of the relative dominance and submissiveness of two individuals who are interacting. The *visual dominance ratio* is the ratio of the percentage of looking in two modes—the percentage of looking while speaking relative to the percentage of looking while listening (Dovidio, Ellyson, Keating, Heltman, & Brown, 1988). As your level of looking while speaking increases and your level of looking while listening decreases, your visual dominance ratio goes up. The perceived dominance of females in particular has been found to increase markedly as their visual dominance ratio increases (Iizuka, 1992a).

We now know that communicators who exhibit a high visual dominance ratio (55 percent looking while speaking versus 45 percent looking while listening) are perceived as significantly more powerful than communicators who exhibit a moderate visual dominance ratio (40 percent versus 60 percent) or a low visual dominance ratio (25 percent versus 75 percent). Not only do communicators relatively high in status, expertise power, and desire for interpersonal control display higher visual dominance ratios, visual dominance behavior is also reliably and accurately decoded by observers (Dovidio & Ellyson, 1985).

We know too that the more expert people are perceived to be, the more visual dominance they exhibit, and women generally have a lower visual dominance ratio than do men (Dovidio, et al., 1988). In short, the eyes encode power and dominance powerfully. In general, communicators with high levels of eye contact are perceived to be more powerful or potent (Knackstedt & Kleinke, 1991). If you think about the people you consider to be weak, you may well recall that they have a low visual dominance ratio and frequently avert their eyes when you look at them.

The Impression Management Function

Eye behaviors frequently assume a central role in the formation of impressions and in impression management. This subject is addressed in detail in separate chapters of this book. Communicators who wish to exercise conscious control over their communicative behaviors in order to make a desired impression would be well advised to begin by monitoring their eye behavior. In fact, eye behaviors do exercise a social control function that is managed, intentional, and situational. Thus, eye behaviors have proven to be important in impression management efforts because they can be used to ingratiate, deceive, dominate, and avoid other human beings, as well as to suggest that one is extroverted (Iizuka, 1992b; Kleinke, 1986).

Public figures such as General George Patton and former President Richard Nixon have been very concerned about the impact of their eye behaviors on their public image. Although

Patton was notably successful, and Nixon notably unsuccessful, in trying to cultivate the "look" of the powerful leader, both men recognized that impression management begins with the eyes.

Our self-concept and self-esteem are vitally important parts of impression management. Communicators with a negative self-concept and low self-esteem are obviously limited in the images they may credibly claim for themselves. Significantly, then, we now know that the longer we sustain eye contact with those with whom we interact, the greater self-esteem we are perceived to have (Droney & Brooks, 1993). In this study, an interviewee maintained eye contact with an interviewer for durations of 5, 30, and 50 seconds, respectively. Self-esteem scores of the interviewee increased significantly as her eye contact increased for each of the 10 scales that make up the Multidimensional Self-Esteem Inventory.

Using the Communicative Potential of Eye Behaviors

Communicators should be aware of the potential value of eye behaviors as an aid in attaining rather specific communicative objectives. Successful communication requires a maximum amount of information about the perceptions of others, their feelings, and their expectations. We must recognize that eye behaviors have the potential to provide us with precisely these kinds of information.

Message senders should be sensitive to the fact that *much of the information communicated by their own eyes operates out of their own level of awareness and is, therefore, beyond their ability to consciously control* (pupil dilation is probably a case in point). Because of this, our eyes may reveal much highly personal information about us that we would not choose to reveal if we could consciously control all of our eye behaviors. Our eyes might show that we are uninterested in the message of a superior, even as we consciously control nonverbal cues to suggest interest. Our eyes could reveal that our level of self-esteem and self-confidence is dissipating rapidly, even though we exude confidence through our verbal communication. Our eyes might reflect an attitude of indifference to an intimate, even when we are whispering words of love in the intimate's ear.

To avoid the constant transmission of inconsistent, unintended, and undesired meanings via our eyes, we may wish to exercise conscious control over selected eye behaviors that will help us make a desired impression. Such efforts are called *impression management.* For example, we could eliminate the downcast and shifty eye movements that are associated with ineffective persuasion. We could carefully monitor the eye behaviors of those with whom we communicate, in order to be sensitive to their turn-signaling prerogatives. We might seek to enhance our perceived power, status, and leadership potential by avoiding sustained visual attentiveness to individuals who compete with us for leadership. We recognize the paradox: The prize for sustaining visual attention is often to be unflatteringly characterized as a low-power and low-status individual

There are no absolute principles or truths you can rely on to make the most effective use of your eyes as a medium of communication. However, let me suggest several reasonable guidelines that seem to be soundly based on the eye behavior research I have just discussed.

First, beware of exhibiting eye behaviors that seem to confirm negative cultural stereotypes. Our society has well-developed eye behavior stereotypes both for the evasive and deceptive person and for the weak and submissive person. You are probably as familiar with those stereotypes as I am. You might be the most truthful person in your neighborhood, but if you exhibit shifty eyes and gaze aversion when the truthfulness of your statements is at issue your chances of being perceived as a liar are excellent. Similarly, you may be a person of great personal and moral courage, but if you characteristically exhibit a low visual dominance ratio when interacting with other persons you run a very high risk of being seen as weak and submissive.

Second, you should recognize that any given eye behavior you exhibit is susceptible to multiple interpretations. If most of those possible interpretations are negative, you might wish to suppress or eliminate those eye behaviors. Let us assume that you almost always look away from people when you are greeting them. The individuals with whom you interact may infer, as you hope they will, that you look away because you are so shy. Alternatively, your listeners may come up with other less favorable interpretations for your averted eyes, such as you do not find them interesting or important enough to look at them, something else or someone else in the room is more important, or you simply do not care. In any event, your position is loosely analogous to that of the football coach who has just called a pass play. At best, one good thing can happen to you; at worst, a number of bad things are possible.

Finally, strive to conform to the rules of eye etiquette that are implicit in your social group(s), community, and culture. Keep in mind that if you are multilingual the rules of eye etiquette may change as you move from one language to another. Some rules of eye etiquette are obvious. Do not stare at the erogenous body zones of a stranger unless you relish being branded as a deviant. Do not exhibit obvious visual inattentiveness in the presence of your boss unless you are overwhelmed with the desire to interview for a new job. To determine the rules of etiquette for a given group, you might observe the eye behaviors that members of that group characteristically exhibit. With regard to your own eye behaviors, I am almost tempted to say, "When in Rome do as the Romans do."

Message receivers should exhibit some of the same information-seeking concerns as message senders but, in addition, they must be concerned with the role of their own eye behaviors in providing visual feedback to the message sender. Abele (1986) maintained that monitoring another person's eye behaviors is more important than the message content of the eye behaviors itself. Thus, *feedback* in the forms of eye behavior may be more valuable than *messages* sent via eye behaviors.

Message senders should recognize that their eyes might reveal more about their affective reaction to the message receiver and about their cognitive state than about anything else. Rasicot (1986) maintained, for example, that the direction of a person's eye gaze may reveal from what areas of the brain a person is gaining information. To look up and to the left is thought to indicate that a person is trying to figure out an appropriate response or answer—the part of the brain used in this instance is concerned with visual construction. The look up and to the left might also indicate deception; by contrast, a person who looks up and to the right is merely trying to recall factual information by accessing visual memory.

If perception is, literally and figuratively, in the eye of the beholder, individuals should recognize that their perceptual responses might be most accurately reflected in their own eyes. Their eyes may not mirror their souls, but they will probably mirror the depths and intensity of their innermost feelings.

Summary

The eyes have been a source of fascination for many centuries. Throughout the ages, many cultures have retained a belief in the inspiration of "the divine eye" and in the insidious power of "the evil eye." Even today, the language of the eyes is a powerful form of communication. This language is defined in part by descriptive labels used to identify various types of eye behaviors: eye contact, face-gaze, eye-gaze, mutual gaze, mutual eye contact, gaze avoidance, gaze omission, eye shifts, staring, and blinking.

Because the eyes are the center of visual attention for the decoder, their importance as a source of information is enhanced. Empirical research has established that eye behaviors serve the following communicative functions: (a) the attention function, (b) the persuasive function, (c) the intimacy function, (d) the regulatory function, (e) the affective function, (f) the power function, and (g) the impression management function.

The eyes have great communicative potential. Message senders should be sensitive to the fact that much of the information communicated by their own eyes operates out of their level of awareness and is beyond their conscious ability to control. Thus, our eyes may reveal much highly personal information about us that we would not choose to reveal if we could consciously control all of our eye behaviors.

To make the most effective use of your eyes, you should consider several reasonable guidelines. You should beware of exhibiting eye behaviors that seem to confirm negative cultural stereotypes. You should recognize that any given eye behavior that you exhibit is susceptible to multiple interpretations. Finally, you should strive to conform to the implicit rules of eye etiquette that apply to you and those with whom you interact.

References

Abele, A. (1986). Functions of gaze in social interaction: Communication and monitoring. *Journal of Nonverbal Behavior, 10,* 83–101.

Argyle, M., & Cook, M. (1976). *Gaze and mutual gaze.* Cambridge, MA: Cambridge University Press.

Burgoon, J. K., Coker, D. A., & Coker R. A. (1986). Communicative effects of gaze behavior: A test of two contrasting explanations. *Human Communication Research, 12,* 495–524.

Burgoon, J. K., Manusov, V., Mineo, P., & Hale, J. L. (1985). Effects of gaze on hiring, credibility, attraction, and relational message interpretation. *Journal of Nonverbal Behavior, 9,* 133–146.

Burgoon, J. K., & Saine, T. (1978). *The unspoken dialogue: An introduction to nonverbal communication.* Boston: Houghton.

Cranach, M. von (1971). The role of orienting behavior in human interaction. In A. H. Esser (Ed.), *Behavior and environment: The use of space by animals and men* (pp. 217–237). New York: Plenum Press.

Dovidio, J. F., & Ellyson, S. L. (1985). Patterns of visual dominance behavior in humans. In S. L. Ellyson & J. F. Dovidio (Eds.), *Power, dominance, and nonverbal behavior* (pp. 129–149). New York: Springer-Verlag.

Dovidio, J. F., Ellyson, S. L., Keating, C. F., Heltman, K., & Brown, C. E. (1988). The relationship of social power to visual displays of dominance between men and women. *Journal of Personality & Social Psychology, 54,* 233–242.

Droney, J. M., & Brooks, C. I. (1993). Attributions of self-esteem as a function of duration of eye contact. *Journal of Social Psychology, 133,* 715–722.

Ellsworth, P. C., & Ludwig, L. M. (1971). Visual behavior in social interaction. *Journal of Communication, 22,* 375–403.

Exline, R., & Fehr, B. J. (1982). The assessment of gaze and mutual gaze. In K. R. Scherer & P. Ekman (Eds.), *Handbook of methods in nonverbal behavior research* (pp. 91–135). Cambridge: Cambridge University Press.

Exline, R. V., Ellyson, S. L., & Long, B. (1975). Visual behavior as an aspect of power role relationships. In P. Pliner, L. Krames, & T. Alloway (Eds.), *Nonverbal communication of aggression.* New York: Plenum Press.

Harper, R. G., Wiens, A. N., & Matarazzo, J. D. (1978). *Nonverbal communication: The state of the art.* New York: Wiley.

Henley, N. M. (1977). *Body politics: Power, sex, and nonverbal communication.* Englewood Cliffs, NJ: Prentice-Hall.

Henley, N. M., & Harmon, S. (1985). The nonverbal semantics of power and gender: A perceptual study. In S. L. Ellyson & J. F. Dovidio (Eds.), *Power, dominance, and nonverbal behavior* (pp. 151–164). New York: Springer-Verlag.

Hess, E. H. (1975). *The tell-tale eye: How your eyes reveal hidden thoughts and emotions.* New York: Van Nostrand Reinhold.

Hornik, J. (1987). The effect of touch and gaze upon compliance and interest of interviewees. *Journal of Social Psychology, 12,* 681–683.

Iizuka, Y. (1992a). Evaluation of gaze pairs by female observers. *Japanese Journal of Experimental Social Psychology, 31,* 231–239.

Iizuka, Y. (1992b). Extraversion, introversion, and visual interaction. *Perceptual & Motor Skills, 74,* 43–50.

Iizuka, Y. (1992c). Eye contact in dating couples and unacquainted couples. *Perceptual & Motor Skills, 75,* 457–461.

Janik, S. W., Wellens, A. R., Goldberg, M. L., & DeLosse, L. F. (1978). Eyes as the center of focus in the visual examination of faces. *Perceptual and Motor Skills, 26,* 34–35.

Kalma, A. (1992). Gazing in triads—a powerful signal in floor apportionment. *British Journal of Social Psychology, 31,* 21–39.

Kellerman, J. L., Lewis, J., & Laird, J. D. (1989). Looking and loving: The effects of mutual gaze on feelings of romantic love. *Journal of Research in Personality, 23,* 145–161.

Kendon, A. (1967). Some functions of gaze direction in social interaction. *Acta Psychologica, 26,* 34–35.

Kleinke, C. L. (1986). Gaze and eye contact: A research review. *Psychological Bulletin, 100,* 78–100.

Knackstedt, G., & Kleinke, C. L. (1991). Eye contact, gender, and personality judgments. *Journal of Social Psychology, 131,* 303–304.

Leathers, D. G., & Hocking, J. E. (1982, November). An examination of police interviewer's beliefs about the utility and nature of nonverbal indicators of deception. Paper presented at convention of the Speech Communication Association, Louisville, KY.

Malandro, L. A., Barker, L., & Barker, D. A. (1989). *Nonverbal communication* (2nd ed.). New York: Random House.

Massie, R. K. (1967). *Nicholas and Alexandra.* New York: Laurel.

Metalis, S. A., & Hess, E. H. (1982a). Pupillary response/semantic differential scale relationship. *Journal of Research in Personality, 16,* 201–216.

Metalis, S. A., & Hess, E. H. (1982b). Pupillometric analysis of two theories of obesity. *Perceptual and Motor Skills, 55,* 87–92.

Metalis, S. A., & Hess, E. H. (1986). Pupillometric assessment of the readability of two videoscreen fonts. *Perceptual and Motor Skills, 52,* 279–282.

Mitchell, G., & Maple, T. L. (1985). Dominance in nonhuman primates. In S. L. Ellyson & J. F. Dovidio (Eds.), *Power, dominance and nonverbal behavior* (pp. 49–66). New York: Springer-Verlag.

Rasicot, J. (1986). *Silent Sales.* Minneapolis, MN: AP Publications.

Schlenker, B. R. (1980). *Impression management.* Monterey, CA: Brooks/Cole.

Webbink, P. (1986). *The power of the eyes.* New York: Springer.

Williams, G. P., & Kleinke, C. L. (1993). Effects of mutual gaze and touch on attraction, mood, and cardiovascular reactivity. *Journal of Research in Personality, 27,* 170–183.

Chapter *4*

Kinesics
Bodily Communication

Movement communicates meaning. Although human beings have accepted this general proposition through the ages, they have rarely examined its implications in detail. If movement communicates meaning, it follows that different movements serve different kinds of communicative functions by communicating different kinds of meanings. Some of the meanings communicated by bodily cues help us attain specific communicative objectives, and other movements communicate highly dysfunctional meanings.

Certain bodily movements do create lasting impressions. Think of the number of friends or acquaintances you remember because of the way they move or use movement to communicate. My own memories are filled with individuals who moved in distinctive ways. Two stand out in particular: Old swivel-hips Becker, the local elevator man, is probably still shuffling down the streets of my hometown and moving with the awkward but fluid grace that suggested that his hip joints had not been greased recently. One college professor also stands out because his incredibly deliberate gestures drew attention to pauses of remarkable length in his speech. The gestures and pauses convinced the students that he was terribly profound.

The efforts of rock stars to mould their own images and manipulate their audiences begin and end with their bodily communication. The same bodily movements by the same rock star may of course be perceived quite differently by fans and disinterested observers. Thus, the dancing of some rock stars may seem distinctive to the initiated and weird to the uninitiated. One individual may be turned on at the thought of Ozzie Osbourne eating a bat on stage, whereas another person may be repulsed by the same thought. You might stand in line to see the Grateful Dead, but your friend would not walk across the street to see them. You might find the sexually explicit movements of the 2 Live Crew titillating, even though police in more than one major metropolitan area found them sufficiently obscene to justify arrest. Whatever your personal response to the bodily communication of the rock stars and rock groups just identified, however, you will probably agree that their bodily communication serves at minimum to gain attention and to elicit strong emotional responses.

These examples focus attention on the functional importance of the gestures and postures that make up bodily communication. Thus, Collier (1985) wrote:

These [bodily] cues provide information about the people speaking, their attitude toward what they are saying, and their relationship to those being addressed. When we meet people for the first time, we form an immediate impression about their character and their current emotional state. Without thinking, we take into account numerous minute details about how they stand, move, and position themselves. (p. 45)

Gesture and speech communication are quite different in a number of respects (Marschark, 1994). First, gesture is a communicative medium that employs space and time, whereas speech uses only time. When the spatial dimension of communication is missing, misunderstanding often results. Let us assume, for example, that you are in England and have just asked an English citizen "Have you seen the Sunday *New York Times*?" Your intended meaning (that the Sunday *New York Times* is a very large/thick newspaper when compared with the Sunday *London Times*) would most likely be unclear. However, if you placed your two hands forward with your palms facing each other and put them tight together (depicting a thick oblong object), the English citizen would understand instantly that Sunday newspapers in the United States are much thicker than in England (Kendon, 1986).

In addition, gestures are defined by that fact that they may be used to disambiguate ambiguous words, to describe action sequences more efficiently than words, and as a more discreet substitute for words in situations where words would be offensive (Kendon, 1986). If, for example, you told a friend that "you just got done using your Mitsubishi," the friend might not know whether you were referring to you car or to your big-screen TV; but by pretending to be driving a car with your hands, you would clarify your meaning immediately. Secondly, individuals such as dance instructors often use gestures rather than words to represent desired movement patterns more efficiently. Finally, you may not be able to tell an inebriated guest at your party that it is time for you to drive him or her home, but you can communicate the same meaning delicately by your gestures. A subtle, beckoning gesture of the index finger should suffice.

Hewes (1992) has argued that human language had its basis in hand and arm gestures rather than vice versa. Thus, bodily communication in the form of a preexisting gestural language seems to have provided the basis for the subsequent development of spoken languages. This theory in turn is based on extensive study of the early use of tools and the actions of primates.

Significantly, gestural communication not only predates verbal communication in a historical sense. Streeck (1993) contends that gestures frequently come before speech when two or more people interact. Gestures thus serve the function of "framing" an interaction that is about to start. Streeck writes that

while there seems to be a parallelism between the delivery of speech and gestures, gestures in fact more often than not precede the units of talk to which they are semantically or otherwise tied. . . . Thus, the stroke of the gesture (the gesture's "accent") often falls on the last accented syllable prior to the 'speech-affiliate'. . . . In other words, while gestures and speech are synchronized at the level of form they are organized into co-extensive units among others things, their semantic position vis-a-vis one another is more properly described as 'syncopation': the words as a rule come only as the gesture is about to decay (the word 'closes the gestalt'). (1993, p. 280)

We know that bodily movements assume important roles in successful interpersonal communication. They often are strong determinants of how likable, assertive, and powerful we are judged to be, for example. Nonetheless, most research efforts have been designed to identify bodily movements that are normative rather than specifying which kinds of bodily cues can be used to attain specific communicative objectives. This chapter deviates from conventional practices. We shall specific not only how various bodily cues are typically used and what major communicative functions they serve, but also how bodily cues should be used. In the past, little effort has been devoted to sensitizing individuals to the functional and dysfunctional uses of bodily cues.

The contrast between nonverbal communication and written communication is striking. Students in writing classes spend many hours trying to improve their ability to transmit their meanings clearly. Similarly, law students spend hours trying to determine the exact meaning of laws or court decisions on pornography, integration, or pollution in order to increase their capacity to encode and decode written messages.

The following example should help make the point: We have studied communication by oral and written discourse intensively, and we assume that we will improve those communication skills by practice. In contrast, we have not expended comparable energy to distinguish between the functional and dysfunctional uses of bodily cues, or to develop our sensitivity to bodily cues. Consequently, this chapter focuses on useful perspectives for conceptualizing different kinds of bodily cues, the major communicative functions they serve, and their functional and dysfunctional uses.

The need to know more about the meanings of bodily movements has resulted in a body of research called *kinesics*. Kinesics is the study of observable, isolable, and meaningful movement in interpersonal communication. Birdwhistell (1970) wrote that "kinesics is concerned with abstracting from the continuous muscular shifts which are characteristic of living physiological systems those groupings of movements which are of significance to the communication process and thus to the interactional systems of particular groups" (p. 192).

Kinesic research begins with the *kine,* the smallest identifiable unit of motion, and emphasizes the *kinemorph,* that combination of kines in any part of the body which conveys a given meaning. Thus, "droopy-lidded" eyelids combined with "bilaterally raised median" brows have an obviously different meaning from "droopy-lidded" combined with a "low unilateral brow lift," (Birdwhistell, 1960). The combination of very specific movement of the eyelids and brow into one larger unit, the kinemorph, conveys a meaning that is consistently recognized in our culture.

Movements that convey meaning are hardly limited to the brows. Many parts of the body convey meanings singly and in combination. In the strictest anatomical sense, the sources of movement in the human body are almost unlimited. From a more practical perspective, Birdwhistell (1952) identifies eight sources of potentially significant bodily movement: (a) total head, (b) face, (c) neck, (d) trunk, (e) shoulder–arm–wrist, (f) hand, (g) hip joint–leg–ankle, and (h) foot.

Most basically, movement consists of the displacement of body parts in space and time. Rosenfeld (1982) provides useful descriptions of body part taxonomies, spatial frames of reference, and temporal frames of reference. As we shall see, some areas of the body have greater functional significance than others. Hand movements are more important than foot movements, for example, in part because of their visibility; the importance of hand movements is also accentuated by the fact that the relatively large area of the brain that is concerned with hand movements is much larger than the parts of the brain that are associated with other types of bodily movements. At the same time, we should recognize that hand movements may be a less reliable source of information than foot movements because they are more frequently subject to conscious control for purposes of deception.

In our society, the communicative significance of the hands is not confined to the ways we use them. "Handedness" is also very important because assumptions commonly made about right-handers and left-handers are quite different. This is a subject of more than passing interest to me because my son, Greg, eats, writes, and bats left-handed but throws, kicks balls, fishes, and plays the trombone right-handed. Is he right-handed or left-handed?

Lee and Charlton (1980) have developed an instructive but amusing test to determine what type of handedness is dominant for a given individual. Among the tasks they use to determine handedness are the following:

1. When you draw the profile of a dog or a horse, which way is it facing?
2. Imagine that you are locked in a room and tied with your hands behind you to a chair. Which foot will you use to try to pull the phone closer?
3. On which side do you chew your food?
4. When you applaud a performer, which hand is on top?

Left-handers will draw the profile of a dog or a horse with the head facing to the right; reach out for the phone with their left foot; chew on the left side of their mouth; and clap with their dominant left hand on top, into the palm of their right hand. Everything is reversed for right-handers.

The Nature of Bodily Cues

Much like facial expressions, bodily cues have been conceptualized as both categorical and dimensional in nature. The categorical perspective is based on the assumption that bodily cues are best understood by classifying them with regard to: (a) the *level of awareness* and *intentionality* with which they are used; (b) the type of *coding* employed; and (c) the *communicative function* served. By contrast, the dimensional perspective is based on the assumption that bodily cues are best described by rating them on scales that represent the dimensions of meaning communicated by the bodily cues. The theory and research of Paul Ekman and associates best illustrate the categorical perspective, whereas the dimensional perspective is most closely associated with the work of Albert Mehrabian.

Classification of Bodily Cues

Ekman and Friesen (1969) developed what is probably the most frequently cited conceptual framework for classifying bodily cues. They emphasized that bodily cues vary not only with regard to their *usage* and the *code* employed but with regard to the *functions* they serve.

The way a bodily cue is used is significant because it involves two questions of particular importance: (a) Was the communicator aware of exhibiting a specific kind of bodily cue? and (b) Was the bodily cue used with conscious intent to communicate a particular kind of information? Communicators who are aware that they are exhibiting certain bodily cues have the capacity to exert conscious control over those types of cues.

This capacity is a necessary, but not a sufficient, condition for individuals who wish to be successful as impression managers. Do you remember Iraqi President Saddam Hussein patting the heads of the young hostages? Impression management tactics such as these did not work well with the American television audience. Those movements were quite different from the movements he reportedly used when he personally assassinated Iraqi soldiers who refused to invade Kuwait. The gestural communication with his young hostages was designed to combat the negative image that resulted from his assassination of his own soldiers.

Similarly, the individual who does not wish to be perceived as deceiving and untrustworthy must take pains to eliminate or minimize the shifty eye behaviors, hand-to-face gestures, and nonfluencies that are part of the cultural stereotype for the deceiver. Determining whether bodily cues of the sender are used without awareness and intentionality is extremely important for message receivers. This is so because bodily cues of this type are apt to reveal much about the sender's attitudes, feelings, and level of self-esteem that he or she may not wish to reveal.

The coding of bodily cues is also extremely important because the type of code determines the relationships between the bodily cue and that which it signifies (Ekman & Friesen, 1969). Nonverbal messages in the form of bodily cues may use *arbitrary, iconic,* or *intrinsic codes.* Although arbitrary coding is much more frequently used in verbal than in nonverbal communication, some bodily messages use an arbitrary code. The hand raised in greetings and departures is an example of arbitrary coding because the raised hand is not directly related to that which it signifies.

Bodily cues that are iconically coded carry some clue to their meaning because of their appearance. A person's finger running under his or her throat is using iconic coding, because the figurative and literal acts of throat cutting bear a resemblance to each other. Finally, acts that are intrinsically coded are visually related to the message they signify. Angry individuals who tremble, turn red in the face, and shake their fist use intrinsic coding because the symbolic meaning and physical manifestations of anger are inseparable.

Individuals who wish to refine their skill in decoding bodily cues must be sensitive to the type of code employed. Certain kinds of bodily cues frequently combine more than one type of coding. For example, confident individuals who are receptive to the ideas of those with whom they communicate frequently exhibit "open" gestures and postures, by way of uncrossed arms and legs. Such bodily cues combine elements of both arbitrary and iconic coding, which make it easier to determine their meaning. Even those bodily cues that are coded exclusively via the arbitrary code are susceptible to accurate decoding when a *set* of bodily cues (such as downcast eyes and hand-to-face gestures) and an indirect bodily orientation is consistently associated with an inferred psychological state such as a decreasing level of self-confidence.

Bodily cues are perhaps most clearly defined and differentiated by the functions they serve. We will highlight all of the major communicative functions of bodily cues in a separate section of this chapter. The five categories of nonverbal behavior identified by Ekman and Friesen (1969) are particularly useful in describing the different kinds of bodily cues that provide different information and meanings: *emblems, illustrators, affect displays, regulators,* and *adapters.*

Emblems

Emblems are bodily cues that have a direct verbal translation, consisting of a word or two, and that have a precise meaning that is known by most of the members of a given culture. They are used with the conscious intention of communicating a particular message. The receiver recognizes that the message was deliberately encoded, and the message sender takes direct responsibility for the message (Ekman & Friesen, 1972).

Most middle-class Americans have command of about a hundred gestural emblems. Gestural emblems are used to communicate interpersonal directions or commands ("Come here"), information about one's own physical state ("I've got a toothache"), insults ("Shame on you"), replies ("Okay"), and greetings and departures ("Good-bye" and "Hello"), among other things (Johnson, Ekman, & Friesen, 1975).

Emblems are used most frequently where speech communication is not possible because of noise or distance barriers. When a substantial number of emblems are organized in a form that might almost be called an emblematic language, we have a *gesture system.* Specialized gesture systems are used by grain merchants, individuals who work the floor of the stock exchange in New York City, airline employees who direct the big jets to their respective gates at airports, truck drivers, hitchhikers, directors of television shows, and baseball umpires (Argyle, 1988; Kendon, 1984).

The term *sign language* refers to highly developed gestural systems that include the primary sign languages of the deaf and alternate sign languages used by groups such as the Aborigines of Australia, the Trappist monks in Europe, and the women of Australia (Kendon, 1984). These examples of sign language systems draw attention to an important fact. Emblems serve as substitutes for words. Emblems by their very nature are the most easily understood class of nonverbal cues. *Perhaps because emblems are used so much more intentionally than other nonverbal behaviors, they are apt to provide little personal information about the person who uses them.*

As we shall see when we discuss the cross-cultural aspects of nonverbal communication, many emblems carry culture-specific meaning. For example, the "chin flick" is a gestural emblem used in Italy, France, and other parts of Europe to indicate annoyance and a desire for the offending person to "bug off," but it has no generally recognized meaning in England and the United States (Lee & Charlton, 1980).

Illustrators

Illustrators are like emblems in that they are used with awareness and intentionality. Illustrator gestures may be used to augment what is being said and to reinforce or deintensify the perceived strength of emotions being experienced by the communicator. Illustrators include *batons, diectic movements, rhythmic movements,* and *pictographs.* Batons are movements that accent or emphasize a particular word or phrase, and diectic movements point to an object, place, or event. Rhythmic movements suggest the rhythm of an event being described, and pictographs draw a picture in the air of the shape of the referent.

Illustrators are typically used to increase the clarity of verbal expressions. The desire for clarity seems to be greater in face-to-face interaction. Thus, the initial portions of a narrative are accompanied by a higher rate of illustrator gestures; the objective here is to establish clarity of communication as one begins a narrative (Levy & McNeill, 1992). Similarly, Cohen (1977) found that subjects giving directions on how to get from one place to another used significantly more hand illustrators in a face-to-face situation than when giving directions over an intercom. Finally, Goldin-Meadow, Wein, and Chang (1992) reported that the reasoning of children who use illustrator gestures as a co-occurring phenomenon with their speech is easier to comprehend than the reasoning of children who do not use illustrator gestures.

Illustrators also can give emphasis to the message being communicated. Movements of the arms/hands and of the head are used most frequently to emphasize a message. Although no single type of gesture seems to be of overriding importance for giving emphasis, the outstretched arm with the pointing index finger and the double head nod are frequently used for purposes of emphasis (Bull & Connelly, 1985).

Illustrators facilitate effective communication for a number of reasons. Visual information may logically be communicated most easily by visual means, some illustrator gestures are like representative pictures in that they at least partially represent the visual appearance of an object or even a person, and illustrators serve to punctuate conversation by providing intensity cues (Bull & Connelly, 1985).

Although illustrators are used with a fairly high level of awareness and intentionality, they can provide valuable information about a communicator's mood, self-confidence, and power in a given situation. They also accurately reflect the difficulty the communicator is experiencing in communicating clearly by verbal means. Ekman and Friesen (1972) wrote:

> *Changes in the frequency of illustrator activity in any given individual depend upon mood and problems in verbal communication. When a person is demoralized, discouraged, tired, unenthusiastic, concerned about the other person's impression, or in a nondominant position in a formal interaction and setting, the rate of illustrators is less than is usual for that person. . . . When difficulty is experienced in finding the right words, or when feedback from the listener suggests he is not comprehending what is being said, illustrators increase.* (p. 359)

Finally, we know that a drop in the number or rate of illustrator gestures exhibited by a communicator can be an indication of deception (Ekman, 1985).

Clearly, gestural illustrators serve a number of useful communicative functions. Their chief function, however, is probably to aid the listener in the comprehension of the spoken word. Rogers (1978) found that gestural illustrators can result in a significant increase in comprehension of the spoken word, even in the absence of facial cues. Gestural illustrators are increasingly useful as noise is introduced, and their value as aids to comprehending the meaning of the spoken word increases as the ideational content of the spoken message becomes more complex.

Affects Displays

The communication of affect displays or emotions is much more closely linked with facial expressions than with bodily cues. As we have already indicated, the face is the primary site for the display of emotions. The communication receiver would be well advised, therefore, to *look to the face to determine the kind of emotion the communicator is experiencing and rely on bodily cues to determine the intensity of the emotion being experienced.*

Posture seems to be more important in communicating emotion than gestures. We know, for example, that a strong expression of contempt is associated with a clearly discernible head tilt. A stiff or even frozen bodily posture may be taken as a sign of fear, acute anxiety, or, if exhibited over long periods of time, as indicative of mental illness. The frequency or infrequency of bodily movements seems to be a much more reliable indicator of general emotional arousal (or lack of it) than an indicator that the communicator is experiencing a specific emotion (Collier, 1985). As we shall see, it is typically difficult and unrewarding to communicate with individuals who show a lack of affect or feeling.

Affect displays are used with less awareness and intentionality than either emblems or illustrators. As a result, they are apt to provide some personal information about the communicator that the individual would be reluctant to disclose voluntarily. Anyone who observed John Dean's testimony during the Watergate hearings will agree that a relative absence of bodily movement and facial expression makes it very difficult to determine what emotions the communicator is experiencing.

Regulators

Regulators are bodily cues used by interactants to exercise a mutual influence over the initiation, length, and termination of spoken messages. Regulators usually seem to be used with a low level of awareness and intentionality. But it is vitally important that interactants be sensitive to each other's turn-taking prerogatives. A lack of sensitivity in the use of regulators is likely to be attributed to rudeness or unmannerliness (Ekman & Friesen, 1969).

Knapp (1978) has developed a particularly useful classification of turn-taking behaviors. He notes that speakers use *turn-yielding* and *turn-maintaining* cues, and listeners use *turn-requesting* and *turn-denying* cues. Examples of turn-yielding cues are the cessation of illustrator gestures and a relaxed bodily posture. Turn-maintaining cues are manifested when we sustain our illustrator activity or touch the other person to indicate we wish to continue. For the listener, an upraised index finger and rapid head nodding represent particularly effective turn-requesting cues. Finally, when we do not wish to make a comment, we may use such turn-denying cues as a relaxed listening pose, or we may stare at something in the surrounding environment.

Regulators assume more importance when we greet other individuals and bid them farewell because greetings and farewells are such important determinants of successful interpersonal relationships. The individual who is successful in initiating and developing interpersonal interactions with others must rely heavily on the proper use of nonverbal cues.

Bull (1983) gave us a more detailed treatment of how bodily cues should be used in conversational management. He noted that effective conversational management requires appropriate use of and response to turn-yielding cues, attempt-suppressing signals, back channels, within-turn-signals, and speaker-state signals. Back-channel cues such as "uh-huh," "yeah," "right," and head nods are certainly important in conversational management because they indicate to the speaker the level of the listener's attentiveness at any given point during the conversation.

A study by Krivonos and Knapp (1975) suggests that acknowledging the other person's presence with a *head gesture,* indicating a desire to initiate communication with *mutual glances,* and suggesting with a *smile* that you anticipate a pleasurable experience are the most important nonverbal cues used in successful greetings. In contrast, *eyebrow flashes,* a sweeping hand gesture in the form of a *salute,* an *open mouth,* and *winking* are nonverbal behaviors which should be avoided. These nonverbal cues are not used in the successful greeting; they deviate markedly from what has been found to be normative behavior in this kind of communicative situation.

An insightful study by Knapp, Hart, and Friedrich (1973) established leave-taking norms which formed the basis for identifying nonverbal behaviors that were both "proper" and "improper" for guiding, controlling, or regulating departures in communication situations that were rather task oriented. The study suggested that (a) *breaking eye contact,* (b) *left-positioning* (pointing your legs or feet away from the person with whom you are communicating and toward the door), (c) *forward leaning,* and (d) *nodding behavior* all represent socially acceptable means of initiating the leave-taking step that is a central part of farewells. In contrast, the following were found to be inappropriate nonverbal means of initiating a farewell: (a) *leveraging* (placing hands on knees or legs in such a manner as to suggest a desire to rise from your chair); (b) *major trunk movements* (postural shifts in your chair, straightening up, and standing up); (c) *explosive hand contact* with some part of your body; and (d) a *handshake.*

Reflection on the nonverbal behaviors associated with successful, as opposed to unsuccessful, greetings and farewells suggest that subtlety and restraint in movement are particularly desirable. Sweeping hand gestures, winking, and gross postural shifts, for example, are such explicit and manipulative forms of behavior that they are apt to be associated with social insensitivity. To consistently use such nonverbal behaviors in greetings and farewells is to invite the influence that you are rude and tactless.

Adaptors

As a potential source of information about an individual's attitudes, anxiety level, and self-confidence, bodily cues in the form of adaptors are apt to be more useful than emblems, illustrators, affect displays, or regulators. Communicators who exhibit adaptors do not use them with the intent to communicate, and they are usually unaware that they are using them. As a result, *adapters are a potentially rich source of involuntary information about the psychological states of individuals who exhibit them.*

In their original form, adaptors were learned adaptive actions used to satisfy bodily needs. The itch was scratched, the unruly hair was groomed, or the tears were wiped away from the eyes (Ekman & Friesen, 1969). Through socialization, the form of many adaptors has been changed, and they have become more important. Currently, their importance is based on what they may reveal about communicators' psychological rather than physiological needs.

Nespoulous and Lecours (1986) use the label "extracommunicative gestures" as a synonym for adaptor gestures. They include bodily movements reflective of degree of comfort/discomfort, autistic gestures (finger tapping, nail biting, etc), and manipulations (smoking a cigarette or playing with it) as subcategories of extracommunicative gestures. The term *extracommunicative gestures* seems to be a singularly inappropriate label for adaptor gestures, however, because they communicate more valuable, personal information about interacting communicators than any other type of gesture.

The two most important kinds of adaptors are *self-adaptors* and *object-adaptors*. Self-adaptors that involve hand-to-face movements are the easiest to decode because of the symbolic significance of the face. For people in the United States, the face symbolizes the self. As a result, hand-to-face gestures are apt to provide reliable information about a person's current level of self-esteem and self-confidence. Ekman and Friesen (1969) wrote that when

> *a person touches his face, the action can be conceived in terms of what the person has had done to him, what he wants done to him, or what he is doing to himself. Activities such as picking or scratching may be forms of attacking the self; holding may be giving nurture or support; rubbing or massaging may be caress or reassurance.* (p. 87)

Whenever a communicator covers his or her eyes with one hand, listeners will usually conclude that the communicator finds the content of the communication unpleasant and wishes to prevent further sensory input of the same sort.

Object-adaptors, as the term implies, refer to the use of the hands to touch or hold objects in one's immediate environment. One study (Sousa-Poza & Rohrberg, 1977) has suggested that object-adaptors are used less frequently to reflect uncertainty on the part of the encoder than are self-adapters. As we shall see in our treatment of the use of nonverbal cues to detect deception, however, police interviewers report that, at the moment of deception, lying criminal suspects frequently play with objects in the interview room.

A later chapter of this book will examine the implications of gestural adaptors for impression management. We know that a variety of bodily messages are interpreted negatively by decoders (Manusov, 1990). More specifically, we know that many gestural adapters (both self- and object-) are interpreted as signs of anxiety or discomfort. Interestingly, results from a recent study by Goldberg and Rosenthal (1986) indicated that job interviewees touch their hair and their upper torso/neck more than job interviewers and that female job interviewees exhibited more gestural adapters of those types than male job interviewees. In a positive sense, the female interviewees' more frequent self-touching might simply be dismissed as a preening action designed to accentuate their femininity. The more likely interpretation, however, is that female job interviewees exhibited more gestural adapters than their male counterparts because they felt more nervous and less secure.

We now have one operational definition of gestural adaptor activity in the form of an instrument designed to measure fidgeting. Mehrabian and Friedman (1986) define fidgeting as "engaging in manipulations of one's own body parts or other objects with such actions being peripheral or nonessential to central or focal ongoing events or tasks" (p. 425).

Their 40-item fidgeting questionnaire asks respondents to choose a number on a 9-point scale, with numbers indicating response options from very strong agreement to very strong disagreement. Sample items include "I frequently rub my neck," "I hardly ever rub my scalp," "I don't fondle or play with my clothes," and "I don't tap or drum on things."

Factor analysis indicates that the fidgeting measure is composed of the two dimensions of localized self-stimulation, or self-manipulation and object manipulation. Importantly, a high level of fidgeting is suggestive of both anxiety and hyperactivity, and fidgeting seems to be an indicator of such psychological states as discomfort, tension, frustration, and irritation.

Dimensions of Meaning

The categorical approach to bodily cues assumes that the meanings we communicate and the information we convey are best understood by classifying bodily cues as to usage, coding, and function. In contrast, the dimensional approach to bodily cues assumes that bodily cues can best be described by three independent dimensions of meaning, labeled by Mehrabian (1981) as *pleasure–displeasure, arousal–nonarousal,* and *dominance–submissiveness.* Any bodily cue or nonverbal act can be measured by separate sets of scales that reflect the degree of pleasure, arousal, and dominance communicated by the nonverbal cue. Thus, pleasure is measured by scales labeled with bipolar adjectives such as "pleasant–unpleasant" and "satisfied–unsatisfied." Similarly, scales used to measure degree of arousal and dominance, respectively, would be "excited–calm" and "assertive–unassertive," and "controlling–controlled" and "dominant–submissive." The communicator's attitudes and the emotional tone of his or her nonverbal messages are thought to be accurately reflected by ratings on scales representing each of these three independent dimensions of meaning.

In nonverbal or implicit communication, three metaphors are used to describe the distinct types of meaning represented by the dimensions of pleasure, arousal, and dominance: (a) *the approach metaphor,* (b) *the arousal-activity metaphor,* and (c) *the power metaphor.* Proponents of the dimensional perspective believe that these metaphors suggest the full range of meanings that can be communicated by nonverbal means.

Nonverbal researchers do not, however, use the metaphor terminology. Instead they have modified Mehrabian's language in such a way as to focus on the three dimensions of meaning communicated clearly and forcefully by bodily communication: (a) *like–dislike,* (b) *assertiveness–unassertiveness,* and (c) *power–powerlessness.*

In his fascinating treatment of this subject, Collier (1985) indicated that people who like each other communicate different types of bodily messages than those who dislike each other. People approach, get more involved with, and exhibit more immediacy behaviors in the presence of individuals they like. Similarly, individuals who like each other stand closer together, assuming the most direct bodily orientation possible while making themselves accessible to the person with whom they are interacting. Because there are a limited number of socially acceptable ways to verbally express strong feelings of pleasure and displeasure, nonverbal communication becomes the primary medium for the expression of this dimension of meaning.

Although the nonverbal assertiveness behaviors do not represent a perfect operationalization of the arousal metaphor, they represent the essence of the idea. Assertiveness behaviors tend to reflect via overt expression the intensity or strength of a communicator's feelings and attitudes and, perhaps more importantly, they frequently serve as accurate indicators of a communicator's current level of self-confidence. Confidence in turn is reflected in messages in which verbal and nonverbal components are consistent, the strength of feelings is communicated directly rather than masked, and attentiveness and interest are accurately expressed.

Finally, communicators get high ratings on the power dimension if their bodies are relaxed, they are relatively uninhibited in their movements, and they exhibit postures that are both open and relatively expansive. In fact, knowledge of the three major dimensions of meaning communicated by bodily communication—likability, assertiveness, and power—can help you make more effective use of this type of nonverbal communication. In the concluding section of this chapter, what you should and should not do if you wish to be perceived as more likable, assertive, and powerful is addressed in the form of three sets of behavioral indicators.

Gestures versus Postures

In discussing the two perspectives used to describe nonverbal behaviors, we have not differentiated between gestures and postures. A number of definitional benchmarks can be used to differentiate between the two basic types of bodily cues. We may, of course, communicate with our entire body or only with some part of it. Thus, Lamb (1965) defined a gesture as an action confined to a part or parts of the body, and posture as an action involving a continuous adjustment of every part of the body, with consistency, in the process of variation.

The amount of bodily involvement in communication is not the only basis for distinguishing between gestures and posture, however. The amount of time used in communicating is also an important factor. Usually, an individual moves quickly from one gesture to another but maintains a given posture for a much longer period of time. The second or split second is the unit of time for gestures. In contrast, individuals often assume a given posture for a matter of several seconds and sometimes several minutes.

Scheflen's penetrating research on bodily communication (1964) helps clarify the relationship between gesture and posture. He maintained that the three basic units of bodily movement are the *point,* the *position,* and the *presentation.* The point is the nonverbal equivalent of an individual's trying to make a point in discussion. While trying to make the point,

> an American speaker uses a series of distinctive sentences in a conversation, he changes the position of his head and eyes every few sentences. He may turn his head right or left, tilt it, cock it to one side or the other, or flex or extend his neck so as to look toward the floor or ceiling. (p. 321)

Because one part of the body is usually involved for a short time, the point may be seen as a gesture.

In contrast, when several points or gestures are combined, we have the position. The position is marked by a gross postural shift involving at least half the body. A typical position is assumed by the discussant who leans toward the person on the opposite side of the conference table.

Finally, the presentation "consists of the totality of one person's positions in a given interaction. Presentations have a duration from several minutes to several hours, and the terminals are a complete change of location" (Scheflen, 1964, p. 323).

Kendon (1986) used the term *gesticulation* to refer to those situations where one or more of our bodily movements are interacting with our verbal utterances. Communication of maximum clarity and forcefulness requires a "synchrony" in the kinds and intensity of meanings communicated verbally, bodily, and vocally. In order to understand the role of gesture in synchronized communication, Kendon said that we must understand the meaning of a *gesture phrase* as a nucleus of movement having some definite form which is preceded by a preparatory movement and succeeded by a movement that either moves a limb back to a rest position or repositions it for the beginning of a new gesture phrase.

With regard to the synchrony of gestures, words, and vocal cues, Kendon (1986) wrote that "there is a close fit between the phrasal organization of gesticulation and the phrasal organization of the speech. . . .The association between Gesture Phrases and Tone Units arises because Gesture Phrases, like Tone Units, mark successive units of meaning" (p. 34). The implication for persons who wish to be successful communicators is clear: We must strive to synchronize the channels through which we communicate in terms of rhythm, phrasing, and, ultimately, meaning.

Rather than three units of bodily communication, Ekman and Friesen (1967) identified two—*body acts* and *body positions.* Body acts are readily observable movements, with a definite beginning and end, which could occur in any part of the body or across multiple body parts simultaneously. Body positions are identified by a lack of movement for a discernible period of time—two seconds or more—with any body part. Scheflen (1964) and Ekman and Friesen (1967) defined the position as a fixed configuration of the parts of the body; therefore, the position might be properly identified as postural communication. Gestural communication is more properly associated with the point (Scheflen's term) and the body act (Ekman and Friesen's term), because both concepts involve movements of one or more parts of the body, with rapid changes to other movements.

Postures by definition represent a more limited medium of communication than gestures. Because they are more limited in number than gestures, they are probably most effectively used to communicate such general attitudes as one's desire to increase, limit, or avoid interaction with another individual; a positive or negative reaction to someone; current level of self-confidence; and the general presentation of self. In addition to their impact on perceptions of presumed status and power, the number and kinds of postures accurately reflect a person's power and degree of responsiveness to another person, as well as the strength of a desire to establish a closer or more immediate relationship with another person.

The film *An Officer and a Gentleman* provides instructive examples of the communicative functions of postures. To watch Lou Gossett, Jr. playing the drill sergeant, is to realize that his "command presence" and "command look" were communicated forcefully by his postures. His words served merely to reinforce the emotional intensity of his commands, which were communicated by his postures.

Scheflen has provided a particularly satisfying answer to the most basic question that might be asked about postures: What meanings can be communicated by variation in posture, when communicators can choose freely from their postural repertoire? Scheflen (1964) identified three basic types of postures, which convey distinctive meanings. In the Type 1 postural orientation, an individual communicates inclusiveness or noninclusiveness. When your body is placed in such a way as to exclude another person, you are clearly communicating your intent to limit or avoid interaction with that individual. In the Type 2 postural orientation, the individual may assume the vis-à-vis or parallel bodily orientation. The vis-à-vis orientation is associated with the exchange of rather intimate feelings, and the parallel bodily orientation conveys a desire to communicate with the entire group rather than with any individual in it. Finally, with the Type 3 postural orientation, the individual assumes a congruent or incongruent posture. When you assume a posture similar to that of the person with whom you are communicating, you are probably suggesting that you agree with the individual and that the person is your equal in status. Postural mirroring—that is, assuming the same posture as your interaction partner—also facilitates cooperation (LaFrance, 1985). Hence, through postural orientation the individual may communicate involvement or withdrawal, feeling or unresponsiveness, and agreement or disagreement.

In the final section of this chapter, we will identify both functional and dysfunctional kinds of gestures and postures. The difficulty of this task is highlighted by Lee and Charlton's (1980) tongue-in-cheek guidelines specifying nonverbal behaviors that should not be exhibited in public. Among other things, they warn against sticking a finger or a hand into an orifice—especially someone else's. They stress that one should not diddle, fiddle, or twiddle in public. Flossing your teeth, pecking a forefinger on someone's shoulder, playing a drum solo on your teeth with a pencil, grooming your fingernails, or cracking your knuckles are also viewed as equally egregious types of nonverbal behavior that should not be displayed in public.

Major Communicative Functions of Bodily Cues

The chapter's emphasis to this point has been on defining the types of gestures and postures that are important in interpersonal communication. Although a good deal of information on the communicative functions of bodily cues has already been presented, these functions are so important that they deserve to be treated in a separate section of this chapter also.

Chapter 2 featured the face as the major medium for the communication of emotions. Chapter 3 stressed that the language of the eyes serve many communicative functions of which the attention, intimacy, and persuasive functions stand out. We would be speaking metaphorically if we said that the eyes are the windows of the soul. In contrast, we would be speaking literally if we said that our bodily cues—gestures and postures—serve as an accurate barometer to many of our internal, psychological states. All four major communicative functions served by our bodily cues are in fact based on the assumption that changes in the internal states of our body are in turn reflected in communicatively significant movements in the form of our gestures and postures.

Bodily cues do of course serve many communicative functions. These functions include *framing* communicative interaction and helping synchronize it. Gestures in particular are integrally tied to the speech process; therefore, gestures function with speech to communicate ideas of great complexity. Finally, we know that our bodily communication may reveal how we feel about ourselves (Streeck, 1993). Although important, the functions of bodily communication just cited are of secondary importance.

Our bodily cues serve at least four major communicative functions. They communicate (a) attitudinal information; (b) highly personal information about a communicator's psychological state(s); (c) the intensity of emotions being experienced; and (d) relational information.

Gestures and postures surely help to reflect how we are predisposed to react to subjects and issues we encounter in our interpersonal interactions with others. These bodily cues typically reveal much more, however, about our attitude toward the person(s) with whom we interact and our attitudes toward self. The kinds of bodily cues that communicate particular attitudes have already been identified in this chapter. We should recognize too that certain gestures and postures may reflect how we feel about ourselves at a given point in time. Thus, communicators who exhibit closed postures experience an increase in unpleasant emotions (Rossberg-Gempton, 1993).

Undeniably, bodily cues provide rather precise information about our psychological states. They accurately indicate not only whether we are confident but how confident we are. They often reveal whether and when we are being deceptive. They also reveal negatively toned psychological states, which range from frustration to discomfort to anxiety and ultimately to fear. Although a rigid posture frequently suggests anxiety, adaptor gestures in the form of self-adapters and object-adapters tend to pinpoint more accurately the nature of a given psychological state we may be experiencing.

The face most accurately communicates particular types of emotions, but it is our bodily cues that indicate what our general level of emotional arousal is and how intensely we feel the emotion we may be displaying facially. Needless to say, intensity cues are vitally important if we are to respond in an appropriate way to the emotions displayed by our interaction partners.

Finally, our bodily cues serve a major relational function. This point is obvious when we realize that our gestures and postures are central determinants of how likable, assertive, powerful, or dominant we are perceived to be. Thus, our chances of experiencing many unsatisfying interpersonal relationships are excellent unless we familiarize ourselves with the relational functions of our gestures and postures.

The functions just identified are not the only communicative functions of bodily cues. In fact, we have already written about the importance of hand gestures, for example, in conversational management. Because the face, eyes, and vocal cues are also important in conversational management, however, the regulatory function of bodily cues seems to be less important than the functions already identified. Gestural emblems in the form of the sign language used by the deaf are also important to a specialized audience. Finally, the roles of bodily cues in indirect suggestion and in gaining attention are not inconsequential ones but simply of less importance than the major functions.

Functional and Dysfunctional Uses of Bodily Cues

Bodily cues can communicate meanings and information that are both functional and dysfunctional from the perspective of the communicator. Also, as stated earlier, such cues frequently play a central role in determining how likely another person is to perceive the communicator as confident, likable, assertive, or powerful. Although it is difficult to generalize about bodily cues, certain types of cues typically have a much more positive impact than other cues on the perceptions, attitudes, and behaviors of those with whom we communicate.

In this section, we will identify bodily cues that have been found to be desirable in a variety of communicative situations, as well as those cues that are undesirable.

When considered from the perspective of the categoric approach to bodily communication, bodily cues that communicate a sense of *openness* and *confidence* have been found to be highly desirable. Communicating a sense of openness in interpersonal communication is very important. It signals the other person(s) that you are making a sincere effort to convey your feelings honestly. *Gestures of openness frequently trigger reciprocal gestures of openness in others* (Nierenberg & Calero, 1973). In one sense, gestures that communicate openness are the nonverbal equivalent of words that are self-disclosing. Both forms of communication eliminate or diminish behavior that is calculated to withhold or distort personal information.

Openness gestures stimulate interaction. Openness gestures seem to be a necessary condition for individuals to reach agreement. Thus, Nierenberg and Calero (1973) write that openness gestures are exhibited whenever

> *individuals unbutton their coats, uncross their legs, and move up toward the edge of the chair and closer to the desk or table that separates them from their opposer. This gesture-cluster is in most instances accompanied by verbal language that communicates a possible agreement, solution, or generally a positive expression of working together.* (p. 46)

Open hands, the unbuttoning of coats or loosening of ties, and the general relaxation of limb discipline often communicate openness. In contrast, crossed arms, crossed legs, and related gestures often communicate inaccessibility and defensiveness.

Confidence gestures are also important for the individual who wishes to be perceived as poised and in control of the communicative situation. Confidence gestures may be identified in two ways. First, a person who does not exhibit gestures that would tend to contradict a feeling of confidence is presumed to be confident. Hand-to-face gestures such as covering the mouth and nose and scratching the head are strong signals that the communicator lacks confidence. Among the most representative of confidence gestures are: (a) steepling (the individual joins fingertips on both hands to form the shape of a church steeple); (b) hands joined together at the back, with chin thrust upward; (c) feet on the table; and (d) leaning back, with both hands supporting the head (Nierenberg & Calero, 1973).

Openness and confidence gestures are generally desirable, but defensiveness and nervousness gestures are not. Defensiveness gestures take many forms, but often they suggest a literal attempt to block out unpleasant ideas or individuals. If you have seen a baseball umpire retreat from an infuriated manager, you will recognize that crossed arms are a traditional gesture of defensiveness. Downcast eyes, indirect bodily orientation, and closed bodily postures are among the most notable of defensiveness gestures.

Finally, nervousness gestures take many forms but usually are exhibited unintentionally. Nervousness gestures are usually manifested in the form of adapters that are associated with an increasing level of anxiety. Twiddling, fiddling, and fidgeting all suggest that a person is becoming more nervous. In fact, any extraneous movement that serves no instrumental purpose will probably be interpreted as a sign of nervousness. Tugging at clothing and ears, as well as playing with objects in the room (object–adapters), are among the many bodily movements that quite clearly suggest "I am nervous."

When considered from the dimensional perspective, bodily movement can be used to communicate meanings on three dimensions: liking–disliking, assertiveness—nonassertiveness, and power–powerlessness cues. We will concentrate on those kinds of bodily cues that represent the particularly strong manifestations of meaning associated with likability, assertiveness, and power. Other kinds of nonverbal cues associated with those dimensions of nonverbal meaning will be considered as well.

Nonverbal Indicators of Liking Versus Disliking

Liking is not the only label to identify the types of nonverbal cues that communicate pleasantness. *Interpersonally attractive, immediacy, intimacy,* and *pleasantness* are all terms that have been used to describe clusters of nonverbal cues that communicate similar, but not precisely the same, kinds of information. To simplify matters, we have decided to use the inclusive terminology of liking–disliking cues.

Certainly, the desire to be liked is almost universal. To communicate your desire to be liked is not of course to assure that you will be. Nor is an expression of liking for another person certain to produce a reciprocal response. Nonetheless, those desires are closely related because we tend to like those who like us.

To establish that you like another person you must express your desire for *high immediacy* by exhibiting your interest in that person. Positive indicators of liking include, but are not limited to, the following nonverbal cues:

1. forward-leaning during encounters
2. body and head orientations that directly face the other individual
3. open-body positions
4. affirmative head nods –listening
5. moderate amounts of gesturing and animation ·
6. close interpersonal distances
7. moderate body relaxation
8. touching
9. initiating and maintaining eye contact
10. smiling
11. postural mirroring (exhibiting similar or congruent postures) (Maxwell & Cook, 1985; Mehrabian, 1981; Schlenker, 1980)

Nonverbal indicators of disliking are, of course, associated with a relative absence of positive indicators of liking, or they may take the reverse form. Nonverbal indicators of disliking include the following cues:

1. indirect bodily orientations
2. eye contact of short duration
3. averted eyes
4. unpleasant facial expressions

5. a relative absence of gestures
6. bodily rigidity
7. visual inattentativeness
8. closed bodily posture
9. incongruent postures
10. bodily tension

As we have already indicated, dislike—or its weaker manifestation, disinterest—may result when individuals violate social norms in their overzealous efforts to be liked. Individuals who use sweeping gestures, nod too much, smile too much, sit too close, stare, and use gross postural shifts may think that they are communicating liking cues. Actually, such unsubtle, manipulative efforts may have the unintended effect of promoting dislike.

Nonverbal Indicators of Assertiveness and Unassertiveness

Social sensitivity is absolutely necessary for the development of satisfying interpersonal relationships. If individuals are to be perceived as socially sensitive, they must take pains to communicate that they are standing up for their rights, but without violating the rights of others. To communicate in a socially sensitive way, a person must be assertive without being aggressive.

Individuals who wish to be perceived as assertive must take special care to monitor their nonverbal cues. Positive nonverbal indicators of assertiveness include the following cues:

1. nonverbal and verbal components of the message used consistently
2. relaxed gestures and postures, with a forward-lean preferred
3. firm but not expansive gestures
4. sustained eye contact, although staring is avoided
5. illustrator gestures and vocal inflection used to emphasize key words and phrases
6. an appropriately loud voice
7. touching used when appropriate

Nonverbal indicators of unassertiveness are more numerous, although some are simply the opposite of the indicators of assertiveness. To avoid the inference that you are unassertive, you should seek to eliminate the nonverbal cues that are indicators of unassertiveness:

1. nervous gestures such as hand wringing and lip licking
2. clutching the other person as the assertive remark is made
3. out-of-context smiling
4. hunching the shoulders
5. covering the mouth with the hand
6. wooden posture (bodily rigidity)
7. frequent throat clearing
8. deferentially raised eyebrow
9. evasive eye contact
10. pauses that are filled with nonfluencies (Lange & Jakubowski, 1976)

Nonverbal Indicators of Power and Powerlessness

The desire to be perceived as powerful may not be as universal as the desire to be liked, but for many people it is compelling. Some people let their desire get out of control, of course. You may have seen politicians as well as personal acquaintances strutting around, using overly expansive gestures and laying claim to your territory in the errant belief that they would be perceived as more powerful.

Schlenker (1980) illustrated that efforts to obtain power can reach the point of absurdity. He recalls that in Charlie Chaplin's famous movie *The Great Dictator* Hitler and Mussolini are trying to gain dominance over each other by finding some way to assert their superiority. In one scene, both dictators are seated in chairs in a barber shop while getting shaves. Because they are seated, the only way they can think of to elevate their status is to elevate their chairs. Predictably, both begin pumping up their chairs furiously. Their wild efforts to enhance their power stop only after they reach the ceiling and crash to the floor.

Nonverbal indicators of power, status, and dominance are not always clearly differentiated in the research literature, so we will identify them under the single label of *power* cues. The following nonverbal cues have proved to be positive indicators of perceived power:

1. relaxed posture
2. erect rather than slumped posture
3. dynamic and purposeful gestures
4. steady and direct gaze
5. variation in speaking rate and inflection
6. variation in postures
7. relative expansiveness in postures
8. the option to touch
9. the option to stare
10. the option to interrupt
11. the option to approach another person closely (Archer, 1980; Harper, 1985; Schlenker, 1980)

As Schlenker (1980) pointed out, cues that communicate a sense of powerlessness or submissiveness are not always dysfunctional. In many instances, we encounter individuals with superior power and status whose self-presentation of relative submissiveness is expected. Everyone is accountable to someone else. For example, the general who takes pride in cultivating the "command look" and the "command voice" is apt to think twice about asserting such prerogatives of power when in the presence of a higher-ranking general. The use of nonverbal cues that communicate power in the presence of a more powerful person is to risk confrontation and even reprimand.

In general, however, the desire to be perceived as powerless is not a strong one. A relative lack of power is associated with the following indicators of powerlessness:

1. body tension
2. excessive smiling
3. continuous visual attentiveness while others are speaking

4. not looking directly at others

5. looking down frequently

6. arriving early for parties

7. sitting in the 11-o'clock position at conference tables (power moves clockwise from 12 o'clock around to 11 o'clock)

8. exhibiting distracting foot movement

9. not exposing the soles of your shoes

10. assuming closed postures

11. elevating your eyebrows frequently

12. never touching another individual (Archer, 1980; Korda, 1975; Schlenker, 1980)

In retrospect we should keep at least two facts in mind: First, although judgments of a person's likability, assertiveness, and power are strongly affected by their bodily communication, these judgments are affected by other types of nonverbal behaviors as well. Secondly, different cultures may attach different priorities to the importance of being perceived as likable, assertive, and powerful. Matsumoto and Kudoh (1987) found, for example, that the Japanese attach the highest priority to being perceived as powerful, whereas Americans attach the highest priority to being perceived as likable.

Summary

This chapter concentrated not only on how bodily cues are typically used but on how they should be used. In pursuit of this objective, the two major perspectives for conceptualizing bodily cues were discussed, the major functions of bodily cues identified, and functional and dysfunctional uses of specific kinds of bodily cues illustrated.

Bodily cues have been conceptualized from both the categorical and dimensional perspectives. The categoric perspective is based on the assumption that the informational potential of bodily cues is best understood by classifying them with regard to level of awareness and intentionality, code used, and functions served by the cues. The five types of nonverbal behavior identified by proponents of the categoric approach are emblems, illustrators, affect displays, regulators, and adaptors. Because communicators frequently use adaptors without awareness and intentionality, they are a particularly valuable source of information about the communicator's attitudes, feelings, and self-confidence.

The dimensional perspective is based on the assumption that the meanings communicated by nonverbal cues are best described by three independent dimensions: pleasantness, arousal, and dominance. These dimensions of meaning are best understood by considering the communicative implications of the approach, arousal, and power metaphors.

Our bodily cues serve four major communicative functions. They communicate attitudinal information, personal information about a communicator's psychological state, the intensity of emotions being experienced, and relational information. Bodily cues also serve other communicative functions of secondary importance.

To enhance communicative effectiveness, individuals should cultivate the use of gestures and postures of openness and confidence. On the other hand, bodily cues that communicate defensiveness and nervousness are dysfunctional. In order to gain more effective control over the meanings they communicate by bodily cues, individuals should carefully consider the nature of the nonverbal indicators of liking–disliking, assertiveness–nonassertiveness, and power–powerlessness.

References

Archer, D. (1980). *How to expand your social intelligence quotient.* New York: Evans.

Argyle, M. (1988). *Bodily communication* (2nd ed.). London: Methuen.

Birdwhistell, R. L. (1952). *Introduction to kinesics.* Louisville, KY: University of Kentucky.

Birdwhistell, R. L. (1960). Kinesics and communication. In E. Carpenter & M. McLuhan (Eds.), *Explorations in communication.* Boston: Beacon.

Birdwhistell, R. L. (1970). *Kinesics and context.* Philadelphia, PA: University of Pennsylvania Press.

Bull, P. (1983). *Body movement and interpersonal communication.* New York: John Wiley.

Bull, P., & Connelly, G. (1985). Body movement and emphasis in speech. *Journal of Nonverbal Behavior, 9,* 169–187.

Cohen, A. A. (1977). The communication functions of hand illustrators. *Journal of Communication, 27,* 54–63.

Collier, G. (1985). *Emotional experience.* Hillsdale, NJ: Erlbaum.

Ekman, P. (1985). *Telling lies: Clues to deceit in the marketplace, politics, and marriage.* New York: Norton.

Ekman, P., & Friesen, W. V. (1967). Head and body cues in the judgment of emotion: A reformulation. *Perceptual and Motor Skills, 24,* 713–716.

Ekman, P., & Friesen, W. V. (1969). The repertoire of nonverbal behavior: Categories, origins, usage, and coding. *Semiotica, 69,* 49–97.

Ekman, P., & Friesen, W. V. (1972). Hand movements. *Journal of Communication, 22,* 353–374.

Goldberg, S., & Rosenthal, R. (1986). Self-touching behaviors in the job interview: Antecedents and consequences. *Journal of Nonverbal Behavior, 10,* 65–80.

Goldin-Meadow, S., Wein, D., & Chang, C. (1992). Assessing knowledge through gestures: Using children's hands to read their minds. *Cognition & Instruction, 9,* 201–209.

Harper, R. G. (1985). Power, dominance, and nonverbal behavior: An overview. In S. L. Ellyson & J. F. Dovidio (Eds.), *Power, dominance and nonverbal behavior* (pp. 29–48). New York: Springer-Verlag.

Hewes, G. W. (1992). Primate communication and the gestural origin of language. (1992). *Current Anthropology, 33,* 65–84.

Johnson, H. G., Ekman, P., & Friesen, W. V. (1975). Communicative body movements: American emblems. *Semiotica, 15,* 335–353.

Kendon, A. (1984). Did gesture have the happiness to escape the curse of the confusion of Babel? In A. Wolfgang (Ed.), *Nonverbal behavior* (pp. 75–114). Lewiston, NY: D. J. Hogrefe.

Kendon, A. (1986). Current issues in the study of gesture. In J. L. Nespoulous, P. Perron, & A. R. Lecours (Eds.), *The biological foundations of gestures* (pp. 24–45). Hillsdale, NJ: Erlbaum.

Knapp, M. L. (1978). *Nonverbal communication in human interaction,* (2nd ed.). New York: Holt.

Knapp, M. L., Hart, R. P. & Friedrich, G. W. (1973). Verbal and nonverbal correlates of human leave-taking. *Communication Monographs, 40,* 182–198.

Korda, M. (1975). *Power!: How to get it and how to use it.* New York: Random.

Krivonos, P. D., & Knapp, M. L. (1975). Initiating communication: What do you say when you say hello. *Central States Speech Journal, 26,* 115–125.

LaFrance, M. (1985). Postural mirroring and intergroup relations. *Personality and Social Psychology Bulletin, 11,* 207–217.

Lamb, W. (1965). *Posture and gesture.* London: Duckworth.

Lange, A. J., & Jakubowski, P. (1976). *Responsible assertive behavior.* Champaign, IL: Research Press.

Lee, L., & Charlton, J. (1980). *The handbook: Interpreting handshakes, gestures, power signals, and sexual signs.* Englewood Cliffs, NJ: Prentice-Hall.

Levy, E. T., & McNeill, D. (1992). Speech, gestures, and discourse. *Discourse Processes, 15,* 277–301.

Manusov, V. (1990). An application of attribution principles to nonverbal behavior in romantic dyads. *Communication Monographs, 57,* 104–118.

Marschark, M. (1994). Gesture and sign. *Applied Psycholinguistics, 15,* 209–236.

Matsumoto, D., & Kudoh, T. (1987). Cultural similarities and differences in the semantic dimensions of body postures. *Journal of Nonverbal Behavior, 11,* 166–179.

Maxwell, G. M., & Cook, M. W. (1985). Postural congruence and judgements of liking, and perceived similarity. *New Zealand Journal of Psychology, 14,* 20–26.

Mehrabian, A. (1981). *Silent messages* (2nd ed.). Belmont, CA: Wadsworth.

Mehrabian, A., & Friedman, S. L. (1986). An analysis of fidgeting and associated individual differences. *Journal of Personality, 54,* 406–429.

Nespoulous, J. L., & Lecours, A. R. (1986). Gestures: nature and function. In J. L. Nespoulous, P. Perron, & A. R. Lecours (Eds.), *The biological foundations of gestures* (pp. 49–61). Hillsdale, NJ: Erlbaum.

Nierenberg, G., & Calero, H. H. (1973). *How to read a person like a book.* New York: Pocket Books.

Rogers, W. T. (1978). The contribution of kinesic illustrators toward the comprehension of verbal behavior within utterance. *Communication Research, 5,* 54–62.

Rosenfeld, H. M. (1982). Measurement of body motion and orientation. In K. R. Scherer & P. Ekman (Eds.), *Handbook of methods in nonverbal behavior research* (pp. 199–286). Cambridge: Cambridge University Press.

Rossberg-Gempton, I. (1993). The effect of open and closed postures on pleasant and unpleasant emotion. *Arts in Psychotherapy, 20,* 75–82.

Scheflen, A. E. (1964). The significance of posture in communication systems. *Psychiatry, 27,* 320–323.

Schlenker, B. R. (1980). *Impression management.* Monterey, CA: Brooks-Cole.

Sousa-Poza, J. F., & Rohrberg, R. (1977). Body movement in relation to type of information (person- and nonperson-oriented) and cognitive style (field independence). *Human Communication Research, 4,* 19–29.

Streeck, J. (1993). Gestures as Communication I: Its coordination with gaze and speech. *Communication Monographs, 60,* 275–299.

$C\ h\ a\ p\ t\ e\ r$ 5

SPACE
Proxemic Communication

The way we use space clearly communicates meaning. Different meanings are communicated in many different ways throughout the world. The beliefs, the values, and, ultimately, the meaning of a culture are communicated by the way people handle space. The German culture, for example, has long emphasized orderliness and clearly defined lines of authority. The felt need for privacy is a strong need which in turn is manifested in the impulse to define and defend well-marked territories. Hence, Germans object to individuals who literally "get out of line" or those who disregard signs such as "Keep Out" and "Authorized Personnel Only," which are intended to stipulate the approved use of space (Hall, 1969).

Americans are inclined to think of space, and to react to it, as "empty." In contrast, in Japan it is space—and not objects—that communicates meaning. The Japanese customarily assign specific meanings to specific types of spaces. For this reason, intersections are given names in Japan, but not streets. The particular space, with its functional characteristics, is the thing of importance in Japan. The space available in a single room serves a number of functions because the Japanese use movable walls and separators to create the kinds of spaces that serve specific functional objectives. In fact, the Japanese cope with the problem of limited available space by miniaturizing parts of their environment. The gardening practices that produce bonsai plants are a case in point (Altman, 1975).

Whereas Americans covet privacy by demanding their own offices and maintain their distance from others through the use of large and elevated desks, the Arabs know no such thing as privacy in public, and they are offended by anything less than intimacy of contact while carrying on a conversation. Such conversations (Hall, 1969) characteristically feature "the piercing look of the eyes, the touch of the hands, and the mutual bathing in the warm moist breath during conversation [which] represent stepped up sensory inputs to a level which many Europeans find unbearably intense" (p. 158). In effect, the Arab's use of space and olfactory stimuli communicates two meanings. It invites and demands intense involvement in interpersonal communication, and it assures the withdrawal of those who reject that method of relating.

Meanings communicated by the use of space are not confined to the sometimes gross differences among cultures. Differences within cultures are probably of more practical importance, and they abound. Spatial needs seem to vary dramatically among citizens of a nation, residents of a city, and even members of a family. To satisfy those needs, some people define and protect a set of spatial boundaries with a persistence and vigor that would put the family dog or cat to shame. The stone wall around one's property may be interpreted by some to be the narcissistic attempt of a socially alienated person to find privacy; others may interpret the wall as an enlightened response to the overcrowding of urban living. The fact that one person's spatial boundaries might intrude on another person's territory accounts for the distinctive type of communication problem that is associated with spatial needs and their frustrations.

In our use of space, we must remember that there is often a great disparity between the meanings we intend to communicate and the meanings we actually do communicate. For example, a professor who engaged my wife in conversation at a cocktail party stood so close to her that she became extremely uncomfortable and, unconsciously, began backing away. She was eventually backed up against a wall on the other side of the room and, in her continuing attempts to maintain a comfortable distance, made a run in one of her stockings. By this use of space, the professor probably intended to communicate a sense of involvement, pleasure, and vigor; however, by his inadvertent violation of my wife's invisible spatial boundaries, he had communicated a drastically different set of meanings—most noticeably, an unseemly aggressiveness.

We must recognize too that our proxemic or spatial behavior seems to be most strongly affected by two competing needs, the *need for affiliation* and the *need for privacy*. In general, we signal our desire to have contact with people and develop closer relationships with them through closer physical proximity. Thus, physical proximity when combined with touching clearly serves a central communicative role in close interpersonal encounters. In contrast, we seek to satisfy our privacy needs by maintaining greater distance from others while often seeking by physical means to assure our separation from them; we may, for example, use our elbows to keep individuals from getting too close to us. Burgoon (1988) wrote that "there are times when we wish to distance ourselves from the group, to achieve greater physical security, to escape stimulation and stress, to gain a greater sense of personal control, or to permit greater psychological freedom and self reflection" (p. 351).

The ways to use space, as well as the ways we react to others' use of space, can have a profound impact on the impression we make on others. The judgments people make about how friendly, likable, dominant, honest, and empathic we are may be strongly affected by the way we relate to people spatially. As we shall see in subsequent chapters, our success in the job interview, in the selling situation, and in cross-cultural communication can be affected in important and readily identifiable ways by our use of space. In short, the impression manager must carefully consider which proxemic behaviors should and should not be exhibited in various contexts because such behaviors are often important in impression management.

Edward T. Hall, the pioneer of proxemic research, coined the term *proxemics* because it suggests that proximity, or lack of it, is a vitally important factor in human interaction. In its broadest perspective, Hall defines proxemics as the study of how people structure and use microspace (1968). Proxemics focuses not only on the ways individuals orient themselves to other individuals and objects in their immediate physical environment, but also on the perceptual and behavioral impact of these spatial orientations. Burgoon, Buller, and Woodall (1989) defined proxemics as the perception, use, and structuring of space as communication. For our purposes, *proxemics* is defined as the study of how individuals use space to communicate.

The Proximate Environment

We use space to communicate. When we use the space that can be perceived directly, we are communicating within the *proximate environment.* The proximate environment includes everything that is physically present to the individual at a given moment. The proximate environment of a student in a classroom includes the student's desk, the other students, the teacher, the chalkboard, the windows, and the doorway. The student's proximate environment does not include the soccer team practicing outside or students in another classroom (Sommer, 1966).

No single concept adequately describes how we communicate in our proximate environment. Because terms such as *space, distance,* and *territory* are clearly related in a conceptual sense, there is a tendency to treat them as synonyms. They are not synonyms, however, and should not be treated as such. *To understand what and how we communicate via our proxemic behavior, we must understand the meaning of five interrelated concepts: space, distance, territory, crowding, and privacy.*

This chapter is built upon the ideational foundation those five concepts provide. More specifically, this chapter is designed to illustrate the communicative uses of space, distance, territory, crowding, and privacy and to demonstrate why each concept is important, to identify the major communicative functions served by proxemic behavior, and to describe the effects and assess the implications of the violation of proxemic norms and expectations.

Space

The concept of visual space in nonverbal communication is somewhat analogous to the concept of silence in verbal communication. Though both are, in a sense, devoid of content, the ways we use them may be rich in communicative significance. Edward Hall, for example, contended that our culture places severe constraints on the ways we use space. In fact, he maintained that there are basically three types of space: *fixed-feature, semifixed-feature, and informal* space (1969). Rapoport (1982) amplified Hall's classifactory scheme and modified his terminology. He identified three major types of space that have communicative significance in our society: *fixed-feature, semifixed-feature, and nonfixed-feature* space.

Fixed-feature space refers to the characteristic arrangement of rooms by function. Within the home, for example, formal meals are rarely served in the bedroom and bookcases rarely line the walls of the bathroom. Ironically, the fixed features that define how space is to be used in the home are often quite dysfunctional. Hall (1969) cites the kitchen as a particular problem. He emphasizes that "the lack of congruence between the design elements, female stature and body build (women are not usually tall enough to reach things), and the activity to be performed, while not obvious at first, is often beyond belief" (p. 105).

The problem may not be as severe as it seems for the upwardly mobile woman in our society because it is important that she foster the perception that she spends little time in the kitchen. As Rapoport (1982) emphasized:

In the case of the Puerto Rican culture, status is gained during a party through a hostess being seen to produce food, being seen in the kitchen, and "performing" in front of an audience of her peers; in Anglo culture, a woman is seen as a good hostess when she apparently does no work, yet food appears as though by magic. (p. 94)

Semifixed-feature space refers to the placement of objects in the home, office, conference room, and other proximate environments. The objects we use in these types of spaces may include furniture, plants, screens, paintings, plaques, and even birds and animals. The objects we choose—to demarcate the boundaries and to accent the meanings of the semi-fixed-feature spaces in which we interact—are important because often they are direct extension of our personality. Our choices of curtains, interior colors, shutters, mailboxes, and decorative planting may reveal more about us than our handwriting or our IRS file.

The semifixed objects we choose to use do more than shape perceptions of presumed personality characteristics. The choice of objects and their placement in semifixed-feature space can have a strong impact on the credibility of the occupant of a home or office. Important as those communicative functions are, perhaps the most important communicative function of semifixed-feature space is the degree to which it promotes *involvement* or *withdrawal* among the individuals who are using the space.

Nonfixed-feature space is a concept with which all of us should be rather familiar. This is the space, immediately surrounding our body, that each of us perceives to be ours. We use no physical objects to mark the boundaries of our "personal space" because these boundaries are invisible. The amount of personal space that we claim as ours may vary, depending on our size, current emotional state, status, and sex. Malandro and Barker (1983) also emphasized that people claim varying amounts of personal space to be theirs, both in front of and in back of them.

As we consider the communicative implications of the three major kinds of space, we should pay particular attention to semifixed-feature and nonfixed-feature space. We have little opportunity to modify the nature of most fixed-feature environments. In contrast, we can consciously consider the communicative implications of the objects we choose to place in semifixed-feature space, and we can contemplate the advantages and disadvantages of claiming and defending a personal space of a given size and dimension.

Semifixed- and nonfixed-feature space can be used in a variety of ways to transmit meanings. Although the uses vary widely, they frequently serve one of two communicative functions. Either they bring people together and stimulate involvement (in which case they are serving a *sociopetal* function) or they keep people apart and promote withdrawal (in which case they are serving a *sociofugal* function). The sociopetal use of space satisfies the affiliative needs of individuals by promoting interaction. By contrast, the sociofugal use of space is well suited to satisfy privacy needs.

Sommer, who has been a leader in research on the sociopetal and sociofugal uses of microspace, maintains that we transmit very different connotative meanings by the way we use space. He refers to the sociofugal function as "sociofugal space," and finds that sociofugal spatial arrangements or conditions suggest the following meanings: (a) large, (b) cold, (c) impersonal, (d) institutional, (e) not owned by an individual, (f) overconcentrated, (g) without opportunity for shielded conversation, (h) providing barriers without shelter,

(i) isolated without privacy, and (j) concentrated without cohesion (1967; 1974). By contrast, the sociopetal use of space promotes involvement, communicative interaction, and a feeling of involvement. Figure 5.1 illustrates the contrasting uses of space. The opposing sets of chairs in the doctor's waiting room represent a sociofugal use of space, and the conversation pit in the home satisfies the sociopetal use of space.

Before you consider how you can and should use space to be a more effective communicator, you should recognize that perceptions and definitions of space tend to be culture-specific. Consider, for example, my personal experience in Mexico City, where usable living space has become extremely difficult to find. Not surprisingly, available space for new houses is at a premium, with the result that new houses tend to be small by U.S. standards and must necessarily be built on a number of levels in order to conserve space. Mexicans' perceptions of what constitutes a "large" space may be affected by their strong need to

FIGURE 5.1

conserve space. Recently, my family was visiting some friends in Mexico City. One of our Mexican friends suggested that my two sons take their soccer balls to a local park for a workout; the park was described as spacious and very large in size. When my sons arrived at the park, they discovered that it sat atop a steep, small hill. In fact, the park was so small that almost every time they practiced their corner kicks, the soccer ball soared far out of the park and rolled for several blocks down the side of the steep hill.

Distance

At least in theory, space has no finite barriers and becomes a tangible concept only when people or objects occupy space and when individuals attempt to define its boundaries. In contrast, distance is a relational concept and is usually measured in terms of how far one individual is from another.

Once again, Hall (1968) has done pioneering work in attempting to identify and classify the distances people use to separate themselves from others in order to satisfy their various needs. Hall identified four types of informal distance: *intimate, personal, social-consultative,* and *public.*

Type 1, or intimate distance (0–18 in.), is easily distinguishable because of the number and intensity of sensory inputs, of which the communicators are intensely aware. Intimate distance is considered inappropriate in public by the typical middle-class American (Hall, 1969).

Type 2, or personal distance (1½–4 ft), is the distance that individuals customarily place between themselves and others. Communication used in close interpersonal relationships typically occurs at this distance. Personal distance is important for several reasons. The personal distance we characteristically assume might be a reliable clue to our self-confidence as well as our felt privacy needs. Successful communicators will be sensitive to the personal distances that others maintain when interacting with them.

Type 3, or social distance (4–12 ft), is the distance that typically separates individuals engaged in a business transaction or consultation and is also appropriate for a range of social gatherings that are informal in nature. Actual separation for Type 3 or social distance will obviously depend on such important factors as whether you are standing or seated and whether you are communicating with one other person or with a group of persons.

Finally, the shift from social to public distance (12 ft or more) has tangible and important implications for interpersonal communication. At the close phase of public distance (12–25 ft), the types of nonverbal meanings that can be perceived vary rather dramatically. Alert communicators can give the appearance that they have received no message, or they can remove themselves physically from the situation. If individuals do communicate at this distance, they will find that the interaction is of a very formal nature.

The far phase of public distance (25 ft or more) can have a particularly disruptive impact on interpersonal communication. Beyond 25 ft the voice loses much of its potential to transmit meanings accurately, and facial expressions and movements must be rather expansive in order to be recognized. As Hall (1969) emphasized, "much of the nonverbal part of communication shifts to gestures and body stance" (p. 125).

Hall's distance zones have been widely cited as the guidelines we should use to assume proper spatial orientations vis-à-vis other individuals, but Burgoon's research suggests that those distance zones should be subjected to more careful scrutiny. In fact, Burgoon and Jones (1976) argued convincingly that *distance zones or "expected distancing" are determined not only by the normative expectations of our culture but by the idiosyncratic preferences of individual communicators.* They contend that "Expected distancing in a given context is a function of (1) the social norm and (2) the known idiosyncratic spacing patterns of the initiator" (p. 132).

Burgoon (1982; Burgoon & Hale, 1988) subsequently developed, and subjected to a number of empirical tests, a theoretical model of proxemic violations that is designed to predict the effects of violating the kinds of proxemic norms just discussed. Not surprisingly, Burgoon concluded that distance violations—violation of proxemic norms and expectations—are arousing and distracting, and they communicate messages. Her three most innovative and important conclusions are derived from empirical tests of her model:

1. The characteristics and behaviors of a person who violates proxemic norms can be interpersonally rewarding to the person who is the object of the proxemic violation.
2. High-reward "initiators" seem to achieve the most desirable communication outcomes when they violate distance norms rather than conforming to them.
3. Nonrewarding or low-reward initiators are more likely to achieve desirable communication outcomes by conforming to rather than violating distance norms.

Burgoon's proxemic violations model is unique because it suggests that the violation of distance norms, that is, norms that specify ranges for personal or social distance, can produce positive effects in some instances. If the response to a violation of proxemic norms is to be positive, it is important that the "violator" of proxemic norms be a high-reward source in terms of such characteristics as personal appearance and that the violation be followed by other positively valued actions such as compliments (Burgoon, 1982).

Communicators with high interpersonal reward potential in the form of apparent status, attractiveness, purchasing power, and expertise seem to be more persuasive and to induce more favorable interaction with their "violated" interaction partner than communicators with low interpersonal reward potential. However, results such as these are far from clear-cut or conclusive to date (Burgoon & Aho, 1982).

Proxemic norms are influenced not only by the beliefs and values that define a particular culture but also by demographic variables or personal characteristics of the communicator that differentiate one person from another. These variables make up the "idiosyncratic" component of proxemic norms that helps explain why different individuals have different preferences with regard to the distance(s) they prefer to be separated from other individuals when interacting with them. Among the more important of such variables are *gender, age, ethnicity* or *race, status, personality, degree of acquaintance,* and *area of residence.* Burgoon and her colleagues (Burgoon, 1988; Burgoon et al., 1989) did a good job of describing the contribution of most of those variables to proxemic norms in the United States.

Within our culture, females sit and stand closer to each other than males. Men respond negatively to face-to-face invasion by strangers, whereas females respond negatively to side-by-side invasion by strangers. Although opposite-sex pairs in the United States consistently adopt closer interaction distances than male dyads, the available evidence does not conclusively establish that opposite-sex dyads usually interact at closer distances in public than female dyads, although that frequently seems to be the case (Burgoon et al., 1989).

The tendency for opposite-sex dyads in the United States to interact at close interpersonal distance could be a culture-specific proxemic practice, however. In some cultures, opposite-sex pairs maintain a greater interaction distance than any other gender combination. Thus, a female in Turkey characteristically maintains a greater distance when interacting with a male than when interacting with a female; separation distance in Turkey for opposite-sex pairs is also greater than the distance for two interacting males (Hortascu, Duzen, Arat, Atahan, & Uzer, 1990; Rustemli, 1986). We also know that "traditional" women experience the sensation of crowding significantly sooner than either androgynous men, androgynous women, or traditional men, and only traditional women—of the four groups—experience a decrease in their task performance when they feel crowded (Lombardo, 1986).

Generally, people maintain greater distances from other people as they get older. This is true from preschool through middle age, although closer contact is characteristic of the very old and young. Not surprisingly, we tend to maintain closer distances when interacting with people who are approximately our own age. Age interacts with status on occasion to dictate that greater interaction distances between people are appropriate.

The contribution of race or ethnicity to distance norms has not been clearly determined. Baxter's (1970) observation of the proxemic behaviors of dyads in the Houston city zoo suggested that Mexican Americans of all age and sex groupings interacted "most proximally"—were consistently closest together, whites were intermediate, and African Americans stood most distant. However, black women appear to interact at closer distances than either white females or white males. In short, any generalizations contrasting whites and blacks in terms of normative interaction distances must be so carefully qualified as to be of doubtful informational value.

The impact of status on distance norms, in contrast, is clear-cut. Preferred separation distance increases as the status differential between two interactants increases. Lower-status persons seem to be particularly aware of the need to "keep their distance" from high-status persons, whereas an increase in people's status is usually associated with their desire to decrease the amount of distance that separates them from the people with whom they are interacting.

The personality profile of individuals also has an impact on the distance they prefer to maintain when interacting with intimates, friends, business associates, or casual acquaintances. We know, for example, that extroverts approach others more closely and maintain shorter communicating distances than do introverts. We know also that people with a high level of communication apprehension and a low level of self-confidence and self-esteem prefer to maintain much greater separation when communicating than do their more confident counterparts.

Degree of acquaintance with the person with whom we interact clearly also exerts an impact on proxemic norms. Predictably, we tend to stand closest to intimates and close friends, stand further away from acquaintances, and maintain the greatest distance from strangers. Burgess (1983) found that we tend not only to stand closest to individuals we know best and who are closest to us in age, but also to avoid or ignore strangers. Interestingly, there is some evidence to suggest that we can generalize across cultures about the impact of degree of acquaintance on distance norms. For example, students at the University of Rajasthan, Jaipur, India, had the sensation of feeling "crowded" first when approached by strangers and last when approached by friends (Kamal & Mehta, 1987).

Finally, area or region of residence can clearly shape people's spatial preferences. Thus, Pedersen and Frances recently reported (1990) that persons from the mountain states (Utah) scored higher than those on the West Coast (Los Angeles) in their preferences for isolation, anonymity, and solitude. People from the Southeast were similar to those on the West Coast in their low preference for isolation but resembled people in the mountain states in their high preference for anonymity. The findings for the West Coast residents of Los Angeles can be explained in part by the fact that low preferences for isolation and solitude are necessary in Los Angeles in order to avoid the frustration of frequent violation of proxemic expectations. Both isolation and solitude are in short supply in an area of such high population density.

The culturally determined distancing zones identified by Hall do not necessarily represent comfortable interaction distances for all communicators. Thus, Hayduk (1981) found that subjects experienced extreme discomfort at an interaction distance of 11.7 in., moderate discomfort at 19.5 in., and only slight discomfort at 27.3 in. More importantly, Hayduk found that preferred interaction distances for individual communicators vary. Individuals who prefer greater interaction distances become uncomfortable much sooner as a stranger approaches them than individuals who prefer shorter interaction distances. Of the former group, 50 percent became moderately uncomfortable at a distance of 4.4 ft. Of the latter group, 50 percent became moderately uncomfortable at a distance of 1.3 ft.

We should therefore beware of encouraging communicators to assume normative separation distances in our society. Demographic variables such as age, gender, and degree of acquaintance may affect culturally determined proxemic norms in such a way that comfortable interaction distances for two individuals may be quite different. Thus, an interaction distance is comfortable for one communicator and agonizingly uncomfortable for another. The best criterion in judging the appropriateness of separation distance for two or more people seems to be how comfortable they are with a given spatial orientation (Burgoon, 1988).

In short, results from research designed to determine desirable separation distances "generally suggest that people seek an *optimal range of distance* for interaction, and departures from this range that leave either too large or too small distances result in discomfort and dissatisfaction" (Sundstrom & Altman, 1976, p. 54). If we know and like an individual, for example, we are apt to prefer an interaction distance that is closer than the culturally prescribed norm. When we interact with an individual we dislike, preferred interaction distance is usually greater than that indicated by the cultural norm.

Territory

The concept of *territory* has vast implications for interpersonal communication, and many of these implications remain unexplored. Much of our knowledge of the concept comes from studies that illustrate how animals identify and defend clearly delineated territories by means of instinct. Territoriality in this sense is a basic concept in the study of animal behavior; it is defined as behavior by which an organism characteristically lays claim to an area and defends it against members of its own species and in so doing assures the propagation of the species by regulating density (Hall, 1969).

Sommer (1966) recognized that the concept of territoriality now has great relevance for the study of human behavior, even if humans do not define their territories exclusively or even primarily by instinctual means. He saw territory as an *area controlled by an individual, family, or other face-to-face collectivity, with the emphasis on physical possession, actual or potential, as well as defense.*

The biggest and best territories since time immemorial have been controlled by the most powerful, the most influential, and often the wealthiest members of a society. The two sets of walls that surround Windsor Castle in England clearly demarcate this type of choice territory. William the Conqueror chose to build Windsor Castle on a large, steep hill that is directly above the Thames River. His motivation was straightforward. He built not a residence but a fortress. The result was an impregnable stronghold that could be used to monitor and control the activities of the hostile population that lived below the castle. William the Conqueror selected eight other choice sites on high hills overlooking the English countryside, and he built eight other castles that were used for similar purposes. Windsor Castle, which has served as the home of kings and queens for nearly nine centuries, is still used as a summer residence by Queen Elizabeth.

The essential nature of territoriality is captured by Sommer's delightfully homespun ruminations on the concept:

> *Since human communication is based largely on symbols, territorial defense relies more on symbols such as name plates, fences, and personal possessions than on physical combat, or aggressive displays. . . . Salesmen have, and actively defend, individual territories. One criterion of territoriality is . . . the home team always wins . . . [and] an animal on its own territory will fight with more vigor. . . . [Hence] a male on its own territory is almost undefeatable against males of the species. (Sommer, 1966, p. 61)*

Territorial behavior, therefore, is defined by attempts to mark the boundaries of territories that are "owned" by individuals or groups. Through the use of personalized markers, we strive either to regulate social interaction within territories perceived as ours or to prevent unauthorized individuals from entering or using the territory.

Sometimes people get a bit carried away in their use of territorial markers. For example, the owner of an antique shop in Santa Monica, California, has posted a sign on his front door that says "No Browsing. Stay out unless you plan to make a purchase today." Some owners of souvenir shops near the Eiffel Tower in Paris will slap the hands of children who touch their merchandise. In an expensive store in Grindewald, Switzerland, stickers are attached to hand-carved music boxes that say "You drop it. You pay for it." Although the insensitive use of personal markers may have undesirable side effects, *the more personal the markers used to delineate territorial boundaries, the more effective they are in controlling or preventing interaction* (Altman, 1975).

If territories serve so central a function in regulating human interaction, the obvious question is: What types of territories are typically defined and defended? Writing from a broad perspective, Lyman and Scott (1967) observe that there are four kinds of territories: *public, home, interactional,* and *body.*

Public territories are areas individuals may enter freely. Great constraints are placed on human interaction within public territories, however, because of explicit laws and social traditions. The fact that individuals are often anonymous when they use certain public territories means that they might be treated in ways that are impersonal and even rude.

The young men who serve as the Swiss Guard at the Vatican in Rome, for example, vigorously enforce rules about what territories visitors may and may not enter and what may be done within different Vatican areas. They do so with an unseemly curtness that they might not exhibit if the visitors they encountered were not anonymous. Similarly, the struggles to desegregate buses, restaurants, and beaches suggest that the term *public territory* can have a very restricted connotation for some individuals who choose to enter and attempt to interact with others within the territory.

By contrast, home territories feature freedom of interaction by individuals who claim the territory. If Mom and Dad want to make love in front of the television set in their own den, who is going to stop them? Surely neither the Swiss Guard nor the local authorities will interfere. Of course, their home territory quickly becomes a public territory if they fail to draw the blinds. How many of you recall the bizarre incident in which a couple made love in a private box in the Houston Astrodome? They did so without drawing their shades while a baseball game was being played and thousands of spectators watched their close encounter. Was this uninhibited couple making love in a public or a home territory?

Home territories are defined in part by the distinctive markers used to assure boundary maintenance. Examples include reserved chairs, personalized drinking mugs, and even the cat's litter. Fraternities, private clubs, and gay bars constitute home territories. In each of them, distinctive territorial markers are used to limit usage by outsiders.

Interactional territories are areas where individuals congregate informally. A party, a local pool hall, and an informal meeting on campus are all interactional territories. Although every territory has boundaries that are maintained, interactional territories are unique in that they have movable boundaries.

Finally, body territories consist of space that is marked as reserved for use by our bodies. Goffman developed and supported the provocative thesis that "eight territories of self" exist, and their changeable boundaries are a function of variability in both individual behavior and environmental conditions. These territories of self are (a) personal space, (b) stalls, (c) use-space, (d) turns, (e) sheaths, (f) possessional territory, (g) informational preserves, and (h) conversational preserves (Goffman, 1971).

Of the eight territories of self identified by Goffman, five seem particularly relevant and important for interpersonal communication. First, the *stall* is space with clear-cut boundaries that individuals claim exclusively for their own use. Telephone booths, public toilets, and parking places are obvious examples of stalls. Unlike personal space, stalls have highly visible and fixed boundaries that can easily be protected from intruders.

Whereas stalls identify themselves by their structure, use-space identifies itself by its function. *Use-space* is the space immediately surrounding us that we must have in order to perform personal functions such as lighting our cigarette or swinging at a golf ball. Our claim to use-space is usually respected by others in close proximity to us because they realize that they would require similar space to perform similar functions.

The *turn* represents a territorial claim based on both structure and function. Expressions such as "Take your turn" and "Get in line, Bud" suggest the nature of this type of territorial behavior. We have been socially conditioned to expect that such territorial claims will be honored.

The *sheath,* which consists of both our skin and the clothes we wear, functions to afford us with the desired degree of privacy. Much like the sheath, *possession territory* is closely identified with the human body. Rather than skin or clothes, which cover the body, possessional territory consists of objects that we claim as our own and that we array around us wherever we are. Objects such as gloves and handbags often function as markers to delineate the boundaries of possessional territory. Only the most insensitive individual will attempt to move such territorial markers.

Crowding

Crowding is a concept of central importance to the study of proxemic communication. To begin, crowding should be clearly differentiated from density. *Density* is a concept that is defined strictly in physical terms. Density refers to the number of people per unit of space. *Crowding,* in contrast, is a psychological concept. Crowding is the condition that exists when an individual's attempts to achieve a desired level of privacy have been unsuccessful, in the sense that more social contact continues to occur than is desired (Altman, 1975).

Common sense seems to suggest that there is a strong relationship between objective measures of crowding and the subjective feeling of being crowded. However, the actual relationship between objective and subjective crowding is not strong (Edwards, Fuller, Sermsri, & Vorakitphokatorn, 1994). For example, objective measurement indicates that four individuals forced to share a single room in a household are crowded. These individuals may not all feel equally crowded, however. In this instance, the lower the level of a person's perceived control of space, the stronger the feeling of being crowded and of psychological distress (Lepore, Evans, & Schneider, 1992). Conversely, the sensation of feeling crowded can be greatly reduced by giving a person exclusive *control* over the small amount of space in which they find themselves (Edwards et al., 1994).

A number of factors enhance the feeling of being crowded, for example, a collectivist orientation, membership in a noncontact culture, and high population density when combined with a high crime rate (Iwata, 1992). As we shall see, the sensation of being crowded is associated with some highly undesirable effects.

Jails constitute one environment in which both subjective and objective overcrowding are chronic and the control of the inmates over most of the space in the jail is minimal. Accordingly, the potential for serious problems is great. Predictably, a national sample of 189 sheriffs reported that every one of the 13 problems they viewed as most important increased significantly as the sensation of crowding increased (Kinkade, Leone, & Semond, 1995). The sensation of being crowded is subjective in that it depends on *who else* is involved, *when* and *where* it occurs, and *why* and *how* it occurs. Regardless of the circumstances, when we experience the sensation of crowding, we usually find interpersonal communication to be less than satisfying. We may or may not have the opportunity to modify our own proxemic behavior (or the proxemic behavior of persons with whom we interact) in ways that will minimize or eliminate the sensation of crowding.

Crowding clearly makes many people uncomfortable. We can now document that crowding negatively affects both health and behavior. Evans and Lepore (1992) maintained that three major mechanisms account for these negative effects: behavioral constraint, diminished control, and stimulus overload/arousal. High temperatures are a good example of a type of stimulus overload that contributes to the perception of overcrowding. Interestingly, the negative effects of high temperatures are reduced when individuals feel that they have some control over the space in which they find themselves (Ruback & Pandev, 1992).

The sensation of crowding is related to dysfunctional behaviors and health problems, whereas objective crowding is not (Fuller, Edwards, Vorakitphokatorn, & Sermsri, 1993). Household crowding has consequences that are selective and modest in North America and Europe but stronger in Southeast Asia. In Bangkok, Thailand, for example, crowded households are associated not only with martial instability, more arguments, and parent–child tensions but also with more frequent disciplining of children. The greater behavioral impact of crowding in Southeast Asia may be explained in part by the fact that people living in this part of the world often have limited control over the space that is available to them. This may be particularly true in the People's Republic of China. In this country three or four generations of a family frequently "share" a small living area.

Individuals who feel crowded also report a higher incidence of health problems. Health problems in turn seem to result at least in part from increased psychological distress that results from crowding (Fuller, Edwards, Sermsri, & Vorakitphokatorn, 1993). Further research must be done before precise relationships between overcrowding and personal health are known.

The feeling of being crowded seems to have a negative impact on our ability to establish and maintain satisfying relationships with others. Not surprisingly, people tend to cope much more successfully with crowding when it occurs in the presence of friends rather than when it occurs among strangers (Kamal & Mehta, 1987).

Our ability to cope with crowding and develop satisfying interpersonal relationships is also affected by the nature and amount of space that is available to us. McCarthy and Saegert (1978) compared the behaviors of individuals living in a 14-story apartment building and in a 3-story walk-up; the residents of the high-rise building felt much more crowded than residents of the walk-up. The individuals who reported that they felt crowded had greater difficulty establishing relationships with their neighbors, were less socially active, felt more detached from their places of residence, belonged to fewer voluntary groups, and felt they had less power to exercise influence on the decisions made by the management of the apartments. In fact, there is even some evidence to indicate that dorm residents who experience an uncomfortable degree of crowding make more frequent visits to their physicians and do not perform as well academically as individuals who do not feel crowded (Stokols, Ohlig, & Resnick, 1989).

The potential for perceptions of crowding to negatively affect our feelings about, and our relationship with, other individuals should not be overemphasized, however. Although feelings of overcrowding do typically result in some elevation in anxiety and stress levels (Altman, 1975), there are at least some indications that the feeling of being crowded is cathartic in some situations and helps to free up inhibitions in others.

A person may or may not experience the sensation of feeling crowded when in a large crowd. Interestingly, many individuals seem to seek out large crowds, such as those who attend football games, because of the intra-audience effects that they experience. Hocking (1982) maintained that the dynamics of crowd behavior tend to be distinctive and that the reactions that members of a large audience or crowd have to other members of the collectivity are "a major factor contributing to the excitement, the arousal, and ultimately the entertainment value" that results when large numbers of people interact with one another (p. 101).

The crowding associated with a large gathering clearly has persuasive implications. This is particularly true of crowd dynamics as they affect the response to an evangelists's persuasive message at a televised religious rally. I have argued (Leathers, 1989) that televangelist Jimmy Swaggart skillfully uses intra-audience effects in large crowds to his own advantage. Presumably he recognizes that his ability to draw large crowds and make mass appeals to the anonymous members of the crowd greatly increases the susceptibility of his religious audience to his persuasive message (Newton & Mann, 1989).

Privacy

Joe Montana, former quarterback of the San Francisco 49ers, is currently experiencing the agonizingly painful effects of an almost total lack of privacy. His celebrity status provides him with a face and name recognition that are matched by few athletes, and for that matter by few Americans in any field. As a result, Montana finds that he has little privacy. Montana has said that "I feel almost like a prisoner in our house. The privacy's really kind of caved in more than we ever thought about. It's become more of a microscope. We didn't think it was possible but it has become that way" (*The Atlanta Constitution,* September 20, 1990, p. E1).

Unidentified individuals have shot windows out of Montana's house, his garage, and the back of one of his cars. People ride by on tour buses and gawk, unknown passersby come up for autographs, and some people pull into his drive and simply sit and admire his house. On one occasion a group of unauthorized and uninvited people invaded the Montana household when the family was gone. They proceeded to throw a party that featured heavy beer drinking and their use of Montana's jacuzzi. The repeated invasions of Montana's privacy have become so painful that he has considered hiring a private security force. Ultimately, he feels he will be driven from his house and forced to seek greater privacy elsewhere.

Altman (1975) clearly connects the importance of privacy to an understanding of the communicative implications of our proxemic behaviors. He wrote that

> *the concept of privacy is central to understanding environment and behavior relationships; it provides a key link among the concepts of crowding, territorial behavior and personal space. Personal space and territorial behavior function in the service of privacy needs and, as such, are mechanisms used to achieve desired levels of "personal or group privacy."* (p. 6)

He went on to emphasize that crowding results from ineffective or unsatisfactory use of space, distance, and territory, with the result that individuals achieve inadequate levels of privacy.

Privacy may be defined as selective control of access to one's self or to one's group (Altman, 1975). To a considerable degree, we control access to ourselves and to groups that are important to us by our use of space. Our needs for privacy must, of course, be balanced against our needs to be perceived as friendly and outgoing individuals who seek interaction with others. Neither the hermit nor the member of the commune has achieved the balance necessary for most of us to be effective communicators in the real world.

As Figure 5.2 suggests, some individuals place a high premium on privacy. Rare indeed is the individual who views the bathroom as the appropriate place for social interaction in the home. On the other hand, some individuals make a practice of walking around nude in their own homes. Privacy, therefore, is defined by the felt needs of those who assert specialized types of claims to it.

There is little doubt that there are different types of privacy. Westin's (1970) classification of privacy into four types—*solitude, intimacy, anonymity,* and *reserve*—is still being used by proxemic researchers. The concepts of solitude and anonymity were used in the study cited earlier in this chapter in which regions of the country were compared in terms of preferences for different types of privacy.

A person who has achieved a state of *solitude* when he or she is completely isolated from other human beings, cannot be observed by others, and is alone. *Intimacy* exists when two or more people are able to minimize sensory inputs from outsiders in order to maximize

FIGURE 5.2

personal contact in their interpersonal relationships. *Anonymity* exists when people are assured that no one will recognize them and they are free from direct personal observation or scrutiny even though they are in a public setting. Finally, *reserve* simply means that you are able to shut yourself off from others by signaling that you do not want to risk the disclosure of potentially embarrassing information about yourself by interacting with others at a given point in time.

The most penetrating and comprehensive effort to compare and contrast types of privacy has been done by Burgoon (1982), however. She properly uses the term *dimensions of privacy* rather than *privacy categories* in recognition of a simple fact: A person rarely experiences complete privacy or a complete lack of privacy, rather, people experience varying degrees of privacy.

The major dimensions of privacy with their contrasting definitions are as follows:

1. *Physical privacy:* a measure of the degree to which one person is physically inaccessible to others
2. *Social privacy:* both an individual and a group state in which the option to withdraw from social interaction with another person(s) exists
3. *Psychological privacy:* people's ability to exercise control over both thoughts and feelings that can be expressed by them and to them
4. *Information privacy:* people's capacity to prevent the gathering and dissemination of information about themselves, their group(s), or their organization(s) without their knowledge or permission

In one sense the experiences of crowding and privacy are polar opposites. Thus, Burgoon (1982) wrote that

> *if personal space invasion or crowding can be seen as one end of a distancing continuum, then physical privacy is the opposite end, since it involves freedom from intrusion on one's self-defined 'body buffer zone' and freedom from the discomfiture of too many people for the available space.* (p. 211)

Significantly, privacy is one of the most powerful needs that human beings experience. Because crowding frustrates and often blocks efforts to achieve a desired level of privacy, the consequences of feeling crowded can be severe.

On the positive side, knowledge of other persons' privacy needs and preferences is vitally important. Such knowledge can greatly enhance our potential for successful communication. This is particularly true when we use this information to respond in sensitive and socially appropriate ways to the expressed or implied privacy needs of those with whom we interact.

We must recognize two things at minimum. The strength of the privacy needs experienced by different individuals and groups is often quite different. Individuals and groups also vary markedly in terms of the importance they attach to different types of privacy. Thus, the person who seeks absolute isolation from others places the highest priority on solitude. By contrast, the person who places the highest priority on anonymity might even savor contact with others as long as personal identity is concealed.

We do know that individuals are most apt to seek privacy when they are distressed (Newell, 1994). We know too that where we choose to sit in a room in public may make a statement about our privacy preferences. Thus students who choose to sit in the back of a classroom receive significantly higher scores on the Privacy Preference Scale (PPS) than students seated in other parts of the classroom. The students seated in the back also scored significantly higher on the "Not Neighboring" and "Seclusion" scales of the PPS (Pedersen, 1994). Finally, we know that both adults and children have certain "places" they prefer when they seek privacy. The bedroom is the preferred place of privacy for adults because it is associated with activities that require peace and quiet (Oseland, 1993). Children ages 3 to 5 report that the places where they seek privacy in a day care center are a cubby, a chair, or a concealed space underneath a playhouse (Zeegers, Readdick, & Hansen-Gandy, 1994).

Finally, the relative importance of physical, social, psychological, and informational privacy is strongly affected by the nature of the activities we undertake at a given point in time. When I am seated at my computer working on this book, for example, I place the highest priority on complete physical privacy. When I am interacting with a member of my family, physical privacy is less important than the social privacy I gain when I am assured that outsiders will not interrupt my efforts to communicate with family members. If I do not want to reveal my innermost thoughts and feelings to intimates or have them disclose their innermost thoughts and feelings to me, then psychological privacy takes precedence over social privacy. Finally, if I want to make sure that certain governmental or private agencies will not have access to my medical or personnel records, I will attach the highest priority to the protection of my informational privacy.

The Communicative Functions of Proxemics

The functional importance of proxemics is undeniable. In fact, Patterson and Edinger (1987) maintained that our proxemic behaviors have at least some impact on the communicative functions of providing information, regulating interaction, and expressing intimacy. They highlight the importance of proxemic behaviors in persuasion and impression management, which in turn serve the social control function of communication.

Even though proxemics may have some impact on a number of communicative functions, *proxemic behaviors are particularly important when individuals are concerned with the impression management, affiliation, and privacy functions of communication.* While serving those functions, proxemic behaviors serve as a sensitive barometer that reflects the relative strength of the competing tendencies to both seek and avoid closer interaction with other individuals.

The Impression Management Function

Impression managers are concerned with many of the defining features of the images they project to others. Two of the most important dimensions of those images—likability and dominance—can be strongly affected by our proxemic behaviors.

In general, the closer you move to another person, the more that person is apt to like you (Andersen, 1988). The relationship between close physical proximity and liking is a strong one. Consider the people you know and ask yourself this question: Do I like best the individuals who stand or sit closest to me when I am interacting with them?

Liking is not apt to increase if a person moves so close to you as to be threatening or if you see the person as physically unattractive, however. Because the majority of the people we encounter are neither physically unattractive nor do they attempt interaction at distances that are so close as to be unseemly, communicating at close distances with most of the people you encounter should involve little risk for you. Research already cited in this chapter supports the conclusion that people will probably like you more as you move closer to them, even if you are violating their distance preferences; the qualifier here is that the "violatee's" general perception of you as "violator" must be favorable.

Judgments of how dominant you are will also probably be affected by your proxemic behavior. Dominant people typically interact with other individuals at closer interaction distances and claim more personal territory than submissive individuals. The impact of proxemics on judgments of dominance is particularly strong in the small group (Andersen, 1988). In small-group contexts, dominant individuals typically choose to sit at the head of the table (Riess, 1982), and the greatest degree of dominance is attributed to the person seated highest, who sits in front of the interaction partner, or who stands (Schwartz, Tesser, & Powell, 1982).

The Affiliation Function

The need for closer affiliation with other human beings is a strong one. The term *closer* in turn suggests that we communicate the strengths of our affiliative needs via our physical proximity to other human beings. We do know that persons who move closer to others are often viewed as more friendly and extroverted, whereas they tend to be perceived more negatively as they move away (Patterson & Sechrest, 1970). Relatedly, if we assume a sociopetal spatial orientation, we signal our desire to develop closer interpersonal relationships with others. If we assume a sociofugal orientation, we signal our desire for greater separation in both a literal and a symbolic sense.

In some instances, individuals seem to experience strong needs for affiliation and privacy at the same time. A physically intimate couple, for example, might communicate in public in such a way as to make clear their wish to be maximally involved with each other whereas they want minimal contact with anyone else. Similarly, groups such as nudists might live in a remote, walled area in order to satisfy their need to affiliate with each other. At the same time, their need for privacy dictates that they exhibit a type of territorial behavior that assures that they will be protected from intrusion by and affiliation with outsiders.

The Privacy Function

The privacy need is also a strong one for many people. As we have already indicated, our attempts to satisfy that need are apt to begin and end with the ways we use space, distance, and territory. Although definitions of privacy are culture specific, the need for some degree of privacy seems to be a universal one.

We communicate the strength of our desire for privacy in many ways. They include the way we relate to others spatially, the placement of furniture in our offices, and the use of territorial markers inside and outside of our home. Although the strength of our needs for privacy may vary, we should recognize that our proxemic behavior represents an effective way of communicating and satisfying our needs for privacy.

The Effects of Violating Proxemic Norms and Expectations

Whether we are talking about the concept of space, distance, territory, crowding, or privacy, individuals have well-developed expectations. Those expectations specify what is acceptable proxemic behavior in a given situation. Because many of those expectations are sufficiently stable and enduring and are shared by so many people, they might be called *proxemic norms.* Although it is difficult to generalize about proxemic behavior, one generalization has been consistently supported in the past by empirical research. Simply put, *the violation of proxemic expectations, or norms, results in consistently disruptive effects on the communication between two or more people.*

Burgoon's (1976; 1988) development and test of a model of proxemic violations suggests that qualification of this generalization is now necessary. As we have indicated, the violation of proxemic norms might result in positive effects under certain conditions. At the same time, we must recognize that the negative consequences that are associated with the strong and sustained violations of proxemic norms are well documented.

So long as we maintain a distance perceived as "comfortable" or appropriate by persons with whom we interact, we know that close physical proximity is consistently associated with positive affect, friendship, and attraction. Close physical proximity that does not violate the interactants notion of "comfortable interaction distance" serves to signal liking and is viewed as a sign of friendliness. However, both the violated and the violator become visibly uncomfortable when interaction is attempted at inappropriately close distances (Sundstrom & Altman, 1976).

Individuals who perceive the violator as someone who is apt to provide them with negative rewards will react negatively when the violator moves closer to them than the proxemic norm dictates. Violators seen as possessing negative-reward power are judged to be threatening at much great distances than violators possessing positive-reward power. As a result, negatively rewarding individuals would be well advised to maintain a communicating distance greater than that specified by the proxemic norm.

Unfortunately, many of the studies of the effects of proxemic violations that have been undertaken were conducted in the somewhat antiseptic and unreal environment of classrooms, libraries, and mental hospitals. In the classroom and library studies, a "plant" is typically used and one or more unsuspecting subjects is approached. In one typical library study, in which a person trained by the experimenter violated the spatial expectations of library users, only 18 of 80 subjects actually left during the 10-minute period of the intrusions (Patterson, Mullens, & Romano, 1971). Although a relatively small number of individuals resorted to "flight" when their proxemic expectations were violated, many used elbows, knees, books, and personal artifacts as barriers to preserve further violations of their personal space.

The communicative impact of violating (or conforming) to spatial expectations has been measured largely in quantitative terms. The questions are straightforward. How many people will physically withdraw from a social situation if their spatial boundaries have been violated? How many people in rather closely proximity to a person will that person tolerate? How much space do people require to separate themselves from others? At what point does the violation of proxemic norms lead to the sensation of crowding and resultant efforts to achieve greater privacy?

Distance between individuals seems to have its greatest impact on the development of interpersonal relationships. Individuals who use mutually preferred interaction distances facilitate the development of satisfying interpersonal relationships. Beware of increasing the distance between yourself and another individual as you interact. This practice will probably create a negative impression and could destroy interpersonal trust (Patterson & Sechrest, 1970).

As we have already pointed out, personal characteristics of the proxemic violator such as age, sex, and ethnicity help shape the way violatees react to a violation of their proxemic expectations and preferences. Two studies (Kmiecik, Mausar, & Banziger, 1979; Smith & Knowles, 1979) support the view that physically unattractive persons should attempt more distant communication than physically attractive persons. Subjects waiting at a stoplight to cross a street were "threatened" by the approach of a physically unattractive pedestrian; they crossed the street more quickly as the physically unattractive pedestrian approached.

The important point to remember is that the violation of proxemic norms is typically disruptive unless the violator has some highly desirable personal qualities or qualifications. In general, violation of proxemic norms is a sort of "noise," because it diverts the attention of the interactants from their communicative objectives. In fact, we know that the violation of proxemic norms is almost always uncomfortable for both the violator and the invadee. Violations are particularly discomforting and stressful when the invadee neither expects nor desires interaction with the invader (Sundstrom & Altman, 1976).

If the violations of preferred spatial orientations typically produce identifiably disruptive effects on interpersonal communication, then certain types of violations seem to be particularly disruptive. Having one's territory invaded, being crowded, and having one's right to privacy violated are uncomfortable at best and threatening at worst.

The boundaries of public, home, and interactional territories are clearly delineated by personal markers. Violations of territorial boundaries are disruptive. Territorial encroachment usually results in defensive reactions designed to defend or to reestablish territory. Fences, hedges, Private Property signs, and guards are all examples of markers used to identify the boundaries of home territories. Reaction to the violation of home territory is so strong that on numerous occasions violators have been shot. Violations of public and interactional territories are typically handled by more subtle means. Books and clothing are used to reserve spaces in public; hostile glances and unpleasant facial expressions are used to warn violators that they are not welcome; groups might resort to in-group jargon or in-group languages to signal intruders that they have violated territorial boundaries; and the ultimate response to territorial encroachment is aggression and fighting (Altman, 1975).

The sensation of overcrowding can produce many disruptive effects. Burgoon (1982) documents that the feeling of being crowded can produce anxiety, excessive stress, illness, feelings of helplessness, impaired cognitive functioning, loss of self-identity, and withdrawal. Indeed, people living in crowded conditions not only tend to withdraw socially from their housemates, but they tend also to be less supportive of them (Evans & Lepore,

1993). High-density environments tend to be associated with the sensation of crowding and negative effects. Thus, employees in a high-density environment in an "open office" felt more crowded than colleagues in a low-density "partitioned office," with the result that they felt a perceived lack of task and communication privacy and reported lower "office satisfaction" (Oldham, 1988).

Finally, the violation of a person's privacy preferences can result in more intense social stimulation than a person desires. When the desired level of privacy exceeds the actual level of privacy, the sensation of crowding results. Baldassare (1978) emphasized that if "there is not enough room or privacy to conduct desired roles alone and with others, competition for space use may occur. Undoubtedly, the possibilities of incomplete role performances, intrusions, and the blocking of desired role enactments are heightened" (p. 47).

Resentment, conflict, and withdrawal frequently result when individuals' felt need for privacy is frustrated by the violation of their proxemic expectations. In our society, certain groups of individuals have difficulty maintaining desired levels of privacy. For example, the personal space of short people is much more frequently violated than the personal space of tall people. In one study (Caplan & Goldman, 1981), the personal space of short males (5ft 5in.) was invaded 69 percent of the time, and the space of tall males (6ft 2in.) was invaded only 31 percent of the time. Furthermore, women are at a disadvantage when they use space to try to achieve desired levels of privacy. This is true in part because the "private territory" claimed by males as their own is significantly larger than that claimed by females (Mercer & Benjamin, 1980).

In short, our use of space represents an important communicative medium. When we conform to the proxemic expectations of those with whom we interact, we enhance our capacity to communicate successfully. When we violate proxemic expectations, we can anticipate resentment, resistance, and conflict in our interpersonal relationships. Successful communicators exhibit the capacity to interpret accurately the spatial expectations of other persons and adjust their own proxemic behaviors so that they are compatible with those expectations.

Summary

Proxemics is defined as the study of how individuals use space to communicate. To understand the communicative effects and implications of our proxemic behaviors, we must understand the significance of space, distance, territory, crowding, and privacy. The successful communicator must be able to recognize and adjust to the normative expectations that have been developed for each type of proxemic behavior.

The three major types of space that have communicative significance are fixed-feature, semifixed-feature, and nonfixed-feature space. Because semifixed-feature and nonfixed-feature space can be controlled by the communicator, they are especially important. Those two types of space can be used to satisfy the sociopetal function of promoting communicative interaction or to satisfy the sociofugal function of inhibiting communicative interaction.

Normative distances have been established for intimate, personal, social-consultative, and public communication. Beyond respective cultural norms, comfortable distances for individual communicators vary. To determine comfortable interaction distances, we must take into account both cultural norms and the idiosyncratic preferences of persons with whom we communicate.

The boundaries of public, home, interactional, and body territories are delineated by personal markers. To disregard such markers is to risk being perceived as both insensitive and inept. Violations of body territory have a particularly disruptive impact on interpersonal communication.

Privacy is defined as selective control of access to one's self or to one's group. Privacy must be classified into four types: solitude, intimacy, anonymity, and reserve. Because individuals desire various degrees of privacy, it is particularly important to understand the nature and uses of the four major dimensions of privacy: physical privacy, social privacy, psychological privacy, and informational privacy.

When proxemic expectations are violated, individuals frequently experience the sensation of crowding. One result might be that a person's needs for adequate privacy are frustrated. In general, the consequences of overcrowding are undesirable.

Our proxemic behaviors are relevant to and have an impact on a number of important functions of communication. However, the most important communicative functions of proxemics are the impression management function, the affiliation function, and the privacy function.

Finally, the violation of proxemic norms and expectations is associated with a substantial number of undesirable effects. Thus, the person who violates proxemic norms and expectations often makes negative impressions, runs the risk of personal rejection, promotes conflict, and contributes to the deterioration of interpersonal relationships. On the other hand, the violation of proxemic norms can produce positive effects if the violator is a high-reward person who compensates for the proxemic violation with appropriate adjustments in other proxemic behaviors.

References

Altman, I. (1975). *The environment and social behavior.* Monterey, CA: Brooks/Cole.

Andersen, P. (1988). Nonverbal communication in the small group. In R. S. Cathcart & L. A. Samovar (Eds.), *Small group communication: A reader.* (5th ed., pp. 333–350). Dubuque, IA: Wm. C. Brown.

Baldassare, M. (1978). Human spatial behavior. *Annual Review of Sociology, 4,* 29–56.

Baxter, J. C. (1970). Interpersonal spacing in natural settings. *Sociometry, 33,* 449–454.

Burgess, J. W (1983). Developmental trends in proxemic spacing behavior between surrounding companions and strangers in casual groups. *Journal of Nonverbal Behavior, 7,* 158–168.

Burgoon, J. K. (1982). Privacy and communication. In M. Burgoon (Ed.), *Communication yearbook, 6* (pp. 206–249). Beverly Hills, CA: Sage.

Burgoon, J. K. (1988). Spatial relationships in small groups. In R. S. Cathcart & L. A. Samovar (Eds.). *Small group communication: A reader* (5th ed. pp. 351–366). Dubuque, IA: Wm. C. Brown.

Burgoon, J. K., & Aho, L. (1982). Three field experiments on the effects of violations of conversational distance. *Communication Monographys, 49,* 71–88.

Burgoon, J. K., Buller, D. B., & Woodall, W. G. (1989). *Nonverbal communication: The unspoken dialogue.* New York: Harper & Row.

Burgoon, J. K., & Hale, J. L. (1988). Nonverbal expectancy violations: Model elaboration and application to immediacy behaviors. *Communication Monographys, 55,* 58–79.

Burgoon, J. K., & Jones, S. B. (1976). Toward a theory of personal space expectations and their violations. *Human Communication Research, 2,* 131–146.

Caplan, M. E., & Goldman, M. (1981). Personal space violations as a function of height. *Journal of Social Psychology, 114,* 167–171.

Edwards, J. N., Fuller, T. D., Sermsri, S., & Vorakitphokatorn, S. (1994). Why people feel crowded: An examination of objective and subjective crowding. *Population & Environment: A Journal of Interdisciplinary Studies, 16,* 149–173.

Evans, G. W., & Lepore, S. J. (1992). Conceptual and analytic issues in crowding research. *Journal of Environmental Psychology, 12,* 163–173.

Evans, G. W., & Lepore, S. J. (1993). Household crowding and social support: A quasiexperimental analysis. *Journal of Personality & Social Psychology, 65,* 308–316.

Fuller, T. D., Edwards, J. N., Sermsri, S., & Vorakitphokatorn, S. (1993). Housing, stress, and physical well-being: Evidence from Thailand. *Social Science & Medicine, 36,* 1417–1428.

Fuller, T. D., Edwards, J. N., Vorakitphokatorn, S., & Sermsri, S. (1993). Household crowding and family relations in Bangkok. *Social Problems, 40,* 410–430.

Goffman, E. (1971). *Relations in public.* New York: Harper.

Hall, E. T. (1968). Proxemics. *Current Anthropology, 9,* 83.

Hall, E. T. (1969). *The hidden dimension.* New York: Doubleday.

Hayduk, L. A. (1981). The permeability of personal space. *Canadian Journal of Behavioral Science, 13,* 272–287.

Hocking, J. E. (1982). Sports and spectators: Intra-audience effects. *Journal of Communication, 32,* 100–108.

Hortascu, N., Duzen, E., Arat, S., Atahan, D., & Uzer, B. (1990). Intrusion upon same-sex or different-sex dyads in a Turkish university dining hall. *International Journal of Psychology, 25,* 33–37.

Iwata, O. (1992). Crowding and behavior in Japanese public spaces: Some observations and speculations. *Social Behavior & Personality, 20,* 57–70.

Kamal, P., & Mehta, M. (1987). Social environment and feeling of crowding. *Indian Psychological Review, 32,* 25–29.

Kinkade, P., Leone, M., & Semond, S. (1995). The consequences of jail crowding. *Crime & Delinquency, 4,* 150–161.

Kmiecik, C., Mausar, P., & Banziger, G. (1979). Attractiveness and interpersonal space. *Journal of Social Psychology, 108,* 227–279.

Leathers, D. G.. (1989). *Jimmy Swaggart: The histrionics of piety.* Paper presented at the convention of the Southern States Communication Association, Louisville, KY.

Lepore, S. J., Evans, G. W., & Schneider, M. L. (1992). Role of control and social support in explaining the stress of hassles and crowding. *Environment & Behavior, 24,* 795–811.

Lombardo, J. P. (1986). Interaction of sex and sex roles in response to violations of preferred seating arrangements. *Sex Roles, 15,* 173–183.

Lyman, S. M., & Scott, M. B. (1967). Territoriality: A neglected sociological dimension. *Social Problems, 15,* 237–241.

Malandro, L., & Barker, L. L. (1983). *Nonverbal communication.* Reading, MA: Addison-Wesley.

McCarthy, D., & Saegert, S. (1978). Residential density, social overload, and social withdrawal. *Human Ecology, 6,* 253–272.

Mercer, G. W., & Benjamin, J. L. (1980). Spatial behavior of university undergraduates in double-occupancy residence rooms: An inventory of effects. *Journal of Applied Social Psychology, 10,* 32–44.

Newell, P. B. (1994). A systems model of privacy. *Journal of Environmental Psychology, 14,* 65–78.

Newton, J. W., & Mann, L. (1980). Crowd size as a factor in the persuasion process. A study of religious crusade meetings. *Journal of Personality and Social Psychology, 39,* 874–883.

Oldham, G. R. (1988). Effects of changes in workspace partitions and spatial density on employee reactions: A quasi-experiment. *Journal of Applied Psychology, 73,* 253–258.

Oseland, N. (1993). The evaluation of space in homes: A facet study. *Journal of Environmental Psychology, 13,* 251–261.

Patterson, M. L., & Edinger, J. (1987). A functional analysis of space in social interaction. In A. W. Siegman & S. Feldstein (Eds.), *Nonverbal behavior and communication* (pp. 523–562). Hillsdale, NJ: Erlbaum.

Patterson, M. L., Mullens, S., & Romano, J. (1971). Compensatory reactions to spatial intrusion. *Sociometry, 34,* 116–120.

Patterson, M. L., & Sechrest, L. B. (1970). Interpersonal distance and impression formation. *Journal of Personality, 38,* 106.

Pedersen, D. M. (1994). Privacy preferences and classroom seat selection. *Social Behavior & Personality, 22,* 393–398.

Pedersen, D. M., & Frances, S. (1990). Regional differences in privacy preferences. Psychological Reports, 66, 731–736.

Rapoport, A. (1982). *The meaning of the built environment.* Beverly Hills, CA: Sage.

Riess, M. (1982). Seating preferences as impression management: A literature review and theoretical integration. *Communication, 11,* 85–113.

Ruback, R. B., & Pandev, J. (1992). Very hot and really crowded: Quasi-experimental investigations of Indian "tempos." *Environment & Behavior, 24,* 527–554.

Rustemli, A. (1986). Male and female personal space needs and escape reactions under intrusion: A Turkish sample. *International Journal of Psychology, 21,* 503–511.

Schwartz, B., Tesser, A., & Powell, E. (1982). Dominance cues in nonverbal behavior. *Social Psychology Quarterly, 45,* 114–120.

Smith, R. J., & Knowles, E. S. (1979). Affective and cognitive mediators of reactions to spatial invasions. *Journal of Experimental Social Psychology, 15,* 437–452.

Sommer, R. (1966). Man's proximate environment. *Journal of Social Issues, 22,* 60–61.

Sommer, R. (1967). Sociofugal space. *American Journal of Sociology, 72,* 65.

Sommer, R. (1974). *Tight spaces: Hard architecture and how to humanize it.* Englewood Cliffs, NJ: Prentice-Hall.

Stokols, S., Ohlig, W., & Resnick, S. M. (1978). Perception of residential crowding, classroom experiences, and student health. *Human Ecology, 4,* 46–47.

Sundstrom, E., & Altman, I. (1976). Interpersonal relationships and personal space: Research review and theoretical model. *Human Ecology, 4,* 46–47.

Westin, A. (1970). Privacy and freedom. New York: Atheneum.

Zeegers, S. K., Readdick, C. A., & Hansen-Gandy, S. (1994). Daycare children's establishment of territory to experience privacy. *Children's Environments, 11,* 265–271.

C h a p t e r **6**

Tactile Communication

Touch is the communicative medium of close encounters. The closest, most intimate encounters of all are of course sexual in nature. We are all acutely aware that we signal sexual interest in another person by touching them, we acknowledge our readiness for the sex act by specific kinds of touching, and we consummate a sexual relationship by limb-to-limb tactile contact. Encounters with other individuals that develop into close interpersonal relationships are hardly limited to intimate sexual contact, however. You will recognize without extended thought that touch also plays a central role in your relational communication with such close contacts as your parents, your brothers and sisters, your good friends, and other acquaintances with whom you would like to develop close relationships. Therefore, Collier (1985) simply stressed what surely has already occurred to you when he wrote that "Touching is one of the most powerful means for establishing and maintaining social contact" (p. 27).

When you think about touch as a medium of communication, there are probably some things you do know and some things you do not know. You probably do not know that a large part of your brain is devoted to receiving and interpreting messages communicated by the skin. Similarly you may not know that your skin accounts for 20 percent of your body weight, or that there are more than a half-million receptor sites on your skin that pick up tactile contact made by others and transmit a signal to your brain as to the type of touch made.

If you are honest, you will probably admit that on more than one occasion you have encountered a person at work, in a classroom, or in another social context who instantly struck you as physically appealing. Once you established verbal contact with this person you probably devoted a good deal of thought to when you should first attempt intimate touching, what the nature of the touching would be, and what part of the body you would touch. You recognized also, if you are a reasonably sensitive person, that the decisions you made were important for at least two reasons. First, your decision to initiate some type of intimate touching of another person at a particular time meant that you would be transmitting "undeniable messages" because your decisions were made consciously. Second, you probably recognized that your tactile messages would have to be compatible with the touching and touch avoidance preferences of the person to whom they were directed if they were to be successful.

Touch communicates many different meanings. Touch has substantial communicative potential, but this potential has not been fully explored. Our lack of knowledge about touch can be attributed to a number of factors. First, many individuals have accepted the misconception that touch is a primitive sense and, therefore, has limited value in the transmission and reception of meanings in interpersonal communication. Second, ironic as it may seem, in an age that has seen the rise of the Esalen Institute—with its nude encounter and sensitivity-training sessions—ours is a society with strong inhibitions and taboos about touching others. Finally, much less empirical research has been done on touch than on other types of nonverbal communication such as facial expressions and eye behaviors. Consequently, we lack a sufficiently precise and detailed terminology to describe the modalities used to touch others, to define the more particularized meanings communicated by touch, and to pinpoint the impact of a variety of personality and demographic variables on the quantity and quality of touching done in interpersonal contexts.

We should not underestimate the important impact of touch on successful interpersonal communication, however. Touch cannot communicate the highly specialized emotions that can be communicated by facial expressions or vocal cues, but this should not obscure the fact that touch often serves as the last medium available to the elderly and to the critically ill to communicate feelings. As a means of communicating caring, comfort, affection, and reassurance, touch is the preeminent sense. As we shall see, touch can also serve important power and affiliative functions in interpersonal communication, functions which are not served at all, or frequently are not served as well, by any other nonverbal medium of communication.

The Nature of Touch

We are just beginning to realize that the skin is a sense organ of great value in interpersonal communication. Scott (1973) maintained that:

> *the skin is the greatest sense of all. There are those physiologists, in fact, who consider touch the only sense. Hearing begins with sound waves touching the inner ear; taste with a substance touching the taste buds; and sight with light striking the cornea. All the other senses are therefore really derivations of touch as an expression of stimulation to the skin, muscles, and blood vessels.* (p. 12)

The great applied communication value of touch can be illustrated by the experience of Helen Keller. More than one authority has argued that if Helen Keller had lost her sense of touch, even while regaining hearing and sight, it is doubtful whether her spirit and talent would have left such a mark (Montagu, 1971).

Until recently, we knew little about what could be communicated by touch. For some time, however, serious students of the skin have known that the amount and kind of touching received by both animals and humans as they matured have a great impact on their behavior. The effect of touching on behavior is strongly associated with the fact that

> *the sense of touch, "the mother of the senses," is the earliest to develop in the human embryo. When the embryo is less than an inch long from crown to rump and*

less than eight weeks old, light stroking of the upper lip or wings of the nose will cause bending of the neck and trunk away from the source of stimulation. (Montagu, 1971, p. 1)

The skin is such a sensitive organ because its surface area has a tremendous number of sensory receptors that receive stimuli of heat, cold, pressure, and pain (Collier, 1985). Montagu (1971) estimated that there are 50 receptors per 100 sq mm; that tactile points vary from 7 to 135 per sq cm, and that the number of sensory fibers which connect the skin with the spinal cord is well over half a million. The number and importance of sensory stimuli experienced through the skin is much greater than most people realize. The acuteness and variety of sensations experienced via the skin is explained in part by the surprising size of the tactile areas of the brain. A disproportionate amount of cerebral space is devoted to the processing of sensory stimuli that come from the lips, the index finger, and the thumb.

We have known for some time that baby monkeys do not develop properly without physical intimacy and that lack of caressing is positively associated with a high death rate among nursery babies (Young, 1973). Harlow (1958), in his famous experiments, exposed baby monkeys to two types of surrogate mothers. One "mother" was made of wire and provided milk and protection to the infant monkeys; the other "mother" was made of rubber and terry cloth but provided no milk or protection. The infant monkeys consistently chose the terry cloth "mother," so it seems obvious that the need to be touched was overriding. Harlow concluded, therefore, that a monkey's access to physical contact was a crucial variable in the development of normal adult behavior—assuring normal affectional responsivity and normal sexual behavior. Subsequent studies on other monkeys, rats, lambs, and other animals have supported the same central conclusion: *Touching is a requirement for the healthy development of animals.*

Many of the animal experiments seemed to be designed to support the inference that suitable maturation of human beings also requires an extensive amount of touching, in the form of fondling, stroking, caressing, or even licking. Hence, when we speak of "skin (cutaneous tactile) stimulation, we are quite evidently speaking of a fundamental and essential ingredient of affection and equally clearly of an essential element in the healthy development of every organism" (Montagu, 1971, p. 31).

Adult behavior is also markedly affected by one's tactile history. For example, Hollender (1970) found that in some women the need to be held is so compelling that it resembles addiction. Those deprived of tactile stimulation earlier in their lives used both direct and indirect means (i.e., sexual enticement and seduction) to obtain the holding or cuddling desired. Not surprisingly, half of Hollender's sample was composed of female psychiatric patients. Their behavior supported his conclusion that the need or wish to be held is a relevant consideration in the treatment of several psychiatric disorders. Similarly, Hollender, Luborsky, and Scaramella (1969) studied the correlation between the intensity of the need to be held or cuddled and the frequency with which sexual intercourse is bartered for this satisfaction. They found that every high scorer on the body-contact scale (those with a great need to be touched) used sex in order to be held, whereas not a single low scorer did so.

The behavioral effects of quantitative and qualitative insufficiency of touch in childhood are numerous and generally accepted. The communicative potential of the skin has remained a mystery until recently, however. Slowly, we have begun to recognize that the skin is not only our most sensitive organ, but also our first means of communication.

As a reader, you may remain skeptical. You may think that it is fine to talk of touch as a mode of communication, but can anything of importance really be communicated solely through the medium of touch? Using electrodes attached to the fingers, to monitor the electrical messages which the skin transmits to the brain, Brown (1974) has demonstrated the remarkable capacity of the skin as a communication *sender.* In contrast, Geldhard (1968) has documented the skin's great value as a communication *receiver.* In so doing, he has established that the skin is capable of decoding a set of electrical impulses into specific symbols, words, and thoughts. He has developed a language of the skin.

The Skin as a Communication Sender

Can the skin send or transmit meaning? Barbara B. Brown answers yes, emphatically. The mind boggles at the possibility that the skin may be capable of sending messages that convey rather specific information and meaning. Nevertheless, she noted:

> All that is necessary to listen to the skin's emotional talk is several small electrodes taped to the skin, and a proper recording instrument. Then you listen. The skin will tell you when there is emotion, how strong the emotion is, and even just how emotional a person you are. It also will very likely tell you when you are lying. (Brown, 1974, p. 52)

Polygraphers and medical researchers have long recognized the potential of the human skin as a communication sender. The polygraph exam is based on the assumption that changes in the liar's internal states at the moment of deception will be reflected in machine-monitored changes in skin-conductance, in pulse, and in heart rate, for example. Similarly, physicians and medical technicians monitor the condition of the heart, brain, and other bodily organs by decoding the electrical messages that are transmitted via the skin (Collier, 1985).

A series of experiments have been conducted that suggest that the skin will much more accurately than the eye, for example, signal the brain as to what events are being perceived in the environment. Because the skin operates at the subconscious level, it is not biased by group-conformity pressures and other external stimuli that might affect the accuracy with which our various senses perceive events and stimuli in our external environment.

The skin's sending capacity, when aided by machines, has perhaps best been demonstrated in the area of subliminal perception. In one experiment, "naughty" and "emotion-arousing" words were flashed on the screen so briefly that the subjects could not report what they had seen. Neutral words were mixed in with the arousing words. Although the subjects could neither see the words nor recognize them consciously, the skin reflected the difference in the emotional meaning of the words. There was an orienting response by the skin to every naughty word, but an absence of tactile response to neutral or bland words (Brown, 1974).

Such research and the results seem astounding. Nonetheless, Brown reports that simple electrodes attached to an individual's fingers will pick up the electricity of the skin and separate the slow from the fast activity. Slow activity is converted into a signal that represents the level of emotional response; fast activity reflects the type of emotional response. Obviously, this newly discovered communicative capacity of the skin has many practical applications.

One seemingly trivial though not unprofitable application is a machine you will see in virtually any large food supermarket, the Stress Test. The large sign on the machine says that by simply attaching a small sensor to two of your fingertips, your current level of stress will be revealed, that is, the machine may indicate that you are calm, normal, or under stress. Psychotherapists make a far more important use of the machine-read messages of the human skin; they interpret the messages sent by the skin to pinpoint emotional difficulties. Obviously, many other applications are possible, including the determination of whether and when the communicator is lying and whether the emotion the skin indicates an individual is really experiencing is consistent with the emotion he or she attempts to convey by some other means such as facial expressions.

In most real-world situations, we do not have the luxury of attaching machines to various parts of a person's body in order to decode the electrical messages being sent by the skin. Obviously, our potential for highly effective and efficient tactile communication would be greatly enhanced if we could accurately perceive—unaided by machine monitoring—the electrical messages sent to us by the touch of other individuals whom we encounter.

The potential of communication by electrical impulses or charges, is limited at the moment for several reasons. First, the electrical charges transmitted by the skin are so weak, typically only a few millivolts, that they are far below a person's threshold or ability to perceive. Second, even if some supersensitive person could detect such weak electrical impulses, that person would most likely be confused by the fact that electrical messages are transmitted from almost every organ of the body (Collier, 1985).

The skin also communicates many unintentional messages that do not require machine reading for accurate interpretation. Most notably, the skin communicates important messages by its appearance, for example, skin color, skin temperature, and perspiration (Collier, 1985). Such "appearance" cues can be the source of much personalized information about a communicator because communicators are generally not aware of the tactile messages they communicate by the appearance of their skin; they cannot consciously control these unintentional but undeniable messages.

Think for a moment about the information communicated to you by the skin color of persons with whom you have communicated. If a person is habitually "pasty-faced," what might you infer about his or her state of health? Have you been in a situation in which you noticed that an individual suddenly became "pale as a ghost"? What conclusion did you draw? What was your response when you noted that your interaction partner's skin felt "cold" even as you wrapped your partner in a passionate embrace? Finally, have you considered the possibility that there is a difference in the way people smell as a function of the type of task to which they address themselves as well as their current emotional state?

Recently, I attended the first meeting of the year for a high school debate team. The assistant debate coach talked with conviction about the benefits of debate and with humor about his memories of traveling to debate tournaments with young debaters. Somehow, I was not surprised when he turned to the young male members of the debate team and urged them to "bring plenty of deodorant to this year's first debate tournament. When you are under the stress that comes from competitive debate and intense concentration on an intellectual task you will sweat. Your sweat will smell different than the sweat of football players," he said.

Unintentional tactile messages are communicated most often and most accurately by three types of cues:

1. changes in temperature
2. changes in muscular tensions
3. changes in the amount of moisture on the skin

Collier (1985) has provided the most detailed and insightful analysis of the specific types of emotional information communicated by the appearance of the skin. Moreover, he spells out the practical value of this type of information for practitioners such as police interrogators and physicians.

Changes in skin temperature reflect the amount of blood flow to the skin. Thus, our skin is typically hot when we are emotionally aroused and cold when we are depressed. Blood flow increases when we become angry, skin temperature goes up, and we typically become red in the face. Blood flow decreases during fear and sadness with the result that skin temperature decreases. Interestingly, blood flow both alternately increases and decreases when we are embarrassed, and as a result a person may blush one moment and turn pale the next.

Muscular tension, in contrast, reveals less about the emotion a person is experiencing than about how hard a person is working to suppress or control certain emotions. Thus, Collier (1985) wrote:

> *Anxious people tend to tense their muscles, rigidify their movements, and overelevate their shoulders in an attempt to block the expression, and in some cases the experience, of an unpleasant or threatening emotional state. In extreme cases, this defense may develop into an enduring pattern of muscular rigidity.* (p. 36)

More specifically, such muscular tension has been found to be associated with the anxiety experienced when a person is lying.

Finally, sweat has consistently been found to be associated with negative emotions such as fear and stress. Visible perspiration is, therefore, a particularly unwelcome sight for the communicator who wishes to be perceived as cool, calm, and confident. Unlike a number of other types of tactile messages, sweating is a phenomenon that cannot be consciously controlled or suppressed. The unfortunate fact for impression managers is that to sweat or not to sweat is not the question—sweating is simply not a conscious choice available to them.

The Skin as a Communication Receiver

Few people would argue that the skin has no communicative value. Is there anyone who does not receive a message from the bite of an insect, from an angry jab in the ribs, or from a light touch on the thigh? We can and do recognize that the skin functions as a crude form of communication. Furthermore, as the examples suggest, most of us tend to think of the skin as a communication receiver. It is doubtful, however, whether very many of us have thought of the skin as a sophisticated receiving instrument capable of deciphering complex ideas and emotions transmitted by an outside source.

Thanks to the research of Frank A. Geldhard, at Princeton's Cutaneous Communication Laboratory, we now know that the skin does have amazing communicative capabilities as well as potential. Geldhard (1960) emphasized that the skin is the body's only communication receiver that can handle both spatial and temporal distinctions fairly effectively; the skin

> *can make both temporal and spatial discriminations, albeit not superlatively good ones in either case. It is a good "break-in" sense; cutaneous sensations, especially if aroused in unusual patterns, are highly attention-demanding. It is possible, therefore, that the simplest and most straightforward of all messages—warnings and alerts—should be delivered cutaneously.... If we add the clear superiority of touch (when vision and hearing are lacking or impaired) to the remaining modalities, the chemical senses, smell and taste, we have a formidable set of properties to utilize in cutaneous message processing—a list that ought to challenge us to find ways to capitalize on it.* (pp. 1583–1584)

In order to make reasonably effective use of the skin's communicative potential, it soon became obvious to Geldhard and his associates that a means for sending electrical impulses to different parts of the body would be necessary. In effect, these electrical impulses would symbolize thoughts and emotions that the skin would have to decode by assigning meanings to groups of symbols. Given this means of message transmission, the central question became how many different ways could the electrical impulses be used to transmit messages? In a very real sense, the problem was analogous to that faced by Morse as he contemplated telegraphic communication. Morse's deductions were simple but important. Variation in the length of time the telegraph key was held down and in the periods of time between keystrokes could be used to send messages by a code that was understandable to a communication receiver on the other end of the telegraph line.

Geldhard developed a language of the skin—*Vibratese*—consisting of electrical impulses transmitted to the skin that vary in intensity, duration, and frequency. Each letter in Geldhard's *Optohapt Alphabet* is represented by an electrical impulse with distinctive stimulus properties. An *Optohapt* (an instrument with a standard typewriter keyboard) is used to transmit cutaneous messages, in the form of electrical vibrations, to the skin of a receiver. Electrodes are attached to nine different places on the body (Geldhard, 1968).

The details of Geldhard's tactile communication system are explored in detail in his own research reports; however, the essence of the system can be described concisely. Letters of the alphabet are

> *each assigned a signal representing a unique combination of duration, intensity and location. The times were kept short—0.1, 0.3, 0.5 second for short, medium, and long, respectively. The most frequently occurring language elements were assigned shorter durations, enabling the system to "fly" at a rapid pace. This proved*

quite efficient, since the all-important vowels were assigned each to its own vibrators, and since letters followed each other promptly, with none of the wasteful silences that are built into International Morse. (Geldhard, 1968, p. 45)

Although research continues, the use of machines such as the Optohapt to transmit messages to the skin suggests that the skin is capable of decoding at least simple ideas as well as differentiating between emotions. The full potential of the skin as a communication receiver has clearly not been explored, however.

Although readers might marvel at the ingenuity and attention to detail reflected in the research of Geldhard and his associates, they could be bothered by two unanswered questions. First, does Vibratese as transmitted by the Optohapt have much practical, communicative value? Second, can the process of transmitting messages to the skin be modified in such a way that human beings can transmit as well as receive messages by Vibratese?

The first question can probably be more readily answered than the second. Certainly Vibratese can have great value in accurately communicating to individuals whose major senses, such as sight and hearing, are temporarily impaired. The most obvious example is the airplane pilot. Consider the commercial jet that plunged into the Pacific Ocean upon takeoff from Los Angeles International Airport, killing all aboard. Both the main and auxiliary generators ceased to function, and all lights in the airplane went out, including those in the cockpit. Suddenly, bereft of his primary means of determining distance, the pilot apparently became highly disoriented and flew the plane straight into the ocean. There is good reason to believe that he could have averted the disaster had his body been equipped with the nine vibrators that are used to receive tactile messages. The vibrators would have enabled the air traffic controller at Los Angeles to use his radar screen to give the pilot specific flight directions via electrical impulses sent by remote control; a pilot trained in Vibratese could easily have understood such tactile messages and maintained level flight while in a darkened cockpit. This is hardly a far-fetched idea. During World War II, research was conducted to determine if warning signals could be built into seat cushions so that pilots could literally hear and fly by the seat of their pants.

Clearly, Vibratese can be used as a warning system; as a means of supplementary information about one's environment; as a sophisticated language for the blind or deaf; and as a command system for pilots, auto drivers, and others. Of course, the possible applications in the area of surveillance and spying are enough to make an intelligence agent's mouth water. All of the foregoing applications are based on the assumption that a wireless means of activating the vibrators on the body will be developed. Such an invention should hardly tax the creativity of the modern engineer.

The greatest deficiencies of Vibratese, as a language of the skin, are that an individual must be wired, and impulses transmitted to a human receiver in order for communication to take place. Obviously, this places great restrictions on the receiver's mobility, and the wires and vibrators may be so distracting as to alter the nature of the perceived messages. In addition, it is obvious that Vibratese gives an individual only a receiving capacity; he or she has no independent capacity to transmit messages to the skin. Solutions to these problems are not presently available, but they should not take long in coming. Anyone who has seen police officers communicating by walkie-talkie or radio will realize that the same principles can be applied to tactile communications. There is no reason that messages in the form of electrical impulses cannot be sent by remote control and received by another individual who is not hampered by wires. Once that goal is achieved, tactile communication by electrical impulse will have almost the same flexibility as kinesic communication. Certainly, the potential for practical application will be greatly expanded.

Touching Norms

Tactile and proxemic communication are similar in one important respect, and they are interrelated conceptually. Both tactile and proxemic behavior are governed by an implicit set of norms that specify what types of behavior are acceptable in our society. When we violate either touching or proxemic norms, we usually make those with whom we interact uncomfortable. The absence of touching by others may be taken as a sign that the untouched person is insignificant and unimportant. Paradoxically, one who is touched too much is apt to be labelled as a person of inferior status.

Proxemic and tactile behavior are obviously interrelated in the sense that people must be close enough to one another for touching to be possible. Obviously, two individuals must be no further separated from each other than intimate distance (0 to 1½ ft if touching is to occur comfortably). Touching and close proximity both signal a desire for closeness and immediacy, although the physical act of touching may require greater physical proximity than is appropriate in public. A number of professionals such as nurses, gynecologists, masseurs, and beauticians are allowed to communicate at a distance known as *intimate distance* because the kind of touch they employ is defined as nonsocial rather than personal.

Finally, the interrelationships of tactile and proxemic communication can result in some unintended humor. For example, one of the many instructors who used the first edition of this book noted an apparent contradiction. In the chapter on proxemics, I reported results from a study that indicated that members of one ethnic group stood further apart when conversing than members of another ethnic group. In the chapter on tactile communication, I reported results from another study that indicated that members of the first ethnic group did more touching than members of the second ethnic group. The instructor reported that one of his students, a member of the first ethnic group, said jokingly "Do not be concerned. The results from the two studies are perfectly consistent. We just have longer arms."

Ours is a noncontact society, where limited touching in public is the norm. Touching norms dictate that even friends and intimates are expected to refrain from anything beyond perfunctory touching in public; touching among strangers is deemed to be deviant. Walker (1975) demonstrated the strength of touching norms in our society by asking strangers to touch each other during encounter-group exercises. He found that strangers who were forced to touch each other perceived the tactile contact as difficult, stress producing, and psychologically disturbing.

Touching norms that have developed in our society have been most strongly influenced by two factors: the region of the body that is touched, and the demographic variables that differentiate one communicator from another (i.e., gender, race, age, status, and culture). Successful communicators will not only exhibit an awareness of what regions of the body may be touched in specific contexts but will also understand that the gender, race, age, status, and culture of the interactants dictate what type and how much touching is socially acceptable.

Jourard (1966) has divided the body into the 24 regions that may be touched. His research indicates that opposite-sex friends may touch nearly all body regions. Touching of the head, shoulders, and arms occurs most frequently, but touching in other regions of the body is also acceptable. In general, touching of same-sex friends should be confined to shoulders, arms, and hands. Touching norms for males and females differ, however, and this difference seems to be reflected in their tactile behavior. Walker (1975) found, for example, that the amount of nonreciprocal touching exhibited by female pairs in sensitivity groups increased as the groups continued to meet, but touching of male pairs decreased over time. Males are reluctant to touch or to be touched by another male because their masculinity is threatened by the homosexual connotations of tactile contact.

Although touching norms dictate that intimates may touch "personal regions" of the body, nonintimates must confine touching to "impersonal regions" of the body. Communicators generally conform to this touching norm (Willis, Rinck, & Dean, 1978). Accordingly, touch among strangers should be confined primarily to the hand-to-hand contact associated with greetings and farewells. Touching norms that specify what regions of the body may be touched by whom seem to have remained relatively constant over time, although recent research suggests that opposite-sex friends are now engaging in an increasing amount of touching in the body areas between the chest and knees (Major, 1980).

Appropriate tactile communication requires familiarity with the demographic variables that exert a major influence on touching norms. These touching norms dictate that the gender, race, age, and status of the interactants must all be considered before we are in a position to exhibit socially appropriate tactile behavior.

Gender is clearly an important variable. The normative expectation is that the most touching should occur among opposite-sex friends. In both intimate and professional relationships, men are expected to touch women much more frequently than they are touched by women, and they do so. A decade ago, Major & Williams (1981) found that male-to-female touch was the most frequent type of touch (females touched children of both sexes more frequently than did men). In same-sex interaction, touch among women has previously been found to be more frequent than it is among men. Whatever the sex of the interactants, however the cultural norm dictates that the amount of touching be increased as their relationship becomes more personal (Major, 1980).

In their recent study on gender patterns in social touch, Major, Schmidlin, and Williams (1990) provided support for results from some earlier studies that had come under increasing challenge, and they greatly expanded our knowledge of the relative frequency with which men and women touch and are touched when interacting with members of their own gender and with each other. In particular, they found the following to be true:

1. Females are significantly more likely to be the recipients of touch than males,
2. Male-to-female touch is significantly more frequent than female-to-male touch,
3. Females have more positive attitudes toward same-sex touching than do males,
4. Touch between females, by far the most frequent type of touch, is more frequent than touch between males,
5. Cross-sex touch is more frequent than same-sex touch,
6. Females more frequently touch children than do males.

Clearly the attitudes of men and women toward touching and their actual tactile behavior vary substantially. Since interpersonal touch is very important in both opposite-sex and same-sex communication, gender differences deserve particular attention. We must recognize, for example, that women in the United States consistently report more positive attitudes to same-gender touch than do their male counterparts (Willis & Rawdon, 1994). In fact, men have much more homophobic attitudes toward same-gender touch than do women, which in turn seem to affect their touching behavior directly. Men touch their same-sex acquaintances less frequently than do women (Roese, Olson, Borenstein, Martin, & Shores, 1992). The touching pattern that emerges then reflects a gender asymmetry that confirms early findings that high-status individuals are more likely to touch low-status individuals than vice versa.

Henley (1977) maintained that the different touching norms for men and women perpetuate the idea that men have superior power and status. Women who touch men in professional settings must be aware that such touching is often interpreted as a sign of unseemly sexual advance. In contrast, the disproportionate amount of touching of women by men gives men the edge in asserting their dominance over women.

Race is also a potentially important determinant of touching norms. Because so little research has been done on this subject, firm generalizations are not really justified. There is some evidence to suggest that tactile contact is much more frequent among blacks than among whites. In one study of racial touching patterns (Smith, Willis, & Gier, 1980), blacks touched each other on the average 29.03 times per hour and whites touched each other only 9.87 times per hour. Consistent with previous findings, white males touched each other less frequently than any other sex-race dyad. However, black males touched each other more frequently than any sex-race dyad. Black females touched each other almost twice as often as white females. The available evidence does seem to point to a discernible touching pattern. When interacting with each other, blacks prefer and exhibit more touching than whites. However, both blacks and whites touch members of their own race much more frequently than they touch members of the other race (Smith et al., 1980; Willis et al., 1978).

Age has also proved to be an important factor in the development of touching norms. Age-related touching norms specify that high rates of touching are most appropriate for the young and the old. As might be expected, rates of touching are high during the first five years of a child's life. Frequency of touching has been observed to decrease from kindergarten through junior high, however. This finding may be attributed in part to the fact that the identity crisis experienced by young people makes the initiation of tactile communication difficult. Because tactile communication is one of the most intimate forms of communication, the initiation of tactile contact may be doubly difficult. During high school years, opposite-sex touch becomes more frequent, presumably because of the important functions of such touch in courtship and in sexual relationships. Finally, the amount of touching characteristically exhibited during the adult years seems to remain relatively constant until retirement age approaches. At that point, frequency of touching behavior increases markedly (Major, 1980).

Status also exerts a major influence on touching norms. High-status individuals touch low-status individuals much more frequently than they are touched by low-status individuals. Henley (1977) maintains that the "touching privilege" not only reliably identifies the high-status person but is reserved almost exclusively for their use.

The status of touchers seems to affect directly the amount of nonreciprocal touching they initiate. Watson (1975) studied the amount of touching of patients by staff members in a home for the elderly. He found *that the higher the rank of the nursing person, the greater the amount of touching of the patients.* Nurses touched patients much more frequently than aides, and aides touched patients much more frequently than orderlies. Low-status individuals seem intuitively to recognize that the touching norm specifies that the amount of touching they initiate should be limited. Thus, Watson (1975) concluded that "the frequent omissions of touching behavior by orderlies suggested a clear relation between low status in the nursing hierarchy and social constraint against touching" (p. 107).

Finally, the *culture* of communicators is an important determinant of the frequency of the various types of touching they exhibit and receive. Cultures are divided on the basis of those that are noncontact and those that are contact. Touching occurs more frequently in contact than in noncontact cultures. As one moves from north to south in Europe, for example, the amount of tactile contact increases. Whereas a young female from the United States might be shocked if she received a pinch on a buttock from a decorous British male her own age, she would probably anticipate this type of tactile contact from a same-aged Italian male. Touching is considerably more frequent in contact cultures that include Arabs, Latin Americans, and southern Europeans than in noncontact cultures such as northern Europeans and Americans (Collier, 1985).

Touching norms are in turn closely related to the concept of *touch avoidance.* Andersen, Andersen, and Lustig (1987) defined touch avoidance as a measure of a person's attitude toward touching, where being touched produces varying degrees of discomfort; "touch-avoidant individuals" touch when they are required to do so, but they find the touching to be an unpleasant experience. Their survey of the touch-avoidance practices of almost 4,000 subjects nationwide produced one finding of particular relevance to touching norms: Opposite-sex touch avoidance was higher for females than males. Thus, males appear to seek actively to touch females, whereas females exhibit a significantly greater tendency to avoid touch with males than vice versa.

Interestingly, the frequency or infrequency with which we touch and are touched seems to have important implications for our self-concept. Results from the touch-avoidance study just identified indicate that as people's predisposition to be touch-avoidant increases their desire to communicate with others decreases, their communication style becomes less open, and, most importantly, they tend to have lower self-esteem. A recent study by Fromme and colleagues (1989) supported and amplified those findings. Individuals who reported a high level of "touch comfort" were also found to be better socialized and less reticent and shy than their touch-avoidant counterparts. Touch comfort was found to be associated with effective interpersonal skills, assertiveness, an absence of negative affective states, and an effective style of self-presentation. In short, individuals who are comfortable giving and receiving touch, as opposed to those who are touch-avoidant, seem to exhibit a more active interpersonal style and have more satisfactory social relationships.

Normative touching practices and patterns within a given culture should not be equated with what is desirable. The distinction here is between what is and what ought to be. Until we expand our knowledge of tactile communication, a detailed set of guidelines that spell out desirable, culture-specific touching behaviors is probably not realistic. At the same time, a communicator who is thoroughly familiar with the touching norms in her or his society should be in a much better position to use tactile communication in a way that is both sensitive and socially appropriate.

The Semantics of Touch

The semantics of touch is not a simple matter. In a professional setting, for example, a man touching a woman can communicate a distinctively different meaning than would result from a woman touching a man. The meanings of touch are affected not only by who touches whom but by the *type of touch.* Nguyen, Heslin, and Nguyen (1975) identified four different types of touches: a *pat,* a *squeeze,* a *brush,* and a *stroke.* The squeeze and the brush seem to communicate meaning that varies with the context. In contrast, a pat is usually interpreted to mean that the toucher is playful and friendly, whereas the stroke signals affection and sexual desire.

Jones and Yarbrough (1985) deserve great credit for conducting a carefully conceived study designed explicitly to identify all of the meanings that can be communicated by humans. They found that touch communicates 12 distinct meanings which in turn can be classified into four major types of communicatively significant touch:

1. positive-affect touches
2. playful touches
3. control touches
4. ritualistic touches

Positive-affect touches include touches that communicate the meanings of support, appreciation, inclusion, sexual interest or attraction, and affection. *Playful touches* in turn communicate the meanings of playful affection and playful aggression. The kinds of meanings communicated by *control touches* are compliance, gaining attention, and announcing a response. Finally, *ritualistic touches* communicate the meanings associated with greeting and departure.

Not only have Jones and Yarbrough (1985) greatly expanded our knowledge of the semantics of touch, but their research also identifies the frequency with which particular types of touch are used to communicate each of the 12 meanings. Also noteworthy is the fact that once we understand the nature of the meanings that can be communicated by touch, we can write with more precision and insight about the major communicative functions served by touch.

The Communicative Functions of Touch

Touch serves a number of communicative functions of considerable importance, such as the communication of affection, commitment, control, intimacy, and sexual interest (Guerrero & Anderson, 1994). In the broadest sense, touch functions to express interpersonal attitudes (Argyle, 1986). From the perspective of the toucher, attitudes expressed may range from a mother's tender love for her infant to the unseemly aggression of an angry person.

We know too that touch plays a role in persuasion. Studies have repeatedly shown that communicators who touch those persons they are trying to persuade are more successful than those who do not (Patterson, Powell, & Lenihan, 1986). Kleinke (1977) found that subjects returned a dime left in a phone booth significantly more often to the caller who touched them than to the caller who did not. Similarly, Willis and Hamm (1980) report that touching behavior is linked to persuasive effectiveness. Experimenters asked consumers at a shopping center in Kansas City to either complete a brief rating scale or to sign a petition; half of the shoppers were touched lightly on the upper arm and half were not touched. The shoppers who were touched complied with the requests significantly more often than those who were not touched.

The three most important communicative functions associated with touch, however, are the support, power, and affiliation functions. Therefore, these functions deserve closer scrutiny.

The Support Function

Tactile communication assumes primary importance when we wish to emphasize feelings of *warmth, reassurance,* or *comfort* (Marx, Werner, & Cohen-Mansfield, 1989). Tactile messages have been found to be particularly effective in providing reassurance to those who need emotional support. Tactile messages seem to serve the therapeutic function better than any other means of communication. Jourard (1966) wrote with conviction that the therapeutic function of touch is the most important of all.

In their insightful book, *Nonverbal Communication with Patients: Back to the Human Touch* (1977), Blondis and Jackson made quite clear that in nursing touch can serve a more important therapeutic role than any other kind of nonverbal communication. They emphasize that our "first comfort in life comes from touch—and usually our last, since touch may communicate with the comatose, dying patient when words have no way of breaking through" (p. 6). Patients who have lost all verbal capacity can ordinarily feel a gentle touch and be moved by the message of caring and reassurance that it represents. Some terminal patients lose the power to speak. When this is the case, a tactile code is sometimes worked whereas the patient squeezes the nurse's hand once to mean yes and twice to mean no. In these instances the tactile message represents the patient's sole surviving means of communicating with the outside world.

Whether working in pediatrics, geriatrics, or the emergency receiving room, the nurse and other members of a medical team recognize that touch is frequently their most effective medium of emotional communication. This is probably true because the trauma associated with birth and critical illness strongly reinforces the patient's insecurities and fears while placing a premium on the emphatic response, which provides reassurance. Thus, a

> *patient may reach out to grasp the nurse's hand, seeking comfort and reassurance through the sense of touch. The positive feelings of sympathy, reassurance, understanding, and compassion are transmitted through touch—just as are the negative feelings of anger, hostility, and fear. To be truly therapeutic, tactile communication must be used at the appropriate time and place.* (Blondis & Jackson, 1977, p. 9)

Previous research has established that touching between individuals can play an important role in the maintenance of health. In reference to their current research, Lewis and her colleagues (1995) wrote:

One particular emphasis, however, has been on the impact of touch initiated by nurses and other health providers in influencing how well patients cope. Nurses may pat, hold, or shake a patient's hand as they seek to convey comfort, and they also touch patients as part of hospital procedures (while giving intravenous medications or monitoring a patient's blood pressures). The question then emerges about the circumstances when the use of touch by a health provider is perceived as appropriate. (p. 101)

The answer to that question is not simple. On the one hand, nurses are rated as more supportive and competent the more they exhibit touching when interacting with the patient. However, the sex of the patient clearly affects how the nurse's touching is perceived. Female patients, compared to males, perceive nurse-initiated touch more positively. This finding in turn may be linked at least in part to sex-role stereotyping. Stereotypically, females prefer supportiveness whereas males may "react less favorably to a nurse who uses touch because the touch implies vulnerability and dependency for the patient" (Lewis et al., pp. 110–111).

The role of touch in providing support and nurturance in parent-child relationships is well established. With increasing concern about child sexual abuse, more attention is being given to assessing the relative appropriateness of different kinds of intrafamily touching. Thus, Harrison-Speake and Willis (1995) discovered reasonably clear overall norms for parent-child touch. They found, for example, lower approval ratings for touching older as opposed to younger children; higher approval ratings for mothers than for fathers when applied to lap-sitting, kissing, and bathing their children; and higher approval ratings for lap-sitting and kissing when applied to girls as opposed to boys.

The need for touching that provides support continues to be strong for many adults. Thus, the types of "body awareness therapy" associated with Rolfing and the Esalen Institute at Big Sur in California are based on the same premise. Supportive touch by other persons is important in attaining and maintaining good health both physically and psychologically. In our increasingly cynical society, however, one runs the risk that touching intended to be supportive may be interpreted as sexual in nature.

Given the therapeutic power of touch, it is a sad fact that many individuals who most need touch are the least likely to receive it. Results from one study indicate that severely impaired patients are touched much less frequently by members of a medical team than are those with less severe impairments. Similarly, patients who have had a breast removed or who have undergone a sex-change operation are less likely to be touched than those who have received less drastic medical treatment (Watson, 1975).

The Power Function

Touch probably functions most effectively to delineate the relative power, dominance, and status of interacting individuals. Henley's fascinating research (1977) has established quite clearly that the frequency with which we touch and are touched by others is a reliable indicator of our perceived power. Results from her research show that

> *people reported more likelihood of their touching subordinates and coworkers than bosses; of touching younger or same-age people than older ones; and of touching sales clerks than police officers. Likewise, their expectations of others' touching them also reflected their hierarchical relationship: for example, they reported more probability of boss and coworker touching them than of a subordinate doing so.* (p. 104)

In short, the powerful person is apt to be the toucher and the powerless person the touched. Because of this relationship, the power of touch is a privilege reserved for the powerful. This relationship applies even to the "untouchable" castes of India. They are called untouchable because their low status dictates that they may not touch members of a higher caste.

Touch is so effective a medium for the communication of power cues that touchers are perceived to have more power and status than the touched, regardless of the gender of the toucher or the touched (Scroggs, 1980). To touch enhances one's perceived power; to be touched diminishes perceived power. Touchers have consistently been perceived as more dominant and assertive than nontouchers (Major, 1980). Finally, observers who have looked at photographs of male–female dyads, some who were touching and some who were not touching, rated the touchers as significantly more powerful, strong, superior, and dominant (Summerhayes & Suchner, 1978).

In her insightful summary of research on the meaning of touch, Major (1980) emphasized that touch strongly and reliably shapes perceptions of one's power. She wrote that empirical research strongly supports Henley's theory that

> *touching implies power. Across experiments, the initiator of touch is seen as more powerful, dominant, and of higher status than the recipient. Furthermore, it appears that touch affects the balance of power in a relationship by simultaneously enhancing that of the toucher and diminishing that of the recipient.* (p. 26)

Although aggression has been treated by one scholar as a separate function served by touch (Argyle, 1986), it surely represents an extreme effort by one person to dominate another person. Thus, pushing, kicking, and outright physical attack may be socially inappropriate forms of tactile communication, but they are undertaken with the objective of dominating another individual. Aggressive touch, therefore, serves the power function.

Quite clearly, touchers are perceived as more powerful than the touched, and that relationship holds without regard to the gender, age, or status of the interactants. Furthermore, the failure to touch others consistently results in a diminution of one's perceived power.

The Affiliation Function

We have already discussed the importance of human touch in forming close interpersonal relationships with other people. In fact, the amount of reciprocal touching done by two people is usually a reliable indicator of how much they like each other (Collier, 1985).

Touch is important in the courtship behaviors that start with sexual interest and end in some cases with sexual intercourse (Pisano, Wall, & Foster, 1986). In our society, the courtship process consists of a sequence of touching steps, defined by the part of the body that is touched, that must be followed. Engaging in mouth-to-breast contact on a second date, for example, would probably be judged as "fast." Not advancing beyond hand-holding after a year, however, might be regarded as "slow." In an intimate relationship, the physical messages communicated by your partner's skin may be your best guide as to whether and when you should proceed with more intimate touching. If your partner's skin is cold, tense, and clammy, you need not be an Ivy League graduate to know that you should not proceed.

The person contemplating the use of touch for sexual purposes would be well advised to check Chapter 5 in a new book by Jones entitled *The Right Touch: Understanding and Using the Language of Physical Contact* (1994). The author has identified the following types of sexual touches in the suggestively titled chapter, "Touch and Sexuality: Attracting and Finding Pleasure With a Partner": *explicitly sexual touches (type #1 being the casual sexual touch and type #2 being the intense sexual touch), seduction touches, flirtation touches, and the "this one is mine" touch.* The author also has made clear that prudent individuals should exercise great care in using any type of touch that is intended to communicate sexual meanings or that may be so interpreted (see his insightful discussion of 10 touching taboos in the office in Chapter 10).

We should recognize that individuals who are romantically involved with each other may interpret their touch quite differently. Thus, females tend to associate progressively intimate touches with greater commitment, although males do not necessarily do so; a woman's association of touching with commitment seems to become stronger as the touching becomes highly intimate (Johnson & Edwards, 1991). Relatedly, men initiate touch significantly more often in casual romantic relationships and during courtship, whereas women initiate touch more frequently in married relationships (Willis & Briggs, 1992; Guerrero & Anderson, 1994). The authors suggested that social control may be more important for men in casual relationships, whereas intimacy may become more important than social control in a stable, long-term relationship.

Finally, we recognize that the functional importance of touch is not confined solely to support, power, and affiliation. Argyle (1986), for example, maintained that touch serves important functions as an interaction signal in greetings and farewells, in congratulations, and in ceremonies. Touch seems to assume a less important role here, however, because touch must interact with eye behaviors and gestures to determine the effectiveness of such specific kinds of communication as greetings.

Summary

Touch can and frequently does play a central role in our maturational development from cradle to grave. The sending and receiving capacity of the human skin, when accentuated with the use of machines, is remarkable. With the aid of electrodes attached to the skin, tactile messages reveal when a person is experiencing an emotion, how strong the emotion is, and even whether the person is lying. When aided by machines, the skin as a communication receiver is capable of decoding both ideational and emotional messages. Those messages can serve vitally important functions when other senses are impaired or inoperative.

Rather detailed touching norms have developed in our society, and those norms specify who may touch whom and in what context. Touch-avoidance data reveal how strongly predisposed members of different groups in society are to avoid being touched by others. The nature of touching norms depends not only on the region of the body that is being touched, but also on the sex, race, age, status, and culture of the interactants.

Touching norms shaped by sex dictate that opposite-sex friends should touch the most, and males should touch each other the least. Men often use the touching privilege—which allows them to touch women more frequently than they are touched by women—to assert their dominance over women. Racial touching norms result in a higher rate of touching among blacks than whites but a lower rate of interracial touching. Touching norms based on age specify that it is appropriate for the young and old to engage in the most frequent tactile contact. Finally, status norms dictate that the high-status person is the toucher and the low-status person the touched.

Twelve different meanings can be communicated by touch: support, appreciation, inclusion, sexual interest or attraction, affection, playful affection, playful aggression, compliance, gaining attention, announcing a response, greeting, and departure. In a general sense, these tactile meanings are used to express interpersonal attitudes. More specifically, they are to be used singly or in combination to serve the three primary functions of touch: the support function, the power function, and the affiliation function.

References

Anderson, J. F., Anderson, P. A., & Lustig, M. W. (1987). Opposite sex touch avoidance: A national replication and extension. *Journal of Nonverbal Behavior, 11,* 89–109.

Argyle, M. (1986). *Bodily communication* (2nd ed.). London: Methuen.

Blondis, M. N., & Jackson, B. E. (1977). *Nonverbal communication with patients: Back to the human touch.* New York: Wiley.

Brown, B. (1974). Skin talk: A strange mirror of the mind. *Psychology Today, 8,* 52–74.

Collier, G. (1985). *Emotional experience.* Hillsdale, NJ: Erlbaum.

Fromme, D. K., Jaynes, W. E., Taylor, D. K., Hanold, E. G., Daniell, J., Rountree, J. R., & Fromme, M. A. (1989). Nonverbal behavior and attitudes toward touch. *Journal of Nonverbal Behavior, 13,* 3–16.

Geldhard, F. A. (1960). Some neglected possibilities of communication. *Science, 131,* 1583–1587.

Geldhard, F. A. (1968). Body English. *Psychology Today, 2,* 45.

Guerrero, L. K., & Anderson, P. A. (1994). Patterns of matching and initiation. Touch behavior and touch avoidance across romantic relationship stages. *Journal of Nonverbal Behavior, 18,* 137–153.

Harlow, B. F. (1958). The nature of love. *American Psychologist, 13,* 678–685.

Harrison-Speake, K., & Willis, F. N. (1995). Ratings of the appropriateness of touch among family members. *Journal of Nonverbal Behavior, 19,* 85–100.

Henley, N. M. (1977). *Body politics: Power, sex, and nonverbal communication.* Englewood Cliffs, NJ: Prentice-Hall.

Hollender, M. H. (1970). The need or wish to be held. *Archives of General Psychiatry, 22,* 445–453.

Hollender, M. H., Luborsky, L., & Scaramella, T. J. (1969). Body contact and sexual enticement. *Archives of General Psychiatry, 20,* 188–191.

Johnson, K. L., & Edwards, R. (1991). The effects of gender and type of romantic touch on perceptions of relational commitment. *Journal of Nonverbal Behavior, 15,* 43–55.

Jones, S. E. (1994). *The right touch: Understanding and using the language of physical contact.* Cresskill, NJ: Hampton.

Jones, S. E., & Yarbrough, A. E. (1985). A naturalistic study of the meanings of touch. *Communication Monographs, 52,* 19–56.

Jourard, S. M. (1966). An exploratory study of body-accessibility. *British Journal of Social and Clinical Psychology, 5,* 221–231.

Kleinke, C. L. (1977). Compliance to requests made by gazing and touching experimenters in field settings. *Journal of Experimental Social Psychology, 13,* 218–223.

Lewis, R. J., Derlega, V. J., Nichols, B., Shankar, A., Drury, K. D., & Hawkins, L. (1995). Sex differences in observers' reactions to a nurse's use of touch. *Journal of Nonverbal Behavior, 19,* 101–113.

Major, B. (1980). Gender patterns in touching behavior. In C. Mayo & N. M. Henley (Eds.), *Gender and nonverbal behavior.* New York: Springer-Verlag.

Major, B., Schmidlin, A. M., & Williams, L. (1990). Gesture patterns in social touch: The impact of setting and age. *Journal of Personality and Social Psychology, 58,* 634–643.

Major, B., & Williams, L. (1981). Frequency of touch by sex and race: A replication of touching observations. Unpublished paper, State University of New York at Buffalo.

Marx, M. S., Werner, P., & Cohen-Mansfield, J. (1989). Agitation and touch in the nursing home. *Psychological Reports, 64,* 1019–1026.

Montagu, A. (1971). *Touching: The human significance of the skin.* New York: Perennial.

Nguyen, T., Heslin, R., & Nguyen, M. L. (1975). The meanings of touch: Sex difference. *Journal of Communication, 25,* 92–103.

Patterson, M. L., Powell, J. L., & Lenihan, M. G. (1986). Touch, compliance, and interpersonal affect. *Journal of Nonverbal Behavior, 10,* 41–50.

Pisano, M. D., Wall, S. M., & Foster, A. (1986). Perceptions of nonreciprocal touch in romantic relationships. *Journal of Nonverbal Behavior, 10,* 29–40.

Roese, N. J., Olson, J. M., Borenstein, M. N., Martin, A., & Shores, A. L. (1992). Same-sex touching behavior: The moderating role of homophobic attitudes. *Journal of Nonverbal Behavior, 16,* 249–259.

Scott, B. (1973). *How the body feels.* New York: Ballantine.

Scroggs, G. F. (1980, April). *Sex, status, and solidarity: Attributions for nonmutual touch.* Paper presented at meeting of the Eastern Psychological Association, Hartford, CT.

Smith, D. E., Willis, F. N., & Gier, J. A. (1980). Success and interpersonal touch in a competitive setting. *Journal of Nonverbal Behavior, 5,* 26–34.

Summerhayes, D. L., & Suchner, R. W. (1978). Power implications of touch in male-female relationships. *Sex Roles, 4,* 103–110.

Walker, D. N. (1975). A dyadic interaction model for nonverbal touching behavior in encounter groups. *Small Group Behavior, 6,* 308–324.

Watson, W. H. (1975). The meanings of touch: Geriatric nursing. *Journal of Communication, 25,* 104–112.

Willis, F. N., & Briggs, L. F. (1992). Relationship and touch in public settings. *Journal of Nonverbal Behavior, 16,* 55–63.

Willis, F. N., & Rawdon, V. A. (1994). Gender and national differences in attitudes toward same-gender touch. *Perceptual & Motor Skills, 78,* 1027–1034.

Willis, F. N., Rinck, C. M. & Dean, L. M. (1978). Interpersonal touch among adults in cafeteria lines. *Perceptual and Motor Skills, 47,* 1147–1152.

Willis, F. N., Jr., & Hamm, H. K. (1980). The use of interpersonal touch in securing compliance. *Journal of Nonverbal Behavior, 1,* 49–55.

Young, M. G. (1973). The human touch: Who needs it? *Bridges not walls.* Reading, MA: Addison-Wesley.

Chapter 7

Personal Appearance

Appearance communicates meaning. In an age when our society gives lip service to the cliché that beauty is only skin deep, one might surmise that personal appearance represents a secondary and superficial value, one to which few people devote attention or time. Exactly the reverse is true. Our personal appearance has a pervasive impact on our self-image and on the image we communicate to others. As such, it is a major factor in shaping our behavior and the behavior of those with whom we interact.

Bloch and Richins (1993) recognize that many advantages accrue to physically attractive individuals in our society. They write that "attractive individuals are better liked, get better jobs, have increased self-esteem, and have more social power as compared with unattractive persons" (p. 467). In fact, physical attractiveness may well be thought of as a valuable commodity that enhances the personal and financial value of those who possess it. For a moment, consider physical attractiveness from a marketing perspective:

> *In their exchange with consumers, marketers go beyond tangible objects and also provide images of beauty and its benefits. Advertising constantly reinforces the notion that physical attractiveness is a highly important characteristic. Such messages also suggest ways in which consumers may successfully increase their level of attractiveness. . . . Looking at the other side of the exchange process, consumers offer financial resources in return for beauty. Spending for cosmetics alone accounts for $20 billion per year. Consumers also offer faith. In their exchanges, consumers subscribe to the belief that attractiveness is worthwhile and that it can be increased through consumption.* (Bloch & Richins, 1993, p. 468)

In *Orpheus Descending,* Tennessee Williams wrote that "we're all of us sentenced to solitary confinement inside our own skins for life." For many Americans, that can be a severe sentence. Our "skin" or overall appearance, does, in many cases, dictate that we cannot date or marry a person more attractive than we are. If our personal appearance is subnormal, our childhood peers ridicule and ostracize us. Our social and sexual successes are heavily dependent on our physical attractiveness. Moreover, personal appearance can be used to predict vocational success.

There is a well-developed physical-attractiveness stereotype in our society that is based on the assumption that beauty is good (Dion, Berscheid, & Walster, 1972; Patzer, 1985). Adams and Crossman (1978) captured the essence of the physical-attractiveness stereotype when they wrote that

> *Enough information is available to support the existence of a wide ranging physical attractiveness stereotype.... The message is that beauty implies goodness, talent, and success. Therefore, attractive people should be able to walk with their heads held high since everyone sees them in a socially desirable way. Also, when they are perceived as failing, this is construed merely as a case of stumbling but not falling.* (p. 17)

Certainly many members of the general public, and some academicians, are resistant to the idea that physical attractiveness is a major component of successful communication. In fact one of the reviewers of this book urged me to put a disclaimer in this chapter that says that I am not advocating that Americans should make a big fuss over personal appearance but simply reporting that they do so. This resistance in turn may be attributable to several factors. In the first place, beauty may be defined in many ways in addition to physical attractiveness, such as beauty as an aspect of nature or beauty as intuition. What is moral might also be considered beautiful, as well as what is useful (as in the design of a product). Secondly, Vacker & Key (1993) argued that conceptualizing beauty strictly in terms of physical attractiveness tends to decontextualize beauty:

> *Because a younger or more youthful individual, all other things being equal, likely possesses more elements of purely physical beauty or health, an individual adhering to the purely physical attraction standard of beauty will then evaluate the younger or youthful individual as embodying the (physical) beauty ideal.... In other words, individuals older than those considered youthful are evaluated in beauty terms that are out of context with the span of their lives. One example of this is female fashion models at age 24 being considered, by some experts, too old for their profession.* (p. 489)

Understandably, a voluminous body of research that strongly affirms the importance of personal appearance in our daily lives makes people uncomfortable. Denigrating such research or refusing to consider its obvious importance is somewhat analogous to killing the messenger who brings bad news. Patzer (1985) wrote insightfully that people who become defensive about physical attractiveness research claim that such research is unethical or improper, or ignore the strong and widespread effects of personal appearance might be well advised to expose themselves to reality therapy. Patzer noted pointedly that the "problem with such reactions is that ignorance of the person's environment is promoted. Such ignorance does not make the physical attractiveness phenomena disappear, nor does such action minimize the impact of physical attractiveness on our lives and within our interpersonal relations. In fact it maximizes the impact" (p. 13).

A multibillion-dollar cosmetics industry testifies to the fact that millions of Americans recognize the importance of accentuating the attractive features of their personal appearance. In fact, the increasing prominence of plastic surgeons in our society highlights the importance of personal appearance. Kurt Wagner, a plastic surgeon, and Gould (1972) wrote that "it used to be the great truism that it was the inner qualities that counted and the outer ones were superficial—as in the old saying that beauty is only skin deep. But we know now that there is no such thing as separating the mind from the body" (p. 22).

There is no more intimate form of communication than personal appearance. *Our visible self functions to communicate in the eyes of others, a constellation of meanings that define who we are and what we are apt to become. In interpersonal communication, the appearance of the participants establishes their social identity.* By our appearance cues, we often send messages designed to construct a social reality or social identity for ourselves that we could not and would not want to construct by verbal means (Kaiser, 1990). Thus, the judicious person will not say to another person, "I am trying to impress you" or "I am trying to dominate you," but the same person will routinely and repeatedly communicate such messages visually by the kinds of clothing he or she chooses to wear.

Our visible self plays a major role in shaping our social identity. Once established, our social identity—as perceived by others and by us—places identifiable limits on how, when, and where we are expected to engage in interpersonal communication. Our social identity carries with it the implicit responsibility to communicate in such a way as to meet the expectations of those for whom that identity has meaning. When we violate those expectations, our communication with others is apt to become ineffective and unsatisfying.

The impact of personal appearance on social identity became even more obvious to me when I walked into one of my classes dressed in a bathrobe and tennis shoes. My hair, which had just received a wild treatment from a dryer, was sticking out in all directions; much of it was combed down to obscure my face. I was wearing sunglasses and smoking a long, black cigar. Placing my bare legs and tennis shoes ostentatiously on my desk, I began my remarks to the students by asserting that "appearance communicates meaning."

Because the meanings communicated by my altered appearance conflicted so strikingly with the meanings associated with my social identity, the students became rather disoriented. They were at first uncertain and seemed not to know whether to laugh or refuse to acknowledge the incongruous sight in front of them. A few laughed, many squirmed, and the rest tried to be cool. Later, when they realized that they were being put on, my appearance triggered an intense and fascinating discussion of the communicative functions of personal appearance.

This chapter begins by identifying those facial and bodily features that are almost universally recognized by our society as physically attractive. The perceptual and behavioral effects of personal appearance are then examined. These effects in turn are used to highlight the major communicative functions served by personal appearance. Finally, the study of personal appearance begins and ends, as does this chapter, with a recognition of the fact that body concept is a central determinant of self-concept.

As I mentioned before, our society has a commonly accepted perspective that suggests that what is beautiful is talented, good, and socially desirable. We have little difficulty in judging objectively the level of physical attractiveness of those with whom we interact. Accurately assessing our own level of physical attractiveness is another matter, however. Why are our self-descriptions of our own bodies and the appearance of the physical features of our bodies so frequently distorted?

We should probably begin with the fact that body concept strongly affects self-concept. Because we recognize that we are apt to suffer severe perceptual and behavioral penalties if our personal appearance is much below normal, we often distort our own image (our physical features) so that, in our mind, they approximate the cultural ideal.

Features of Physical Attractiveness

The societal stereotype for personal appearance dictates what is and is not beautiful. Adams (1977) emphasized the strength of the stereotype and the implicit guidelines for judging physical attractiveness when he wrote that "the evidence suggests the stereotype is seldom mediated by environmental contexts, and that physically attractive persons are differentiated from their less attractive peers across a variety of experiences which are typical of various stages in the life cycle" (p. 219).

As we consider the defining features of physical attractiveness, three facts should be kept in mind. Americans have a much more detailed stereotype, or mental picture, of the physical features that define beauty for women than for men. Cross-cultural ratings as to what features constitute a beautiful female face are highly consistent (Cunningham, Roberts, Barbee, & Druen, 1995). Americans are much more precise in identifying physical features associated with facial beauty than in identifying physical features associated with bodily attractiveness.

Facial Attractiveness

The *ideal* face has been described objectively and in specific detail. The noted plastic surgeon, Dr. Kurt Wagner, and Helen Gould (1972) wrote that the German sculptor Gottfried Schadow (1764–1850) geometrically laid out his ideal of facial beauty in the nineteenth century. In so doing, Schadow

> *formulated the facial proportions for a prevailing standard of symmetry which the occidental world accepts as the ideal.... Our own eyes automatically accept the standard of what is aesthetically pleasing. Take any super example—from Greta Garbo to Rock Hudson—to even any example of the good-looking individual, and you know they pass the Schadow test before you apply the calipers.* (p. 45)

Schadow's model of perfect facial features and proportions has been adopted by plastic surgeons because it accurately reflects the detailed standards in our society that are used in assessing facial attractiveness. Whenever clients approach a plastic surgeon with a request that they undergo facial surgery, for example, they begin their treatment with profile analysis. The term *profile analysis* correctly suggests that plastic surgeons agree on a very specific ideal for beauty. The profile analysis "indicates the necessity for a definite proportion between the forehead, nose, lips, and chin. To correct a nose alone, without considering the related features, is going on a fool's journey" (Wagner & Gould, 1972, p. 47).

By using the profilometer to determine exactly how far a patient's facial features deviate from the perfect profile or ideal face, the plastic surgeon can project with precision the degree of correction needed on one or more facial features. The *profilometer,* a special instrument that resembles and functions like the protractor, is used to measure the length and angles of the nose, from the tip, through the bridge, to the top in centimeters.

The ideal nose for a man . . . is straight with a bridge angle of 30 to 35 degrees and an 8- to 12-degree tip angle. As to length, the nose should roughly correspond to the man's height measured in feet. Thus, a 6-foot man would ideally have a nose of about six centimeters (2.35 inches) in length. (Routh, 1974, p. 39)

The larger your facial features the more unattractive they will probably be perceived. *Large facial features are typically considered less attractive than smaller facial features* (Staat, 1977). A fascinating study by Cunningham (1986) on the sociobiology of female facial beauty suggests that for facial features the small is good and big is bad distinction may need qualification or at least amplification. For male subjects in this study, female facial beauty was defined by the "neonate" features of large eyes, small nose area, small chin, and widely spaced eyes. Female beauty was also defined by the "mature" facial features of wide cheekbones and narrow cheeks and the "expressive" features of highly set eyebrows, wide pupils, and a large smile. This profile for female facial beauty is augmented by a recent study that identifies three facial features as most central to facial attractiveness: widely separated eyes, a short nose, and high placement of features. When considered together, these features on a female's face were judged attractive even with low placement. With low placement, however, a narrow mouth is particularly undesirable (Mckelvie, 1993).

Interestingly, females whose faces met the definition of beautiful were consistently perceived by male subjects to have more desirable personal qualities than females whose faces were not beautiful. Thus, females with greater eye height, small nose area, greater cheekbone width, and a wider smile were seen as *brighter* than females with less attractive faces. Secondly, females with greater eye height and width, small nose area, wider cheekbones, higher eyebrows, wider pupils, and wider smiles were perceived to be more *sociable*. Finally, females with greater eye height, smaller nose area, and wider smiles were seen as more *assertive* (Cunningham, 1986). In short, in American society, females with attractive faces start with a definite advantage in terms of the impressions they might want to make and are capable of making on individuals with whom they interact.

A single unattractive facial feature does not, of course, mean that you have a physically unattractive face. Dr. Kurt Wagner stressed this point during a tape-recorded interview done with me in his home in the Hollywood Hills. If most of your facial features conform to the ideal profile for facial attractiveness, you may still be perceived as a winner. Dr. Kurt Wagner claimed that

the reasons that you know [what the ideal model or profile for beauty] is that people still have a good idea of what is beautiful. OK. Now you might not like Elizabeth Taylor, or her lifestyle, or what she stands for, but nobody is going to deny that Elizabeth Taylor is beautiful. OK. You take the males and push them in the profile. . . . We tend to go for real antiheroes now. Right now, it is just a rebellion against male beauty—where you have Charles Bronson or Richard Boone. Yet, they have strong, square faces, except their nose is a little weird, but even their nose isn't too weird. Redford, very popular. James Coburn, very popular. OK. . . . There never has been a successful leading man who has no chin. (K. Wagner, personal interview, May 10, 1973)

Bodily Attractiveness

The physical features that differentiate one human body from another often differ drastically. Both common and uncommon persons have recognized this fact for centuries. Shakespeare, a man of uncommon insight, expressed in *Julius Caesar* what common people have long recognized.

> *Caesar* Let me have men about me that are fat; Sleek-headed men, and such as sleep o'nights: Yond Cassius has a lean and hungry look; He thinks too much: such men are dangerous.

> *Anthony* Fear him not, Caesar; he is not dangerous; He is a noble Roman, and well given.

> *Caesar* Would he were fatter!

People have known for centuries that human bodies differ in appearance, but they made few systematic efforts to measure the differences. Ernst Kretschmer, a professor of psychiatry and neurology, probably made the first comprehensive effort to record differences in bodily appearance. In 1925 Kretschmer published the first edition of *Physique and Character: An Investigation of the Nature of Constitution and of the Theory of Temperament* (1970). Kretschmer concluded that individuals who share morphological similarities may be classified into three major groups: (a) *asthenic* (skinny, bony, narrow body), (b) *athletic* (muscular body), and (c) *pyknic* (fat body).

Sheldon's follow-up research established the empirical practice of *somatyping*— classifying people as to body type. Sheldon's classification is now widely used. According to Sheldon (1954), there are three body types: (a) *endomorphic* (soft, fat, and so on), (b) *mesomorphic* (bony, athletic, and so on), and (c) *ectomorphic* (thin, fragile, and so on).

When we classify individuals by body type, it is easiest to conjure up simplistic images of someone such as football star Herschel Walker, who is clearly mesomorphic, or a *Vogue* fashion model, who is clearly ectomorphic. To accurately describe a person's body type, however, you need to assign them three numbers on a seven-point scale. The numbers refer to the degree of endomorphy, mesomorphy, or ectomorphy. Herschel Walker would probably get a rating of 1/7/1, and the skinny fashion model would be rated 1/1/7.

Sheldon theorized that there is a relationship between body type and temperament, or personality characteristics. In Sheldon's view, the person with the endomorphic body type will probably exhibit a *viscerotonic* temperament—a laid-back, relaxed, and even indolent personality. Mesomorphic body types are associated with a *somatotonic* temperament—a highly confident, task-oriented, aggressive person. Finally, the ectomorphic body type is associated with the *cerebrotonic* temperament—individuals who are tense, fussy, and critical of others (1954).

Although Sheldon's theory and his system for body typing have both been criticized, body typing (or somatyping) represents an undeniably useful way of describing a dominant set of physical features that differentiate one body from another. As we shall see, the impact of a person's body type on his or her self-perceptions and behaviors, as well as on the perceptions of those with whom they interact, is substantial.

In our society, it is more important for a woman than for a man to have bodily features that are physically attractive (Patzer, 1985). Relatedly, Americans seem to have a more detailed notion of what constitutes bodily beauty for women than for men. *For females, slenderness is a particularly important feature of bodily attractiveness, and waist width and hip width correlate negatively with perceptions of physical attractiveness* (Horvath, 1979). *The bigger a woman's waist and the hippier she is, the less attractive she is perceived to be.* When considered either from the perspective of male or female perceivers, female physiques that emphasize great curvature (e.g., very large breasts and a very small or a very large waist) are seen as less physically attractive than breasts and waists of moderate size.

For women, waist-to-hip ratio (WHR) is critically important. In fact, Singh (1994) identifies body fat distribution as reflected in WHR as the most important determinant of female bodily attractiveness. Normal-weight females figures with low WHR are judged most attractive. Significantly, females with low WHR have many desirable image qualities attributed to them. Not surprisingly, depressed women with high WHR report higher levels of dissatisfaction with their own bodies than depressed women with low WHR (Joiner, Schmidt, & Singh, 1994).

The ideal body type for men features reasonably broad shoulders and a muscular chest (Horvath, 1981). Ideally, men should be tall with an average body mass (Melamed, 1994). The "traditional female" places a high priority on such stereotypically masculine features as well-muscled upper arms and a tapering upper trunk. Nontraditional females attach much less importance to muscle development. But traditional and nontraditional women agree, however, that males who have small chests and arms, an "unmasculine physique," are physically unattractive (Lavrakas, 1975).

In short, there is nothing ambiguous about the proportions of the face and body that distinguish the physically attractive from the unattractive person. The profile for physically attractive women is more complete than the profile for physically attractive men, and, partially as a result of this fact, women attach a higher priority to physical attractiveness than do men.

Body Image

Body image, or body concept, is the mental picture we have of our own body. This mental picture consists of our estimate of the size, shape, and appearance of each of the parts of our body as well as the body as a whole. Our body image is vitally important because it is a central component of self-concept and ultimately of the communicative behaviors that we exhibit.

As we shall see, the behaviors exhibited by individuals who have a positive body image are strikingly different from the behaviors of individuals with a negative body concept (Zahr, 1985; Domzal & Kernan, 1993). In his insightful book, *Development and Structure of the Body Image* (1986), Fisher stresses that body image has been linked with a wide array of behaviors that include achievement, sexual arousal patterns, clothing choice, authoritarianism, tolerance for stress, sociability, hostility, delinquent behavior, drug usage, and drug addiction. As you might expect, it is a negative body image rather than a positive body image that is linked to such socially unacceptable behaviors as delinquency and drug usage.

Although our own body concept is often quite distorted, our body image is strongly affected by how physically attractive others judge us to be. Not surprisingly, the impact of body image on self-concept is most pronounced for individuals who are either extremely attractive or extremely unattractive and for individuals who have a high public self-consciousness. Adolescents, for example, have a high public self-consciousness about their personal appearance. They are, therefore, particularly susceptible to the striking deterioration in self-concept that often results as their body image becomes more negative (Patzer, 1985).

We do not all use the same *body image dimensions* to form a mental picture of our own body. However, the following body image dimensions are widely used by individuals to describe and evaluate their own body:

1. *degree of overall awareness of one's body*
2. *body boundary articulation*
3. *distribution of attention to the major parts of the body*
4. *evaluation of the attractiveness of one's body and its parts*
5. *perception of the size of the overall body and its parts*
6. *perceived degree of masculinity-femininity of one's body*
7. *amount of anxiety experienced about one's overall body and its subdivisions.* (Fisher, 1986)

The image dimensions that we use to form our body image are both descriptive and evaluative in nature. The evaluative judgments we make about our body tend to be disproportionately important because they reflect how satisfied or dissatisfied we are with our own body. *Body-cathexis* is the degree of feeling of satisfaction or dissatisfaction with the various parts or processes of our body (Secord & Jourard, 1953). Empirical research has confirmed the hypothesis that body-cathexis or image is integrally related to the self-concept.

Empirical researchers have repeatedly confirmed the existence of a strong positive relationship between a high level of body satisfaction and a high level of social self-esteem (McCaulay & Glenn, 1988). People with a negative body image are predisposed to be anxious; concerned with pain, disease, and bodily injury; and are insecure (Secord & Jourard, 1953). By contrast, individuals with a positive body concept (based in part on their self-perceptions as mesomorphs) have a much more sophisticated conception of their own body (Sugerman & Haronian, 1964). From such findings, we might infer that individuals with a negative body image attempt to avoid the negative connotations of such an image by deliberately maintaining a fuzzy or incomplete image of their own body.

The image we have of our own body is often quite inaccurate. Our distorted body image might be attributed in part to the fact that we rarely carefully observe our own body and its features. We know, for example, that only 10 percent of a sample of subjects in one study correctly identified a front-view photograph of their own face. People have also had great difficulty when exposed to a distorted mirror image of themselves in adjusting the image to its true proportions. Finally, we know that individuals estimate their own heart rate highly inaccurately (Fisher, 1986).

We cannot be sure how often we intentionally distort our conception of our body. Authorities such as Fisher suggest that much of the distortion is intentional, however. He writes that "people are endlessly engaged in defensive strategies to cope with body experiences that are complex, threatening, confusing, and even alien. . . . When asked publicly to rate their body, people are more positive than negative—but numerous sources tell a different story" (1986, p. 626).

Persons with negative body images have understandable reasons for developing an inaccurate image of their own body. The practice of distorting one's physical features in one's own mind is known as *body distortion* (Malandro, Barker, & Barker, 1989). People with negative body concepts experience unusual difficulty in visualizing accurately the physical features of their personal appearance and often have unrealistic notions about their personal appearance.

Gender seems to play an important role in body distorting. To begin, we know that women are more likely to express dissatisfaction with their bodies than men (McCaulay & Glenn, 1988). We are not surprised by such a finding, in view of a physical-attractiveness stereotype in our culture that stipulates that physical attractiveness is more important for women than for men.

Women are also more likely than men to engage in body distortion. Race does not seem to be an important variable here, however, since the body image concerns of black and white women seem to be quite similar (Thomas & James, 1988). When women do distort their descriptions of their own bodies, their distortions might not operate at the conscious level, because they are hardly self-promotional in nature. Thus, McCaulay & Glenn (1988) found that women typically saw themselves as larger than their actual size, whereas men saw themselves as smaller than their actual size. They wrote that

> There was a fairly consistent pattern with women typically seeing themselves as one weight category larger than their actual size. Men were, on the whole, more accurate in their perceptions . . . with the greater distortion [exhibited] as a tendency to perceive themselves as smaller than their actual size. (p. 388)

Interestingly, both women and men distorted their descriptions of their own body away from the ideal body concept. Thus, the women sampled wanted to weigh about 8.5 lbs less, whereas the men wanted to weigh about 3 lbs more. These findings once again are consistent with the physical attractiveness stereotype, which suggests that physically attractive women should be slender and their male counterparts should be muscular. Then too, narcissistic males, but not narcissistic females, are more likely to overestimate their own physical attractiveness (Gabriel, Critelli, & Ee, 1994). Indeed, Stonebraker (1989) found that both women and men may become compulsive in their efforts to achieve an idealized body image but that they use different means to achieve their goals. Women dieted to become slim, whereas men exercised to become muscular.

The impact of gender on body-cathexis and body distortion is reflected in two other findings of note. First, feminine females evaluate their physical appearance less favorably than androgynous females (Jackson, Sullivan, & Rostker, 1988). Second, body image dissatisfaction is more pronounced among single women (Thomas & James, 1988). In our society it would seem that both feminine females and single females would be inclined to attach a high priority to being perceived as physically attractive. Both groups might, therefore, be inclined to make harsh judgments about their self-perceived level of physical attractiveness.

Obese individuals represent another group who do not have to search for reasons for engaging in body distortion. The obese person probably recognizes that "once the endomorphic phenotype is firmly established, stigmatization sets in and blocks the exit to normal acceptance in interpersonal relationships" (Cahnman, 1968, p. 297). If you realized that overweight persons are frequently characterized as uninteresting, lazy, and unsocial (Worsley, 1981), you might subconsciously engage in some body distortion in order to slim down your bodily proportions—at least in your own mind.

There is little disagreement as to what the physically attractive females and males *should* look like; this is *ideal body image.* There is also a good deal of evidence to suggest that most persons can make accurate judgments about how physically attractive *other* individuals are. People seem to encounter the most difficulty in describing accurately how they appear in the eyes of others.

Body Image: Self, Other, and Reflective

The communicator must be prepared to deal with at least three types of body image. Each of us has an image of our own body that varies both with respect to our feelings about our personal appearance and with regard to how detailed that image is. As indicated, the more positive our feelings about our body image, the more detailed that image is apt to be. Moreover, our friends, associates, and others with whom we interact also have an image of our bodies. Finally, there is the *reflective* image. The reflective image represents a completely objective and accurate description of our facial and bodily features, as measured by instruments such as the profilometer and the X ray.

Mike and Marvin Westmore recognize the importance of making individuals completely aware of the features of their reflective image. (The Westmore brothers are sought-after consultants to the movie industry in Hollywood; they own and operate their own cosmetic studio.) When I taped an interview with the Westmore brothers in their office, they emphasized that they begin a series of consultations with a client by describing in detail a client's reflective image. They do so because the reflective image reveals, in an objective and precise manner, the undistorted features of the individual's personal appearance. Mike Westmore told me that they "are interested in the impact of the reflective image on the self-image. And we are dealing with, we are working on a reflective image but the impact is on the self-image. And the self-image determines our place in society" (1973, May 29).

Effective communication based on fact rather than fantasy puts a premium on our ability to perceive accurately the defining features of our personal appearance. We must recognize that our actual (or reflective) body image may be different in important respects from our own image of our body or the image our friends and associates have of our body. We must have an objective basis for comparing and contrasting those three images of our body before we decide whether to modify our appearance. Procedures for measuring them already exist (Leathers, 1976).

The Matching Hypothesis

Success in the development of intimate relationships seems to be based, at least in part, on the ability to seek out opposite-sex individuals who match your own level of physical attractiveness. In fact, individuals who have a realistic image of their body frequently seek to associate with others with similar levels of physical attractiveness. This is particularly true for dating relationships.

The *matching hypothesis* has been developed to explain the role of physical attractiveness in the selection of dating partners. This hypothesis is based on the assumption that individuals of similar levels of physical desirability seek each other out as dating partners and, eventually, as marriage partners (Adams & Crossman, 1978; Patzer, 1985). There is considerable empirical evidence to support the validity of the matching hypothesis. In fact, we can safely conclude that *individuals are likely to be attracted to other individuals who are similar to them in body build or type, dress, facial and bodily features, and overall physical attractiveness* (Archer, 1980).

Patzer (1985) concluded, after a detailed review of studies examining the physical attractiveness of long-term dating couples and marriage partners, that evidence supporting the matching hypothesis is conclusive. The matching hypothesis might seem counterintuitive in view of a physical-attractiveness stereotype that suggests that males should seek out females of maximum attractiveness. At the same time, males expect a much greater probability of rejection when they approach the most attractive females. In the real world, then, the dominant tendency is for the level of physical attractiveness of married couples to be similar. Kalick and Hamilton (1986) recently raised questions about the methods used in studies designed to test the matching hypothesis, but their own methods were, in turn, indicted as flawed (Aron, 1988).

The matching hypothesis may not apply when other factors prove to be more important than physical attractiveness. The physically attractive person may be drawn to the physically unattractive person who is wealthy, or who has a compensating virtue. There is evidence to suggest, however, that even among friends of the same sex, similarity in degree of physical attractiveness exceeds chance expectations (Cash & Derlega, 1978).

Do you have the ability to match up dating couples by assessing their level of physical attractiveness? Will the matching hypothesis be supported if we consider the physical attractiveness of dating couples at a major university? The Matching Test that follows is not intended to be a comprehensive and valid test of the matching hypothesis. It is intended, however, to increase your awareness of the matching hypothesis and its implications for the development of intimate relationships.

Your task is to determine which of the individuals in the photographs of Figure 7.1 on pages 142 and 143 are dating couples. The photographs are of University of Georgia students who were waiting to see a movie at the Tate Student Center. Study the physical features of Female A and decide which of the males is her partner. In Table 7.1, put the appropriate number for the male you chose in the blank across from Female A. Follow the same procedure as you consider Female B, C, and so on. Photographs of the couples are shown in the Appendix.

Do not look at the Appendix at this time. You may wish to provide yourself with a further test of your ability to classify individuals by level of physical attractiveness. Please look at the 15 males in Figure 7.1. Write down the numbers for the five males whom you consider to be most attractive, the five males you would classify at a lower level of physical attractiveness, and the five you would classify at the lowest level of physical attractiveness. Go through the same procedures for the 15 females in Figure 7.1, but use letters rather than numbers. See how your classification matches up with the keyed answers in the Appendix.

TABLE 7.1   The Matching Test

	COUPLE #1	
Female A		Male_____
	COUPLE #2	
Female B		Male_____
	COUPLE #3	
Female C		Male_____
	COUPLE #4	
Female D		Male_____
	COUPLE #5	
Female E		Male_____
	COUPLE #6	
Female F		Male_____
	COUPLE #7	
Female G		Male_____
	COUPLE #8	
Female H		Male_____
	COUPLE #9	
Female I		Male_____
	COUPLE #10	
Female J		Male_____
	COUPLE #11	
Female K		Male_____
	COUPLE #12	
Female L		Male_____
	COUPLE #13	
Female M		Male_____
	COUPLE #14	
Female N		Male_____
	COUPLE #15	
Female O		Male_____

Effects of Personal Appearance

When we consider the effects of personal appearance, we should recognize that a number of the studies done on physical attractiveness exhibit both conceptual and methodological problems. Although Morrow (1990) focused on research designed to examine the impact of physical attractiveness in employment selection, his critique included many of the common criticisms of physical attractiveness research: Many studies of physical attractiveness have compared only extremely attractive and unattractive subjects; laboratory rather than field studies are the norm; the ratings of judges who assess level of physical attractiveness may be biased if they are aware of what is being studied; and physical attractiveness is often operationalized in a limited and unrealistic way (for example, facial photographs are used). The fact that studies of physical attractiveness can and should be improved does not negate the powerful and pervasive effects of physical attractiveness, however.

FIGURE 7.1

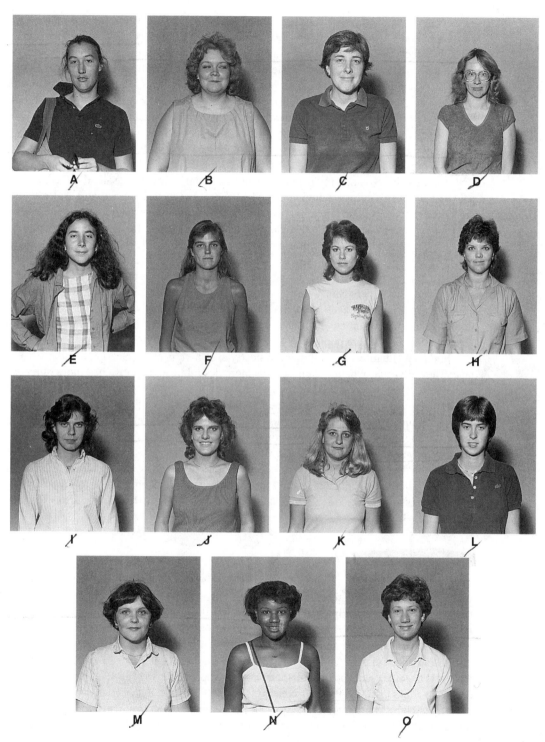

FIGURE 7.1   (Continued)

Personal appearance has repeatedly been found to exert a major influence on impression formation in a wide variety of social contexts (Patzer, 1985). <u>Our personal appearance strongly affects the personality traits and personal qualities that are attributed to us</u>. As a result, personal appearance is an influential determinant not only of first impressions we make on others but also of more enduring impressions as well.

We know that personal appearance exerts a significant impact on perception and behavior in almost every setting in which its effects have been studied; physically attractive persons consistently receive preferential treatment. As we shall see, <u>*physically attractive persons seem to be discriminated against only when they take obvious advantage of their personal appearance.*</u>

Adams and Crossman (1978) have identified some of the more salient effects of appearance in school, family, dating, and clinical contexts. Physical attractiveness clearly affects the expectations and perceptions of teachers and parents. In school settings, teachers seem to expect physically attractive children to be more successful, academically and socially. As a result of this expectation, a physically attractive child often becomes "teacher's pet." In the family setting, too, parents' perceptions are often affected by their child's level of physical attractiveness. Thus, parents are inclined to attribute the misbehavior of unattractive children to personality flaws but dismiss the misbehavior of physically attractive children as a temporary aberration. Such parental behavior may reflect a general expectation: that physically attractive children will have better attitudes toward school and life in general and will be more popular.

In dating situations as well, the physically attractive persons clearly have the advantage. They are usually better liked, seen as more desirable, and approached more often. In fact, Patzer (1985) emphasized the counterintuitive research finding that the impact of physical attractiveness on interpersonal attraction does not decline as time passes. In contrast to popular opinion, <u>"physical attractiveness remains a major determinant of mutual romantic attraction regardless of the elapse of time, the number of meetings, and even competing negative information"</u> (1985, p. 82).

Even in the clinical setting, the physically attractive person is apt to receive preferential treatment. Thus, physically unattractive individuals are more likely than their physically attractive peers to be referred to a psychiatrist and are more likely to be diagnosed as extremely maladjusted.

Perceptual Effects

The perceptual impact of our level of physical attractiveness begins with our self-concept. As we have already stressed, there is a strong positive relationship between physical attractiveness and self-concept. In simple terms, <u>*the more physically attractive we are perceived to be, the more positive our self-concept is apt to be.*</u> The impact of physical attractiveness on self-concept is particularly pronounced for adolescents. In view of the rapid growth spurts and skin disturbances that are characteristic of the teenage years, it is not surprising that many teenagers become preoccupied with their personal appearance. However, mature college students and adults also find that self-concept is strongly affected by personal appearance.

Research by Martin and Kennedy (1993) highlights the fact that many young people are preoccupied with their self-concept and their belief that their level of physical attractiveness is perhaps the central determinant of their self-concept. This seems to be particularly true for young females. Their research findings support four conclusions of central importance: (a) the socialization period between the 4th and 12th grades is critical for female preadolescents and adolescents in terms of self-perceptions of their physical attractiveness; (b) the young female's perception of her own level of physical attractiveness tends to decrease during this time period; (c) the tendency of female preadolescents and adolescents to compare themselves to fashion models in ads not only increases with age but this tendency is greater for those with more negative self-perceptions of their physical attractiveness or with lower self-esteem; (d) a single exposure to highly attractive advertising models raises the standards for physical attractiveness from the perspectives of female adolescents in the 8th through the 12th grades.

Physical attractiveness affects not only self-perceptions but the ways others perceive us. Dion, Berscheid, and Walster (1972) found, for example, that physically attractive individuals were more likely to be perceived as sexually warm and responsive, sensitive, strong, and sociable than less attractive persons. Similarly, physically attractive counselors have been viewed as more intelligent, competent, trustworthy, assertive, and likable than less attractive counselors (Cash, Begley, McCown, & Weise, 1975).

The way we choose to dress clearly affects the way others perceive us. Thus, Behling and Williams (1991) found that dress affected both perception of intelligence and academic potential of students in secondary school settings. The greatest disparity in perceptions was for students who wore "the hood look" as opposed to "the dressy look." These styles were the most extreme and seemed to represent a good/bad dichotomy. The hood look was viewed as indicative of both lower intelligence and lower academic achievement by students and teachers in all of the high schools studied. Even though suits are not a traditional type of attire in a high school, male subjects who wore a suit and tie were perceived much more positively than those who did not.

Physical features over which a person can exert little if any control may strongly affect the way one is perceived. Height is a good example. Height is positively related to perceptions of dominance for both men and women and interpersonal attractiveness for men (Hensley, 1994). Children perceive taller males and females as stronger and more dominant than their shorter counterparts. Interestingly, taller females are judged to be stronger, more dominant, and smarter when they are in the presence of shorter males (Montepare, 1995). The next time you see a woman towering over her male companion perhaps you will consider the implications of this finding.

A person's level of physical attractiveness also markedly affects the judgments that are made about the person's behavior. A number of studies have shown a relationship between an individual's personal appearance and the judgments made about the quality of work he or she produces. Landy and Sigall (1974) found, for example, that male readers of essays gave comparable grades to high-quality essays written by physically attractive and unattractive females. When the quality of the essay was inferior, however, unattractive females received significantly lower grades. Anderson and Nida (1978) found that physically attractive essay writers received the highest evaluations from members of the opposite sex, but individuals of moderate physical attractiveness received the highest ratings from members of their own sex.

Perhaps most importantly, essay writers of the lowest level of physical attractiveness received the lowest evaluations of all. Finally, attractive female essay writers have been judged, by male judges, to be significantly more "talented" than less attractive female essay writers (Kaplan, 1978). In short, the physically unattractive woman who does high-quality work may find that she receives relatively objective evaluations by men. When the physically unattractive woman produces work of marginal or low quality, however, she can expect much more negative evaluations by males than her more attractive female counterpart.

Physical attractiveness seems also to affect the dispensation of justice. This is particularly true when the plaintiff or defendant is a woman. Jurors, at least in a mock trial, who are exposed to an attractive plaintiff and an unattractive defendant more often find in favor of the plaintiff. They also award more money to the physically attractive as opposed to the physically unattractive plaintiff (Kulka & Kessler, 1978). Furthermore, attractive women are convicted less often for crimes they are accused of committing and in general receive more lenient sentences. Physically attractive female defendants seem to lose their edge in court only when they have taken advantage of their personal appearance to commit a crime. Thus, physically attractive females convicted of swindling receive stiffer sentences than their less attractive counterparts. If the conviction is for burglary, the unattractive female is apt to receive the harsher sentence (Adams, 1977).

Finally, there is some evidence to suggest that the morality of a person's behavior is affected by his or her level of physical attractiveness. In one interesting study, subjects were shown photographs of Barb and John. They were told that John invited Barb to his apartment and asked her to have sexual intercourse. Barb accepted the invitation. No matter what their attitude toward "casual sex," subjects judged the sexual behavior of the "highly attractive Barb" to be *less* moral than the behavior of the "quite unattractive" Barb. The study represents one of those rare instances in which physical attractiveness seems to be a disadvantage. Because the attractive female might be viewed as having more opportunities for socially acceptable sexual outlets than the unattractive female, she is apparently expected to set and meet higher standards of morality in her sexual conduct (Hocking, Walker, & Fink, 1982).

Behavioral Effects

Our level of physical attractiveness affects not only our own behavior but the behavior of those with whom we interact. Ultimately, the nature of our relationships with other individuals is affected in important ways by our level of physical attractiveness.

The impact of our level of physical attractiveness is perhaps manifested most strongly in its effect on our self-concept. As I have already indicated, the more physically attractive we are, the more positive our self-concept is likely to be. Adams (1977) has examined the physical attractiveness/self-concept relationship in detail, and has found that the behavioral profiles for physically attractive and physically unattractive persons do differ significantly in effectiveness of communication. For example, both physically attractive females and physically attractive males exhibit greater resistance to conformity pressure, more independence, and more self-disclosure than their less attractive peers.

Attractive facial features have a particularly pronounced effect on the behaviors of those who possess such features. Females with attractive facial features are more confident, experience little anxiety about having their own actions evaluated, and are less likely to be critical of self and others (Adams, 1977; Patzer, 1985). Moreover, physically attractive females are more popular than their less attractive counterparts (Adams & Roopnarine, 1994).

The potential of personal appearance to affect an individual's behavior is strikingly illustrated by the case of Rebecca Richardson. Becky Richardson came from a family with a history of congenital cleft palates. Her own condition was so bad that she had undergone 17 operations on her face to correct both articulatory and appearance problems associated with her cleft palate. After the final operation, she went to Mike and Marvin Westmore for professional cosmetic treatment of her face. When the Westmores began their cosmetic treatment, Becky Richardson's self-confidence was very low, she was withdrawn, and it was difficult to sustain communicative interaction with her. In the words of Mike Westmore (personal interview, May 29, 1973), "She was twenty-two years old and obviously not getting her share of social intercourse with male members of society."

After she received a full set of aesthetic cosmetic treatments from the Westmore brothers, which produced a dramatic improvement in the attractiveness of her facial features, Becky Richardson's behavior changed dramatically. She was once withdrawn and uncommunicative, and she became a confident and sought-after young woman who assumed an active role in many social activities. She developed to the point where she actually became socially aggressive in some situations. In Becky Richardson's case, the change in her reflective image produced a significant, highly beneficial change in her self-image and, consequently, in her behavior. She became not only a much more effective communicator, but also a much more effective and satisfied human being.

The body's physical appearance also seems to have important behavioral implications. We expect people with given body types to behave in distinctive ways. For example, the stereotypical expectation is that mesomorphs will be more assertive, mature, and self-reliant than individuals with other kinds of body types. Endomorphs are stereotyped as relatively lazy, warm-hearted, sympathetic, good-natured, and dependent. Ectomorphs are viewed stereotypically as suspicious, tense, nervous, pessimistic, and reticent. Although not conclusive, there is evidence to support the view that persons with each of these body types do indeed behave in ways that conform to their stereotypes (Wells & Siegel, 1961).

The behavioral impact of body type may be stronger for children than for adults; we know that teenagers are particularly concerned about their personal appearance. In one study, Walker (1963), who had reliably classified children by body type, was able to confirm two-thirds of the predictions he made about the children's behavior, based solely on their body types. Girls' behaviors could be predicted from body type much more accurately than boys' behaviors. This finding is understandable in view of the fact that society attaches more importance to the physical attractiveness of females than males.

Parents' actual description of their children's behaviors indicated that endomorphic girls are eager to please, even-tempered, friendly, and relaxed. By contrast, ectomorphic girls are tense, jealous, unpredictable, moody, suspicious, worried, and afraid of failure. The behaviors of mesomorphic children could not be predicted with a high degree of accuracy (Walker, 1963). Subsequent research indicates, however, that adolescents with mesomorphic body builds have a much stronger achievement need than either endomorphs or ectomorphs (Cortes & Gatti, 1966, 1970).

In short, individuals who are perceived to be physically attractive do behave differently. In general, persons who are physically attractive have a more positive self-image than persons who are not. Their behavior is characterized by self-confident and assertive efforts to achieve demanding goals, by an independence of thought and action, and by an ability to resist the kinds of conformity pressure that would diminish their uniqueness as individuals.

Because our physical attractiveness has such marked effects on our self-perceptions, behaviors, and on the perceptions of those with whom we interact, it is not surprising that physical attractiveness also affects our interpersonal relationships and interpersonal communication with others. The fact that the physically attractive are more highly regarded in our society means that they have greater opportunity for developing satisfying heterosexual relationships.

Physically attractive persons of both sexes have more opportunities to interact with members of the opposite sex. They have more dates; they go to more parties; they spend more time conversing with members of the opposite sex; and they spend less time on non-social, task-oriented activities. Perhaps most importantly, both physically attractive females and physically attractive males report that they are more satisfied with their opposite-sex relationships over an extended period of time than their less physically attractive peers (Reis, Nezlek, & Wheeler, 1980).

Physical attractiveness in turn is strongly affected by the ability to purchase socially appropriate clothing. Francis (1992) found that high school students who experienced "perceived clothing deprivation" (reflected in the inability to buy clothes or in clothing inadequacy relative to peers) suffered two negative consequences: They were perceived as less socially competent and experienced less social participation.

Whether an individual is a casual or a serious dater, the more physically attractive a person is, the greater the availability of opposite-sex partners. Also, attractive persons are less inclined to worry about the involvement of their partner with members of the opposite sex (White, 1980). In short, not only do physically attractive persons have more social interaction with members of the opposite sex, but the quality of that social interaction tends to be superior, from their perspective (Reis, Wheeler, Spiegel, & Kernis, 1982).

The physical-attractiveness stereotype emphasizes that physically attractive individuals are more socially desirable. As a result, many of us exhibit a desire to identify with, to associate with, and to be similar to physically attractive persons. The net result is that physically attractive persons receive preferential treatment in the initiation and development of interpersonal relationships.

We know, for example, that more positive personality characteristics are attributed to a female when she is associated with a physically attractive male (Strane & Warts, 1977). We are more self-disclosing when in the presence of a physically attractive person. We exhibit a greater willingness to reward physically attractive individuals monetarily (Mathes & Edwards, 1978). We are more willing to extend help to those who are physically attractive (Wilson, 1978). We view our attitudes as being more similar to physically attractive than to physically unattractive persons (Mashman, 1978).

Finally, we tend to judge the physically attractive as more credible and, ultimately, as more persuasive. Because you are viewed as being physically attractive does not, of course, assure that you will always be more persuasive than a less attractive person (Chaiken, 1979; Whaley, 1983), but it provides you with a decided advantage in a great variety of communicative situations. As I will emphasize in the chapter on impression formation, personal

appearance is frequently a major determinant of both first impressions and the more enduring impressions that we make on others.

The Nature of Artifactual Communication

Personal appearance is clearly a powerful medium of communication. Appearance cues include not only a person's overall level of physical attractiveness, body type, size, shape, and
weight, but also the clothing and other artifacts used to control personal appearance. Indeed, many groups in our society rely almost exclusively on the visual medium of appearance cues to establish their social identity, for example, inner-city gangs, punks, skinheads,
heavy metal rockers, and military units.

When I use the term *artifact*, I do not refer to the esoteric findings that came from an
archaeological dig. I refer instead to *those things that humans can wear on their body, do
to their bodies, or use as an extensions of their bodies for purposes of exercising conscious
control over their personal appearance.* Chief among such artifactual means are clothing,
accent items, hairstyles (as well as hair care and treatment), eyeglasses, contact lenses, rain-
coats, and purses and briefcases.

The distinctive features of artifactual communication as a specialized code were treated insightfully by Kaiser in the second edition of her *The Social Psychology of Clothing:
Symbolic Appearances in Context* (1990). She noted that the effectiveness of an artifactual
message is determined by the degree to which it conforms to implicit aesthetic rules or standards; that is, the appropriateness of clothing choice at the present time is determined in
large part by the degree to which the choice meets the dress expectations of the groups or
individuals with whom we interact.

Appearance messages by their nature are nondiscursive, inflexible, and multidimensional in terms of the meanings they communicate. As Kaiser pointed out, individuals cannot use their appearance to *discuss* when they are interacting with someone else in a social
context, nor can they use their appearance to move from one topic to another. In contrast to
verbal messages, appearance messages do not fade but tend to sustain their impact over
time. Appearance messages at the same time are inflexible because they cannot be adapted
to meet the changing demands of a given communicative context. Finally, the complex nature of appearance messages is reflected in the fact that they typically communicate multiple meanings:

> *Seldom is only one meaning associated with an appearance message. More com-
> monly, a range of possible meanings exist or meanings are layered on one another,
> almost creating a rainbow effect of meaning. Some meanings are derived from cul-
> tural experience, some are negotiated during social transactions, and some are
> conjured independently in the minds of participants. For two-way, meaningful
> communication to occur, the meaning intended by a programmed appearance
> should roughly coincide with that reviewed and interpreted by a perceiver.* (Kaiser,
> 1990, p. 238)

Clothing as a Medium of Communication

Clothing represents a particularly important type of artifactual communication. The clothing choices we make frequently exert a strong impact on the impressions that we make on others. More specifically, the clothing we wear has been proven to be a strong determinant of four "image dimensions" that define the impressions that we make on others:

1. credibility
2. likability
3. interpersonal attractiveness
4. dominance (Molloy, 1988; Rasicot, 1983; Rasicot, 1986; Smith & Malandro, 1985)

Image dimensions are the components or defining features of the impression(s) we make on others.

Authorities seem to agree that the most potent effect of clothing is on the credibility judgment of how competent or authoritative we are judged to be. Molloy (1988) and Rasicot (1986) agreed that our clothing is a major determinant of not only how competent we are judged to be but also how likable we are in the eyes of those with whom we interact. Ironically, the clothing choices that have the effect of enhancing our perceived competence often have the effect of depressing our likability and vice versa. The big, tall person may gain authoritativeness because of size but actually seem so unapproachable as to lose likability. One way to cope with the problem is to sacrifice some authoritativeness by wearing less conservative, lighter-colored clothing in order to be seen as more approachable and likable.

Clothing also clearly communicates one's degree of power or powerlessness. This is particularly true of the uniform. Thus, there seems to be a proliferation of uniforms in countries and regions where a high priority is placed on differentiating groups of people on the basis of their power or status. In Rome, for example, the large number of different uniforms worn by different kinds of law enforcement officers is almost overwhelming.

Nathan (1986) emphasized how clothing is used to control power judgments when he wrote that:

> A basic relationship read into clothing is that of power, or 'who controls whom' in the realm of clothing. The powerful, or controllers, include the parent of the child, the master of the servant, or the husband of the well-dressed traditional wife. (pp. 39–40)

Finally, the impact of uniforms on impressions formed of the wearer is not confined to impact on power judgments. Generally, people who wear uniforms seem to have more desirable personal qualities attributed to them. Hewitt and German (1987) found that a male marine sergeant and a male navy lieutenant were perceived as more attractive when in uniform than when dressed casually. Similarly, police officers were perceived as more competent, reliable, and intelligent when dressed in their uniforms (Singer and Singer, 1985). In contrast, air force enlisted personnel and officers viewed counselors in civilian attire as more expert, and they were more willing to cooperate with counselors when the counselors were dressed in civilian attire than when they were dressed in uniform (Huddleston & Engels, 1987). How would you account for the contrasting responses to individuals in uniform?

Cosmetics as a Medium of Communication

Cosmetics are clearly an important type of artifactual communication. They consist of things we put on our ourselves—particularly our face—that are intended primarily to serve the impression management function of nonverbal communication. Cosmetics include makeup, skin creams, perfume, aftershave lotion, and tattoos. Incidentally, the potential impact of tattoos on self-perceptions and interpersonal perceptions is often powerful and long-lasting. This is true in part because tattoos, a highly inflexible body message that is very difficult to change or eliminate, often tap into societal stereotypes that communicate a number of highly negative, connotative meanings (Rubinstein, 1985). However, makeup is the most important type of cosmetic because of its unsurpassed potential to shape the impressions made by those who use it.

What is makeup? Makeup consists of products that are used to give color to the human face, such as lipstick, eye shadow, blush, mascara, eyeliner, foundation, and powder (Fabricant & Gould, 1993). Because makeup is used primarily to enhance the physical attractiveness of the female face, its use raises issues of profound psychological importance for many women (Cash, 1987). When considering whether and how to use makeup, the contemporary woman may have to resolve a number of issues: (a) Does the use of beauty-enhancing makeup help perpetuate sex-role stereotyping of women? (b) Is it appropriate to use makeup for identity construction or impression management? (c) How are women to deal with the paradoxical and oxymoronic overtones of using something that is artificial—makeup—to make them appear natural? (d) Can ideologically feminist women avoid wearing any makeup without appearing to be situationally inflexible (Fabricant & Gould, 1993)?

Questions such as these are addressed in some recent, creative research. Respondents in this study suggested that the frequency with which women wear makeup, the amount of makeup used, and the kinds of makeup applied depend on the role a woman assumes at a given point in time. As Fabricant and Gould wrote:

> A woman's trajectory and predominant style of makeup use are tied in directly to her identity construction and reflection. Makeup is a means by which women may construct aspects of their selves consistently over time, at least their visible self-images. It is also one very visible sign by which they may be seen to reflect who they are to other people or at least whom they want to be seen as. (1993, p. 538)

More specifically, the authors stress the choices women make with regard to the use of makeup are affected by the time of day, the nature of the occasion, and the most central role being assumed. In constructing their desired identity through the use of makeup, women are aware of the differences between night versus day makeup, sexy versus nonsexy makeup, and makeup that emphasizes or deemphasizes sex role and gender identity.

Other Artifacts as Communicative Messages

The choice of highly personalized artifacts, such as cosmetics, hairstyle, eyeglasses or contact lenses, and even orthodontal devices clearly requires the aid of a professional image consultant. Molloy (1988) did not hesitate to provide guidelines for artifact choice. He did so at times with a sense of humor that is hardly self-deprecating. In his test of "Your Image

I.Q." he asked "For which professionals are bow ties acceptable—and often preferred—attire?" Molloy's answer is waiters, clowns, college professors, and commentators.

Finally, plastic surgery is perhaps the most drastic means of modifying unattractive features. Plastic surgery is no longer undertaken exclusively for therapeutic purposes—reconstructing the face of the victim of an automobile crash or rebuilding the skin of a burn victim. Each year, millions of Americans now elect to have aesthetic plastic surgery because they are not satisfied with their physical image.

Almost without exception, individuals who seek plastic surgery have a negative image of their own body. They may be upset by the social stigma of ethnic facial features, excessive fatty tissue, or sagging skin. Their own sense of identification, or self-definition, is fuzzy at best and extremely self-deprecating at worst. Many of these individuals start with a negative personal sense of identification and seem to take conscious steps to make others aware of their feelings of inferiority. Thus, Dr. Kurt Wagner, who served part of his residency performing plastic surgery on inmates in a prison in Oklahoma, has observed that "many inmates feel ugly, or they don't feel accepted or they have been made fools of.... With tattoos, they go out of their way to mark themselves and further isolate themselves" from society (Wagner & Gould, 1972).

The motivation of those who seek plastic surgery, the resultant changes in their image, and the impact on their communicative behavior is a subject I have treated in detail elsewhere (Leathers, 1976). The considerable expense that is usually associated with plastic surgery and the pain and discomfort that sometimes result seem to emphasize the high priority that many Americans attach to an acceptable personal appearance.

The Communicative Functions of Personal Appearance

You will recall that different kinds of nonverbal communication serve different kinds of communicative functions. Eye behaviors, for example, serve no less than seven major communication functions: the attention, intimacy, persuasive, regulatory, affective, power, and impression management functions. Proxemic behaviors, by contrast, are particularly important whenever individuals are concerned with the impression management, affiliation, and privacy functions of communication.

Personal appearance has an undeniable impact on a number of communicative functions. The importance of personal appearance in defining the societal role, occupation, class, gender, status, nationality, and age of the persons with whom we interact is undeniable. Moreover, personal appearance is also functionally important in the initiation and maintenance of romantic relationships. In fact, the sustained impact of personal appearance on romantic relationships is much greater than people might think. Patzer (1985) wrote that

> the research findings do not support the notion of subsiding effects and reveal instead enduring effects of surprising strength. Physical attractiveness remains a major determinant of mutual romantic attraction regardless of the elapse of time, the number of meetings, and even competing negative information. (p. 82)

In short, there are an almost unlimited number of communicative functions that are affected in some way by our personal appearance.

The two major communicative functions of personal appearance, however, are the *self-concept function* and the *impression management function.* Consider for a moment the integral and inseparable relationship of self-concept and body concept. As we have already demonstrated, numerous studies have confirmed the significant body image/self-concept/behavior linkage. When an investigator recently found that the academic performance of physically attractive schoolchildren in Lebanon was superior to that of their less physically attractive counterparts (Zahr, 1985), how did he interpret the results? Not surprisingly, the author's cited the body image/self-concept/behavior linkage. He concluded that because they were physically attractive, one group of schoolchildren had a more positive body concept. Their more positive body concept contributed to a more positive self-concept which in turn resulted in superior grades.

The impact of body concept on self-concept and ultimately on behaviors has been illustrated in so many ways in this chapter that further amplification is hardly necessary. At minimum, we should remember that the impact of our body concept on our self-concept is manifested not only in our perception of self and others but also in the interpersonal perceptions and behaviors of those with whom we interact.

Finally, the impression management function of nonverbal communication begins and ends with personal appearance. I will cover this important function in detail in the chapter on impression management. You may wonder, for example, what clothing choices you should and should not make if your major concern is maximizing your own credibility. On the other hand, you might wish to know whether you should wear different kinds of clothes if you are putting a premium on being judged to be interpersonally attractive. Professionals such as doctors and attorneys now recognize the importance of such questions. Indeed, the importance they attach to the impression management function of appearance helps explain the rise of the well-paid image consultant.

Summary

In our society, a well-developed physical attractiveness stereotype suggests that what is beautiful is talented, good, and socially desirable. Persons who deviate from the cultural ideal for physical attractiveness frequently suffer severe penalties in terms of self-concept, the undesirable personal traits attributed to them, and the relatively limited social rewards they are able to derive from interpersonal relationships.

The facial and bodily features that differentiate the physically attractive from the physically unattractive person are almost universally recognized in our society. Societal standards that are used to define beauty are more detailed for women than for men; and definitions for facial features are more detailed than those for bodily features. A precise profile exists that identifies the facial features that define facial attractiveness. In general, the smaller our facial features, the more attractive they are judged to be. Bodily attractiveness depends in part on whether one's body type is mesomorphic, ectomorphic, or endomorphic. For women, slenderness of body and body parts is an important feature of bodily attractiveness. For males, the physique that lacks muscles and muscle tone is viewed as particularly unattractive.

Body image, or the mental picture we have of our own body, is extremely important because body image strongly affects self-concept. Self-concept in turn has a powerful impact on our own perceptions and behaviors as well as on the way others perceive us and interact with us.

Body-cathexis is the concept that reflects how satisfied or dissatisfied we are with our own body. To the extent that we are unsatisfied with the appearance of our own body, or parts of it, we are apt to engage in body distortion. Body distortion is the distortion of our own estimates of the size of certain of our physical features, usually those that deviate from the cultural ideal.

The perceptual impact of personal appearance is perhaps strongest on self-concept; the more physically attractive we are perceived to be, the more positive our self-concept is apt to be. From a perceptual perspective, physical attractiveness also affects the kind of person we are perceived to be; it markedly affects judgments made about the quality of work we produce, and it affects the way we are treated by the judicial system.

The behavioral impact of personal appearance is also striking. Individuals who are viewed as physically attractive *do* behave differently. They are self-confident and assertive in their efforts to attain demanding goals; they exhibit independence in thought and action; and they exhibit an ability to resist conformity pressure, which is not characteristic of the physically unattractive person. When mingling with others, the physically attractive person has greater opportunities to interact with the opposite sex, and the nature of the interaction tends to be more satisfying.

Persons who do not meet the standards used to define acceptable personal appearance may wish to modify their personal appearance with artifacts. Artifacts are the things humans wear on their bodies, or do to their bodies, in order to modify their personal appearance. Clothing, cosmetics, hairstyle, eyeglasses and contact lenses, and plastic surgery are among the major artifactual means that can be used to exercise control over personal appearance.

Finally, personal appearance serves two major communicative functions—the self-concept function and the impression management function. These functions are integrally related. The impression management efforts we would like to undertake, and are capable of undertaking, are controlled to a considerable extent by how positive or negative our self-concept is.

References

Adams, G. R. (1977). Physical attractiveness research: Toward a developmental social psychology of beauty. *Human Development, 20,* 217–239.

Adams, G. R., & Crossman, S. M. (1978). *Physical attractiveness: a cultural imperative.* Roselyn Heights, NY: Libra.

Adams, G. R., & Roopnarine, J. L. (1994). Physical attractiveness, social skills, and same-sex peer popularity. *Journal of Group Psychotherapy, Psychodrama & Sociometry, 47,* 15–35.

Anderson, R., & Nida, S. A. (1978). Effects of physical attractiveness on opposite- and same-sex evaluations. *Journal of Personality, 46,* 410–413.

Archer, D. (1980). *How to expand your social intelligence quotient.* New York: Evans.

Aron, A (1988). The matching hypothesis reconsidered again: Comment on Kalick and Hamilton. *Journal of Personality and Social Psychology, 54,* 441–446.

Behling, D. W., & Williams, E. A. (1991). Influence of dress on perception of intelligence and expectations of scholastic achievement. *Clothing and Textiles Research Journal, 9,* 1–7.

Bloch, P H., & Richins, M. L. (1993). Attractiveness, adornments, and exchange. *Psychology & Marketing, 6,* 467–470.

Cahnman, W. J. (1968). The stigma of obesity. *Sociological Quarterly, 9,* 297.

Cash, T. F. (1987). The psychology of cosmetics: A review of the scientific literature. *Social and Behavioral Science Documents, 17,* 1–62.

Cash, T. F., Begley, P. J., McCown, D. A., & Weise, B. C. (1975). When counselors are heard but not seen: Initial impact of physical attractiveness. *Journal of Counseling Psychology, 22,* 237–239.

Cash, T. F., & Derlega, V. (1978). The matching hypothesis: Physical attractiveness among same-sexed friends. *Personality and Social Psychology Bulletin, 4,* 240–243.

Chaiken, S. (1979). Communicator physical attractiveness and persuasion. *Journal of Personality and Social Psychology, 37,* 1387.

Cortes, J B., & Gatti, F. M. (1966). Physique and motivation. *Journal of Consulting Psychology, 30,* 408–414.

Cortes, J. B., & Gatti, F. M. (1970). Physique and propensity. *Psychology Today, 4,* 42.

Cunningham, M R. (1986). Measuring the physical in physical attractiveness: Quasi-experiments on the sociobiology of female facial beauty. *Journal of Personality and Social Psychology, 59,* 925–935.

Cunningham, M. R., Roberts, A. R., Barbee, A. P., & Druen, P. B. (1995). "Their ideas of beauty are, on the whole, the same as ours": Consistency and variability in the cross-cultural perception of female physical attractiveness. *Journal of Personality & Social Psychology, 68,* 261–279.

Dion, E., Berscheid, E., & Walster, E. (1972). What is beautiful is good. *Journal of Personality and Social Psychology, 24,* 285–290.

Domzal, T. J., & Kernan, J. B. (1993). Variations on the pursuit of beauty: Toward a corporal theory of the body. *Psychology & Marketing, 10,* 495–511.

Fabricant, S. M., & Gould, S. J. (1993). Women's makeup careers: An interpretive study of color cosmetic use and "face value." *Psychology & Marketing, 10,* 531–548.

Fisher, S. (1986). *Development and structure of body image,* Vol. 2. Hillsdale, N. J.: Erlbaum.

Francis, S. K. (1992). Effect of perceived clothing deprivation on high school students' social participation. *Clothing and Textiles Research Journal, 10,* 29–33.

Gabriel, M. T., Critelli, J. W., & Ee, J. S. (1994). Narcissistic illusions in self-evaluation of intelligence and attractiveness. *Journal of Personality, 62,* 143–155.

Hensley, W. E. (1994). Height as a basis for interpersonal attraction. *Adolescence, 29,* 469–474.

Hewitt, J & German, K. (1987). Attire and attractiveness. *Perception & Motor Skills, 64,* 558.

Hocking, J E., Walker, B. A., & Fink, E. L. (1982). Physical attractiveness and judgments of morality following an immoral act. *Psychological Reports, 51,* 111–116.

Horvath, T. (1979). Correlates of physical beauty in men and women. *Social Behavior and Personality, 77,* 145–151.

Horvath, T. (1981). Physical attractiveness: The influence of selected torso parameters. *Archives of Sexual Behavior, 2.*

Huddleston, J E., & Engels, D. W. (1987). Influence of male military counselor attire on Air Force members' perceptions and preferences. *Military Medicine, 152,* 512–515.

Jackson, L. A., Sullivan, L. A., & Rostker, R. (1988). Gender, gender role, and body image. *Sex Roles, 19,* 429–443.

Joiner, T. E., Schmidt, N. B., & Singh, D. (1994). Waist-to-hip ratio and body dissatisfaction among college women and men: Moderating role of depressed symptoms and gender. *International Journal of Eating Disorders, 16,* 199–203.

Kalick, S. M., & Hamilton, T. E. (1986). The matching hypothesis re-examined. *Journal of Personality and Social Psychology, 51,* 673–682.

Kaiser, S. (1990). *The social psychology of clothing: Symbolic appearances in context* (2nd ed.). New York: Macmillan.

Kaplan, R M. (1978). Is beauty talent? Sex interaction in the attractiveness halo effect. *Sex Roles, 4,* 195–204.

Kretschmer, E. (1970). *Physique and character* (2nd ed.). New York: Cooper Square.

Kulka, R A., & Kessler, J. B. (1978). Is justice really blind? The influence of litigant personal attractiveness on juridical judgment. *Journal of Applied Social Psychology, 88,* 366–381.

Landy, D., & Sigall, H. (1974). Beauty is talent: Task evaluation as a function of the performer's physical attractiveness. *Journal of Social Psychology, 29,* 299–304.

Lavrakas, P. J. (1975). Female preferences for male physiques. *Journal of Research in Personality, 9,* 324–344.

Leathers, D. G. (1976). *Nonverbal communication systems.* Newton, MA: Allyn.

Malandro, L. A., Barker, L., & Barker, D. A.(1989). (2nd ed.). *Nonverbal communication.* Reading, MA: Addison-Wesley.

Martin, M. C., & Kennedy, P. F. (1993). Advertising and social comparison: Consequences for female preadolescents and adolescents. *Psychology & Marketing, 10,* 513–530.

Mashman, R. C. (1978). Effect of physical attractiveness on the perception of attitude similarity. *Journal of Social Psychology, 106,* 103–110.

Mathes, E. W., & Edwards, L. L. (1978). Physical attractiveness as an input in social exchanges. *Journal of Psychology, 98,* 267–275.

McCaulay, M. M., and Glenn, A. A. (1988). Body image, self-esteem, and depression-proness: Closing the gender gap. *Sex Roles, 18,* 381–391.

Mckelvie, S. J. (1993). Effects of feature variation on attributions for schematic faces. *Psychological Reports, 73,* 275–288.

Melamed, T. (1994). Correlates of physical features: Some gender differences. *Personality & Individual Differences, 17,* 689–691.

Molloy, J. T. (1988). *New dress for success.* New York: Warner.

Montepare, J M. (1995). The impact of variations in height on young children's impressions of men and women. *Journal of Nonverbal Behavior, 19,* 35–47.

Morrow, P. C. (1990). Physical attractiveness and selection decision making. *Journal of Management, 16,* 45–60.

Nathan, J. (1986). *Uniforms and nonuniforms: Communication through clothing.* New York: Greenwood Press.

Patzer, G. L. (1985). *The physical attractiveness phenomena.* New York: Plenum.

Rasicot, J. (1983). *Jury selection, body language and the visual trial.* Minneapolis: AB Publications.

Rasicot, J. (1986). *Silent sales.* Minneapolis: AB Publications.

Reis, H T., Nezlek, J., & Wheeler, L. (1980). Physical attractiveness in social interaction. *Journal of Personality and Social Psychology, 38,* 604–617.

Reis, H. T., Wheeler, L., Spiegel, N., & Kernis, M. H. (1982). Physical attractiveness in social interaction: II. Why does appearance affect social experience? *Journal of Personality and Social Psychology, 43,* 979–996.

Routh, J. R. (1974, April 7). Cosmetic surgery is for men, too. *The Atlanta Journal and Constitution Magazine,* 39.

Rubinstein, R. P. (1985). Color, circumcision, tattoos, and scars. In M. R. Solomen (Ed.), *The psychology of fashion* (pp. 243–254). Lexington, MA: Lexington Books.

Secord, P. F., & Jourard, S. M. (1953). The appraisal of body-cathexis: Body-cathexis and self. *Journal of Consulting Psychology, 17,* 347.

Sheldon, W. H. (1954). *Atlas of man: A guide for somatyping the adult male at all ages.* New York: Harper.

Singh, D. (1994). Is thin really beautiful and good? Relationship between waist-to-hip ratio (WHR) and female attractiveness. *Personality & Individual Differences, 16,* 123–132.

Singer, M. S., & Singer, A. E. (1985). The effect of police uniform on interpersonal perception. *Journal of Psychology, 119,* 157–161.

Smith, L. J., & Malandro, A. (1985). *Courtroom communication strategies.* New York: Kluwer Law Book.

Staat, J. C. (1977). Size of nose and mouth as components of facial beauty. *Dissertation Abstracts International.* Doctoral dissertation, University of Oklahoma, Norman, Oklahoma.

Strane, K., & Warts, C. (1977). Females judged by attractiveness of partner. *Perceptual and Motor Skills, 45,* 225–226.

Stonebraker, P. M. (1989). Biocultural influences to male and females body images, eating, and activity behaviors. *Dissertation Abstracts International.* Doctoral dissertation, Howard University, Washington, DC.

Sugerman, A. A., & Haronian, F. (1964). Body type and sophistication of body concept. *Journal of Personality, 32,* 393.

Thomas, V. G., & James, M. D. (1988). Body image, dieting tendencies, and sex role traits in urban black women. *Sex Roles, 18,* 523–529.

Vacker, B., & Key, W. R. (1993). Beauty and the beholder: The pursuit of beauty through commodities. *Psychology & Marketing, 10,* 471–494.

Wagner, K., & Gould, H. (1972). *How to win in the youth game: The magic of plastic surgery.* Englewood Cliffs, NJ: Prentice-Hall.

Walker, R. N. (1963). Body build and behavior in young children: II. Body build and parents' ratings. *Child Development, 34,* 20–23.

Wells, W. E., & Siegel, B. (1961). Stereotypes somatypes. *Psychological Review, 8,* 78.

Whaley, L. J. (1983). The effects of physical attractiveness on persuasion. Unpublished master's thesis, University of Georgia, Athens, GA.

White, G. L. (1980). Physical attractiveness and courtship progress. *Journal of Personality and Social Psychology, 39,* 660–668.

Wilson, D. W. (1978). Helping behavior and physical attractiveness. *Journal of Social Psychology, 104,* 313–314.

Worsley, A. (1981). In the eye of the beholder: Social and personal characteristics of teenagers in their impressions of themselves and fat and slim people. *British Journal of Medical Psychology, 54,* 231–242.

Zahr, L. (1985). Physical attractiveness and Lebanese children's school performance. *Psychological Reports, 56,* 191–192.

Chapter 8

Vocalic Communication

Sounds communicate meaning. The meanings exchanged by sound are vitally important in communicating the emotional state, the perceived personality characteristics, and, ultimately, the impressions made by a communicator. If you doubt the truth of this assertion, listen to the audiotapes of President Franklin Roosevelt's Fireside Chats during World War II.

The expressed purpose of Roosevelt's extemporaneous speeches was to allay the fears of the nation, and FDR's consummate use of sound as a communication medium was highly instrumental in helping him achieve his purpose. Imagine for a moment the following situation: Roosevelt's voice comes over the radio; he is speaking in a high-pitched, quavering voice, at an extremely rapid rate. He stutters repeatedly and fills his frequent pauses with perceptible sighs. If this had been the case, the nation might have experienced a real panic. Americans might have been as fearful of an emotionally distraught president as they were of the Nazis.

In fact, Roosevelt recognized what many subsequent studies have verified. The voice can be a powerful instrument for transmitting the emotional state of the communicator. Perhaps more important to the person concerned with making a desired impression, the voice can be used as a major force in shaping the impressions other people form of a communicator. FDR used his voice to communicate the image of a vigorous, confident, and decisive leader who was completely in control of his emotions. Not so incidentally, he used his voice to mold a political personality that successfully withstood the critical scrutiny of four presidential campaigns.

At least intuitively, most individuals recognize the role of the voice in shaping the impressions they make. The point was demonstrated graphically in my class on communication and conflict, in which former Secretary of State Dean Rusk was once a guest. As the students proceeded to ask him many questions, it was obvious that they wished to put their best personalities forward. Significantly, the students' vocal patterns were very different when addressing Rusk from their usual in-class patterns. Almost invariably, each student paused before addressing Rusk. Usually, the pitch of the voice was much lower, the rate was much slower, the cadence more measured, and the nonfluencies less frequent. Clearly, the students wanted to be perceived as serious and thoughtful observers of the international scene who were in control of their emotions. They knew that Rusk's perception of them would be significantly affected by their use of voice.

Vocal cues can serve many functions. The sound of the voice can be used to signal extroversion or introversion, dominance or submission, and liking or disliking; to reveal turn-taking preferences; and to provide information on gender, age, and race (Scherer, 1982). The voice also informs others about our interpersonal attitudes. We know that we use the sounds of the voices of those with whom we interact to determine their social class. In fact, our own dialect and accent strongly affect judgments of how much prestige we are perceived to have (Argyle, 1988).

Although vocal cues certainly have some impact on a number of functions of communication, they assume a vitally important role in serving three communicative functions:

1. the emotion function
2. the impression management function
3. the regulatory function

This chapter focuses on those primary functions of vocalic communication, and it begins with a consideration of the fundamental nature of vocalic communication.

The Semantics of Sound

The semantics of sound is not a simple matter. Siegman (1987) maintained that no generally accepted system exists that can be used to define and classify the vocal features of extralinguistic cues. We do know, however, that the vocal cues of communicators can be differentiated on the basis of attributes of sound uniquely associated with each communicator's vocal cues. Vocal cues consist of all attributes of sound that can convey meanings and that have some measurable functions in interpersonal communication. The sound attributes that give any vocal cue its unique characteristics are (a) loudness, (b) pitch, (c) rate, (d) duration, (e) quality, (f) regularity, (g) articulation, (h) pronunciation, and (i) silence.

Loudness, or the power of the human voice, is perhaps the most basic attribute, because if a voice cannot be heard, none of its other attributes can be used to convey meaning. Loudness is defined in terms of *decibels,* a measure of the acoustic energy reaching the receiver at a given second. The terms *loudness* and *amplitude* may be used interchangeably (Argyle, 1988).

The quiet whisper, at 10 decibels, can be just as disruptive to interpersonal communication as the construction worker's hammer blows on steel plate, at 114 decibels. Very often, as individuals experience anxiety while they are delivering a speech or engaging in interpersonal communication, the power of their voice drops quickly and they begin talking in a whisper that is unintelligible to the individuals with whom they are trying to communicate. On one occasion, I had a student who might very aptly have been nicknamed Whispering Smith. A prominent and affluent businessman, the student (whom we shall simply call "Smith") experienced great anxiety when giving a public speech. As his anxiety increased, Smith's volume dropped until he was whispering, and his audience was left in silent exasperation.

In spite of the fact that studies have been conducted on a great variety of conditions in big companies that use the assembly-line technique, few have focused on the damaging effects of excessive noise. The noise level in an average factory is 10 decibels above the noise level of a big-city street. This fact was dramatically emphasized for me when, with a group of my students, I toured an assembly plant of one of the world's largest auto manufacturers. The personnel director indicated that he had no idea what the noise level on the assembly line was, but that he knew for certain that his assembly line was really rather quiet and that his company had never been sued for job-related hearing disability. Interestingly, communication with the personnel director, who was 3 to 6 ft away as we toured the assembly line, was often impossible because of the noise level.

Anyone who has played a musical instrument is familiar with the concept of pitch. *Pitch* is the musical note that the voice produces. When you strike middle C on the piano, the C-string is vibrating at the rate of 256 times per second. Likewise, a human voice that produces the middle C is conveying the same pitch. Communicators have a *modal* pitch, that is, one that occurs more frequently than any other pitch in their extemporaneous speech. You can easily identify your own modal pitch by recording a brief sample of your speech and matching the pitch of the sound that occurs most frequently with the appropriate note on your piano keyboard.

The communicator should note that a number of factors affect modal pitch. Most importantly,

> *emotion affects modal pitch. A person who is sad or stunned is likely to use a lower modal pitch. Excitement and gaiety are normally shown by higher modal pitch. The quietly angry individual may use a low pitch, but the volatile type of anger may be high-pitched. We tend to associate low pitch with affection between sexes, but higher pitch with talking to babies.* (Fisher, 1975, p.155)

Your speaking or communicating *pitch range* is a measure of the musical interval (the number of notes) between the high and low pitches you use in speaking. Fisher notes that the ranges we employ in speaking depend on both our intent, and the content of what we are attempting to communicate. Factual communication has a much more limited pitch range than emotional communication, and emotional communication is apt to be high-pitched because most of it falls above your modal speaking range. Apathetic and apparent monotone speech both have a very narrow range (Fisher, 1975).

Rate is the third sound attribute of vocal cues that may facilitate or disrupt the transfer of meaning. Rate refers to the number of sounds emitted during a given unit of time—usually one second. Of course, when the communicator uses sounds to produce speech, speaking rate can have a vitally important impact on the quality of communication. Irregular rate may result in the communicator's combining words into units that are unconnected phrases rather than thought units.

Intelligibility and/or comprehension decline when rate of utterance exceeds 275 to 300 words per minute, although individuals can learn to comprehend material presented at faster rates through training in simple listening routines (Orr, 1968). Although we recognize that the average individual's thought rate is considerably faster than his or her speech rate, an accelerated rate of utterance is not always desirable. People differ substantially as to the optimum rate of utterance that they as listeners prefer. If the rate is too slow or the pauses too long, communicators will lose the attention of the persons with whom they are trying to communicate.

Finally, rate is a variable of primary interest to the paralinguistic not only because it helps determine how fluent or dysfluent the communicator is and, hence, how effective the communicator is but also because speaking rate is positively related to the perceived intensity of a speaker's speech (Bond, Feldstein, & Simpson, 1988). In short, a person is typically seen as speaking with greater intensity as his or her speaking rate increases.

The attributes of rate and *duration* are integrally related because the length of time a communicator takes to emit a given sound or sounds is a major factor in determining the short-term, and often the long-term, rate at which sounds are emitted. Duration is sometimes treated as a component of rate, but it is treated separately here because duration is an identifiable attribute of sound and, as such, may either hinder or help the communicator in attempts to transmit distortion-free meanings.

Quality, the fifth attribute of sound, has a variety of connotations and is difficult to define precisely. Certainly the modal pitch and the loudness of a person's voice are important determinants of its quality (Argyle, 1988). In a broader sense, students of vocalic communication generally agree that voice quality refers to those dominant vocal characteristics that allow you to differentiate one person's voice from another.

Several authorities now maintain that an individual's voice qualities are so distinctive that an expert can identify a given individual's voice from a tape that includes the voices of many other individuals. In the past few years, *voiceprints* have been used increasingly in criminal trials in an attempt to provide positive identification of a suspect. More attention is now focused on the attempt to identify those sound attributes that are most helpful in facilitating "earwitness identification" (Read & Craik, 1995).

The dominant quality of a person's voice strongly affects the impression that person makes. Addington's research (1968), for example, indicated that individuals with flat voices are apt to be perceived as masculine, sluggish, cold, and withdrawn. The breathy female voice reinforces the stereotypical conception that females having such voice quality are superficial and shallow. The nasal voice makes a particularly bad impression because it is associated with a substantial number of socially undesirable personal qualities.

The sound attribute of *regularity* refers to whether your production of sound has a rhythmical, and possibly even a predictable, quality. If you have ever listened to newscaster Tom Brokaw, you know what is meant by *regularity of sound* and *sound pattern*. In contrast, comedian Tom Smothers has made a sizable amount of money by emphasizing the arrhythmic or irregular nature of his sound production. Depending on the communicative situation, the sound attribute of regularity can be highly desirable or undesirable.

Articulation involves the use of movable parts at the top of the vocal tract such as tongue, jaw, and lips to shape sounds and, in speech communication, to make transitions between individual sounds and words. Although primarily physiological, articulation represents an attribute of sound, much like loudness, that must be present in acceptable form or communication virtually creases to exist. If you remember saying "Peter Piper picked a peck of pickled peppers" in your grade-school days, you know that very careful articulation was necessary or the listener would not be able to determine the exact nature of Peter's task.

Pronunciation is defined by specific vowel or consonant sounds in words and by the syllable that is emphasized. If you pronounce a word in a way that is inconsistent with general usage, or usage among the social groups with which you associate, it almost surely will result in confusion, at minimum. Perhaps more importantly, in terms of its long-range effect on the communicator, consistently mispronouncing words may impair a speaker's credibility and communicative effectiveness. For example, *irrelevant* is probably one of the most commonly mispronounced words in our society. Often *irrelevant* is pronounced "irrevelant." If such mispronunciation occurs frequently, this will markedly lower the quality of an individual's communication.

In the strictest technical sense, *silence* is not an attribute of vocal cues because silence assures that none of the eight defining attributes of vocal cues can be present. On the other hand, any sensitive observer of interpersonal communication recognizes that silence is a variable that is closely related to the other eight attributes of vocalic communication; therefore, silence serves important functions in interpersonal communication. We might give someone the "silent treatment" if we do not wish to acknowledge his or her presence; we sometimes become silent when we are unbearably anxious; or we may remain silent in order to exhibit emotions such as defiance or annoyance (DeVito, 1983).

Many other important vocal variables cannot and should not be dissociated from the sound attributes just defined, such as vocal intensity, response latency, type of turn-maintaining or -relinquishing cue, turn duration, dialect, and accent (Street, 1984). Although these vocal variables are important individually and collectively, they are defined by the interaction of one or more of the sound attributes of vocal cues that were just discussed.

The Communicative Functions of Vocal Cues

The Emotion Function

Vocal cues represent an important medium of emotional communication (Frick, 1985; Fukushima & Aoyagi, 1994). Mehrabian (1981), for example, maintained that 38 percent of the emotional information transmitted by a given message can be attributed to vocal cues. Facial expressions, as the predominant medium of emotional communication, account for 55 percent of the total feeling in a message, and words account for only 7 percent.

In order to assess the potential of vocal cues as a medium of emotional communication, researchers have used a number of techniques to eliminate the effective impact of the words uttered. Subjects have been asked to read ambiguous passages from texts that have no readily identifiable meaning, to utter nonsense words and syllables, and to speak in a foreign language. Electronic "filters" have also been applied to speech samples, to eliminate the sounds of higher frequencies. This practice renders the verbal message unintelligible and leaves the vocal message relatively intact.

Fairbanks and Pronovost (1939) were among the earliest experimenters in speech communication who attempted to determine whether individuals could communicate significant emotions solely by vocal cues, and if so, how accurately various emotions could be communicated. They used the technique of an ambiguous text in an attempt to assure that the communicated meanings were solely the result of the sound attributes of the vocal cues used in reading the passage. Six competent actors were asked to read the following passage repeatedly:

> *You've got to believe it in time to keep them from hanging me. Every night you ask me how it happened. But I don't know! I can't remember. There is no other answer. You've asked me that question a thousand times, and my reply has always been the same. It always will be the same. You can't figure out things like that. They just happen, and afterwards you're sorry. Oh, God, stop them ... quick ... before it's too late.*

As the actors repeated the passage to a group of 64 student judges, they were to vary the nature of the vocal cues in such a way that they believed they were accurately conveying the emotions of contempt, anger, fear, grief, and indifference.

The experiment demonstrated not only that *all emotions could be conveyed accurately by vocalic communication, at a level that greatly exceeded chance,* but also that *the vocal cues that conveyed the different emotions had readily identifiable and distinctive sound attributes.* Average accuracy of identification for the five emotions was 88 percent for indifference, 84 percent for contempt, 78 percent for anger and grief, and 66 percent for fear.

Contempt was communicated by extreme variations in inflections at the ends of phrases, a low median pitch level, and a wide total pitch range. Anger was associated with the greatest variability in all sound attributes, the widest mean extent of all pitch shifts, and the most downward pitch shifts. Fear was associated with the highest median pitch level, the widest total pitch range, and the fewest pauses within phrases at which shifts of pitch were not made. Grief exhibited the least variability among the attributes of sound, the presence of vibrato, the shortest duration of sound, and the slowest rate of pitch change. Indifference was communicated by the lowest pitch, the narrowest total pitch range, and shortest duration of sound when downward or upward inflections occurred.

Research by Scherer & Oshinsky (1977) identified similar but not identical relationships between specific emotions and the sound attributes that are used to express them. For example, sadness is expressed by downward inflections, low pitch, and slow speaking rate. Anger is expressed by wide variations in pitch, downward inflections, and fast speaking rate.

We should recognize that we sometimes communicate an attitude toward an event or individual at the same time that we use vocal cues to communicate emotions. Thus, anger and contempt are emotional states that can be expressed vocally but they can also serve to communicate attitudes toward specific individuals (Argyle, 1988). Second, it is important to note that the voice rarely communicates emotion by means of a single sound attribute. Thus, Frick (1985) noted in his enlightening discussion of sound attributes and the communication of emotion that pitch alone is not sufficient to express emotion vocally, but instead it is the interaction of pitch and loudness that is critical.

Probably the most detailed and enlightening contemporary research on the use of vocal cues to communicate specific emotions was done by Davitz and Davitz. They gave graduate students at Columbia University a list of 10 emotions and asked them to communicate those emotions by reciting the alphabet. Subjects were then asked to identify the emotions communicated via separate recitations of the alphabet delivered by the graduate students. Judges were asked to make 240 total judgments. The number of correct identifications expected by chance would be 24. The number of correct identifications for each emotion expressed was anger, 156; nervousness, 130; sadness, 118; happiness, 104; sympathy, 93; satisfaction, 74; fear and love, 60; jealousy, 59; and pride, 50 (Davitz & Davitz, 1959).

Subsequent research by Davitz (1964) and by Scherer (1979); an extensive review and assessment of this type of research by Harper, Wiens, and Matarazzo (1978); and a detailed study by Frick (1985) clearly support the conclusion that vocal cues are an effective medium for the communication of specific emotions. In fact, the human voice has the potential to communicate specific kinds of information about emotions experienced by individual communicators that is exceeded only by the human face.

The fact that the human voice can be used as a powerful medium for the communication of emotions does not mean that everyone uses it effectively for this purpose. In fact, we know that *individual ability to encode and decode emotional information via vocal cues varies substantially.* Levy (1964) found significant differences among individuals in terms of the accuracy with which they were able to encode and decode vocally expressed emotions. Individuals even differed significantly in their ability to identify their own feelings, which had previously been expressed in their own voice on audiotape.

The practical implications of this finding are clear for the person who wishes to be a successful communicator. We must be able to use our own voice effectively to express our emotions. We must also be able to identify accurately the emotions that others express vocally.

The Impression Management Function

Vocalic communication assumes a central role in the formation and management of impressions. Zuckerman and Driver (1989) emphasized the importance of vocalic communication in impression management when they wrote that "there is a large literature showing that both voice cues (e.g., pitch, intensity, etc.) and speech cues (e.g., nonfluencies, speech rate, etc.) are rich sources of interpersonal impressions" (1989, p. 68). Some recent evidence (Zuckerman, Hodgins, & Miyake, 1990) suggests that vocal cues have a greater impact on impression formation than does physical attractiveness. Although the impact of vocal cues on impression management and formation takes a number of forms, it begins with the impact of our vocal cues on the personality traits that are attributed to us.

Communicators can make marked changes in their personality, as it is perceived by others, by their use of vocal cues. The implications of this finding are striking for individuals who wish to emphasize or de-emphasize certain perceived characteristics of their personality. This is true in part because there is a detailed vocal attractiveness stereotype in our society that specifies what is and is not vocally attractive communication (Zuckerman et al., 1990).

This statement could, of course, be misinterpreted. A course or two in voice training is not apt to result in a startling transformation of your actual personality. It might, however, result in marked differences in the ways others perceive your personality.

Interest in the possible relationship between vocal cues and personality characteristics can be traced to the early days of radio, when massive national audiences were first attracted to it. Not surprisingly, many radio listeners became convinced that they could form accurate personality profiles of radio performers simply by listening to their voices. Other listeners were convinced that they could also accurately predict announcers' appearances by listening to them.

Stimulated by the intense curiosity of radio listeners, Pear (1931) analyzed the reaction of more than 4,000 radio listeners to nine trained radio voices and concluded that listeners consistently identified certain patterns of vocal cues with certain occupations such as clergymen and judges. Pear also found, however, that listeners consistently agreed that certain "vocal stereotypes" identified certain professions, although they made a number of errors in the application of such stereotypes.

In 1934, Allport and Cantril conducted the first major study specifically designed to examine whether, and to what extent, the natural voice is a valid indicator of personality. Their results strongly affirmed a positive relationship. The authors wrote that the voice definitely conveys "correct information concerning inner and outer characteristics." Specifically, they found that the sound attributes that comprise vocal cues are accurate indicators of the important personality dimensions of introversion–extroversion and ascendance–submission.

Although the pioneering study by Allport and Cantril did suggest a strong relationship between the nature of vocal cues and dimensions of the speaker's personality, the authors were bothered by the apparent fact that a limited number of vocal cues seemed to create a stereotype of the speaker in the mind of the listeners. Initially, the tendency of listeners to deal in stereotypes suggested that the listeners took a limited number of vocal cues and erroneously concluded that a large group of people, who conveyed vocal cues with the same sound attributes, had the same personality characteristics.

The concern that "vocal stereotypes" might invalidate research that attempts to predict personality characteristics from vocal cues has persisted up to the present. Such concern seems unwarranted for a number of reasons: (a) Stereotypes, although sometimes inaccurate, are often accurate. (b) When the vocal stereotypes are inaccurate, the judges typically make the same error. Thus, Crystal (1969) wrote that

> *such consistency in error may well be indicative of the existence of unformulated but none the less systematic voice-quality/trait correlations, or* vocal stereotypes, *as they are usually called in the literature, and is an importance piece of evidence justifying the psychologists' optimism that a systematic basis for personality in vocal cues does exist.* (p. 70)

(c) The accuracy of an audience's or individual's inferences about a speaker's real personality characteristics is not as important as an audience's agreement about a speaker's perceived personality characteristics.

As Pearce and Conklin (1971) wrote:

> *it should be noted that the accuracy of audience inferences about a speaker is not particularly important in this context. Experienced public speakers develop characteristic manners of presentation that lead audiences to draw desired or undesired inferences about them which,* whether accurate or not *[author's italics], affect the continuation and effectiveness of the communication situation. If a speaker is perceived as effeminate, arrogant, unscrupulous, or incompetent because of vocal cues . . . his actual personality and credibility may be superfluous.* (p. 237)

In spite of the great promise of the Allport and Cantril research, World War II, and perhaps the cyclical rhythms of researchers, resulted in a period of almost 25 years during which little effort was made to examine the relationship between vocal cues and perceived personality characteristics.

Addington conducted perhaps the most exhaustive research on the question of which specific attributes of sound are indicators or predictors of specific personality characteristics. In work for his doctoral dissertation (1963), he attempted to simulate a number of vocal qualities ("breathy," "thin," "flat," "nasal," "tense," "throaty," and "orotund") to manipulate rate and to introduce variety in pitch. Judges consistently agreed on the personality attributes associated with the different sound attributes in the vocal cues. Judges' agreement was highest on the feminine–masculine ratings of personality (0.94) and lowest for the extroverted–introverted ratings (0.81). The most uniformly perceived personality dimensions were feminine–masculine, young–old, enthusiastic–apathetic, energetic–lazy, good-looking–ugly, cooperative–uncooperative, unemotional–emotional, talkative–quiet, intelligent–stupid, interesting–uninteresting, and mature–immature.

Male communicators were seen as varying along four relatively unique personality dimensions: (a) lanky–dumpy, (b) hearty–glum, (c) potent–impotent, and (d) soft-hearted–hard-hearted. In contrast, female communicators were seen as varying along five personality dimensions: (a) social–antisocial; (b) aggressive–unresisting; (c) urbane–coarse; (d) passionate–dispassionate, and (e) wise–foolish. Thus, personalities of males were perceived, from vocal cues, in terms of physical characteristics, and females were evaluated in more social terms.

Pitch, rate, and the distinctive overall quality of communicators' voices are attributes of vocal cues that determine which personality characteristics are attributed to the communicators. For both male and female speakers, those who use greater variety in *pitch* are thought to be dynamic and extroverted. Both male and female speakers who use variety in *rate* are thought to be extroverted; males are also seen as *animated,* but females are seen as high-strung, inartistic, and uncooperative (Addington, 1963).

Specific sound attributes seem, in the minds of the listeners, to be associated with very specific personality characteristics. For example, both males and females with flat voices were evaluated as sluggish, cold, and withdrawn, and both males and females with nasal voices were evaluated as unattractive, lethargic, and foolish. Other vocal qualities were associated with very different personality characteristics for males and females. For example, males with breathy voices were perceived as youthful and artistic, and females with breathy voices were viewed as feminine but callow and high-strung. Males with tense voices were perceived as cantankerous, but females with tense voices were perceived as high-strung and pliable. Even more strikingly, the male with a throaty voice was evaluated as suave, but a female with a throaty voice was evaluated as "oafish," or a "clod"; males with orotund voices were perceived as vigorous and aesthetic but the female with an orotund voice was perceived as a "club-woman." Certainly,

> *this study has made it quite evident that it is possible for a speaker, through a variety of vocal changes, to make gross or subtle alterations in his personality as it is perceived by listeners cued only by a sample of the speaker's speech.... For those speakers interested in creating a perceived personality they would be*

pleased to claim as their own, and for those interested in character interpretation, vocal dexterity is a mandatory skill. (Addington, 1963, p. 163)

Research conducted since Addington's comprehensive efforts has consistently confirmed the idea that the nature of vocalic communication materially affects the personality characteristics that listeners identify with the communicator (Miyake & Zuckerman, 1993). In addition, listeners consistently associate specific sound attributes—such as rate, pitch, or nasality—with the same specific personality traits. In further interpreting and refining his earlier research, Addington (1968) concluded that "judgments of listeners ascribing personality from samples of speakers' voices tended to be uniform," and that this relationship was "well supported in the present findings" (p. 498).

When considered from a somewhat broader perspective, we know that "the attractive voice" is defined as sounding more articulate, lower in pitch, higher in pitch range, low in squeakiness, nonmonotonous, appropriately loud, and resonant (Zuckerman & Miyake, 1993). People with attractive voices in turn have greater power, competence, warmth, and honesty attributed to them than people with unattractive voices. Individuals with "babyish" vocal qualities are usually perceived to be less powerful and less competent but warmer and more honest than people with mature-sounding voices (Berry, 1992). We know too that vocal cues can have a significant impact on the most important image dimensions that define the impressions we make on other people: *competence, interpersonal attractiveness, and dominance.* As we shall see, different sound attributes affect each of these image dimensions in different ways.

Our society has a well-developed vocal stereotype that specifies how communicators must sound if they are to be viewed as *credible* (Thakerar & Giles, 1981). The dimension of credibility most apt to be affected by the sound of our voice is competence. We know, for example, that individuals who exhibit standard or prestigious accents, pause only briefly before responding, speak fluently, exhibit suitable variation in pitch and volume, and speak at a relatively fast rate are usually perceived as more competent than individuals who are associated with contrasting vocal cues (Street & Brady, 1982).

To speak with the "voice of competence," you must pay particular attention to those attributes of sound that are known to markedly affect judgments of credibility. Dialects and accents are known to be particularly important in affecting such judgments. Thus, communicators who speak with a general American dialect are viewed as more competent than those who do not. Standard dialects tend to enhance credibility in formal settings, whereas ethnic and in-group dialects are preferable in informal contexts such as homes and bars. Moreover, when the degree of accent is an important consideration for stereotyping and categorizing people, the more intense the accent, the more negative the impact on credibility (Street & Hopper, 1982).

Finally, we know that competence seems to be enhanced by considerable variation in pitch and volume (Sherer, London, & Wolf, 1973) and that competence increases as speaking rate increases. There obviously is a point at which speaking rate becomes so fast as to have a negative effect on competence, but there is no current consensus on what that rate is (Siegman, 1987). We also know that short, purposeful pauses positively affect perceived competence but that both "hesitation pauses" and nonfluent speech depress perceived competence (Erickson, Lind, Johnson, & O'Barr, 1978).

In separate chapters on selling yourself nonverbally, impression formation, and impression management, I will identify in detail the sound attributes that you should and should not exhibit if you wish to speak with the voice of competence. In a variety of applied contexts, such as the sales and selection interviews, it is clear that the sound of your voice will go a long way to establish or destroy your personal credibility (Gray, 1982).

We have already indicated that vocal cues strongly influence judgements of *interpersonal attractiveness.* For example, communicators who sound alike, or whose speech "converges" in terms of similarity in dialect, speaking rate, and response latency, are apt to perceive each other as more interpersonally attractive (Street, 1984). Indeed, the person who wishes to be judged to be interpersonally attractive must speak with the "voice of social attractiveness." The socially attractive voice is one that at the same time sounds confident and does not sound tense (Zuckerman, Hodgins, & Miyake, 1990).

The confident voice is defined by substantial but not excessive volume, a rather rapid speaking rate, expressiveness, and fluency. Cross-cultural research shows that appropriate loudness has a positive impact on perceptions of power in all groups studied (Peng, Zebrowitz, & Lee, 1993). Self-confidence and self-assurance are encoded in a clear and powerful manner by the confident voice (Kimble & Seidel, 1991). Communicators who exhibit a "confident" as opposed to a "doubtful" voice are perceived as significantly more *enthusiastic, forceful,* and *active* (Scherer, London, & Wolf, 1973).

Conversely, we attribute unacceptable levels of tension and anxiety to individuals who speak nonfluently. Nonfluencies include expressions such as "ah," sentence changes, word repetitions, stuttering (repeating the first syllable of a word), incomplete sentences, tongue slips, and intruding incoherent sounds, such as tongue clicks (Prentice, 1972). From a perceptual perspective, nonfluencies are, in the mind of the perceiver, strongly associated with high levels of anxiety (Jurich & Jurich, 1974).

Finally, the voice assumes a central role in shaping judgments of how dominant an individual may be. Indeed, recent empirical research suggests that the voice is more important than the face in affecting judgments of dominance, whereas the face is more important than the voice in affecting judgments of liking (Zuckerman & Driver, 1989). More particularly, dominant individuals speak with a loud voice, whereas submissive individuals speak with a soft voice. Relatedly, dominant and powerful individuals exhibit speech that is relatively free from hesitations and hedges, but these vocal phenomena are characteristic of the speech of submissive and low-power people (Hosman, 1989).

A moderately fast rate, high volume, and full resonance all reinforce perceptions of power and status (Burgoon & Saine, 1978). Schlenker (1980) emphasized

> that an image of power can be communicated to an audience through paralanguage in several ways. When people are anxious and lacking in confidence, they speak with lower volume and exhibit more speech disturbances, such as stuttering, omitting portions of a word or sentence, failing to complete a sentence, and taking longer pauses between words and sentences—seeming to grope for the correct word but unable to find it. People who are self-confident do not display such awkward paralanguage. (p. 252)

Vocal cues clearly have the potential to play a major role in helping an individual make a desired impression. They are major determinants of first impressions (Kleinke, 1975), true in part because listeners intuitively distrust the calculated first impression that communicators try to project through the words that they utter. More importantly, lasting impressions can be strongly affected by our vocal cues.

The Regulatory Function

Vocal cues clearly serve a central role in regulating the communicative interaction that takes place in interpersonal communication. They interact with a number of kinesic behaviors, particularly gestures and eye behaviors, to signal the turn-taking desires of interacting individuals. In a definitional sense, Knapp put the matter clearly (1978) when he noted that speakers use turn-yielding and turn-maintaining cues whereas listeners use turn-requesting and turn-denying cues.

Cappella (1985) provided us with a particularly insightful treatment of the classes and kinds of vocal cues that are used to regulate conversational exchange between two people. The use of vocalic cues to manage conversations can take one of two general forms: first, the conscious control or alteration of sound attributes such as volume and pausing in order to impose turn-taking preferences on a conversation and, second, exploiting certain regularities in the sequencing of utterances that characterize the vocal component of conversation, for example, recognizing that your partner will generally increase rate or increase mean duration of pauses to match the rate or mean duration of pauses (Cappella & Planalp, 1981).

How successful you are in the use of vocal cues to regulate or manage interaction depends on the criterion measure that you use. Because Coker and Burgoon (1987) attach a positive value to "involvement," they define "better interaction management" as the use of vocal cues that promote involvement, such as fewer silences/latencies and more coordinated speech. Recognize that in some instances that the objective might be *not* to promote the involvement of one's interaction partner but to inhibit it.

If we wish to have favorable image traits attributed to us, we should modify our vocal cues so that we sound more like the individual with whom we are communicating. To reap the potential impression management benefits that "convergence" or "matching" may provide them, speakers often seek to make their vocal cues similar to the vocal cues of the person with whom they interact. Vocal cues that are particularly important in this regard include dialect choice, accent, and pausing. In general, the more we sound like the person with whom we interact, the more favorable the impression that we make (Street, 1982).

Cappella (1985) recognized that the regulatory and impression management functions of vocalic communication are interrelated when he wrote that "the evidence is overwhelming in its support of the relationship between holding the floor and observers' rating of control and power (leadership, dominance, and so forth) and associativity (attraction, social evaluation, and so forth)" (p. 402). We know, for example, that courtroom attorneys use the loudness and cadence of their speech with the explicit intent of becoming the dominant figure in the proceedings. We also know that such attorneys seek to attain dominance in the courtroom not only for purposes of controlling conversation but also to define the impression they make in terms of high power.

At minimum, two people engaged in conversation must be concerned with three types of turns: within-turn interaction, simultaneous turns (when two people speak at the same time), and the management of turn taking when two individuals are sharing turns. The vocal behaviors of greatest importance in regulating interaction are duration of vocalization, pause duration, switching pauses, utterance length, latency (length of time taken to respond), and intensity or amplitude. The person who wants to maintain a turn, for example, will typically sustain vocalization, use short pauses, and maintain or increase loudness. It is interesting to note that when simultaneous turns occur—two people speak at the same time—the person who speaks the loudest will typically win the floor (Cappella, 1985).

Individuals often speak with an unusually loud voice whenever they wish to command or order other persons to act in a certain way. The louder a person's voice the more dominant that person is apt to be perceived to be (Siegman, 1987). The "command voice" of the drill sergeant is legendary, and more than one parent has used it to regulate a child's behavior. For sheer stridency and volume, I have never heard anything that matches the vocal commands of the Beafeaters who guard the Queen's jewels, housed in a basement vault in the Tower of London. The Beafeaters, who are middle-aged men of some degree of distinction, are apparently charged with keeping the tourists moving. They cry out in almost unbelievably loud and aggressive tones, "Keep it moving. We can't let you stop. Other people want to see." The command voice seems to work in this instance, but it also seems to make a lot of tourists mad as hell.

Developing the Ability to Encode and Decode Vocalic Messages

The ability to encode and decode vocalic messages represents an important nonverbal communication skill. As an encoder, you must develop this skill to an acceptable level if you are to make effective use of the great functional potential of vocalic communication. We have already established the functional importance of vocalic cues in conveying emotions, making first and long-term impressions, and in regulating communicative interaction. Similarly, you must develop your skill in decoding vocalic messages to an acceptable level if you are to interpret accurately the important kinds of information that are being communicated to you.

The Vocalic Meaning Sensitivity Task (VMST) has been developed both to test and to develop the accuracy with which individuals can communicate and perceive emotional meanings conveyed solely by vocal cues. The personal testimony of many classroom instructors who have used the VMST suggests that it is a useful training tool. Individuals who use the VMST almost always become very involved in the learning experience it provides. Many of those same individuals have emphasized that the VMST gives them a much better appreciation of the functions of vocalic communication, and with repeated use it significantly improves their encoding and decoding abilities.

To use the VMST in its simplest form you must do two things. First, have a friend or acquaintance attempt to communicate disgust, happiness, interest, sadness, bewilderment, contempt, surprise, anger, determination, and fear solely by using different vocal cues in reading the following sentences: "There is no other answer. You've asked me that question a thousand times, and my answer is always the same."

Your friend should repeat the two sentences 10 times, trying to communicate a different meaning each time by varying sound attributes such as pitch, loudness, and rate. Randomize the order in which attempts are made to communicate each class of vocalic meaning. For example, sadness could be the first meaning and determination the second.

To separate one reading from another, your friend should begin each reading by saying, "This is vocal message number 1," then, "This is vocal message number 2," and so on.

For communication of the highest possible quality, you might have your friend record the sentences on audiotape. Then, rather than listening to the communicator speaking in person, you will listen to the tape. When attempting to communicate vocally before a live audience, the communicators should sit with their chairs turned away from the audience. Ideally, communicators should sit behind a screen, to prevent the audience from seeing kinesic or other nonverbal cues.

Second, follow the directions for the VMST exactly in order to produce accurate measurements. When you identify the vocal message of others, your own decoding skill is being measured; when others attempt to identify your vocal messages, your own encoding skill is being measured.

The Vocalic Meaning Sensitivity Task (VSMT)

The communicator you are listening to—either live or on a tape recording—is attempting to communicate ten different classes or kinds of meaning to you. Each attempt to communicate a class of meaning will begin with the words "This is a vocal message number _____." You are to listen very carefully, then in Table 8.1 place the number of the vocal message in the blank across from the word, such as *disgust* or *happiness,* that comes closest to representing the meaning just communicated to you vocally. Follow the same procedure for each of the 10 vocal messages.

To test your ability to communicate meanings accurately as opposed to testing your ability to perceive meanings transmitted by vocal cues, you should attempt to communicate

TABLE 8.1   Vocalic Meaning Sensitivity Task (VMST)*

Class of Vocalic Meaning	Number of Vocal Message
Disgust	_____
Happiness	_____
Interest	_____
Sadness	_____
Bewilderment	_____
Contempt	_____
Surprise	_____
Anger	_____
Determination	_____
Fear	_____

*You may use an expanded form of the VMST if you desire. The 10 terms here were used for two reasons: They have previously been used in research on vocalic communication, and they are the same terms used in Step 1 of the FMST. Therefore, you can make direct comparisons between your ability to perceive and communicate meaning by facial and vocal means. Simply compare accuracy of identification scores for Step 1 of the FMST with scores on the VMST. If you want to make a more extended test of your ability to perceive and transmit meanings vocally, however, you should add the following 10 terms to the task, which also are frequently used in tests of vocalic communication: *indifference, grief, anxiety, sympathy, pride, despair, impatience, amusement, satisfaction,* and *dislike.* By adding these terms to the VMST, you have a more comprehensive and demanding measure of vocalic skills.

the 10 emotions that comprise the VMST by making a tape recording and then giving the test to a group of people of your own choice.

Students' ability to communicate the 10 emotions of the VMST vary dramatically (6 correct choices out of 10 is 60 percent accuracy of identification). The scores of the vocal communicators in my classes have ranged from 85 to 30 percent; the scores of the vocal perceivers have been in approximately the same range. As a rule of thumb, you can assume that a score of 70 percent or above is excellent; 69 to 50 percent is average; and below 50 percent is poor.

Repeated use of the VMST usually leads to marked improvement in both the ability to encode and the ability to decode messages conveyed by sound. You have the potential to improve your scores on the test by at least 20 percent. If you set realistic goals for yourself, the VMST can be a great help in attaining them.

The use of the VMST, or your own experiences in real-world contexts of importance to you, may indicate that you are vocally expressive or that you have specific problems. Let us assume, for example, that others perceive your voice to be unpleasantly nasal, harsh, or hoarse; that you exhibit a high nonfluency rate; or that you speak with a soft voice. Specific voice-training exercises have been developed to deal with such problems. You may wish to use such exercises on your own or to work with a voice-training coach (Linver, 1983).

Summary

Vocal cues consist of all attributes of sound that can convey meanings and have some measurable functions in interpersonal communication. The sound attributes that differentiate one person's vocal cues from another's are loudness, pitch, rate, duration, quality, regularity, articulation, pronunciation, and silence.

Vocal cues serve many functions. They assume a particularly central and important role in serving three communication functions, however: the emotion function, the impression management function, and the regulatory function.

Vocal cues are an important medium of emotional communication. Their potential to provide specific information about a communicator's emotional states is exceeded only by facial expressions. We do know, however, that individuals' ability to encode and decode emotional information via vocal cues vary substantially.

Vocal cues serve the impression management function in two ways. First, the voice sound is a major determinant of the personality traits that are ascribed to a person. Vocal cues strongly affect the specific kinds of personality characteristics and personal qualities that are attributed to the communicator. Pitch, rate, and the overall quality of a person's voice determine which personality characteristics are attributed to that person. Individuals who exhibit little variation in pitch and rate, for example, are typically viewed as introverts, lacking dynamism and assertiveness. Persons who exhibit a nasal quality are likely to have a wide array of undesirable personality characteristics attributed to them.

Second, vocal cues serve the impression management function by exerting a major impact on three image dimensions—credibility, interpersonal attractiveness, and dominance—that in turn define the impressions we make on others. Specific sound attributes are associated with "the voice of competence" and "the voice of social attractiveness." Also, the sound of our voice is very important in judgments people make about how dominant or submissive we are.

The regulatory function of vocalic communication has been receiving increasing attention recently. In order to engage in enlightened conversational management, we must understand how vocal variables such as duration of vocalization, pause duration, utterance length, latency of response, and amplitude can be used to regulate interaction. We typically will use not only vocal cues but also eye behaviors and gestures in our attempts to regulate communicative interactions.

Successful communication puts a premium on the development of important nonverbal communication skills. The Vocalic Meaning Sensitivity Task (VMST) presented in this chapter should be used both to test and to develop the accuracy with which individuals can communicate and perceive emotional meanings conveyed solely by vocal cues.

References

Addington, D. W. (1963). The relationship of certain vocal characteristics with perceived speaker characteristics. Doctoral dissertation, University of Iowa, 1963.

Addington, D. W. (1968). The relationship of selected vocal characteristics to personality perception. *Speech Monographs, 35,* 492–503.

Allport, G. W., & Cantril, H. (1934). Judging personality through voice. *Journal of Social Psychology, 5,* 40–51.

Argyle, M. (1988). *Bodily communication* (2nd ed.). Methuen: London.

Berry, D. W. (1992). Vocal types and stereotypes: Joint effects of vocal attractiveness and vocal maturity on person's perception. *Journal of Nonverbal Behavior, 16,* 41–53.

Bond, R. N., Feldstein, S., & Simpson, S. (1988). Relative and absolute judgments of speech rate from masked and content-standard stimuli: The influence of vocal frequency and intensity. *Human Communication Research, 14,* 548–568.

Burgoon, J. K., & Saine, T. (1978). *The unspoken dialogue.* Boston: Houghton.

Cappella, J. N. (1985). The management of conversations. M. L. Knapp & G. R. Miller (Eds.). *Handbook of Interpersonal Communication* (pp. 393–435). Beverly Hills, CA. Sage.

Cappella, J. N., & Planalp, S. (1981). Talk and silence sequences in informal conversations III: Interspeaker influence. *Human Communication Research, 7,* 117–132.

Coker, D. A., & Burgoon, J. K. (1987). The nature of conversational involvement and nonverbal encoding patterns. *Human Communication Research, 13,* 463–494.

Crystal, D. (1969). *Prosoic systems and intonation in English.* Cambridge, MA: Cambridge University Press.

Davitz, J. R. (1964). (Ed.). *The communication of emotional meaning.* New York: McGraw-Hill.

Davitz, J. R., & Davitz, L. J. (1959). The communication of feelings by content-free speech. *Journal of Communication, 9,* 9.

DeVito, J. A. (1983). *The interpersonal communication book* (3rd ed.). New York: Harper.

Erickson, B., Lind, E. A., Johnson, B. C., & O'Barr, W. M. (1978). Speech styles and impression formation in a court setting: The effects of "powerful" and "powerless" speech. *Journal of Experimental Social Psychology, 14,* 266–279.

Fairbanks, G., & Pronovost, W. (1939). An experimental study of the durational characteristics of the voice during the expression of emotion. *Speech Monographs, 6,* 88–91.

Fisher, H. B. (1975). *Improving voice and articulation* (2nd ed.). Boston: Houghton.

Frick, R. W. (1985). Communicating emotion: The role of prosoic features. *Psychological Bulletin, 97,* 412–429.

Fukushima, O., & Aoyagi, S. (1994). Learning to decode vocally encoded emotions. *Japanese Journal of Counseling Science, 27,* 37–45.

Gray, J., Jr. (1982). *The winning image.* New York: AMACOM.

Harper, R. B., Wiens, A. N., & Matarazzo, J. D. (1978). *Nonverbal communication: The state of the art.* New York: Wiley.

Hosman, L. A. (1989). The evaluative consequences of hedges, hesitations, and intensifiers: Power and powerless speech styles. *Human Communication Research, 15,* 383–406.

Jurich, A. P., & Jurich, J. A. (1974). Correlations among nonverbal expressions of anxiety. *Psychological Reports, 34,* 199–204.

Kimble, C. E., & Seidel, S. D. (1991). Vocal signs of confidence. *Journal of Nonverbal Behavior, 15,* 99–105.

Kleinke, C. L. (1975). *First impressions.* Englewood Cliffs, NJ: Prentice-Hall.

Knapp, M. L. (1978). *Nonverbal communication in human interaction* (2nd ed.). New York: Holt.

Levy, P. K. (1964). The ability to express and perceive vocal communications of feeling. In J. R. Davitz (Ed.), *The Communication of Emotional Meaning.* New York: McGraw-Hill.

Linver, S. (1983). *Speak and get results.* New York: Summit.

Mehrabian, A. (1981). *Silent messages* (2nd ed.). Belmont, CA: Wadsworth.

Miyake, K., & Zuckerman, M. (1993). Beyond personality impressions: Effects of physical and vocal attractiveness on false consensus, social comparison, affiliation, and assumed and perceived similarity. *Journal of Personality, 61,* 411–437.

Orr, D. B. (1968). Time compressed speech—A perspective. *Journal of Communication, 18,* 288–291.

Pear, T. H. (1931). *Voice and personality.* London: Chapman and Hall.

Pearce, W. B., & Conklin, F. (1971). Nonverbal vocalic communication and perception of a speaker. *Speech Monographs, 38,* 235–241.

Peng, Y., Zebrowitz, L. A., & Lee, H. K. (1993). The impact of cultural background and cross-cultural experience on impressions of American and Korean male speakers. *Journal of Cross-Cultural Psychology, 24,* 203–220.

Prentice, D. S. (1972). The process effects of trust-destroying behavior on the quality of communication in the small group. Doctoral dissertation, University of California at Los Angeles.

Read, D., & Craik, F. I. M. (1995). Earwitness identification: Some influences on voice recognition. *Journal of Experimental Psychology: Applied, 1,* 6–18.

Scherer, K. R. (1979). Nonlinguistic vocal indicators of emotion and psychopathology. In C. E. Izard (Ed.), *Emotions in personality and psychopathology.* New York: Plenum.

Scherer, K. R. (1982). Methods of research on vocal communication: Paradigms and parameters. In K. R. Scherer & P. Ekman (Eds.), *Handbook of methods in nonverbal behavior research.* Cambridge, MA: Cambridge University Press.

Scherer, K. R., London, H., & Wolf, J. J. (1973). The voice of confidence: Paralinguistic cues and audience evaluation. *Journal of Research in Personality, 7,* 31–44.

Scherer, K. R., & Oshinsky, J. S. (1977). Cue utilization in emotion attribution from auditory stimuli. *Motivation and emotion, 1,* 331–346.

Schlenker, B. R. (1980). *Impression management.* Monterey, CA: Brooks/Cole.

Siegman, A. W. (1987). The telltale voice: Nonverbal messages of verbal communication. In A. W. Siegman & S. Feldstein (Eds.), *Nonverbal behavior and communication* (2nd ed.). Hillsdale, NJ: Erlbaum.

Street, R. L. (1982). Evaluation of noncontent speech accommodation. *Language & Communication, 2,* 13–31.

Street, R. L. (1984). Speech convergence and speech evaluation in fact-finding interviews. *Human Communication Research, 11,* 139–169.

Street, R. L., & Hopper, R. (1982). A model of speech style evaluation. In E. B. Ryan & H. Giles (Eds.), *Attitudes towards language variations: Social and applied contexts* (pp. 175–188). London: Arnold.

Street, R. L., Jr., & Brady, R. M. (1982). Speech rate acceptance ranges as a function of evaluative domain, listener speech rate, and communication context. *Communication Monographs, 49,* 290–308.

Thakerar, J., & Giles, H. (1981). They are—So they spoke: Noncontent speech stereotypes. *Language and Communication, 1,* 255–261.

Zuckerman, M., & Driver, R. E. (1989). What sounds beautiful is good: The vocal attractiveness stereotype. *Journal of Nonverbal Behavior, 13,* 67–82.

Zuckerman, M., Hodgins, H., & Miyake, K. (1990). The vocal attractiveness stereotype: Replication and elaboration. *Journal of Nonverbal Behavior, 14,* 97–112.

Zuckerman, M., & Miyake, K. (1993). The attractive voice: What makes it so? *Journal of Nonverbal Behavior, 17,* 119–135.

Developing the
Successful Communicator

Impression Formation

The chapters in Part 2 of this book focus on the subject of impression management, illustrating and demonstrating how knowledge of impression management can be used to give us social control over individuals we wish to control. We will see how and why the social control function of nonverbal communication is exercised in order to achieve specific impression management goals. Any time you seek to control the behavior of the person or persons with whom you are interacting, you are exercising the social control function of communication. We can, for example, exercise control over other individuals by using persuasive messages and by providing feedback. However, the nature of the control we seek might in some instances be viewed as quite negative by other people. We could, for example, communicate for purposes of deceiving other individuals. Because I consider deception to be both unethical and undesirable, the chapter on deception focuses on ways to develop skills in detecting deception but excludes methods for individuals to become more effective deceivers.

Attempts to communicate how powerful or dominant we are, to provide feedback and reinforcement, to be deceptive, and to be persuasive all share one common denominator. The common denominator is the attempt to manage impressions. Thus, Edinger and Patterson (1983) wrote that all of those kinds of communication "involve impression management. That is, in attempting to exert power, persuade others, provide feedback, or deceive, individuals are at least indirectly managing impressions" (p. 43).

Collectively, the five chapters in Part 2 of this book are designed to give you the potential to become a more successful communicator by developing your understanding and your skills of impression management. Separate chapters are devoted to impression formation and to impression management, although emphasizing the complex ways they are conceptually interrelated. Chapter 10 on impression management asserts that credibility is the most important of the four image dimensions that control the impressions we make on others—credibility, likability, interpersonal attractiveness, and dominance. All of Chapter 11 (Selling Yourself Nonverbally) then is devoted to the role of nonverbal behaviors and cues in the development of one's personal credibility. The importance of the final two chapters in Part 2—Detecting Deception and Communicating Consistently—will become apparent as you read them.

Do you recall the first time you called someone on the telephone and asked for a date? Do you recall being highly conscious of the ways you were behaving on early dates? Do you remember interviewing for a job that was extremely important to you? Have you ever appeared in a courtroom as a litigant, witness, or member of the jury? Were you ever a candidate in a beauty pageant? Do you recall being stopped by a police officer and asked to walk along a white line painted on the road? Have you ever tried to get elected to an office or position that was important to you?

In all likelihood, you answered yes to a number of these questions. If you did, you will undoubtedly admit that impression formation is a subject of great importance to you. In fact, an almost endless number of situations or contexts exist in which the impression you make on other people is the key to your success. If you are honest, you will probably admit at least two other things. First, you have spent many hours trying to figure out how you could make a favorable impression on a first date or make a good impression in such a vitally important communicative situation as a job interview. Thus, you were doing some heavy thinking not only about impression formation but also about impression management. Second, you recognize that you have a strong need to increase your understanding of how other people form impressions of you and what you can do to exercise conscious control over those impressions. This chapter is designed to help you increase your understanding of impression formation. Chapter 10 is written for the person who wants to become an effective impression manager.

The Importance of Nonverbal Cues in Interpersonal Perception

The kind of person you are judged to be is much more heavily influenced by nonverbal than verbal cues. Argyle, Salter, Nicholson, Williams, and Burgess (1970) found that nonverbal cues have 4.3 times the impact on the impression we make than do verbal cues. Walker (1977) found that, to express confidence, nonverbal cues were 10 times more important than verbal cues. Schlenker (1980) put it succinctly:

> *A picture is worth a thousand words. When face-to-face we get the complete moving picture. We see the look in their eyes, the expression on their faces, the way their bodies lean, how closely they are willing to approach, the way they sit, the tenseness or relaxedness of their gestures. We hear the tones of their voices and the speed of their speech. We may not even be conscious at the time of the impact this information has on our overall impressions, but there is no doubt that it plays a major role in shaping our views of others. The other person's "style" comes through to form images that can mean more than the specific words he or she speaks.* (p. 235)

Chapters 2 through 8 in this book clearly document the importance of nonverbal communication in impression formation. Those chapters make quite clear that we often rely to an extraordinary degree on nonverbal sources of information in forming our impressions of other people. Think back for a moment and you will probably agree that when you make evaluative judgments about individuals, you typically give disproportionate weight to the nonverbal behaviors and cues that they exhibit, rather than to their actions.

Consider what you already know about the highly personalized information we obtained from the nonverbal communicative behaviors and cues of persons whom you observe and with whom you interact. You look to their face if you want to make precise judgments about the emotions they are experiencing. You look to their eye behaviors to judge the degree of their emotional arousal, how competent they are, and how dominant they are in your interaction. You observe their gestures and postures to identify their interpersonal attitudes, to assess their level of self-confidence, and to determine how close or distant a relationship they wish to develop with you. You look to their personal appearance to make judgments about their self-concept and personality traits. You observe their spatial behavior to determine the strength of their needs for affiliation and privacy. You listen to their voice in order to ascribe a wide array of presumed personality traits to them and to determine how assertive they are. Finally, you watch how, where, and how often they touch you and others in order to determine how emotionally supportive they are.

Not only do we rely heavily on nonverbal cues in attributing personal traits and qualities to others; we now know that *nonverbal cues do provide accurate information about personal traits* (Paunonen & Jackson, 1979). We rely heavily on nonverbal cues in forming our impressions of other individuals because we recognize intuitively that people's words provide information about their actions but their nonverbal cues provide information about them as individuals.

The impressions we make on others are heavily influenced by our nonverbal communication (Manusov, 1990). We will emphasize in the next chapter on impression management that the impressions we make on another person are defined by how positively or negatively we are perceived on each of four image dimensions: credibility, likability, interpersonal attractiveness, and dominance. We now know not only that our nonverbal messages often exert a controlling impact on these image dimensions but also that certain types of nonverbal messages have a much stronger impact on one type of image dimension than another. Although these four image dimensions are the most important components of the impression we make on others, there is more to impression formation. Our level of self-confidence, attitudes, and emotional states—as perceived by others—all interact to shape the impression others form of us.

Factors That Affect Interpersonal Perceptions

Interpersonal perception is the complex process by which individuals select, organize, and interpret stimuli, or sensory stimulation, into a meaningful view of the world (Sereno & Bodaken, 1975). If every perceiver attended to the same stimuli, organized the stimuli from the same perspective, and interpreted the stimuli in the same way, interpersonal perception would be a simple and completely predictable matter. In practice, however, interpersonal perception is a subjective matter. *We frequently rely on subjective impressions of people and events to try to explain what kind of people they are and why they behave as they do* (Schrader, 1994). Whenever we try to explain individuals' behaviors, we must make *attributions*. Shaver recognized that the attributions we make are often subject to error because we "are not dispassionate observers of human behavior, watching without evaluation. On the contrary, we try to understand behavior, to explain it, to determine what it means for us, and to make value judgments about it" (Shaver, 1975, p. v).

Whenever we make judgments about people's past behavior or predict their future behavior, we make attributions about the reasons for their behavior. We make either *situational* or *dispositional* attributions. To illustrate the point, consider the case of Congressman Jeremy Funkhouser (a hypothetical congressman), who was apprehended in the Abscam investigation and convicted of taking one million dollars in bribe money from FBI agents posing as Arab oil sheiks. The situational attribution would be that Funkhouser took the money because of the pressures of his family situation—his terminally ill wife was running up huge medical bills. The dispositional attribution would be that Funkhouser took the money because of the kind of person he really is—unethical, weak, unprincipled, sneaky, and exploitative.

The perceptual judgments we make about other people and their actions are *made more difficult by the fact that our perceptual judgments may be unduly influenced by the following:*

1. stereotypes
2. the primacy effect (first impressions)
3. selective perceptions
4. the recency effect (last impressions)

Because these factors play a central role in shaping the impressions others have of us, it is easy to understand why nonverbal cues are so important in impression formation and management.

Stereotypes

The impressions other people have of us are often controlled to a startling degree by stereotypes. An individual who belongs to a particular group is expected to exhibit certain personal characteristics and attitudes and to act in certain ways.

The O. J. Simpson trial certainly gave us graphic examples of negative stereotyping. Mark Furhman, who retired as a detective in the Los Angeles Police Department during the Simpson trial, clearly developed a highly negative stereotype of African Americans. He characteristically referred to them by means of a derogatory racial epithet, the "*N* word." The Furhman tapes hardly prove that his stereotypical conception of African Americans is at all representative of the attitudes of the typical police officer. However, Vru and Winkel (1994) concluded that

> *Black nonverbal behavior (indirect answers and many speech disturbances) was assessed more negatively than White nonverbal behavior (direct answers and fewer speech disturbances). Results provided empirical support for the occurrence of nonverbal communication errors in cross-cultural police–citizen interactions: Typical Black nonverbal behavior displayed by Black citizens will be interpreted as suspicious, tense, and unpleasant behavior by White police officers.* (p. 290)

Particularly when someone meets you for the first time, he or she might stereotype you, primarily on the basis of how you look and sound. If you are shifty eyed, appear nervous, engage in frequent postural shifts, and exhibit many nonfluencies during a police interrogation, for example, you will fit the "liar stereotype." Regardless of whether convicted hijackers actually confirm the accuracy of the hijacker profile, your own chances of being stopped by security personnel at an airport certainly increase when your appearance and behavior differ markedly from those of the typical, middle-class American.

The physical-attractiveness stereotype and vocal-attractiveness stereotype both exert a profound impact on interpersonal perception. Adams and Crossman (1978) emphasized that there exists in our culture a well-developed physical-attractiveness stereotype that has a perceptual impact matched by few, if any other, stereotypes. They wrote that physical attributes

> *are the most salient characteristics individuals have in presenting themselves. Although you can put on different masks or self-images for different situations, it is difficult to alter physical attributes.... However, since we can't change our physical characteristics from moment to moment, our body image messages are likely to be relatively constant over a variety of social situations.* (p. 3)

Ironically, a college professor once told some of the students in my nonverbal communication class that "this physical attractiveness stuff is all bunk." Perhaps this college professor was trying to escape the stigmatizing impact of his own lack of physical attractiveness, or perhaps he was blindly committed to the old myth that the quality of a person's mind is all that matters and that personal appearance is a superficial matter of no consequence. In fact, the research shows quite clearly that college professors, like virtually every other group in our society, cannot escape the impact of the physical-attractiveness stereotype.

The college professor who dismissed the behavioral and perceptual impact of physical attractiveness as "bunk" would undoubtedly be mortified by the results of a recent study. Romano and Bordieri (1989) found that physically attractive, as opposed to physically unattractive, college professors were viewed as better teachers who were more likely to be asked by their students for additional assistance, more likely to be given positive recommendations to other students, and less likely to receive blame for failing course grades.

Individuals who deviate from the normative profile for the physically attractive person suffer severe perceptual penalties; there is some evidence that stereotyping is less important for nationalities that place a heavy emphasis on communal values (Dion, Pak, & Dion, 1990). Consider the impact of a female's bust size on the personal traits attributed to her, for example. Kleinke and Staneski (1980) found that females with medium, as opposed to small or large, busts were perceived as more likable and as having greater personal appeal. In addition, big-busted women were judged to be relatively less intelligent, competent, moral, and modest, but small-busted women were viewed as most intelligent, competent, and moral. In short, the big-busted woman who wishes to be perceived as highly intelligent and moral must take action to cope with the perceptually unflattering portion of her physical stereotype. As we have already seen, the endomorphic male with excessive body weight must also deal with the negative connotations associated with his stereotype.

The unfavorable stereotype of the big-busted woman may be singularly American, however. Members of the Latino, South American, and Mediterranean cultures, in particular, seem to value highly the amply built, big-busted woman. In contrast, those cultures tend to have a negative view of the flat-chested, hipless, bony fashion models who can command staggering fees in America. In fact, the flat-chested woman seems to viewed in a number of cultures as uninteresting and lacking desirable womanly qualities.

Body weight is another aspect of the physical-attractiveness stereotype. In our culture, we consistently attribute very unflattering characteristics to individuals who are seriously overweight; we stigmatize the obese. Worsley (1981) conducted a study in which subjects were asked to look at silhouette figures of four 18-year olds: a slim young woman (SYW), a slim young man (SYM), a fat young woman (FYW), and a fat young man (FYM). After looking at the silhouettes, the subjects were asked to identify the personality characteristics they associated with the SYW, SYM, FYW, and FYM.

Because physical attractiveness and body image are more important for women than for men (Adams & Crossman, 1978), it is not surprising that the FYW was viewed more negatively than the FYM. Both the FYW and the FYM were perceived to have personality characteristics that would be a decided handicap in almost any social situation, however. The FYW was viewed as underconfident, sad, bored, tense, submissive, weak willed, easily embarrassed, and a poor social mixer. Several of the same (but not as many) negative personality characteristics were attributed to the FYM. The stereotypical description for the FYM was less complete than it was for the female, although he was dismissed by subjects as an uninteresting person—slothful, lazy, and lacking physical agility (Worsley, 1981).

The physical attractiveness we are judged to possess quite clearly affects in striking ways the dispositional attributions made by the perceiver. Thus, subjects who viewed photographs of physically attractive boys with whom they had never interacted believed that the boys would be more popular, have more pleasant personalities, and be more active in extracurricular activities than their less physically attractive counterparts (Tompkins & Boor, 1980). Perceivers anticipated that physically unattractive students would behave more aggressively than their physically attractive peers (Langlois & Downs, 1970). The attributional power of the physical-attractiveness stereotype even extends to the predicted performance of classroom instructors. Subjects who viewed physically attractive and unattractive instructors predicted that the former would be better instructors, in part because they would be more sensitive and have greater communication skills (Lombardo & Tocci, 1979).

Adams and Crossman provided detailed empirical support for their claim that the physical-attractiveness stereotype has a significant impact on the personal qualities attributed to the interactants in almost every conceivable social situation. They wrote that the "numerous studies completed by social scientists across the country suggest that attractiveness is influential in almost *every* social setting in which it has been investigated (the exception perhaps being those studies conducted in absolute darkness)" (1978, p. 4). They added that the contexts in which physical attractiveness strongly affects the images projected by the interactants include the school classroom, the home, heterosexual dating, performance appraisal, and clinical settings. We should not be surprised, therefore, that an individual's appearance affects not only our perceptions of the kind of person he or she is, but also the quality of that individual's performance as a member of organizations (Ross & Ferris, 1981).

The vocal-attractiveness stereotype also strongly affects the perceptual judgments we make. Few would deny that Walter Cronkite's vocal image helped to make him a popular and trusted newscaster (Gray, 1981). Franklin Roosevelt's vocal image, one of his major assets, perhaps helped him to become our only four-term president. Because they sounded the way competent, trustworthy, and confident individuals are supposed to sound, Cronkite and Roosevelt were placed in a preferred perceptual category.

The vocal-attractiveness stereotype is important because notions of who we are and how we are likely to behave are based heavily on the sound of our voices. We use the sound of people's voices to make judgments about their sex, age, race, occupation, and socioeconomic state. Above all, *we rely heavily on voice sound to develop the personality profiles we attribute to individuals.*

The sound of our voice is particularly important in shaping judgments of how powerful we are perceived to be. In a perceptual sense, the defining features of powerful versus powerless talk are well established. Powerful people talk in a rather loud, fluent voice. In contrast, powerless people hesitate, hedge ("I guess," "I think"), and become dysfluent by filling their pauses with "uh," "um," "ah," "well," and "you know." Johnson and Vinson (1990) found that powerless speech has a strikingly negative impact on impression formation. As expected, individuals who speak with a powerless voice are viewed as less credible than those who speak with a powerful voice. More importantly, the serious attributional consequences of speaking with a powerless voice cannot be overcome by switching back to the use of a powerful voice.

Vocal cues are also a major source of information in making predictions about how individuals will behave in the future. When the truthfulness of their current statements is at issue, the anxious voice may raise questions about the propriety of both past and future actions.

First Impressions

Our image in the eyes of others is strongly affected by the *primacy effect,* or first impressions, on interpersonal perception. First impressions may affect all subsequent perceptions; they are resistant to change. First impressions create a "cognitive category" in the mind of the perceiver. Attitudes and evaluative judgments formed during the creation of such categories are extremely difficult to change later (Shaver, 1975).

First impressions account for a disproportionate amount of the information used in the formation of all impressions, and nonverbal cues exert a controlling influence on the development of first impressions. When we meet someone for the first time, we know that "conversation is not a very good source of initial information. When we are first introduced to someone, talk is frequently limited to social amenities and topics such as the weather. We have to rely heavily on nonverbal cues" (Burgoon & Saine, 1978, p. 145). We must rely on a limited amount of information to make the evaluative judgments that form first impressions; initial impressions are formed by treating others as objects, with an emphasis on how they look and sound; and our first impressions are strongly affected by the stereotypic expectations we bring to a social encounter.

Because of the importance of the physical-appearance and the vocal-attractiveness stereotypes in interpersonal perception, it is not surprising that our appearance and our vocal cues are two important nonverbal determinants of first impressions. Remember that during the critically important seconds when we first meet people, their guarded speech communication is unlikely to reveal very much about their personal qualities. Thus, *people's visual and vocal cues assume dominant, perceptual roles in the formation of first impressions.*

Selective Perception

Selective perception is the tendency to attend to and interpret only those stimuli or perceptual cues that are consistent with past experiences and concerns. To put it another way, individuals frequently see and hear only what their own beliefs and values will let them see and hear. Therefore, because our perceptions are filtered through our beliefs and values, it is not surprising that most of us are highly susceptible to selective perception.

When we wish to make a favorable impression, it is particularly important that we be aware of the perils of selective perception. If the person with whom we are communicating likes us, we need not be overly concerned that we avoid exhibiting eye behaviors, gestures, and postures that might ordinarily damage our credibility. The person who likes us will probably de-emphasize those cues that could provide negative information about our personal qualities and emphasize those cues that would provide positive information. When dealing with an unfriendly person or with someone who does not like us, however, selective perception works in reverse. The unfriendly person is predisposed to single out and emphasize those nonverbal cues that are least flattering to us.

Last Impressions

The *recency effect,* or the last impression a person makes, can also be extremely important in impression formation. Perceptual distortion often seems to result from the disproportionate influence of an individual's most recent actions or from our last contact with that individual. General George Patton obviously recognized the importance of last impressions. He took pains to make sure that the last impression he left with his soldiers and the public before a military battle was the impression that Patton was moving aggressively to the front rather than retreating hastily to the rear.

If you were aloof, unfriendly, and stolid the last time you saw Person X, Person X is likely to remember you as an aloof, unfriendly, and stolid person. The recency effect has proven to be a strong force in shaping perceptions of top Soviet leaders, for example. At least until Mikhail Gorbachev arrived on the scene, we had been conditioned to expect that each Soviet leader would exhibit the same personality characteristics as those of his immediate predecessors. Leonid Brezhnev and Yuri Andropov had both served as general secretaries of the Communist Party. Whether fairly or not, both men were characterized by the media as conservative, dull, phlegmatic, and too cautious to "make waves." Not surprisingly, the widespread expectation was that Konstantin U. Cherenko, Andropov's successor, also would be conservative, dull, phlegmatic, and too cautious to "make waves." This expectation was nurtured by the recency effect, even before Cherenko had officially assumed his duties as leader of the former Soviet Union.

Defining Components of Impression Formation

As a student of impression formation, you will recognize that impression formation and impression management are inseparably interrelated but nonetheless distinguishable phenomena. The central players in efforts to manage impressions are the impression former (decoder) and the impression manager (encoder). Thus, Burgoon, Buller, and Woodall (1989) noted that "impression formation is studied from a decoder perspective and is concerned with how we form impressions of a communicator.... Impression management takes on an encoder perspective and is concerned with what we, as communicators, can alter and control intentionally to present ourselves positively" (p. 221).

Professional groups such as courtroom attorneys now recognize that their ability to understand how juries form impressions and to determine what impressions have been formed is critically important. Smith and Malandro devoted almost 170 pages to the subject of impression formation in the courtroom in their fascinating book, *Courtroom Communication Strategies* (1985).

Smith and Malandro did an insightful job of applying relevant knowledge of impression formation to the dynamics of communication in the courtroom. They emphasized that courtroom attorneys too often assume an "I" orientation rather than a "we" orientation in trying to figure out how a jury will form its impressions of a given witness, for example. The authors wrote that

> *if we want the jurors to have the perception of our client as being trustworthy, likable and responsible we must first consider (1) how the jurors perceive these traits and (2) their exposure to people who have these characteristics. . . . The psychological persuasion of another person depends on the extent to which information can be presented and linked to the ways in which this individual thinks. This demands a "they" focus, not an "I" focus.* (1985, pp. 17–18)

Before we actually consider the defining features of impression formation, you might want to think of the ways you form impressions. When you shake a person's hand and it is cold and clammy, what kind of an impression do you form? When the person with whom you are communicating consistently uses nonstandard grammar, what do you think of the person? When you learn that an acquaintance went to an expensive preparatory school, how is your impression of that individual affected? When the person with whom you are communicating talks in a soft, nearly inaudible voice, how is your impression affected?

As you consider your answer to those questions, you will realize that your understanding of the defining components of impression formation is limited. Of course, you are probably already aware of some generalizations about the nature of impression management. Smith and Malandro (1985) identify six principles that focus on the way communication and perception interact; for example, they noted that people use stereotypes in order to organize their perceptions. Similarly, Burgoon and associates (1989) offer five principles of impression formation, including the evaluations people make of other individuals are based on limited external information.

Hamachek (1982) identified a set of principles that help focus attention on some of the general forces that strongly affect the dispositional attributions that impression formers make. Among the most important principles identified are the following:

1. We tend to give more weight to negative information about others than to positive information.
2. We tend to be influenced by the stimuli that are most obvious.
3. We tend to judge others on the assumption that most people are like us.

The first principle is an important one. Because people seem to be inclined to look for negative information about others, we must take pains to consciously control the nonverbal cues that reflect negatively on the judgments others make about our self-confidence, self-esteem, likability, power or status, and, certainly, our credibility. We know, for example, that the anxious voice is strongly associated with the attribution of a low level of self-confidence. We know also that individuals who exhibit closed and defensive postures are perceived to have less status and power than individuals who exhibit open and confident postures.

Clearly, people do tend to be influenced by the aspect of our communication that is most obvious. As we shall see in Chapter 10, George Bush's soft voice contributed strongly to the widespread public perception that he was a "wimp." Impression managers must identify the most strikingly positive and negative features of their own communication, because those are the features the perceiver is likely to remember. The *principle of association* dictates that the most strikingly positive features should be highlighted and the negative features eliminated or attention directed away from them (Schlenker, 1980).

Finally, perceivers tend to judge others on the assumption that most people are like them. When our nonverbal communicative behaviors are different from the nonverbal communicative behaviors of those with whom we interact, our behaviors are seen as less socially desirable. Fiorello LaGuardia is frequently considered to have been a skillful impression manager. While he was mayor of New York City, he visited its various ethnic sections, and he not only spoke the languages of the people there, but also used the kinds of gestures that were distinctively associated with the ethnic groups he was addressing. In short, successful impression managers will not confine their efforts to establishing a common ground or to making statements that stress their similarities in interests and background. They will also take pains to suppress those nonverbal communicative cues that make them seem discernibly different from those with whom they interact.

General principles such as those just identified are a good place to start. However, we need to go further, by identifying and defining the most important components of impression formation. Impression formation is defined most centrally by the set of interacting factors that affect the attributions of the person who is the target of impression management.

Several scholars have provided illuminating discussions of the major components that define impression formation (Gardner and Martinko, 1988; Patterson, 1995). Patterson (1994) also applied his detailed perspective on interpersonal perception to the challenging environment of the small group. In the small group, impressions formed are jointly shaped by the competing forces of individual and group goals and motivations.

Leathers and Ross (1990) built on the effort of Gardner and Martinko to do two things: to identify and define the most important components of the impression formation process and to develop a set of principles that highlight the potential impact of each of those components of impression formation as they interact with each other.

Impression formers are defined by their

1. self-concept, self-definition, and self-identification
2. cognition (cognitive scripts, expectations, attitudes, beliefs, and values)
3. personal characteristics (personal appearance, abilities, and personality traits)
4. motives

The defining features of the context in which communicative interaction occurs are also known to strongly affect attributions. Such contextual features as favorability, ambiguity, formality, and novelty may affect attribution, but attributions are most strongly affected by whether communicative interaction occurs in public or in private.

Principles of Impression Formation

In our exhaustive review of the attributional and impression formation literature, we derived a large number of principles of impression management. In this section, however, I will identify only a limited number of those impression formation principles that I think are particularly useful.

Impression formation principles are most easily understood and their implications more readily explored if we understand that certain defining features of the impression former and of the communicative context exert a particularly powerful impact on the attributions made. The impression former's self-concept, for example, has repeatedly been shown to have a strong impact on her or his dispositional attributions.

Schlenker (1985; 1986) has developed a provocative theory of self-identification in which he pinpoints the attributional consequences of the impression former's self-concept. Self-identification involves the attempt to contribute to a positive self-concept by claiming "desirable identity images." The identity images a person claims can have a great impact not only on what interpersonal information is perceived and recalled but also on what attributions are made from it. Schlenker (1985) wrote that

> *Like a template or filter, [identify images] screen out some types of information and transform other types to provide the best possible fit to existing images, selectively coloring interpretation and recall. People are more likely to notice and attend to image-relevant information, process such information more quickly and easily, and organize and interpret supporting or ambiguous information in image-consistent ways. (p. 70)*

The cognitions of the impression former are also an important attributional force. The expectations of the impression former, with regard to what constitutes socially acceptable and desirable actions on the part of the impression manager, exert influence on attributions that are both powerful and complex. Attributions tend to become more negative when the impression former's expectations are violated.

Interpersonal context, too, is a major determinant of communicative interaction between an impression former and manager. The nature of interpersonal attributes made in public and private is qualitatively different, and sometimes the differences are dramatic in terms of the implications for the communicative interaction between or among the concerned individuals.

Let us consider some of the principles of impression formation that apply to four of the defining features of the impression former: self-concept, cognition, personal characteristics, and motives.

Self-Concept of the Impression Former

Principle 1

Impression formers who are high in self-monitoring attach greater weight to the personal appearance of individuals they observe and with whom they interact than do impression formers low in self-monitoring (Whitehead & Smith, 1986). The impression a person makes is apt to be strongly affected by his or her personal appearance if the impression former is a high self-monitor. High self-monitors monitor their own self-presentational efforts carefully and are particularly sensitive to the impact of appearance cues in impression formation.

Principle 2

Impression formers high in social anxiety make more modest self-attributions while attributing greater causality to themselves for failure than for success (Arkin, 1981; Schlenker & Leary, 1982). Impression formers high in social anxiety tend to form positive impressions of others while showing a tendency to excuse doubtful actions for which those persons might be "blamed." In short, it is unlikely that socially anxious impression formers will form impressions of others that are harshly judgmental or accusatory.

Principle 3

Impression formers are more concerned with dissociating themselves from information that suggests they have a negative self-concept than they are with associating themselves with information that suggests they have a positive self-concept (Ogilvie, 1987). Beware of anything you do or say that is directly or indirectly critical of the self-concept of a person who is forming an impression of you. People strongly resent criticism of their self-concept. If you wish to be positively perceived by impression formers, you must take pains not to do anything that might suggest that their self-concept is negative.

Cognitions of the Impression Former

Principle 4

Expectancy disconfirmation promotes attributional search on the part of the impression former; that is, to violate the impression former's expectations is to invite closer scrutiny of your motives and careful evaluation of the claims you have made about yourself, and ultimately you run the risk of having negative image qualities attributed to you (Harvey & Weary, 1984). If the impression former begins with positive expectations about you, it is particularly important that you behave in a way that confirms those expectations. For example, the impression former may be initially predisposed to view you as a straightforward and honest person. If you suddenly begin to exhibit shifty eyes and nonfluencies, the impression former might begin to view you as a deceiver.

Principle 5

When individuals behave in ways that suggest two traits that are inconsistent (e.g., truthfulness and deceptiveness), the impression former will try to resolve the seeming inconsistency (Casselden & Hampson, 1990). Impression managers should seek to control the attribution made by the impression former so that the positive rather than the negative personal trait is attributed to the impression manager.

Principle 6

Impression formers will prefer the individuals who seem most like themselves, as long as the behavior of those individuals falls within socially acceptable limits. This important principle emphasizes the value of two individuals being able to identify with each other. We established in the chapter on personal appearance that communicators who meet the dress expectations of those with whom they interact will be better liked. Also, the chapter on vocalic communication established that individuals who "sound" like us tend to be better liked by us.

Personal Characteristics

Principle 7
The most important judgment an impression former will make about you is how credible are you (Leathers, 1988; Tedeschi, 1981). In order to be an effective impression manager, you should exhibit communicative behaviors that build credibility but avoid communicative behaviors that damage personal credibility (examined in detail in Chapter 11).

Principle 8
Impression formers frequently examine the direct or implied self-presentational claims of individuals with whom they interact or whom they observe to determine whether those claims are accurate (Leathers, 1988). Individuals who make demonstrably false claims about their personal qualities or achievements risk the destruction of their personal credibility.

Motives

Principle 9
The strongest motivation for impression formers whenever they are in private is the need to maintain or to enhance self-esteem (Arkin, 1981). Communicators should avoid exhibiting any behaviors that threaten or negatively affect the self-esteem of an impression former.

Principle 10
Impression formers will judge impression managers' positive or negative signals according to the four image dimensions of credibility, likability, interpersonal attractiveness, and dominance (Leathers & Ross, 1990).

Finally, the actions of impression managers tend to be quite different in public and in private. Impression managers tend to be more strongly motivated to make favorable impressions in public, but they recognize that the risk of being exposed as a deceitful manipulator is greater in public. Thus, it is important to consider these final impression formation principles:

Principle 11
Impression formers tend to discount claims made in public that cannot be checked for accuracy because individuals will claim more credit for their successes than for their failures when they do not expect their self-promotional claims to be evaluated in public by experts (Harvey & Weary, 1984).

Principle 12
Impression formers evaluate an individual who is self-effacingly modest most favorably when other people are aware of this person's accomplishments (Schlenker, 1985).

Principle 13
Impression formers are more likely to attribute desirable image traits to an individual to the extent that the individual behaves in a manner that is congruent with the impression former's definition of the situation (Gardner & Martinko, 1988).

Summary

This chapter examines the important role of nonverbal cues in interpersonal perception. Nonverbal cues are vitally important in interpersonal perception because they are the primary source of information used to attribute personality traits and personal qualities to individuals. In making judgments about a person's level of self-confidence, we rely much more heavily on their nonverbal than on their verbal cues.

The impressions we form of others are strongly affected by stereotypes, first impressions, selective perception, and last impressions. Each of these factors is strongly affected by a communicator's nonverbal cues. Impression managers recognize the perceptual importance of nonverbal cues. They attempt to exercise conscious control over their own communicative cues for purposes of projecting a winning image.

The defining components of impression formation are identified in this chapter. Impression formers are defined by their self-concept, cognition, personal characteristics, and motives. Each of these major components of impression formation is in turn defined by a set of subcomponents.

A set of principles of impression formation is presented in the last section of this chapter. These principles help identify and illustrate the individual and collective impact of a communicator's self-concept, cognition, personal characteristics, and motives on the impressions formed about this individual. The principles of impression formation are designed not only to increase one's understanding of the fundamental nature of impression formation but to enhance one's potential to manage impressions effectively.

References

Adams, G. R., & Crossman, S. M. (1978). *Physical attractiveness: A cultural imperative.* Roslyn Heights, New York: Libra.

Argyle, M., Salter, V., Nicholson, H., Williams, M., & Burgess, P. (1970). The communication of inferior and superior attitudes by verbal and nonverbal signals. *British Journal of Social and Clinical Psychology, 9,* 222–231.

Arkin, R. M. (1981). Self-presentation styles. In J. T. Tedeschi (Ed.), *Impression management theory and social psychological research* (pp. 311–333). New York: Academic.

Burgoon, J. K., Buller, D. V., & Woodall, W. G. (1989). *Nonverbal communication: The unspoken dialogue.* New York: Harper & Row.

Burgoon, J. K., & Saine, T. (1978). *The unspoken dialogue: An introduction to nonverbal communication.* Boston: Houghton.

Casselden, P. A., & Hampson, S. E. (1990). Forming impressions from incongruent traits. *Journal of Personality and Social Psychology, 59,* 353–362.

Dion, K. K., Pak, A. W.-P., & Dion, K. L. (1990). Stereotyping physical attractiveness: A sociocultural perspective. *Journal of Cross-Cultural Psychology, 21,* 378–398.

Edinger, J. A., & Patterson, M. L. (1983). Nonverbal involvement and social control. *Psychological Bulletin, 93,* 30–56.

Gardner, W. L., & Martinko, M. J. (1988). Impression management in organizations. *Journal of Management, 14,* 321–338.

Gray, J., Jr. (1982). *The winning image.* New York: AMACOM.

Hamachek, D. E. (1982). *Encounters with others: Interpersonal relationships and you.* New York: Holt.

Harvey, J. H., & Weary, G. (1984). Current issues in attribution theory and research. *Annual Review of Psychology, 35,* 427–459.

Johnson, C., & Vinson, L. (1990). Placement and frequency of powerless talk and impression formation. *Communication Quarterly, 38,* 325–333.

Kleinke, C. L., & Staneski, R. A. (1980). First impressions of female bust size. *Journal of Social Psychology, 110,* 123–134.

Langlois, J. H., & Downs, A. C. (1970). Peer relations as a function of physical attractiveness: The eye of the beholder of behavioral reality. *Child Development, 50,* 409–418.

Leathers, D. G. (1988, November). *Impression management training: Conceptualization and application.* Top four paper presented on a program of Applied Communication Section, Convention of Speech Communication Association, New Orleans, LA.

Leathers, D. G., & Ross, C. S. (1990). *Theoretical conceptualization of the functions of nonverbal communication in impression management.* Unpublished manuscript.

Lombardo, J. P., & Tocci, M. E. (1979). Attribution of positive and negative characteristics of instructors as a function of attractiveness and sex of instructor and sex of subject. *Perceptual and Motor Skills, 48,* 491–494.

Manusov, V. (1990). An application of attribution principles to nonverbal behavior in romantic dyads. *Communication Monographs, 57,* 103–118.

Ogilvie, D. M. (1987). The undesired self: A neglected variable in personality research. *Journal of Personality and Social Psychology, 52,* 379–385.

Patterson, M. L. (1994). Interaction behavior and person perception: An integrative approach. *Small Group Research, 25,* 172–188.

Patterson, M. L. (1995). Invited article: A parallel process model of nonverbal communication. *Journal of Nonverbal Behavior, 19,* 3–29.

Paunonen, S. V., & Jackson, D. N. (1979). Nonverbal trait inference. *Journal of Personality and Social Psychology, 37,* 1645–1659.

Romano, S. T., & Bordieri, J. E. (1989). Physical attractiveness stereotypes and students' perceptions of college professors. *Psychological Reports, 64,* 1099–1102.

Ross, J., & Ferris, K. R. (1981). Interpersonal attraction and organizational outcomes: A field examination. *Administrative Science Quarterly, 26,* 617–632.

Schlenker, B. R. (1980). *Impression management.* Monterey, CA: Brooks/Cole.

Schlenker, B. R. (1985). Identity and self-identification. In B. R. Schlenker (Ed.), *The self and social life* (pp. 65–99). New York: McGraw-Hill.

Schlenker, B. R. (1986). Self-identification: Toward an integration of the private and public self. In R. F. Baumeister (Ed.), *Public self and private self* (pp. 21–62). New York: Springer-Verlag.

Schlenker, B. R., & Leary, M. R. (1982). Social anxiety and self-presentation: A conceptualization and model. *Psychological Bulletin, 92,* 642–669.

Sereno, K. K., & Bodaken, E. M. (1975). *Trans per understanding human communication.* Boston: Houghton Mifflin.

Shaver, K. G. (1975). *An introduction to attribution processes.* Cambridge, MA: Winthrop.

Schrader, D. C. (1994). Judgments of acceptable partners for social goals based on perceptions of nonverbal behavior. *Journal of Social Behavior & Personality, 9,* 353–368.

Smith, L. J., & Malandro, L. A. (1985). *Courtroom Communication Strategies.* New York: Kluwer.

Tedeschi, J. T. (Ed.). (1981). *Impression management theory and social psychological research.* New York: Academic Press.

Tompkins, R. C., & Boor, M. (1980). Effects of students' physical attractiveness and name popularity on student teachers' perceptions of social and academic attributes. *Journal of Psychology, 106,* 37–42.

Vru, A., & Winkel, F. W. (1994). Perceptual distortions in cross-cultural interrogations: The impact of skin color, accent, speech style, and spoken fluency on impression formation. *Journal of Cross-Cultural Psychology, 25,* 284–295.

Walker, M. B. (1977). The relative importance of verbal and nonverbal cues in the expression of confidence. *Australian Journal of Psychology, 29,* 45–57.

Whitehead, G. I., III, & Smith, S. H. (1986). Competence and excuse-making as self-presentational strategies. In R. F. Baumeister (Ed.), *Public self and private self* (pp. 161–177). New York: Springer-Verlag.

Worsley, A (1981). In the eye of the beholder: Social and personal characteristics of teenagers and their impressions of themselves and fat and slim people. *British Journal of Medical Psychology, 54,* 231–242.

Chapter *10*

Impression Management

Not long ago, a criminal attorney contacted me regarding a client who was accused of making sexual advances to two young boys. The attorney's overriding concern was the undesirable image he felt his client was apt to project to the jury. In the attorney's opinion, his client was a decent, hardworking person, who was not guilty of the charge. The problem, he said, was the man "looks and sounds effeminate. To a jury in a small town in southern Georgia he will be seen as queer as a three-dollar bill." The attorney was concerned that the negative impact of his client's visual and vocal image would be greater than the positive impact of the exonerating evidence. To deal with his client's problem, the attorney proposed that I work as a trial consultant with the defense team. My proposed task was to use my knowledge of impression management to make the necessary changes in the defendant's projected image.

The importance of managing impressions in the courtroom has been apparent to attorneys for some time. As a result, the legal profession has led the way in the use of image consultants to try to control, consciously, the impressions made by a legal team and their client when facing a jury. Not surprisingly, impression management has emerged as an important topic for legal scholars. In the pages of scholarly journals in both communication and law, for example, articles on the applied value and implications of impression management are becoming increasingly prominent (Anthony & Vinson, 1987; LeVan, 1984; Linz & Penrod, 1984: Pryor & Buchanan, 1984; Sannito, 1983). These articles focus directly on how impressions are made by members of legal teams and their clients in the courtroom.

The importance of impression management is hardly limited to the courtroom, however. The dividends derived from the use of impression management skills in the classroom (Gorham, 1988; Plax, Kearney, McCroskey, & Richmond, 1986), in medical communication (Harrigan & Rosenthal, 1983; Heath, 1984), in the family (Fry & Grover, 1983), in counseling (Friedlander & Schwartz, 1985), in the police interview (Leathers, 1986), in intercultural communication (Almaney & Alwan, 1982; LaFrance & Mayo, 1978), and in the job interview (Gifford, Ng, & Wilkinson, 1985) are becoming increasingly apparent.

Edinger and Patterson (1983) maintained that "impression management may be seen as an actor's behavioral strategy designed to create some beneficial image of presentation for the individual" (p. 43). As we indicated in the last chapter on impression formation, Patterson conducted influential research on the role of nonverbal behaviors in impression formation and management. He asserted that impression management is associated with and helps to serve the social control function of nonverbal communication. The social control function, nonetheless, is only one of a number of functions served by nonverbal communication; at the same time, Patterson maintained that efforts to exercise power over others, to give them feedback, to deceive them, and to persuade them all involve impression management.

Recently, Patterson added two functions of nonverbal communication to sets of functions he identified previously. These functions are of considerable importance for impression managers: the presentational function and the affect management function (Patterson, 1987). Ordinarily, the impression manager attempts to exercise conscious control over the impression he or she makes on the person with whom he or she is communicating. By contrast, the impression manager who exercises the presentational function is trying to make a given impression on a third party as a result of communication with the interaction partner.

> *For example, a person may wish to be seen as a loving spouse, the considerate parent, or the patient and understanding friend. Under such circumstances, close attention to one's partner by holding gaze and maintaining a direct orientation . . . [could] contribute to creating the desired impression in a group of observers.* (1987, p. 115)

The impression manager who exercises the affect management function consciously controls his or her emotional response to what someone else has done. When you encounter your married friend at a party with someone else's spouse, for example, you might decide to suppress a look of contempt because you think that would be a socially inappropriate expression. Instead you give your friend an embarrassed smile.

This chapter draws on the insights of Patterson (1994; 1995) and a number of other nonverbal and impression management researchers (DePaulo, 1992; Schlenker, Diugoleckie, & Doherty, 1994). My own perspective is fundamentally different from Patterson's in several fundamental respects, however. He is concerned with how nonverbal communication affects impression management, which is narrowly conceived as serving a single function. My broader concern is to identify the different impressions we may make, or the images we may claim, and to describe the particular kinds of nonverbal communicative behaviors and cues that are most useful in making a given impression.

To begin, *impression management* is defined as an individual's conscious attempt to exercise conscious control over selected communicative behaviors and cues—particularly nonverbal cues—for purposes of making a desired impression. We acknowledge that impression managers may affect some of the impressions they make on others without consciously intending to do so, but impression management that does not involve the conscious intent or awareness of the impression manager falls outside the scope of this chapter.

As the last chapter indicated, impression formation and impression management are conceptually interrelated phenomena that cannot profitably be considered in isolation. The impression former generally assumes the role of the decoder whereas the impression manager assumes the role of the encoder, but those roles are interchanged often and instantaneously. In fact, you would be well advised to recheck relevant concepts in Chapter 9 on impression formation as you read this chapter.

In order to make a desired impression, impression managers must carefully consider which impressions are consistent with their current reputation, known abilities, and attitudes. In short, the impression manager must consider not only which impressions can be emphasized and de-emphasized, but which impressions will be believable.

In seeking to make a desired impression by consciously controlling their nonverbal cues, communicators should be guided by the association principle: They must, through their communication, seek to associate themselves with desirable image traits while disclaiming association with undesirable image traits (Schlenker, 1980).

The principle of association can be illustrated by the actions of successful magicians. Successful magicians are by definition extremely skillful impression managers. They are masters of the art of misdirection; they draw our attention to movements that have no relevance to the performance of a certain trick while diverting our attention from those movements that are absolutely necessary to perform the trick. Magicians practice "magic by misdirection," through the use of simulation, dissimulation, ruse, disguise, and maneuver (Fitzkee, 1975).

Harlan Tarbell, a legendary magician, understands that the principle of association must be used to focus an audience's attention on the details of a presentation that will make an individual look good and divert an audience's attention from details of a presentation that will make an individual look bad. Thus, Tarbell (1953) wrote, "Do not look at your hands. Watch your hands in the mirror. Never look at them directly. If you watch your hands when performing, your audience will not get your effect" (p. 50). In short, magicians attempt to present an image of mystification by diverting attention from the sometimes simple movements essential to perform the trick to flashy hand movements, which serve only to distract and impress.

This chapter is divided into three parts. The first part identifies and defines the four types of image dimensions that are components of the impressions we make on others. It also describes the types of motives that impel us to prioritize one type of image dimension over another. The second part provides a complete conceptualization of the four stages in the impression management process. Finally, the last section illustrates how impression management can work in the real world with an analysis of the efforts of George Bush and his image handlers to fight the "wimp" factor. The analysis of Bush's impression management efforts is based on the original conceptualizations developed in the first two parts of this chapter.

The Nature of Impression Management

Although you might agree that knowledge of impression management can be very valuable to you, a careful look at the impression management literature could cause you to become frustrated. You will discover that there has been no clear and comprehensive attempt to identify the defining components of the impressions we make on other individuals or to determine whether we should exhibit different types of nonverbal communicative behaviors if we wish to make one type of impression as opposed to another. No one to date has developed a theoretical perspective that explains what motivates impression managers to claim specific images by exhibiting particular types of communicative behaviors and cues in certain contexts.

This section presents some of the essential parts of a new theoretical conceptualization being developed (Leathers & Ross, 1990). This conceptualization is designed to provide you with a fundamental understanding of the types of impressions you might wish to make and how you can most effectively use your own nonverbal communication to make one type of impression as opposed to another.

Schlenker (1980), in his innovative treatment of impression management, contends that impression mangers are most directly concerned with claiming images that are useful to them in achieving their goals. Tedeschi and Riess (1981) amplify that position by maintaining that both impression formers and impression managers have been socially conditioned to believe that certain image dimensions are desirable and positively valued in our culture.

The Defining Components of an Impression: Image Dimensions

Impression is the broad and all-encompassing term that is made up of, or defined by, four basic components called image dimensions. Careful reading, synthesis, and evaluation of current impression management theory and research suggests that each impression we make is defined by these four image dimensions: credibility, likability, interpersonal attractiveness, and dominance (Ross, 1991). These image dimensions, which are part of an impression that you make on another person, are universal in at least one sense: Each one is important in almost any context that might be important to you. The context you are in will, of course, affect how you prioritize their importance. If you are going out on a date, likability or interpersonal attractiveness might be more important to you than credibility. On the other hand, if you are being interviewed by the admissions officer of a prestigious law school, you might feel that credibility is much more important than either likability or interpersonal attractiveness.

The image dimension of *credibility* has repeatedly been identified as centrally important to impression managers who attempt to control attributions about their believability in public. In addition, there is a consensus among impression management researchers that competence and trustworthiness are two defining dimensions of credibility. Theorists Tedeschi and Norman (1985), for example, have asserted that whenever individuals seek to claim a positive public image, credibility overrides all others in importance. They concluded that "holding all else constant, the more believable the source's communication, the more success the source will have in influencing the target" (p. 236). Similarly, Schlenker (1985) theorized that the standard of overwhelming importance in judging the desirability of an "identity image" is its credibility or believability.

Likability is the second image dimension that is a central, defining component of any given impression you make. You will probably agree that as an impression manager you must be concerned with communicating in such a way that your interaction partner will judge you to be likable and that you must be concerned with being perceived as likable in a wide variety of contexts. Schlenker (1980) theorized that likability is one of the two most important of image dimensions. DeMeuse (1987) came to a similar conclusion.

Interpersonal attractiveness is the third image dimension that is an important part of the impressions we make on others. When we make perceptual judgments about individuals seeking to make positive impressions in public, those judgments are almost invariably made on the dimension of interpersonal attractiveness (Albright, Kenney, & Malloy, 1988; Alicke, Smith, & Klotz, 1987). Although the evidence is far from conclusive at the moment, interpersonal attractiveness seems to be defined by three subdimensions: *interestingness* (Muehlenhard & Scardino, 1985); *emotional expressivity* (Riggio & Friedman, 1986); and *sociability* (Albright, et al., 1988; Dion & Dion, 1987).

Finally, *dominance* is the fourth image dimension that is a defining component of the impression (DeMeuse, 1987; Ellyson & Dovidio, 1985; Henley & Harmon, 1985). Although a number of factors might be viewed as subdimensions or defining parts of the central image dimension of dominance, *power* and *assertiveness* seem to be the two most important.

In this theoretical conceptualization, positive labels have been used to identify each of the universal image dimensions—"credibility," "likability," "interpersonal attractiveness," and "dominance." However, negative labels might have been used to identify each of the universal image dimensions with equal accuracy—"noncredible," "unlikable," "interpersonally unattractive," and "submissive." The essential point is that the judgment made of impression managers by impression formers on each image dimension is not categorical but, rather, a judgment of degree; for example, a judgment is made about the *degree* to which an impression is or is not credible.

You must decide how you wish to prioritize these image dimensions. I would guess that an attorney might prioritize them from most to least important in the following way: credibility, dominance, interpersonal attractiveness, and likability. In comparison, a politician might prioritize the image dimensions differently: likability, interpersonal attractiveness, credibility, and dominance. The nonverbal communication that can have the strongest positive impact on your perceived credibility will be quite different from the nonverbal communication that will help you most in achieving your aim of being judged to be dominant in a given communicative context.

Major Motives of the Impression Manager

Impression management scholars have given little attention to the motives of the impression manager. This inattention to the motivational bases of impression management is unfortunate. Such an understanding is essential if we are to develop a sound explanation as to how and why impression managers decide on the relative importance of each of the four major image dimensions to them. Furthermore, understanding why impression managers are motivated to prioritize the four image dimensions from most to least important in a given interpersonal context greatly enhances the ability to predict what communicative behaviors or cues impression managers will actually exhibit in order to be positively perceived on one or more image dimensions. Significantly, Jones and Pittman (1982) contended that "We believe strongly that a theory of strategic self-presentation must be anchored in identifiable social motives. Self-presentation involves the actor's linkage of particular motives to his or her strategic resources" (p. 235).

Brembeck and Howell (1976) developed one of the most insightful treatments of the classes of social motives that can be used to explain the communicative behaviors individuals exhibit and predict how they will behave communicatively in the future. The classificatory framework presented in this chapter draws directly on their treatment of classes of motives.

The definitional relationship between *drives* and *motives* must be understood at the outset. Individuals experience drives when they are aroused and tense because they are suffering from a failure to satisfy one or more of their needs. Motives, in contrast, are socially conditioned drives. Both physiological motives and social motives combine to impel or compel an individual to behave in given ways. Thus, Brembeck and Howell (1976) viewed "some motives as *physiological motives* (those leading to the reduction of a drive based on a physiological need) and others as *social motives* which lead to the satisfaction of our socio-psychological needs" (p. 90).

An understanding of how an individual is motivated at a given point in time enhances our potential to predict how that individual will behave, because motives guide a person's behaviors in ways that person judged effective in reaching one or more goals. Motives serve not only a valuable predictive function but also a useful explanatory function, in part because the names of motives tend to identify the communicator's immediate goal, for example, the "hunger motive," the "social approval motive," and the "conformity motive."

Passing reference has been made in the impression management literature to such social motives as self-esteem, fear of failure, achievement, and approval (Tedeschi & Norman, 1985). McClelland's research (1987) on how categories of motives are measured and defined is brilliant. The major classes of motives he identified—the achievement, affiliation, avoidance, and power motives—are similar to the types of motives described here. However, McClelland and other researchers focusing on motives have not made systematic efforts to identify the major classes of social motives that shape the communicative behavior of impression managers. This book asserts that four major classes of motives are of overriding importance for the impression manager:

1. achievement motives
2. affiliation motives
3. social approval motives
4. mastery motives

The achievement motive is characterized by the felt need to meet high standards of excellence, to set and meet challenging goals, to be viewed as an achiever, and often to be viewed as an expert. Impression managers who are most strongly motivated by the achievement motives should ordinarily prioritize the image dimension of credibility as most important. Impression managers who are motivated by achievement will put a premium on claiming an image of competence; they will be uncomfortable if they are not perceived as intelligent and well informed. By exhibiting specific nonverbal behaviors/cues, impression managers can frequently exert a strong influence on the judgments others make about their competence.

The affiliation motive, the second major class of motives, is defined by an individual's felt need to develop relational ties and interpersonal bonds with other human beings, to form friendships, to trigger positive emotional responses from others, and above all else to be liked. Impression managers whose strongest motivation is affiliation will in all probability attach the highest priority to the image dimension of likability.

Social approval is the third major type or class of motive related to impression management. This is a broad-based motivation that is defined by people's need to be perceived positively rather than negatively, as the result of their actions and the kind of people they are judged to be. Perhaps more than the other major class of motives, social approval is tied to societal rules, regulations, norms, and laws. Thus, both the person who meets the expectations of society and the individual with whom interaction occurs will be rewarded with social approval.

Although impression managers who are motivated most strongly by social approval might be concerned with more than one image dimension, most often they will attach the highest priority to being judged interpersonally attractive. Not surprisingly, interpersonally attractive individuals typically have beliefs, values, and attitudes that are similar to those of their interaction partners, and they are perceived to behave in ways that are compatible with the societal norms and the expectations of their interaction partners. Individuals who are perceived to be interpersonally attractive, therefore, virtually assure themselves of a high level of social approval.

The final major class of motives which can be a driving force behind the actions of impression managers is mastery motives. By definition, persons who are motivated by a need to exhibit mastery over others want to lead, to take charge, to control, and in some cases to order others around. In extreme cases, mastery motivation manifests itself in the need to be treated deferentially. Impression managers who are moved by the motivation to exhibit mastery over others will attach the highest priority to being positively perceived on the image dimension of dominance.

The Impression Management Process

In the past decade, empirical knowledge of impression management has expanded rapidly. It is difficult to use, however, because such knowledge has not been synthesized and organized in a way that makes it easily usable by the impression manager. In fact, until recently an explicit conceptualization of the impression management process derived from existing theory and research did not exist. In an attempt to remedy that deficiency, I drew on my experiences as a trainer of corporate salespeople and my own research on impression management to develop my own conceptualization of the impression management process (Leathers, 1988). The following conceptualization was developed with its applicability to sales training in mind, but with minor modification it could also be useful for a wide variety of different groups of impression managers, including readers of this book, attorneys, doctors, diplomats, and politicians.

Impression management can be viewed as a process consisting of four interrelated stages. When used to train or educate individuals to become successful managers, the four stages in the process are treated as steps. The four-step description has proved to be particularly helpful in spelling out the sequence of actions necessary for corporate salespeople to become effective impression managers. The following four stages make up the impression management process:

Stage 1: Familiarization with the communication of successful impression managers

Stage 2: Identification, selection, and application of principles of impression formation and of impression management

Stage 3: Measurement of the impressions made

Stage 4: Modification of undesirable communicative behaviors/cues to control impressions made

Model Impression Managers

Studies of individuals who have become successful impression managers suggest that they typically begin by studying the efforts of other notably successful impression managers (Schlenker, 1980). Whether the successful managers are politicians, auto executives, or attorneys, for example, they usually are voracious readers of autobiographies; autobiographies often reveal not only the major strategies used by the successful impression manager, but also such tactical factors as the gestural nuances and appearance cues that were crucial to success.

General George Patton and J. Edgar Hoover are two good examples of individuals who carefully contemplated their own impression management goals. They consciously controlled their own communication for purposes of accentuating certain image dimensions that defined the impression they made on people who were important to them. Patton and Hoover left little to chance.

In his insightful book, *Impression Management,* Schlenker (1980) noted that

> *Patton recognized the importance of controlling nonverbal activities to create the impressions he desired. . . . He developed hypotheses about what attributes soldiers would most respect in their commander and acted accordingly. For example, he was careful about when he went to and departed from the front lines.* (p. 235)

Thus, Patton practiced his "war face" in front of a mirror so that he would look particularly determined, brave, and powerful. He also believed that a strong leader should be seen going to the front but not returning from it. As a result, Patton frequently went to the front by road during the day but returned at dusk or even after dark, sometimes in a small liaison plane.

Until age and paranoia began to affect his cunning shrewdness, J. Edgar Hoover was a master of the art of cultivating a public image that captivated his admirers and intimidated his detractors. In *Witness to Power: The Nixon Years* (1982), John Ehrlichman provides a fascinating account of the carefully contrived steps Hoover took to make the desired impression.

When Ehrlichman arrived at Hoover's office for a visit, he encountered a staggering array of television monitors, electronic gear, and FBI agents, all of whom had short haircuts, narrow lapels, quiet ties, and shined shoes. As he entered the anteroom to Hoover's office, he noted that every available inch of wall space was used for plaques, framed citations, mounted trophies, medals, and certificates. Many of the awards featured torches, eagles, flags, and gavels. Later, in Hoover's private office, he tried in vain to identify a wavering purplish light that came from behind a segment of the cornice because he was convinced that television cameras were recording his every move.

Ehrlichman went on to describe Hoover's private office, which

> *was about twelve or thirteen feet square and dominated by Hoover himself; he was seated in a large leather desk chair behind a wooden desk in the center of the room. When he stood, it became obvious that he and his desk were on a dais about*

six inches high. I was invited to sit on a low, purplish leather couch to his right. J. Edgar Hoover looked down on me and began to talk. (Ehrlichman, 1982, p. 158)

As you consider the image he projected, can you understand why Hoover was able to intimidate presidents and senators for many decades? Can you imagine yourself challenging the competence of a "legend," whose walls are lined with trophies, medals, and certificates? Would you challenge the authority of a man who controlled the nation's most sophisticated surveillance techniques and who had immediate access to your classified files? Do you believe that a man not vitally concerned with impression management would sit at an elevated desk and seat you below him, to his right?

Former Prime Minister Margaret Thatcher has proved herself to be at least equally astute as an impression manager. She is not only one of the most successful leaders in recent history, but she also overcame serious problems early in her career with the use of professional consultants to help her manage the impressions she made.

In his insightful book *Our Master's Voices* (1984), Max Atkinson provides a detailed account of the impression management problems Thatcher encountered and resolved. For example, Thatcher was particularly concerned by the fact that her modal speaking pitch was

CARTOON 10.1

unpleasantly high. She recognized that this important feature of her vocal image might reinforce stereotypical expectations that she, as a female leader, would be more emotional and less logical than her male counterparts.

Because of her concern, Thatcher moved directly to confront the perceptual problems associated with her high-pitched voice. She hired a voice tutor to put her through a voice training program. The training program included special humming exercises aimed at lowering the modal pitch level at which she formerly spoke. In fact, Thatcher did enough humming to lower her modal pitch significantly. Remarkably, her modal pitch reduction (46 Hz) was almost half the average difference in pitch between male and female voices.

Thatcher and her image consultants were also concerned that she be perceived as feminine. She had always been attractive, but her initial problem, according to Atkinson, was that she "so closely resembled a stereotypically middle-class housewife" (p. 115). The impression management goal, therefore, became to transform her image from that of the dowdy housewife to the image of the worldly and smart professional woman.

In pursuit of that goal, Thatcher hired television producer Gordon Reece as an image consultant. He concentrated on hairstyle, clothes, jewelry, and makeup. Reece's image-building efforts were combined with those of Saatchi and Saatchi, the Conservative party's advertising agents. The image consultants' activities included, but were not confined to, regularly tinting Thatcher's blond hair, capping her front teeth, and carefully selecting her clothing and accessories. These actions were calculated to nurture the visual image of a professional woman.

Ironically, the Soviets may unwittingly have been the biggest help to Thatcher and her image consultants. The Soviets referred to her as the "Iron Lady." This not necessarily flattering term was exploited by Thatcher and her consultants to cultivate a public image that stresses that she is a tough and decisive leader but undeniably feminine. Thus, Max Atkinson (1984) wrote:

> *The aptness of the "Iron Lady" as a nickname for Mrs. Thatcher can be seen to derive from the way it captures the two most visible and contrasting characteristics of her public image—toughness and femininity. And it is arguable . . . that when these two qualities are exhibited in the conduct and appearance of the same woman, she will have found a workable way of deferring, resisting, and neutralizing attacks based on male-chauvinist assumptions.* (pp. 116–117)

Max Atkinson, who is now a full-time image consultant and counts some of England's top politicians among his clients, recently elaborated on his analysis of Thatcher's impression management activities. Atkinson and I appeared in Dublin, Ireland, on a program of the annual conference of the International Communication Association; the program was entitled "Heads of State Confront Impression Management Problems." The title of Atkinson's paper was "The Other Thatcher Revolution: Impression Management and the Transformation of Political Communication in Britain"; my paper on George Bush's effort to "Fight the Wimp Factor" will receive treatment later in this chapter.

Atkinson, who had recently returned from doing a presentation for President Bush's speech writers, proved in person not only to be a man of impressive insight but a delightful raconteur. During his presentation in Dublin (Atkinson, 1990), he stressed that Thatcher

CARTOON 10.2

and her image handlers sought to balance their desire to make her appear "tough" with their desire to make her appear feminine. Atkinson emphasized that

> *the neat thing about Margaret Thatcher is that no one could question her tough-ness. In fact her problem as we shall see is the opposite of the one Dale Leathers will be talking about. She has never had a "wimp problem" since the early days. So no one could seriously question her toughness. On the other hand, you couldn't say that this woman is so tough that she is not a proper woman. The trappings are there in terms of her appearance. Unequivocally, she is 120 percent female.* (Atkinson, 1990)

Image consultants such as Atkinson must concentrate on getting flattering news coverage for their political clients on television because TV spots or ads for politicians are not allowed in England. In Thatcher's case, her image handlers did encounter some impression problems in the campaign of 1983 and later, because a number of prominent male politicians seemed to resent the fact that the top politician in England was a woman. Accordingly, male politicians gave Thatcher such unflattering nicknames as "The Leaderee," "Attilla the Hen," "The Blessed Margaret," and "The Immaculate Misconception." However, Thatcher's image handlers were able to transcend such sexist slurs, and in her most recent campaigns they cultivated an image of her that made her appear more and more like the Queen.

Principles of Impression Management

Step 2 in the impression management process requires that you identify, select, and apply relevant principles of impression management. The impression management principles in Figure 10.1 should prove to be useful to you. They should be used in conjunction with the set of impression formation principles provided in Chapter 9. You will recognize that the four sets of impression management principles have been classified respectively under the four major image dimensions of credibility, likability, interpersonal attractiveness, and dominance.

The sets of impression management principles in Figure 10.1 draw on a substantial amount of the most recent empirical information on the subject. In addition, they are set up in such a way as to try to make them of maximum value. You might note three things before you begin to use the impression management principles in Figure 10.1: First, you may consistently view one of the image dimensions as particularly important to you; for example, likability. Second, the communicative contexts in which you communicate most often might make some principles more valuable than others. Third, you might want to concentrate on controlling or eliminating negative nonverbal communicative behaviors; we already indicated in the last chapter that impression formers tend to give disproportionate weight to negative information.

The principles of impression management would seem to require little explanation, but let us look briefly at the principles under the image dimension of dominance to illustrate how some of them might be used. These principles suggest that a person's eye behaviors and vocal cues have a particularly strong impact in affecting judgments of dominance. Note, for example, that you will want to spend less time looking at interaction partners when they are speaking than the amount of time you spend looking at them while *you* are speaking—see Principle 4, which defines the visual dominance ratio. You must also avoid speaking with a soft voice, or a voice that lacks volume, because individuals who speak with a soft voice are typically judged to be unassertive.

Measurement of the Impressions Made

Impression managers who are equipped with the principles of impression management in Figure 10.1 clearly have the potential to make the desired changes in the impressions they are making. Before they become actively engaged in trying to modify the impressions they make on others (or the impressions formed of them by others), however, they must obtain

FIGURE 10.1   Impression Management Principles

Principles of Impression Management

Image Dimension I: Credibility

P1 Communicators who maintain a high level of eye contact with their interaction part-
    ner, but not continuous eye contact, are perceived as more competent (Kleinke,
    1986; Webbink, 1986).

P2 Vocal cues such as relatively fast rate, substantial volume, and short, purposeful
    pauses are related to perceptions of increased competence (Street & Brady, 1982).

P3 Communicators who meet the personal appearance expectations of the person(s)
    with whom they interact will be judged to be more competent (Rosenberg, Bohan,
    McCafferty, & Harris, 1986).

P4 Communicators who speak General American dialect with standard accent are
    viewed as more competent than those who do not (Burgoon & Saine, 1978; Street
    & Hooper, 1982).

P5 Competence is negatively affected by looking down before responding to a question,
    characteristically downcast eyes, and a low level of eye contact (Burgoon,
    Manusov, Mineo, & Hale, 1985; Kleinke, 1986).

P6 Communicators whose verbal and nonverbal messages are inconsistent are viewed as
    less trustworthy than communicators whose multichannel messages are consistent
    (Leathers, 1986; Mehrabian, 1981).

P7 Individuals who exhibit insincere smiles at inappropriate times will probably be
    viewed as less trustworthy than individuals who smile sincerely in context
    (Ekman, 1985; Ekman & Friesen, 1982).

P8 Communicators who exhibit behavioral "tension-leakage" cues in the form of nonflu-
    encies, shifty eyes, and lip moistening will be judged to be less competent than
    those who do not (Exline, 1985).

Image Dimension II: Likability

P1 Communicators who exhibit immediacy behaviors in the form of close interaction
    distances, a direct bodily orientation, forward-leans, socially appropriate touching,
    in-context and sincere smiling, bodily relaxation, and open body positions are
    consistently perceived as more likable than communicators who do not exhibit
    such immediacy behaviors (Andersen, 1985; Richmond, McCroskey, & Payne,
    1987).

P2 Communicators who signal interest and attentiveness via direct body and head orienta-
    tions, direct eye contact, and smiling are typically viewed as more likable than com-
    municators who do not similarly signal interest and attentiveness (Schlenker, 1980).

P3 Communicators who dress in such a manner as to meet the dress expectations of
    those with whom they interact will be better liked (Leathers, 1988).

P4 The interaction of body type and clothing can have a major impact on judgments of
    likability; for example, big persons with endomorphic body types should wear
    softer, lighter shades of blue, gray, or beige in order to be perceived as likable.

P5 Impression managers should recognize that clothing which will make them appear to
    be likable (i.e., lighter-colored and informal clothing) may also make them appear
    to be less credible, and vice versa (Rasicot, 1983; Smith & Malandro, 1985).

P6 Sustained and direct eye contact, and the maintenance of mutual gaze with one's
    interaction partner, are strongly correlated with positive judgments of likability
    (Kleinke, 1986).

P7 Likability is positively associated with a speaking voice which is pleasant, relaxed,
    emotionally expressive, and friendly, and that sounds confident, dynamic, ani-
    mated, and interested (Richmond et al., 1987).

FIGURE 10.1   (Continued)

P8 Nonverbal indicators of disliking, which reinforce the perception that the person exhibiting such behavioral indicators is unlikable, are unpleasant facial expressions, a relative absence of gestures, visual inattentiveness, closed bodily posture, and an incongruent posture (Leathers, 1986).

Image Dimension III: Interpersonal Attractiveness

P1 Communicators whose nonverbal communicative behaviors seem to be spontaneous, disclosing, and uncensored are seen to be more interpersonally attractive (Sabatelli & Rubin, 1986).

P2 There is a strong positive intercorrelation between overall physical, facial, bodily, and interpersonal attractiveness (Alicke, Smith, & Klotz, 1987).

P3 Communicators who exhibit a high level of responsiveness via such nonverbal communicative behaviors as head nodding, positive vocal reinforcement (e.g., saying "uh-huh"), forward-lean, direct body orientation, and direct eye contact with their interaction partner will be perceived as more interpersonally attractive than those who do not (Remland & Jones, 1989).

P4 Nonverbally expressive communicators are viewed as more interpersonally attractive (Friedman, Riggio, & Cassella, 1988; Sabatelli & Rubin, 1986).

P5 Communicators can exhibit emotional expressivity via facial animation, appropriate vocal volume, vocal warmth, smiling and laughing, and gestural and bodily animation (Coker & Burgoon, 1987).

P6 Communicators who choose seating arrangements that provide for decreased interpersonal distance and increased capacity for visual contact with individuals with whom they interact are usually seen as more interpersonally attractive (Riess, 1982).

P7 Communicators who exhibit a low frequency of nonverbal communicative behaviors and cues will be judged to be less interpersonally attractive (Roll, Crowley, & Rappl, 1985).

P8 Communicators who exhibit a narrow pitch and volume range are often perceived to be uninteresting (Leathers, 1986).

Image Dimension IV: Dominance

P1 The eyes serve to define or reveal the distribution of power within social relationships (Webbink, 1986).

P2 Dominance is communicated strongly by staring and submissiveness by gaze avoidance—emotional states associated with gaze aversion include fear, guilt, shame, and social inferiority (Harper, 1985).

P3 Communicators are perceived as increasingly dominant as their amount of eye contact increases (Brooks, Church, & Frazer, 1986).

P4 Communicators become more dominant as their level of looking while speaking increases and their level of looking while listening decreases, that is, their visual dominance ratio goes up (Dovidio & Ellyson, 1985).

P5 Dominance is conveyed by controlling talk time, speaking in a loud voice, and frequently interrupting the interaction partner (Harper, 1985).

P6 Communicators who use hesitations and hedges are perceived as less powerful than those who do not (Hosman, 1989).

P7 Nonverbal indicators of submissiveness include constricted and closed body postures, a limited range of movement, hunched body, downward-turned head, and bodily tension (Harper, 1985).

P8 The soft voice with little volume communicates lack of assertiveness (Montepare & Zebrowitz-McArthur, 1987).

rather detailed and objective information from business associates or significant others about how positive or negative their impressions are. Ken Cooper wrote perceptively in *Nonverbal Communication for Business Success* (1979) that the

> *first step in building a successful image is to determine what your current image is. You may not be aware of your image or you may think others don't have an image of you. You are wrong!... The challenge is to develop an accurate picture of yourself as others perceive you.* (p. 195)

In theory, at least, there are a number of ways to measure the impressions you are making; I will describe two ways. The first measure is a general one that gives you an overall picture of the positive and negative image traits that others are attributing to you. The second measure is set up to provide a precise quantitative reading of how positive or negative is the impression you are making, based on each of the four image dimensions described previously.

The personality traits and personal qualities that others attribute to you are called *image traits*. Image traits identified in Figure 10.2 should be useful to the impression manager for at least two reasons. First, each of these traits has been repeatedly identified in empirical research as a trait that perceivers frequently used in forming their impressions of others. Second, specific nonverbal cues have been shown to be strongly linked, perceptually, to each of those image traits.

FIGURE 10.2   Image Traits

confident–anxious	honest–deceitful
friendly–unfriendly	expressive–unexpressive
sensitive–insensitive	mature–immature
spontaneous–unspontaneous	direct–evasive
active–passive	powerful–weak
forceful–tentative	relaxed–tense
wise–foolish	flexible–rigid
feminine–masculine	honest–dishonest
dominant–submissive	interesting–uninteresting
extroverted–introverted	uninhibited–inhibited
strong-willed–weak-willed	intelligent–unintelligent
happy–sad	patient–impatient
likable–unlikable	tactful–tactless
strong–weak	unaffected–affected
assertive–unassertive	comfortable–uncomfortable
considerate–inconsiderate	artistic–inartistic
sociable–unsociable	warm–cold
poised–flustered	agile–awkward
opinionated–unopinionated	competent–incompetent
modest–immodest	pleasant–unpleasant
vigorous–lazy	energetic–sluggish
tolerant–intolerant	sophisticated–naive
emotional–unemotional	gregarious–withdrawn
conventional–unconventional	selfish–unselfish
dependable–undependable	perceptive–dull

To obtain a complete description of your own image, ask individuals with whom you frequently interact in social or business situations to use Figure 10.2. They should place a check mark by each trait that they feel is clearly a defining feature of your image. Pay particular attention to the five positive and five negative image traits that are checked most frequently. By simply tabulating the check marks, you will know what the dominant positive and negative features of your image actually are.

In order to get a more precise reading of how positive or negative the impressions you made are in regard to each of the four image dimensions, use Figure 10.3. In fact, you can simply run multiple copies of this figure and then ask individuals who have been the target of your impression management activities to fill out the form. When the evaluation forms are returned to you, compute a mean or average score for each of the 28 scales.

Let us assume that you receive the following mean ratings for the sets of scales in Figure 10.3:

Credibility
Competence: 6.4, 6.2, 5.7, 5.8;
Trustworthiness: 2.3, 2.5, 2.1, 1.8
Likability: 1.3, 1.5, 2.2, 1.7
Interpersonal Attractiveness: 1.8, 1.6, 1.3, 2.1, 1.3, 1.2, 2.0, 1.9
Dominance: 5.8, 6.6, 6.8, 6.4, 5.9, 6.5, 6.7, 6.4.

You will quickly see that your credibility is defined in terms of high competence but low trustworthiness, that you are seen as quite unlikable and interpersonally unattractive, and that you are perceived to be highly dominant.

Making a Favorable Impression by Modifying Communication

You have discovered from the measurements you have undertaken that the impression you are making with regard to trustworthiness, liking, and interpersonal attractiveness is unacceptably negative. You must now decide what changes you can make in your communicative behaviors and cues in order that the individuals with whom you interact will see you as more trustworthy, likable, and interpersonally attractive. You need to do two things at minimum: You must carefully assess the nonverbal communicative behaviors/cues you consistently exhibit to determine which ones reinforce the impression that you are untrustworthy, unlikable, and interpersonally unattractive. Then you should study the impression management principles in Figure 10.1 to determine which of them would be most useful in helping you deal with your impression management problem.

Let us concentrate on the fact that you are perceived to be untrustworthy, for purposes of illustration. Many factors might, of course, contribute to the perception that you lack trustworthiness, but you could start by considering impression management Principle 7 under "Credibility." I know from personal experience as a trainer of corporate salespeople that phony smiles exhibited out of context negatively affect a salesperson's trustworthiness. On a number of occasions, I have observed a salesperson exhibit a phony smile when a sales

FIGURE 10.3

Impression Management Evaluation

Name of Impression Manager _____

Name of Evaluator _____

The communicative behaviors and cues that differentiate the impression(s) made by one person as opposed to another are often quite subtle. In order to determine how favorable or unfavorable an impression a given impression manager makes on each of the four image dimensions—credibility, likability, interpersonal attractiveness, and dominance—you will have to observe the impression manager's communicative behaviors live or on videotape. Then you will have to rate the impression manager on scales that define each of the image dimensions. The scales for each dimension and subdimension are listed below. Before you actually use these scales, you should reorder them randomly. Also, change the polarity on half the scales; for example, move the "Competent" label to the right end and the "Incompetent" label to the left end of Scale 1. Then assign a number between 7 and 1 to each scale as you observe the communicative behaviors of a given impression manager. If, for example, you believe the impression manager you are evaluating is extraordinarily competent, that person should receive a rating of 7 on Scale 1. When your ratings are complete, you will have a profile that indicates how favorable or unfavorable an impression the impression manager made on each of the four universal image dimensions.

Credibility

Competence
1. Competent/Incompetent
2. Qualified/Unqualified
3. Well-informed/Poorly-informed
4. Intelligent/Unintelligent

Trustworthiness:
1. Honest/Dishonest
2. Straightforward/Evasive
3. Trustworthy/Untrustworthy
4. Sincere/Insincere

Likability

1. Likable/Unlikable
2. Pleasant/Unpleasant
3. Agreeable/Disagreeable
4. Lovable/Hateful

Interpersonal Attractiveness

1. Interesting/Uninteresting
2. Desirable/Undesirable
3. Sociable/Unsociable
4. Attentive/Unattentive
5. Expressive/Unexpressive
6. Emotional/Unemotional
7. Social/Unsociable
8. Physically attractive/
   Physically unattractive

Dominance

1. Active/Passive
2. Assertive/Unassertive
3. Powerful/Powerless
4. Dominant/Submissive
5. Confident/Anxious
6. Relaxed/Tense
7. Direct/Evasive
8. Strong/Weak

---

prospect announced that the salesperson's six-figure sales proposal was being rejected. In a situation that should be painful to the salesperson, the smile is out of context. In addition, it is visibly phony because no crow's-feet appear around the salesperson's eyes, the smile is slightly asymmetrical, the smile appears too quickly, and the 15-s duration of the smile makes it seem less than believable (Ekman & Friesen, 1982).

When we consider how we should modify our communicative behaviors and cues to make a more favorable impression, we should remember the importance of first impressions. Successful impression managers pay particular attention to first impressions. They do this because first impressions create images in the mind of the perceiver that are highly resistant to change. First impressions assume a central role in interpersonal perception because they tend to be lasting impressions. First impressions are critically important in defining your personal qualities and traits in the eyes of others.

The impression manager who wishes to make a favorable first impression must recognize at least two facts: (a) nonverbal cues are the major determinants of the kind of first impression that we make, and (b) personal appearance and vocal cues are known to make a strong impact on first impressions. By exercising conscious control over our visual and vocal images, we greatly enhance our chances of making a favorable first impression.

When considering the way you would like to look and sound, remember the importance of the physical-attractiveness stereotype and the vocal-attractiveness stereotype. These stereotypes dictate that individuals who look and sound unappealing pay a stiff perceptual penalty. These stereotypes provide a rather detailed picture of the look and the sound that are widely viewed as desirable in our culture. Because we also know that perceivers give more weight to negative rather than to positive information, the impression manager begins with an advantage. The message is clear: We should be less concerned with cultivating idealized visual and vocal images and more concerned with eliminating those undesirable features of our image that perceivers use to make unflattering attributions about us.

The importance of appearance cues and vocal cues is not, however, confined to first impressions. Both types of cues also are known to exert a major impact on the long-term impressions we make. The guidelines presented in Figures 10.4 and 10.5 are designed to help you become a more successful impression manager.

Personal Appearance Guidelines

Most communicators may exercise a number of options to modify, conceal, or eliminate negative features of their personal appearance. The obese individual can diet; the individual with a physical deformity can undergo plastic surgery; the individual with acne can use medicinal ointments; and the individual with crooked teeth can seek orthodontal treatment. In practice, however, those options might not be feasible, because they either are time-consuming and costly or will not correct the physical deformity.

Clothing choice represents the most effective and efficient means of controlling your personal appearance (Damhorst, 1990). When you consider the implications of the association principle, you will realize that you must dress so as to concentrate attention on the most flattering features of your personal appearance, while diverting attention from the features that might be used to make negative attributions about your personal qualities (Francis, 1992).

No one set of appearance guidelines will serve the impression management goals of all people in all situations all of the time (Gray, 1993). Nevertheless, there are basic guidelines that can be useful to many different people communicating in a wide variety of contexts (Roach-Higgins & Eicher, 1992). The guidelines in Figure 10.4 are drawn from some of the most valuable references on the subject.

FIGURE 10.4   Personal Appearance Guidelines

1. Strive to meet the dress expectations of the person (or group) with whom you interact by noting such factors as their age, education, class, gender, ethnicity, and region or specific area of residence. In general, it is important that your clothing and other appearance items such as jewelry not be markedly different in quality or level of sophistication from the same items worn by the person with whom you are communicating.

2. Consider the way you have prioritized the image dimensions of credibility, likability, interpersonal attractiveness, and dominance. If the credibility dimension of competence or authoritativeness is of major concern to you, you should wear dark-colored, conservative clothing. If likability is most important, you may wish to sacrifice some perceived competence by choosing to wear the lighter-colored clothing that is known to enhance perceptions of likability and friendliness.

3. Your body type should exert a major influence on your choice of clothing and other appearance items. If you are a large and tall person, you could intimidate individuals with whom you interact, due to your size. In order to be seen as less overpowering and more approachable, you would be well-advised to choose softer, lighter shades of blue, gray, or beige. Conversely, you might wish to wear darker-colored clothing in order to seem more powerful and authoritative if you are a short and thin person.

4. Color choice strongly affects the overall impression we make on others. More specifically, color choice has been shown to affect how professional other persons judge us to be. Outer garments tend to be seen as a reliable indicators of our status, whereas our accent items are used to make judgments about our personality traits. The color of our main items of clothing—for example, our suits—strongly affects judgments as to whether our clothing is sufficiently conservative for a given occasion; the color of our accent items—for example, ties and scarves—communicates information about our personality.

5. You should be sure that your clothing and other appearance items are sufficiently formal and conservative for your first meeting with another individual. In many business and social situations, a first meeting with another person or group requires that you have maximum credibility. Your appearance is one of the most important determinants of the first impression you will make, and you should recognize that although you can "dress down" when you meet a person for a second time in a business context, you cannot credibly "dress up."

6. You should avoid wearing glasses with heavily tinted or photosensitive lenses. Not only do such items limit the number of people who can identify with you, but also the eye-behavior stereotype dictates that people want to be able to see your eyes. If you are to be trusted, persons with whom you interact must be able to see your eyes.

7. Avoid designer clothing or accessories.

8. Avoid clothing choices which communicate inconsistent messages and, consequently, damage personal credibility—for example, a high-power suit with a low-power pair of shoes.

9. You should not wear any item (class ring, lapel pin, religious symbol, etc.) that serves to highlight your affiliation with a given civic, political, or religious organization. Such personalized accessories may, on occasion, be used to establish common ground with a person of similar background. However, they are more apt to trigger an emotional reaction that will make it more difficult for you to establish common ground with a person who notices that you have chosen to personalize your appearance in such a manner.

10. You should recognize that you will lose authority in the eyes of members of many professional groups if the length of your hair exceeds the norm for such groups. For males in particular, excessive facial hair is sometimes viewed as either expressing an unwillingness to conform to conventional societal standards or expressing a preoccupation with a machismo image.

From *The Professional Image* by S. Bixler, 1984, New York: Putnam: *The Social Psychology of Clothing* (2nd ed.) by S. B. Kaiser, 1990, New York: Macmillan: *New Dress for Success* by J. T. Molloy, 1988, New York: Warner; *Jury Selection, Body Language and the Visual Trial* by J. Rasicot, 1983, Minneapolis: AB Publications; *Silent Sales* by J. Rasicot, 1986, Minneapolis: AB Publications; and *Courtroom Communication Strategies* by L. J. Smith and L. A. Malandro, 1985, New York: Kluwer.

FIGURE 10.5   Vocal Guidelines

Desirable Vocal Cues

1. Strive for a conversational speaking style of 125 to 150 words per minute. If you are engaging in persuasive communication, then a moderately fast rate has been shown to be effective. Individuals who use a conversational speaking style are viewed as more pleasant, likable, and friendly than those who do not.

2. Emphasize the most important points you are making with appropriate changes in volume and pitch; the monotone voice has been found to be very damaging to credibility.

3. The voice that is judged most credible is fluent, low-pitched, varied, moderately paced, and general American in dialect and accent.

4. Individuals with a narrow pitch range are viewed as unassertive, uninteresting, and lacking in confidence.

5. Speaking with appropriate variation in rate and pitch will make you appear more dynamic, animated, and extroverted.

6. Faulty or sloppy articulation and improper pronunciation are apt to have a highly negative impact on your perceived competence.

7. Inconsistent messages have a particularly damaging impact on the first impression you make. If you tell someone that you like them or their ideas, be sure to use your voice to reinforce the point you are making so that it sounds believable.

8. Deliberate pauses before the most important points you are making will make you seem more competent and will increase the likelihood that the point you are making will be remembered.

Undesirable Vocal Cues

1. To make a favorable first impression, try to eliminate nonfluencies such as "ah," incomplete words, and incomplete sentences. The nonfluent individual is usually perceived as underconfident, anxious, and less competent.

2. Avoid lengthy pauses before responding to a question, because such pauses raise questions about your competence and make you seem indecisive.

3. The excessively loud voice is associated with unseemly aggressiveness.

4. Seek to eliminate or minimize flatness, nasality, and tenseness in your voice. Those vocal qualities reinforce perceptions that an individual is nondynamic, uninteresting, and withdrawn.

5. Do not speak at a rate of over 200 words a minute, because an accelerated speaking rate is associated with an unacceptable level of anxiety.

6. Avoid interruptions, because they help to create the impression that you are socially insensitive.

These personal appearance guidelines may perhaps prove to be most useful in combatting or neutralizing features of personal appearance that are associated in a negative way with the physical-attractiveness stereotype. For example, what are the implications of the clothing guidelines for the big-busted woman with an endomorphic body type who is overweight? If she chooses to wear bright colors, she accentuates those physical features that have been linked perceptually with low self-confidence, below-average intelligence and competence, and submissiveness. Such a perceptual penalty could be avoided or minimized by the choice of neutral colors, which divert attention from bust size, body weight, and body type.

Consider also the importance of making choices that minimize the possibility that the perceiver will obtain other kinds of negative information from your personal appearance. Why should the salesperson who is a graduate of Southeastern Institute of Technology not wear a class ring when making a sales call? The reason is obvious. The sales prospect might be a graduate of another university and have negative feelings about SIT. Also, the skillful impression manager should avoid wearing deeply tinted contact lenses or glasses. To hide or obscure your eyes is to perpetuate the part of the eye-behavior stereotype that suggests that untrustworthy individuals wear dark eyeglasses.

Your specific situation might require that you obtain much more specialized information on a subject such as the psychological impact of the color of clothing, the kinds of accent items you should wear, or the choice of a briefcase or an umbrella. The sources cited in Figure 10.4 provide highly specialized information and guidance on those appearance items.

Vocal Guidelines

Vocal cues play a central role in shaping the first impression that you make. Chapter 11 emphasized that the vocal cues of a communicator have been found to affect all three dimensions of credibility—competence, trustworthiness, and dynamism. Perhaps more importantly, we know that vocal cues are a major source of information that perceivers use to make judgments about the other three image dimensions that are defining components of the impressions. For example, we know that vocal cues are major determinants of judgments made about how dominant or submissive you are.

Figure 10.5 provides specific guidelines, grounded in empirical research; see Chapter 8 for supporting references. By carefully considering the nature of desirable vocal cues, you increase the probability that others will attribute a flattering personality profile to you. As the guidelines suggest, positive personality traits and personal qualities are associated with a conversational speaking style that features substantial but appropriate variations in rate, pitch, and volume.

Because perceivers attach more weight to negative rather than to positive information about a person, you should take pains to minimize or eliminate the use of undesirable vocal cues. If you place a high value on being perceived as confident, you must take pains to avoid nonfluencies and an excessive speaking rate. Both kinds of vocal cues have repeatedly been found to communicate the impression that the communicator has an unacceptably low level of self-confidence and an unacceptably high level of anxiety.

The guidelines in Figure 10.5 should help you to use your voice in such a way that you associate yourself with the flattering features of the vocal-attractiveness stereotype and dissociate yourself from the unflattering features. When combined with the information contained in Chapter 11, these guidelines give you the potential to control the sound of your voice in ways advantageous to you.

The Impression Manager in Action

George Bush as "Wimp"

As George Bush approached the presidential election of 1992, he should have been confident that he could deal effectively with any impression management problems he might encounter. In fact, Bush and his image handlers successfully confronted a formidable image problem in his victory over Michael Dukakis in 1988. The images of presidential candidates Bush and Clinton were much less an issue in 1992 than in 1988, however. As candidate Bill Clinton took pains to point out, "It is the economy–stupid." An incumbent president is usually blamed for unfavorable economic conditions, and the United States economy was in bad shape in 1992. Bush was blamed. He lost. Thus, the preceeding presidential campaign of 1988 tells us much more about how presidential candidates may effectively exercise control over their own image by the careful control of their own nonverbal communication.

As George Bush approached the presidential election of 1988, he faced impression problems of major proportions. Bush's verbal gaffes, memory lapses, high nonfluencey ratio, and a tendency to become verbally incoherent were only surface manifestations of a much more serious problem. The big problem for Bush was that he was repeatedly and continually characterized by the media as a "wimp." Worse yet, national public opinion polls confirmed the accuracy of this judgment.

For the student of impression management, two questions are of most central importance: What factors contributed to the public's impression of Bush as a "wimp" and how did Bush and his image handlers fight the "wimp factor" in the presidential campaign of 1988 (Leathers, 1990)?

The public perception that Bush was a wimp was firmly established by 1988. What was not so clear was why Bush had made such an unsavory impression in the minds of so many Americans. Although many factors may have contributed to the widespread and enduring impression that George Bush was a wimp, six seem particularly important: (a) Bush's wealthy parents stressed the importance of self-effacing modesty and sharing. (b) Bush had the mind-set of the privileged preppy—he seemed preoccupied with the most trivial concerns of the wealthy and well educated. (c) Bush was viewed by some people as willing to sell out his principles to please his superiors or to win over a political constituency. (d) Bush was constrained by institutionized subservience as vice president. (e) The media accentuated the wimp image. (f) Bush's communication style suggested a lack of dominance.

In view of the importance of the last two factors, let us consider them separately. Bush's treatment by many members of the media had the effect of accentuating the most unattractive features of the wimp image. Gary Trudeau's visual characterization of George Bush in his "Doonesbury" comic strip seemed to have been particularly damaging. Although Trudeau's view of Bush as a wimp was influential in part because his cartoon reached millions, it was even more influential because people on the street discussed the strip.

In the presidential campaign of 1988, Trudeau characterized Bush as a wimp who was totally lacking in assertiveness and substance. Trudeau's Bush was such an insubstantial person that he would say anything in the interests of political expediency. In fact, Bush was such an insubstantial person that only his disembodied voice was heard.

Trudeau delighted in contrasting the macho, aggressive, maniacal presidential candidate Al Haig with the weak and devious wimp he pictured as George Bush. The idea seemed to be that Crazy Al would do anything for a little publicity, but at least Haig was a man. In the February 2, 1988, "Doonesbury," one of Haig's fanatical young followers asked him to describe his "program." Haig replied, "Son my program is all stick and no carrot! My program has all the manly saber-rattling of Reaganism without any of the weenie waffling of Bush-style pragmatism."

CARTOON 10.3

Finally, communication style probably contributed most to the impression that Bush was a wimp. Bush's biggest problem with his communication style was that his nonverbal communication functioned to make a very negative impression on the image dimension of dominance. His communication style—particularly in high-stress public appearances such as press conferences, interviews, and debates—was defined by many of the nonverbal behaviors that communicate submissiveness. Bush's eye behaviors, for example, surely reinforced the public perception that he was a submissive wimp. Especially when under pressure, Bush often blinked rapidly and shifted his eyes from side to side (Suplee, 1988).

Sometimes his eye shifting was quick enough to create the impression that he was flicking his eyeballs back and forth or that he was suffering from eye flutter. Bush's serious eye-behavior problems were particularly evident in his vice-presidential debate with Geraldine Ferraro at the Philadelphia Civic Center in 1980. His eyes were shifting back and forth at a high speed in such a manner as to suggest that he was quite anxious.

In general, Bush's eye behaviors are those of an unassertive, anxious, and submissive person; he often looks down or away before answering a question. He is notably shifty eyed, and he does not try to achieve dominance over an opponent by staring at the opponent. He rarely looks at an opponent directly, and when he does he often averts his eyes.

Second, a person strongly communicates dominance by speaking in a loud and expressive voice, by interrupting an opponent, and by fluent speech—characteristics Bush does not always display. He has long been known for speaking with a soft voice (described by Trudeau's version of President Reagan in a "Doonesbury" cartoon of January 27, 1988, as a "tiny," "tinny" voice), his speaking rate has accelerated to more than 200 words a minute (as it did in the debate with Ferraro), he has frequently been the person who is interrupted, and his high nonfluency ratio has frequently been parodied.

Third, Bush has contributed strongly to the perception that he is submissive with his lip-licking, lip-pursing, hand-to-face adaptor gestures (the timid and restrained gestures that his own image analyst said made him look like a "pansy"), rigid posture, and out-of-context smiling that has been described as a "silly grin." (The Bush smile is a phenomenon that deserves analysis in its own right because it surely makes him seem more likable and interpersonally attractive in those situations where he feels confident. It is only when he becomes anxious that his spontaneous and ingratiating smile seems to dissolve into a "silly grin").

George Bush as Impression Manager

George Bush's shrewdest move may have been choosing Roger Ailes to be his chief image advisor for the Presidential campaign of 1988. If it was George Bush who was forced to "fight the wimp factor" in that campaign, then it was Roger Ailes who devised the three-phase impression management strategy that enabled Bush to make the fight.

Ailes emphasized two things of interest to the impression manager in his book *You Are the Message* (1988). The artful impression manager must be assertive, even aggressive, to the point of achieving dominance over an opponent; this emphasis proved to be particularly useful to Bush, who was perceived to be unassertive, weak, and dominated.

If Ailes is convinced that successful impression management requires the communication of a suitable degree of dominance, he is also convinced that the most desirable image quality that can be attributed to a person is likability. He wrote that

> *if you could master one element of personal communication that is more powerful than anything we've discussed it is the quality of being* likable. *I call it the magic bullet, because if your audience likes you, they'll forgive just about everything else you do wrong. If they don't like you, you can hit every rule right on target and it doesn't matter.* (p. 69)

The impression management strategy that Ailes devised to help George Bush fight the wimp factor in the presidential campaign of 1988 went through three phases. Phase 1 featured *attack* in the form of negative television commercials designed to put Michael Dukakis on the defensive and a televised confrontation between George Bush and Dan Rather. Phase 2 focused on George Bush's masterful impression management effort to fight the wimp factor and reconstruct his image via the speech he gave at the Republican National Convention to accept the nomination for president. Phase 3 was the major impression management challenge Bush would confront in the campaign of 1988—the presidential debate with Michael Dukakis.

Phases 2 and 3 deserve particular attention since George Bush's nonverbal communication played a central role in both phases. Phase 2 of Bush's fight against the wimp factor featured his acceptance speech at the Republican National Convention. It was a well-designed and well-executed impression management effort that employed the principle of association (Schlenker, 1980). Primarily through his nonverbal communication, Bush was able to dissociate himself from the most troubling qualities of the wimp image (a dominance deficit and questions about his competence). At the same time, Bush drew attention to his most appealing image assets (likability and interpersonal attractiveness).

George Bush's acceptance speech at the Republican convention was a pivotal event in the fight against the wimp factor, which Bush's image handlers found to be his biggest liability politically. The convention represented the type of controlled communication environment in which the potential for redefining Bush's image in a desired way was great and the risk of further damaging that image was slight. Bush's effort as an impression manager via this acceptance speech was masterful. He exhibited a commendable set of impression management skills that he had not before exhibited.

During that one speech, Bush was able to inhibit or virtually eliminate most of the nonverbal behaviors that had defined him in the public's consciousness as weak, unassertive, and of doubtful competence. Gone were the wildly shifting and downcast eyes that seemed to say "I am not a dominant and confident leader and may not be sufficiently competent to be president"; instead, Bush fixed the camera with a steady and unremitting stare. Gone was the vocal image of weakness and timidity that had been parodied with devastating effect by friend and foe—the soft and high-pitched voice, the rapid speaking rate, the narrow pitch and volume range, and the nonfluencies that are all indicators of the unassertive person, the person who might not have sufficient command of self and subject to speak fluently; in their place was a vocal conviction that has not been heard since then from the man who eventually became President Bush.

Gone were the timid and restrained gestures, the bodily rigidity, and the out-of-context smiles that branded Bush as unassertive, anxious, uncomfortable, and even timid; in their place were firm gestures that exuded confidence, a relaxed posture, and a broad smile that suggested "I am in command." (When Bush commented that his wife suggested that he relax while preparing this speech and put "his silver leg up on the table," Bush's broad grin seemed to suggest "I am so confident that I can make fun even of the fact that I was born to wealth and privilege.") Surely the roaring confirmatory response from the partisan Republican audience had the effect of further emboldening Bush and reinforcing his confidence.

Finally, the verbal content of the speech reinforced the image of the dominant, assertive, and confident leader that Bush was communicating via his nonverbal behavior/cues. Bush challenged his opponent directly ("And someone better take a message to Michael . . . the fact is that they talk and we deliver"). He placed himself in the great American tradition of "the fighter" who would lead the charge to protect rights and privileges of various interest groups. (He kept repeating the phrase "I am not going to let them take it away from you" when he addressed the "gains" of women, the elderly, and other interest groups for which he claimed credit for Reagan and himself). He made sure that everyone would see him as highly assertive by continued use of the personal pronoun "I." ("I will not allow this country to be made weak again—never!") In a repetitive theme, Bush said "My opponent says no but I say yes" as he referred to his stands on abortion, gun control, education, and so on.

The first presidential debate with Michael Dukakis was an impression management event of great importance to George Bush. This debate would be the ultimate test, and Bush and his image handlers knew it. They had put Dukakis on the defensive with highly negative television ads in Phase 1 of their impression management strategy. However, in both Phases 1 and 2 of Bush's impression management efforts, he had worked within communicative contexts that were carefully controlled by his image handlers. In the debate with Dukakis, Bush would be forced to perform adequately but not brilliantly in a communicative context he could not control. From an impression management perspective, Bush simply had to communicate with enough skill to provide an affirmative answer to one question of overriding importance: Would Bush be able to make a sufficiently positive impression on each of the major image dimensions so that he would not lose the momentum generated in Phases 1 and 2 of his impression management strategy?

Bush started with a deficit on the competence dimension of credibility and on the dominance image dimension. Competence was a problem because of his seeming inability to express himself in complete sentences, to sustain thought continuity, and to avoid the high nonfluency rate suggestive of an undisciplined mind, in addition to his disconcerting tendency to make verbal gaffes. Bush presumably did not want to bring back memories of the verbally nonfluent and fumbling Gerald Ford, but he knew it was not necessary to make an impression of extraordinary competence. Bush had only to cultivate the impression that he had sufficient competence to be president.

The image dimension of dominance was where Bush approached the debate with his most serious deficit. Although he had attacked the wimp factor effectively in his acceptance speech at the Republican National Convention, serious doubts lingered in the public's mind about whether Bush was tough and assertive enough to be president. He and his image handlers recognized that he need not come across as Rambo in the debate. He would risk sacrificing his major advantages over Dukakis on likability and interpersonal attractiveness if he communicated with unseemly aggressiveness.

On the positive side, Bush had a clear edge on Dukakis on both the likability and interpersonal attractiveness image dimensions. His edge on likability was important because his own image analyst, Roger Ailes, was on record as arguing that likability is considerably more important to a politician than any of the other image dimensions. His edge on interpersonal attractiveness came more from his opponent's weakness than from his own strength. Bush had the good fortune in debating Michael Dukakis to encounter a man with serious problems in terms of interpersonal attractiveness. The reasons become apparent when we recall that the subdimensions of interpersonal attractiveness are interestingness, emotional expressivity, and sociability.

Bush did many things to make him seem to be more likable than Dukakis. To begin, he smiled more often than Dukakis. Except when he was under direct attack, Bush's smiles

CARTOON 10.4

seemed to be spontaneous and genuine. Dukakis's smile, in contrast, seemed forced, unspontaneous, and condescending when he was responding aggressively to Bush.

Bush's ability to use self-deprecating humor in the debate gave him a great edge in likability. Gardner stressed in his insightful analysis of the humor displayed by past presidents, *All the Presidents' Wits: The Power of Presidential Humor* (1986), that all of the best-liked presidents had well-developed senses of humor. Gardner contended that humor contributes in a powerful way to likability. He wrote that

> *nothing is more effective in creating this impression than a library of self-deprecating humor. No public figure should be without it.... Sad to say, many*

voters don't object to mediocrity in their president but they absolutely insist on a sense of humor. (p. 14)

Even when Bush became flustered in the debate (e.g., when he called the MX missile a Minuteman), he exhibited the ability to ingratiate by using self-deprecating humor (he turned to Dukakis and said "It's Christmas"—a joking reference to a statement Bush had made several months earlier when he mistakenly stated that Pearl Harbor occurred on December 25). Similarly, Bush smiled after another heated exchange with Dukakis and said he had hoped that the debate would be more friendly so that he "could hitch a ride home in his tank."

Bush also made a favorable impression on the image dimension of interpersonal attractiveness. People judged to be interpersonally attractive communicate in such a way as to be perceived as interesting, emotionally expressive, and sociable. Bush exhibited many more gestures and was more relaxed than Dukakis; he exhibited a wide range of emotions, whereas Dukakis was the emotionless "Ice Man"; and Bush exhibited a warm and friendly communication style associated with sociability.

Finally, the image of dominance was of critical importance. Bush's wimp image, after all, was based on the public's perception that he was so lacking in dominance behavior that it was not believable that he could assume the ultimate leadership role of president of the United States. Because dominance is a relational concept, it could be assessed only in the ways the candidates reacted to each other. A split screen was used frequently in coverage of this debate, providing the public with the opportunity of studying the reaction of one candidate to another via sequences of their behaviors.

Bush's passive, unassertive, and nonengaging response behavior was one indication that Dukakis was visually dominant. Bush very rarely looked at Dukakis while Dukakis was speaking, whereas Dukakis almost always looked at Bush while Bush was speaking. Furthermore, Dukakis frequently fixated on Bush with an unremitting stare while Bush was speaking. He often directed a fixed smile at Bush that seemed to take the form of a condescending sneer. On a number of occasions he challenged Bush (with the familiar "George") to respond directly, or he interrupted Bush while he was speaking.

Bush rarely engaged Dukakis directly until later in the debate, and he exhibited a number of nonverbal indicators of unassertiveness—a high nonfluency rate, licking and pursing his lips, and hand-to-face gestures. When Dukakis attacked Bush for questioning his loyalty by calling him a "card-carrying member of the ACLU," the split screen showed Bush putting the cap on his pen and his hand was shaking noticeably.

Significantly, Bush exhibited superior vocal assertiveness even though Dukakis dominated him visually during the debate. Whereas Dukakis spoke in a passionless way with a narrow pitch and volume range, Bush spoke with decided vocal conviction. He added emphasis to important points with an increase in volume and pitch, and he paused for effect.

Bush's success as an impression manager cannot be assessed adequately by public reaction to the debate as measured in public opinion polls. Besides, those results suggested that neither candidate was a decisive winner of the first presidential debate. Gallup poll results showed that 42 percent of the voters thought Dukakis won, whereas 41 percent thought Bush won. In the ABC News poll, 44 percent saw Dukakis as the winner and 36 percent picked Bush; by comparison, 42 percent of the respondents in the CBS News–New York Times poll picked Bush as the winner and 39 percent thought Dukakis won (*Gwinnett Daily News,* 1988, September 27).

If Bush's success as an impression manager is measured in terms of the goals developed by his image handlers, he was extraordinarily successful in fighting the wimp factor by dissociating himself from many of the most damaging defining features. However, this judgment does need to be placed in perspective: Bush had the good fortune of opposing a person with very limited impression management skills.

Summary

This chapter begins by emphasizing the importance of impression management in a variety of real-world contexts. Impression management is defined as an individual's conscious attempt to exercise conscious control over selected communicative behaviors and cues—particularly nonverbal cues—for purposes of making a desired impression.

Impressions are defined by four image dimensions: credibility, likability, interpersonal attractiveness, and dominance. How important each of these image dimensions is to you will depend on your motives, the context in which you communicate, your objectives, and a number of other factors. Impression managers typically prioritize these image dimensions in terms of their importance to them.

An understanding of how an individual is motivated in a particular situation enhances our ability to predict how that individual will behave, because motives serve to guide a person's behaviors in ways that person judges effective in reaching one or more goals. The major classes of motives of most importance to the impression manager are achievement motives, affiliation motives, social approval motives, and mastery motives.

This chapter develops an original conceptualization of the stages in the impression management process. Much of the chapter's second section concentrates on the guidelines that the impression manager can use to implement the stages or steps in that process.

Finally, the last section focuses on the serious impression management problems that George Bush encountered in the presidential campaign of 1988 and the strategy that Bush and his image handlers devised to resolve them. Considerable attention is given to the reasons that Bush was widely perceived to be a wimp. His effort to fight the wimp factor is analyzed from the perspective of the original conceptualization of impression management and the impression management process that is presented in this chapter.

References

Ailes, R. (1988). *You are the message.* Homewood, IL: Dow-Jones-Irwin.

Albright, L., Kenny, D. A., & Malloy, T. E. (1988). Consensus in personality judgments at zero acquaintance. *Journal of Personality and Social Psychology, 55,* 387–395.

Alicke, M. D., Smith, R. H., & Klotz, M. L. (1987). Judgments of physical attractiveness: The role of faces and bodies. *Personality and Social Psychology Bulletin, 12,* 381–389.

Almaney, A. J., & Alwan, A. J. (1982). *Communicating with the Arabs.* Prospects Heights, IL: Waveland.

Andersen, P. A. (1985). Nonverbal immediacy in interpersonal communication. In A. W. Seigman & S. Feldstein (Eds.), *Multichannel integration of nonverbal behavior* (pp. 1–36). Hillsdale, NJ: Erlbaum.

Anthony, P. K., & Vinson, D. E. (1987). Nonverbal communication in the courtroom: You don't say? *Trial Diplomacy, 39,* 35–37.

Atkinson, M. (1984). *Our master's voices: The language and body language of politics.* London: Methuen.

Atkinson, M. (1990, June). *The other Thatcher revolution: Impression management and the transformation of political communication in Britain.* Paper presented at the annual conference of the International Communication Association, Dublin, Ireland.

Bixler, S. (1984). *The professional image: The total program for marketing yourself visually.* New York: Putnam.

Brembeck, W. L., & Howell, W. S. (1976). *Persuasion: A means of social influence.* Englewood Cliffs, NJ: Prentice-Hall.

Brooks, C. I., Church, M. A., & Fraser, L. (1986). Effects of duration of eye contact on judgments of personality characteristics. *The Journal of Social Psychology, 126,* 71–78.

Burgoon, J. K., Manusov, V., Mineo, P., & Hale, J. L. (1985). Effects of gaze on hiring, credibility, attraction and relational message interpretation. *Journal of Nonverbal Behavior, 9,* 133–146.

Burgoon, J. K., & Saine, T. (1978). *The unspoken dialogue: An introduction to nonverbal communication.* Boston: Houghton Mifflin.

Coker, D. A., & Burgoon, J. K. (1987). The nature of conversational involvement and nonverbal encoding patterns. *Human Communication Research, 13,* 463–494.

Cooper, K. (1979). *Nonverbal communication for business success.* New York: AMACOM.

Damhorst, M. L. (1990). In search of a common thread: Classification of information communicated through dress. *Clothing Textiles Research Journal, 8,* 1–12.

DeMeuse, K. P. (1987). A review of the effects of nonverbal cues in the performance appraisal process. *Journal of Occupational Psychology, 60,* 207–226.

DePaulo, B. M. (1992). Nonverbal behavior and self-presentation. *Psychological Bulletin, 111,* 151–161.

Dion, K. L., & Dion, K. K. (1987). Belief in a just world and physical attractiveness stereotyping. *Journal of Personality and Social Psychology, 52,* 775–780.

Doonesbury cartoons, 1988, January 27, February 2, and March 13. *Athens Daily News.*

Dovidio, J. F., & Ellyson, S. L. (1985). Patterns of visual dominance behavior in humans. In S. L. Ellyson & J. F. Dovidio (Eds.), *Power, dominance, and nonverbal behavior* (pp. 129–149). New York: Springer-Verlag.

Edinger, J. A., & Patterson, M. L. (1983). Nonverbal involvement and social control. *Psychological Bulletin, 93,* 30–56.

Ehrlichman, J. (1982). *Witness to power: The Nixon years.* New York: Simon & Schuster.

Ekman, P. (1985). *Telling lies: Clues to deceit in the marketplace, politics, and marriage.* New York: W. W. Norton.

Ekman, P., & Friesen, W. V. (1982). Felt, false, and miserable smiles. *Journal of Nonverbal Behavior, 6,* 238–258.

Ellyson, S. L., & Dovidio, J. F. (1985). Dominance and nonverbal behaviors: Basic concepts and issues. In S. L. Ellyson & J. F. Dovidio (Eds.), *Power, dominance, and nonverbal behavior* (pp. 1–27). New York: Springer-Verlag.

Exline, R. V. (1985). Multichannel transmission of nonverbal behavior and the perception of powerful men: The presidential debates of 1976. In S. L. Ellyson & J. F. Dovidio (Eds.), *Power, dominance, and nonverbal behavior* (pp. 183–206). New York: Springer-Verlag.

Fitzkee, E. (1975). *Magic by misdirection.* Oakland, CA: Magic Limited.

Francis, S. K. (1992). Effects of perceived clothing deprivation on high school students' social participation. *Clothing and Textiles Research Journal, 10,* 29–33.

Friedlander, M. L., & Schwartz, G. S. (1985). Toward a theory of strategic self-presentation in counseling and psychotherapy. *Journal of Counseling Psychology, 32,* 483–501.

Friedman, H. S., Riggio, R. E., & Casella, D. F. (1988). Nonverbal skill, personal charisma, and initial attraction. *Personality and Social Psychology Bulletin, 14,* 203–211.

Fry, P. S., & Grover, S. C. (1983). An exploration of the child's perspective: Children's perceptions of parental treatment, personal anxiety, and attributions of blame in single-parent families. *Journal of Psychiatric Treatment and Evaluation, 5,* 353–362.

Gardner, G. (1986). *All the president's wits: The power of presidential humor.* New York: Beachtree/Morrow.

Gifford, R., Ng, C. F., & Wilkinson, J. (1985). Nonverbal cues in the employment interview: Links between applicant qualities and interviewer judgments. *Journal of Applied Psychology, 70,* 729–736.

Gorham, J. (1988). The relationship between verbal teacher immediacy behaviors and student learning. *Communication Education, 37,* 40–67.

Gray, J. (1993). *The Winning Image.* New York: American Management Association.

Harper, R. G. (1985). Power, dominance, and nonverbal behavior: An overview. In S. L. Ellyson & J. F. Dovidio (Eds.), *Power, dominance, and nonverbal behavior* (pp. 29–66). New York: Springer-Verlag.

Harrington, J. A., & Rosenthal, R. (1983). Physicians' head and body positions as determinants of perceived rapport. *Journal of Applied Psychology, 13,* 496–509.

Heath, C. C. (1984). Participation in the medical consultation: The coordination of verbal and nonverbal behavior between the doctor and patient. *Sociology of Health & Illness, 6,* 311–338.

Henley, N. M., & Harmon, S. (1985). The nonverbal semantics of power and gender: A perceptual study. In S. L. Ellyson & J. F. Dovidio (Eds.), *Power, dominance and nonverbal behavior* (pp. 151–164). New York: Springer-Verlag.

Hopefuls break even in debate aftermath. (1988, September 27). *Gwinnett Daily News,* p. 1A.

Hosman, L. A. (1989). The evaluative consequences of hedges, hesitations, and intensifiers: Powerful and powerless speech styles. *Human Communication Research, 15,* 383–406.

Jones, E. E., & Pittman, T. S. (1982). Toward a general theory of strategic self-presentation. In J. Suls (Ed.), *Psychological perspectives on the self* (Vol. 1) (pp. 213–262). Hillsdale, NJ: Erlbaum.

Kaiser, S. B. (1990). *The social psychology of clothing: Symbolic appearances in context* (2nd ed.) New York: Macmillan.

Kleinke, C. L. (1986). Gaze and eye contact: A research review. *Psychological Bulletin, 100,* 78–100.

LaFrance, M., & Mayo, C. (1978). Cultural aspects of nonverbal communication. *International Journal of Intercultural Relations, 2,* 71–89.

Leathers, D. G. (1986). *Successful nonverbal communication* (1st ed.) New York: Macmillan.

Leathers, D. G. (1988). Impression management training: Conceptualization and application to personal selling. *Journal of Applied Communication Research, 16,* 126–145.

Leathers, D. G. (1990, June). *George Bush as impression manager: Fighting the wimp factor.* Paper presented at the annual conference of the International Communication Association, Dublin, Ireland.

Leathers, D. G., & Ross, C. S. (1990). Theoretical conceptualization of the impression management functions of nonverbal communication. Unpublished manuscript.

LeVan, E. A. (1984). Nonverbal communication in the courtroom: Attorney beware. *Law & Psychology Review, 8,* 83–104.

Linz, D. G., & Penrod, S. (1984). Increasing attorney persuasiveness in the courtroom. *Law & Psychology Review, 8,* 83–104.

McClelland, D. C. (1987). *Human motivation.* Cambridge: Cambridge UP.

Mehrabian, A. (1981). *Silent Messages* (2nd ed.). Belmont, CA: Wadsworth.

Molloy, J. T. (1988). *New dress for success.* New York: Warner.

Montepare, J. & Zebrowitz-McArthur, L. (1987). Perceptions of adults with childlike voices in two cultures. *Journal of Experimental Social Psychology, 23,* 331–349.

Muehlenhard, C., & Scardino, T. (1985). What will he think? Men's impressions of women who initiate dates and achieve academically. *Journal of Counseling Psychology, 32,* 560–569.

Patterson, M. L. (1987). Presentational and affect-management functions of nonverbal involvement. *Journal of Nonverbal Behavior, 11,* 110–122.

Patterson, M. L. (1994). Interaction behavior and person perceptions: An integrative approach. *Small Group Research, 25,* 171–188.

Patterson, M. L. (1995). A parallel process model of nonverbal communication. *Journal of Nonverbal Behavior, 19,* 3–29.

Plax, T. G., Kearney, P., McCroskey, J. C., Richmond, V. P. (1986). Power in the classroom VI: Verbal control strategies, nonverbal immediacy and effective learning. *Communication Education, 35,* 54–55.

Pryor, B., & Buchanan, R. (1984). The effects of a defendant's demeanor on your perception of credibility and guilt. *Journal of Communication, 34,* 92–99.

Rasicot, J. (1983). *Jury selection, body language and the visual trial.* Minneapolis, MN: AB Publications.

Rasicot, J. (1986). *Silent sales.* Minneapolis, MN: AB Publications.

Remland, M. S., & Jones, T. S. (1989). The effects of nonverbal involvement and communication apprehension on state anxiety, interpersonal attraction, and speech duration. *Communication Quarterly, 37,* 170–183.

Richmond, V. P., McCroskey, J. C., & Payne, S. K. (1987). *Nonverbal behavior in interpersonal relations.* Englewood Cliffs, NJ: Prentice-Hall.

Riess, M. (1982). Seating preferences as impression management: A literature review and theoretical integration. *Communication, 11,* 85–113.

Riggio, R. E., & Friedman, H. S. (1986). Impression formation: The role of expressive behavior. *Journal of Personality and Social Psychology, 30,* 421–427.

Roach-Higgins, M. E., & Eicher, J. B. (1992). Dress and identity. *Clothing and Textiles Research Journal, 10,* 1–8.

Roll, S. A., Crowley, M. A., & Rappl, L. E. (1985). Client perceptions of counselors' nonverbal behavior: A reevaluation. *Counselor Education and Supervision, 24,* 234–243.

Rosenberg, S. W., Bohan, L., McCafferty, P., & Harris, K. (1986). The image and the vote: The effect of candidate presentation on voter preference. *American Journal of Political Science, 30,* 108–127.

Ross, C. S. (1991). *Image dimensions and impression managers' perception of nonverbal behavior.* Unpublished Ph.D. dissertation, University of Georgia, Athens, GA.

Sabatelli, R., & Rubin, M. (1986). Nonverbal expressiveness and physical attractiveness as mediators of interpersonal perceptions. *Journal of Nonverbal Behavior, 10,* 120–133.

Sannito, R. (1983). Nonverbal communication in the courtroom. *Trial Diplomacy Journal, 35,* 35-37.

Schlenker, B. R. (1980). *Impression management.* Monterey, CA: Brooks/Cole.

Schlenker, B. R. (1985). Identity and self-identification. In B. R. Schlenker (Ed.), *The self and social life* (pp. 65–99). New York: McGraw-Hill.

Schlenker, B. R., Diugoleckie, D. W., & Doherty, K. (1994). The impact of self-presentations on self-appraisals and behavior—The power of public commitment. *Personality and Social Psychology Bulletin, 7,* 79–100.

Smith, L. J., & Malandro, L. A. (1985). *Courtroom communication strategies.* New York: Kluwer.

Street, R. L., Jr., & Brady, R. M. (1982). Speech rate acceptance ranges as a function of evaluative domain, listener speech rate, and communication context. *Communication Monographs, 49,* 290–308.

Street, R. L., Jr., & Hooper, R. (1982). A model of speech style evaluation. In E. B. Ryan & H. Giles (Eds.), *Attitudes toward language variation: Social and applied contexts* (pp. 175-188). London: Arnold.

Suplee, C. (1988, July 10). Sorry, George, but the image needs work. *The Washington Post,* pp. C1–C4.

Tarbell, H. (1953). *The Tarbell course in magic.* New York: Louis Tannen.

Tedeschi, J. T., & Norman, W. (1985). Social power, self-presentation, and the self. In B. R. Schlenker (Ed.), *The self and social life* (pp. 293–322). New York: McGraw-Hill.

Tedeschi, J. T., & Riess, M. (1981). Identities, the phenomenal self, and laboratory research. In J. T. Tedeschi (Ed.), *Impression management theory and social psychological research* (pp. 3–22). New York: Academic Press.

Webbink, P. (1986). *The power of the eyes.* New York: Springer.

Chapter *11*

Selling Yourself Nonverbally

In an interview presented by CBS television on November 4, 1979, CBS correspondent Roger Mudd asked Senator Ted Kennedy, "What's the present state of your marriage, Senator?" Kennedy replied, "Well, I think that, uh, it's a, uh, uh, we've had um, some uh, difficult uh, uh, times but I think we uh, have uh, oof, I think been able to make some uh, very good progress and uh, uh, it's uh, uh, I would say that it's uh, uh, it's it's um delighted that we're able to, to share, share the time and the, the relationship that we do share" (CBS Television, 1979).

The vocal image Kennedy projected was highly undesirable for a man trying to sell himself as a credible presidential candidate. Consider for a moment how Kennedy's vocal message might have affected his credibility in your eyes. Did his frequent hesitations, stammering, and speech errors make him seem more or less competent, trustworthy, and dynamic? Did his vocal message help convince you that he was seeking to give Mudd a forthright and honest answer?

Kennedy's credibility was seriously damaged because he projected an image he quite clearly did not wish to project. Students of mine who have analyzed Kennedy's interview with Mudd approach unanimity in the judgments they make: Kennedy's vocal cues assumed a central role in communicating an image of evasiveness and indecision that is unacceptable for a presidential candidate. The student analysts became convinced that the negative impression that Kennedy made was shaped primarily by his nonverbal communication rather than by the words that he uttered.

If you disagree with those judgments, think once again about Senator Kennedy's response to Roger Mudd's question. Kennedy did not say that the question made him uncomfortable to the point of being anxious; he did not say that he would be forced to be indirect, evasive, and untruthful in his response; and he did not say that his marriage was irreparably broken. Nonetheless, those messages were all clearly communicated. They were communicated unintentionally and implicitly through the communicative medium of Kennedy's vocal cues.

Senator Ted Kennedy is not the only contemporary political figure whose credibility has been seriously damaged as a result of a single appearance on national television. Consider the cases of former President Ronald Reagan and Senator Joseph Biden. President Reagan's credibility was so high before the Contragate controversy that it was probably unequaled by any previous president. However, President Reagan's credibility dropped precipitously after his fateful press conference of November 19, 1986; Reagan never succeeded in restoring his personal credibility to its previous heights after that press conference. Senator Biden destroyed his own credibility as a presidential candidate by his response to a single question in a single interview.

On July 19, 1988, Senator Biden appeared in a private home in New Hampshire to give a short political speech and to be interviewed by the people assembled in the home; his appearance was being recorded for later rebroadcast by C-SPAN II. Biden seemed both animated and relaxed as he began by delivering an extemporaneous campaign speech. Then about halfway through a question-and-answer session, a person in the crowd said, "Senator, I have one real quick follow-up question. What law school did you attend and where did you place in your class?" The tension generated by this question seemed to be reflected in cries of "Who cares?" from Biden's supporters. Biden appeared to freeze for a minute; he licked his lips and then replied in a voice that was noticeably strident:

> *I think that I have a much higher IQ than you do. I was the only one in my class to have a full academic scholarship. . . . [I] ended up in the top half of my class. I was the outstanding student in the political science department in the end of my last year, I graduated with three degrees from undergraduate school, I graduated with 165 credits and only needed 123 credits, and I would be delighted to sit down and compare my IQ with yours if you like, Frank.* (C-Span II, 1988)

Within a short time it became apparent to reporters who checked the record that Senator Biden had lied repeatedly in responding to the question about his academic credentials; virtually every statement he made was verifiably false. For example, Biden finished 76th out of 85 in his law school class rather than in the top half as he claimed, he received two rather than three college degrees, and he did not win an award as the outstanding student in his political science department. In this case, the verifiably false statements in his answer to a single question so damaged his credibility that Senator Biden was forced to withdraw a short time later as a candidate for the democratic nomination for president.

The nonverbal portion of Biden's message seemed to be particularly damaging to a man trying to make a favorable impression as a credible presidential candidate. Senator Biden had been charming, animated, and affable up to the point that he responded to the question about his academic credentials. He smiled, he gesticulated, and he pontificated but in a pleasant way. In short, he communicated nonverbally in such a way as to be likable and interpersonally attractive. The question about Biden's academic credentials triggered a dramatic change in his nonverbal communication style, however. He suddenly became nonverbally aggressive. He became the attacker. Indeed, Senator Biden's physical tenseness, strident voice, direct attack on his questioner, and defensive manner provided a clear signal to those attending the press conference in New Hampshire and those who watched it on television that Biden's trustworthiness had become the matter of overriding concern.

Next, consider the case of President Ronald Reagan. Reagan had been called the "Teflon President" because the American public seemed disinclined to hold him personally responsible for the misdeeds of his subordinates, or even for his own misdeeds. Throughout his first four years in office and well into his second term, President Reagan's personal credibility had never been seriously challenged. The Contragate crisis, and Reagan's own efforts to mislead the public with regard to his role in Contragate, soon became so controversial, however, that President Reagan's personal credibility came under repeated and sustained attack.

Reagan and his advisors recognized that the threat to the President's personal credibility was serious. Although the president had avoided holding a press conference for many months, his advisors realized that they would soon have to schedule one. The press conference was finally scheduled for November 19, 1986 (CBS Television, 1986). As President Reagan approached the podium at the press conference, he undoubtedly recognized two things, at minimum: This would be the most important press conference he had ever held, and the central issue in question was his personal credibility.

President Reagan had earned the title of the "Great Communicator" because he had repeatedly demonstrated an ability to communicate in a poised and confident manner in a variety of public situations. He was particularly effective because he used the nonverbal channels of communication to reinforce and make more believable the words that he uttered. He shook his head from side to side to emphasize his disagreement with an action or a policy, and he nodded his head up and down if he wished others to agree with him. He used seemingly spontaneous gestures, well-timed pauses, and appropriate vocal modulation to add emphasis and believability to the points that he made.

His air of confidence started with a seemingly genuine smile. Friends and foes agreed that the smile and the low-key but expressive bodily communication helped make him one of the most likable presidents of all time. He rarely exhibited the adaptor gestures that have been previously identified as indicators of anxiety. In short, President Ronald Reagan, the Great Communicator, seemed to personify the confident public man as he prepared for the press conference of November 19, 1986.

The press conference had hardly begun when it became apparent that Reagan was not performing well as a communicator. He hesitated verbally, clear idea development seemed to be beyond his grasp, he rarely uttered a complete sentence, and at times he seemed to be virtually incoherent. At one point during the press conference, NBC news reporter Chris Wallace came close to calling the President a liar. Wallace noted that in spite of Reagan's denial that he was trading arms for hostages, the United States always seemed to make a major arms shipment to Iran immediately before a hostage was released. Chris Wallace turned to the President and asked, "Are we all to believe that that was just a coincidence?" President Reagan replied:

Chris...I didn't know anything about that until I saw the press on it because we certainly never had any contact with anything of the kind. And, ah. So [Reagan pauses and shakes his head back and forth horizontally as if to deny that the United States had been shipping arms to Iran]. There's. It's just—ah. Ah. So. But, ah. It's just that—ah—we did something for—ah—a particular [reason].

CBS reporter Bill Plante also addressed a question to President Reagan. Plante prefaced his question to Reagan by noting that President Reagan had said that the equipment that the United States shipped to Iran did not alter the military balance, but Plante wanted to touch on "several things." Bill Plante said, "The United States apparently condoned shipments by Israel and other countries. So how can you say that it didn't break the law?"

President Reagan replied:

Bill, everything you have said here is based on a supposition that is false. Ah. We did not condone and do not condone the shipment of arms from other countries. And, ah, as to what was the other point that you—ah—made here ah [Reagan pauses with a confused look on his face as if to suggest that he has forgotten Plante's question. He turns to Plante for help and Plante reminds him that the question had to do with the "anti-tank missiles"]. Oh, no. Ah—about that, it didn't ah, that it didn't, ah [pause] that it did violate the law.

The verbal portion of Reagan's communication in this interview can be judged on its own merits. Students of mine who have watched the interview agree that his verbal statements had a devastatingly negative impact on his perceived competence. You can make your own assessments of how Reagan's verbal communication affected your perception of his competence.

Reagan's nonverbal communication probably had an even more negative impact on his perceived credibility—particularly his trustworthiness and dynamism. If you had watched this press conference, you might have wondered if you really were watching the man known as the Great Communicator. Almost all of the old and familiar nonverbal signs of confidence were gone. In their place were a wide array of nonverbal behaviors known to communicate uncertainty, discomfort, and anxiety. President Reagan's eyes frequently shifted from side to side, he typically looked down while beginning to answer a question, he licked his lips frequently and was highly nonfluent, his eyes had a dull appearance, his voice communicated doubt and uncertainty, and, finally, President Reagan frequently had a confused if not befuddled expression on his face.

The interviews just discussed dramatize the potentially powerful impact of nonverbal cues on perceived credibility. Nonverbal factors are known to be particularly important for the person who wishes to be regarded as a leader. In fact, perceptions of leadership potential and leadership qualities are often more strongly affected by nonverbal than verbal cues (Gitter, Black, & Fishman, 1975). Both frequency and specific kinds of nonverbal cues have been shown to exert a strong influence on perceptions of leadership (Baird, 1977).

Successful communication requires the development of an image of personal credibility. As James Gray, Jr., wrote in *The Winning Image* (1982), "your image is a tool for communicating and for revealing your inherent qualities, your competence, abilities, and leadership. It is a reflection of qualities that others associate with you, a reflection that bears long-lasting influence in your bid for success" (p. 6). You need not be a presidential candidate to be concerned about the impact of your credibility on your bid for success.

My work as a communication consultant in a presidential campaign and as a communication trainer of corporate salespeople has convinced me that successful communicators must master the art of selling themselves nonverbally. You will not vote for the politician or buy from the salesperson unless you find that person to be sufficiently credible.

This chapter focuses on the role of nonverbal communication in the development of personal credibility. The nonverbal communication behaviors of presidential candidates and corporate sales representatives are used to illustrate the specific perceptual effects of such behaviors on credibility. Specific guidelines for developing credibility are presented, and the nonverbal profile of the credible communicator is highlighted.

If you doubt the importance of credibility in personal selling, consider the case of the agritech salesperson in the Rio Grande Valley of Texas. The prospect is a vegetable farmer in the valley who has more than 50,000 acres in cultivation. The salesperson must try to persuade the farmer to purchase a liquid hormone that will be sprayed on his vegetables and will allegedly increase his yield by up to 25 percent. Because the liquid hormone is a new product, results from field research are still limited. The farmer recognizes that a decision to use the salesperson's product on all of his vegetables will cost him many thousands of dollars. He does not want to make the wrong decision.

Salespeople in the Rio Grande Valley who actually find themselves in such a selling situation tell me that their personal credibility is frequently the critical issue. Their company's credibility might have been important in arranging the sales call, but it is their personal credibility that is of most concern to the farmers. Do the farmers find them to be knowledgeable and trustworthy enough to buy from them? One farmer told an agritech salesperson, "I can't buy from you. I give old Ned all of my business. He knows what he is doing. I trust him. I give Ned all of my business because he has never done me wrong."

The farmers found "old Ned" to be credible because to them he was believable. Credibility is a measure of how believable you are to those with whom you interact. The development of high credibility does not, of course, provide any assurance that you will achieve your objectives. Many other factors may also affect persuasive effectiveness (Brembeck & Howell, 1976). Generally, however, *the higher your credibility, the greater your chances for success as a persuader (*Burgoon & Saine, 1978).

Dimensions of Credibility

Credibility is a concept that has been studied extensively by communication scholars for at least three decades. These scholars have disagreed about how many dimensions define credibility and about the methodological procedures that should be used to discover such dimensions (Infante, Parker, Clarke, Wilson, & Nathu, 1983; Liska, 1978; Tucker, 1971). There does seem to be a consensus among credibility scholars with regard to two important definitional points, however: (a) the two most important dimensions of credibility are *competence* and *trustworthiness;* (2) *competence* is clearly the more important dimension of credibility.

Although *competence* and *trustworthiness* are clearly the two most important components of credibility, a third component, *dynamism,* is also frequently cited by speech communication scholars (Brembeck & Howell, 1976). Therefore, credibility is defined in this book by the three components just identified.

We should note that Infante (1980) argued that dynamism scales are evaluative scales that measure how "potent" a communicator's behavior is. He maintained that dynamism scales should, therefore, be included in the "general person perception set" that applies to impression formation, whereas competence and trustworthiness scales are properly used as measurements of a communication receiver's attitude toward the communication source.

McCroskey and Dunham's special report (1966) that identified two defining dimensions of credibility—competence or authoritativeness and trustworthiness or character—has proven to be a benchmark for credibility research. Not only did McCroskey and Dunham identify competence and trustworthiness as the two most important dimensions of credibility, but also the figures they cite for variance accounted for by the two factors suggested that competence is almost twice as important as trustworthiness. Although as many as five dimensions of credibility have been identified in empirical research (Burgoon, 1976), the most common finding in subsequent studies has been that competence and trustworthiness are the two central defining dimensions of credibility (Lui & Standing, 1989; McCroskey & Young, 1981; Sternthal, Phillips, & Dholakia, 1978). As was pointed out in Chapter 10 on impression management, the preponderance of impression management researchers also conclude that credibility is defined by the two dimensions of competence and trustworthiness. Because dynamism has also been identified as a third but much less important dimension than competence and trustworthiness, credibility will be treated as three-dimensional in this chapter.

How competent, trustworthy, and dynamic a communicator is judged to be will vary, depending on such factors as personal reputation, organizational affiliation, personal appearance, and, most importantly, communicative behaviors. Although individuals have the potential to exercise considerable control over their perceived credibility, we should recognize that credibility is not defined by inherent qualities or characteristics of the source. On the contrary, credibility or believability is the perception of the message sender by the *receiver.*

A person's perceived competence, trustworthiness, and dynamism can be positively or negatively affected in a given situation by the person's communication. For example, professors who provide inaccurate information in their lectures will lower their perceived competence. An individual's perceived competence, trustworthiness, and dynamism may vary from extremely high to extremely low in a given situation; therefore, those terms may be properly identified as *dimensions of credibility.*

Competence

Competence is an important dimension of credibility. Individuals who are recognized as experts on a given subject inspire confidence. Conversely, *incompetence* is a word with unflattering connotations. In our society, competence is associated with excellence. For example, universities that are widely recognized for their academic excellence receive such recognition in large part because their faculty members have been judged to be unusually competent.

As Table 11.1 suggests, an individual's perceived level of competence may be assessed by rating that individual on a set of scales that reflect how competent, qualified, well-informed, and intelligent that individual is judged to be. When individuals exhibit communicative behaviors that raise serious doubts about their competence, their competence ratings usually drop sharply.

TABLE 11.1 Measuring Personal Credibility

Dimensions of Credibility	Initial Credibility	Terminal Credibility
Competence		
1. competent/incompetent	_____	_____
2. qualified/unqualified	_____	_____
3. well-informed/poorly informed	_____	_____
4. intelligent/unintelligent	_____	_____
Trustworthiness		
1. honest/dishonest	_____	_____
2. straightforward/evasive	_____	_____
3. trustworthy/untrustworthy	_____	_____
4. sincere/insincere	_____	_____
Dynamism		
1. assertive/unassertive	_____	_____
2. bold/timid	_____	_____
3. forceful/meek	_____	_____
4. active/inactive	_____	_____

Communicator's Name _____

Until recently, competence was thought to be perceived almost solely according to the manifest content of a person's speech communication. The key questions were (a) how much relevant and useful information does an individual have on a given subject, (b) how familiar is the individual with that information, and (c) does the individual use that information effectively to support carefully qualified generalizations? We now know, however, that our nonverbal communication often exerts a dramatic influence on how competent we are perceived to be.

In the 1968 presidential campaign, Richard Nixon's advisors made unprecedented use of the potential of nonverbal cues to enhance Nixon's perceived competence. Nixon's advisors recognized that many Americans do not monitor the content of a politician's speech very closely, but they may be strongly affected by implicit messages communicated visually. Thus, Joe McGinniss wrote that

> *[the] words would be the same ones Nixon always used—the words of the acceptance speech. But they would all seem fresh and lively because a series of still pictures would flash on the screen while Nixon spoke. If it were done right, it would permit television to create a Nixon image that was entirely independent of the words.... The flashing pictures would be carefully selected to create the impression that somehow Nixon represented competence, respect for tradition, serenity.*
> (McGinniss, 1969, p. 85)

Trustworthiness

Not too long ago, a recent acquaintance invited me to go deep-sea fishing with him in the Gulf of Mexico. I raised some questions about the safety of such a venture in a relatively small boat. He understood that my unstated question (Did I trust him enough to go deep-sea fishing with him?) was more important than my implicit questions about his competence as a seaman. I have not yet answered that question in my own mind. I do recognize, however, that my response will be determined by how trustworthy I judge him to be.

As a dimension of credibility, *trustworthiness* is a measure of our character as seen by those persons with whom we interact. Our presumed level of trustworthiness is based on an assessment of our personal qualities, intentions, and attitudes. The dominant sources of information that are used to determine how trustworthy people are judged to be may be nonverbal (McMahan, 1976), because individuals will not usually tell you how honest or sincere they actually are. Their actions are usually more important than their words.

As Table 11.1 indicates, you can assess a person's perceived level of trustworthiness by rating that individual on a set of scales that reveal how honest, straightforward, trustworthy, and sincere you judge that individual to be. Successful communicators almost invariably receive high ratings on this dimension of credibility.

Dynamism

The third dimension of credibility—*dynamism*—defines people's credibility or image in terms of the level of confidence they are perceived to have. The ability to project a feeling of confidence is important because it is apt to trigger a reciprocal feeling of confidence in those with whom we communicate. Further, the more dynamic we are perceived to be, the more credible we are apt to be. According to one authority, the "shy, introverted, soft-spoken individual is generally perceived as less credible than the assertive, extroverted, and forceful individual. The great leaders in history have generally been dynamic people. They were assertive and dynamic people" (DeVito, 1980).

A communicator's level of dynamism can be accurately assessed by rating that individual on a set of scales that reflect how assertive, bold, forceful, and active he or she is judged to be. The meek may ultimately inherit the earth, but for the moment, at least, they have a serious credibility problem. Political satirists who delighted in their caricatures of the 1984 presidential candidate Walter Mondale as weak and indecisive obviously recognized the importance of dynamism in shaping perceptions of credibility. In the 1988 presidential campaign, George Bush was the frequent target of political satirists because of a dynamism deficit so serious that he was widely perceived to be a "wimp." Such caricatures had a humorous impact precisely because of the incongruous and implausible image conjured up by presidential candidates so lacking in dynamism.

The development of a communicator's credibility requires that individual dimensions of credibility be assessed at two points in time: *Initial credibility* is the credibility the communicator possesses *before* communication begins. *Terminal credibility* is the credibility that the communicator is seen to possess *after* communication occurs in a given situation. Terminal credibility is the product of the communicator's initial credibility and the credibility that was derived as a result of the individual's communicative behaviors (DeVito, 1980).

The scales in Table 11.1 should be used to make an accurate evaluation of a person's credibility. Write in the name of the communicator and rate the individual on the 12 scales measuring level of competence, trustworthiness, and dynamism. The initial set of ratings should be in the Initial Credibility column.

Imagine that the 12 sets of terms are on 12 separate bipolar scales. Use a seven-point scale to rate the person, with a 7 to identify the term on the left side of the scale and a 1 to identify the term on the right side of the scale. for example, if you judge an individual to be extremely competent before communication begins, you would put a 7 in the first blank in the Initial Credibility column. If you cannot decide whether the person is competent or incompetent, put a 4 in the same blank. A person perceived as extremely incompetent would receive a rating of 1. Any value from 7 through 1 may be used.

After the communication is completed, cover up the first column and rate the person again in the Terminal Credibility column. You should then have a before-and-after profile of the communicator's credibility.

Illustrating the Impact of Nonverbal Cues on Credibility

Presidential candidates engage in the type of personal selling that has generated widespread interest in this country. Millions of people study the candidates' efforts to sell themselves; those people then make their own judgments as to how the candidates' communication affected their credibility. Because of the high visibility of the candidates' communicative efforts, the presidential debates represent a useful vehicle for illustrating how nonverbal cues can affect credibility.

After the first televised presidential debate between Jimmy Carter and Gerald Ford in 1976, I was contacted by Rafshoon Advertising. Rafshoon was Carter's media advisor in that campaign. As the Rafshoon representative viewed the situation, Carter had a problem. All the public opinion polls showed Carter with a substantial lead over Ford *before* their first debate. Carter's advisors thought he had done well in the first debate, in terms of the traditional factors that are usually thought to affect credibility. He was well-informed on the major issues, he had good command of his information, and he took pains to qualify the generalizations he made.

In terms of his *speech communication,* Carter appeared to have been at least the equal of Gerald Ford. Nonetheless, the polls showed that Carter had lost the first debate, and a loss in the second debate would be a serious and possibly catastrophic blow to Carter's chances. The request from the Rafshoon representative was simple. Would I analyze Carter's nonverbal cues in the first debate in order to develop a nonverbal profile that might be used to enhance Carter's credibility in the second debate?

The Selling of Presidential Candidates

It was actually Gerald Ford who approached the first presidential debate with some serious image problems. Both friends and foes raised questions about his competence. Political satirists wondered aloud whether Ford was smart enough to think and chew gum at the same time. He was pictured on *Saturday Night Live* as an amiable but uncoordinated bumbler who fell off a ladder onto the White House Christmas tree while trying to trim it. Few had forgotten the satisfaction Lyndon Johnson seemed to get from saying that Gerald Ford had played much too much football "without a helmet."

Ford's own actions seemed to suggest that he might have been competent enough to have been a U.S. congressman from Michigan but raised doubts about his competence as president. Newspaper photographs frequently showed Ford hitting his head on the door of the presidential helicopter when exiting or falling on the ski slopes of Colorado. Some photos even showed one of his golf balls bouncing off the head of a spectator after an errant tee shot. Ford made matters even worse by his propensity for making such gaffes as appearing before a political rally in Nebraska and solemnly remarking how pleased he was to be in Kansas. Things were so bad at one point that Ford reportedly said he really enjoyed "watching" something on radio (Schlenker, 1980).

As the candidates approached the first presidential debate, there seemed good reason to believe that Gerald Ford had a serious credibility problem. The media had frequently depicted Ford as marginally competent, at best. In contrast, his opponent, Jimmy Carter, was thought to possess a first-rate mind. Aside from an admission that he was occasionally overcome by "lustful" thoughts, Carter had done little to damage his personal credibility, which had not been challenged as frequently or persistently as Ford's. Although one of Carter's opponents in the presidential primaries had run a television spot that showed Carter talking out of both sides of his mouth, his trustworthiness had not become an issue.

My careful analysis of the videotape of the first Ford–Carter debate resulted in some unanticipated conclusions (CBS Television, 1976). Gerald Ford projected an image of superior credibility. He did so by skillful use of visual cues. In contrast, Jimmy Carter's nonverbal communication was so ineffective as to raise serious questions about his competence, trustworthiness, and dynamism. Because I assessed the candidates' eye behaviors, gestures, postures, and vocal cues to be the nonverbal factors that most strongly affected the images they projected, my analysis of Ford's and Carter's nonverbal behaviors focused on those factors.

As I have already indicated in Chapter 3, eye behaviors are known to affect strongly the way we are perceived. The eye behaviors of the two candidates contrasted strikingly in the first debate. Carter almost always paused and looked down or away before answering a question. The characteristic direction of Carter's gaze was downcast when not speaking; instead of looking at Ford when Ford was speaking, Carter stared off into space or down at his notes. Carter also exhibited a high blink rate and often appeared shifty eyed. Ford, in contrast, sustained direct eye contact with the reporters when answering their questions and looked at Carter when Carter was speaking.

In my recommendations to Carter's media advisors, I emphasized that Carter must stop looking down at the beginning of each answer, must sustain eye contact with Ford while Ford is speaking, and must avoid the downcast eyes in all situations during the second presidential debate. To look down before answering a question and to exhibit shifty eyes while answering would likely affect Carter's perceived competence and trustworthiness negatively (Burgoon & Saine, 1978). The unwillingness to establish or maintain eye contact with Ford during the first debate quite clearly suggested a lack of assertiveness and even timidity, both of which are associated with the nondynamic individual. Worst of all, Carter's characteristically downcast eyes connoted qualities inconsistent with the desired image of a man trying to sell himself as the nation's leader. For those reasons, I concluded that Ford's eye behaviors, when compared with Carter's, played an important role in the first debate and helped Ford to project an image of superior competence, trustworthiness, and dynamism.

Ford and Carter exhibited gestures that differed noticeably, with regard to both number and kind. Many, but not all, of Ford's gestures seemed calculated to create the impression that he was a powerful person. His frequent hand gestures were so forceful that they resembled a subdued karate chop. Ford combined his forceful hand gestures with frequent head nodding and shoulder movement to add emphasis and feeling to the points that he was making verbally. In short, Ford used illustrator gestures purposefully to make him seem more dynamic.

In contrast, Carter used few gestures. The gestures he did use were weak and tentative, for the most part, and took the form of adaptor gestures. Carter's gentle hand gestures suggested a lack of confidence and an elevated level of anxiety. For example, Carter licked his lips, moved his hands in and out of his pockets, and sometimes put his hands together in a prayerful position. The aggregate effect was to depress Carter's perceived dynamism and make him appear to be anxious.

In my recommendations, I stressed that Carter should use many, and more forceful, hand gestures to emphasize the points about which he felt deeply. At the same time, he would have to eliminate the gestures that suggested he was hesitant, uncertain, or tentative about his answers. Ford's gestures gave him an additional advantage over Carter, although eye behaviors were more important than gestures in the candidates' efforts to sell themselves nonverbally.

Posture is very significant for individuals who wish to be perceived as credible leaders, because it is known to be a potent source of information about another person's power. In the Ford–Carter debate, Ford made skillful use of the image-building potential of certain types of postures. If you have viewed videotapes of the debate, perhaps you noticed that Ford's characteristic posture was that of standing with his feet and arms spread widely, gripping the opposite sides of the podium. He usually leaned forward as he began to answer a question and increased the forward lean during the answer. Ford's widespread stance helped him to project an image of superior power; as he spoke, the forward lean communicated a sense of confidence and immediacy; and his fairly frequent postural shifts made him seem responsive to the reporter's questions. Although Ford's postures were somewhat exaggerated, they were synchronized with his gestures in such a manner as to suggest quite clearly that this was not a man who was apt to fall out of his helicopter or onto the family Christmas tree.

Carter, in contrast, rarely if ever spread his arms expansively in front of him or leaned forward. In fact his relative bodily rigidity, when combined with hands clasped in what appeared to be almost a prayerful pose, suggested a passivism that was not useful for a person trying to project the image of a dynamic leader and man of action. Leaders are usually viewed as active rather than passive.

In short, Ford exhibited many of the positive indicators of perceived power identified in Chapter 4, and Carter exhibited a distressing number of nonverbal cues that are known to be indicators of powerlessness. My recommendation to Carter was to accentuate the gestures and postures associated with perceptions of power and to de-emphasize those gestures and postures associated with powerlessness.

Neither candidate used the image-molding potential of vocal cues to good effect. Ford's voice lacked the orotund quality that would make it pleasing, and his tendency to give vocal emphasis to unimportant words, as opposed to thought units, hardly had the effect of accentuating his intellectual capacity. At the same time, Ford's substantial volume helped him communicate a sense of emotional intensity.

Carter's use of his voice was less than desirable for at least three reasons. First, his speaking rate was much too fast. At a number of points in the debate, Carter's speaking rate was in the range of 200 to 260 words per minute. A speaking rate of over 275 words per minute makes comprehension difficult, particularly if the communicator is using a regional dialect. When speaking at 200 to 260 words per minute, Carter had exceeded the range for conversational speech by around 100 words per minute. Such a rapid speaking rate also creates the impression that a person is anxious.

Secondly, Carter exhibited a very narrow pitch and volume range and dropped his voice at the end of sentences. Anything approaching monotone speech makes the communicator seem to be emotionally uninvolved, uninteresting, and nondynamic. The personality traits and personal qualities usually ascribed to a communicator who is vocally unexpressive are primarily negative.

Third, Carter paused frequently, filled a number of his pauses with nonfluencies such as "ah," and repeated certain words. By exhibiting those vocal phenomena, Carter reinforced the impression that he lacked confidence. *To be persuasive, the communicator must sound confident.* We know that

> *[the] ideal voice is smooth, free of hesitation, and clear, possesses good tone and volume, and varies in speech rate. Public speaking experts and coaches agree that speakers who control loudness, pitch, fluency, resonance, and rate of speech are thought to be more active and dynamic, more persuasive.* (Gray, 1982, pp. 85–86)

I recommended that Carter take the necessary actions to develop a more confident speaking voice in the second presidential debate with Gerald Ford. To communicate greater emotional involvement and commitment to the positions he was taking, Carter had to use greater variation in pitch and volume. To become more conversational, he would have to slow down his speaking rate. Finally, he would have to minimize nonfluencies because nonfluencies are usually perceived to be strong and reliable indicators of an elevated level of anxiety.

Although some of Carter's media advisors were concerned about the impact of his personal appearance in the debates, I do not believe the candidates' personal appearances strongly affected the images they projected. Personal appearance is particularly important in shaping the first impression an individual makes, but both candidates were already well-known by the electorate.

Carter was subsequently briefed on the probable perceptual impact of specific kinds of communicative behaviors before his second debate with Gerald Ford. Polls showed that Carter won the second debate, in the opinion of the American electorate. However, a Gallup poll conducted for *Newsweek* magazine (Cooper, 1979) indicated that 50 percent were not sure. Those polled also felt that Carter was better informed than Ford and that Carter would be more honest and open with the public about his foreign policy. In short, Carter was judged to be more credible on the important dimensions of competence and trustworthiness. Ken Cooper (1979) concluded that "the NVC [nonverbal communication] information these two candidates transmitted in the debates explains the results of the poll, and ultimately the choice Americans made for President" (p. 185).

I certainly would not claim that Carter's nonverbal communication in the second debate with Ford was responsible for his victory in that debate. During the second debate, however, Carter controlled his eye behavior and used gestures, postures, and vocal cues much more skillfully than he had done in the first debate—for the purpose of selling himself nonverbally. His media advisors apparently also felt that nonverbal factors played an important role in the second debate. After Carter was elected, I got another call from a Rafshoon representative. He generously offered to contribute all of the television videotapes and radio audiotapes of commercials used in the primaries and the presidential campaign to me, and through me to the University of Georgia, as a gesture of appreciation for my analysis of the role nonverbal factors played in affecting Jimmy Carter's image in his debates with Ford.

During the presidential campaign of 1988, I was asked by *The Washington Post* to analyze the impact of then-Governor Michael Dukakis's nonverbal cues on his personal credibility. Other analysts of political communication also contributed to an article written by Lloyd Grove that was titled "Dukakis: If He Only Had a Heart (His Video-Image Scorecard—Brains 10, Warmth 0)" (1988). I subsequently expanded that brief analysis reported in the newspaper article for a convention paper in which I compared Dukakis and Bush not only with regard to how well they did on the important image dimension of credibility, but also on the three other image dimensions of likability, interpersonal attractiveness, and dominance. Part of that analysis is provided in Chapter 10 on impression management.

My analysis of the first Dukakis–Bush debate (1988) led me to conclude that Dukakis's "greatest strength is his communication of competence." As I have already noted, a number of studies indicate that people tend to key in on eye behaviors as an indication of how well candidates know what they are talking about. Dukakis's eye contact in the first presidential debate with George Bush was remarkable by almost any standard. When asked a question, he maintained eye contact with the questioner; he almost never looked down before he responded; and whenever Bush was talking, he maintained eye contact with Bush.

Only Dukakis's high blink rate and slightly accelerated speaking rate (up to 195 words a minute, or a bit beyond the conversational norm) suggested that he was nervous or lacked confidence; these behaviors could have had a negative impact on the dynamism dimension of credibility. Bush, by contrast, seldom maintained eye contact, looked down often before answering a question, and occasionally rolled his eyes upward, all probably indicators of discomfort. Finally, Dukakis had minimal *response latency* (the time it take to begin to answer), whereas Bush's performance was marked by long pauses and false starts. *The less time people take to respond to a question, the more competent they will be perceived to be.* Nonverbally, as well as verbally, Dukakis clearly communicated the impression that he had a decided edge in competence over George Bush.

Trustworthiness was the credibility dimension with which Dukakis had a serious problem. It has already been established that we tend to trust most those individuals who are open, straightforward, and emotionally disclosing. Governor Dukakis was called the "Ice Man" for a reason—there was almost nothing in his nonverbal communication (the primary means of expressing emotion) to suggest that he had feelings. When you express a feeling, you run a risk—you might be rejected. If you do not communicate any emotion, you avoid the risk of rejection, but you run a different type of risk—you might not be trusted. The unfortunate fact for Dukakis was that many of the things he did nonverbally reinforced the idea that he is an emotionally undisclosing man who lacks spontaneity. His voice was monotonous, and with his mechanical hand gestures, he almost looked like a toy soldier.

Dukakis's biggest liability in terms of trustworthiness was probably his smile. When Dukakis smiled during the first debate with Bush, viewers saw a lot of teeth but no crow's-feet around the eyes. Dukakis's smile is a lower-face phenomenon; there is reason to doubt the sincerity of a smile that isn't reflected throughout the face. Because his smile was fixed in the lower part of his face, Dukakis often appeared to mask emotions rather than exhibiting the felt happy smile that is associated with the emotionally disclosing person.

In short, Dukakis was extraordinarily strong on the competence dimension of credibility, but he had a definite deficit in terms of trustworthiness. We have already seen that he had another advantage over George Bush in that he dominated him visually. However, Dukakis had such a serious deficit on two of the other image dimensions—likability and interpersonal attractiveness—that the overall impression made by George Bush in the first presidential debate was more favorable than the impression made by Michael Dukakis.

Finally, let us consider the presidential campaign of 1996. Assume for the moment that this campaign is upcoming. Assume also that you have been asked by Senator Robert Dole's campaign manager to work for Dole as an image analyst. Your primary task is to study the defining features of Dole's nonverbal communication style. More specifically, you are to identify those nonverbal cues and behaviors exhibited by Dole that affect his credibility in strongly positive and negative ways. Dole's campaign manager has asked you to answer the following question: How do Senator Dole's eye behaviors, gestures, postures, and vocal cues affect his personal credibility? Although you have been asked to focus on the impact of Dole's nonverbal communication on his personal credibility, you will also comment briefly on President Bill Clinton's nonverbal communication style by way of comparison.

On the positive side, Senator Dole has risen to one of the most prestigious leadership positions in the United States after serving 35 years in Congress and serving as Senate majority leader; for a number of years he served as Senate minority leader for the Republican party. Dole is perceived as a pragmatic politician, a Washington insider who is skilled at the art of vote counting, compromise, and dealmaking. In fact, some critics have labeled him "The Great Equivocator" because of his propensity to compromise.

There is reason to think that Dole is viewed as a man of experience, character, and brave determination. His image as a courageous person is undoubtedly attributable in large part to his military service and to the fact that after he was severely wounded in Italy during World War II he was sent home in a body cast to die. Dole's wounds crushed his vertebrae and mangled his right arm, leaving his right arm and hand virtually useless. Because he has very limited use of his right arm today, he places a pen or pencil in his right hand so that his fingers will not splay and he greets individuals with his left hand. (Duffy & Gibbs, 1995). In spite of his rather severe physical disability, Dole managed to emerge as a major figure in national politics.

Political insiders identify four image problems with which Dole must cope successfully in the 1996 presidential campaign: his relatively advanced age in a culture that values youth, his abrasive personality, his status as a Washington insider at a time when the mood of the country favors the outsider, and the perception by the right wing of the Republican party that Dole's middle-of-the-road pragmatism is much too distant from their own zealous brand of conservatism. Because of his pragmatism and his willingness to compromise on the issues, Dole—like President Clinton—has been criticized as a man without convictions who vacilitates on the issues (Kilgore, 1995).

Dole and his advisors are particularly concerned with his image as a septuagenarian. They could not have been pleased when *Time* magazine (Duffy & Gibbs, 1995), in an issue that featured Dole in its lead article, raised this ominous question next to his photograph on the front cover: "Is Dole Too Old for the Job?"

An early effort by Dole's advisors to cope with the age issue was not promising. They started by getting a photograph of Dole published in many leading newspapers that showed him walking on a treadmill. Alas, Dole was incongruously attired in a formal, long-sleeved shirt along with black-and-white striped shorts that looked like they might be his underwear rather than his running shorts. The unintended and silent message that this posed photograph communicated was not helpful: Senator Dole is in fact too old and too old-fashioned to be president. The further inference is surely that Dole is totally out of contact with yuppies and the younger generation.

Dole's image advisors tried to recover by issuing detailed results from a medical exam that showed Dole to be in very good health for a man of his age. They released a nine-page document on Dole's 72nd birthday that offered the most detailed and complete medical information ever released on a presidential candidate. Dole himself tried to blunt the age issue by saying, "I'll put Strom Thurmond on the ticket for age balance." At the same time, Dole probably recognizes that although countries like Japan venerate the old, the United States tends to celebrate youth.

The other part of Dole's image that is most problematic is his reputation for being abrasive. His penchant for putting down political opponents with what has been seen as mean-spirited humor and a glowering, dour demeanor has resulted in some persisting nicknames that suggest the nature of this part of Dole's image problem: "Nixon's Doberman pinscher," "hatchet man," and "Nasty Bob." During the 1988 presidential campaign, Dole delighted in referring to the ideas of Democratic candidate Michael Dukakis as "Du-cockeyed." His biting humor is also reflected in the way he has greeted female acquaintances on the streets of his hometown of Russell, Nebraska: "So you just visited the beauty parlor today, eh? Obviously it was closed" (Harzog, 1995).

The nonverbal communicative behaviors that Senator Dole and President Clinton exhibit during the presidential campaign of 1996 will undoubtedly play a central role in minimizing or exacerbating the image problems they brought to the campaign. Surely, the dominant features of their nonverbal communication styles will strongly affect their personal credibility. The following analysis is based on close observation of videotapes of Senator Robert Dole's appearances on ABC's *Nightline* on June 29 and on November 29, 1994, and on CBS's *Face the Nation* on October 7, 1995.

Dole's eye behaviors should help to enhance perceptions that he is a competent person. He does an excellent job sustaining eye contact while both listening and speaking. In addition, he rarely pauses and looks down before responding to a question.

In other respects, however, Dole's eye behaviors are a disaster. The most outstandingly negative feature of his eye behaviors is a blink rate so high as almost to defy belief. In three recent television appearances Dole's blink rate ranged from 150 to 160 blinks per minute. In addition, some of his eye blinks come with such machine-gun rapidity that they suggest that Dole is about to have some type of seizure. This blink rate is apt to strongly depress his ratings on the dynamism dimension of personal credibility. Dynamism, as reflected by a more midrange blink rate, tends to correlate highly with the perception that an individual is confident. As the blink rate increases, however, perceived confidence tends to decrease. As you will recall, one of the nonverbal factors judged to have the most negative impact on Jimmy Carter's confidence level in his debate with Gerald Ford was his high blink rate. Without a doubt, Dole's blink rate is much faster than Carter's.

In his two appearances on *Nightline,* Dole exhibited almost no tendency to be shifty eyed. In his appearance on *Face the Nation,* however, Dole was extremely shifty eyed; he has also been observed to be shifty eyed in other public appearances. During his appearance on *Face the Nation,* Dole's eye-shift rate ranged from 130 to 156 shifts a minute. With an accelerated eye-shift rate such as this, Dole's eyes appear to be darting from side to side, giving the effect that they are almost dancing. Harzog (1995), who observed Dole's video-taped appearance at the 1988 Republican convention, also concluded that Dole is highly shifty eyed. She noted that Dole's shifty-eyed behavior detracts from perceptions of trustworthiness, and hence, from perceptions of credibility. If Dole's eyes exhibit a high degree of shiftiness during the intense pressure he will experience during the 1996 presidential campaign, the shifting eyes will surely make observers perceive him much more negatively on the trustworthiness dimension of credibility. Our society has a strong eye behavior stereotype that specifies that shifty-eyed people are untrustworthy.

In terms of gestures and posture, Dole is strikingly impassive, unexpressive, and unassertive. A good part of his problem may be attributed to his serious war injuries. In the three televised appearances studied, the cameras were sufficiently close up that only Senator Dole's face and shoulders and about six inches of his upper torso were visible. Perhaps there is an unwritten agreement among television people that Dole's crippled right arm and hand will rarely be shown on the air. In one sense, this may be an advantage to Dole because it tends to divert attention from his physical disability. On the other hand, Dole loses the great potential to be expressive and assertive that hand gestures would give him.

If presidential candidate Michael Dukakis was called the "Ice Man" because he communicated so little about his emotions, Senator Dole might be called the "Immobile Man" because of his lack of bodily movement. Dole is unusually stiff on television. Because of the relatively tight close-ups, the only bodily movement that Dole is observed to exhibit with some degree of frequency is a slight but perceptible head nod as if to affirm the point he is making. Very rarely Dole's left hand will appear briefly on screen making a gesture of limited intensity. Thus, Dole's absence of gestures enhance the perception that he lacks dynamism. Dynamism, or assertiveness, in turn is viewed as essential to projecting the visual image of a leader. Dole uses few gestures and the occasional gesture he does use is not particularly firm.

Posture is, of course, extremely important in shaping judgments of dynamism, particularly the power dimension. Harzog (1995) argued that Dole's upright posture helps him "exude a great deal of presence." The salient point, however, is that Dole's posture appears to be fixed, rigid, and unchanging. Such immobility tends to define one as lacking dynamism. Indeed, communicators who are perceived as dynamic assume an open and relaxed posture, use postural shifts to communicate interest in what they are saying or in those with whom they are communicating, and lean forward to emphasize a point they are making. Senator Dole, the Immobile Man, does none of these things.

Finally, what about Senator Dole's vocal cues? He speaks with a deep, orotund voice, at a conversational rate (a slightly elevated 195 words per minute), and he pauses effectively to give emphasis to the points he is making. In addition, he sometimes emphasizes his points by slightly increasing his speaking rate or volume. These factors should enhance judgments made of Dole on the competence dimension of credibility.

The fact that Dole's "gravelly" voice sometimes sounds flat, nasal, and harsh means that he is apt to be perceived as a somewhat unpleasant individual. Vocally, Dole's greatest deficiency is that he speaks with a very limited pitch range. His near monotone delivery usually reinforces the impression that he is unexciting and surely uninteresting.

Finally, Dole is generally fluent but when under pressure he has a tendency to become dysfluent. When Forrest Sawyer told Dole on *Nightline* that 70 percent of those polled disapprove of what the Republicans are doing on health care, Dole because noticeably dysfluent. He replied after a pause, "Well, it's, ah, it's [pause] a different poll than I have seen." Under the extreme pressure he will experience during the presidential campaign, therefore, Dole exhibits a predisposition that may result in high dysfluency. High dysfluency, in turn, can negatively affect the way one is perceived on both the competence and trustworthiness dimensions of credibility.

The features of Senator Dole's nonverbal communication style just identified will in all probability result in him being perceived by the public and caricatured by the media as a would-be leader sorely lacking in dynamism. His stiff and unexpressive public demeanor is not likely to be useful as he tries to defuse the age issue. In addition, because of his nonverbal cues Senator Dole is apt to be perceived as a person lacking in likability. He may certainly be perceived as dour, forbidding, and unapproachable. If so, this part of his image may be attributed to the fact that he almost never smiles in public, has extremely heavy and bushy eyebrows that make his dour expressions even more forbidding if not threatening, has deep lines permanently etched across his forehead, and perhaps most importantly, lacks bodily movements. Thus, he fails to display many of the nonverbal behaviors that correlate strongly with positive perceptions that a person is likable.

If Senator Dole might justifiably be called the Immobile Man, President Clinton might be called the "Friendly Man." In this instance the striking contrast in the images that the public may claim for each candidate may not of course be the decisive factor that determines the outcome of the presidential race. First, victory or defeat may well primarily result from situational factors that neither presidential candidate can control, such as the state of the economy, the degree of conflict at the international level, and so forth. Then too the objective analyst will recognize that "candidate" Bill Clinton must also confront serious image problems. Like Dole he has been criticized as being a vacillator who waffles on the issues when under pressure. His ultraconservative opponents have pilloried him in the media by claiming almost unbelievably negative images for him, such as identifying Clinton as an immoral philanderer who cheats on his wife, a draft dodger, a liar, someone with direct links to the underworld, one who panders to public opinion, and so on.

You are working as an image analyst for Senator Dole so you must take a realistic look at the communicative assets President Clinton brings to the 1996 presidential campaign in terms of his nonverbal communication style. First, you recognize that Clinton has revolutionized campaigning by using interactive media for the first time. He relishes the opportunity to appear live before a small audience in a television studio and interact with members of the audience in an informal, unrehearsed manner without using notes. Second, you recognize that Clinton is strong precisely where Dole is weak—he uses nonverbal communication skillfully to make himself appear to be a highly likable, sincere, and dynamic person.

As Senator Dole's image analyst, you would be well advised to study a videotape of Clinton's appearance on MTV's "Music Television—Choose or Lose." Clinton appeared live on this program during the 1992 presidential campaign and interacted with a small audience in the television studio.

Clinton is a confident and skilled communicator. Unlike Senator Dole, he does not exhibit highly distracting nonverbal behaviors that suggest that he lacks confidence. Whereas Dole exhibits an almost unbelievably high blink rate as well as shifty eyes, Clinton sustains direct eye contact with his audience. Clinton blinks a low two to three times a minute, for example.

In contrast to Senator Dole, the Immobile Man, President Clinton uses bodily movements forcefully and naturally to emphasize the most important points he is making. Significantly, his bodily movements are synchronized with vocal cues such as the pause for effect and an increase in the rate or volume of his voice for emphasis. During his appearance on MTV, Clinton said, "We have quadrupled the national debt in 12 years." While making this statement, Clinton spread his arms wide in an expansive gesture as if to emphasize how fast the national debt has increased. In addition, when Clinton wants to emphasize a point or focus the audience's attention, he holds up a finger.

In contrast to Senator Dole, Clinton's posture is open and relaxed. Moreover, Clinton looks like he is enjoying himself while interacting with an audience. If you had to choose a single word to characterize Clinton's nonverbal communication style, it would probably be "pleasant." In contrast, Senator Dole often looks stern, serious, and unapproachable during his appearances in public. Clinton's great edge in pleasantness and likability may certainly be traced to the fact that he seems to minimize the distance between himself and those with whom he interacts, and he does so with a style that accentuates informality and close personal contact. Dole in contrast appears to cultivate a stiff informality that makes it difficult for people to get close to him at least in a figurative sense.

In short, Senator Dole may bring a number of political assets to the 1996 presidential campaign that President Clinton cannot match. In terms of building his personal credibility, however, Dole's nonverbal communication style is not one of those advantages.

The Selling of Corporate Sale Representatives

Nonverbal factors quite clearly do play a central role in determining how successfully presidential candidates and others sell themselves nonverbally. Although most of you are not likely to be a presidential candidate, you may someday be in a situation in which the selling of your abilities is important. Most of us attach importance to success in the job interview, where the ability to sell oneself is pitted against the abilities of competing job applicants.

Modern corporations recognize that you must sell yourself to potential customers before they will buy from you. The sales training manual of one corporation, Burst Inc., identifies "Sell Yourself First" as a principle of overriding importance in sales training. Sales trainees are reminded to sell themselves first, even though some "people think it's an old worn-out cliche, but it's not worn out. It's absolutely essential for success in selling or any other occupation."

My own experience in presenting sales and communication programs to corporate sales representatives has convinced me that nonverbal factors are vitally important in personal selling. The case of Omar Johnson helped to convince me. Omar is a sales representative for a pharmaceutical company. He has been reasonably successful because he works hard and has good product knowledge. He does not make a good first impression, however, primarily because he stutters, fills his frequent pauses with nonfluencies, and is vocally unexpressive.

Recently, a sales manager received a telephone call from a salesman who wanted to discuss an upcoming visit he was to make with a sales prospect. After talking to the salesman for five minutes, the sales manager realized he did not know to whom he was talking, so he asked, "Who is this?" The caller replied in a carefully modulated voice, which was free of stutters or nonfluencies, "Why this is Omar Johnson. Don't you know who I am? I have worked for you for 10 years." The sales manager was amazed because Omar projected such a totally different image, by vocal means, that he was unrecognizable. "What have you done, Omar?" said the sales manager. "You have changed dramatically. You now seem to be confident and forceful." Omar explained, it "is the sales and communication program that I recently attended. I saw myself on the six-foot television screen for the first time, and I listened to myself. I looked and sounded like a fool. Since then, I've practiced my sales presentation on a tape recorder, and I'm a new man."

The sales manager subsequently accompanied Omar when he made a sales presentation to a prospect. Omar used his newly acquired communication skills to project an image of a much more competent, trustworthy, and dynamic salesperson. He persuaded the prospect to use a large quantity of the product that he was selling. Omar's sales manager was so impressed that he recommended that all of his company's salespeople be required to take a sales and communication training program. The company is currently implementing the sales manager's recommendation. The training program emphasizes the central role of nonverbal cues in developing the credibility of the corporate sales representative.

I have had the opportunity to observe and analyze the persuasive efforts of individuals who were selling products that ranged from wine to electrical appliances to fertilizer. Although product salespeople and politicians must both sell themselves first, the selling situations they encounter are different in important respects. Politicians who attempt to sell themselves on television via a persuasive speech have control over many situational variables. Their captive audiences have no opportunity to provide immediate feedback, therefore the politician need not make any on-the-spot adjustments in a preplanned message. The well-known politician need not be concerned about exercising the listening skills associated with effective communicative interaction, because no direct interaction with another individual occurs.

But corporate sales representatives engage in interpersonal rather than public communication. Because they interact directly with prospective customers, they cannot adhere rigidly to a preplanned text. They frequently encounter sales resistance that is both unanticipated and unwelcome or questions that directly challenge their credibility. To be successful, they must be able to adjust to the continually changing demands of distinctive kinds of communicative situations over which they can exercise only partial control.

Because of the distinctive situational demands of successful product selling, the development and maintenance of a corporate salesperson's personal credibility are particular challenges. To meet the constant threats to their credibility, less successful salespeople often communicate in ways that are either inappropriately aggressive or unassertive. The aggressive salesperson, for example, seems to take pride in cultivating an image of irreverence, toughness, and insensitivity that limits sales.

The development of a salesperson's credibility places a premium on the ability to communicate in an assertive, as opposed to an unassertive or aggressive, manner. Judgments of a salesperson's level of assertiveness are strongly affected by the nature of his or her visual and vocal communication.

The Nonverbal Unassertive Salesperson

Many corporate sales representatives are so unassertive visually and vocally that they damage their credibility. Visually unassertive salespeople rarely look at the prospect during the greeting or the close of a sale, and they fail to sustain eye contact during the sales presentation. They tend to reveal their anxiety by means of hand-to-face gestures and other extraneous movements, and they use few gestures to emphasize the selling points they do make. Their rigid bodily posture makes them seem unresponsive to what the customer is saying. *Nonverbally unassertive sales representatives frequently respond in inappropriate nonverbal ways when they encounter sales resistance or receive negative feedback from the customer.* When encountering sales resistance, many salespeople become defensive; they cross their arms over their chest, smile nervously, and laugh at inappropriate times.

The nonverbally unassertive salesperson usually does not sound convincing. I was dismayed when I heard one salesman ask a client, "Can I send out five cases of our product, then?" in such a timid and unassertive tone of voice as to almost assure noncompliance. If you do not sound convinced that you are selling a product with many tangible benefits, how can you expect the sales prospect to be convinced?

Vocally unassertive salespeople often try to let their product sell itself. They tend to read to the prospective customer from company literature in an unexpressive voice that suggests a lack of enthusiasm about the product. Their speaking rate is too fast to allow purposeful pauses just before they make their most important selling points. Although they may not speak in a monotone, their pitch and volume ranges are narrow. Their anxiety is reflected not only in an excessive speaking rate but also in the nonfluencies they utter.

I made the following recommendations to one vocally unassertive salesperson, after listening to his sales presentation:

> *Avoid dropping the pitch of your voice at the end of sentences, since this practice makes you seem less enthusiastic about the product you are selling—and indecisive. Your fast speaking rate and many filled pauses will have the effect of eroding your perceived competence. When you asked the customer whether you could "send out five cases of our product?" you said it with a lack of conviction that might make it more likely that the customer would hesitate, or say no. Be sure to enunciate clearly and speak with vocal conviction. You must sound convinced that*

you are selling a superior product. Work for greater variation in pitch, rate, and volume. Practice your sales presentation with a tape recorder, in order to develop a persuasive voice.

The Nonverbally Aggressive Salesperson

Nonverbally aggressive salespeople have a different problem that threatens their perceived trustworthiness. They act and sound aggressive. Their apparent confidence borders on arrogance. Their visual and vocal image is such that customers can hardly avoid the feeling that they are being coerced rather than persuaded.

The aggressive salesperson frequently fixes the prospect with an unremitting stare, assumes a belligerent posture, and shakes a finger in the prospect's face in order to emphasize a selling point. Exaggerated gestures and postures are often combined with manipulative questions and judgmental statements, such as: "Why ask me?"; "Don't you agree?"; "Isn't that right?"; and "That's a false economy, son." *Unassertive salespeople become defensive when they encounter sales resistance, but the aggressive salesperson often becomes condescending.* The stare becomes more pronounced, the tone of voice becomes sarcastic, and volume becomes excessive. Nonverbal condescension is reinforced

CARTOON 11.1

by statements such as, "It would be a serious mistake not to use our product" or "Did you really buy that product?"

In their zeal to sell their product, aggressive salespeople appear to be insensitive to the needs and feelings of the prospect. They not only dominate the prospect visually, vocally, and verbally, but they are poor listeners. Unknowingly, they parody the hard-sell image of the used-car salesperson, who is commonly believed to have a credibility problem of gigantic proportions.

After evaluating the unsuccessful sales presentation of one aggressive salesman, I made the following recommendations to him:

> *In your sales presentation, you were so forceful that you ran the risk of being perceived as aggressive. Avoid putting the customer down, sounding argumentative when the customer raises objections, and pointing and shaking your finger at him. Note that at times your unremitting eye contact, your strident and condescending tone of voice, and your emotionally loaded gestures made you seem aggressive and less empathic than you actually are. The ring of conviction in your voice can be a real selling asset, but do not get carried away so that you sound like Mr. Hardsell. Given your ability to establish rapport with the customer, I am not sure why you lost this advantage by becoming aggressive. Rather than drawing the customer out and letting him do the talking, it seemed that you were determined to control the conversation from your frame of reference. In short, seek to be nonverbally assertive rather than aggressive.*

Developing Personal Credibility

The foregoing examples were designed to illustrate the impact of nonverbal cues on credibility. A careful reading of the previous section should give you a rather good idea of what you should and should not do if you wish to sell yourself nonverbally. Nonetheless, you might find it helpful to have a specific set of guidelines to use for developing your own credibility. Figure 11.1 presents such a set of guidelines. The guidelines focus on the four classes of nonverbal cues that are known to have the strongest potential for affecting personal credibility. Study the guidelines carefully, for they represent the nonverbal profile of the credible communicator.

You will recognize that the potentially powerful impact of nonverbal cues on perceived credibility is not confined to presidential candidates and corporate salespeople. The impact of individuals' communicative behaviors/cues has been proved to be greater than the impact of their verbal communication in many different interpersonal contexts. Significantly, the impact of nonverbal communication is most pronounced on the most important dimension of credibility, competence (Barak, Patkin, & Dell, 1982). You also should note that the impact of a person's nonverbal communicative behaviors/cues on perceived competence is greater during the early part of interaction with another person (Exline, 1985).

Eye behaviors are treated first because they play a central role in the development of personal credibility. We spend much more time monitoring the eye region of persons with whom we interact than any other part of their body; therefore, eye behaviors strongly affect judgments of credibility.

FIGURE 11.1   Guidelines for Developing Your Nonverbal Credibility

Eye Behavior

Eye behaviors represent particularly important cues that are used to make judgments about individuals' credibility. A well-developed cultural stereotype for Americans specifies the kinds of eye behaviors that will raise and lower a communicator's credibility.

Positive Eye Behaviors: Sustained eye contact while talking to others; sustained eye contact while others talk to you; and the maintenance of direct but not continuous eye contact with the individual(s) with whom you are communicating.

Negative Eye Behaviors: Looking down before responding to a question; exhibiting shifty eyes; looking away from the person with whom you are communicating; keeping your eyes downcast; excessive blinking; and eye-flutter.

Gestures

Positive Gestures: Gestures should be used to add emphasis to the points you are making; gestures should appear spontaneous, unrehearsed, and relaxed; gestures should be used to signal whether you wish to continue talking or wish another individual to begin talking; hands and elbows should be kept away from the body; and gestures should be used to communicate the intensity of your feelings and emotions.

Negative Gestures: Gestures that suggest a communicator lacks confidence, is defensive, or is nervous should be avoided. Hand-to-face gestures, throat-clearing, fidgeting, tugging at clothing, visible perspiration on face or body, lip-licking, hand-wringing, finger-tapping, extraneous head movements, out-of-context smiling and grimacing, and weak and tentative gestures should be avoided, as they are apt to undermine a communicator's credibility.

Postures

Posture is particularly important in communicating an individual's status or power; how responsive the communicator is; and how strongly a communicator desires to establish a warm rapport with interaction partners.

Positive Postures: Communicators who wish to be perceived as powerful will spread their arms expansively in front of them, will assume an open and relaxed posture, and will walk confidently. Responsiveness is communicated by frequent and forceful postural shifts while communicating. Rapport is established in part by leaning forward and smiling (when appropriate) as you begin to answer a question.

Negative Postures: Communicators should avoid constricted postures that suggest that they are timid or lack assertiveness. Bodily rigidity, crossed arms and legs, arms and legs kept close to the body, and overall bodily tension are apt to impair a communicator's credibility.

Voice

Communicators' vocal cues frequently play a major role in shaping their credibility. The personality characteristics communicators are presumed to have are often determined by the sound of their voices. Vocal qualities shape impressions about credibility, status, and power.

Positive Vocal Cues: A communicator should strive for a conversational speaking style while recognizing that a moderately fast rate will enhance perceived competence. Appropriate variation in pitch, rate, and volume is particularly important in projecting the image of a confident, competent, and dynamic person. Monotone delivery should be avoided. Sufficient volume has been found to be important for individuals who wish to be perceived as competent and dynamic.

Negative Vocal Cues: Communicators should avoid speaking in such a way that their voices sound flat, tense, or nasal. Nasality is a particularly undesirable vocal quality. Communicators should also avoid speaking at an excessive rate and should not use frequent, lengthy pauses, which suggest lack of confidence and sometimes a lack of competence. The following nonfluencies have been shown to have a markedly negative impact on credibility: "ahs," repeating words, interruptions or pauses in mid-sentence, omitting parts of words, and stuttering. Persons who wish to enhance their credibility should strive to eliminate the use of such nonfluencies.

Chapter 3 discussed in detail some of the reasons our eye behaviors play such a central role in developing or damaging our personal credibility. Perhaps the most important reason is that our eye behaviors directly reflect the amount of self-confidence we are perceived to have. We know that communicators who exhibit behavioral "tension-leakage" cues in the form of nonfluencies, shifty eyes, and lip moistening will be judged to be less competent than those who do not (Exline, 1985). Jurich and Jurich (1974) found that failure to sustain eye contact correlated more highly with traditional measures of a communicator's level of anxiety than any other type of nonverbal cue. In short, *failure to sustain eye contact is the most damaging thing you can do nonverbally if you are particularly concerned about being perceived as confident.*

Eye behaviors are important determinants of credibility (Beebe, 1974; Burgoon, Coker, & Coker, 1986; Burgoon, Manusov, Mineo, & Hale, 1985; Burgoon & Saine, 1978; Edinger & Patterson, 1983; Harper, Wiens, & Matarazzo, 1978; Hemsley & Doob, 1978; Kleinke, 1975). They are important because we are simply not believable unless we exhibit certain types of eye behaviors (Webbink, 1986). Figure 11.1 specifies which eye behaviors should and should not be exhibited in developing personal credibility. As you study Figure 11.1 recall Jimmy Carter's eye behaviors in his first debate with Gerald Ford and how they affected his credibility. Think also of the visually unassertive and aggressive salespeople who damaged their credibility by exhibiting too few positive eye behaviors and too many negative eye behaviors. Do you have any doubt that your own eye behaviors have a major impact on your credibility?

Gestures and postures can also exert a strong impact on our credibility. Before considering Figure 11.2, you may want to return to Chapter 4. Think about the kinds of nonverbal cues that communicate liking versus disliking, assertiveness versus nonassertiveness, and power versus powerlessness. You will recognize that the development of your personal credibility depends to a considerable degree on how likable, assertive, and powerful others perceive you to be. As you become actively engaged in developing your own credibility by nonverbal means, you must seek to eliminate the gestures and postures that have the potential to negatively affect your perceived competence, trustworthiness, and dynamism.

Finally, vocal cues are an important nonverbal determinant of credibility. As I indicated in Chapter 8, the sound of one's voice strongly affects the personality traits and personal qualities that person is presumed to have. Scherer, London, and Wolf (1973) emphasized that the "confident voice" exhibits considerable variation in pitch and volume, has high energy, and uses pauses of short duration infrequently. Communicators who use the "confident voice" are perceived as more competent, forceful, active, and enthusiastic than those who use the "doubtful voice." *The development of personal credibility requires the development of a confident voice.*

The "doubtful voice," which suggests a low level of self-confidence and a high level of anxiety, must be eliminated (Cooper, 1979; Erickson, Lind, Johnson, & Barr, 1978; Miller, Beaber, & Valone, 1976). Speech errors or nonfluencies in the form of stuttering, tongue slips, incoherent sounds, sentence changes, incompletions, and pauses filled with "ah," repetitions, and phrases such as "you know," are strong and reliable indicators of anxiety.

The individual who pauses and stutters before answering a question will probably be seen as less competent. The individual who pauses at length and uses many sentence

FIGURE 11.2   Nonverbal Cue Evaluation

Communicator _____ **Evaluator** _____

Please monitor the communicator's nonverbal cues very carefully to determine which cues had a positive and negative impact on credibility. The communicators should use these evaluations to make the adjustments in persuasive communication that are necessary to develop personal credibility.

During the sales presentation, did the salesperson:

Eye Behaviors	Yes	No
(+)1. Sustain eye contact with customer?	____	____
(+)2. Look directly at the customer?	____	____
(-)3. Look down or away before making a point?	____	____
(-)4. Exhibit shifty eyes?	____	____
(-)5. Blink excessively?		

Gestures

(+)1. Use hand and head gestures to emphasize points?	____	____
(+)2. Use gestures to signal a desire to continue talking?	____	____
(+)3. Keep hands and elbows out and away from the body?	____	____
(+)4. Avoid using distracting hand-to-face gestures?	____	____
(-)5. Exhibit any weak and tentative gestures?	____	____
(-)6. Clear throat?	____	____
(-)7. Smile out of context?	____	____
(-)8. Fidget?	____	____
(-)9. Put hand in pockets or on objects in the room?	____	____

Posture

(+)1. Assume an open and relaxed posture?	____	____
(+)2. Use postural shifts to indicate interest?	____	____
(+)3. Lean forward while making a point?	____	____
(+)4. Face the customer directly?	____	____
(-)5. Exhibit bodily tension?	____	____
(-)6. Appear rigid?	____	____
(-)7. Communicate with crossed arms and/or legs?	____	____

Vocal Cues

(+)1. Use a conversational speaking style?	____	____
(+)2. Emphasize important points with change in pitch and volume?	____	____
(+)3. Communicate with sufficient volume?	____	____
(+)4. Speak at an appropriate rate?	____	____
(-)5. Speak with a limited pitch rate?	____	____
(-)6. Sound flat, tense, or nasal?	____	____
(-)7. Pause at length before answering questions?	____	____

FIGURE 11.2   (Continued)

(-)8. Use nonfluencies such as "ah" and word repetitions?   _____   _____

(-)9. Interrupt the customer?   _____   _____

Write an evaluation of the persuasive communication. Begin by reviewing the assessments you have made on page 1. Then identify each of the communicative cues that you felt had a positive or negative impact on credibility. Be sure to identify points not covered on the evaluation sheet.

Desirable Aspects of Communication:

Undesirable Aspects of Communication:

Suggestions for Improvement:

fragments in trying to answer a question will probably be seen as untrustworthy; because such vocal cues are frequently associated with evasiveness. Finally, the individual who exhibits many nonfluencies will probably be seen as less than dynamic. Nonfluencies correlate highly with the perceived anxiety level of a nonfluent communicator (Jurich & Jurich, 1974).

Communicators' credibility can also be affected by whether they speak with an accent or dialect and by what kind of accent or dialect they exhibit. Regional accents have been rated in terms of their credibility; in general, the closer you come to speaking a standard midwestern dialect, the more competent you will be judged to be. Although individuals who speak a regional accent may judge you to be more trustworthy if your own accent sounds like theirs, they will see you as less competent if that accent gets moderate to low marks on the competence dimension of credibility (Giles & Street, 1985).

Senator Ted Kennedy's strikingly nonfluent responses to Roger Mudd's questions illustrate dramatically the powerfully negative impact that nonfluencies can have on a person's credibility. What did Kennedy say when Roger Mudd asked him if he thought that anybody would ever really believe his explanation of Chappaquiddick? Kennedy replied:

Well there's the, the problem is, is from that night uh, I found, the, the the, uh, conduct of behavior almost beyond belief myself. I mean that's why it's been uh (pause) uh, but I think that that's that's the way it was. That that's, that happens to be the way it was. Now, uh, I find as I've stated it, that I've found that the conduct that uh, in that evening and in, in the uh, as a result of the impact of the accident and the, the sense of loss, the sense of tragedy and the, the whole set of circ, circumstances the uh, that the uh, behavior was inexplicable. So I find that those, uh, those types of questions as they apply to that are questions of my own, uh, could as well ut uh, that, that happens to be the way it was. (CBS Television, 1979)

Figure 11.1 spells out in detail what you should and should not do if you are to use the full potential of your voice to develop your own credibility. As we have seen, the cultivation of the persuasive voice is a major responsibility of individuals who wish to develop their personal credibility.

Monitoring the Communicator's Nonverbal Cues

In order to make full use of the potential of nonverbal cues in developing their personal credibility, individuals must be able to monitor the nonverbal cues they exhibit in specific persuasive situations. Figure 11.2 should be used to make a record of the nonverbal cues you actually do exhibit.

The form provided in Figure 11.2 may be used to make a record of the nonverbal cues you exhibit in either a real or a simulated situation. You might try to sell a product to a potential customer in a real situation where other individuals can unobtrusively observe your persuasive effort, or you could make a sales presentation in a role-playing situation. In either case, it is easy enough to ask a third party to make a record of your nonverbal cues. Perhaps you could have the session videotaped. In that case, either you or another person could record your visual and auditory cues by placing check marks in the appropriate blanks while the videotape was being replayed.

Students and trainees who have used the monitoring and evaluation form provided in Figure 11.2 have found it to be valuable. The completed form provides a detailed profile of the nonverbal cues you actually have exhibited in a persuasive situation. The guidelines in Figure 11.1 identify the profile of nonverbal cues you should exhibit in order to be most credible. By comparing your actual profile with the desired profile, you should have a clear idea of the modifications you will have to make in your nonverbal communication if you wish to sell yourself more effectively.

Summary

Selling yourself is essential for successful persuasive communication. Selling yourself successfully requires the development of your personal credibility. Your credibility, in turn, is defined by how competent, trustworthy, and dynamic others judge you to be. Competence and trustworthiness are the most important dimensions of credibility; competence has repeatedly been found to be more important than trustworthiness.

Traditional treatments of credibility have been based on the assumption that our perceived competence, trustworthiness, and dynamism are controlled almost exclusively by the words we utter. This chapter provides information that challenges that assumption. In fact, we now know that nonverbal cues have the potential to exert a controlling influence on our personal credibility in many instances.

The persuasive efforts of presidential candidates and corporate sales representatives analyzed in this chapter illustrate how and why specific kinds of nonverbal cues affect our credibility. Eye behaviors, gestures, postures, and vocal cues are highlighted as the most important determinants of credibility.

In order to make maximum use of the image-building potential of nonverbal cues, careful attention should be given to the guidelines in Figure 11.1. The nonverbal profile presented in the figure spells out in detail what you should and should not do to develop personal credibility. Figure 11.2 provides you with a systematic means of identifying the nonverbal profile you actually do exhibit. By carefully comparing the nonverbal cues you exhibit with the nonverbal cues you should exhibit, you can determine what changes must be made in your nonverbal communication in order to sell yourself successfully.

References

ABC Television (1994, June 29). *Nightline, Interview with Senator Robert Dole.*

ABC Television (1994, November 29). *Nightline, Interview with Senator Robert Dole.*

Baird, J. E., Jr. (1977). Some nonverbal elements of leadership emergence. *Southern Speech Communication Journal, 42,* 352–361.

Barak, A., Patkin, J., & Dell, D. M. (1982). Effects of certain counselor behaviors on perceived expertness and attractiveness. *Journal of Counseling Psychology, 29,* 261–267.

Beebe, S. A. (1974). Eye contact: A nonverbal determinant of speaker credibility. *Communication Education, 23,* 21–25.

Brembeck, W. L., & Howell, W. S. (1976). *Persuasion: A means of social influence* (2nd ed.). Englewood Cliffs, NJ: Prentice-Hall.

Burgoon, J. K. (1976). The ideal source: A reexamination of source credibility measurement. *Central States Speech Journal, 27,* 200–206.

Burgoon, J. K., Coker, D. A., & Coker, R. A. (1986). Communicative effects of gaze behavior: A test of two contrasting explanations. *Human Communication Research, 12,* 495–524.

Burgoon, J. K., Manusov, V., Mineo, P., & Hale, J. L. (1985). Effects of gaze on hiring, credibility, attraction and relational message interpretation. *Journal of Nonverbal Behavior, 9,* 133–145.

Burgoon, J. K., & Saine, T. (1978). *The unspoken dialogue: An introduction to nonverbal communication.* Boston: Houghton Mifflin.

CBS Television (1976, September 23), *The first Ford–Carter presidential debate.*

CBS Television (1979, November 4). *CBS reports: Teddy.*

CBS Television (1986, November 19). *President Ronald Reagan press conference.*

CBS Television (1995, October 7). *Face the Nation, Interview with Senator Robert Dole.*

Cooper, K. (1979). *Nonverbal communication for business success.* New York: AMACOM.

C-SPAN II (1988, July 19). *Senator Joseph Biden press conference.*

DeVito, J. A. (1980). *The interpersonal communication book* (2nd ed.). New York: Harper.

Duffy, M., & Gibbs, N. (1995, July 31). Is Dole too old for the job?: The G. O. P. presidential front runner says he's 72 years young, but the age issue won't fade away. *Time, 146,* 26–31.

Edinger, J A., & Patterson, M. L. (1983). Nonverbal involvement and social control. *Psychological Bulletin, 93,* 30–56.

Erickson, B., Lind, E. A., Johnson, B. C., & Barr, W. M. (1978). Speech style and impression formation in a court setting: The effects of "powerful" and "powerless" speech. *Journal of Experimental Social Psychology, 14,* 266–279.

Exline, R. V. (1985). Multichannel transmission of nonverbal behavior and the perception of powerful men: The presidential debates of 1976. In S. L. Ellyson & J. F. Dovidio (Eds.), *Power, dominance, and nonverbal behavior* (pp. 183–206). New York: Springer-Verlag.

Giles, H., & Street, R. L., Jr. (1985). Communicator characteristics and behavior. In M. L. Knapp & G. R. Miller (Eds.). *Handbook of interpersonal communication* (pp. 205–261). Beverly Hills, CA: Sage.

Gitter, G., Black, H., & Fishman, J. E. (1975). Effect of race, sex and nonverbal communication on perceptions of leadership. *Sociology and Social Research, 60,* 46–57.

Gray, J., Jr. (1982). *The winning image.* New York: AMACOM.

Grove, L. (1988, October 9). Dukakis: If he only had a heart. *The Washington Post,* pp. D1, D4.

Harper, R. G., Wiens, A. N., & Matarazzo, J. D. (1978). *Nonverbal communication: The state of the art.* New York: Wiley.

Harzog, B. B. (1995). *An analysis of Senator Robert Joseph Dole: The impact of nonverbal cues on the credibility dimension of impression management.* Unpublished paper, University of Georgia, Athens, GA.

Hemsley, G. D., & Doob, A. N. (1978). The effect of looking behavior on perceptions of a communicator's credibility. *Journal of Applied Social Psychology, 8,* 136–144.

Infante, D. (1980). The construct validity of semantic differential scales for the measurement of source credibility. *Communication Quarterly, 28,* 19–26.

Infante, D., Parker, K., Clarke, C., Wilson, L., & Nathu, I. (1983). A comparison of factor and functional approaches to source credibility. *Communication Quarterly, 31,* 43–48.

Jurich, A. P., & Jurich, J. A. (1974). Correlations among nonverbal expressions of anxiety. *Psychological Reports, 34,* 199–204.

Kilgore, M. (1995). *Senator Bob Dole: Impression management analysis.* Unpublished paper, University of Georgia, Athens, GA.

Kleinke, C. L. (1975). *First impressions.* Englewood Cliffs, NJ: Prentice-Hall.

Liska, J. (1978). Situational and topical variations in credibility criteria. *Communication Monographs, 45,* 85–92.

Lui, L., & Standing, L. (1989). Communicator credibility: Trustworthiness defeats expertness. *Social Behavior and Personality, 17,* 219–221.

McCroskey, J. C., & Dunham, R. E. (1966). Ethos: A confounding element in communication research. *Speech Monographs, 33,* 456–463.

McCroskey, J. C., & Young, T. (1981). Ethos and credibility: The construct and its measurement after three decades. *Central States Speech Journal, 32,* 24–34.

McGinniss, J. (1969). *The selling of the president, 1968.* New York: Trident.

McMahan, E. M. (1976). Nonverbal communication as a function of attribution in impression formation. *Communication Monographs, 43,* 287–294.

Miller, N., Beaber, R. J., & Valone, K. (1976). Speed of speech and persuasion. *Journal of Personality and Social Psychology, 34,* 615–624.

Scherer, K. R., London, H., & Wolf, J. J. (1973). The voice of confidence: Paralinguistic cues and audience evaluation. *Journal of Research in Personality, 7,* 31–44.

Schlenker, B. R. (1980). *Impression management.* Monterey, CA: Brooks/Cole.

Sternthal, B., Phillips, L. W., & Dholakia, R. (1978). The persuasive effect of source credibility: A situational analysis. *Public Opinion Quarterly, 42,* 285–314.

Tucker, R. K. (1971). On the McCroskey scales for the measurement of ethos. *Central States Speech Journal, 22,* 127–129.

Webbink, P. (1986). *The power of the eyes.* New York: Springer.

$$C \; h \; a \; p \; t \; e \; r \;\; 12$$

Detecting Deception

From the beginning of recorded history, society has placed a premium on the detection of deception. In part, the fascination with deception may be attributed to the fact that it occurs so often in so many forms. Thus, "white lies, cover-ups, bluffing, euphemisms, masks, pretenses, tall-tales, put-ons, hoaxes, and other forms of falsehoods, fabrications, and simulations have coexisted with truthfulness and honesty in human communication for centuries" (Knapp & Comadena, 1979, p. 270).

Some of the ancient methods used to detect deception seem humorous today, but they reflect societal determination to ferret out the liar. In King Solomon's day, a rather unusual method was used to resolve a dispute between two women who both claimed to be the mother of the same child. An order was given to cut the child in two by a sword. The woman who cried out against the order was presumed to be telling the truth and the woman who remained silent was presumed to be lying. The ancient Chinese also used a rather novel method to detect deception. A suspected deceiver was required to chew on rice powder while being questioned. If, after it was spit out, the rice powder was dry, the person was judged to be deceptive. The theory was that the anxiety associated with lying would block off the salivary glands, resulting in a dry mouth (Larson, 1969).

Law enforcement officials have been particularly concerned with refining methods and techniques for detecting deception. Their efforts have always been based on the same fundamental assumption: *Deceivers will experience an elevated level of arousal or anxiety at the moment of deception, which will be reflected in changes in one or more of the internal states of the body.*

The polygraph was developed to monitor changes in heart rate, blood pressure, skin resistance, and other presumed physiological indicators of deception (Podlesny & Raskin, 1977). Israeli police have begun using a device that measures palpitations of the stomach to detect deception of terrorist suspects whom they are interrogating. A number of corporations now require that the Psychological Stress Evaluator be used when job prospects are being interviewed. This device is designed to pick up microtremors of the voice that indicate that deception is occurring (Goodwin, 1975).

CARTOON 12.1

The fact that physiological measures indicate that an individual is aroused or anxious does not, of course, prove that the person is being deceptive. Proponents of voice stress analysis start with the fundamental assumption that the elevated level of anxiety that deceivers experience at the moment of deception will in turn be manifested in a measurably higher level of vocal stress. Those same proponents admit, however, that an elevated level of vocal stress has not proved to be a consistently accurate predictor or indicator of deception. The fundamental problem seems to be that communicators may become aroused for many different reasons. Arousal in the absence of tell-tale behavioral indicators is an insufficient reason for believing that a person is lying.

Researcher Dan O'Hair has led the effort to determine whether a person's level of vocal stress is a reliable indicator of deception. Recently O'Hair, Cody, Wang, and Chao (1990) concluded that "vocal stress scores cannot be used to detect deception *in general*" (p. 159). They add that there is some evidence to suggest vocal stress can be used to detect prepared lies, as opposed to spontaneous lies. However, vocal stress can be used to detect this one, specialized type of deception only if the deceiver is prone to exhibit high levels of stress or arousal. In short, a *high level of arousal might be a necessary condition for deception to take place but it is not a sufficient condition by itself to justify a judgment that someone is engaging in deception.*

Although deceivers might always experience some degree of arousal when they lie, it is quite possible that other individuals experience comparable levels of arousal when they tell the truth. In a recent study, deTurck and Miller (1985) stimulated both truthful and deceitful communicators so that they experienced similar levels of arousal. They concluded that the "six cues (adapters, hand gestures, speech errors, pauses, response latency, and message duration) that distinguished deceivers from unaroused nondeceivers *also* differentiated deceivers from aroused nondeceivers" (p. 195). Thus, a heightened level of arousal or anxiety is not enough to explain the fact that deceivers and nondeceivers exhibit distinctively different types of behaviors. We are almost forced to conclude that deceivers experience a distinctive deception-induced type of arousal that truthful communicators do not experience. In fact, the most basic difference in arousal between deceptive and truthful communicators may be that deceptive communicators feel guilty whereas truthful communicators do not.

In a general sense, societal concern with deception has never been more evident. Our form of government requires that we trust our elected public officials to represent us in ways that are both straightforward and truthful. Such trust seems misplaced whenever we view such tawdry spectacles as government officials being forced out of office for allegedly soliciting the sexual favors of minors, laundering money from the drug syndicate in order to remain financially solvent, and peddling influence to foreign agents for no reason other than greed.

In the face of repeated acts of deception by governmental officials, it is not surprising that only 16 percent of a group of one thousand citizens surveyed in the San Francisco Bay area described their national government as "trustworthy" (Sniderman, 1981). Quite clearly, members of society must be able to determine if and when elected public officials are lying if they are to have a defensible basis for trusting those officials who are not lying.

Most of us, however, are most immediately concerned about possibly being deceived by the individuals with whom we interact on a personal and face-to-face basis. In order to make accurate assessments of the attitudes, feelings, and motivations of friends, business associates, and intimates, we must develop the capability to detect deception when it occurs. As we shall see, familiarity with the nonverbal profiles of deceivers provides us with the potential to develop that capacity.

Nonverbal Indicators of Deception

Deception in interpersonal communication is difficult to detect. We know that untrained individuals can detect the deception of strangers at, or just above, an accuracy level that would be expected by chance (Knapp, Hart, & Dennis, 1974). The question of how accurate the accuracy figures actually are has been disputed by some investigators. Kalbfleisch (1990), for example, maintained that a number of the accuracy figures that have been reported for human lie detectors might be somewhat inflated because of persisting measurement problems.

The finding that untrained individuals do little better than chance in their efforts to detect deceivers is hardly a damaging or counterintuitive finding, however. There is little reason to expect untrained persons to perform very well. We should focus our attention on a much more relevant and important question: How accurate are trained observers in the use of nonverbal indicators to detect deception?

We now know that trained lie detectors can identify deception at accuracy levels well above chance. The performance of trained judges in 16 deception studies (DePaulo, Zuckerman, & Rosenthal, 1980) indicated that the judges' accuracy level was significantly better than chance in all but three of the studies. Druckman, Rozelle, and Baxter (1982) reported significant gains in the accuracy with which judges were able to differentiate between honest, evasive, and deceptive communication after the judges were trained in the use of the nonverbal profile for each of those three types of communication. Finally, nearly two-thirds of a group of trained police interrogators reported that their judgments of deception on the part of criminal suspects are "highly accurate" when they rely solely on the suspects' nonverbal cues to make their judgments (Leathers, 1982).

The value of skills training for human lie detectors has been clearly established. For example, deTurck and Miller (1990) conclude that "people can be trained to use successfully a universal set of behavioral cues for detecting deception across a variety of communicators" (p. 617). Similarly, as deTurck, Harszlak, Bodhorn, and Texter (1990) emphasized:

> *Results obtained in the current study clearly indicate that training social perceivers to detect deception enhances their accuracy in judging the veracity of communicators' messages. . . . Stated differently, the training enhanced social perceivers' ability to judge when communicators were lying and when they were telling the truth in a context that is highly arousing to deceivers.* (pp. 196–197)

In the latter study, trained females were able to achieve an impressive detection accuracy of 77 percent.

We also know that a person's speech communication is not apt to reveal, in a consistent and reliable way, whether that person is engaging in deception. *Nonverbal cues have primacy for human lie detectors.* Thus, results from empirical research indicate that nonverbal communicative cues are the most important source of information that human lie detectors use in making veracity judgments. In addition, the established primacy of nonverbal cues in identifying deception has one other practical consequence. Human lie detectors rely primarily on nonverbal cues in making judgments of deception and veracity when the verbal and nonverbal portions of a communicator's message are inconsistent or contradictory (Hale & Stiff, 1990). As a result, analyses of communicators' verbal behavior for purposes of identifying indicators of deception are uncommon (Knapp & Comadena, 1979).

You should consider the relationship between deceptive and inconsistent messages carefully if you put a premium on increasing your ability to use a communicator's behavioral cues to detect deception. The multichannel messages communicated by all deceivers must be inconsistent to some degree or in some way if the human lie detector is to have the realistic hope of detecting deception when it occurs. By definition, liars must maintain, via their spoken words, that they are telling the truth. In rare instances, liars inadvertently reveal their deception by making verbal statements that are mutually contradictory. Unless they suddenly confess that they are lying or contradict themselves, however, their deception will be detectable only if the information they communicate through one or more of the nonverbal channels is inconsistent with, or seems to contradict, their claim that they are telling the truth.

In his enlightening book, *Telling Lies: Clues to Deceit in the Marketplace, Politics, and Marriage,* Ekman (1985) made clear that deceivers reveal their deception only when their verbal and nonverbal messages become inconsistent in some way:

> *There are only clues that the person is poorly prepared and clues of emotions that don't fit the person's line. These are what provide leakage or deception clues. The lie catcher must learn how emotion is registered in speech, voice, body, and face, what traces may be left despite a liar's attempts to conceal feelings, and what gives away false emotional portrayals. Spotting deceit also requires understanding how these behaviors may reveal that a liar is making up his line as he goes along.* (p. 81)

The lie detector must decide which communication channel is the most useful source of information whenever inconsistent messages are being transmitted. Those channels that are most susceptible to conscious control by the deceiver are the least "leaky," whereas the channels least suspectible to conscious control are the most "leaky." The face, for example, leaks least because it is most susceptible to the conscious control of the communicator. "Since the face is more controllable, it is less likely to give away deception. Stated differently, the channel that is most informative when the communicator is truthful is most misleading when the communicator is deceptive" (Zuckerman, DePaulo, & Rosenthal, 1981, p. 5).

When you consider the relationship between deceptive and inconsistent messages, it is important to remember that the conscious intent of the liar is to deceive. By definition, deception is a type of communication intended to gain acceptance by another person of a belief or understanding which the deceiver recognizes consciously to be false (Zuckerman et al., 1981). As Chapter 13 will establish, the deceptive message is only one type of inconsistent message. The intentions of individuals who communicate inconsistently are often multiple in nature and sometimes they are unknown. In short, all deceptive messages that are potentially detectable as deceptive are inconsistent to some degree, and they serve a wide variety of purposes in addition to deception.

The potential of verbal messages as useful indicators of deception is limited because many deceivers can consciously control their verbal presentation of self. The skillful impression manager will presumably consciously control verbal statements that might lead the listener to infer deceit. In view of the fact that human lie detectors give primacy to the deceiver's nonverbal behaviors, deceitful impression managers must work very hard to make sure that their nonverbal messages are consistent with their verbal messages that emphasize that they are telling the truth. The carefully formulated verbal message of a deceiver should minimize rather than maximize's the chances that deception will be detected.

Although deception is difficult to detect, the development of successful interpersonal relationships depends to a considerable extent on our ability to detect deception when it occurs. Rare indeed is the individual who would wish to develop a personal or business relationship that is not based on interpersonal trust. Interpersonal trust is, in turn, based on the anticipation that the individuals with whom we interact will be honest and straightforward in their dealings with us. In order to have a defensible basis for assessing an individual's level of trustworthiness, we must be able to determine whether and when that person chooses to be deceptive.

We now know that lying is apt to have disastrous consequences for interpersonal relationships. Results from one study (McCornack & Levine, 1990) show that

> *more than two-thirds of the subjects who reported that their relationship had terminated since the time that the lie was discovered reported that the discovery of the lie played a direct role in their decision to end the relationship. Nearly all of these breakups were reported as being unilateral, initiated by the recipient of the lie.* (p. 131)

Without question, the discovery that one of the partners in a relationship has been deceptive typically results in an emotional experience for those involved that is traumatic, intense, and negative. If you doubt the negative emotional impact of lying by a partner in an intimate relationship, recall how you felt the last time an intimate lied to you.

Those with whom we interact must also be concerned about their ability to determine whether we are engaging in deception. We must recognize that even when we are being completely truthful, we might be perceived as being deceptive because there is a well-developed *deceiver stereotype* in our society that leads us to expect that deceivers will behave in certain ways. One survey suggests that the most striking feature of the deceiver stereotype is the belief that deceivers will exhibit more bodily movements than truthful communicators. Those surveyed believed that, on more than two-thirds of the 45 behavioral indicators that were identified, deceivers will exhibit more movements than their truthful counterparts (Hocking & Leathers, 1980). The implication is clear: If you do not wish to be perceived as a deceiver, you must make sure that your nonverbal behaviors do not conform to the defining features of the deceiver stereotype.

The human lie detector in turn must be aware of the fact the a number of the cues that are commonly *perceived* to be indicators of deception are not accurate indicators. In our society, for example, lie detectors have consistently expressed the *belief* that deceivers will sustain eye contact for shorter periods of time, smile less, speak more slowly, exhibit more postural shifts, take longer to respond to questions, speak with a higher pitch, hesitate more, and exhibit more speech errors than truthful communicators. Interestingly, the correlation between perceived and actual indicators of deception has been identified as around 0.50 (Zuckerman et al., 1981).

Of course, no foolproof method exists for detecting deception. Even when time-tested machines such as the polygraph are used, the accuracy with which deception is detected may fall as low as 64 percent (Lykken, 1974). Furthermore, the use of machines (such as the polygraph or the Psychological Stress Evaluator) to detect deception is not feasible in the typical interpersonal communication situation. The use of such machines to detect deception may also be unethical and illegal in many situations.

Deception that occurs in interpersonal communication must be detected without the aid of machines. We can detect this sort of deception without the use of mechanical monitoring devices if we become thoroughly familiar with the nonverbal profiles that differentiate lying from truthful communicators. We now know that liars exhibit a number of identifiable nonverbal cues at the moment of deception that are distinctively different from the nonverbal cues exhibited by truthful communicators. Recent research on deception clearly documents that the guilt and the resultant anxiety associated with deception are reflected not only in changes in such internal physiological factors as the deceiver's heart and breathing rate. Deceivers also behave differently nonverbally because of an elevated level of anxiety that markedly affects their nonverbal communication. These external nonverbal indicators of deception have proved to be very valuable to the human lie detector.

Nonverbal Profile of the Deceptive Communicator—Type I

The nonverbal behaviors of laboratory liars, who are asked to lie by an experimenter, have been examined in detail. Results from laboratory studies cannot, of course, be used to develop the nonverbal profile of all types of deceivers in the real world. These results are most useful in developing the nonverbal profile of the real-world deceiver who is exposed to conditions fundamentally similar to conditions experienced by laboratory liars.

Consider the following examples of deception: You lie to the telephone caller about your real reason for not accepting a date. You lie to your boss's secretary when you call in and say you are sick. You lie to your children about the depth of your religious convictions in order to get them to attend Sunday School. You lie to a job interviewer in order to pad your credentials. You lie about your business expenses to an IRS income tax auditor. Each of these lies might be labeled "Type I deception." Such deception represents the kind of lying that occurs frequently in the real world, as well as in the laboratory.

Type I deception can be identified by three defining features. From the perspective of the deceiver, (a) the level of anxiety experienced at the moment of deception is typically fairly low; (b) the consequences of being detected as a deceiver are not severe; and (c) deception occurs for a short period of time. As we shall see, Type I and Type II deceptions are quite different. In fact, Type II deceivers typically experience a high level of anxiety in their long-term efforts to deceive, because they recognize that the consequences of being detected may be catastrophic.

Type I deceivers can consciously control at least some of the nonverbal cues that serve as tell-tale signs of their deception. Because their level of anxiety is relatively low, they have the opportunity to concentrate on their presentation of self without being overly distracted by their guilt feelings. Zuckerman and colleagues (1981) emphasized that "the extent to which deception fosters guilt, anxiety and/or duping delight varies according to the purposes of the deception, its social context, and the characteristics of the deceiver" (p. 9).

In addition, Type I liars are not ordinarily faced with the prospect of the gas chamber or a long jail sentence if their deception is detected. They can concentrate on what they perceive to be credible actions as they engage in impression management. In short, they are impression managers who are not distracted from their goal of monitoring the nonverbal cues that they believe will reveal their deception or from taking the necessary actions to suppress those cues that might reveal deception.

Finally, Type I liars are usually required by an experimenter to lie for only a short period of time. Conventional wisdom suggests that deceivers may effectively control their presentation of self for limited periods of time, but lying convincingly for extended periods of time is much more difficult. The longer deception must be sustained, the greater the level of anxiety the deceiver is likely to experience. As we shall see, the nonverbal profiles for Type I and Type II deceivers differ in some important respects. The differences may be attributed to the contrasting conditions experienced by the two types of deceivers.

To develop the nonverbal profile for the Type I deceiver, I have concentrated on those nonverbal cues that have most frequently and consistently been found to be indicative of deception. The cues identified in Table 12.1 have, therefore, been recognized as particularly reliable indicators of deception. No single cue will always be exhibited at the moment of deception, however. Nonetheless, the patterns of cues exhibited by Type I deceivers are quite consistent.

You should be aware of the importance of baseline data, or of being familiar with the "truthful baseline," as you consider the information in Table 12.1. A number of researchers have found that lie detectors are much more accurate in identifying deceivers when they have had a chance to observe the same person engaging in truthful communication (Zuckerman et al., 1981). Without the truthful baseline for purposes of comparison, you might be misled by some stereotypical assumptions you have made about deceivers. For example, I recall the time I was asked to observe a young woman on videotape before deciding whether she was lying or telling the truth. I was immediately struck by the fact that her eyes were

TABLE 12.1   Nonverbal Indicators of Deception: Type I

	Deceivers Exhibit	
	More	**Less**

Vocal cues	Pausing
	    Pauses
	    Time before pausing
	    Lengthy pauses
	    Hesitations
	Nonfluencies
	    Sentence changes
	    Word repetitions
	    Intruding sounds
	Rapid speaking rate
	Overall vocal nervousness:
	    Voice sounds tense or stressed
		Lengthy answers

Gestures	Self-adaptors (touching face and body,
	    hand shrugs)
	Object-adaptors (touching or playing
	    with objects in room)
	Overall bodily nervousness
		Head movement
		Head-nodding
		Foot movements
		Illustrators
		Leg movements

Eye Behaviors	Time spent looking away Averted gazes Pupil dilation Blinking	Eye-contact duration
Smiling[a]	Masked smiles	Felt happy smiles

Note: Rather than concentrating on a single cue that might indicate deception, the lie detector should concentrate on classes of indicators. When trying to determine whether an individual is engaging in some sort of low-risk deception, vocal cues are probably the most useful indicators, followed, in order of their potential value, by gestures, eye behaviors, postures, and facial expressions.

[a]In general, facial expressions do not reliably differentiate deceitful from honest communicators.

darting wildly from side to side. If I had not already seen the same young woman in the truthful condition, I might have erroneously concluded that her "shifty eyes" were indicative of deception. Because I knew that her eyes also shifted wildly from side to side when she was telling the truth, I recognized that I should rely on behaviors other than eye shifts to determine whether she was lying.

You also should recognize that we are focusing on micro-indicators of deception. A group of researchers (O'Hair, Cody, Goss, & Krayer, 1988) is now attempting to develop macro-assessments of honesty and deceit. So far, results lack specificity, but the approach does have considerable promise. Much additional research must be done, however, to determine the potential of the "macro" detection of deception.

To be successful in detecting deception, you must decide which type or class of nonverbal cue will receive your closest scrutiny. Vocal cues have proved to be a particularly rich source of deception cues. A number of studies have found that *deceivers exhibit more speech errors than honest communicators* (deTurck & Miller, 1985; Druckman et al., 1982; Knapp et al., 1974; Mehrabian, 1971). *Deceivers also consistently hesitate and pause more frequently and for longer periods of time* than their truthful counterparts (Harrison, Hwalek, Raney, & Fritz, 1978; Kraut, 1978; O'Hair et al., 1990). Speech errors or nonfluencies associated with deception take the form of sentence changes, word repetition, and intruding sounds. The speaking rate of deceivers has been found to be both abnormally fast and slow, although a preponderance of studies have found that *liars speak faster than truthful communicators* (Hocking & Leathers, 1980; Zuckerman et al., 1981).

Finally, *overall vocal nervousness* has been identified as a particularly reliable indicator of deception (deTurck et al., 1990; Hocking & Leathers, 1980; Zuckerman et al., 1981). Because you are well-advised to avoid relying on a single vocal cue in your efforts to detect deception, available evidence suggests that a stressed or tense voice could be a reliable warning that deception is taking place.

Gestures have also been found to be reliable indicators of Type I deception. To make optimal use of gestural cues you should *be alert for any abnormality in the rate or frequency with which certain kinds of gestures are exhibited* (DePaulo et al., 1980). *Self-adaptors,* in the form of hand-to-face gestures and hand shrugs, and *object adaptors,* in the form of touching or playing with objects in the room, are exhibited with abnormal frequency by deceivers (Cody & O'Hair, 1983; Ekman and Friesen, 1972; O'Hair, Cody, and McLaughlin, 1981). Because gestural adaptors are known to reflect anxiety, we should not be surprised that even Type I deceivers exhibit an abnormal number of adaptors. Type I deceivers exhibit much less anxiety than Type II deceivers, but they are more anxious when lying than when telling the truth. The deceiver's adaptor rate is understandably accelerated because of the increased anxiety level.

Although deceivers exhibit more gestural adaptors, they exhibit fewer gestural illustrators. A number of studies have found that deceivers reduce the number of head movements, foot movements, and leg movements. In short, deceivers may seem abnormally unexpressive because of their reduced illustrator rate (Ekman & Friesen, 1972; Hocking & Leathers, 1980; Mehrabian, 1971; Zuckerman et al., 1981).

Ekman (1985) agreed that illustrators decrease when deception occurs. He seems to stand alone, however, in his contention that "emblematic slips" may increase at the moment of deception. The most notorious emblematic slip is giving someone "the finger." We do not include emblematic slips in Table 12.1 for several reasons. First, emblematic slips have not been identified in multiple studies as reliable indicators of deception. Second, the term *emblematic "slip"* is almost a contradiction in terms because the individuals who uses gestural emblems should be fully aware that they are using them and do so with conscious intent.

Postural indicators of deception are more limited in number. However, in a number of instances deceivers have exhibited a preference for more distant seating, with little trunk swiveling, and an indirect bodily orientation (Druckman et al., 1982). When the characteristic gestures and postures of Type I deceivers are considered together, the image projected is one of unusual impassivity, immobility, and bodily rigidity.

The eye behaviors of Type I liars have been found to be different in different studies (Matarazzo, Wiens, Jackson, & Manaugh, 1970; McClintock & Hunt, 1975). A number of studies have found, however, that *the eye contact of deceivers is more limited* than it is for truthful communicators (Exline, Thibaut, Hickey, & Gumpert, 1970; Hocking & Leathers, 1980), and that averted gazes and *substantial time spent looking away from the person with whom the deceiver is communicating* might be indicative of deception (Druckman et al., 1982). *Blinking and pupil dilation* have also repeatedly been identified as reliable indicators of deception (O'Hair et al., 1990; Zuckerman et al., 1981).

Finally, the utility of facial expressions in identifying deception is open to serious question. For example, Ekman and Friesen (1969) theorized that facial expressions are apt to be less useful indicators of deception than bodily cues because facial cues are more susceptible to effective conscious control. Subsequent research by Ekman and Friesen (1974) did support the view that bodily cues are more accurate indicators of deception than facial expressions.

Hocking and Leathers (1980) also theorized that facial expressions are less reliable indicators of deception than bodily cues, although their theoretical perspective is based on different assumptions than Ekman and Friesen used to form their theory. In fact, recent evidence suggests that facial expressions of lying and honest communicators do not differ in ways that are consistently and reliably identifiable (Cody & O'Hair, 1983; Hocking & Leathers, 1980).

One type of facial message has been cited as a reliable indicator of deception, however: smiling. We have already indicated that the stereotypical belief in our society is that deceivers smile less than their truthful counterparts. There is some evidence that deceivers actually do smile less than truth tellers although the difference only approaches statistical significance (Zuckerman et al., 1981). Interestingly, deceivers smile significantly less than truthful communicators only when their motivation to lie successfully is low. Are we to conclude that highly motivated deceivers are so eager to please that they also throw in a smile?

The kind of smile rather than the frequency of smiling seems to be the important factor. Thus, Ekman, Friesen, and O'Sullivan (1988) reported that the type of smiles used by liars and truthful communicators can be used to differentiate between them. Liars more frequently use a "masking smile," whereas truthful individuals are more apt to display a "felt happy smile." When people use a masked smile, they do so to try to conceal the fact that they are experiencing strong, negative emotions such as fear or disgust. Deceivers are known to experience such emotions.

Ekman (1988) called the "felt smile" a Duchenne smile. Duchenne smiles in turn are strongly associated with honest as opposed to deceptive communication. Duchenne smiles "involve the muscle around the eye, in addition to the muscle which pulls the lip corners up" (p. 171). Masked smiles in contrast are reliable indicators of deception. Masking smiles,

> *smiles in which there are muscular traces of disgust, anger, fear, sadness, or contempt in addition to the smile, as expected, occurred more often when the subjects were actually trying to conceal such negative feelings than when they were actually enjoying themselves.* (p. 171)

The Duchenne and the masked smiles are, respectively, reliable indicators of honesty and deception. In one study, Ekman, O'Sullivan, Friesen, and Scherer (1991) used only three kinds of measures to differentiate between lying and truthful communicators: Duchenne smiles, masked smiles, and vocal pitch. Their overall accuracy, or "hit rate," was an extremely high 86 percent.

Both types of smiles should be identifiable by the untrained observer. The two most valuable clues to the masked smile associated with deception are traces of negative emotions on the face and the absence of the crow's-feet around the eyes; crow's-feet are defining features of the felt happy smile. The two types of smiles can also be differentiated on the basis of how long it takes for them to appear, how long they remain on the face before fading, and how quickly they disappear.

To the human lie detector, the face should be considered primarily as a source of noise, however. Concentrating on the suspected deceiver's facial expressions will divert attention from nonverbal cues that are known to be much more useful indicators of deception. When considered in the aggregate, vocal cues and bodily cues are the most useful nonverbal indicators of Type I deception.

Finally, Burgoon and Buller's creative research on deception deserves attention. Their research attempts not only to identify the major kinds of nonverbal indicators of deception and to prioritize them in terms of their utility. Their research also explores the implications of deception in terms of the interpersonal perceptions of the interactants. Thus, Burgoon and Buller focus on deception as an important type of impression management. Burgoon in particular has been a leader in assessing how the purposeful act of deception affects the interpersonal perceptions of those involved. Burgoon and Buller have identified four communication objectives that deception strategies are designed to achieve: impression management, relational communication, emotion management, and conversation management. They wrote:

> *The twin functions of impression management and relational communication concern, respectively, the kinds of images people project for a general audience and the images or "messages" tailored to specific partners that have implications for defining the interpersonal relationship along such dimensions as trust, receptivity, and involvement. Emotion or affect management concerns how people regulate emotional experiences and expressions, including the appropriate revelation or suppression of emotional displays in social contexts. Conversation management concerns how interactants regulate conversational activities such as topic initiation and turn-taking.* (Burgoon & Buller, 1994, pp. 157–158)

Using this perspective, Burgoon and her colleagues (Burgoon & Buller, 1994; Buller, Burgoon, Buslig, & Roiger, 1994) have compared deceptive and truthful communicators in terms of such collective and individual variables as nonverbal involvement, dominance, and formality cues. Whether using the perceptions that deceivers and their partners have of their own behaviors or direct observations of the deceivers' behaviors, certain results stand out. Deceivers, in contrast to truthful communicators, exhibit fewer immediacy behaviors and are more reticent, are more nervous particularly in the first part of the time period when deception occurs, leak some negative affect in that they are perceived as more unpleasant kinesically, and are less composed and more formal (Burgoon & Buller, 1994).

In order to use the nonverbal profile of the Type I deceiver to develop our capacity to detect deception, we must understand why these deceivers behave as they do. A colleague and I (Hocking & Leathers, 1980) developed a theoretical perspective designed to explain the distinctive behaviors of Type I deceivers. This perspective focuses exclusively on the behaviors of deceivers who are using prepared, as opposed to spontaneous, lies. We currently know little about the behavioral profile of the spontaneous liar. Because the spontaneous lie will probably induce less anxiety than the prepared lie, however, individuals engaging in the two types of lying might manifest somewhat different nonverbal behaviors (O'Hair et al., 1981).

The theoretical perspective is grounded in three explanatory propositions. The Type I deceivers are apt to (a) attempt to exercise conscious control over the nonverbal behaviors that they believe to be important defining features of the cultural stereotype for deceivers, (b) exercise conscious control over the nonverbal behaviors that can be most directly and easily monitored at the moment of deception, and (c) exercise effective conscious control over those behaviors that are most susceptible to conscious control.

As already indicated, the cultural stereotype of the deceiver fosters the expectation that deceivers will exhibit more bodily movements than truthful communicators. For example, deceivers are expected to exhibit *more* defensiveness gestures, *more* extraneous movements suggestive of anxiety, and *greater* bodily nervousness. Clearly, skillful deceivers will not wish to be associated with the deceiver stereotype. Therefore, in order to avoid that association, they will presumably attempt to suppress the number of bodily movements they exhibit. The theoretical perspective developed by Hocking and Leathers (1980) predicts that Type I deceivers will exhibit an abnormal lack of bodily movements. The perspective also provides a basis for understanding the facial expressions and vocal cues that Type I deceivers exhibit.

The perspective focuses on the three classes of nonverbal cues that have most frequently been examined as potentially useful indicators of deception: bodily movements, facial expressions, and vocal cues. Bodily cues in the form of head, foot, and leg movements can be easily monitored and controlled by the deceiver. Vocal cues are most difficult to monitor and, therefore, are difficult to control consciously.

Two recent studies provide support for the explanatory value of this theoretical perspective. In fact, these two studies produced detailed information that can be used to develop fully the nonverbal behavioral profile of the Type I deceiver. The first study (Hocking & Leathers, 1980) supports the conclusion that bodily movements and vocal cues are particularly useful indicators of deception and facial expressions are not. Results from the second study (Cody & O'Hair, 1983) "support the Hocking and Leathers perspective" and provide additional information about the nonverbal profile of the Type I deceiver.

If you wish to increase the accuracy with which you can detect Type I deception, consider carefully the nonverbal indicators of deception identified in Table 12.1. Certain kinds of vocal cues are strongly indicative of deception. In contrast to truthful communicators, deceivers exhibit more hesitations, longer pauses, word repetitions, intruding sounds, and an accelerated speaking rate. Most importantly, deceivers are apt to *sound* nervous.

Bodily cues that may reveal deception require careful scrutiny. Type I deceivers have been found consistently to exhibit fewer of the bodily movements that they can consciously control than their truthful counterparts. Thus, deceivers, when compared with nondeceivers, exhibit *less head movement, foot movement, leg movement, and illustrator activity.* They also exhibit a *less direct bodily orientation and do less trunk swiveling.* Deceivers exhibit *more self-adaptors and object-adaptors* than truthful communicators. Most importantly, deceivers exhibit *greater overall bodily nervousness.*

Eye behaviors are less useful indicators of Type I deception. This may be true because some eye behaviors are susceptible to effective conscious control and others are not. We do know that deceivers seem to have *eye contact of relatively limited duration.* Pupil dilation and blinking have been used to identify deceivers. In addition, deceivers exhibit a propensity to avert their gaze and more frequently look away from individuals with whom they are communicating than honest communicators.

Finally, facial expressions of deceitful and honest communicators do not seem to differ consistently. For this reason, human lie detectors would be well advised to pay little attention to a suspected deceiver's facial expressions and concentrate instead on vocal and bodily cues.

Nonverbal Profile of the Deceptive Communicator—Type II

The lying criminal suspect who is interviewed by the police interrogator is clearly a Type II deceiver. Most Type II deceivers do not of course experience a level of stress comparable to a person undergoing police interrogation. Nonetheless, the typical Type II deceiver is a highly anxious person. Type II deceivers experience a high level of anxiety for at least two reasons: The probable consequences of being detected as a deceiver are severe, and the deceivers must successfully sustain their deception for a considerable period of time.

A number of the government officials who were indicted in the Watergate and Wall Street scandals were Type II deceivers. They faced public disgrace, the loss of important positions, and jail sentences if their long-term efforts to deceive were detected. Additional examples of Type II deceivers abound. Consider the many married persons who have been cheating on their spouses, the athletes who have been surreptitiously using hard drugs, employees who have been stealing from their employers, or alcoholics who struggle to conceal their affliction from friends and associates. All of those individuals experience high levels of anxiety in their long-term efforts to deceive because the consequences of being detected are hardly trivial.

Do Type II deceivers exhibit an identifiable nonverbal behavioral profile that can be used as an aid in detecting their deception? There is now considerable evidence to suggest that they do. The evidence comes primarily from the reports of police interrogators who have interviewed lying criminal suspects. Because all Type II deceivers are apt to experience a high level of anxiety and fear the consequences of being detected as a deceiver, there seems good reason to believe that different kinds of Type II deceivers will exhibit similar nonverbal behaviors at the time of deception.

Knowledge of the nonverbal behaviors of Type II deceivers comes primarily from law enforcement agencies. Law enforcement agencies continue to have extensive exposure to Type II deception. Those agencies are committed to detecting criminal deception when and where it occurs. Investigators receive highly specialized training that is designed to detect deception, and trained interviewers have many opportunities to study the behaviors of criminal suspects under the controlled conditions of the police interview.

The police interview is ideally suited to the study of Type II deception. If criminal suspects do exhibit identifiable nonverbal cues at the moment of deception, the probability of occurrence and of detection should be enhanced in this setting. In contrast to the low levels of guilt and anxiety typically experienced by the Type I deceiver, guilt and anxiety levels for the lying criminal suspect should be exceptionally high.

Researcher Paul Ekman's (1985) creative conception of autonomic nervous system (ANS) clues may prove to be particularly useful in predicting which nonverbal behaviors Type II deceivers exhibit and in explaining why they exhibit them. Although Ekman did not distinguish between Type I and II cues, his ANS clues are clearly more applicable to Type II deception because he assumed that the deceiver was highly aroused.

The ANS clues include noticeable changes in the pattern of breathing and in the frequency of swallowing, as well as blushing, blanching, and pupil dilation. Interestingly, Ekman believed that deceivers exhibit particular autonomic cues for different emotions. For example, Ekman noted that when his actors exhibited facial anger and fear, "different things happened to their skin temperature. Their skin became hot with anger and cold with fear" (p. 119).

As a result of my research on deception, I have established personal contact with interrogators who work for the Georgia Bureau of Investigation. The GBI, as well as other police agencies in various parts of the country, attaches much importance to the value of nonverbal cues as indicators of deception.

Mike Smith is one of the GBI's most experienced and respected interrogators. He is convinced that nonverbal cues are reliable indicators of deception. In a guest lecture to one of my classes in nonverbal communication, Smith revealed which nonverbal cues he uses to detect Type II deception and why he uses them (Smith, 1979).

In Smith's view, the anxiety level of the Type II deceiver is so high that a substantial number of nonverbal cues are readily discernible to the trained observer. For example, during his many years as a police interrogator, Smith said that he observed suspects who were undergoing interrogation do the following: (a) bite their lips until they bled; (b) foam at the mouth; (c) make clicking sounds while talking (because of a dry mouth); (d) bend their feet beneath their chair, at a painful angle; and (e) give a "weak, wet, and clammy" handshake. (These particular suspects were proved to have been lying.) Smith emphasized, however, that he relies on no single cue in making an inference of deception; instead, he is alert for *sets of cues,* in the form of eye behaviors, gestures, and vocal cues, all of which seem to support a judgment that deception is taking place.

To determine whether police interrogators agree on the defining features of the nonverbal profile for Type II deceivers, a colleague and I conducted a survey of all active interrogators employed by the Georgia Bureau of Investigation. The survey was designed to accomplish two objectives. We wanted to determine to what extent police interviewers rely on a suspect's nonverbal cues to detect deception. We also wanted to identify the nonverbal cues that are viewed as the most important in the nonverbal profile for the lying suspect (Leathers & Hocking, 1983).

Results from the survey indicate that the nonverbal cues of the lying criminal suspect represent a major source of information used by police interrogators to make a judgment of deception or truthfulness. Of the 86 police interrogators interviewed, 76.7 percent indicated that they either relied equally on both verbal and nonverbal behaviors to detect deception or relied more heavily on nonverbal than verbal behaviors to detect deception. When forced to rely solely on nonverbal cues, 64 percent of the agents indicated that their judgments would be proved "highly accurate."

Police interviewers in this study strongly endorsed the value of nonverbal cues as indicators of deception. They not only believe that nonverbal cues are a valuable and accurate source of information about Type II deception, but also have a nonverbal behavioral profile of the deceiving criminal suspect that is both detailed and internally consistent.

To begin, each GBI interrogator was asked to describe, in two or three words, each of the nonverbal behaviors that deceivers exhibit when lying in the police interview. Their responses were illuminating. Many of the nonverbal cues seem directly linked to the Type II deceiver's elevated level of anxiety (e.g., noticeable perspiration; fidgeting and twitching; pupil dilation; dry mouth, reflected in lip licking; unusual breathing; and abnormal swallowing).

Police interviewers clearly believe that eye behaviors and bodily movements are the two most important kinds of indicators of deception. Poor eye contact was identified as a distinctive and identifiable behavior of lying criminal suspects by a much higher percentage of police interviewers (82.6 percent) than the next most frequently identified variable, hand movement (50 percent). The importance of specific kinds of bodily movements as indicators of deception is reflected in part by the number of specific bodily movements identified. Of the 15 most frequently identified nonverbal cues, 11 involved some form of bodily movement, such as hand movements, foot movements, fidgeting, posture shifts, and object-adapters.

The nonverbal profile for the Type II deceivers encountered by police interrogators is presented in Table 12.2. Results were obtained by asking police interrogators to rate 20 variables (identified in previous deception research as potential indicators of deception) on a 10-point scale as to their usefulness as indicators of deception (a rating of 10 indicated high usefulness, and a 1 indicated very little usefulness). Directional ratings, using a 5-point scale, indicated whether police interrogators believed lying criminal suspects exhibit more or less of a given nonverbal variable at the moment of deception. Interrogators reported that Type II deceivers exhibit eye contact of more limited duration (mean = 0.14) and more overall body nervousness (mean = 1.33) than their truthful counterparts.

Results in Table 12.2 indicate that the eye behaviors and bodily movements of Type II deceivers are the most useful kinds of specific nonverbal cues that indicate deception. Type II deceivers are thought to be identifiable in part by their limited eye contact and by their shifty eyes. In conversations with me, almost all interrogators reported that the pupils of Type II deceivers dilate at the moment of deception.

Type II deceivers interviewed by police interrogators clearly exhibit an abnormal number of specific kinds of bodily movements. Whereas Type II deceivers exhibit more bodily movements than truthful communicators, Type I deceivers exhibit fewer bodily movements

TABLE 12.2   Nonverbal Indicators of Deception: Type II

Variable	Usefulness (1 to 10)			Direction (−1 to +2)		
	Mean	Standard Deviation	Mode	Mean	Standard Deviation	Mode
Eye contact duration	8.12	1.70	10.0	−0.14	1.68	−2.0
Overall body nervousness	7.79	1.60	7.0	1.33	0.70	1.0
Eye movement	7.44	2.07	7.0	1.33	0.70	1.0
Defensiveness gestures	7.07	1.74	7.0	1.07	0.66	1.0
Overall vocal nervousness	6.89	1.84	7.0	1.04	0.70	1.0
Posture shift	6.94	1.86	8.0	1.08	0.73	1.0
Overall facial nervousness	6.89	1.84	7.0	1.04	0.70	1.0
Length of time pausing	6.82	2.09	7.0	1.04	0.70	1.0
Leg movement	6.75	1.93	7.0	1.01	0.69	1.0
Hand movement	6.55	1.78	8.0	0.92	0.59	1.0
Number of pauses	6.54	2.05	5.0	0.88	0.77	1.0
Hand-to-face gestures	6.25	2.05	8.0	0.81	0.77	1.0
Foot movement	6.52	2.05	8.0	1.01	0.72	1.0
Head movement	6.20	2.09	5.0	0.77	0.74	1.0
Number of "ahs"	6.19	2.15	5.0	0.81	0.64	1.0
Number of stutters	6.04	1.85	5.0	0.69	0.72	1.0
Speaking rate	5.90	1.82	5.0	0.52	0.85	1.0
Illustrating gestures	5.53	2.15	5.0	0.65	0.73	1.0
Facial pleasantness	5.09	2.20	5.0	0.09	0.84	0.0
Number of smiles	4.94	2.30	5.0	0.10	0.85	0.0

than their truthful counterparts. The difference may be attributed to the fact that Type II deceivers cannot effectively suppress bodily movement at the time of deception because of the high level of anxiety they experience. In contrast, Type I deceivers do suppress the number of bodily movements they exhibit in their attempts to escape detection. They have the opportunity to consciously control a number of the bodily movements they exhibit because of the relatively low level of anxiety they experience.

As you study the nonverbal profile for the Type II deceiver, you should recognize that any single nonverbal cue that seems indicative of deception could be misleading. Police interrogators repeatedly emphasized that they relied on their overall impression of the suspect's nonverbal behaviors rather than on a single cue. Thus, overall body nervousness, overall vocal nervousness, and overall facial nervousness were viewed as particularly useful indicators of deception.

The nonverbal profile presented in Table 12.2 may not, of course, apply to all Type II deceivers because it is a profile for one specific kind of deceiver. Opportunities for effective impression management are minimal in the high-stress conditions of the police interview. At the same time, there seems good reason to believe that the factors that exert a controlling impact on the nonverbal behaviors of Type II deceivers, both within and outside the context of the police interview, are fundamentally similar. For this reason, the nonverbal profile presented in Table 12.2 should certainly be helpful to you as you seek to identify Type II deception in the real world.

The Deception Process

So far we have concentrated on the two major types of deception that occur and on the specific kinds and relative utility of the nonverbal behaviors that can be used to detect deception. As the title of this chapter suggests, the emphasis has been on detecting deception. We should recognize, however, that just as interpersonal communication is a process consisting of a set of interacting components, deception is a special type of communication consisting of those same components: the message sender (the deceiver), the message, the channel, the context, and the message receiver (the lie detector). In order to understand the nature of deception, it is important to know what variables affect each part of the process and how the parts of the process interact with each other.

The Deceiver

Because lying is an activity I do not condone, my objective in this section is not to provide the deceiver with a blueprint for becoming a more effective deceiver. Instead I will simply attempt to identify some of the more important variables that positively and negatively affect the performance of the deceiver.

Planning and age might be thought to contribute in a positive way to a deceiver's success. However, being better prepared and becoming older hardly ensure success for a deceiver. In fact, if well-prepared liars are also highly motivated, the chances of being detected actually increase (Burgoon, Buller, & Woodall, 1989).

Similarly, the relationship between a deceiver's age and successful lying is so complicated as to almost defy precise generalization. Deception ability does seem to increase with age, but how much it increases depends on the sex of the deceiver, the channel of communication, and the type of lie (Zuckerman et al., 1981).

Three factors can strongly affect a deceiver's performance in a positive way:

1. level of deceiving skill
2. honest demeanor bias
3. personality factors of high Machiavellianism and high self-monitoring

Let us consider each factor separately.

Level of Deceiving Skill

The deceiver's level of skill is very important. In particular, highly successful deceivers are differentiated from their less successful counterparts on the basis of their ability to identify and control the types of communicative behaviors that are most likely to reveal their deception. Control of, or suppression of, behaviors that are an important part of the deceiver stereotype is particularly important. "In fact, deceivers may hold to certain shared beliefs concerning the nonverbal cues that we stereotypically associate with deception and they may give particular attention to monitoring and controlling these 'known' cues of deception (i.e., controlling for lack of eye contact, or attempting to control nervous behaviors)" (Riggio, Tucker, & Widaman, 1987, p. 126).

Honest Demeanor Bias

Secondly, skillful deceivers will make *the honest demeanor bias* work to their advantage. They will recognize that certain types of nonverbal behaviors are typically perceived by potential lie detectors to be more believable than other kinds of behavior. For example, deceivers who exhibit fluent speech and sustained eye contact are making effective use of honest demeanor bias. However, deceivers may lose the advantage of the honest demeanor bias if they act in nonnormative ways that are perceived as "weird" or "fishy" (Bond et al., 1992).

High Machiavellianism and High Self-Monitoring

Finally, a number of personality factors might affect the performance of the deceiver. However, the two personality variables that have consistently been found to have the most positive impact on deception efforts are high Machiavellianism and high self-monitoring (deTurck et al., 1990). The idea is simple: Individuals with these personality types not only tend to be more skilled at assessing the feedback they get from those they are attempting to deceive, but they also can deceive with few, if any, tell-tale signs of guilt.

On the other hand, deceivers must recognize that a number of variables, including those that follow, can negatively affect their efforts to deceive others:

1. a high level of motivation to deceive successfully
2. the associated problems of the need to control certain behaviors—a heightened level of arousal, signs of guilt, and the cognitive complexity of lying
3. high public self-consciousness
4. emotionality

Counterintuitive though the finding may be, a high level of motivation has been found to negatively affect the efforts of individuals to deceive:

> *As the pressure to perform well increases, performers pay closer attention to the processes of performance; however, if the components of the task that they are performing are not consciously known to them, then their efforts at deliberate control backfire, leading to a decrement rather than an increment in task performance.* (DePaulo, Stone, & Lassister, 1985, p. 1201)

In short, the harder some deceivers try, the greater the likelihood that they will give themselves away. The breakdown of a highly motivated liar's performance is reflected partially in the findings that lies told to opposite-sex targets are easier to identify than lies told to same-sex targets, ingratiating lies are easier to detect than noningratiating lies, and senders addressing attractive targets are perceived as less sincere than those addressing unattractive targets (DePaulo et al., 1985). In short, deceivers do least well in trying to deceive the kinds of individuals they most want to deceive.

The effort to control certain behaviors can at times become a disadvantage because controlled behavior often appears to be premeditated, rehearsed, and unspontaneous. A high level of arousal and guilt are related problems in at least one sense. The more aroused a deceiver becomes, the greater the sense of guilt. The feeling of guilt, in turn, often causes a deceiver to lose the ability to control or suppress nervousness behaviors that reveal deception. Finally, the more cognitively complex a lie is, the greater the level of concentration that is required; the result might be an increase in speech pauses or hesitations and increased pupil dilation, with the ultimate result being that the deception is detected (Zuckerman et al., 1981).

For reasons that are probably obvious, lying successfully in public is more difficult than lying successfully in private. In particular, deceivers who exhibit a high degree of "public self-consciousness" are less effective liars than their less self-conscious counterparts. Have you ever seen a bowler who threw gutter balls when people were watching, but who bowled well when they were not watching? If so, you will probably understand that high public self-consciousness negatively affects a liar's performance (Riggio et al., 1987).

Finally, emotionality is negatively correlated with successful lying. The primary reason for this finding is that effective lying requires a carefully controlled presentation of self. Because we expect liars to be upset emotionally, we are more likely to judge them to be deceptive if they express a high level of emotionality.

Because the chapter has focused in detail on the specific nonverbal characteristics that are associated with truthful and deceptive messages, let us turn briefly to the subject of channel. Knowledgeable deceivers will recognize that the nonverbal channels have primacy for most individuals who try to detect deception. For deceivers there are, therefore, at least two critically important questions: How believable is information transmitted by a deceiver over one nonverbal communication channel as opposed to one or more other nonverbal communication channels? How effectively can a deceiver exercise conscious control over one type of nonverbal communication channel as opposed to another?

For the lie detector, the channel variables of major importance are *deception accuracy* and *leakage accuracy* (Zuckerman et al., 1981). The lie detector who is most concerned with deception accuracy must focus on the communication channel of the deceiver that provides the most useful cues for determining whether deception is occurring. We have already established, for example, that the face provides the least reliable information about the occurrence of deception.

The lie detector who is concerned with determining what type of emotion the deceiver is experiencing must decide which nonverbal channel leaks the most information about the deceiver's emotions. For the lie detector concerned with accurately interpreting the deceiver's leakage cues, the choice of communication channel is critically important. Even if they choose the leakiest channel, untrained observers find it almost impossible to interpret a deceiver's leakage cues accurately unless they have access to the truthful baseline, that is, unless they have also seen the deceiver telling the truth.

The context is another important component of the deception process (Millar & Millar, 1995). In fact, the context in which the lying occurs is a vitally important difference between Type I and II deception. Contextual features that maximize the deceiver's arousal, require that the lying be sustained for a long period of time, and involve serious consequences if the deception is detected (defining features of Type II deception) put a great strain on the deceiver. In such contexts it is more likely that deception will be detected. Finally, we have already established that successful lying in public is much more difficult than lying done in private.

The lie detector is the last component of the deception process. Because much of this chapter has focused on the lie detector, you might want to review what has already been said. In summary, at least four important factors have been shown to positively affect the performance of a lie detector:

1. basing deception judgments on information obtained from the deceiver's leakiest channel
2. familiarizing yourself with the deceiver's truthful baseline
3. starting with well-developed skills
4. using deception detection training to further develop skills

Successful lie detectors must deal with at least three negative factors. First, *the truthful judging bias* means that lie detectors are more likely to judge a person's communication as truthful than deceptive. This is true because there seems to be "a general inclination toward trusting the information that others provide. It would be socially awkward to challenge the veracity of another's communication—we tend to give people 'the benefit of the doubt'" (Riggio et al., 1987). Second, the lie detector has to be wary of the honest demeanor bias, which is manifested in a tendency for lie detectors to see individuals with a certain demeanor as more believable, such as those who speak fluently and have direct eye contact. Finally, lie detectors must guard against relying too heavily on stereotypical cues of deception as opposed to cues that have been verified as accurate indicators. For example, the stereotype is that Type I deceivers will exhibit more bodily movements than truthful people. In fact, the reverse is true.

Summary

The development of successful interpersonal relationships requires that individuals develop the ability to detect deception. Successful interpersonal relationships are built on mutual trust. In order to have a defensible basis for determining our level of trust for another person, we must be able to determine if and when that person chooses to be deceptive.

Nonverbal cues have proven to be useful indicators of deception in interpersonal communication. In order to make optimal use of the informational value of nonverbal indicators of deception, however, the human lie detector must be thoroughly familiar with the nonverbal profile for Type I and Type II deceivers. Type I and Type II deceivers differ with regard to the level of anxiety they experience, their fear of the consequences of being detected, and in the length of time they are required to sustain their deception.

Nonverbal cues characteristically exhibited by Type I deceivers seem to be controlled by three factors. Type I deceivers attempt to (a) exercise conscious control over those nonverbal behaviors that they believe to be the defining features of the cultural stereotype for deceivers, (b) exercise conscious control over those nonverbal behaviors that can be most directly and easily monitored at the moment of deception, and (c) exercise effective conscious control over those behaviors that are susceptible to conscious control.

Type I deceivers characteristically exhibit greater overall vocal nervousness, more nonfluencies, and more pauses, and they speak faster than their truthful counterparts. They also exhibit less overall bodily nervousness, and they use fewer of the bodily movements that they can control, such as head, foot, and leg movements. However, they exhibit more self-adaptors and object-adaptors, bodily movements that cannot be consciously controlled, than their truthful counterparts. Facial expressions do not provide a reliable basis for differentiating deceiving from truthful communicators.

Type II deceivers differ from Type I deceivers in that they exhibit many more bodily movements than truthful individuals. Bodily movements and eye behaviors of Type II deceivers are particularly useful cues to their deception. However, we, as human lie detectors, should concentrate on collective measures, such as overall bodily nervousness and overall vocal nervousness, in order to maximize our chances of detecting Type II deception.

In order to understand the complexities of nonverbal deception, it is important to identify and define the components of the deception process: the deceiver, the message, the channel(s), the context, and the lie detector. Your understanding of the deception process will be based on your knowledge of those variables which positively and negatively affect each of the components of the process as those components interact with each other.

References

Bond, C. F., Jr., Omar, A., Pitre, U., Lashley, B. R., Skaggs, L. M., & C. T. Kirk. (1992). Fishy-looking liars: Deception judgment from expectancy violation. *Journal of Personality and Social Psychology, 63,* 969–977.

Buller, D. B., Burgoon, J. K., Buslig, A., & Roiger, J. F. (1994). Interpersonal deception: VIII. Further analysis of the nonverbal correlates of equivocation from the Bavelas et al. (1990) research. *Journal of Language & Social Psychology, 13,* 396–417.

Burgoon, J. K., & Buller, D. V. (1994). Interpersonal Deception: III. Effects of deceit on perceived communication and nonverbal behavior dynamics. *Journal of Nonverbal Behavior, 18,* 155–183.

Burgoon, J. K., Buller, D. B., & Woodall, W. G. (1989). *Nonverbal communication: The unspoken dialogue.* New York: Harper & Row.

Cody, M. J., & O'Hair, H. D. (1983). Nonverbal communication and deception: Differences in deception cues due to gender and communicator dominance. *Communication Monographs, 50,* 175–192.

DePaulo, B. M., Stone, J. I., & Lassiter, G. D. (1985). Telling ingratiating lies: Effects of target sex and target attractiveness on verbal and nonverbal deceptive success. *Journal of Personality and Social Psychology, 48,* 1191–1203.

DePaulo, B. M., Zuckerman, M., & Rosenthal, R. (1980). Humans as lie detectors. *Journal of Communication, 30,* 129–131.

deTurck, M. A., Harszlak, J. J., Bodhorn, D. J., & Texter, L. A. (1990). The effects of training social perceivers to detect deception from behavioral cues. *Communication Quarterly, 38,* 189–199.

deTurck, M. A., & Miller, G. R. (1985). Deception and arousal: Isolating the behavioral correlates of deception. *Human Communication Research, 12,* 181–201.

deTurck, M. A., & Miller, G. R. (1990). Training observers to detect deception: Effects of self-monitoring and rehearsal. *Human Communication Research, 16,* 603–620.

Druckman, D., Rozelle, R. M., & Baxter, J. C. (1982). *Nonverbal communication: Survey, theory, and research.* Beverly Hills: Sage.

Ekman, P. (1985). *Telling lies: Clues to deceit in the marketplace, politics, and marriage.* New York: Norton, 1985.

Ekman, P. (1988). Lying and nonverbal behavior: Theoretical issues and new findings. *Journal of Nonverbal Behavior, 12,* 163–175.

Ekman, P., & Friesen, W. (1969). Nonverbal leakage and clues to deception. *Psychiatry, 32,* 88–106.

Ekman, P., & Friesen, W. (1972). Hand movements. *Journal of Communication, 22,* 353–374.

Ekman, P., & Friesen, W. (1974). Detecting deception from the body and face. *Journal of Personality and Social Psychology, 29,* 288–298.

Ekman, P., Friesen, W. V., & O'Sullivan, M. O. (1988). Smiles when lying. *Journal of Personality and Social Psychology, 54,* 414–420.

Ekman, P., O'Sullivan, M., Friesen, W. V., & Scherer, K. R. (1991). Invited article: Face, voice, and body in detecting deceit. *Journal of Nonverbal Behavior, 15,* 125–135.

Exline, R. V., Thibaut, J., Hickey, C. B., & Gumpert, P. (1970). Visual interaction in relation to Machiavellianism and an unethical act. In R. Christie & F. L. Geis (Eds.), *Studies in Machiavellianism* (pp. 53–75). New York: Academic.

Goodwin, G. L. (1975). PSE: New security tool. *Burroughs Clearing House, 59,* 29.

Hale, J. L., & Stiff, J. B. (1990). Nonverbal primacy in veracity judgments. *Communication Reports, 3,* 75–83.

Harrison, A. A., Hwalek, M., Raney, D. R., & Fritz, J. G. (1978). Cues to deception in an interview situation. *Social Psychology, 41,* 158–159.

Hocking, J. E., & Leathers, D. G. (1980). Nonverbal indicators of deception: A new theoretical perspective. *Communication Monographs, 47,* 119–131.

Kalbfleisch, P. J. (1990). Listening for deception: The effects of medium on accuracy of detection. In R. N. Bostrom (Ed.), *Listening behavior: Measurement and application* (pp. 155–177). New York: Guilford.

Knapp, M. L., & Comadena, M. E. (1979). Telling it like it isn't: A review of theory and research on deception communications. *Human Communication Research, 5,* 270–285.

Knapp, M. L., Hart, R. P., & Dennis H. S. (1974). An exploration of deception as a communication construct. *Human Communication Research, 1,* 15–29.

Kraut, R. E. (1978). Verbal and nonverbal cues in the perception of lying. *Journal of Personality and Social Psychology, 36,* 380–391.

Larson, J. A. (1969). *Lying and its detection.* Montclair, NJ: Patterson Smith.

Leathers, D. G. (1982, November). An examination of police interviewers' beliefs about the utility and nature of nonverbal indicators of deception. Paper presented at the annual convention of the Speech Communication Association, Louisville, KY.

Leathers, D. G., & Hocking, J. E. (1983). *An examination of police interviewers' beliefs about the utility*

and nature of nonverbal indicators of deception. Unpublished manuscript.

Lykken, D. T. (1974). Psychology and the lie detector industry. *American Psychologist, 29,* 725-727.

Matarazzo, J. D., Wiens, A. N., Jackson, R. H., & Manaugh, T. S. (1970). Interviewer speech behavior under conditions of endogenously-present and exogenously-induced motivational states. *Journal of Clinical Psychology, 26,* 148.

McClintock, C. C., & Hunt, R. G. (1975). Nonverbal indicators of affect and deception in an interview setting. *Journal of Applied Social Psychology, 5,* 62–66.

McCornack, S. A., & Levine, T. R. (1990). When lies are uncovered: Emotional and relational outcomes of discovered deception. *Communication Monographs, 57,* 119–138.

Mehrabian, A. (1971). Nonverbal betrayal of feelings. *Journal of Experimental Research in Personality, 5,* 64–75.

Millar, M., & Millar, K. (1995). Detection of deception in familiar and unfamiliar persons: The effects off information restriction. *Journal of Nonverbal Behavior, 19,* 69–84.

O'Hair, D., Cody, M. J., Goss, B., & Krayer, K. J. (1988). The effect of gender, deceit orientation and communicator style on macro-assessments of honesty. *Communication Quarterly, 36,* 77–93.

O'Hair, D., Cody, M. J. & McLaughlin, M. L. (1981). Prepared lies, spontaneous lies, Machiavellianism, and nonverbal communication. *Human Communication Research, 7,* 325–339.

O'Hair, D., Cody, M. J., Wang, X-T, & Chao, E. Y. (1990). Vocal stress and deception detection among Chinese. *Communication Quarterly, 38,* 158–169.

Podlesny, J. A., & Raskin, D. C. (1977). Physiological measures and detection of deception. *Psychological Bulletin, 84,* 784–785.

Riggio, R. E., Tucker, J., & Widaman, K. F. (1987). Verbal and nonverbal cues as mediators of deception ability. *Journal of Nonverbal Behavior, 11,* 126–145.

Smith, M. (1979, May). Nonverbal indicators of deception: The lying suspect. Lecture given at University of Georgia, Athens, GA.

Sniderman, P. M. (1981). *A question of loyalty.* Berkeley: University of California Press.

Zuckerman, M., DePaulo, B. M., & Rosenthal, R. (1981). Verbal and nonverbal communication of deception. In L. Berkowitz (Ed.), *Advances in experimental social psychology* (Vol 14, pp. 1–60). New York: Academic.

Chapter 13

Communicating Consistently

Interpersonal communication frequently features inconsistent messages that represent serious problems for both the message sender and the message receiver. Message senders who communicate inconsistently invite others to infer that they are inept communicators, untrustworthy, or duplicitous. The message sender who uses inconsistent messages is also apt to be perceived as less sincere, honest, straightforward, genuine, and credible than one who does not. When inconsistent messages are used repeatedly in interpersonal communication, they virtually assure that a relationship of mutual trust will not develop.

Inconsistent messages also represent serious problems for the receiver or decoder. Decoders find it unpleasant to respond to messages that contain inconsistent or mutually contradictory meanings. Decoders are forced to bear the burden of attributing intent to a message sender when the message sender's intent is unclear at best and unknown and unknowable at worst. They must decide which of the contradictory meanings is most believable, and why. They must face the fact that an ethically responsible and honest response to an inconsistent message might necessitate a direct challenge to the message sender to resolve the inconsistencies that define a given message. Understandably then, individuals who must cope frequently with inconsistent messages often find that they become anxious. Moreover, individuals who are frequently the target of inconsistent messages over an extended period of time in a specific context, such as in husband–wife communication, have been known to develop mental illness.

With the exception of the sadists or masochists in our midst, individuals rarely make conscious attempts to communicate inconsistently. When they do use inconsistent messages, they usually do so unintentionally, although *intent* is a term that is difficult to define (Stamp & Knapp, 1990). People often communicate inconsistently when they experience one emotion but feel, at least subconsciously, that it is socially appropriate to convey a different emotion.

Consider, for example, the times when someone has called you on the telephone and asked you for a date. Did you respond by saying, "I will not go because I find you to be physically unattractive?" You probably did not, because it seems to be an insensitive way to respond. You might have said, "There is nothing I would rather do, but I have a previous commitment." If you really did not wish to accept the date, it is likely that your words and vocal cues communicated inconsistent messages. Your spoken words probably suggested that the date would have been a highly pleasurable experience, but your unenthusiastic tone of voice probably suggested your conviction that such a date would be anything but pleasurable.

Inconsistent messages are particularly dysfunctional when they create or reinforce an impression quite different from the impression the message sender intended to make. For example, Mehrabian (1981) cited the example of the department head who was welcoming a new employee. The department head wanted to make clear that both department heads and members of the department were treated as equals in the firm and that all employees were encouraged to express their feelings openly to their department heads.

> When the department head actually speaks with the new employee, however, his posture, facial expression, and vocal expressions convey his awareness of his dominant relationship relative to the new member of his department, who comes away from this pep talk with the feeling that the boss is a bit of a phony, that he is trying to be a nice guy, but that he doesn't really mean what he says. In other words, the new man feels that he will be wise not to be critical of anything the boss says or does. (p. 81)

This chapter examines the nature of multichannel messages that communicate inconsistent meanings, as well as the attitudinal, perceptual, and behavioral impact of such messages on decoders, those who must assume the unwelcome burden of coping with inconsistent messages. It becomes clear that multichannel messages that communicate inconsistent or contradictory meanings are a formidable barrier to successful communication. The major reasons that individuals communicate inconsistently are identified not only so that we can better understand the causes of inconsistent messages but also so that we can eliminate such dysfunctional messages from our own communication. Finally, a set of guidelines is provided that communicators can use to help assure that they communicate consistently.

The Nature of Inconsistent Messages

The study of inconsistent communication is based to a large extent on the double-bind theory of interpersonal communication. Not surprisingly, this theory evolved from a study of schizophrenic patients. Schizophrenic patients frequently express themselves in inconsistent ways. Indeed, "where double-binding has become the predominant pattern of communication, and where the diagnostic attention is limited to the overtly most disturbed individual, the behavior of this individual will be found to satisfy the diagnostic criteria of schizophrenia" (Watzlawick, Beavin, & Jackson, 1967, pp. 214–215).

A double-bind is a situation in which: (a) two or more ego-involved individuals are attempting to communicate on matters of substantial physical or psychological value for them (parent–child and husband–wife interactions are examples); (b) a message is transmitted that asserts something and asserts something about its own assertion, and these two assertions are mutually exclusive (the meanings of the messages appear to be undecidable in the traditional sense); and (c) the recipient is often so tied to a particular frame of reference that he or she is unwilling to seek, or is incapable of obtaining, clarification as to the *intended* meaning of the message. Therefore, even though the message may be mildly contradictory, at best, or logically meaningless, at worst, it is communicational reality.

Paradoxical messages illustrate why the decoder may experience a double-bind. Consider the popular paradoxical injunction "Be spontaneous!" or the road sign that reads, "Ignore This Sign." Both messages are paradoxical because they require contradictory responses. To respond to the first command—to be spontaneous—requires a deliberative effort, which is by definition nonspontaneous. To respond to the second command—to ignore the sign—requires obedience within a perceptual framework that assures disobedience.

Paradoxical expressions represent an extreme type of inconsistent message. Such expressions force addressees to respond with behaviors that are incompatible. When employed repeatedly, paradoxical messages might threaten the sanity of the individuals to whom they are addressed. Thus, Watzlawick and coworkers emphasized that

> there is something in the nature of paradox that is of immediate pragmatic and even existential import for all of us; paradox not only can invade interaction and affect our behavior and our sanity but it challenges our belief in the ultimate soundness of our universe. (p. 187)

The double-bind message and response are both forms of maladaptive behavior. As such, they have assumed major importance in the diagnosis and treatment of mental illness. Another type of inconsistent message is much more important to the reasonably well-adjusted individual, however. The object of increasing attention at present is the multichannel message, which conveys conflicting meanings through the verbal and nonverbal channels.

Mehrabian (1981) maintained that the messages we communicate exhibit varying degrees of pleasure–displeasure, arousal–nonarousal, dominance–submissiveness, and like–dislike. *Our messages are inconsistent when our words and nonverbal cues communicate different degrees of pleasure, arousal, dominance, and liking.* For example, the individual who encounters a business associate who is held in low esteem might express pleasure in a verbal greeting but displeasure through such nonverbal cues as averted eyes, frowning, and an unenthusiastic tone of voice. The fast-talking tour guide may communicate high arousal with his or her speaking rate but low arousal with a bored facial expression. The department head welcoming the new employee stressed verbally that the department head and all employees were equals, but contradicted this message with his high-power visual cues. Finally, the wife may verbally express her unqualified affection for her husband while displaying nonverbal indicators of unhappiness or even contempt.

In practice, our inconsistent messages can be either negatively inconsistent or positively inconsistent. A message is *negatively inconsistent* when the nonverbal channel(s) communicates meaning with a negative connotation while the verbal channel communicates a positive connotation. Consider the person with a contemptuous look on his or her face who says, "That was a very perceptive statement." In contrast, a message is *positively inconsistent* when the nonverbal channel(s) communicates meanings with a positive connotation while the verbal channel communicates a negative connotation (e.g., a person nods his or her head, as if to signify understanding, while saying, "Now you've got me totally confused").

When we express ourselves inconsistently, there is frequently a strong predisposition to use negatively inconsistent messages because most communicators are reluctant to express negative emotions and attitudes verbally. As a result, we are inclined to say relatively positive things about individuals with whom we interact, even though our true feelings about that person, or at least about their actions, are rather negative. When our words express an emotion quite different from the one we are actually experiencing, we run a high risk of communicating an inconsistent message. In a high proportion of cases, the type of inconsistent message we do communicate is negatively inconsistent.

Decoding Inconsistent Messages

Because inconsistent messages contain meanings that are ambiguous or contradictory, it is not surprising that such messages are a formidable barrier to successful communication. We know, for example, that parents of disturbed children are more likely to use inconsistent messages than the parents of normal children (Bugental, Love, Kaswan, & April, 1971). Relatedly, the children of parents who communicate inconsistently seem to be less pleasant and more anxious than children of parents who communicate consistently (Hall & Levin, 1979).

Counselors who use inconsistent messages are perceived as less attractive, sincere, and genuine than those who do not (Graves & Robinson, 1976). Both quality of communication and quality of outcomes in negotiating sessions may be negatively affected when negotiators communicate inconsistently (Johnson, McCarthy, & Allen, 1976). The fact that inconsistent messages can represent a serious threat to our personal credibility is illustrated by a study that shows that teachers who communicate inconsistently raise serious doubts in their students' minds about the authenticity and truthfulness of their verbal statements (Feldman, 1976).

Finally, we now know that laboratory researchers can introduce experimenter bias into their own experiments by the use of multichannel messages that are inconsistent (Duncan, Rosenberg, & Finkelstein, 1969). Rosenthal (1966) found that experimenters who introduced bias into their experiments were perceived by subjects as less honest than experimenters who did not introduce bias, because of the tell-tale information provided by their vocal cues.

In short, the impact of the use of inconsistent messages on a communicator's image is usually highly negative. Successful communication reinforces the perception that we are trustworthy, sincere, honest, empathic, and caring individuals. By contrast, the habitual use of inconsistent messages results in the attribution of undesirable image traits that are apt to damage our personal credibility.

Decoders have repeatedly reported an aversion to coping with inconsistent messages. Decoders find inconsistent messages to be anxiety producing. They frequently force the decoder to make negative inferences about the person who uses them, and it is difficult to respond to inconsistent messages in socially acceptable ways. When decoders are forced to respond to inconsistent messages, they prefer to do so in informal as opposed to formal situations (Mehrabian, 1970). Formal situations presumably invite closer scrutiny of the ways decoders actually respond to inconsistent messages.

When decoders are asked to resolve the apparent contradictions in the meanings of multichannel messages that are inconsistent, they must decide which communication channel is the most reliable source of information. Decoders typically rely much more heavily on nonverbal, as opposed to verbal, cues to determine the dominant meaning of an inconsistent message (Argyle, Salter, Nicholson, Williams, & Burgess, 1970). Mehrabian (1981) emphasized that the nonverbal portion of inconsistent messages exerts a disproportionate impact on the decoder when determining the meanings of such messages. Mehrabian wrote that when nonverbal communication

> *contradicts speech, it is more likely to determine the total impact of the message. In other words, touching positions (distance, forward lean, or eye contact), postures, gestures, as well as facial and vocal expressions, can all outweigh words and determine the feelings conveyed by a message.* (p. 78)

The central importance of visual information is undeniable (Argyle, 1988); this is particularly true when a person's task is the decoding of an inconsistent message. In order to emphasize the predominant importance of visual information to individuals who must decode inconsistent messages, some researchers (Burgoon, Buller, & Woodall, 1989) now refer to "visual cue primacy." As we shall see, however, visual cues assume primacy under certain circumstances, but in other circumstances they lose their primacy.

Research has shown that visual communication in the form of facial expressions, gestures, and postures is the dominant source of emotional meaning (Fujimoto, 1972). When a communicator's words and visual cues convey contradictory information about the emotions the communicator is experiencing, the decoder typically relies on the visual cues as the accurate source of information. Empirical research also supports the formula Mehrabian (1981) developed to show the relative importance that decoders attach to words, facial expressions, and vocal cues when they are trying to determine the meaning of inconsistent messages. Of the "total feeling" communicated by a message, decoders attribute 7 percent to words, 38 percent to voice, and 55 percent to facial expressions.

DePaulo and Rosenthal (1979) conducted some fascinating research that further clarifies the weight that decoders attach to different communication channels as sources of information whenever messages are discrepant or inconsistent. Decoders who took their Nonverbal Discrepancy Test (DePaulo & Rosenthal, 1979) quite clearly established the primacy of the visual channel as the source of information they used to resolve contradictions of meaning in inconsistent messages. *Decoders place particular reliance on visual cues when they are trying to determine whether the message sender is experiencing a positive or a negative emotion. However, decoders are more likely to rely on vocal, as opposed to visual, cues in determining the message sender's level of assertiveness.* This finding might be attributed in part to the fact that visual communication is a particularly effective medium for conveying information about the type and intensity of emotions a communicator is experiencing, and the loudness (volume) with which we speak is known to be a particularly effective way of communicating degrees of dominance or submissiveness.

When messages become highly inconsistent, however, visual cues become less important and vocal cues more important as sources of information. In cases where the face communicates a highly pleasant emotion and the voice communicates an unpleasant emotion, for example, decoders tend to discount the reliability of the face as a source of information. Decoders may recognize intuitively that facial expressions are more easily controlled for purposes of deception than vocal cues. "When a communication becomes more and more discrepant, the overall message may begin to seem more and more like a deceptive one, and subjects may begin to weight the audio information relatively more heavily" (DePaulo & Rosenthal, 1979, p. 222).

In fact, Bugental (1974) contended that the weight a decoder attaches to information provided by a given communication channel when messages are inconsistent depends on the credibility of the information. If the information provided by each communication channel is equally credible, the decoder will place primary emphasis on visual cues, with decreasing degrees of emphasis given to vocal cues and to the verbal content of the message. *If the decoder has reason to believe that the information provided by one communication channel lacks credibility, however, a discounting process occurs wherein less weight is attached to the information provided by that channel.*

Context also plays a central role in determining the believability of information communicated by different communication channels. The communication context interacts with the communication channel to determine how credible the information obtained from that channel is and to what degree the information might be discounted. For example, the famous filmmaker Eisenstein showed the same equivocal facial expression to different audiences. He found that the audiences interpreted the same facial expression as horror, love, or concentration, depending on whether the facial expression was juxtaposed on film with a shot of a corpse, a baby, or a machine (Archer & Akert, 1984).

In contrasting the informational value of verbal and vocal cues in inconsistent messages, Bugental (1974) stressed that *the verbal content is disregarded if the vocal cues seem believable.* She emphasizes that what

> *appears to be occurring is a channel-discounting process; that is, if the intonation is convincing, the content is disregarded. If, on the other hand, the speaker has a slow, deliberate, polished delivery (which was found here to be associated with noncongruence between facial expression and voice), the approval or disapproval with the voice fails to have any significant direct effects on the interpretation of the message.* (p. 131)

This same channel-discounting process helps explain why vocal cues become more important and facial expressions less important whenever messages are highly inconsistent. Decoders clearly attach the greatest importance to visual cues as the source of information used in determining the dominant meaning of an inconsistent message. Their commitment to visual cues is qualified, however. If decoders have reason to believe that visual cues are providing counterfeit or deceptive information, they tend to discount that information and place a higher priority on information obtained from other communication channels. However, although facial expressions are used most frequently to deceive, the voice also may be used deceptively.

In considering the importance of sound attributes that might be indicative of deception in inconsistent messages, silence should not be overlooked. *When* a communicator becomes silent and *for how long* the communicator remains silent can affect the credibility of information communicated by vocal cues. Although silence may serve a number of communicative functions (Ehrenhaus, 1988; Lippard, 1988), judgments of deception are often strongly affected by the type of pausing that occurs; pausing phenomena as indicators of deception were discussed in Chapter 12.

Research cited to this point reveals the priorities that decoders attach to different communication channels as sources of information that can be used to interpret inconsistent messages. What this research does not reveal, however, is what communicative behaviors decoders exhibit in responding to inconsistent messages. I addressed that subject in a study designed to determine the impact of inconsistent messages on verbal and nonverbal decoding behaviors (Leathers, 1979).

In that study, subjects were assigned to 20 separate problem-solving groups. Each group was asked to discuss what, if anything, should be done to promote better relations between black and white students at the University of Georgia. Subjects in 10 of the groups had to respond to inconsistent messages introduced by a Confederate who was a member of those groups; subjects in the other 10 groups had to respond to consistent messages introduced by a Confederate.

Both negatively and positively inconsistent messages were introduced into the discussion of the experimental groups. For example, Confederates introduced a negatively inconsistent message when they addressed other discussants with a look of contempt while saying, "That was a very perceptive statement." Confederates introduced a positively inconsistent message when they responded to discussants while leaning forward (as if to signify interest) and saying, "I find that to be a very uninteresting statement." Discussants in this experiment were required to respond to four types of negatively inconsistent, and four types of positively inconsistent, messages.

Detailed analyses of the verbal and nonverbal behaviors that discussants used to respond to inconsistent messages lends support to the following conclusions: (a) discussants decoded consistent messages with ease, but inconsistent messages had a highly disruptive impact on their decoding behaviors; (b) discussants responded to inconsistent messages in a way that is seemingly inconsistent; and (c) discussants responded to positively inconsistent messages in a much more guarded and negative manner than they responded to negatively inconsistent messages.

The highly disruptive impact of inconsistent messages is reflected in the fact that decoders responding to inconsistent, as opposed to consistent, messages were more uncertain, withdrawn, confused, displeased, and hostile. However, they were also more deliberative, analytical, responsive, and interested than decoders responding to consistent messages. It is curious that a decoder could be withdrawn and interested at the same time or exhibit both deliberative behavior and hostility.

In fact, the videotapes of the discussions reveal that the behavioral response to inconsistent messages appears to be defined characteristically by a sequence made up of three phases. In Phase 1, the receiver exhibits confusion and uncertainty about how to decode the inconsistent message. In Phase 2, the receiver's level of concentration seems to increase markedly as he or she becomes more deliberative and interested in the inconsistent message; the receiver frequently stares thoughtfully at the Confederate, as if searching for additional clues to clarify the meaning of the inconsistent message. In Phase 3, the receiver seems to move from expressions of displeasure and hostility, directed to the message sender, to outright withdrawal.

To illustrate the sequential nature of the decoder's behavioral responses to inconsistent messages, a representative response from the experiment is provided here:

Inconsistent Message

(*Contempt*) Ron, that was a very perceptive statement.

Response

Verbal Channel: (*Pause*) Huh? What are you referring to?

Nonverbal Channel: Ron's eyebrows move up, his mouth drops open, and he gets a quizzical and confused expression on his face. Ron bites his lower lip with his teeth, jabs nervously at his belt with his left hand, and turns away from the Confederate to the other discussant, with his palms upturned, as if seeking their help in dealing with the inconsistent message. [Phase 1 decoding behavior signals confusion with uncertainty.] Ron then turns back toward the Confederate, leans forward, rubs his forehead with the middle fingers of his right hand, as if deep in thought, and stares intently at the Confederate. [Phase 2 decoding behavior signals a high degree of deliberation and interest in the message just transmitted.] At this point, Ron scowls at the Confederate and, after brief thought, his scowl changes to a sneer. Finally, Ron completely abandons his attempt to interpret the meaning of the inconsistent message and stares down into his notes. [Phase 3 decoding behavior has moved from expressions of displeasure and hostility to withdrawal from the discussion.]

Decoders who were forced to respond to positively inconsistent, as opposed to negatively inconsistent, messages became quite uncertain and tentative in their actions, although they expressed displeasure, both facially and bodily. The obvious question is why did decoders find it more difficult and more unpleasant to cope with positively inconsistent than negatively inconsistent messages? There might be a number of reasons, but two seem particularly important. First, because decoders encounter negatively inconsistent messages much more frequently than positively inconsistent messages, they are more accustomed to dealing with that type of message. Secondly, decoders may prefer sarcastic messages (e.g., a compliment accompanied by a look of contempt) to insincere messages (e.g., a verbal expression of disinterest accompanied by a nonverbal expression of interest).

Results of this study (Leathers, 1979) support the double-bind theory, which predicts that individuals will respond to inconsistent messages in one of the following ways:

1. They will attempt, unsuccessfully, to determine the literal meaning of the inconsistent message.
2. They will increase their level of concentration as they search diligently for what they believe to be overlooked clues that will clarify the meaning of the message.
3. They will withdraw from further involvement with the message sender.

The results of the study support the conclusion that decoders responding to inconsistent messages employ not one but all three of these behavioral alternatives.

The decoding of inconsistent messages focuses our attention on how decoders use the message sender's nonverbal behaviors in making attributions about the message sender's intentions, motivations, and goals. Although no study has focused directly on the role of nonverbal behaviors in shaping the attributions that receivers use to resolve inconsistent messages, Manusov (1990) studied the role of nonverbal behaviors in shaping attributions in a general sense.

Reasons for Inconsistent Messages

In view of the fact that inconsistent messages are so often dysfunctional and disruptive, the successful communicator should try to avoid using such messages. The first step in any attempt to eliminate inconsistent messages is to understand why messages are or become inconsistent. Put most succinctly, what are the major reasons for inconsistent messages? Although there are many reasons why individuals communicate inconsistently, the following are particularly important:

1. A communicator's intent may be unclear or undecipherable.
2. There could be a disparity between the stated and actual intent of the message.
3. Inconsistent messages might be motivated by multiple intentions that, in turn, are incompatible or contradictory.
4. Individuals might be made uncomfortable by the necessity of communicating unpleasant or bad news to another person.
5. There is often a striking difference between the impression we are trying to make in public and our internal states and feelings.

In order to understand why individuals communicate inconsistently, we begin with the important concept of intent. Motley (1990) maintained that two of the most fundamental assumptions made about communication are (a) one cannot *not* communicate and (b) communication requires a sender's intention to transmit a message. Watzlawick and coworkers (1967) are responsible for the first axiom, whereas countless communication scholars might claim credit for the second. Note that two fundamental axioms about communication are in themselves inconsistent. Motley (1990) captured the essence of the debate over whether a communicator's intent is a central defining feature of communication when he wrote:

> *Generally, those who claim that communication requires intention would say that since some behaviors are not accompanied by intent, then one* can indeed *not communicate. Those, on the other hand, who do not require communication to be intentional include virtually all behavior as communicative, and thus would say that one* cannot *not communicate.* (p. 3)

In their enlightening discussion of intent, Stamp and Knapp (1990) noted that *intentionality* suggests to many scholars that communication should be defined as an intentional effort that takes place at varying degrees of consciousness with the ultimate objective of attaining a given goal or set of goals. In effect, the notion of intentionality provides a rational basis for constructing messages that are clear and unambiguous. By contrast, inconsistent messages often result when the intent of the message is unclear or implied, or when the intentions of the message sender are multiple in nature.

Remember the central role that a communicator's intent plays in the formulation of clear and consistent messages as we turn now to the reasons individuals communicate inconsistently. First, messages are frequently inconsistent if a message sender's objective or intent is less than clear to the message sender. Moreover, if the message sender attempts to formulate a message that is nonintentional, in the sense that it has no apparent purpose or goal, the chances that the message will be inconsistent are even greater.

Let us assume, for example, that a young couple encounters each other for the first time after they have had a bitter fight. The person who speaks first may still be trying to clarify the intent or purpose of the original message, that is, to apologize, to criticize, to equivocate, and so on. Because the message sender's intent is unclear to the message sender, it is quite likely the message sender will communicate inconsistently. The verbal content of the greeting might be affectively positive, whereas the nonverbal portion is affectively negative, just as the nonverbal message conveys the latent resentment which the message sender still feels.

Manusov and Rodriguez (1989) indicated that individuals attribute intent to any given message at a rate greater than chance. The attribution of intentionality to a message is far from a simple matter, however. The nature of the nonverbal behaviors also affects the types of attributions made. Thus perceivers are more likely to attribute intent to nonimmediate behaviors than to nonverbal immediacy behaviors directed toward them (Manusov, 1991). Interestingly, Manusov's research suggests that subjects usually interpret positively labeled nonverbal messages as intentional, but negative messages are often viewed as unintentional. Negative messages in turn may more frequently be viewed incorrectly as unintentional so that the recipient of the message can more effectively protect her or his self-image.

Second, messages are apt to be inconsistent when there is a disparity between a person's stated and real intent, or between the message sender's publicly identified and real feelings about a person. Societal pressures and norms are such that we frequently find it undesirable or imprudent to reveal our true intentions, feelings, and motivations in public. Whereas my real intention may be to get the position my boss now holds for myself, my stated intention in public might necessarily be a steadfast desire to be supportive of my boss. In order to avoid revealing my true intentions, I may carefully control my facial expressions when in the presence of my boss via a technique of facial management such as falsification. When there is a disparity or even incompatibility between our stated and real intent, the verbal and nonverbal portions of our messages are likely to become inconsistent. If we consciously control the content of our verbal messages, we may continue to communicate our stated intent in public. Because the nonverbal portion of our message is much more difficult to control consciously, however, one or more of the nonverbal channels of communication could leak our real intent to the message receiver.

Third, the message sender who has multiple intentions and multiple goals will find it difficult to avoid using inconsistent messages. (Stamp & Knapp, 1990). President George Bush is a good example of a communicator whose multiple intentions and goals have resulted in inconsistent messages. Bush expressed a desire to be well liked at the same time that he has expressed a desire to be perceived as a strong leader. As you discovered in Chapter 10, those goals can be inconsistent. George Bush cultivated the image of the tough-talking, macho leader during the presidential campaign, but during budget conferences with members of Congress in 1990 he became the victim of his own weak and inconsistent messages. Thus, *Newsweek* magazine stressed that after "20 months of building a presidential image, George Bush suddenly reverted to caricature. Repeatedly, flip-flopping on the budget bill, placating his enemies, shouting incomprehensible wisecracks, and taking no stand on principle, he looked goofy" ("Bush League," 1990).

Fourth, our messages can become inconsistent whenever we are forced to communicate bad news or unpleasant information to other individuals. I know very few people who would not be uncomfortable saying to someone, "You are a pompous ass," "You have no social life because you are ugly," or "You are universally recognized as a pathological liar." Instead we use euphemisms to express such unpleasantries. We try to soften the impact of the bad news by qualification, indirection, or even equivocation. The pompous ass may become a person who is a "bit stiff" or "occasionally preoccupied with self." The ugly person may be transformed verbally into a person who "has chosen not to use modern beauty aids." Verbally, the pathological liar may be transformed into a person who "exaggerates on occasion." When we use euphemisms, we do so because being the bearer of bad news makes us uncomfortable. The result is often that there is an inconsistency in the tone if not the actual meanings communicated by our verbal and nonverbal messages.

Finally, our messages can be inconsistent because there might be a great difference between the feelings we are experiencing internally and the feelings we would like others to believe we are experiencing. In many public situations, for example, we find it important to stress how confident we feel. At the same time that we say we are feeling confident, we may be experiencing the dry mouth, accelerated heart rate, and sweaty palms so indicative of anxiety. We begin to communicate inconsistently at the point where our level of anxiety becomes high enough to be manifested in external, nonverbal behaviors that are recognized as nervousness behaviors. In short, we begin to communicate messages of confidence and anxiety simultaneously.

Guidelines for Communicating Consistently

Inconsistent messages represent a major deterrent to successful communication. They deter communication for several reasons: In the first place, they reflect negatively on the communicator's skill. They suggest that the communicator is unwilling to, or does not have the capacity to, communicate clearly. Multichannel messages that communicate inconsistent or contradictory meanings are by definition unclear. As a result, they place an unwelcome burden on the individuals who must decode them. In contrast, results from a number of studies have demonstrated "that when nonverbal cues convey consistent meanings, the availability of greater numbers of these cues facilitates communicational accuracy" (DePaulo & Rosenthal, 1979).

Second, inconsistent messages are undesirable because they deprive communicators of the valuable opportunity of exercising effective conscious control over their communicative behaviors—for instance, to project a particularly desirable image. The perceptual impact of inconsistent messages on the image we project is almost always undesirable. The primary reason for this is that the defining features of the image we wish to project are not accepted by the decoder as believable. The desirable features of our image are often discounted or rejected, because the inconsistent messages invite inferences about our personal qualities and image traits which are far from flattering.

Although I maintain that the impact of inconsistent messages is usually undesirable, I do recognize the growing number of theorists who argue that purposeful ambiguity is a strategy in organizational communication. Eisenberg (1984) stressed that *"clarity is only a measure of communicative competence if the individual has as his or her goal to be clear"* (p. 230).

Successful communication usually places a premium on the ability to communicate consistently. We must, therefore, make a special effort to assure that the communication channels we use do in fact communicate similar, or at least mutually compatible, meanings. When our words, facial expressions, and vocal cues all function to provide the same kinds of information, there is a minimal probability that our message will be misinterpreted. In contrast, the communication of inconsistent messages via two or more of the human communication channels invites unflattering inferences about our communication skills and about the kind of person we are perceived to be.

To communicate consistently, we must carefully monitor our cues to make sure they are sending essentially the same kinds of meanings. If they are not, we must make adjustments in the messages communicated by one or more of the channels we are using. The following guidelines should be useful in helping to assure that we do communicate consistently.

Guideline #1

Because our facial expressions are the major medium for the expression of our emotions, we must make a special effort to display genuine facial emotions that are compatible with the type and intensity of emotions that we express verbally.

Guideline #2

The level of attentiveness, interest, and arousal communicated via our eye behaviors must be consistent with the level of those same attitudes and emotions that are communicated through other channels.

Guideline #3

We should strive to communicate similar degrees of liking, assertiveness, and power via our spoken words and bodily cues.

Guideline #4

The level of involvement we communicate via our spatial orientation to other persons should be comparable to the level of involvement we communicate by other nonverbal as well as verbal behaviors.

Guideline #5

In order to project an image that emphasizes a set of personality traits and personal qualities that are mutually reinforcing, we must carefully consider the decisions we make with regard to clothing and other items that define our personal appearance.

Guideline #6

We must carefully monitor our vocal cues to help assure that the personality traits that are inferred from such cues are consistent with the personality traits that are inferred from the words that we utter.

Guideline #7

The level of intimacy, reassurance, or emotional support we seek to communicate via our touching behavior, and other nonverbal and verbal behaviors, must be compatible.

Guideline #8

To avoid the inference that we are being deceptive, our verbal, vocal, and visual cues must communicate similar levels of self-confidence, self-assurance, and immediacy.

Summary

Multichannel messages that are inconsistent may take one of two forms. A message is negatively inconsistent when the nonverbal channels communicates meanings with a negative connotation while the verbal channel communicates a positive connotation. In contrast, a message is positively inconsistent when the nonverbal channel communicates meanings with a positive connotation while the verbal channel communicates a negative connotation. Both types of inconsistent messages represent formidable barriers to successful communication to the message sender as well as to the message receiver.

Decoders typically rely much more heavily on visual cues than on other types of nonverbal or verbal cues in resolving the meaning of inconsistent messages. Visual cues are a particularly important type of cue whenever the inconsistent message communicates contradictory information about the type of emotion the message sender is experiencing. Vocal cues are given greater weight when different degrees of assertiveness are communicated by nonverbal and verbal means. Ultimately, the importance attached to information provided by different communication channels (when the message is inconsistent) depends on the believability of the information provided by a given communication channel.

The use of inconsistent messages is highly undesirable. The first step in any attempt to eliminate inconsistent messages is to understand why messages are or become inconsistent. The primary reasons that individuals communicate inconsistently are (a) a communicator's intent may be unclear or undecipherable; (b) there might be a disparity between the stated and actual intent of the message; (c) inconsistent messages could be motivated by multiple intentions that, in turn, are incompatible or contradictory; (d) individuals might be made uncomfortable by the necessity of communicating unpleasant or bad news to another person; and (e) there may be a striking difference between the impression we are trying to make in public and our internal states and feelings.

To use inconsistent messages repeatedly is to invite unflattering characterization of your communication skills and undesirable attributions about your personality traits and personal qualities. The communicator who is to be successful must attach the highest priority to the goal of communicating consistently. To help assure consistent communication, the guidelines presented at the end of this chapter should be carefully considered.

References

Archer, D., & Akert, R. M. (1984). Problems of context and criterion in nonverbal communication: A new look at the accuracy issue. In M. Cook, (Ed.), *Issues in person perception* (pp. 114–144). New York: Methuen.

Argyle, M. (1988). *Bodily communication* (2nd ed.). London: Methuen.

Argyle, M., Salter, V., Nicholson, H., Williams, M., & Burgess, P. (1970). The communication of inferior and superior attitudes by verbal and nonverbal signals. *British Journal of Social and Clinical Psychology, 9,* 230.

Bugental, D. E. (1974). Interpretations of naturally occurring discrepancies between words and intonation: Modes of inconsistency resolution. *Journal of Personality and Social Psychology, 30,* 125–133.

Bugental, D. E., Love, L. R., Kaswan, J. W., and April, C. (1971). Verbal-nonverbal conflict in parental messages to normal and disturbed children. *Journal of Abnormal Psychology, 77,* 9.

Burgoon, J. K., Buller, D. B., & Woodall, W. G. (1989). *Nonverbal communication: The unspoken dialogue.* New York: Harper & Row.

Bush league: The president stumbles, Congress bumbles, boooo! (1990, October 22). *Newsweek,* p. 3.

DePaulo, B. M., & Rosenthal, R. (1979). Ambivalence, discrepancy, and deception in nonverbal communication. In R. Rosenthal, (Ed.), *Skill in nonverbal communication: Individual differences* (pp. 204–248). Cambridge, MA: Oelgeschlager.

Duncan, S. D., Rosenberg, M. J., & Finkelstein, J. (1969). The paralanguage of experimenter bias. *Sociometry, 32,* 217.

Ehrenhaus, P. (1988). Silence and symbolic expression. *Communication Monographs, 55,* 41–57.

Eisenberg, E. M. (1984). Ambiguity as a strategy in organizational communication. *Communication Monographs, 51,* 227–242.

Feldman, R. S. (1967). Nonverbal disclosure of teacher deception and interpersonal affect. *Journal of Educational Psychology, 68,* 807–816.

Fujimoto, E. K. (1972). The comparative communicative power of verbal and nonverbal symbols (Doctoral dissertation, Ohio State University, Columbus, 1971). *Dissertation Abstracts International, 32,* 7A.

Graves, J. R., & Robinson, J. D., II (1976). Proxemic behavior as a function of inconsistent verbal and nonverbal messages. *Journal of Counseling Psychology, 23,* 336–337.

Hall, J. A., & Levin, S. (1979). *Affect and verbal-nonverbal discrepancy in schizophrenic and normal family communication.* Unpublished manuscript.

Johnson, D. M., McCarthy, K., & Allen, T. (1976). Congruent and contradictory verbal and nonverbal communication of cooperativeness and competitiveness in negotiations. *Communication Research, 3,* 288–289.

Leathers, D. B. (1979). The impact of multichannel message inconsistency on verbal and nonverbal decoding behaviors. *Communication Monographs, 46,* 88–100.

Lippard, P. V. (1988). The rhetoric of silence: The society of friends' unprogrammed meeting for worship. *Communication Quarterly, 36,* 145–156.

Manusov, V. (1990). An application of attribution principles to nonverbal behavior in romantic dyads. *Communication Monographs, 57,* 104–118.

Manusov, V. (1991). Perceiving nonverbal messages: Effects of immediacy and encoded intent on receiver judgments. *Western Journal of Speech Communication, 53,* 235–253.

Manusov, V., & Rodriguez, J. S. (1989). Intentionality behind nonverbal messages: A perceiver's perspective. *Journal of Nonverbal Behavior, 13,* 15–24.

Mehrabian, A. (1970). When are feelings communicated inconsistently? *Journal of Experimental Research in Personality, 4,* 206–211.

Mehrabian, A. (1981). *Silent messages* 2nd ed. Belmont, CA: Wadsworth.

Motley, M. T. (1990). On whether one can(not) not communicate: An examination via traditional communication postulates. *Western Journal of Speech Communication, 54,* 1–20.

Rosenthal, R. (1966). *Experimenter effects in behavioral research.* New York: Appleton.

Stamp, G. H., & Knapp, M. L. (1990). The construct of intent in interpersonal communication. *Quarterly Journal of Speech, 76,* 282–299.

Watzlawick, P., Beavin, J. H., & Jackson, D. D. (1967). *Pragmatics of human communication: A study of interactional patterns, pathologies, and paradoxes.* New York: Norton.

Successful Communication in Applied Settings

Nonverbal Determinants of Successful Interviews

Much like death and taxes, interviews are unavoidable. Because interviews play such a central role in our professional and personal lives, we attach a high priority to the successful interview. Rare indeed is the job applicant who does not prefer to approach a selection interview with a feeling of confidence and the anticipation of success. The married couple who bring the accumulated problems of a troubled marriage to a counseling interview can, or should, have a desire to resolve their problems.

In spite of the high aspirations we may bring to an interview, this kind of communication is often associated with a high level of anxiety. Such high anxiety can be attributed to at least two factors. Interviews have the potential to reveal much highly personal information about our self-definition, self-esteem, and self-confidence. Interviews are also a high-risk endeavor; unsuccessful interviews could have immediate and unpleasant consequences.

Consider the case of Mark Harrington, job applicant. Harrington is about to have a selection interview. He is being interviewed for a position as a sales representative for a major firm which manufactures and sells electrical appliances. As he contemplates the interview, he realizes that recent Equal Employment Opportunity legislation provides him with a measure of protection. He can no longer be asked certain types of questions that might reflect negatively on the impression he creates. For example, he cannot legally be asked to provide a picture of himself, to describe what kind of discharge he received from service, to reveal whether he is married or is living with someone, or indicate what fraternity he belonged to in college (Stewart & Cash, 1994).

At the same time, Harrington realizes that he faces a paradoxical situation as a communicator. Professional interviewers have traditionally attached much importance to the interviewee's ability to communicate effectively. He must communicate in an assertive, self-confident, enthusiastic, and pleasant manner, one which serves to enhance the interviewer's perceptions of his intelligence, leadership potential, and sociability. He also recognizes that the pressures of the job interview have the potential to minimize the probability that he will

"I FIND YOUR DOSSIER TO BE MOST UNUSUAL."

CARTOON 14.1

communicate in such a manner. In fact, he fears that the interview may prove to be disastrous, in view of the fact that he stutters, is 40 pounds overweight, and has never been able to sustain direct eye contact. If you were Mark Harrington, what would you do to improve your chances for a successful interview?

Harrington would be well advised to familiarize himself with the nonverbal profile of successful job interviewees. There is now a substantial body of research to support the view that an interviewee's nonverbal cues frequently function as major determinants of success in the job interview. In Harrington's case, most of the communicative cues that he can effectively control in his upcoming job interview will probably be nonverbal in nature.

Harrington's communicative liabilities are likely more numerous and severe than yours. Nonetheless, the example may focus attention on the *critically important role that nonverbal cues frequently assume, not only in shaping an interviewer's perceptions, but also in affecting a decision to hire.*

Nonverbal communication assumes added importance in the context of the interview because nonverbal cues can provide the kinds of highly personal information frequently sought by interviewers. Stewart and Cash (1994) recognized the functional importance of nonverbal communication in the job interview when they wrote that the "intimate and personal nature of the interview (the parties are often a mere arm's length apart and are directly involved in the topic and outcome of the interview) tends to magnify the importance of nonverbal communication" (p. 33).

There are many kinds of interviews in addition to selection and counseling interviews, of course. Exit interviews, informational interviews, performance-appraisal interviews, and sales interviews are all important in our society. This chapter will concentrate on only two types of interviews, however. Successful communication in the selection and the counseling interviews is probably important to the largest number of people because of the frequency with which those kinds of interviews occur in their lives.

The central objective of this chapter is to specify the kinds of nonverbal cues that are consistently associated with both successful and unsuccessful communication in selection and counseling interviews. By providing detailed nonverbal profiles of the successful job interviewee and the successful counselor, we do not mean to de-emphasize the importance of more traditional kinds of performance criteria. The following remain important: (a) express yourself verbally in a clear and logical manner, (b) adapt to the interests and concerns of the interviewer, and (c) demonstrate your mastery of relevant information. As the following sections will demonstrate, however, the cultivation of the foregoing is necessary but may not be sufficient to ensure success in an interview.

The Job Interview

Success in a job interview can be defined in various ways. Interviewees could consider an interview successful simply because they acquired interviewing experience or because they met or exceeded their own performance standards. They might even consider the interview successful if they resisted the temptation of accepting a position with dubious merits. The interviewer, on the other hand, may consider an interview successful if it elicited the information necessary to make a defensible decision.

Critical Interviewer Decisions

The most critical decision made by a selection interviewer is whether to accept or reject the job applicant; the interviewer can also place the interviewee in a "reserved" category, pending follow-up interviews (Kinicki & Lockwood, 1985). In addition, the interviewer must make critical decisions with regard to ratings of the applicant's qualifications, relative acceptability for a given position, and, perhaps, starting salary (Anderson, 1991; Anderson & Shackelton, 1990).

These critical decisions are in turn affected by the interviewer's judgments about the effectiveness of the interviewee's performance in the job interview. McGovern and Tinsley (1978) maintained that the following factors are critical in affecting a job interviewer's judgments about the interviewee:

1. ability to communicate
2. aggressiveness and initiative
3. self-confidence
4. enthusiasm and motivation
5. intelligence
6. leadership potential

7. maturity
8. persuasiveness
9. pleasant personality and sociability
10. positive attitude

Because most of those abilities and personal qualities are difficult to measure by objective means, interviewers must rely heavily on their own perceptions.

The prospective job interviewee would be justified in asking at least two questions, at this point. First, are the interviewee's nonverbal cues likely to exert a major influence on the judgments the interviewer makes about specific abilities and personal characteristics such as ability to communicate, self-confidence, and sociability? Second, does the available evidence suggest that accept and reject decisions are affected in consistent and predictable ways by the nonverbal cues exhibited by the interviewee? As we shall see, the answers to both questions seem to be yes.

Nonverbal Profile of Successful Interviewees

McGovern and Tinsley (1978) provided solid support for the claim that an interviewee's nonverbal cues can be important determinants of success in the job interview. In their research, two groups of interviewees were labeled, respectively, "high nonverbal interviewees" and "low nonverbal interviewees," on the basis of the distinctive kinds of nonverbal cues they exhibited in a videotaped interview. The high nonverbal interviewees maintained steady eye contact; used varied voice modulations to express appropriate affect; demonstrated appropriately high energy level by hand gestures, smiling, and general body movement; and responded to interviewer questions with fluidity and little hesitation. By contrast, the low nonverbal interviewees avoided eye contact; displayed little or no affect; had a low energy level; and spoke in a broken, nonfluent manner.

Fifty-two professional interviewers from business and industry rated the two groups of subjects on the 10 interviewee characteristics previously identified as particularly important to professional interviewers. They also classified interviewees on the basis of which ones they would invite for a second interview.

The results provide strong endorsement for the importance of nonverbal cues as determinants of successful interviews. Thus, the professional interviewers gave significantly higher ratings to the high as opposed to the low nonverbal interviewees on 39 of 40 ratings they made of factors such as enthusiasm/motivation, confidence in self, persuasiveness, and pleasant personality. Moreover, the ratings of the interviewees' effectiveness were made after each of four 4-minute excerpts from the interview. The strong positive impact of the desirable nonverbal cues on the interviewers' perceptions remained constant during the full 16 minutes of the interview.

Finally, the nonverbal behaviors of the two groups of interviewees had a dramatic impact on the interviewers' decisions to invite interviewees for a second interview. Fully 89 percent of the interviewers who saw the high nonverbal interviewees would have invited them back for a second interview, but 100 percent of those who saw the low nonverbal interviewees would *not* have invited them for a second interview. The researchers noted that it would be hard to overstate the impact of nonverbal communication on the degree of success experienced in the job interview. They concluded that "it would be safe to say that the candidate who avoids eye contact, stutters and stammers, and is generally unemotional and flat will match a common stereotype of a 'reject' candidate" (p. 171).

A second study (Forbes & Jackson, 1980) is perhaps even more illuminating, in two respects. It focused on *real* as opposed to *simulated* job interviews, and examined the impact of desirable and undesirable interviewer nonverbal profiles on the reject and accept decisions of professional interviewers. In this instance, 101 recent engineering graduates were interviewed for real jobs by professional interviewers with extensive education and experience in engineering. The authors hypothesized that favorable decisions to employ would be associated with the interviewees who exhibited positive nonverbal styles, and reject decisions would be associated with the job candidates who exhibited unfavorable nonverbal styles.

The results strongly supported the hypothesis. Eye behavior seemed to be the most reliable nonverbal indicator of success or failure in those job interviews. Thus, direct eye contact occurred significantly more often in the accept interview than in the reserve or reject group; interviewees were either accepted or rejected for available jobs or placed in a reserve category, where follow-up interviews were possible. Gaze avoidance and eye wandering occurred much less frequently in the accept than in the reserve or reject group.

Although body position did not differentiate reliably between the three groups of interviewees, both smiling and frowning were important. Interviewees who were accepted for jobs smiled much more frequently than those who were placed on reserve or were rejected; those who were rejected frowned more than those who were accepted. Moreover, previous chapters have reported that individuals who smile "appropriately" are perceived as more credible (Bugental, 1986), and that individuals who exhibit "felt" smiles tend to be perceived as honest, whereas those who exhibit "masking" smiles that hide true feelings tend to be viewed as deceptive (Ekman, Friesen, & O'Sullivan, 1988).

Finally, interviewees who were accepted exhibited more head movement (in the form of affirmative nodding) and less frequently held their head in a static position than interviewees who were either rejected or placed on reserve. In short, eye behaviors, facial expressions, and head movements—both individually and collectively—proved to be good predictors of success or failure in the "real job" interview situation.

Eye behaviors, high-immediacy behaviors, and vocal cues have all been repeatedly identified as important determinants of success in the job interview. Physical attractiveness, in contrast, has not at this point been found to exert a strong and uniformly positive impact on the perceptions of job interviewers.

Eye behaviors clearly play a central role in the job interview. They are known to exert a significant impact on the perceived effectiveness of both the interviewee and the interviewer. Interviewees who sustain eye contact for the shortest amount of time have consistently been viewed as lowest in self-confidence (Tessler & Sushelsky, 1978). Similarly, interviewers who have received particularly unfavorable ratings from interviewees have been found to exhibit minimum amounts of eye contact (Kleinke, Staneski, & Berger, 1975). Conversely, individuals who sustain eye contact in a job interview are viewed as more persuasive (Hornik & Ellis, 1988). Interviewees who look directly at the interviewer not only are more likely to be hired, but also make a much more favorable impression, in that they are viewed as more assertive, confident, and as having more initiative (Arvey & Campion, 1984; Tullar, 1989).

Exhibiting high-immediacy behaviors is also extremely important in the job interview. Interviewees who communicate *high immediacy* (via sustained eye contact, smiling, attentive posture, direct body orientation, illustrator gestures, and relatively close physical proximity to the interviewer), as opposed to low immediacy, seem to markedly increase their chances of being hired. Imada and Hakel (1977) found that 86 percent of the interviewees who exhibited high-immediacy behaviors were recommended by the interviewers for the jobs for which they applied, but only 19 percent of the interviewees who exhibited low-immediacy behaviors received a similar recommendation.

You should note that adaptor gestures are one of the most damaging types of low-immediacy behaviors you can exhibit in a job interview. One of the critical factors job interviewers use in assessing a job interview is level of self confidence. Adaptor gestures such as hand wringing, hand-to-face gestures, and fidgeting all indicate nervousness, and, conversely, that the interviewee's level of self-confidence is eroding. Fidgeting is particularly undesirable because sometimes it is associated stereotypically in the interviewer's mind with the excessive movement that deceivers exhibit (Ruback & Hooper, 1986).

Although nonverbal cues are frequently powerful determinants of success in the job interview, their relative importance has rarely been compared directly with the impact of verbal behaviors. Hollandsworth, Kazelski, Stevens, and Dressel (1979) did conduct a study desired to yield estimates of the relative contributions of verbal and nonverbal behaviors to employment decisions. They found that verbal behaviors were the most important determinant of success in a job interview, and fluency of speech also contributed strongly to the employment decision. The most important verbal behaviors were (a) expressing oneself concisely, (b) answering questions fully, (c) stating personal opinions when relevant, and (d) keeping to the subject at hand.

The ability to speak fluently was clearly the most important nonverbal determinant of success in the job interview. Indeed, the use of nonfluencies proved so damaging to the job applicants that the researchers advocate the use of training designed to decrease speech disturbances and to improve speech fluency. Composure, as communicated via nonverbal cues, was also very important. Other less important nonverbal factors contributing to employment decisions (listed here in the order of their importance) were eye contact, body posture, loudness of voice, and personal appearance.

More specifically, a premium is placed on the ability to speak what is perceived to be standard English in the job interview. Consider the study done by Atkins (1993). In her study, 65 employment recruiters who visited West Virginia University were to assume that they were interviewing job applicants who spoke either "Black English" (BE) or "Appalachian English" (AE). These job recruiters gave negative ratings to 93 percent of the job applicants speaking BE and to 58 percent speaking AE. Although individuals speaking both dialects were positively perceived in terms of some image qualities, they were also viewed as pessimistic, disreputable, dependent, and unintelligent.

Physical attractiveness seems to be a less important determinant of success in the job interview than other kinds of nonverbal variables. In one study (Greenwald, 1981) social performance, previous experience, and qualifications were all found to be influential in affecting the interviewer's accept or reject decisions in a job interview. However, the study found no significant effect for the physical attractiveness of the interviewee. Results from this study should be interpreted with caution, however, because of the way physical attractiveness was manipulated—posed photographs from college yearbooks were used.

Heilman and Saruwatari (1979) found that *the impact of physical attractiveness in the job interview depends on the sex of the applicants and the nature of the jobs they seek.* Although physical attractiveness was advantageous for male applicants seeking white-collar organizational positions, it was useful for female applicants only when the position they sought was a nonmanagerial one.

On the basis of the job interview, the physically attractive woman who applied for a managerial position was less likely to be hired than the physically unattractive woman. This finding has serious implications with regard to the consequences of sex-role stereotyping for the female interviewee. Heilman and Saruwatari (1979) described the problem graphically when they wrote that this finding "implies that women should strive to appear as unattractive and masculine as possible if they are to succeed in advancing their careers by moving into powerful organizational positions. Surely giving up one's womanhood should not be a prerequisite for organizational success" (p. 371).

We should keep in mind that the nonverbal behaviors that an interviewee exhibits are not necessarily accurate indicators of the interviewee's actual social skills. Some nonverbal behaviors seem to reflect more accurately the social skills of interviewees than others. One study (Gifford, Ng, & Wilkinson, 1985) showed that the interviewee's social skill was most accurately inferred from the amount of gesturing and talking and from the formality of dress. In each instance, more seemed to be better than less.

There is some evidence to indicate that interviewers tend to discount some of the nonverbal behaviors of interviewees because the interviewees are victims of a social stigma or are being so manipulative as to damage their credibility. In the first instance, Cipolli, Sancini, Tuozzi, and Bolzani (1989) found that interviewees who were "anorexic" looked less frequently and more briefly toward the eyes of the interviewer than did control subjects, and mutual gazing was less frequent. Even if interviewees do not stigmatize themselves by their appearance, they could be stigmatized by exhibiting gender-inappropriate behaviors. Rachklowski and O'Grady (1988) found that female interviewees who exhibit male behaviors tend to be stigmatized. In addition, interviewers tend to discount nonverbal behaviors of interviewees whom they perceive to be manipulative. Baron (1986) found that male interviewers perceived a female interviewee who *both* exhibited positive nonverbal behaviors and used a clearly detectable perfume less favorably than a female interviewee who exhibited *only* positive nonverbal behaviors. The impression management implications are obvious. When the interviewee's self-presentation goes so far as to be perceived as unappealing or manipulative, the interviewee makes a more negative impression.

The nonverbal profile that is associated with job applicants' success and failure in the selection interview is presented in Table 14.1. This profile is based entirely on results from empirical research. In view of the demonstrated importance of the interviewee's nonverbal cues as determinants of success in the job interview, this profile should be studied carefully by prospective job applicants.

The Counseling Interview

The counseling interview places a premium on the communicative skills of the interactants because counseling interviews are designed to solve problems. The problems addressed are not usually susceptible to resolution unless clients modify their attitudes and behaviors as

TABLE 14.1   Nonverbal Profile of Successful Job Interviewees

Should Exhibit	Should Not Exhibit
High-immediacy behaviors: sustained eye contact; smiling; attentive posture; direct body orientation; illustrator gestures; close physical proximity	Low-immediacy behaviors: intermittent eye contact; frowning; inattentive posture; indirect body orientation; adaptor gestures; distant seating

Smiling	
Appropriate smiling	Inappropriate smiling
Felt smiles	Masked insincere smiles

Vocal Cues	
Voice modulation to express appropriate affect; suitable variation in pitch, rate, and volume	Monotone voice
Fluency	Nonfluencies—hesitation; stuttering, word repetition; sentence fragments; filled pauses (e.g., "ah")
Substantial volume	
No hesitation in responding to interviewer questions	Soft voice—inadequate volume

Eye Behaviors	
Steady eye contact	Gaze-avoidance
Sustained eye contact	Wandering eyes
Substantial amount of eye contact	Limited amount of eye contact
	Eye contact of short duration

Bodily Cues	
Affirmative head nodding	Immobile head
Hand gestures communicating high energy levels	Hand gestures communicating low energy levels or anxiety
Responsive postural shifts	Rigid posture
Confidence gestures	Nervousness gestures
Open posture	Closed and defensive posture
	Hand-to-face gestures
	Extraneous bodily movements

a result of the confidence and trust they place in the counselor. In short, effective counselors must be able to promote self-disclosure and active problem-solving involvement on the part of clients. To achieve this objective, counselors must be perceived to be unusually sensitive individuals who are highly credible, empathic, and trustworthy.

Counseling takes many forms. People seek counseling to deal with problems of emotional instability, physical health, marriage, morals, work performance, alcoholism, and child abuse, for example. Contrary to popular belief, many counseling interviews are conducted by individuals who are not professionally trained as counselors. Many counselors—doctors, teachers, supervisors, fellow workers, students, friends, and family members—may be "professionals" but most are not professionally trained counselors (Stewart & Cash, 1982).

The acquisition of effective counseling skills is important, because all of us will, at some time, assume the role of counselor, whether as a parent, a friend, or a coworker. It is even likely that we will find ourselves in the role of client in a counseling interview. In either case, we are apt to put a premium on achieving success in the counseling interview. The degree of success achieved is often determined, to a striking degree, by the counselor's nonverbal behaviors.

You may still wonder why you should familiarize yourself with the nonverbal profile of an effective counselor. In one sense, the answer is obvious: Inevitably you will find yourself in contexts where your ability to be empathic will be valuable. In this regard, consider the empathic listening situations you frequently encounter with friends, coworkers, intimates, or family members. In those same situations, is it not very important that you also have the capacity to *behave nonverbally* in an emphatic and sensitive manner? If your answer is yes, pay careful attention to the following discussion and to Table 14.2.

Critical Objectives

The success of a counseling interview is much more difficult to measure than the success of a job interview. From the perspective of the job applicant, the success or failure of the employment interview can be assessed directly and immediately. Job applicants are either accepted or rejected for the position for which they apply, but the success of the counseling interview must be assessed in terms of both short-range and long-range objectives.

TABLE 14.2   Nonverbal Profile of Successful Counseling Interviewers

Should Exhibit	Should Not Exhibit
High-Immediacy Behaviors	*Low-Immediacy Behaviors*
High level of eye contact; close physical proximity (sit within three feet of client); head and body oriented toward client	Low level of eye contact; distant seating; head and body oriented away from client
Responsive Behaviors	*Unresponsive Behaviors*
Open posture and gestures; head nodding; postural shifts; illustrator gestures; appropriate touching of client	Closed and defensive postures; gestures with arms crossed over chest and legs crossed at the ankles; immobile head and body; lack of touching
Consistent Messages	*Inconsistent Messages*
Vocal cues, gestures, postures, close distancing, and appropriate touching should be used to reinforce the meaning(s) of verbal messages that communicate liking, acceptance, empathy, warmth, and a genuine regard for the client's feelings, concerns and problems	Vocal cues, gestures, postures, physical separation, and inappropriate touching, which contradict the meaning(s) of verbal messages, with the result that a lack of liking, acceptance, empathy, and warmth and an unauthentic regard for the client's feelings, concerns, and problems are communicated
Sets of nonverbal behaviors that enhance the counselor's perceived competence and trustworthiness	Sets of nonverbal behaviors that lower the counselor's perceived competence and trustworthiness

In most cases, the overriding short-term objective of the counselor is to inspire sufficient trust on the part of the client so that he or she will become actively involved in the problem-solving process. Well-trained counselors are probably sensitive to the fact that clients tend to form their basic impressions of them during the first four minutes of a counseling interview. This finding becomes even more important in view of the related finding that clients are better able to differentiate between the counselor's positive and negative nonverbal behaviors during the early part of the interview (Uhlemann, Lee, & Hasse, 1989).

The long-range objective usually focuses on the attempt to solve problems regarding alcoholism, drug abuse, marital discord, or sexual incompatibility, for example. Because successful resolution of such problems can take months or even years, much of the research on counseling interviews has focused on how successfully the counselor attains short-range objectives.

The short-term goals of the counselor are to exhibit interpersonal skills and to develop sufficient credibility in the eyes of the client so as to inspire trust in the counselor's therapeutic actions and methods. To inspire this trust, counselors must be perceived as empathic, warm, and genuine (Sherer & Rogers, 1980). You cannot persuade a client to modify the attitudes and behaviors that are causing a specific problem unless the client finds you to be a believable and caring person, one who will address problems in a sensitive manner.

Imagine for a moment that you are about to have your initial counseling session with a psychiatrist. You suffer from depression. You have been so depressed for the last six months that you cannot sleep, you suffer from extreme fatigue, and you are convinced that you have a life-threatening heart disorder. As you enter the office of I. M. Cold, psychiatrist, you notice that she is talking on the telephone, with her back turned to you and her feet on the desk. She motions you to take a seat on the other side of the room and resumes her phone call. When, 10 minutes later, she finally finishes her phone conversation, she scowls, leans back in her chair and thumbs casually through your medical records. She then says to you, "I am positive that your symptoms can be easily treated. You are a hypochondriac who feels sorry for herself. I have already written you a prescription for antidepressant pills. Take the pills for two months and call my secretary in the unlikely event that you still think you are depressed."

How would you react to such a counseling interview? In view of the fact that your psychiatrist is nationally recognized as an expert in the treatment of depression, does it really matter that you did not like her because she lacked empathy and warmth? Do you believe that her effectiveness as a psychiatrist will be measurably affected by the communicative behaviors she exhibited?

Nonverbal Profile of Successful Counselors

The level of expertness or competence attributed to the counselor by the client is perhaps the most important perceptual determinant of the counselor's effectiveness. Interestingly, Siegel (1980) found that a client's perception of the counselor's level of expertise was determined both by objective evidence of expertise and by the counselor's nonverbal behaviors. Counselors who displayed objective evidence of expertness (in the form of diplomas on the office wall) were judged as significantly more credible than those who did not. Less obvious but perhaps equally important is the finding that counselors who exhibited desirable nonverbal behaviors were judged more "expert" than counselors who did not exhibit such behaviors. Relatedly, Lee, McGill, and Uhlemann (1988) found that both counselors and clients rely more heavily on verbal cues in judging the others' competence but on nonverbal cues in judging attractiveness and trustworthiness.

Counselors' nonverbal behaviors have been found to have a strong impact not only on their perceived competence but also on their perceived trustworthiness. A study by Fretz, Corn, Tuemmler, and Bellet (1979) focused on three types of counselor nonverbal behaviors. One group of counselors maintained high levels of eye contact with the client, used a direct bodily orientation, and leaned forward while conversing. The other group of counselors exhibited an opposite set of nonverbal behaviors. Counselors in the first group were judged to be significantly more effective than those in the second group. Clients also judged them to be superior with in terms of their level of regard for the clients and empathy.

This study clearly showed, in addition, that the display of just three types of desirable nonverbal behaviors by the counselors significantly enhanced their perceived competence and trustworthiness. Clients rated the counselors who exhibited the desirable nonverbal behaviors as significantly more poised, friendly, trusting, warm, attentive, intelligent, patient, capable, considerate, concerned, and expressive and significantly less critical, cold, and aloof than the other group of counselors.

The two kinds of nonverbal behaviors that seem to have the most positive impact on the counselor's perceived credibility and effectiveness are immediacy and responsiveness behaviors. Sherer and Rogers (1980) found that counselors who exhibited high-immediacy behaviors (i.e., sat within 36 in. of the client, maintained eye contact, and oriented the head toward the client 90 percent of the time) were rated much more effective than counselors who exhibited low-immediacy behaviors. The group of effective counselors were not only better liked but they were viewed as more empathic, warm, and genuine. Sherer and Rogers concluded that

> *the present results strongly supported the prediction that a therapist who uses high-immediacy nonverbal cues, which communicate liking and acceptance, would be rated as possessing superior therapist interpersonal skills and as being a more effective therapist.... Because people are more likely to approach and become involved with someone who likes and accepts them, the use of immediacy cues may produce a variety of beneficial therapeutic outcomes (including continuation in therapy so that the therapist will have the opportunity to work on symptomatic complaints, disruptive behaviors, etc.). These results clearly support the assumption that the use of appropriate nonverbal cues may facilitate therapy.* (p. 699)

The counselor's nonverbal responsivity is also very important. Counselors who exhibit appropriate bodily movements are viewed as more responsive, warmer, and more empathic than those who do not. Arms crossed over the chest and crossed legs, with one leg resting on the other ankle, have been viewed by clients as particularly unresponsive forms of counselor behavior, and the counselor is typically viewed as cold and nonempathic (Smith-Hanen, 1977). In contrast, appropriate client touching by the counselor is viewed as a desirable form of responsive behavior (Alagna, Whitcher, Fisher, & Wicas, 1979). In short, counselors who exhibit responsive nonverbal cues are viewed as more expert, trustworthy, and attractive than those who do not (Claiborn, 1979).

Finally, counselors who wish to be perceived as effective must make sure that their messages are consistent. The counselor who tells the client how interested he or she is in the client's problems while exhibiting low-immediacy behaviors, for example, runs the risk of alienating the client. Clients have a much lower level of regard for counselors who use inconsistent as opposed to consistent messages and see them as less effective (Reade & Smouse, 1980).

The impact of the counselor's nonverbal behaviors on the client can be so powerful that they stimulate the self-fulfilling prophecy. In one study (Vrugt, 1990) therapists communicated their negative attitudes and expectancies toward the clients by exhibiting more ah-filled pauses, making more speech disturbances, and looking at the interviewees less. The clients reciprocated by increasing in their pauses, adding speech disturbances, and averting the counselor's gaze. In short, the clients fulfilled the therapists' prophecy by exhibiting discomfort and acting less competent communicatively.

The nonverbal profile associated with successful and unsuccessful counselors is presented in Table 14.2 This profile is also based on results from empirical research. Counselors who wish to increase their effectiveness must, quite clearly, exhibit both high-immediacy and responsive behaviors, and they must exercise special care to assure that their multichannel messages are consistent.

The Interviewer's Perspective

Biasing Factors

In the section on the job interview, we examined behavioral data from the interviewee's perspective. The reason is obvious. A much higher proportion of the individuals who read this book are apt to be job interviewees than job interviewers. At the same time, we should recognize that the job interview is a process in which interviewee and interviewer exert mutual influence on the behaviors they exhibit and, ultimately, on the results of the interviewer. Even if you never become a professional interviewer, you can become a more successful interviewee by learning something about the interviewer's perspective.

The interactive and interdependent relationship between interviewer and interviewee is illustrated by some recent research that focuses on the potential impact of the interviewer's preinterview impressions of the interviewee. First, research by Macan & Dipboye (1990) emphasized the strong positive relationship between a job interviewer's preinterview and postinterview impression. By definition this means that preinterview impressions are resistant to change. It also suggests that making a positive first impression in the job interview is vitally important for at least two reasons. A positive first impression is potentially advantageous for all of the reasons discussed in Chapter 9. Secondly, a positive first impression can be used to combat the tendency for an interviewers' preinterview impression and postinterview impression to remain essentially unchanged.

The second, related type of research focuses attention on a fascinating finding. An interviewer's first impression of an interviewee tends to have a strong, predictable set of effects on the interviewer's behaviors throughout the job interview. Moreover, the interviewer's first impression of the interviewee may also affect the interviewee's behavior during the interview. Research by Dougherty, Turban, and Callender (1994) indicates that job interviewers who form a positive impression of the job interviewee tend to act in positive ways during the actual interview such that their positive impression is "confirmed." Thus, job interviewers with a positive first impression of the interviewee exhibit "positive regard" toward the interviewee, actively "sell" their own company, give more information about the job and gather less information from the job applicant, and alter their communication style in an attempt to establish greater rapport. Relatedly, the multiple nonverbal signals from the interviewer that the interviewee made a favorable first impression have a reciprocal, positive impact of the nonverbal behavior of the interviewee; for instance the interviewee's vocal style becomes more positive, the individual extends his or her available speaking time, the applicant's rapport with the interviewer increases, and so on.

No attempt will be made to build a separate nonverbal profile for the successful interviewer here. This subject is handled in a detailed and enlightening manner elsewhere (Gallois, Callan, & Palmer, 1992; Gorden, 1987; Harris, 1989). Although the desirable nonverbal behaviors for the interviewer and the interviewee are somewhat different, to compare them here would be an exercise in redundancy.

Instead let us focus briefly on some of the perceptual biases that may affect the judgments that the interviewer makes of the interviewee. The most insightful treatment of this subject that I have seen is by Arvey and Campion (1984). According to Arvey and Campion, a number of factors strongly affect interviewers' judgments and may lead to biased judgments. Interviewers are influenced

1. by their own attitudes in interpreting the interviewee's responses
2. more strongly by unfavorable than favorable information
3. by interaction that takes place early in an interview
4. by the stereotypes they bring to the interview
5. by "first impression error"
6. by racial and gender biases

Of course, not all job interviewers are affected by the same biasing factors. Some may be relatively free from bias. Interviewers are prevented by recent legislation not only from exhibiting certain biases but also from posing insensitive questions. In any event, the objective here is not to impugn the integrity of professional job interviewers. My experience suggests that most are highly ethical and skilled professionals who set high standards for themselves. The point to remember is that you give yourself an edge over your competitors if you are aware of the factors that have the potential to bias an interviewer's judgments.

Factors That Prevent Bias

Robert Half wrote an interesting book which he modestly titled *Robert Half on HIRING* (1985). Because he has devoted a lifetime to professional interviewing and finding jobs for people, his opinions carry some weight. In one chapter of his book—On "Reading" the Candidate—Half provided some guidance for job interviewers who want to guard against making biased judgments. Half stressed:

Most personnel professionals will tell you that trying to get an accurate reading of a candidate's personality in one (or even two or three) interviews is all but impossible even for highly experienced interviewers. The problem, they point out, isn't only the limited amount of time you have to make the assessment. The personality that many candidates reveal during the interview may not be what you're likely to see once they're on the job. (p. 129)

In Half's view, job interviewers would be well advised to rely on general impressions of the interviewee rather than making highly specialized judgments. The interviewer should try to make judgments about no more than those two or three image qualities or personality traits that are most relevant to job performance and should rely heavily on the kinds of nonverbal behaviors exhibited by the interviewee that cannot be consciously controlled. He also stresses the importance of not being unduly influenced by first impressions and not being misled by your prejudices.

In retrospect, you should recognize that most professional interviewers are well aware of the behavioral and perceptual factors that have the potential of biasing their judgments of interviewees. They may not have seen it all, but they have seen enough to differentiate with relative ease between the skillful and unskillful use of nonverbal behaviors to manage impressions in the job interview.

Summary

Nonverbal cues frequently are major determinants of success or failure in job and counseling interviews. The critically important role of nonverbal cues in the job interview has been clearly established. The interviewee's nonverbal cues are known to affect not only the interviewer's perceptions of the quality of the interviewee's performance, but also the critically important decision to accept or reject the interviewee for a job.

In the counseling interview, counselors must be perceived not only as credible but also as empathic if they are to be effective. The client's perception of the counselor's credibility and empathy are influenced to a striking degree by the counselor's nonverbal behaviors.

The nonverbal profile for job applicants, which is associated with success and failure in the selection interview, is presented in Table 14.1. Successful job interviewees typically exhibit high-immediacy behaviors, use voice modulation to express appropriate affect, maintain a high level of sustained eye contact, and use affirmative head nodding accompanied by responsive gestures and postures. In contrast, unsuccessful job interviewees frequently exhibit low-immediacy behaviors; speak in a broken and nonfluent manner; avoid eye contact; and are easily identifiable because of lack of head movements, rigid and defensive postures, and nervousness gestures.

Table 14.2 provides the nonverbal profile of successful counseling interviewers. Successful counselors consistently exhibit specific kinds of high-immediacy and responsive behaviors while communicating consistent messages. Counselors who wish to enhance their perceived credibility and cultivate their interpersonal communication skills should study the nonverbal profile of successful counseling interviewers.

Finally, consideration of the interviewer's perspective is important, because the interview is a process in which the interviewee and the interviewer exert mutual influence on the behaviors they exhibit and on the outcomes of the interview. Interviewees should note that a number of factors may bias the judgments that interviewers make about them. At the same time, there are a number of guidelines that interviewers can follow to guard against making biased judgments.

References

Alagna, F. J., Whitcher, S. J., Fisher, J. D., & Wicas, E. W. (1979). Evaluative reaction to interpersonal touch in a counseling interview. *Journal of Counseling Psychology, 26,* 465–472.

Anderson, N. R. (1991). Decision making in the graduate selection interview: An experimental investigation. *Human Relations, 44,* 403–417.

Anderson, N. R., & Shackleton, V. J. (1990). Decision making in the graduate selection interview: A field study. *Journal of Occupation Psychology, 63,* 63–76.

Arvey, R. D., & Campion, J. E. (1984). Person perception in the employment interview. In M. Cook (Ed.), *Issues in person perception* (pp. 202–241). New York: Methuen.

Atkins, C. P. (1993). Do employment recruiters discriminate on the basis of nonstandard dialect? *Journal of Employment Counseling, 30,* 108–118.

Baron, R. A. (1986). Self-presentation in job interviews: When there can be "too much of a good thing." *Journal of Applied Social Psychology, 16,* 16–28.

Bugental, D. B. (1986). Unmasking the 'polite smile': Situational and personal determinants of managed affect in adult-child interaction. *Personality and Social Psychology Bulletin, 12,* 7–16.

Cippoli, C., Sancini, M., Tuozzi, G., & Bolzani, R. (1989). Gaze and eye-contact with anorexic adolescents. *British Journal of Medical Psychology, 62,* 365–369.

Claiborn, D. D. (1979). Counselor verbal intervention, nonverbal behavior, and social power. *Journal of Counseling Psychology, 26,* 378–383.

Dougherty, T. W., Turban, D. B., & Callender, J. C. (1994). Confirming first impressions in the employment interview: A field study of interviewer behavior. *Journal of Applied Psychology, 79,* 659–665.

Ekman, P., Friesen, W. V., & O'Sullivan, M. O. (1988). Smiles when lying. *Journal of Personality and Social Psychology, 54,* 414–420.

Forbes, R. J., & Jackson, P. R. (1980). Non-verbal behavior and the outcome of selection interviews. *Journal of Occupational Psychology, 53,* 65–72.

Fretz, B. R., Corn, R., Tuemmler, J. M., & Bellet, W. (1979). Counselor nonverbal behaviors and client evaluations. *Journal of Counseling Psychology, 26,* 304–311.

Gallois, C., Callan, V. J., & Palmer, J-A. M. (1992). The influence of applicant communication style and interviewer characteristics on hiring decisions. *Journal of Applied Social Psychology, 22,* 1041–1060.

Gifford, R., Ng, C. F., & Wilkinson, M. (1985). Nonverbal cues in the employment interview: Links between applicant qualities and interviewer judgments. *Journal of Applied Psychology, 70,* 729–736.

Gorden, R. L. (1987). *Interviewing: Strategy, Techniques, and Tactics* (4th ed.). Chicago: Dorsey.

Greenwald, M. A. (1981). The effects of physical attractiveness, experience, and social performance on employer decision-making in job interviews. *Behavioral Counseling Quarterly, 1,* 275–287.

Half, R. (1985). *Robert Half on HIRING.* New York: Crown.

Harris, M. M. (1989). Reconsidering the employment interview: A review of recent literature and suggestions for future research. *Personnel Psychology, 42,* 691–726.

Heilman, M. E., & Saruwatari, L. R. (1979). When beauty is beastly: The effects of appearance and sex on evaluations of job applicants for managerial and non-managerial jobs. *Organizational behavior and human performance, 23,* 360–372.

Hollandsworth, J. G., Jr., Kazelski, R., Stevens, J., & Dressel, M. E. (1979). Relative contributions of verbal, articulative, and nonverbal communication to employment decisions in the job interview setting. *Personnel Psychology, 32,* 359–367.

Hornik, J., & Ellis, S. (1988). Strategies to secure compliance for a mail intercept interview. *Public Opinion Quarterly, 52,* 539–555.

Imada, A. S., & Hakel, M. D. (1977). Influence of nonverbal communication and rater proximity on impressions and decision in simulated employment interviews. *Journal of Applied Psychology, 62,* 295–300.

Kinicki, A. J., & Lockwood, C. A. (1985). The interview process: An examination of factors recruiters use in evaluating job applicants. *Journal of Vocational Behavior, 26,* 117–125.

Kleinke, C. L., Staneski, R. A., & Berger, D. E. (1975). Evaluations of an interviewer as a function of interviewer gaze, reinforcement of subject gaze, and interviewer's attractiveness. *Journal of Personality and Social Psychology, 31,* 115–122.

Lee, D. Y., McGill, M. E., & Uhlemann, M. R. (1988). Counsellor and client reliance on verbal and nonverbal cues in judging competency, trustworthiness, and attractiveness. *Journal of Counselling, 22,* 35–43.

Macan, T., & Dipboye, R. L. (1990). The relationship of interviewers' preinterview impressions to selection and recruitment outcomes. *Personnel Psychology, 43,* 745–768.

McGovern, T. V., & Tinsley, H. W. (1978). Interviewer evaluations of interviewee nonverbal behavior. *Journal of Vocational Behavior, 13,* 163–171.

Rachkowski, R., & O'Grady, K. E. (1988). Client gender and sex-typed nonverbal behavior: Impact on impression formation. *Sex Roles, 19,* 771–783.

Reade, M. N., & Smouse, A. D. (1980). Effect of inconsistent verbal-nonverbal communication and coun-selor response mode on client estimate of counselor regard and effectiveness. *Journal of Counseling Psychology, 27,* 546–553.

Ruback, R., & Hopper, C. H. (1986). Decision making by parole interviewers: The effect of case and interview factors. *Law and Human Behavior, 10,* 203–214.

Sherer, M., & Rogers, R. W. (1980). Effects of therapist's nonverbal communication on rated skill and effectiveness. *Journal of Clinical Psychology, 36,* 696–700.

Siegel, J. C. (1980). Effects of objective evidence of expertness, nonverbal behavior, and subject sex on client-perceived expertness. *Journal of Counseling Psychology, 27,* 117–121.

Smith-Hanen, S. S. (1977). Effects of nonverbal behaviors on judged levels of counselor warmth and empathy. *Journal of Counseling Psychology, 24,* 87–91.

Stewart, C. J., & Cash, Jr., W. B. (1994). *Interviewing principles and practices* (7th ed.). Dubuque, IA: Wm. C. Brown.

Tessler, R., & Sushelsky, L. (1978). Effects of eye contact and social status on the perception of a job applicant in an employment interview situation. *Journal of Vocational Behavior, 13,* 338–347.

Tullar, W. L. (1989). Relational control in the employment interview. *Journal of Applied Psychology, 74,* 971–977.

Uhlemann, M. R., Lee, D., & Hasse, R. F. (1989). The effects of cognitive complexity and arousal on client perception of counselor nonverbal behavior. *Journal of Clinical Psychology, 45,* 661–665.

Vrugt, A. (1990). Negative attitudes, nonverbal behavior and self-fulfilling prophecy in simulated therapy interviews. *Journal of Nonverbal Behavior 14,* 77–86.

Chapter 15

Female–Male Interaction

The communicative styles of men and women are distinctively different in our society. Our stereotypic conceptions of men and women are clearly and consistently reflected in their contrasting communicative styles. Men are stereotyped as active, dominant, aggressive, and insensitive persons who dominate communicative interaction by virtue of their superior status. By contrast, women are perceived stereotypically to be passive, submissive, supportive persons, who are dominated as a result of their desire to adapt to men's needs, and to be accommodating. To a considerable degree, the stereotypes mirror the dominant characteristics of female–male interaction.

Sex-linked stereotypes are strongly reinforced by the use of sexist or exclusionary language, which relegates women to narrowly defined and dependent roles (Thorne & Henley, 1975). The basic differences in male and female communication styles are revealed in implicit nonverbal messages rather than through the use of language, however. Men rarely communicate their desire to dominate women by the words they utter. Similarly, women do not generally use verbal communication to make clear their desire to be interpersonally accommodating. Such messages are communicated most frequently and forcefully by nonverbal cues.

Sex-Role Stereotyping

Strong and enduring sex-role stereotypes have developed in our society; similar sex-role stereotypes have also developed in nations with strikingly different governing systems such as the Soviet Union (Gibson, 1988). Men are expected to assume the *proactive* role. The cultural norm dictates that the proactive person will be active, independent, self-confident, and decisive. Individuals who assume the proactive role place a high priority on accomplishing the task at hand. Women are expected to assume the *reactive* role. Reactive individuals respond to the contributions made by others rather than initiating contributions; they are emotionally expressive and sensitive to the emotional needs of the initiator, and they are interpersonally supportive and accommodating (LaFrance & Mayo, 1978).

The sex-role stereotypes reflected in those roles are quite detailed. The stereotype for women is more detailed than the stereotype for men, although it is less socially desirable. In spite of the fact that women tend to be stereotyped broadly as one large group, a woman's ethnicity may have an impact on the way that she is stereotyped. The stereotype for the black woman, for example, seems to be particularly detailed. The greater detail comes in part from the assumption that black women have suffered from "double domination" from a white society and from males in general (Reid, 1989). The following descriptive labels are typically used to identify the more negative portion of the female stereotype: "submissive," "dependent," "touchy," "moody," "temperamental," "excitable," "frivolous," "talkative," and "timid." The more positive portion of the female stereotype is identified by these descriptive labels: "affectionate," "considerate," "cooperative," "supportive," and "sensitive."

The stereotype for women has been quite resistant to change. Thus, Wood (1994) wrote that the societal view of "femininity in the 1990s is also relatively consistent with earlier views, although there is increasing latitude in what is considered appropriate" (p. 21). She stresses that

> *To be feminine is to be attractive, deferential, unaggressive, emotional, nurturing, and concerned with people and relationships. Those who embody the cultural definition of femininity still don't outdo men (especially their mates), disregard others' feelings, or put their needs ahead of others. Also, "real women" still look good (preferably very pretty and/or sexy), adore children, and care about homemaking. For all of the changes in our views of women and men, the basic blueprint remains relatively constant.* (p. 21)

Males are stereotyped in positive terms, such as "task-oriented," "rational," and "active." More specifically, males are stereotyped by these positive adjectives: "logical," "industrious," "sharp-witted," "shrewd," "confident," "forceful," and "dominant." Descriptive labels typically used to identify the negative portion of the male stereotype are "boastful," "stubborn," "arrogant," "conceited," "hardheaded," and "opportunistic" (Eakins & Eakins, 1978; Heilbrum, 1976).

As we shall see, men and women frequently do behave in ways that are quite consistent with their stereotype. The obvious question is *why*? Biological differences seem to have a relatively limited impact on the contrasting communicative styles of women and men. Some biological differences may, of course, affect communication. Women are usually physically smaller than men, and this difference could account, in part, for the fact that they *claim* less personal space than men. Because they are smaller than men, their vocal cords tend to be shorter, and their shorter vocal cords may help explain why women's modal pitch is significantly higher than men's. However, Thorne and Henley (1975) maintained that the female's characteristically higher pitch is more a function of social learning than of anatomical differences.

The greatest difference between male and female communicative behaviors seems to be attributable to gender differences, as opposed to biologically determined sex differences. *Gender* is defined as the culturally established correlates of sex (Goffman, 1979). The fact that women and men do behave differently, then, might be largely a result of cultural norms that specify appropriate behavior. The characteristic domination of females by males is a socially learned behavior, reinforced by a man's gender rather than by his sex. A man's primary sexual characteristics do not usually dictate that he behave in a particular way, but his gender is associated with well-developed social norms that specify how he should behave.

Gender behavior is clearly learned. Boys and girls are expected to behave in ways that are consistent with their gender. They are expected to conform. If they do not do so, their behavior will be branded deviant. Thus, Wood (1994) wrote that young girls are advised "Don't be selfish—share with others," "Be careful—don't hurt yourself," and "Don't get messy." In contrast, young boys are told "Don't be a sissy," "Go after what you want," and "Don't cry."

Goffman (1979) argued that the contrasting images of men and women have been strongly influenced by gender displays. *Gender displays* are conventionalized portrayals of those behaviors that society has defined as prototypically "masculine" and "feminine." The media have proved to be the strongest force in legitimizing and defining the gender displays that have become associated in the popular mind with so-called feminine and masculine behavior.

Umiker-Sebeok (1981) did the most detailed study of the ways gender displays are used to depict men and women in visual advertisements. She found that the image of women portrayed in magazine advertisements is one of "weak, childish, dependent, completely domestic, irrational, subordinate creatures, the producers of children and little else compared with men" (p. 211). More specifically, she maintained that body size and clothing style are used in magazine advertisements to associate females with smallness and subordination. Members of athletic teams are ordinarily portrayed as male, but females are pictured as primarily concerned with clothing, cosmetics, jewelry, hair products, and fragrances that can be used to enhance physical appearance.

In magazine advertisements, a young woman's high social status is frequently linked to her father's success, but a young man's success results from his own efforts; women are dependent and men are independent. The physical domination and subordination of the female is also frequently communicated clearly by the gender displays of the male. In the case of young lovers, it is the male who exhibits such stereotypic gestures as the "shoulder hold" and the "armlock"; it is the man who grasps the woman's upper arms, and it is the male who grasps the woman's hand, rather than vice versa.

Umiker-Sebeok (1981) indicated quite clearly that the advertising industry consistently portrays the male in the proactive role and the female in the reactive role. In the marriage ceremony, for example, the bride is "given away" and "carried over the threshold" of the couple's new home. Middle-aged women are pictured as "plump" and "passive," but the middle-aged man assumes positions of even greater authority, status, and power. Although Umiker-Sebeok's description of male and female gender displays in visual advertisements may be somewhat selective, it makes the point that the stereotypical images of women and men are deeply embedded in cultural values.

The origin of gender stereotypes is not so clear. In one sense, the notion of gender stereotypes almost seems to conjure up a chicken and egg argument. That is, we might ask whether gender stereotypes reflect the way women and men actually behave or whether men and women behave as they do to validate the stereotype. It seems unlikely that either men or women would behave consciously in a way designed to confirm the negative portion of their stereotype. However, they might behave in ways that seem to affect their image negatively if their behaviors were affected by the self-fulfilling prophecy.

Sex-role stereotyping often forces women and men to make difficult decisions. Take the professional woman, for example. She is probably well aware that many of the personal traits that are associated with managerial success are also defining features of the male stereotype. The professional woman may, therefore, be caught on the horns of a dilemma. Should she exhibit some of the behaviors that are stereotypically associated with male leadership and sacrifice her femininity? Or should she emphasize behaviors stereotypically associated with femininity while disregarding the option of exhibiting selected masculine behaviors? No matter which choice she makes she may not escape criticism.

In this regard I vividly recall overhearing the conversation of two corporate salesmen for General Electric a few years ago. They were discussing a young woman who had been selected as the national salesperson of the year for their division. Her photograph was featured on the front page of the corporate newsletter. On the one hand, these men both admired her great accomplishment and said so. On the other hand, one of them commented snidely to the other that "she dresses like a man." In terms of her own professional goals, this woman had made a proper decision in choosing her attire. Even though she succeeded professionally, however, she still found herself in a no-win situation from a perceptual perspective.

A recent study addressed this very dilemma (Johnson, Crutsinger, & Workman, 1994). The authors noted that women have often been advised to adopt a masculine appearance in order to communicate credibly in an executive role. Their study focused on the question of whether a woman can appear too masculine and consequently negatively affect both her professional credibility and her chances for promotion. In this instance, merchandising majors were asked to view three photographs of a middle-level female manager. Three head and shoulder color photographs were taken of the same female model. In one photograph the "female executive" was wearing a white shirt with a button-down collar and a navy blue jacket; in the second photograph the executive wore a square scarf tied in a flat knot that was placed under the collar; in the third photograph a man's necktie was placed under the collar and tied at the neck.

The female manager wearing either the necktie or the scarf was judged to possess significantly more managerial competence than the female wearing the open-collared shirt. The female executive wearing the necktie was judged as more likely to be determined than the one wearing the open-collared shirt. Importantly, the manager wearing the scarf was rated as significantly more likely to be promoted than the one wearing the necktie or the one wearing the open-collared shirt.

This research seems to suggest that the professional woman need neither dress like a man nor accentuate her femininity to succeed in a managerial positions. The authors concluded that

> *Preference for promotability may be given to females who wear adaptations or feminized versions of masculine symbols rather than the masculine symbol itself. One explanation of this finding may be that women are allowed to adopt some level of masculinity in appearance but not to the extent that their appearance is inconsistent with the gender role. When individuals adopt an aspect of dress that is inconsistent with gender role, they may violate expectations for appearance and*

question existing boundaries concerning what is masculine and what is feminine. (Johnson, Crutsinger, & Workman, 1994, p. 30)

In any event, we continue to accumulate evidence that suggests that men and women do exhibit attitudes and behaviors that confirm the accuracy of at least part of their stereotypes. Thus, Townsend and Levy (1990) found that males are more willing than females to invest in a relationship simply because the heterosexual partner is attractive, and a man's willingness to become involved with a partner increases when the sexual potential of the relationship was emphasized. Women, in contrast to men, are more willing to make a high-level investment in a relationship and are less willing than men to enter a relationship that emphasizes the sexual component unless there is a high level of investment by the partner. Finally, although women see physical attractiveness as less important then men do, they prefer to associate with an attractive man and they agree on the physical features that make a man attractive (Cunningham, Barbee, & Pike, 1990).

Differences in Nonverbal Communication of Women and Men

There are many distinctive differences in the nonverbal communication of men and women. In order to communicate more successfully with each other, men and women must become fully aware of the nature of those differences. They must also understand which nonverbal behaviors must be modified, and why they must be modified, if more successful communication is to result. Gender differences in nonverbal communication are manifested most clearly in contrasting communicative styles and in contrasting levels of encoding and decoding skills.

Nonverbal Profile of Female and Male Communicators

The vocalic communication of women and men is different in important respects. A woman's vocalic communication style is particularly important because it plays a central role in the way she is stereotyped (Kramarae, 1982). Contrary to the stereotype of women as *talkative,* men talk more than women (Mulac, 1989). Men's vocal dominance of women is not confined to the amount of talking they do, however. Men tend to dominate opposite-sex interactions because of the following: (a) the average duration of their talk-turns is longer, (b) the number and rate of their filled pauses is greater, and (c) they interrupt more frequently than women (Vrugt & Kerkstra, 1984).

Males' dominance of women in conversations is achieved in part by interruptions. The "interruption privilege" is one that men exercise frequently. LaFrance and Mayo (1979) emphasized that in same-sex conversations, interruptions, overlaps, and silences are almost evenly distributed between speakers. In male–female interaction, however, the following occurs:

1. Women are frequently interrupted by men.
2. Women are often silent for long periods after being interrupted.

3. Women are often prevented from interrupting men by the exaggerated lengths of mens' "ums" and "hmms."
4. It is unusual for a woman to protest being interrupted by a man.

In contrast to men, women use reactive intonation patterns that may make them seem to be more emotionally expressive. Thus women, when surprised, characteristically use the "high-low down-glide" (as in "Oh, how awful!") and women often answer questions with declarative statements that end with a rising inflection. Those rising inflections can make women seem more emotional than men, but also more uncertain and indecisive.

Women do ask more questions than men and more frequently use justifiers, that is, they justify the statements they make by providing supportive evidence or reasons for their statements. The fact that women, in comparison to men, ask more questions, use more justifiers, more frequently employ intensive adverbs ("I *really* like him") and more frequently begin sentences with adverbials ("Surprisingly . . .") suggests that women use vocal communication as a way of exercising social control by indirect means. In contrast, men use their voice so assertively that they try to exercise direct control over others via the sound of their voice (Mulac, Wiemann, Widenmann, & Gibson, 1988).

Hall (1984) summarized some of the more salient differences in the vocalic communication of women and men when she wrote:

Females' voices are more fluent, softer, slower, higher pitched, and perhaps more variable in pitch; women also talk less in mixed groups, and interrupt less, overall, than men do. . . . It also seems to be the case that for the more sex-typed variables—such as loudness and rated dominance—men also receive more of the same kind of behavior that they themselves engage in. (pp. 139–140)

Finally, it is important to note that women laugh significantly more than men, both when speaking and listening; the total time spent laughing is almost twice that of men. Excessive laughter or out-of-context laughter is frequently interpreted in our society as a sign that a person lacks self-confidence (Frances, 1979; LaFrance & Mayo, 1979).

The visual communication of men and women also differs in important respects. Oscar Wilde reportedly said, "A man's face is his autobiography; a woman's face is her work of fiction." There is limited evidence to support the view that women are more likely than men to control their facial expressions consciously in order to avoid displeasing the person with whom they are communicating.

The fact that women smile almost twice as much as men, and that they smile more frequently when listening, seems to support the inference that female smiles are not always completely genuine. The gender difference in smiling represents an important communicative phenomenon although authorities do not agree as to why women smile more or what the impact of the smiling may be. This finding may or may not be related to the fact that stereotypically women are thought to smile more than men (Briton & Hall, 1995). Hall (1984) suggested that women may smile more than men because they are conforming unconsciously to their sex-role stereotype. To explain the finding that women smile more than men, Vrugt and Kerkstra (1984) wrote that *we may perhaps conclude that smiling in women has a different motivational basis from smiling in men. For men, smiling could be associated with feelings of friendliness, affiliation, and comfort. For women, it could also be an expression of feelings of uneasiness, socially desirable (stereotypical) behavior, and reconciliation.* (p. 19)

Finally, Henley and LaFrance (1984) identified another function of smiling when they wrote that "ethologists have also suggested another function, and that is to signal appeasement and submissiveness. . . . In this sense, smiles are designed to ward off possible competition or assault by indicating that no threat is intended" (p. 364).

Women maintain eye contact with their partners for longer periods of time when listening than when speaking; low-status females sustain eye contact for significantly longer periods of time when listening than do high-status females (Ellyson, Dovidio, Corson, & Vinicur, 1980). Women appear to suffer severe perceptual penalties because of their excessive smiling and visual attentiveness. They not only reinforce their stereotypic image as status inferiors, but also raise doubts about the genuineness of the emotions they appear to be experiencing.

In general, men exhibit more bodily movements, they are more open, and they appear to be more relaxed than women. Women exhibit a disproportionate number of the gestures and postures that were identified in Chapter 4 as cues to nonassertiveness and powerlessness. Eakins and Eakins (1978) highlight fundamental differences in the bodily communication of males and females:

Communicators in general are more relaxed with females than with males. They show less body tension, more relaxed posture, and more backward lean. By their somewhat tenser postures, women are said to convey submissive attitudes. Their general bodily demeanor and bearing is more restrained and restricted than men's. (p. 161)

Men also use space as a means of asserting their dominance over women, as in the following:

1. They claim more personal space than women.
2. They more actively defend violations of their territories, which are usually much larger than the territories of women.
3. Under conditions of high density, they become more aggressive in their attempts to regain a desired measure of privacy.
4. Men more frequently walk in front of their female partner than vice versa.

The characteristic differences of men and women in their tactile behavior has already been treated in detail in Chapter 6. In general, the male is the toucher and the female the touched. Males use the touching privilege to touch females much more frequently than they are touched by them. Women touch others more frequently than men only when they are interacting with children. This is not surprising, considering the stereotypical view that men are emotionally unexpressive individuals who have difficulty in providing comfort and re-assurance, but that women excel in this familiar familial role.

The gender differences in the tactile behavior of women and men is quite pronounced. Although males tend to take liberties in touching women, they seem inhibited when it comes to touching each other. Derlega, Lewis, Harrison, and Costanza (1989) have gone so far as to suggest that homophobia, the fear of appearing or being homosexual, accounts for the limited amount of touching among males. They found that men avoid touching that is suggestive of physical intimacy, that certain types of tactile contact—such as men hugging each other or walking around with their arms around each other's waist—are evaluated as inappropriate, and that such types of male touching lead to an inference of sexual involvement.

Much of the nonverbal profiles for women and men focus on the relational dimension of dominance/submission. The other important relational dimension where the nonverbal profiles of women and men is of central importance is intimacy. In fact, many of the readers of this book may be particularly interested in which nonverbal behaviors of males and females are functional as opposed to dysfunctional in the initiation of a heterosexual relationship. A recent study (Simpson, Gangestad, & Biek, 1993) addressed this topic in a stimulating way.

The authors maintained that *sociosexuality* is a concept of most central importance. This construct concerns "the extent to which individuals require closeness, commitment, and strong emotional bonds prior to having sex" (p. 437). Individuals with an *unrestricted sociosexual orientation* require little closeness and commitment before engaging in sex and, hence, they enter relationships where sex and intimacy occur soon after the initiation of the relationship. In contrast, individuals with a *restricted sociosexual orientation* require more commitment and closeness prior to sex. In this type of relationship, emotional bonds must have formed before sex occurs.

This study produced nonverbal profiles that give some indication as to how men and women with unrestricted and restricted sociosexual orientations behave during initial heterosexual encounters. Males with an unrestricted sociosexual orientation smile more, laugh more, gaze downward less often, and display flirtatious glances more frequently compared to males with a restricted sociosexual orientation. Relatedly, men who are not unrestricted in sociosexuality but who were highly extroverted and self-monitoring were rated as more socially engaging, dominant, and phony. Unrestricted women are more likely to lean forward and cant their head than restricted women.

Results such as these are particularly intriguing because they document that individuals who share social and personality traits or qualities do behave nonverbally in ways that are consistent and predictable. Not surprisingly the nonverbal behaviors exhibited by males and females with an unrestricted sociosexual orientation almost without exception communicated their "contact readiness." The interpretations of individual nonverbal behaviors such as head canting by females is of course not always a simple matter. Interestingly, the authors (Simpson, Gangestad, & Biek, 1993) concluded that

> *Forward lean also accentuates the impact of other nonverbal cues that emanate from the head and face (e. g., smiles, head cants) by drawing interactants closer together. It has been proposed that head canting may function as a flirtatious gesture designed to signal "coy" sexual interest without affect in heterosexual interaction.* (p. 455)

Most of the research done to date has attempted to classify the kinds of nonverbal behaviors that are characteristically exhibited by men in contrast to women. Little attention has been given to how these characteristically "male" or "female" behaviors may be modified as a result of the reaction of the person with whom we are interacting. Weitz (1976) maintained that the sex of the message receiver, as well as the sex of the message sender, affects communicative behaviors in opposite-sex interactions.

Women, but not men, seem to adapt their nonverbal behaviors to make them compatible with the personality traits and attitudes of their opposite-sex partners. Men tend to remain inflexibly committed to a proactive communicative style, but women do modify their nonverbal communicative behaviors. They adapt to meet their male partner's perceived needs, rather than to meet the distinctive requirements of a particular kind of communicative situation, however.

Weitz (1976) found that women are nonverbally adaptive when interacting with a dominant male partner, during the first phase of female–male interaction. Similarly, women exhibit less nonverbal warmth when interacting with a male partner who shows strong affiliative tendencies. In short, women interacting with men seem to adjust their nonverbal behaviors in such a way as to "create an equilibrium in the interaction which would result in maximum interpersonal comfort (especially for the male) in the interaction" (p. 179). In contrast, women who are interacting with other women (in the early stages of interpersonal interaction) do not seem to adapt their nonverbal behaviors in order to be compatible with the dominant personality traits of the female partner.

A similar pattern emerges in male–female interactions as they spend more time together. Women modify their nonverbal behaviors when interacting with a male partner to make their behaviors more compatible with the male's personality characteristics, but men do not make a complementary effort—they do not modify their nonverbal behaviors in order to make their female partner more comfortable. Women's greater willingness to be accommodating to males may be attributable in part to the finding that individuals in general experience significantly more anxiety when interacting with a male than with a female.

Whether they are motivated by a desire to relieve their anxieties or by a desire to be accommodating, women do seem to adjust their nonverbal behaviors when they interact with a male. Females exhibit a higher focus of attention on their male partner and show significantly more sexual interest in him than vice versa. Moreover, career-oriented women communicate significantly more nonverbal warmth when interacting with a male than do family-oriented women. This adjustment in nonverbal behavior may involve an attempt to counteract the stereotypic conception that career-oriented women are colder and less emotionally expressive than their family-oriented counterparts.

Weitz (1976), therefore, emphasized that a woman's nonverbal communication is affected not only by sex-role stereotyping but also by a desire to be supportive and interpersonally accommodating. She noted that

> *[the] finding of a possible female monitoring mechanism shown by the complementary relationship between female nonverbal style and male personality traits reinforces this idea of greater female responsiveness to the other person in the interaction. Of course, one can see this as a positive quality as well, except if this*

responsiveness is done at the expense of the assertion of the women's point of view, which it perhaps might be. (p. 183)

Gender Differences in Nonverbal Skills

We know very little about the relative ability of women and men to encode nonverbal messages. There is, however, some evidence to suggest that women communicate the basic emotions more clearly via their facial expressions than do men. Whereas women seem to be better at encoding negative emotions such as dislike, men are better at communicating positive emotions such as happiness (Wagner, Buck, & Winterbotham, 1993). These differences in encoding performance could be related to the fact that women smile so much more than men. Negative emotions are conveyed by facial expressions that are in striking contrast to the smile so often found on the face of a woman (LaFrance & Mayo, 1979). When men and women communicate more specialized kinds of emotional meaning, it appears that they exhibit comparable levels of encoding skill (Leathers & Emigh, 1980).

Women's decoding skills have consistently proved to be superior to men's, however. An exhaustive review of studies that compared the accuracy with which women and men decode nonverbal messages indicates quite clearly that women are superior decoders. Women's advantage in decoding nonverbal cues is greater when the message contains both visual and auditory cues than visual cues alone (Hall, 1981). The superiority of women over men as decoders has also proved to be greater when they are decoding visual messages rather than vocal messages. Because women spend so much more time looking at men than vice versa, it is not surprising that they decode visual cues with particular skill. In fact, these decoding data support the view that women use the visual channel as their primary nonverbal source of information about others.

Women's decoding superiority is most pronounced whenever they are decoding messages that have been intentionally communicated by the message sender. Women are very good at determining the meanings of messages they believe are intended for them. However, women seem reluctant, or unwilling, to determine the implicit meanings of messages that are not intended for them.

Rosenthal and DePaulo (1979) examined the comparative ability of women and men to decode messages that were communicated through channels that varied with regard to their "leakiness" (i.e., the probability that meanings were being communicated unintentionally). From the least to the most leaky, the channels used were facial expressions, bodily cues, tone of voice, and inconsistent messages (visual-auditory channels combined). Results indicated that women decoders lost their superiority over men when they were asked to decode messages transmitted over increasingly leaky channels. The diminution in decoding performance may be traced to a conscious decision on the part of women not to decode the meanings of messages transmitted through the leakier channels rather than to a relative lack of ability to decode such messages.

Subsequent research suggests that women recognize that it is not in their best interests to be too good at decoding the leaky, or unintended, nonverbal cues. They may simply not wish to know or to acknowledge that their male partner is deceiving them or is becoming unbearably anxious. Women might recognize intuitively that if they are to be supportive and interpersonally accommodating, they should refrain from decoding the meanings of messages that were not intended for them. In our society, the more accommodating a woman is non-verbally, the more likely she is to experience satisfactory interpersonal outcomes (Blanck, Rosenthal, Snodgrass, DePaulo & Zuckerman, 1981).

In short, women's nonverbal skills are superior to men's in a number of important aspects. When decoding messages are sent with a high level of awareness and intentionality by the message sender, women's superiority over men as decoders is quite striking. The fact that women exhibit no greater accuracy than men in decoding the meanings communicated through leaky channels should not be interpreted as evidence that women *cannot* decode such messages, and at high levels of accuracy. The plausible explanation seems to be that women choose not to decode certain unintended messages because they are difficult to cope with in ways that are socially appropriate. In these cases, the desire to be polite and accommodating seems to override the desire to utilize effectively their superior decoding skills.

Dysfunctional Male and Female Nonverbal Behaviors

A careful inspection of the nonverbal communicative behaviors that characterize male–female interaction reveals that many of those behaviors are dysfunctional. They are dysfunctional for the following reasons: (a) many link females and males directly to some of the most negative features of their respective stereotypes, (b) they are not consciously modified to meet the varying requirements for successful communication in different contexts, and (c) they often serve as barriers to satisfying interpersonal outcomes.

Men's nonverbal communicative behaviors seem to change little from one type of communication situation to another. Whether a man is trying to sell himself, to conduct an interview, or to run a business meeting, he exhibits a propensity to cultivate the proactive role. As we have seen, males talk more and for longer periods of time than females, and they inhibit immediate feedback by using long, filled pauses. By their visual inattentiveness, their exercise of the touching privilege, their familiar forms of address, and their bodily relaxation, men also indicate that they perceive themselves as status superiors who can legitimately exercise the right to dominate heterosexual interaction. Even though men may not be aware of the implications of their nonverbal communication, their characteristic nonverbal behaviors serve to legitimate the gender-related image traits that are attributed to them (i.e., forcefulness, dominance, confidence, status, power, insensitivity, and inflexibility).

Women, in contrast to men, are nonverbally adaptive and supportive. Their adaptive and supportive behaviors are frequently dysfunctional, however, because they are misdirected. Rather than adapting their nonverbal behaviors to meet the distinctive requirements of specific communication contexts, women adapt to meet the perceived needs of their male partner. In their self-deprecating efforts to please, appease, and placate their male partners, they frequently lend credibility to the stereotypic terms that are used to describe their actions (i.e., *reactive, submissive, dependent,* and *inferior*).

The nonverbal behavioral profile of males is dysfunctional for three more specific reasons: (a) males become inflexibly committed to a single, unchanging communicative style; (b) males come to accept their unexpressive, nondisclosing, and insensitive communication as the norm; and (c) males cultivate a self-directed intrapersonal orientation that is incompatible with successful female–male interaction.

In one sense, the unchanging "male" style of nonverbal communication seems to have some desirable features in business situations. In a business world dominated by males, the unyielding attachment to the proactive role might seem to be desirable. This seems particularly true for leaders and those who aspire to leadership. Individuals who initiate most of the contributions, control communicative interactions, and enhance perceptions of dominance and status by their nonverbal cues might be thought to have the edge. However, this is also an age that values participative management and quality circles, which puts a premium on a communicative style that encourages flexibility and interaction, minimizes status differences, and accents the uniqueness and intrinsic value of each individual. In the new business climate, the male who remains inflexibly committed to a single, domineering communicative style is at a severe disadvantage.

This is also an age that values the ability to express emotions openly and to read and respond with sensitivity to the feelings of those with whom we communicate. Although "women have been socialized to display their emotions, their thoughts, and ideas" (Thorne & Henley, 1975, p. 209), men continue to be verbally unexpressive, nondisclosing, and insensitive. Men's lack of expressiveness frequently means that their true feelings and emotions remain a mystery in female–male interaction. Their insensitivity is reflected, in part, in their inattentiveness to their female partner. This inattentiveness seems to be linked directly to the fact that men are much less skillful decoders of nonverbal messages than women. Men cannot respond to women emotionally until they have developed the capacity to determine more precisely the nature of their female partners' emotional needs.

Finally, men's characteristic nonverbal communicative behaviors are dysfunctional because they perpetuate a preoccupation with self. Whereas women communicate their concern for others nonverbally, men exhibit a primary concern with self-assertion and self-protection; their preoccupation with short-term sexual relationships is a good example (Townsend & Levy, 1990). Men's nonverbal behaviors focus on a set of goals that are frequently important only to them, but women's nonverbal behaviors focus on their desire to facilitate interpersonal outcomes that are satisfying to *both* the male and female interactants. Until men become less preoccupied with the importance of their own talk, and work actively to solicit the feedback of their opposite-sex partners, men's dysfunctional intrapersonal orientation will continue to be a barrier to successful female–male interaction.

In one sense, the nonverbal communicative behaviors that seem to be prototypically female are desirable. In a family setting, the emotionally sensitive and supportive woman has no peer in providing the comfort and emotional support that is so essential to the development of the cohesive family unit. The intrapersonally oriented father, in contrast, may be as likely to brood about his own concerns as to be concerned about the emotional needs of family members.

In contemporary society, however, women must function effectively in many contexts outside of the home. Whenever they do so, their nonverbal behavioral profile can be dysfunctional because (a) females frequently display nonverbal behaviors that invite the attribution of unflattering image traits, (b) females display adaptive nonverbal behaviors that raise questions about their motivations, and (c) females do not fully utilize their impressive nonverbal communication skills.

Skillful impression managers try to associate themselves with favorable images and dissociate themselves from unfavorable images. Women seem to associate themselves with unfavorable images due to some of the nonverbal behaviors they most frequently display. The fact that women smile and laugh twice as much as men clearly implies that their anxiety is high and their self-confidence is low. Women's polite forms of address, the small amount of personal space they claim as theirs, their visual attentiveness to men, the disproportionate amount of touching they receive, and their constricted and tense bodily postures almost assure that they will be perceived as persons of inferior status and power (Henley, 1977).

Women's repeated efforts to be emotionally supportive and to adapt their behaviors to meet men's need to be made comfortable might seem desirable, in one sense. But a woman's efforts to be interpersonally adaptive and supportive could raise questions about her motivations. How likely is it that a man will interpret a woman's smile as being genuine when it is displayed so frequently? What motivation is a man likely to attribute to a woman who becomes noticeably submissive when interacting with a dominant male? Excessive smiling, laughter, and eye contact seem to invite inferences that a person is insincere, manipulative, and deceptive. Because these nonverbal behaviors are such prominent features of the nonverbal profile for women, it is not surprising that they sometimes reinforce doubts about the wholesomeness of women's motivations in a female–male interactions.

Finally, women do not fully and effectively exercise their ability to decode nonverbal messages. In order to be polite, supportive, and accommodating, women apparently choose not to decode the meanings of messages they believe their male partners did not wish to send. In view of the great informational potential of unintentional messages, women's disregard of such messages represents a sacrifice of major proportions.

Guidelines for Successful Female–Male Interaction

The messages communicated nonverbally through female and male gender displays are both powerful and resistant to change. These messages frequently serve as barriers to successful communicative interaction between males and females; therefore, the need for change is apparent. But the extent to which the dysfunctional features of female–male communication can be modified is a debatable question.

Potential for Modifying Nonverbal Cues

In their penetrating essay on the potential of nonverbal communication as an agent for modifying the dysfunctional features of gender displays, Mayo and Henley (1981) argued that gender-defining nonverbal cues are resistant to change for these reasons: (a) nonverbal behaviors that are out-of-awareness obviously will not be changed, (b) nonverbal behaviors characteristic of gender displays are reinforced by powerful social forces such as the media, and (c) nonverbal behavior that is gender-deviant is frequently punished.

These arguments clearly have merit. Neither males nor females can modify their undesirable nonverbal communication behaviors unless they know that those behaviors *are* undesirable. At the same time, we must recognize that individuals can be trained to become aware of nonverbal behaviors that are demonstrably dysfunctional or undesirable. Recent evidence suggests that many dysfunctional, gender-linked nonverbal behaviors can be eliminated with appropriate training (Brown, Dovidio, & Ellyson, 1990). In fact, some sensitivity training is based on the proposition that individuals learn to communicate more effectively by increasing sensitivity to their own behaviors.

Clearly, many of the nonverbal behaviors we have come to accept as characteristic of each sex are learned behaviors. Sex-role stereotypes reflect deeply embedded cultural values that are reinforced by powerful communicative forces such as the media. Comprehensive changes in the nonverbal profile for males and females must be preceded by major changes in cultural values. Dysfunctional gender-related behaviors are learned, therefore they can become unlearned. The force of cultural norms is not so strong at present that dysfunctional "male" and "female" nonverbal behaviors cannot be modified. Individuals will attempt such modification, however, only when they become convinced that the advantages of change outweigh the disadvantages of inflexible attachment to fixed communication styles.

Gender-deviant behavior by a woman involves some degree of risk. Such behavior might be punished. Porter and Geis (1981) recognized the double-bind that a woman may encounter when interacting with a male who assumes the traditional proactive role. They wrote that if

> *a woman is ignored when she presents ordinary, moderate demand signals which are effective for men, she may attempt to secure recognition by increasing the intensity of the signal, and end up being recognized, not for achievement, but as overly emotional, arrogant and abrasive. Indeed, from the perceiver's point of view, the strong demand is uncalled for.* (pp. 55–56)

Punishment and negative reinforcement are far from inevitable, however, when males recognize that such reactions on their part are counterproductive.

Although nonverbal behaviors characteristic of gender displays cannot be changed easily, there is an increasing amount of evidence that the most dysfunctional of those behaviors can be changed in specific situations. For example, the psychologically androgynous person has consistently exhibited the ability to add selective opposite-sex behaviors and eliminate the least desirable behaviors associated with his or her own sex (Mayo & Henley, 1981). Androgynous persons have a communicative flexibility not possessed by the person who conforms to the behavioral norms associated with traditional sex-role stereotypes. They have demonstrated the valuable ability of emphasizing or de-emphasizing the male and female traits they display, depending upon the specific requirements of the communication situation. This ability could account for the fact that androgynous individuals experience more satisfying interpersonal outcomes than proactive males and reactive females (LaFrance & Carmen, 1980).

Sensitizing Communicators to Dysfunctional Gender Cues

The first step in modifying, and ultimately eliminating, dysfunctional nonverbal cues that are characteristic of gender displays is making the communicators *aware* of such cues. The success of conventional sensitivity training suggests that individuals can be made aware of behaviors that are dysfunctional. Individuals typically seek to change their own behaviors when they become fully aware that those behaviors serve neither their own ends nor the ends of successful interpersonal communication.

Nonverbal sensitivity training currently takes a variety of forms. For example, a colleague and I conduct a sales and communication training program designed to sensitize salespeople to their communicative behaviors that serve as barriers to effective persuasive communication. In order to make the salespeople aware of their most dysfunctional behaviors, they are videotaped in both simulated and real sales situations. Their dysfunctional behaviors are then identified by their peers and by the trainers during a videotape replay. Similar formats are being used by others to train police officers, politicians, and labor-management negotiators. The objective is to make the trainees fully aware of which of their communicative behaviors are dysfunctional, and why they should be changed.

I believe that similar procedures should be used to sensitize interacting males and females to the nonverbal communicative behaviors that can and should be modified. The rapid growth of assertiveness workshops and seminars suggests that communicators realize that they must become aware of their problems before they can solve them. Women attend assertiveness workshops in disproportionate numbers. This fact may reflect the rapidly growing awareness of a number of women that their relative nonassertiveness is a gender-related problem.

Modifying Gender-Stereotypic Nonverbal Behaviors

Males and females, by virtue of their gender, tend to adopt inflexible communicative styles that limit their potential for successful communication. As I have indicated, those communicative styles cannot be easily modified. The reasons for trying to modify them are compelling, however. Helpful guidelines that can be used to modify stereotypic male and female dysfunctional nonverbal behaviors have begun to appear (Cannie, 1979; Eakins & Eakins, 1978; Hall, 1984; Thorne & Henley, 1975).

The following guidelines are not comprehensive, because our current level of knowledge about the nature of female–male interactions is still incomplete. There is, nonetheless, a basis for a beginning.

Both men and women should begin by examining their own styles of nonverbal communication for sex-stereotypical cues that are dysfunctional. They should recognize that they will probably have to modify some of their gender-related behaviors in order to have a marked impact on the image traits that are attributed to them. Porter and Geis (1981) found, for example, that a woman who sits at the head of a discussion table does not increase her chances of being perceived as the group's leader. The implication is that women must modify more than one nonverbal behavior if they are to enhance their prospects of being perceived as leaders. For a man to become a successful leader in a group that prefers democratic leadership, he must seek to suppress a number of the dominating and autocratic behaviors associated with the traditional male style of communication.

Men in particular must begin by developing a style of communication that features an interpersonal rather than an intrapersonal orientation. Through a modified communication style, men must demonstrate quite clearly that their attention is focused on the needs, concerns, and opinions of their opposite-sex partners. Men must become more physically and psychologically attentive. As Cannie (1979) put it, attending "is the basic nonverbal skill for valuing others. It is a process of showing people you are interested in them, you are listening, and what they say is important to you. This meets their self-esteem need and returns trust to you. Attending can be physical and it can be psychological" (p. 11).

In order to become a more flexible, sensitive, and attentive communicator, the male should do the following:

1. Minimize the use of dominance and power cues that characterize him as an insensitive and condescending person, one who relegates females to the defensive posture of an inferior.
2. Develop his capacity to express clearly, and interpret accurately, a wide range of emotions, in the interest of facilitating emotionally appropriate and satisfying interpersonal communication.
3. Provide his opposite-sex partner with clear and complete feedback that can be used by the female to assess fully the nature of his communicative reactions.

Women should be guided by a different set of guidelines, including the following:

1. Suppress those nonverbal communicative behaviors that associate them with such undesirable traits as weakness, submissiveness, nonassertiveness, and powerlessness.
2. De-emphasize the display of nonverbal gender cues such as excessive smiling and laughing, which reinforce the impression that they are insincere, manipulative, and dishonest.
3. Fully exercise their impressive decoding skills, rather than interpreting only those male messages they believe are intended for them.

These guidelines, when used by both sexes, should help promote successful female–male interaction, which should result in mutually satisfying outcomes. Men and women must be able to adapt their communication styles not only to help satisfy mutual needs, but to make them more responsive to the requirements of various communication situations. The time is past when the Tarzan–Jane model of communication can be anything but a cruel and demeaning caricature of male–female interaction.

Summary

Sex-role stereotyping has had a pervasive impact on female–male interaction in our culture. Men have been stereotyped as confident, dominant, and forceful individuals who, at the same time, are stubborn, arrogant, and inflexibly committed to the accomplishment of specific tasks. By contrast, women are viewed stereotypically as affectionate, supportive, and sensitive persons who are submissive, excitable, dependent, and timid. To a considerable degree, the communicative behaviors of men and women confirm the accuracy of their respective stereotypes.

Nonverbal cues seem to be the most powerful medium for the communication of gender displays that feature prototypically "feminine" and "masculine" behaviors. The distinctive differences in the nonverbal communication of women and men are manifested most clearly in their contrasting nonverbal communicative styles and in the contrasting levels of their encoding and decoding skills.

The most dysfunctional features of the nonverbal communication styles of men and women are examined in detail in this chapter. Men's characteristic nonverbal communication style is dysfunctional because it is inflexible. It is emotionally nondisclosing and insensitive, and it reflects a preoccupation with self. In contrast, women's nonverbal communication style is dysfunctional because it features the display of nonverbal behaviors that invite the attribution of unflattering image traits. It helps create the impression that women are insincere and dishonest, and it prevents women from effectively utilizing their superior decoding skills.

Many of the dysfunctional features of female–male interaction can be modified. Such modification is not easy, however, because gender-defining cues are reflective of cultural values, which are resistant to change. Dysfunctional nonverbal cues must be raised to the individual communicator's conscious level of awareness before they can be successfully modified. When such modification is attempted, the guidelines presented in this chapter should prove to be useful.

References

Blanck, P. D., Rosenthal, R., Snodgrass, S. E., DePaulo, B. M., & Zuckerman, M. (1981). Sex differences in eavesdropping on nonverbal cues: Developmental changes. *Journal of Personality and Social Psychology, 41,* 391–396.

Briton, N. J., & Hall, J. A. (1995). Gender-based expectancies and observer judgments of smiling. *Journal of Nonverbal Behavior, 19,* 49–65.

Brown, C. E., Dovidio, J. F., & Ellyson, S. L. (1990). Reducing sex differences in visual displays of dominance: Knowledge is power. *Personality and Social Psychology Bulletin, 16,* 358–368.

Cannie, J. K. (1979). *The woman's guide to management success: How to win power in the real organizational world.* Englewood Cliffs, NJ: Prentice-Hall.

Cunningham, M. R., Barbee, A. P., & Pike, C. L. (1990). What do women want? Facialmetric assessment of multiple motives in the perception of male facial physical attractiveness. *Journal of Personality and Social Psychology, 59,* 61–72.

Derlega, V. J., Lewis, R. J., Harrison, S., & Costanza, R. (1989). Gender differences in the initiation and attribution of tactile intimacy. *Journal of Nonverbal Behavior, 13,* 83–96.

Eakins, B. W., & Eakins, R. G. (1978). *Sex differences in human communication.* Boston: Houghton Mifflin.

Ellyson, S., Dovidio, J. F., Corson, R. L., & Vinicur, D. L. (1980). Visual dominance behavior in female dyads and situational and personality factors. *Social Psychology Quarterly, 43,* 328–336.

Frances, S. J. (1979). Sex differences in nonverbal behavior. *Sex Roles, 5,* 519–535.

Gibson, J. T. (1988). Sex roles in the family, school and workplace: The Soviet example. *International Journal for the Advancement of Counseling, 11,* 209–218.

Goffman, E. (1979). *Gender advertisements.* Cambridge, MA: Harvard University Press.

Hall, J. A. (1981). Gender effects in decoding nonverbal cues. *Psychological Bulletin, 85,* 845–857.

Hall, J. A. (1984). *Nonverbal sex differences.* Baltimore: Johns Hopkins University Press.

Heilbrum, A. B., Jr. (1976). Measurement of masculine and feminine sex role identities as independent dimensions. *Journal of Consulting and Clinical Psychology, 44,* 183–190.

Henley, N. M. (1977). *Body politics: Power, sex, and nonverbal communication.* Englewood Cliffs, NJ: Prentice-Hall.

Henley, N. M. & LaFrance, M. (1984). Gender as culture: Difference and dominance in nonverbal behavior. In A. W. Siegman (Ed.), *Nonverbal behavior* (pp. 315–317). Lewiston, NY: C. J. Hogrefe.

Johnson, K. K. P., Crutsinger, C., & Workman, J. E. (1994). Can professional women appear too masculine? The case of the necktie. *Clothing and Textile Research Journal, 12,* 27–31.

Kramarae, C. (1982). Gender: How she speaks. In E. B. Ryan & H. Giles (Eds.), *Attitudes towards language variations: Social and applied contest* (pp. 175–188). London: Arnold.

LaFrance, M., & Carmen, B. (1980). The nonverbal display of psychological androgyny. *Journal of Personality and Social Psychology, 38,* 36–49.

LaFrance, M., & Mayo, C. (1978). *Moving bodies: Nonverbal communication in social relationships.* Monterey, CA: Brooks/Cole.

LaFrance, M., & Mayo, C. (1979). A review of nonverbal behaviors of women and men. *Western Journal of Speech Communication, 43,* 96–107.

Leathers, D. G., & Emigh, T. H. (1980). Decoding facial expressions: A new test with decoding norms. *Quarterly Journal of Speech, 66,* 418–436.

Mayo, C., & Henley, N. M. (1981). Nonverbal behavior: Barrier or agent for sex role change? In C. Mayo & N. M. Henley (Eds.), *Gender and Nonverbal Behavior* (pp. 3–13). New York: Springer-Verlag.

Mulac, A. (1989). Men's and women's talk in same-gender and mixed-gender dyads: Power or polemic? *Journal of Language and Social Psychology, 8,* 249–270.

Mulac, A., Wiemann, J., Widenmann, S. J., & Gibson, T. W. (1988). Male/female language differences and effects in same-sex and mixed-sex dyads: The gender-linked language effect. *Communication Monographs, 55,* 315–335.

Porter, N., & Geis, F. (1981) Women and nonverbal leadership cues. When seeing is not believing. In C. Mayo & N. M. Henley (Eds.), *Gender and Nonverbal Behavior* (pp. 39–61). New York: Springer-Verlag.

Reid, E. (1989). Black girls talking. *Gender and Education, 1,* 295–300.

Rosenthal, R., & DePaulo, B. M. (1979). Expectancies, discrepancies, and courtesies in nonverbal communication. *Western Journal of Speech Communication, 43,* 76–95.

Simpson, J. A., Gangestad, S. W., & Biek, M. (1993). Personality and nonverbal social behavior: An ethological perspective of relationship initiation. *Journal of Experimental Social Psychology, 29,* 434–461.

Thorne, B., & Henley, N. M. (1975). Womanspeak and manspeak: Sex differences and sexism in communication, verbal and nonverbal. In B. Thorne & N. M. Henley (Eds.), *Language and sex: Difference and dominance.* Rowley, MA: Newbury House.

Townsend, J. M., & Levy, G. D. (1990). Effects of potential partners' costume and physical attractiveness on sexuality and partner selection. *The Journal of Psychology, 124,* 371–398.

Umiker-Sebeok, J. (1981). The seven ages of woman: A view from American magazine advertisements. In C. Mayo & N. M. Henley (Eds.), *Gender and nonverbal behavior.* New York: Springer-Verlag.

Vrugt, A., & Kerkstra, A. (1984). Sex differences in nonverbal communication. *Semiotica, 50,* 1–41.

Wagner, H. L., Buck, R., & Winterbotham, M. (1993). Communication of specific emotions—Gender differences in sending accuracy and communication measures. *Journal of Nonverbal Behavior, 17,* 29–53.

Weitz, S. (1976). Sex differences in nonverbal communication. *Sex Roles, 2,* 175–184.

Wood, J. T. (1994). *Gendered lives: Communication, gender, and culture.* Belmont, CA: Wadsworth.

Chapter *16*

Successful Intercultural Communication

The communication styles characteristic of given cultures are often distinctively different. To communicate successfully with members of another cultural group, we must be able to identify those behaviors that define the unique communication style of the culture. We must identify specific communicative behaviors, both those perceived as positive and those perceived as negative in a particular culture (Payrato, 1993). Then we can adapt our communication to conform to that culture's norms and rules.

We know, for example, that individuals who communicate nonverbally in a manner that is consistent with the nonverbal communication style of a given culture will be perceived as more interpersonally attractive by members of that culture (Dew & Ward, 1993). Accomplished nonverbal communicators are held in high esteem in Japan, for example. In order to be viewed as an accomplished communicator in Japan, one's nonverbal behaviors must be consistent with the communication style for the Japanese culture. Indeed, conformity to the defining features of Japan's communication style is unusually important because Japanese culture is high context (McDaniel, 1993).

The nonverbal communication style of Native Americans is particularly distinctive. Their communicative style is strongly influenced by central culture values, such as humility, respect for elders, learning through storytelling, intuitiveness, and concern for group harmony. For the Cherokee, Navajo, and Hopi educators studied, these values shaped a distinctive nonverbal communication cultural style defined by the following behaviors: (a) soft talk; (b) gentle handshakes; (c) minimal eye contact, especially with elders; (d) little facial display of emotion, with most facial movement around the eyes; and (e) varying expectations as to appropriate personal distances in different distance zones (Chiang, 1993). Careful study of this nonverbal communication style for Native Americans strongly reinforces the importance of communication style to help establish successful communication within a given culture. Clearly the individual communicator must ask whether it is possible to communicate effectively with members of a culture such as Native Americans without detailed knowledge of the defining features of that culture's communication style.

A culture's communication style is, of course, strongly affected by its language. The potentially powerful impact of language on culture is perhaps most clearly and concisely described in the Sapir-Whorf hypothesis. This hypothesis stipulates that the language of a culture serves not only as a medium of communication but also as a major force in shaping the thought processes and perceptions of members of that culture (Condon & Yousef, 1975). Knowledge of and command of the language of a culture is not apt to be sufficient to assure success in intercultural communication, however. In fact, Almaney and Alwan (1982) maintained that "cultural anthropologists consider nonverbal skills as far more important than verbal skills in determining communication success abroad" (p. 18). For reasons that will be emphasized in this chapter, the centrality of nonverbal message systems in successful intercultural communication has become widely recognized (Barnlund, 1989).

Nonverbal messages are particularly important in intercultural communication because they usually contain sets of implicit rules or "commands" (LaFrance & Mayo, 1978a) that specify what is and what is not acceptable behavior in a given culture. If outsiders are to become successful communicators in a culture other than their own, they must become thoroughly familiar with the socially learned display rules that make the communication style of the culture distinctive. When the nuances of socially sensitive and appropriate behavior within a given culture remain out-of-awareness to the foreigner, the potential for successful intercultural communication remains limited.

Executives and employees of multinational corporations, exchange students, international travelers, and diplomats all need to communicate effectively in cultural contexts that are unfamiliar to them. This chapter is designed to be helpful to those individuals. To begin, cross-cultural similarities and differences in nonverbal communication are compared and contrasted. Then, to demonstrate how a person becomes thoroughly familiar with the communication styles of contrasting cultures, the nonverbal communication styles of the Japanese and Arab cultures are examined in detail. Finally, a set of guidelines is included, which can be used to identify with and adapt to the nonverbal communication style of the culture in which communicative interaction might occur.

Cross-Cultural Similarities in Nonverbal Communication

Darwin (1872/1965) theorized that the "chief" facial expressions will be recognized universally by members of different cultures because the ability to communicate and identify the major classes of facial emotions is innately acquired. Ekman, Friesen, and Ellsworth (1972) conducted research that supports the view that six basic emotions—happiness, fear, surprise, anger, disgust–contempt, and sadness—are communicated via similar facial displays and are decoded at similar levels of accuracy by members of both literate cultures and preliterate cultures such as that of New Guinea.

Eibl-Eibesfeldt (1972) also maintained that members of different cultures use the same facial muscles to communicate emotions such as happiness and anger. For example, he observed the familiar eyebrow flash used in greetings by such diverse cultural groups as Europeans, Balinese, Papuans, Samoans, South American Indians, and Bushmen. He concluded that *similarities in expressive movements between cultures lie not only in such basic expressions as smiling, laughing, crying, and the facial expressions of anger, but in whole syndromes of behavior. For example, one of the expressions people of different cultures may produce when angry is characterized by opening the corners of the mouth in a particular way and by frowning, and also by clenching the fists, stamping on the ground and even by hitting at objects.* (p. 299)

Eibl-Eibesfeldt maintained, as did Ekman and his associates, that facial communication across cultures is similar in that members of different cultures use the same facial muscles to display basic emotions such as happiness or anger. Although different facial muscles are, of course, used to display happiness and anger, for example, the looks of facial happiness and anger are quite similar in all cultures they have examined. As a note of caution, however, Eibl-Eibesfeldt noted that even though members of all cultures may inherit a facial display that features an eyebrow flash to signal pleasure when greeting someone, the eyebrow flash is not a universal feature of greeting behavior. In Japan, the eyebrow flash is suppressed because it is considered indecent.

Izard (1971) has probably done the most detailed examination of the facial communication of emotions in nine national-cultural groups: American, English, German, Swedish, French, Swiss, Greek, African, and Japanese. He concludes that the *ability to encode and decode the basic emotions communicated by facial expressions is innate and universal.*

The different cultural groups that Izard studied were able to identify the basic facial emotions at a level exceeding chance expectation. However, there are some striking differences in the accuracy with which different cultural groups identified given types of facial emotions. For example, the Greeks were much less accurate than the eight other cultural groups in identifying facial interest–excitement; the Africans had difficulty in identifying facial disgust–contempt; and the Japanese were notably inaccurate in their attempts to identify facial shame–humiliation. Because shame is viewed as the most undesirable of emotions in the Japanese culture (Sweeney, Cottle, & Kobayashi, 1980), we might infer that the reluctance to exhibit or acknowledge facial shame in Japan is a socially learned behavior.

There are striking differences in the socialization experiences of the Japanese as opposed to Americans and Europeans, for example (Sherer, Walbott, Matsumoto, & Kudoh, 1988). The cultural experiences of the Japanese shape display rules that dictate which emotions should and should not be communicated nonverbally and ultimately affect the level of accuracy with which one or more emotions are encoded and decoded. (Display rules work similarly in cultures other than the Japanese culture.) Consider the fact that the Japanese experience great difficulty in decoding the facial expression of disgust (Ekman et al., 1987) and that in a recent study Japanese subjects were able to identify disgust expressed by bodily movements only 2 out of 22 times. The problems that the Japanese experience in decoding and encoding disgust can be traced to a cultural display rule that says that disgust should not be communicated in public. Thus, Sogon and Masutani (1989) wrote that

[the] greater accuracy of American subjects in identifying the expression of disgust, and the great difficulty the Japanese had in distinguishing between contempt and disgust, suggest that there may be culture-specific socialization processes influencing recognition of these emotions. In Japanese culture, feelings of disgust

and contempt are mostly suppressed. It is a serious breach of custom to express these emotions overtly even if one is of high status and the expression objectively justifiable. (p. 41)

In short, there is evidence that a limited number of emotions are communicated by similar facial expressions across cultures. However, LaFrance and Mayo (1978b) noted that the pancultural element in facial communication seems to be limited to four or five basic emotions. They contend emotional expression is subject to both cultural and biological influences. More specifically, "the innate elements link particular emotions with particular facial muscles while cultural elements adapt the facial signal to the environment in which it occurs" (p. 77). Thus, members of some cultures appear to experience and communicate sentiments and emotions that members of other cultures neither know nor recognize. For example, the facial blend that North Americans label "smug" is rarely named or recognized in any other culture. Similarly, the "wry smile" of the English, with one corner of the mouth up and the other corner down, may be unique to England.

A study that examined the skill of West German students in decoding of facial expressions (Leathers & McGuire, 1983) suggests that people's cultural experiences can have a dramatic impact on their ability to identify the more subtle kinds of meanings that can be communicated by facial expressions. A colleague and I, using the Facial Meaning Sensitivity Test (FMST) described in Chapter 2, compared the decoding performance of samples of American and West German decoders. Consider the results reported in Table 16.1. Germans were significantly less accurate than Americans in identifying 13 of the 30 highly specific facial meanings in Step III of the FMST (p. 39). Although Germans were more sensitive than Americans to such specific kinds of facial disgust as repugnance and distaste, they were much less sensitive to special kinds of facial sadness, bewilderment, and anger. We attribute the differences in ability to identify subtle nuances of facial meaning not to innately acquired skills but to culturally acquired attitudes about the emotions that are communicated by facial expressions.

The results for the German decoders (see Table 16.1) may be explained at least in part by two forces that may have helped shape the German culture. Leathers and McGuire (1983) contended that the Germans' sense of superiority would seem to encourage the display of, and help to develop sensitivity to, those emotions that would reinforce or be consistent with a feeling of superiority. In addition, the Germans' national sense of shame would seem to discourage the display of shame and prevent the development of sensitivity to those emotions that might be associated with a sense of shame.

The results in Table 16.1 do suggest that Germans are particularly sensitive to such highly specialized facial emotions as repugnance, distaste, and disdain. Those emotions traditionally have been associated with a sense of superiority and a limited tolerance for individuals and actions that are judged to be inferior.

German decoders exhibited striking insensitivity to subtle differences in specific kinds of emotions that might contradict a feeling of superiority or that might reinforce a sense of shame. Germans were particularly insensitive to different kinds of sadness expressed by facial expressions. Sadness, which is a negative emotional state, might be associated in the German mind with the enormous amount of suffering inflicted on the Jews and others by the Germans during World War II, and a sense of shame could have conditioned Germans against the facial display of sadness in public.

TABLE 16.1   Accuracy of Identification of Specific Facial Expressions by German Decoders Within Each Class of Meaning

Class of Meaning		Photo Number	Percentage of Correct Identification		Type of Decoding Error Made by German Decoders	Percentage of Decoders Correctly Identifying All Facial Expressions Within a Class	
			American	German		American	German
Happiness	Laughter	9	98.45	94.37	Amusement (5.63) Love (0.00)	90.27	77.33
	Love	26	91.09	82.67	Amusement (10.67) Laughter (6.67)		
	Amusement	2	90.31	83.56	Love (12.33) Laughter (4.11)		
Fear	Terror	10	98.44	91.78	Anxiety (5.48) Apprehension (2.74)	76.74	68.00
	Anxiety	21	77.43	73.97	Apprehension (19.18) Terror (6.85)		
	Apprehension	27	77.82	76.06	Apprehension (23.94) Terror (0.00)		
Disgust	Aversion	30	78.68	77.46	Repugnance (21.13) Distaste (1.41)	42.25	56.00
	Repugnance	12	49.61	62.50	Aversion (19.44) Distaste (18.06)		
	Distaste	8	45.35	80.56	Repugnance (16.67) Aversion (2.78)		
Anger	Rage	28	95.74	61.11	Hate (23.61) Annoyance (15.28)	94.53	56.00
	Hate	1	94.92	67.12	Rage (28.77) Annoyance (4.11)		
	Annoyance	20	98.96	80.56	Hate (11.11) Rage (8.33)		
Interest	Attention	23	89.92	80.28	Excitement (14.08) Anticipation (5.63)	66.15	48.00
	Anticipation	6	67.05	60.27	Excitement (34.25) Attention (5.48)		
	Excitement	15	71.32	52.06	Anticipation (34.25) Attention (13.70)		
Bewilderment	Confusion	18	86.38	50.73	Doubt (34.78) Stupidity (14.49)	85.66	40.00
	Doubt	4	88.72	50.70	Confusion (43.67) Stupidity (5.63)		
	Stupidity	17	93.39	79.45	Doubt (13.70) Confusion (6.85)		
Contempt	Disdain	24	55.25	66.67	Arrogance (29.17) Superiority (4.17)	43.80	36.00
	Arrogance	13	47.47	41.10	Superiority (30.14) Disdain (28.77)		
	Superiority	29	71.98	65.28	Arrogance (30.56) Disdain (4.17)		

Continued

TABLE 16.1   **(Continued)**

Class of Meaning		Photo Number	Percentage of Correct Identification		Type of Decoding Error Made by German Decoders	Percentage of Decoders Correctly Identifying All Facial Expressions Within a Class	
			American	German		American	German
Determination	Stubborn	11	51.55	38.89	Resolute (36.11) Belligerent (25.00)	37.98	22.67
	Resolute	22	67.05	39.72	Belligerent (31.51) Stubborn (28.77)		
	Belligerent	25	44.19	43.84	Stubborn (31.51) Resolute (24.66)		
Surprise	Amazement	16	45.74	54.92	Astonishment (28.17) Flabbergasted (16.90)	20.62	16.00
	Flabbergasted	19	35.66	32.29	Astonishment (46.48) Amazement (21.13)		
	Astonishment	3	32.17	23.29	Flabbergasted (50.69) Amazement (26.03)		
Sadness	Disappointment	14	56.59	4.11	Distress (93.15) Pensiveness (2.74)	53.91	2.67
	Distress	5	72.48	5.48	Disappointment (39.73) Pensiveness (38.36)		
	Pensiveness	7	68.61	60.27	Disappointment (39.73) Distress (0.00)		

Germans were also highly insensitive to such special kinds of anger as rage, hate, and annoyance. Those emotions also can be linked rather directly in the German mind to a sense of shame, because many of the inhumane acts of Germans during World War II were triggered by emotions such as those. On the other hand, displays of rage would violate the cultural preference for a stoical, controlled, "superior" person.

Finally, the Germans' insensitivity to special kinds of facial bewilderment may be explained by an implicit cultural rule that discourages the public display of bewilderment. Certainly, the Germans' propensity to exercise self-control while cultivating a public image of superiority, or even arrogance, is not consistent with the frequent expression of bewilderment. The most extreme forms of bewilderment suggest uncertainty, and perhaps weakness, which Germans would presumably be reluctant to reveal in public.

In short, the striking differences between German and American decoders in sensitivity to highly specialized kinds of facial emotions seem to be directly related to the impact of different display rules in the two cultures. *Cultural display rules* are a deeply ingrained set of implicit cultural conventions, learned early in life, that specify which emotions should and should not be expressed in public (Ekman & Friesen, 1975). During socialization, an individual learns not only whether the public display of emotions is positively or negatively rewarded, but also "which facial expressions are expected, preferred, or allowed in which circumstances and [communicators] learn to perform accordingly" (Kilbride & Yarczower, 1980, p. 282).

Because German display rules seem to dictate that sadness, bewilderment, and anger should be infrequently displayed in public, these are emotions that the German decoder presumably sees rarely. Infrequently seen facial expressions should be the expressions decoded at the lowest levels of accuracy. In West Germany, at least, cultural display rules seem strongly to affect sensitivity to specialized kinds of facial emotions.

In the broadest perspective, however, the evidence supports the conclusion that individuals from a wide variety of cultures encode and decode a limited number of general classes of facial emotions at similar levels of accuracy. We know much less about the cross-cultural communication of vocal messages. Guidetti (1991) recently did a study on this unexplored field of research. Fifty French adults and 50 German adults were asked to take the vocal emotion recognition test designed by Scherer and Wallbott (1994). This test requires that the subject identify and differentiate among the emotions of fear, anger, joy, and sadness while the encoder relies strictly on vocal cues. The results indicate that German and French subjects decoded these vocally communicated emotions at similar levels of accuracy.

Rosenthal, Hall, DiMatteo, Rogers, and Archer (1979) took cross-cultural comparisons of nonverbal skills a step further by testing the relative sensitivity of different cultural groups to emotional and attitudinal information transmitted through 11 channels and combinations of channels. The Profile of Nonverbal Sensitivity (the "PONS" Test) has been administered by Rosenthal and his colleagues to such diverse cultural groups as Australians, Hawaiians, New Guineans, and Israelis.

The PONS Test is a 45-minute, black-and-white sound film that contains 220 auditory and visual segments. Viewers are asked to respond to two-second excerpts from a scene portrayed by a female. Viewers must make judgments about dominance and submissiveness for five different scenes. The channels are as follows:

1. face alone, no voice
2. body from neck to knees, no voice
3. face and body down to thighs, no voice
4. electronic content-filtered voice, no picture
5. randomized spliced voice, no picture

The other six are mixed channels that use some combination of the first five channels. Interpreting their results, Rosenthal and coworkers wrote that the

> *cultural universality hypothesis, which suggested that all cultures would do equally well due to the universality of nonverbal behavior, can also be considered disproved by the data. There was a wide variation among cross-cultural groups in their levels of accuracy in decoding the PONS film.* (p. 211)

Interestingly, members of those cultures rated most similar to Americans had the highest PONS scores, and those rated least similar had the lowest PONS scores. Australian aborigines, Australian psychiatric patients, and Papuan New Guinea Civil Service trainees received the lowest ratings on similarity to American culture scales and three of the four lowest scores on the PONS test.

When considered in their broadest perspective, cross-cultural similarities in nonverbal communication seem to be primarily limited to affect displays. Similar facial expressions are used across cultures to communicate such broadly defined emotions as happiness and anger. The frequency with which such basic emotions are facially displayed varies from one culture to another, however, depending on how the emotion is valued in the culture. The more specialized the emotional meaning that is being communicated, the greater the cross-cultural differences in encoding and decoding accuracy. Those differences seem to be related directly to cultural display rules that specify which emotions should and should not be expressed.

As we shall see, cross-cultural differences in nonverbal communication seem to become much more pronounced as we move from a consideration of affect displays to emblems, illustrators, and regulators. Cross-cultural differences are also manifested clearly in the contrasting proxemic and tactile behaviors exhibited in different cultures. Finally, chronemics, or the way a culture uses time, also reflects and emphasizes cross-cultural differences in nonverbal communication.

However, even with the nonverbal cues that tend to be culture specific in meaning—emblems, illustrators, and regulators—we should recognize that the greater the similarity between two or more cultures, the greater the probability that the nonverbal communication styles of those cultures will be similar. As Rosenthal and colleagues (1979) speculated:

> *similarities among verbal languages in a given language group may be paralleled by similarities among the nonverbal behaviors of speakers of those languages. Nonverbal similarities within a language group could include paralanguage, as well as other nonverbal behaviors like facial expressions, body movements, gestures, etc.* (p. 223)

Cross-Cultural Differences in Nonverbal Communication

Members of different cultures all experience the same biological drives that motivate them to satisfy their needs to be relieved of tensions associated with hunger, thirst, sexual desire, inadequate protection from the elements, and fatigue. In their attempts to satisfy those needs, members of different cultures all develop rules that are used in courtship, in marriage, in family relations, in division of labor, and in developing codes of ethics, for example.

Although our drives and needs are biologically determined, the ways in which we satisfy our needs are socially learned. For example, if you grew up in China, you would probably eat bird's nest soup, well-aged eggs, and rice, among other foods. Members of other cultures eat snakes, grasshoppers, and lizards. From the perspective of intercultural communication, life would be much less complicated if all cultures developed identical behavioral responses to satisfy the same needs. They do not.

If one word best describes the communication that is characteristic of specific cultural groups, that word is *different*. This is particularly true when we consider cultures with dissimilar values and belief systems. In fact, one culture is differentiated from another on the basis of difference rather than similarity. *A culture is defined as those values, beliefs, customs, rules, laws, and communicative behaviors that can be used to differentiate one societal group from another.*

Cross-cultural differences in nonverbal communication are so numerous as to defy complete description. Suffice it to say that each "culture has its own distinct nonverbal communication system. Children learn this system before they master verbal skills and rely on it as their major vehicle of communication. As they grow up, nonverbal behavior becomes so deeply rooted in their psyche that they engage in it rather unconsciously" (Almaney & Alwan, 1982, p. 16).

Cross-cultural differences in nonverbal communication are manifested in many ways. Gestural emblems are perhaps the most important, and because this is true, gestural emblems are highly susceptible to misinterpretation. Similar gestural emblems have different meanings in different cultures, and different emblems are used in different cultures to communicate the same meaning. For instance, in the United States the head nod signals agreement, but in Japan it signals acknowledgment that the message has been received. In Italy, "up yours" is communicated by the forearm jerk; Americans use the upraised middle finger.

The diversity that is characteristic of cross-cultural gestural communication is documented in the detailed inventory of European gestures compiled by Morris, Collett, Marsh, and O'Shaughnessy (1979). They found that not only do the same gestures have different meanings in different European cultures, but also some cultures consistently use different gestures to communicate the same meanings. Furthermore, in some cases gestures used to communicate specialized meaning in one European culture are not used at all, or are not recognized, in another European culture.

Consider the case of the *hand-purse* gesture—the fingers and thumb of one hand are straightened and brought together in a point facing upwards; held in that posture, the hand may be kept still or moved slightly. In Italy this gesture means "Please be more precise" or "What are you trying to say?"; in Spain the gesture means "good"; in Tunisia the gesture means "Slow down"; in Malta the gesture means "You may seem good, but you are really bad." The hand-purse gesture, interpreted as "Please be more precise," is widely understood throughout the Italian-speaking world, but only 3 percent of the persons surveyed in neighboring southern France knew its meaning.

Cross-cultural differences abound, not only with regard to the kinds of gestural emblems, illustrators, adaptors, and regulators that are used and their culture-specific meanings, but also with regard to cross-cultural proxemic norms and behaviors. We know, for example, that Latin Americans prefer closer interaction distances than do North Americans. We also know that distance preferences vary among Latin Americans. Costa Ricans stand closer to those with whom they interact than do Panamanians or Colombians. Costa Ricans also touch others more frequently than Colombians or Panamanians (Shuter, 1976). When the proxemic behaviors of Italians, Germans, and United States citizens are compared, the finding is that Italians interact with others at the closest distances, Germans communicate at greater distances than Italians, and citizens of the United States are most distant in their interaction with others (Shuter, 1977).

Cross-cultural differences in nonverbal communication are not confined to differences in the visual, proxemic, and tactile behaviors that are exhibited in different cultures, however. Hall (1969) emphasized that different cultures place greater or lesser emphasis on certain sensory modalities that are used to encode and decode nonverbal messages. He stressed that Americans and Arabs live in different sensory worlds much of the time and as a result they attach different priorities to certain kinds of nonverbal communication. Thus, "Arabs make more use of olfaction and touch than Americans. They interpret their sensory data differently and combine them in different ways" (p. 3).

Chronemics is defined by the way members of a given culture define, experience, structure, and use time. From the perspective of a decoder, knowledge of time norms for a given culture can be valuable. Hickson and Stacks (1989) wrote:

> *Culture begins to educate each of us at an early age as to the value of and the means by which we distinguish time. Each culture has its own particular time norms, which are unconsciously followed until violated. When such violations occur, however, they are perceived as intentional messages associated with that particular culture. In this regard each culture teaches its people what is appropriate or inappropriate with regard to time.* (p. 186)

Chronemics is of much more limited value from the perspective of the encoder, however, because the cultural differences in the way time is defined, experienced, structured, and used remain relatively fixed over time. As a result, the culture-bound messages a person may transmit about time norms will remain the same no matter what the nature of the communication situation.

The study of chronemics places much emphasis on Edward T. Hall's distinction between *formal time* and *informal time* (1963). Although Hall now claims that no fewer than eight types of time tend to be used to differentiate certain types of cultures from others (1984), the distinction between formal and informal time remains one of his most enduring and valuable contributions to the study of chronemics.

Formal time is measured by such precise and fixed units of time as minutes, days, weeks, and months. In Western nations formal time is extremely important. Because people are expected to be "on time," the clock assumes a central role in cultures where formal time is given a high priority. If members of a culture become preoccupied with conforming to the rigid norms that formal time imposes on them, they may ultimately become controlled by what has been called "the tyranny of the clock."

Bruneau (1988) maintained that members of a culture who become preoccupied with formal time might suffer from "chronophilia":

> *In a chronophiliac atmosphere, people value clock time very much, they value accuracy highly, and cherish the order assumed to exist under such standards. . . . In such an atmosphere of temporality, clocks are increasingly extended into pacers which regulate the flow and speed of activities. More and more areas of life-space are regulated and punctuated by clocks and their extensions.* (p. 289)

Informal time is different in that the units of informal time are measured not by the precision of the clock but by the much more subjective judgments of people who are interacting. The "instantaneous event" is the shortest unit of informal time, and "forever" is the longest. Additional time distinctions made by individuals using informal time include "very short duration," "short duration," "long duration," "very long duration," and "impossibly long duration" (Hall, 1963).

Hickson and Stacks (1989) maintained that "subcultural informal time" is, in effect, a subcategory of Hall's larger category of informal time. Their notion of subcultural informal time is provocative because it allows for the development of the notion that there are regional differences within a nation in the ways people of a given region view time. They wrote perceptively that

> *we encounter such time orientations as CPT (Colored People's Time), or street time, hauley time, or white person's time (hauley is a derogative Hawaiian term that referred to the early missionary's pallid complexion), is contrasted to Hawaiian time, which is more lax. In each case, the subcultural time orientation (Hawaiian and street time) refers to a more lax and unconscious perception of time.* (p. 188)

When we turn more specifically to international business, two types of time are used: *monochronic* and *polychronic* time (Hall & Hall, 1987). "Monochronic time (M-time) means paying attention to and doing only one thing at a time. Polychronic time (P-time) means being involved with many things at once. Like oil and water, the two systems do not mix" (p. 17).

Western cultures represented by such nations as the United States, Switzerland, Germany, and Scandinavia use M-time to conduct international business. M-Time requires an allegiance to the clock and rather minimal involvement with the persons with whom one does business. P-time, in contrast, stresses maximum involvement with the parties to a business transaction with recognition of the fact that many different personal and business activities might occur at the same time. A number of Latin American and southern European business persons operate on P-time. Needless to say, compromise will probably be necessary if successful intercultural communication is to occur during those business meetings where proponents of both M- and P-time are participants.

In short, "Time talks. It speaks more plainly than words. The message it conveys comes through loud and clear. Because it is manipulated less consciously, it is subject to less distortion than the spoken language" (Hall, 1963, p. 15). Thus, sensitivity to culture-specific time norms and conceptions of time will reveal many intercultural differences (Hall & Hall, 1987). Cultures that share values similar to those of the United States expect rigid adherence to the deadlines and time limits associated with formal time. The past, present, and future are defined precisely, and an emphasis is put on time-bound planning. For contrast, in the Navajo culture there is no conception of the future, so that promises of future actions become meaningless. Latin American and similar cultures prefer an informal conception of time that places a premium on the leisurely development of interpersonal relationships. Finally, the Japanese culture seems to be able to combine the best features of formal and M-time with the best features of informal and P-time.

Culture-specific conceptions of time and time norms can operate very much like display rules. The sensitive observer of a foreign culture can learn what are and are not proper uses of time within that culture. As a result, many of the misunderstandings and misinterpretations associated with culture-bound notions of time could be eliminated or minimized (Bruneau, 1988).

A comprehensive description of the major differences in nonverbal communication that help to define the nonverbal communication styles of existing cultures is not possible at this time; knowledge of that subject is simply not complete enough to warrant such an undertaking. We are beginning to gather information on parts of the communication styles for some cultures and nationalities, however. Two recent examples help make the point that useful information is being produced, but the relationship of one study to another is not always obvious.

Belk, Garcia-Falconi, Hernandez-Sanchez, and Snell (1988) found that the nonverbal style of U.S. couples is assertive and confrontational when compared to Mexican couples. More particularly, Mexican women were much less likely to use nonverbal disapproval and voiced objections in dealing with an intimate than U.S. women were. Those differences in nonverbal communication style may be attributed in part to cultural differences. Masters and Sullivan (1989a; 1989b) have done research in that area with a somewhat different focus. In contrasting the nonverbal communication style of French and U.S. politicians, they found many similarities as well as some differences: French citizens expected more authoritative and aggressive nonverbal behaviors from their political leaders and responded more favorably than U.S. citizens to facial displays of anger and threat from their political leaders. Although our knowledge in this area remains incomplete, we also know that many of the more salient differences in the nonverbal communication systems of major cultures have already been identified (LaFrance & Mayo, 1978a, 1978b).

In retrospect, we can conclude that when two or more cultures are compared there are apt to be *both* cross-cultural similarities and differences in the ways they communicate nonverbally. For example, the Greek and U.S. cultures are quite different in many respects. One would expect, therefore, that there are many differences in the nonverbal communication style for Greeks and Americans. On the other hand, a recent study by Bernieri and Gillis (1995) found a high correlation between Greeks and Americans in terms of the nonverbal behaviors that they believe are most effective in communicating rapport, such as *extent* of gestures, supportive back-channel responses in the form of head nods and "hmms," close physical proximity, forward lean, and synchronized bodily movements.

A fascinating study by Montepare and Zebrowitz (1993) highlights a seemingly anomalous fact. Members of two strikingly different cultures may interpret the same nonverbal behaviors in ways that are both similar and dissimilar (Peng, Zebrowitz, & Lee, 1993). In a study by Montepare and Zebrowitz, separate groups of Korean and American subjects were asked to observe the gaits of different people who were walking along. Interestingly, the different "patterns of gait" exhibited exerted a strong and highly similar impact on the social perceptions of both the Koreans and the Americans. Using "walker's gait" as their sole source of information, there was a high degree of intercultural agreement among Korean and American perceivers in terms of the perception of each walker's age and sex as well as rated happiness, physical strength, and sexiness. The authors concluded that

> *American and Korean perceivers responded similarly to age-related variations in gait. Furthermore, these shared impressions held true independent of the age and sex attributed to walkers, indicating they were directly related to the walkers' patterns of movement and were not simply the result of age- or sex-stereotypic labeling.* (p. 65)

Even though this study revealed many cross-cultural similarities in the way Koreans and Americans interpret a walker's gait, there was one important cross-cultural difference. Walkers with a "youthful gait" were perceived as more dominant than those with an older gait by Americans but not by Koreans. The authors suggested that this finding may be explained by the fact that youthfulness is positively valued in Western cultures, whereas aging is viewed as related to decreasing independence and low social status. In the Korean culture, by contrast, senior citizens are treated deferentially and are seen as sources of enlightenment and strength.

Cross-cultural studies of nonverbal communication have focused in greatest detail on the functions of nonverbal cues in communicating emotions, greetings, status differences, and intimacy. Each of those functions assumes a central role in defining the distinctive nonverbal communication style of a given culture. In order to understand how knowledge of nonverbal communication styles of specific cultures can be used to facilitate more successful intercultural communication, I will compare and contrast the styles of two cultures of particular importance to U.S. citizens: the Japanese culture and the Arab culture.

Communicating Nonverbally with the Japanese and the Arabs

The dominant values of a culture reveal what is important to members of a culture (Shuter, 1983). Cultural values are reflected clearly in the nonverbal communication styles that differentiate one culture from another. Familiarity with a culture's communicative style is absolutely necessary if successful intercultural communication is to occur, because the implicit display rules that suggest how not to behave are an integral part of the nonverbal communication style of a culture.

A comparison and contrast of the nonverbal communication styles of the Japanese and Arab cultures should be useful for at least two reasons. In view of current political and economic realities, American contact with members of those cultures is increasing daily. In addition, we possess more in-depth knowledge of the nonverbal communication that is characteristic of those two cultures than of any other non-Western culture.

The previous statements above the potential utility of this section seem to have even greater force in the 1990s than they did when the first edition of this book was completed in 1986. Indeed, you may have acquired much of your knowledge about the Arab culture during the first few days of the war between the United Nations coalition and Iraq. As you spent countless hours before your television set, you may have recognized that the American and Arab cultures were experiencing a type of forced and sustained contact that had never occurred before. Saudi Arabia alone was faced with the challenge of welcoming over one-half million "Westerners" who were predominantly American. The challenge for Saudi Arabia was to interact with the Americans in a way that was compatible with American culture as well as the Arab culture.

Because Japan is geographically isolated, there is a high degree of homogeneity and uniformity in Japanese values. The cultural values of the Japanese have been shaped by three religious faiths: Confucianism, Shintoism, and Buddhism (Barnlund, 1989). However, the impact of Zen Buddhism on the development of Japanese cultural values has been particularly pronounced. Zen Buddhism values introspection more than action. Partially as a result of that value orientation, the Japanese attach great importance to the value of silence. Nonobvious, subtle, and even indirect expression is also viewed as a cultural ideal. The inscrutable (expressionless) face of a Japanese is understandable in view of this value orientation.

The importance of maintaining self-control in public requires the conscious inhibition of those emotions that might reveal weakness. For example, to openly express an emotion that is as negatively valued as shame is to lose face in Japan. Disgust is also a negatively valued emotion in Japan and should not be displayed in public. Predictably, results from a recent study (Ekman et al., 1987) show that Japanese decoders identified facial disgust at a lower level of accuracy than they identified six other facial emotions. Furthermore, the decoders from the nine other countries in the study, including Greece, Italy, Turkey, and the United States, all identified facial disgust at a higher level of accuracy than the Japanese decoders. As Morsbach (1973) put it, "control of an outward show of pleasant emotions in public is also rarely relaxed in Japan. Women tend to cover their mouth while laughing, and males show true merriment (but also true anger) mainly after hours when their culture allows them greater freedom of behavior while drinking alcohol" (p. 269).

In Japan, it is extremely important to know your place (Lebra, 1976). Commitment and loyalty to the work group and family group are stressed, at the expense of developing the uniqueness of the individual. Indeed "the family not only dominates; it is the prototypic model for society. All large organizations from the school to the corporation, even to the state itself, are modeled upon it" (Barnlund, 1989). A person's individual accomplishments are much less important than the organization with which that person is affiliated (Ouchi, 1981). Interaction in Japan must conform to carefully prescribed "forms." The importance attached to the values of showing respect for superiors and being polite is manifested in cultural rituals that openly emphasize those two values (Barnlund, 1975a). Not surprisingly, the Japanese put a premium on the importance of achieving consensus and avoiding conflict (Barnlund, 1989).

Because the Japanese value subtlety, restraint, indirectness in emotional expression, deference to authority, and politeness, it is not surprising that a rather detailed stereotype of the Japanese communicator has developed. Japanese communicators are viewed by Americans, and by themselves, as silent, reserved, formal, cautious, serious, and evasive. Because of the strength of the stereotype, those stereotypic qualities have become an important part of the "public" communication style of the Japanese (Barnlund, 1975b).

In contrast, many of the values that are dominant in the Arab culture are quite different from Japanese values. In their insightful book, *Communicating with the Arabs* (1982), Almaney and Alwan emphasize that hospitality, pride, honor, rivalry, and revenge are particularly important values to the Arabs. Whereas the Japanese value a public presentation of self that is emotionally nondisclosing and unexpressive, polite, and withdrawn, Arabs attach great value to the uninhibited expression of emotions that exhibit maximum sensory experience and physical contact.

The Islamic faith is obviously an important cultural force in Arab countries. One of the direct effects of the faith is rather stringent prohibitions on what foreigners may not do in Arab countries. Saudi Arabia in particular has explicit rules that dictate what is and is not acceptable in public.

When Bob Hope went to entertain U.S. troops in 1990, his female entertainers were forced to wear pant suits. Similarly, U.S. citizens were told which items they could *not* mail to U.S. troops in Saudi Arabia in 1990: alcohol, pornography or sexual items, any materials depicting nude or seminude people, religious materials that were contrary to the Islamic faith, nonauthorized political material, and pork and pork by-products ("What's OK to Send to U.S. Troops," 1990).

The expansive hospitality of the Arabs has the effect of promoting social interaction rather than inhibiting it. A real or imagined insult to the Arab's well-developed sense of pride and dignity is apt to be met not with silence but with an immediate visceral reaction. The Arabs' preoccupation with honor, rivalry, and revenge means that the public display of emotions is the rule rather than the exception. Almaney and Alwan (1982) noted that the Arabs "are plagued by excessive rivalry, bickering, and backbiting," and that "vengeance murder as a means of settling political disputes is still in evidence throughout the Arab world" (p. 96).

Whereas the Japanese covet privacy, Arabs place no value on privacy in public. Pushing and shoving, crowding, and high noise levels are the norm in Arab states. In fact, Arabs are offended by anything less than intimacy of contact while carrying on a conversation. Such conversations characteristically feature "the piercing look of the eyes, the touch of the hand, and the mutual bathing in the warm moist breath during conversation [which] represent stepped-up sensory inputs which many Europeans find unbearably intense" (Hall, 1969, p. 158).

The obvious question at this point is how do these contrasting values affect the nonverbal communication styles that are characteristic of the Japanese and Arab cultures? That question can perhaps best be answered by a cross-cultural comparison of the use of nonverbal cues in communicating emotions, greetings, status differences, and intimacy.

Communicating Emotions

The nonverbal communication style of the Japanese is relatively expressionless. Implicit display rules seem to dictate that the impulse to display felt emotions via facial expressions should be inhibited and suppressed. Ekman and associates (1972) found that Japanese subjects who were asked to describe stress-inducing films, which they had just watched, displayed fewer negative expressions and more impassive expressions than their American counterparts.

Not only do the Japanese inhibit the expression of emotions, but also they are known to substitute the display of emotions they do *not* feel for those they *do* feel. They do so in order to avoid displaying such socially unacceptable expressions as shame or anger. This use of facial management has undoubtedly reinforced the popular view that the Japanese are evasive. Morsbach (1973) noted that although smiling is viewed universally as an indication of joy, it is used in Japan to hide pressure, anger, and sorrow.

In the Arab culture, in contrast, the open, direct, and uninhibited display of emotion is positively valued. Arabs slurp their coffee to show that they are enjoying it; belching after a meal is not uncommon—it indicates that the diner is full. The emotional richness of conversation with Arabs is also reinforced by their frequent use of gestures. Almaney and Alwan (1982) observe that to "tie an Arab's hands while he is speaking is tantamount to tying his tongue."

The importance that Arabs attach to a sensitive reading of, and response to, the emotions of the person with whom they are communicating is perhaps best revealed in their piercing and unremitting eye contact. Arabs carefully monitor dilation and contraction of the pupils of the eyes, because they believe that pupil dilation accurately reflects the level of interest, as well as information about the emotion being experienced. Japanese communicators, in contrast, do not directly monitor the eyes of the person with whom they are communicating; they look instead at the Adam's apple.

Greetings

In Japan, the "form" or "frame" of interpersonal relationships tends to override the substance of communication in importance. Thus, the *nakōdo,* or go-between, not only arranges marriages in Japan but arranges meetings with a wide array of individuals ranging from government officials to corporation executives to political leaders. Other forms of communication or expression that are important in the Japanese culture include the tea ceremony (*cha-no-yu*), flower arrangements (*ikebana*), and calligraphic representation (*shodo*) (Barnlund, 1989).

For the Japanese, social interaction must begin with the bow. The complex set of rules that govern socially acceptable bowing seem to reflect the importance the Japanese attach to civility, politeness, status, and form in interpersonal communication. In Japan, torso angle is very important. Morsbach (1973) wrote that "reciprocal bowing is largely determined by rank: the social inferior bows more deeply and the superior decides when to stop bowing" (p. 268). Bowing is such an integral part of greeting behavior in Japan that animated bowing dolls with tape-recorded voices have been used to welcome customers to department stores.

When a Japanese businessperson and a foreigner greet each other, a combination of a bow and a handshake may be in order. Circumspection and restraint, with no mutual touching, is expected. Maximum distance should be maintained after the bow–handshake. Native Japanese prefer greater interaction distances than either Americans or Hawaiian Japanese (Engebretson & Fullmer, 1970). Conversation should be kept to a minimum, and business cards should be exchanged.

The nonverbal communication style employed to greet someone in the Arab culture is quite different. Effusive greetings are expected. Pleasantries are encouraged. Considerable verbalization, in the form of "How is the family?," "We pray that you are well," and "We are honored by your presence," is expected. Vigorous handshaking is used in conjunction with the other nonverbal greeting behaviors to "size up" the person being greeted (Almaney & Alwan, 1982).

The Arab also likes to get close enough to the person being greeted to inhale their body aromas. We know that body scent frequently reveals emotional states, therefore this culture-specific greeting behavior certainly seems to be a useful way of obtaining highly personal information. The intimate and physically involving nature of Arab greeting behavior is reinforced by the lavish hospitality that is typically exhibited if the Arab is the host.

Status Differences

The hierarchical nature of both the Japanese and Arab cultures means that both rank and status must be respected. Although both cultures profess to honor women, they treat women as status inferiors. Business is man's work and the family is woman's work. In Japan, a woman is expected to maintain a proper distance behind her spouse—usually two steps. In Arab countries, women are not permitted to drive or to work. Some Saudi Arabian women who recently tried to defy cultural custom by driving their own cars were rebuffed by the authorities. Women also are expected to keep their bodies covered, and when business associates visit the home, women are to be seen but not heard.

In Japan, status is perhaps reflected most clearly in the way people bow and in the artifacts they exhibit. Badges, costumes, and uniforms assume particular importance in status-conscious Japan because they quite clearly reveal status. There are, literally, specific costumes for hiking, biking, and striking. The uniform and costume serve a central role in establishing and maintaining status and in signaling the appropriate type of interaction between two people.

The business card, or *meishi,* also is used to signal rank. In view of the fact that the business organization is the single most important determinant of status in Japan, the name of the organization appears first on the business card, followed by the person's position in the organization, academic degree (if any), family name, first name, and address (Barnlund, 1989; Lebra, 1976; Morsbach, 1973).

Status distinctions are communicated in less formal and ritualistic ways in the Arab culture, where people's status is determined largely by the nature and magnitude of their possessions rather than by the rank of the organization with which they are affiliated. Arabs believe that it is better to give than to receive. As a result, the foreign visitor should be careful about expressing admiration of possessions in the home of an Arab. The Arab will feel duty-bound to give the possession to the visitor as a gift. Although formalized manifestations of status differences are relatively rare in Arab nations, the high status accorded to older people and persons of authority is reflected in a law that forbids smoking in their presence.

Intimacy

The nonverbal communication style of the Japanese clearly prohibits intimacy in public. The characteristic lack of expression, when combined with the Japanese sense of reserve, means that the Japanese expect communication in public to be formal and reserved. Of course, ritualized bowing, costumes that emphasize status differences, and the value placed on reserved and subtle expression all militate against the spontaneity that usually promotes intimate interaction in public.

Barnlund (1975b) emphasized that in Japan, physical intimacy communicated via touch drops off sharply after childhood. Physical inaccessibility due to maximum communicating distances and lack of touching reveal the negative value the Japanese place on intimate interaction in public. In fact, many "observers have noted the serious composure, lack of facial expression, and gestural restraint of the Japanese. Physical intimacies are avoided and even reinforcing gestures rarely accompany remarks" (p. 109).

In the Arab culture, in contrast, a lack of physical contact and involvement is considered aberrant. Arabs frequently communicate with strangers at distances as close as two feet. They encourage reciprocal touching, particularly in greetings, and they like to be breathed on, as well as to breathe on others. The late President Anwar Sadat of Egypt, for example, often placed a hand on the knee of the person with whom he was conversing. In addition, some eyebrows have apparently been raised at dinners for international diplomats by the propensity of representatives of Arab states to touch the persons with whom they are communicating.

Because Arabs do not value or practice privacy in public, it is not surprising that they are emotionally self-disclosing, physically expressive, and uninhibited. The public presentation of self in the Arab countries places a high value on two types of nonverbal communication that play a central role in the development of intimate relationships: touch and olfaction.

Guidelines for More Successful Intercultural Communication

Successful intercultural communication requires that we become thoroughly familiar with a communication style that may be quite different in important respects from the communication style that is dominant within our own culture. In his illuminating book, *Counseling the Culturally Different* (1981), Sue emphasized that the culturally skilled counselor is one who moves from being unaware to being aware of and sensitive to his or her "own cultural baggage." This means that we must begin by rejecting the ethnocentric view that the communication style of our own culture is intrinsically superior.

The centrality of nonverbal behaviors and cues to successful intercultural communication becomes apparent when we recognize that "culture is primarily a nonverbal phenomenon because most aspects of one's culture are learned through observation and imitation rather than explicit verbal instruction or expression. The primary level of culture is communicated implicitly, without awareness, by primarily nonverbal means" (Andersen, 1988, p. 272).

Peter Andersen (1988) maintained that most of the important cultural differences in nonverbal behavior result from variations between cultures along five dimensions:

1. immediacy and expressiveness
2. individualism
3. masculinity
4. power distance
5. high and low context

When one culture has been differentiated from another along these five dimensions, the most important nonverbal behaviors and cues that make up the nonverbal communication style of that culture should be apparent. A closer look at Andersen's ideas emphasizes the importance of his five dimensions to successful intercultural communication.

Immediacy behaviors consist of acts or actions that signal a desire to establish closer contact with another person while exhibiting warmth, closeness, and availability. Importantly, cultures that exhibit a high level of immediacy behaviors are known as "contact cultures" because members of such cultures stand close to each other and touch frequently. Andersen (1988) maintained that contact cultures represented by countries such as Saudi Arabia, France, Greece, and Italy are typically located in "warm" climates. In contrast, "low-contact cultures," which include Scandinavia, Germany, England, the United States, and Japan, have "colder" climates. This is an important dimension because the socially sensitive visitor must know how much contact to exhibit within a given culture.

A second dimension that can be used to distinguish one culture from another is the degree of *individualism* versus *collectivism*. Western cultures are associated with individualism, whereas Eastern cultures are identified with collectivism. Countries with individualistic cultures include the United States, Canada, Belgium, and Denmark; countries with some of the least individualistic cultures include Colombia, Pakistan, Taiwan, and Hong Kong. There are a number of significant differences in the nonverbal behaviors of members of these two types of cultures. For example, members of individualistic cultures are rather distant proximally, but they are more nonverbally affiliative than people from collectivist cultures. Not surprisingly, bodily behaviors tend to be more predictable and more synchronized in collectivist cultures. "In individualistic countries like the United States, affiliativeness, dating, flirting, small-talk, and initial acquaintance are more important than they are in collectivist countries where the social network is more fixed and less reliant on individual initiative" (Andersen, 1988, p. 276).

Third, cultures are differentiated from one another along the dimension of *masculinity*. When you recall the masculine stereotype, you will not be surprised to know that masculine traits that define a masculine culture include assertiveness, competitiveness, and ambitiousness (whereas feminine traits include affection, compassion, and nurturance). If males and females are to be treated similarly within a given culture, androgynous behaviors—rather than masculine or feminine—must be a dominant part of the nonverbal communication style. The negative communicative implications for cultures that are high in either masculinity or femininity are obvious.

Fourth, *power distance* is another important dimension of intercultural communication. The power distance index (PDI) is used to measure the extent to which there is unequal distribution of power, prestige, and wealth within a culture. In effect, PDI measures the distance one group or member of a culture is separated from another in terms of power. The higher a culture's score on the PDI, the more authoritarian that culture will be. Countries with the highest PDI include Mexico, Venezuela, Brazil, and Colombia. Note that all of these countries are highly stratified in terms of class distinctions. In contrast, class distinctions are relatively unimportant in countries such as Austria, Ireland, and Switzerland. If nonverbal cues encode power forcefully, then it is predictable that nonverbal behavioral indicators of both power and powerlessness will be exhibited more frequently in hierarchical than in egalitarian cultures.

Finally, *context* is an important dimension that can be used to differentiate cultures. *High context (HC)* messages are those in which much of the communicated information comes from the context or is not stated verbally. *Low context (LC)* messages, in contrast, contain most of the information in the particular language that is used. Cultures of particularly high context are found in the Orient. China, Japan, and Korea all have cultures of particularly high context. Significantly, members of low context cultures tend to view people with good verbal skills as particularly attractive but "HC cultures are more reliant on and tuned into nonverbal communication than are LC cultures. LC cultures, and particularly the men in LC cultures, fail to perceive as much nonverbal communication as do members of HC cultures" (Andersen, 1988, p. 279).

If we are to succeed in our attempts to communicate with members of another culture, we must try to become aware of which communicative behaviors are, and which are not, acceptable in that culture. We can attain that level of awareness by becoming as familiar as possible with the distinctive features of the nonverbal style of the culture in which we seek to communicate.

Success in intercultural communication can be facilitated by training designed to develop intercultural communication competencies (Ben-Peretz & Halkes, 1987; Westwood & Borgen, 1988). Martin and Hammer (1989) provided a particularly useful profile of the nonverbal behaviors that must be exhibited in order to develop intercultural communication competence. They identified the nonverbal behaviors most strongly associated with intercultural competence when Americans are interacting with members of various cultures. The three nonverbal behaviors most strongly associated with intercultural competence in all of the cultures studied were *direct eye contact, listening carefully,* and *smiling.* Those three nonverbal behaviors were consistently found to be much more important than any other in making a favorable impression in any foreign culture.

Successful intercultural communication requires that we develop skills as impression managers. In a foreign culture, impression managers should seek to do at least two things: *associate themselves with images that are positively valued and dissociate themselves from images that are negatively valued in the culture where communication occurs.* Because more weight is usually given to negative than to positive information, it is particularly important to *avoid* behaving in ways that are considered inappropriate or deviant. One particularly valuable book which spells out in detail what one should and should not do nonverbally in countries and cultures in Europe, the Middle East, Africa, the Pacific and Asia, Central and South America, and the United States and Canada was published recently (Axtell, 1993).

The following guidelines should prove useful to communicators who wish to exhibit appropriate nonverbal behaviors in cultures other than their own.

Guideline #1
Familiarize yourself with the facial expressions of the culture to determine whether the public display of emotions is encouraged or discouraged, determine which kinds of emotions are positively and negatively valued, and make the necessary adjustment in your own facial displays of emotion.

Guideline #2
Learn and follow the rules that govern proper form and interaction sequence for greeting behaviors, with an emphasis on the intricacies of cultural rituals.

Guideline #3
Become familiar with the types of status distinctions that must be acknowledged, and use culturally approved nonverbal behaviors for acknowledging such status distinctions.

Guideline #4
Determine the degree of physical contact, involvement, and accessibility that is expected in public, and act accordingly.

Guideline #5

Try to become sensitive to culture-specific touching, proxemic, eye-behavior, and chronemic norms so that you may act in ways that are nonverbally appropriate.

Guideline #6

Become familiar with the nonverbal regulators that should and should not be used in culturally acceptable conversational management.

Guideline #7

Identify the most important nonverbal behaviors used in cultural ritual so that you can, if necessary, modify your own nonverbal behaviors as a way of identifying with important cultural values.

Guideline #8

Systematically identify, itemize, and avoid the use of culture-specific emblems that communicate meanings that are apt to be interpreted as affronts or as insults.

Guideline #9

Determine the kind of clothing and personal artifacts that are and are not compatible with cultural conventions.

Summary

Successful intercultural communication requires that a visitor to a foreign country acquire an in-depth familiarity with the nonverbal communication style of the culture of that country. This is necessary because the nonverbal communication style of a culture is defined by nonverbal behaviors that contain sets of implicit rules or commands. These implicit display rules, in turn, specify what kinds of communication are and are not appropriate.

Cross-cultural similarities in nonverbal communication are most evident in the use of facial expressions, which communicate a limited number of basic emotions. Cross-cultural differences abound. Those differences are strongly reflected in a great variety of gestural emblems that communicate culture-specific meanings and, as a result, are highly susceptible to misinterpretation by the foreigner. Proxemic, tactile, eye-behavior norms as well as conceptions and uses of time also tend to be distinctively different in cultures with dissimilar value orientations.

In order to demonstrate how knowledge of the nonverbal communication style of specific cultures can be used to facilitate more successful communication, the Japanese and Arab cultures are compared and contrasted in this chapter. The point is made that important differences in the nonverbal styles of the two cultures are manifested most clearly in the communication of emotions, greetings, status differences, and intimacy.

Finally, a set of nine guidelines is included, which can be used to facilitate more successful intercultural communication. These guidelines can be used to increase our awareness of the specific kinds of communicative behaviors that are and are not acceptable in a foreign culture of importance to us. Such awareness is necessary if we are to engage in intercultural communication that reflects a knowledge of and a desire to adapt to the distinctive communication style of a particular culture.

References

Almaney, A. J., & Alwan, A. J. (1982). *Communicating with the Arabs: A handbook for the business executive.* Prospect Heights, IL: Waveland Press.

Andersen, P. (1988). Explaining intercultural differences in nonverbal communication. In L. Samovar & R. E. Porter (Eds.), *Intercultural communication: A reader* (5th ed., pp. 272–282). Belmont, CA: Wadsworth.

Axtell, R. E. (1993). *Gestures: The do's and taboos of body language around the world* (2nd ed.). New York: John Wiley & Sons.

Barnlund, D. C. (1975a). *Public and private self in Japan and the United States: Communicative styles of two cultures.* Tokyo, Japan: The Simul Press.

Barnlund, D. C. (1975b). Communicative styles in two cultures: Japan and the United States. In A. Kendon, R. M. Harris, & M. R. Keys (Eds.). *Organization of behavior in face-to-face interaction.* The Hague, The Netherlands: Mouton.

Barnlund, D. C. (1989). *Communicative Styles of Japanese and Americans: Images and Realities.* Belmont, CA: Wadsworth.

Belk, S. S., Garcia-Falconi, R., Hernandez-Sanchez, J. E., & Snell, W. E. (1988). Avoidance strategy use in the intimate relationships of women and men from Mexico and the United States. *Psychology of Women Quarterly, 12,* 165–174.

Ben-Peretz, M., & Halkes, R. (1987). How teachers know their classrooms: A cross-cultural study of teachers' understanding of classroom situations. *Anthropology and Education Quarterly, 18,* 17–32.

Bernieri, F., & Gillis, J. S. (1995). The judgment of rapport: A cross-cultural comparison between Americans and Greeks. *Journal of Nonverbal Behavior, 19,* 115–129.

Bruneau, T. (1988). The time dimension in intercultural communication. In L. A. Samovar and R. E. Porter (Eds.), *Intercultural communication: A reader.* (5th ed., pp. 282–292). Belmont, CA: Wadsworth.

Condon, J. C., & Yousef, F. (1975). *An introduction to intercultural communication.* Indianapolis, IN: Bobbs.

Chiang, L. H. (1993). Beyond the language: Native American's nonverbal communication, ERIC microfiche document, ED368540, October 1993.

Darwin, C. (1872/1965). *The expression of emotion in man and animals.* London: J. Murray. Reprinted in 1965, Chicago: University of Chicago Press.

Dew, A. M., & Ward, C. (1993). The effects of ethnicity and culturally congruent and incongruent nonverbal behaviors on interpersonal attraction. *Journal of Applied Social Psychology, 23,* 1376–1389.

Eibl-Eibesfeldt, I. (1972). Similarities and differences between cultures in expressive movements. In R. A. Hinde (Ed.), *Non-verbal communication.* Cambridge, MA: Cambridge University Press.

Ekman, P., & Friesen, W. V. (1975). *Unmasking the face.* Englewood Cliffs, NJ: Prentice-Hall.

Ekman, P., Friesen, W. V., & Ellsworth, P. (1972). *Emotion in the human face.* New York: Pergamon.

Ekman, P., & Friesen, W. V., O'Sullivan, M., & Chan, A. (1987). Universals and cultural differences in the judgments of facial expressions of emotion. *Journal of Personality and Social Psychology, 53,* 712–717.

Engebretson, D. E., & Fullmer, D. (1970). Cross-cultural differences in territoriality: Interaction distances of native Japanese, Hawaii Japanese, and American Caucasians. *Journal of Cross-Cultural Psychology, 1,* 261–269.

Guidetti, M. (1991). Vocal expression of emotions—A cross-cultural and developmental approach. *Annee Psychologique, 9,* 383–396.

Hall, E. T. (1963). *The silent language.* Greenwich, CT: Premier.

Hall, E. T. (1969). *The hidden dimension.* Garden City, NY: Anchor.

Hall, E. T. (1984). *The dance of life: The other dimension of time.* New York: Doubleday.

Hall, E. T., & Hall, M. R. (1987). *Hidden differences: Doing business with the Japanese.* Garden City, NY: Anchor.

Hickson, M. I. III, & Stacks, D. W. (1989). *Nonverbal Communication: Studies and applications* (2nd ed.). Dubuque, IA: Wm. C. Brown.

Izard, C. E. (1971). *The face of emotion.* New York: Appleton.

Kilbride, J. E., & Yarczower, M. (1980). Recognition and imitation of facial expressions: A cross-cultural comparison between Zambia and the United States. *Journal of Cross-Cultural Psychology, 11,* 282.

LaFrance, M., & Mayo, C. (1978a). Cultural aspects of nonverbal communication. *International Journal of Intercultural Relations, 2,* 71–89.

LaFrance, M., & Mayo, C. (1978b). *Moving bodies: Nonverbal communication in social relationships.* Monterey, CA: Brooks/Cole.

Leathers, D. G., & McGuire, M. (1983, November). *Testing the comparative sensitivity of German and American decoders to specific kinds of facial meaning.* Paper presented on program of the Commission on International and Intercultural Communication at annual convention of the Speech Communication Association, Washington, DC.

Lebra, T. S. (1976). *Japanese patterns of behavior.* Honolulu, HI: The University Press of Hawaii.

Masters, R. D., & Sullivan, D. G. (1989a). Facial displays and political leadership in France. *Behavioral Processes, 19,* 1–30.

Masters, R. D., & Sullivan, D. G. (1989b). Nonverbal displays and political leadership in France and the United States. *Political Behavior, 11,* 123–156.

Martin, J. N., & Hammer, M. R. (1989). Behavioral categories of intercultural communication competence: Everyday communicators' perceptions. *International Journal of Intercultural Relations, 13,* 303–332.

McDaniel, E. R. (1993, November). *Japanese nonverbal communication: A review and critique of literature.* Conference paper presented at the 79th Annual Meeting of the Speech Communication Association, Miami Beach, FL.

Montepare, J. M., & Zebrowitz, L. A. (1993). A cross-cultural comparison of impressions created by age-related variation in gait. *Journal of Nonverbal Behavior, 17,* 55–67.

Morris, D., Collett, P., Marsh, P., & O'Shaughnessy, M. (1979). *Gestures: Their origins and distribution.* New York: Stein & Day.

Morsbach, H. (1973). Aspects of nonverbal communication in Japan. *The Journal of Nervous and Mental Disease, 157,* 262–277.

Ouchi, W. (1981). *Theory Z: How American business can meet the Japanese challenge.* Reading, MA: Addison-Wesley.

Payrato, L. (1993). A pragmatic view on autonomous gestures: A first report on Cattalan emblems. *Journal of Pragmatics, 20,* 193–216.

Peng, Y., Zebrowitz, L. A., & Lee, H. L. (1993). The impact of cultural background and cross-cultural experience on impressions of American and Korean male speakers. *Journal of Cross-Cultural Psychology, 24,* 204–220.

Rosenthal, R., Hall, J. A., DiMatteo, M. R., Rogers, P. L., & Archer, D. (1979). *Sensitivity to nonverbal communication: The PONS test.* Baltimore: The Johns Hopkins University Press.

Scherer, K. R., & Walbott, H. G. (1994). Evidence for universality and cultural variation of differential emotion response patterning. *Journal of Personality and Social Psychology, 66,* 310–328.

Sherer, K. R., Wallbott, H. G., Matsumoto, D., & Kudoh, T. (1988). Emotional experience in cultural context: A comparison between Europe, Japan, and the United States. In K. R. Sherer (Ed.), *Facets of emotion—Recent research* (pp. 1–30). Hillsdale, NJ: Erlbaum.

Shuter, R. (1976). Proxemics and tactility in Latin America. *Journal of Communication, 26,* 46–52.

Shuter, R. (1977). A field study of nonverbal communication in Germany, Italy and the United States. *Communication Monographs, 44,* 298–305.

Shuter, R. (1983). *Values and communication: Seeing the forest through the trees.* Unpublished paper.

Sogon, S., & Masutani, M. (1989). Identification of emotion from body movements: A cross-cultural study of Americans and Japanese. *Psychological Reports, 65,* 35–46.

Sue, D. W. (1981). *Counseling the culturally different.* New York: Wiley.

Sweeney, M. A., Cottle, W. C., & Kobayashi, M. J. (1980). Nonverbal communication: A cross-cultural comparison of American and Japanese counseling students. *Journal of Counseling Psychology, 27,* 154.

Westwood, M. U., & Borgen, W. A. (1988). A culturally embedded model for effective intercultural communication. *International Journal for the Advancement of Counselling, 11,* 115–125.

What's OK to send to U.S. troops. (1990, August 22). *The Atlanta Journal and Constitution,* A6.

Chapter *17*

Physician–Patient
Interaction

I feared Dr. Lambert when I was five years old. Dr. Lambert was the eye, ear, and nose specialist at the local clinic. Because I had punctured eardrums on several occasions and had chronic infections of my adenoids and tonsils as a preschooler, I suffered through a number of Dr. Lambert's examinations. Dr. Lambert's imperious communication style was what frightened me the most. He would glower at me with his deep-set, penetrating eyes while issuing commands to his nurse in a strident and aggressive tone that seemed to make the nurse wince and then cower. Of course, Dr. Lambert never asked me how I felt or for my opinion. He simply gave me orders while he looked down on me with a penetrating stare so threatening that I would have probably done almost anything he ordered to escape his withering eye contact in the future. On one occasion I remember vividly, Dr. Lambert commanded me to open my mouth wide while he roughly inserted a tongue depressor. Even though I was only five years old, Dr. Lambert exerted so much pressure on the tongue depressor that he snapped it off in my mouth. As empathy was hardly his strength, he did not apologize. Instead he stared at me and said "Well, I broke that stick off in your mouth. If you do not open your mouth wider and keep it open, I will break off another stick in your mouth."

Dr. Lambert personified what has become known as the traditional communication style for a physician. To begin, he was a white male. Also, because he took it for granted that he and he alone had the truly impressive medical expertise that his patient sought, he took it as his right that he would be dominant and the patient would be submissive. He expected immediate and unquestioning compliance with his commands. Dr. Lambert brought only one perspective to a meeting with a patient—his own. He undoubtedly felt that interacting with a patient would be a waste of time. After all, medical knowledge and competency were the only things that mattered. Clearly he possessed virtually all of the valuable information and the patient none. Why bother interacting with the patient in any detailed way?

Dr. Lambert clearly delighted in his dominant position. He may even have seen himself as a benevolent autocrat. He would tell you he acted as he did to bring relief to the patient in the shortest possible period of time. To be fair to him, he was highly respected by his patients for his competence and record of surgical success. Indeed, I must report that he operated on me on several occasions without complications. Thus, Dr. Lambert—and tens of thousands of doctors like him in the middle of the twentieth century—behaved in a way consistent with their medical training. They knew nothing other than the traditional clinical method.

McWhinney (1989) emphasized that:

> *The traditional method is strictly objective: it diagnoses diseases. It does not aim, in any systematic way, to understand the meaning of the illness for the patient or to place it in the context of his life story or culture. Subjective matters, such as feelings and relationships, are excluded from consideration. . . . The objectivity of the traditional method accords well with its origins in the European Enlightenment.* (p. 27)

In all probability, Dr. Lambert is no longer preoccupied with earthly concerns. It is the generations of physicians who have followed him who are the focus of this chapter. The chapter first identifies barriers that may prevent effective communicative interaction between physician and patient. The next section examines the reasons why nonverbal communication is so functionally important in a medical setting. This section also describes the functions of specific kinds of nonverbal communication of particular importance in medical settings. The chapter then profiles the distinctive features of the nonverbal communication style that exists between physicians and patients who are currently interacting in the medical setting. The nonverbal communicative style that characterizes doctor–patient interaction provides the reader with the opportunity to consider doctor–patient communicative interaction as it currently exists. The final section of this chapter *goes a step beyond describing the nonverbal communicative style of interacting doctors and patients as it currently is and projects the style as it ought to be.* Thus, the chapter concludes with a set of recommendations that enumerate the changes that should be made in the nonverbal communication of physicians and patients.

This is an age where U.S. citizens are getting older. Bitter national debate ensues on the subject of health care. In what ways, if at all, should our system of health care be modified? Should Medicare and Medicaid be modified? Abandoned? For these reasons and many others, health care contexts are of great importance.

In spite of the raging national debate, the average citizen might have trouble defining health care. At minimum it is important to identify the full range of professionals that are involved in providing health care. Kreps and Thornton (1992) maintained that "The health care delivery system is like a wagon wheel with many different spokes. . . . The hub of the wheel is the client's role" (p. 4). The spokes of the wheel represent each of the professional categories involved in providing health care: medicine, dentistry, medical administration, therapy, nursing, pharmacy, and social work. Similarly, Northouse and Northouse (1992) provided a somewhat more detailed identification of the health professionals that make up a "health team." They wrote that the following health care professionals all have the primary objective of focusing on patient care: physicians, nurses, social workers, dentists, psychologists, nutritionists, allied health workers, physical and occupational therapists, health scientists, and pharmacologists.

Clearly, the term *health care context* is broader in scope and more numerous in referents than the term *medical context*. Without question, the medical context of greatest importance is that of physician–patient interaction (Northouse & Northouse, 1992). We are not, of course, overlooking the vitally important medical functions provided by the nurse, or for that matter the dietician and the physical therapist. Our knowledge of communicative interaction in medical contexts includes the interaction patients have with their physicians, nurses, members of their family, as well as other members of the medical team. This chapter, however, gives primary attention to the communicative interaction between the physician and patient.

Potential Problems in Physician–Patient Communicative Interaction

The most fundamental problem in physician–patient communicative interaction in past years has been one of control. Physicians refused to treat patients as their equals. In fact, physicians treated patients as inferiors and were more likely to speak down to rather than interacted with them. Stewart and Roter (1989) wrote that their

> *definition of excellent communication in this book arises from underlying principles that communication should be patient-centered; patients should be involved in their own care, and patients should have a sense of control over their own treatment. . . . More important is the conviction that active patient involvement in care will lead to earlier recovery and higher quality of life."* (p. 19)

These authors argue that the most important factor that defines any physician–patient interaction is the degree of *control* that each of the interactants exercise. The four types of physician–patient relationships are based on the degree of control exercised by the two parties: *paternalism* (physician control is high and patient control is low), *consumerism* (physician control is low and patient control is high), *mutuality* (both physician and patient share a high degree of control), and *default* (both patient and physician have a low degree of control).

Paternalism has been the dominant form of physician–patient interaction for many decades. As Stewart and Roter (1989) wrote:

> *If there is a high physician control and low patient control, the physician will dominate making decisions in what he or she perceives to be the patient's best interest. The patient's job is to cooperate with medical advice, that is, to do what he or she is told. This is the traditional form of the doctor–patient relationship and is still the most common.* (p. 20)

Dr. Lambert was comfortable with this dictatorial, paternalistic relationship with his patients. Doctors who cultivate this type of relationship do not give detailed explanations for their diagnosis, do not bring up the possibility of an alternative opinion or different diagnosis, and specify only one type of treatment. Patients who are facing life-threatening illness or life-limiting conditions may prefer this type of relationship. This model requires little effort on the part of the patient. Because it gives almost no emphasis to interactive communication, this model clearly is unlikely to lead to a balanced, mature relationship between physician and patient. "Since the balance of power is obviously imbalanced, this model assumes patient trust and physician altruism, with significant potential for patient exploitation" (Stewart & Roter, 1989, p. 21).

From a communication perspective, the preferred type or model for a physician–patient relationship is called *mutuality.* This is a relationship in which both participants perceive and treat each others as equals. They also bring distinctive resources to the communicative situations where interaction occurs. Because power in this relationship is relatively balanced, decisions made should result from the vigorous and balanced communicative interaction. Rather than simply serving as the submissive vessel into which the physician pours technical information, patients in this type of relationship can justifiably think of themselves as partners.

Northouse and Northouse (1992) identified a number of factors as potential barriers to effective physician–patient communication. Three seem particularly important: (a) *role uncertainty,* (b) *power differences,* and (c) *unshared meanings.* Role uncertainty often becomes a particular problem for the patient who is hospitalized. Patients frequently must give up, at least temporarily, the familiar roles of husband, wife, employer, employee, sports enthusiast, arts aficionado, and so forth. The patient's new role in an unfamiliar setting is vague at best, and the suitable accompanying behaviors are unclear.

This role uncertainty may make the patient hesitant about raising legitimate health concerns with the physician or other health providers. The doctor may misinterpret the patient's relative silence as signaling a lack of concern, and this role uncertainty may result in physicians and patients dealing with each other in stereotypical ways.

Power differences represent a second potential communication problem. Because the physician is generally perceived to be powerful and the patient to be relatively powerless, the resulting relationship is by definition asymmetrical. Asymmetry in the doctor–patient relationship has the potential to affect communicative interaction negatively in a number of ways. Clearly, the physician may simply assume more power than warranted. Secondly, physicians, or other health-care providers for that matter, may abuse their high power by making decisions that the patients should be making for themselves. Then too physicians may simply impose their own values on their patients.

Finally, unshared meanings often serve as a third barrier to effective doctor–patient communication. Physicians who have been trained via the traditional clinical method are apt to bring only a single perspective to meetings with patients—their own. Of course doctors trained in this method have been educated to use a technical medical terminology, which may work with other medical professionals but may make it difficult to exchange consensually shared meaning with patients. To deal with the problem of unshared meaning, physicians obviously need to work harder to understand how their patients perceive themselves, their world, and the physician. They may have to use previously untapped communicative resources to understand the patient's perspective. As you will note later in this chapter, many of these resources are apt to be nonverbal in nature.

In short, there seem to be good and sufficient reasons for more physicians to move toward a patient-centered method of interaction. Stewart and Roter (1989) wrote that such a patient-centered method *demands of physicians that they learn to respond to cues by which patients express their feelings, that they develop enough self-knowledge to respond appropriately to patients' feelings, that they have the ability to organize complex biopsychosocial information from the patient, and that they practice empathy and attentive listening.* (p. 18)

The Functional Importance of Nonverbal Communication in the Medical Setting

The switch from the traditional clinical method of training for doctors to a biopsychosocial model has great communicative implications. By definition, nonverbal communication becomes extremely important. The enhanced importance of nonverbal communication may in turn be traced directly to a model that stresses the ability of the physician to give a sensitive reading of and provide a socially appropriate response to the feelings, moods, emotions, and attitudes of the patient. This puts the focus on the development of the nonverbal decoding skills on the physician. At the same time, the new training model for physicians places particular emphasis on the physician's ability to build rapport with the patient, to respond in an empathic manner, to share control of the medical interview, to be self-disclosing, and to provide the patient with needed confirmation. To a considerable degree, success in achieving these interpersonal objectives is often controlled by the physician's nonverbal encoding skills (Northouse & Northouse, 1992).

Of course, many long-term outcomes may result from the interaction of physician and patient and the treatment that results, including symptom resolution; a modification of physiologic, behavioral, or function status; anxiety reduction; work loss; and a change in quality of life; to name a few. Most communication research seeks to assess the impact of the nature of physician–patient communication on short-term outcomes, however. Short-term outcomes include tension release, intention to comply, acceptance of recommended services, disease knowledge acquisition, tension release, doctor satisfaction, and patient satisfaction (Beckman, Kaplan, & Frankel, 1989). Other short-term outcomes that may be even more important are the patient's judgment as to how credible, interpersonally attractive, and dominant the physician is at a given point in time. In any event, degree of patient satisfaction is currently used most frequently as the central measure of how effective the doctor's behaviors are when she or he interacts with a patient.

Physicians' Nonverbal Skills and Patients' Satisfaction Level

We know that the physician's nonverbal communication is a major determinant of the level of satisfaction a patient experiences. The early, influential research done by Rosenthal (1979) provides perhaps the most convincing support for this relationship. This relationship in turn is based on the finding that a patient's level of satisfaction is strongly affected by how sensitive the physician is perceived to be. Because a physician's perceived sensitivity is communicated most strongly by his or her nonverbal communication, it is predictable that patients consistently report that they experience the highest levels of satisfaction when interacting with physicians who have been determined to have the best nonverbal skills. Based on her own research, DiMatteo (1979) wrote that

> *The physicians' ability to decode nonverbal communicated affect, as well as to encode emotional messages in nonverbal channels, appears related to the physicians' ability to satisfy patients' needs for the socioemotional aspects of care. The results of this research also suggest that nonverbal encoding and decoding skill may, taken together, constitute a large component of a general ability to relate empathically to people in the therapeutic relationship.* (p. 128)

Recent research provides convincing support for the strong, positive impact of a physician's nonverbal communication on a patient's level of satisfaction. Thus, Street (1991) reported that parents' evaluations of their childrens' health care are strongly affected by their perceptions of a physician's interpersonal sensitivity as well as the physician's willingness to be informative and to seek to build a partnership with the patient. A subsequent study (Street, 1992) again confirmed that patients put a very high priority on how sensitive they judge the physician to be.

This finding in isolation would not be particularly significant. What does seem very significant from a communicative perspective, however, is the repeated link between a physician's perceived level of sensitivity and her or his measured level of nonverbal communication skills. Thus, DiMatteo and Taranta (1979) found a relationship between the physician's ability to understand the patient's nonverbal cues and the patient's level of satisfaction. Harrigan, Oxman, and Rosenthal (1985) found that physicians who exhibited appropriate bodily movements were judged by patients to have greater rapport than physicians who did not exhibit such movements. Then too, DiMatteo, Linn, Chang, and Cope (1985) reported that patients prefer physicians who are emotionally expressive; and, as this book has repeatedly emphasized, nonverbal communication is the medium of greatest importance in the communication of emotions.

Finally, a study by DiMatteo (1986) affirmed that the physician's nonverbal communication encoding and decoding skills are the best predictor of patients' satisfaction. Not surprisingly, physicians who have more effective nonverbal skills report fewer unrescheduled appointment cancellations and a heavier workload. Although we do not know how many appointment cancellations Dr. Lambert had, they may have been quite numerous. In short, patients are more inclined to make and keep appointments with doctors they perceive as interpersonally sensitive. In a disproportionate number of instances, the "sensitive" doctors are also the doctors with the most impressive nonverbal communication skills.

Reasons Why Nonverbal Communication Is Important in the Medical Context

Northouse and Northouse (1992) stressed the importance of nonverbal communication in the medical context:

> *Nonverbal communication has special relevance in health care primarily because patients pay close attention to the nonverbal communication of professionals, and*

professionals, on the other hand, rely heavily on the nonverbal communication of patients. (p. 118)

These authors identify some of the major reasons why nonverbal communication is functionally important from the patient's perspective: (a) A health care setting such as the medical interview generates a high level of fear and uncertainty among patients as well as family members; to lessen their uncertainty patients often rely heavily on what they perceive to be the most reliable information available to them, which is often unintentionally communicated by a physician's nonverbal communication. (b) Because patients frequently feel that doctors are being less than completely honest with them, or even lying to them, they tend to rely on the "leakage" cues in the doctor's nonverbal communication to determine the true meanings of the doctor's messages. (c) Patients often rely on nonverbal communication as a source of "preinteraction" information; for example, they study the physician's face to determine how reassuring or threatening are the results from recent tests. (d) Patients often rely heavily on the physician's nonverbal communication as the primary source of information when the doctor is either too busy to communicate with them at any length verbally or is unapproachable.

From the physician's perspective, nonverbal communication has great functional importance for several reasons: (a) The patient's physical or psychological condition may make verbal communication impractical or impossible. (b) Doctors may recognize that a patient's implicit or unstated messages are the best source of information with regard to the patient's moods, feelings, emotions, and attitudes. (c) In moments of crisis the physician's only way of communicating with the patient, or with other physicians, may be by nonverbal means, such as a touch on the hand of a comatose patient or a sharing of concerns among members of the medical team via eye behaviors and facial expressions while working to revive a patient who has suffered cardiac arrest (Northouse & Northouse, 1992).

Enelow and Swisher (1986) emphasized the importance of nonverbal communication in the medical interview when they wrote:

When verbal communication ceases, non-verbal communication continues. Pointing out the non-verbal behavior tends to encourage the verbal expression of the inner experience. For example, a patient who is told that he has a worried and pained look may then describe his chronic, low-grade neck stiffness and headache. Feelings such as sadness or fear, may be first expressed after the non-verbal (behavioral) evidence has been brought to his attention. (p. 20)

In a general sense, nonverbal communication is functionally important in the medical context for many of the same basic reasons identified in Chapter 1. However, some of these reasons take on added importance in an age when many doctors are trying to move from a commitment model—in which they were dominant dictators when interacting with a patient—to a training model—in which they make a commitment to cultivate a "partnership" with the patient. The partnership in turn particularly emphasizes that the physician give a sensitive reading of and response to the patient's feelings, moods, and emotions. Given this perspective, nonverbal communication becomes more important to the physician for several reasons: (a) nonverbal communication is the major medium for the exchange of emotions, (b) nonverbal messages most frequently communicate a person's real intentions in an undistorted manner, (c) the metacommunicative potential of nonverbal messages to clarify meanings of previously unclear verbal messages is vitally important to doctors in moments of crisis, and (d) many of the emblematic gestures used in an operating room greatly enhance the efficiency of exchange among members of a medical team.

Functions of Nonverbal Communication in the Medical Context

Enlightening discussions of the major functions of nonverbal communication in physician–patient interaction are rare. The treatment of this subject by Northouse and Northouse (1992) is a striking exception. They argued incisively that nonverbal communication serves five major functions in the medical context where physicians and patients interact: (a) expression of feelings and emotions; (b) regulation of the interaction; (c) validation of the verbal message; (d) maintenance of the self-image; and (e) maintenance of relationships.

Their emphasis on the use of nonverbal communication to maintain a self-image and relationships seems particularly insightful. The maintenance of an acceptably positive self-image for a patient is an objective that is not easily attained. We have already commented in this chapter, for example, that role uncertainty often becomes a major problem when the patient moves from the familiar territory of his or her own home or office to the unfamiliar territory of the physicians's office or a hospital.

A patient's self-concept is surely threatened in a medical setting not only by a lack of privacy but by repeated, intrusive invasions of privacy. When you enter a hospital, for example, you are literally stripped of the distinctive clothing or uniforms that have designated your achieved status in the real world. You are also stripped of your self-identity in the real world. You are given a medical nightshirt, which may yawn open ominously at the rear with the alarming prospect that some or all of your private parts will be exposed involuntarily to strangers. To make matters worse, a nurse, nurse's attendant, or orderly may enter your room at any moment without your invitation or consent. They may then move briskly to insert a medical device in any one of a number of what have previously been your private bodily orifices. Just when you begin to relax in your room, a medical attendant of the opposite gender may ask you to roll over on your side so that she or he can give you an enema. In short, there is almost no indignity that you may not be forced to endure in your new role as patient.

Northouse and Northouse (1992) skillfully illustrated how nonverbal communication can serve the self-image protection function in a medical setting:

> *In any interaction, individuals have images of themselves they want to maintain. For example, in an extended care facility, an 80-year-old resident who was a banker for 40 years before his retirement may want to be dressed daily in a coat and tie because that is the way bankers dress. His clothes communicate to others that he wants to be seen as a respectable banker. Or consider the newly graduated nurse who wears a stethoscope around her neck during breaks in the coffee shop because she wants to been seen by others as a qualified professional. In both of these examples, the individuals are using nonverbal cues to maintain a role that communicates to others a part of their self-image.* (p. 122)

The second function of nonverbal communication these authors stress is the maintenance of relationships. Although there are of course a number of features that may define a relationship between a physician and a patient, the degree to which physicians and patients *share control* in a medical setting is perhaps most important. We know that nonverbal messages strongly communicate the degree to which we are dominant or submissive in a relationship with another person. As this book has already documented, the loudness of one's voice encodes power powerfully. Strong, dominant individuals tend to speak with a loud voice. Conversely, weak, submissive persons tend to speak with a soft voice. Then too, eye behaviors are particularly important in signaling the degree of control two individuals have in their relationship.

Our discussion in Chapter 1 and in this chapter suggests that nonverbal behaviors or cues can, therefore, be used to serve five major communicative functions in the medical context where physicians and doctors interact:

1. exchange of emotions
2. metacommunication
3. self-concept protection
4. impression formation and management
5. reassurance

The sensitive exchange and interpretation of the meanings of emotions are perhaps the most important functions of nonverbal communication when physicians and patients interact. Repeatedly, authorities cited in this chapter stress that physicians must abandon the traditional, clinical method that was used to train them in order to embrace a new method. That new method puts a premium on the development of a set of skills by physicians which will enable them to give a sensitive reading of the feelings, moods, and emotions of their patients. The open exchange of emotions in the medical interview must therefore be given the highest priority.

We have already documented in this book that the three most effective ways of exchanging emotions are the face (by far the most important), vocal cues, and touching. Therefore, patients and physicians must work not only to develop their encoding and decoding skills when using these three types of nonverbal communication, but they must also be sensitive to cultural norms that pertain to each of them, (such as what types of facial expressions should and should not be exhibited in a medical setting; what combination of sound attributes most effectively communicate such emotions as apprehension, distress, and fear; and what touching norms are operative in a given medical setting).

Metacommunication too is a vitally important communication function in the medical setting that is served mainly and best by nonverbal behaviors and cues. The meanings of the verbal messages of physicians and patients are often unclear. The lack of clarity may of course be affected by many things: physicians may be rushed, they may be reluctant to share disturbing information with the patient, they may get mired down in their own jargon, and so on. The patient in turn may be reluctant to disclose information verbally to a physician who is acting in an imperious or dominant manner, may be quite reticent because of threats to her or his self-concept in the medical environment, or may feel that the doctor is lying to him or her. In all of these instances, the manifest content of a message (the words) may not be adequate to make the intended meaning clear. When this is the case, patients and physicians may have to turn to a second-level order of communicative cues known as metacommunication. The most informative metacommunicative cues tend to be nonverbal in nature. Metacommunicative cues may include an unintended grimace, shifty eyes, a strident voice, or adaptor gestures that express heightened tension.

Clearly, self-concept protection represents an important communication function that is served particularly well by nonverbal cues in the medical setting. The subtle, implicit messages communicated by such things as whether a patient is given reserved places in which to keep prized, personal possessions; whether the doctor cultivates the perception that patient and doctor are "partners" by communicating at eye level with the patient (rather than towering over the patient who is lying prostrate in a hospital bed); or the degree to which the patient is treated in a highly impersonal way may signal to patients whether their self-concept is being threatened or protected. Nonverbal communication variables clearly can play a central role in protecting the patients' self-concept.

Nonverbal communicative behaviors and cues that are particularly relevant to the self-concept protection function of nonverbal communication in the medical setting include a number of things. Successful efforts by the physician to respect the patient's privacy needs, to avoid violating preferred separation distances, and to help the patient preserve "territories of self" that patients perceive as their own are all important in helping the patient protect her or his self-concept. The use of eye behaviors and gestures that signal that the physician wishes to establish a partnership relationship with the patient rather than a superior–subordinate relationship is also important. Finally, physicians have to be careful to avoid using the command voice if the self-concept of the patient is not to be threatened.

The impression formation and management function of nonverbal communication in physician–patient interaction is surely important, because both physicians and patients are concerned with claiming images that are acceptable to them. As we already know, the three image dimensions that define the impression made by a given individual are *credibility, interpersonal attractiveness,* and *dominance.*

The credibility of the physician may of course be the major factor that determined why a patient chose a particular physician or surgeon in the first place. In the interactive context of the medical interview, however, the other two image dimensions of interpersonal attractiveness and dominance may prove to be more important. We know, for example, that interpersonal attractiveness is defined by how likeable, sociable, interesting, and emotionally expressive a person is judged to be. All of these image qualities are seen as highly desirable features of the nonverbal communication style of a physician who has adopted the new, interactive model of associating with the patient.

We are already familiar with the nonverbal behaviors that most positively and negatively affect judgments of interpersonal attractiveness. Likewise, immediacy behaviors in the form of sustained eye contact, direct bodily orientation, forward lean, and appropriate touching have repeatedly been found to enhance interpersonal attractiveness in general and liking in particular.

The image dimension of dominance is obviously of great importance when considering the interaction of physician and patient. Indeed, previous discussion in this chapter clearly documents that the single most important dimension along which physician and patient interaction may be evaluated is the degree of dominance or control exhibited by each of the interactants. Nonverbal communication is known to exert what is frequently a controlling influence over judgments or control, that is, relative dominance and submissiveness.

Nonverbal communicative behaviors and cues of particular importance in shaping impressions of dominance or submission are eye behaviors, vocal variables such as the sound of one's voice, and expansiveness of gestures and posture. In the medical interview, as in other contexts, the interactants may of course be faced with a somewhat painful trade-off. Those nonverbal communicative behaviors and cues that enhance one's perceived dominance tend to depress one's perceived likeability, and vice versa.

Finally, the patient's need for reassurance is undeniably stronger in the medical setting than in any other. Nonverbal means of providing the patient with reassurance are unrivaled by any other type of human communication. Touch in turn is the nonverbal medium with the greatest potential for reassuring patients in the medical context.

Actual Features of Physician–Patient Nonverbal Communication

We should consider two facts at minimum before we describe the actual nonverbal communicative behaviors of physicians and patients. The milieu of the physician is dominated by male values, and medical training places a premium on the authoritativeness of the physician. Let us begin with the focus on male values and attributes in medical contexts. At present, medical students, regardless of gender, continue to be exposed to male values. Hall, Roter, and Rand (1994) emphasized this point when they wrote:

> *The kinds of students selected into the highly competitive world of medicine are characterized by their task orientation, single-mindedness, narrow focus, and quantitative skill, attributes associated with maleness. . . . Moreover, the values and attitudes inculcated during the socialization process have also traditionally been masculine in nature. Medicine has been described as glorifying machismo, with the effect of turning both male and female medical students into macho doctors.* (p. 384)

Secondly, there has been much emphasis recently on the desirability of the physician being less controlling and instead sharing control with a patient to such an extent that a partnership results. Although there are good reasons for adopting this practice, we should recognize that it may not be without its liabilities. In a medical context, a very high priority traditionally has been given to the physician's authoritativeness. Indeed, if the patient does not make a sufficiently positive assessment of the physician's expertise, the patient-physician relationship will be terminated. Furthermore, there is reason to believe that it is perhaps the norm for both physicians and patients to equate dominance and authoritativeness. Street and Buller (1987) emphasized that in the medical context

> *both parties typically approach the encounter with the expectation that the doctor is the primary problem-solver and will presume to exercise (and the patient will allow) considerable influence regarding the content and structure of the interaction. . . .* In most medical interactions we expect physicians and patients to create patterns of communicative exchange, reflecting relatively greater

dominance and control by the physician and relatively less by the patient. [emphasis added] (pp. 236–237)

What would your own reaction be if your physician communicated nonverbally in a way that reminded you of the actor Don Knotts? If you were about to undergo brain surgery, would you prefer that your surgeon in her or his conversations with you exhibited strong, decisive movements or timid, tentative gestures? In the medical context, a physician's communication of nonverbal messages of dominance that connote reassurance as a result of self-assurance, authoritativeness, and being in command of the situation is not necessarily a bad thing.

In short, physicians are trained in a culture that embraces male values and attributes. This culture in turn is undoubtedly strongly influenced by the stereotype that suggests that males are active, dominant, aggressive, and insensitive persons who dominate communicative interaction by taking advantage of their superior status. By contrast, women are stereotypically perceived to be passive, submissive, supportive persons who are dominated as a result of their desire to adapt to men's needs and to be accommodating. Chapter 15 on female–male interaction contrasted the defining features of the nonverbal communication style for men and women. If all medical students are trained in a male-oriented culture, we would expect the nonverbal communication style for physicians in general to more closely resemble the male rather than the female nonverbal communication style.

Physicians themselves report that doctors trained in the traditional clinical method dominate communicative interaction with a patient (McWhinney, 1989). Nonverbally they sometimes communicate their dominance by using the penetrating eye contact with the patient that resembles a stare, whereas on other occasions they exhibit the visual inattentiveness of the high-power person. The physician often speaks in a loud voice, interrupts the patient without apparent qualm, and dominates interaction with long talk-turns.

Empirical studies of physicians' nonverbal communication reveal that physicians' dominance is expressed by similar means, that is, physicians frequently interrupt the patient (Lane, 1983) and they dominate the patient with their vocal cues (Hall et al., 1981). Research consistently shows that physicians dominate and control interaction with patients by asking more questions, interrupting more often, changing the topic, and talking for longer periods of time. Street and Wiemann (1988) stressed that dominant communicators exhibit domineering and controlling acts such as holding the floor longer, interrupting frequently, and engaging in nonreciprocal touch. Furthermore, dominant communicators are allowed to communicate nonverbally in such a way that they align themselves with the behaviors that are associated with high-power persons, such as relaxed, open, and expansive posture; relatively slow speaking rate; steady and direct eye contact; dynamic and purposeful gestures; and purposeful pausing (see the section in Chapter 4 that discusses the nonverbal indicators of power and powerlessness).

In their study of 44 English-speaking patients, Street and Buller (1987) confirmed that physicians dominate patients by their nonverbal communication. In this instance, physicians dominated patients by speaking for longer periods of time and exhibiting more social touch, which was not reciprocated by their patients. The authors concluded that "of the two participants physicians emerged more dominant nonverbally by exercising greater communicative control and displaying more status markers" (p. 246).

Although the primary emphasis in this chapter is on physician–patient interaction, it is important to stress that the issue of control is also of great importance in the interaction of dentists (and their assistants) and their patients. As Street (1990) wrote:

> *One of the more difficult communicative objectives for the dentist is to establish an acceptable level of communicative control during interactions with patients. On one hand, patient's satisfaction has diminished when dentists were perceived as domineering, or critical of the patient's behavior. On the other hand, because of the dentist's expertise and status, patients typically allow dentists substantial control over the interaction.* (p. 335)

Significantly, Street's research suggests that as the dentist's level of control over the patient increases, the patient's degree of liking for the dentist decreases. This finding seems to generalize to physicians as well as some other health care providers. When visiting my local dentist, for example, I noted how this relationship works in practice. As soon as the dental hygienist had me strapped down in the dentist's chair, she began to laser beam me with fear appeals: "If you do not brush your teeth regularly using my prescribed brushing technique and meet my flossing schedule, you are facing orthodontal disaster." In this case, my dentist seems to use the good guy/bad guy technique. He leaves the fear appeals up to his surrogates. Interestingly, I found my liking for this dentist decreasing as I became the object of more and more domineering acts in his dental chair.

In short, the role demands of "the competent physician" seem to place a premium on nonverbal communication that is dominant and controlling (Hall, Irish, Roter, Ehrlich, & Miller, 1994). Again, the training of physicians embraces the values of a macho culture, therefore it is not surprising that the nonverbal communication style of today's physician rather closely resembles many of the defining features of the male nonverbal communication style.

The nonverbal communication style of today's physical should not, however, be treated as if it is unidimensional, that is concerned exclusively with using the physician's communication to exercise the desired degree of control over a patient. There is some evidence to suggest that physicians may now be increasingly concerned with how interpersonally attractive they are perceived to be by their patients. Street and Buller (1987) found that the body orientations, gaze behavior, gestures, and response latencies of physicians and patients are relatively congruent. This congruence or similarity in the nonverbal behaviors exhibited by patients and physicians as they are interacting suggests that their affiliative efforts are mutually acceptable. Their findings also revealed a higher level of expressiveness on the part of physicians than expected. Although much more research needs to be done, there is at least some evidence to suggest that physicians are now making a greater effort to balance their felt need to claim an image for themselves of dominance and control with the need to claim an image of greater interpersonal attractiveness. Such a shift in emphasis will presumably serve two ends at minimum. The medical interview will become more interactive, and the patient will become more satisfied with the interview.

Any attempt to characterize the nonverbal communication style of today's physician would be incomplete if the impact of gender is not taken into account, however. Thanks in large part to a recent study by Hall and her colleagues (1994), we now have definitive evidence that reveals how the nonverbal communication style of female and male physicians differ.

The nonverbal communication style of the female physician differs from the style for male physicians in at least the following respects. Female MDs (a) elicit significantly more utterances from patients than do male MDs; (b) more evenly distribute the ratio of MD-to-patient speech than occurs when male physicians are interacting with patients; (c) exceed male MDs in "positive talk" (laughing, approving, and agreeing); (d) emit more back-channel responses than do male MDs (mm-hmmm, yeah, okay, and right); (e) have a voice quality that is rated as more anxious than the voice quality of male MDs; (f) are rated as more submissive than male MDs; and (g) smile more than male MDs and smile more to male patients than do male MDs.

The nonverbal communication profile of the female physician that emerges from this study is in many respects highly desirable. Thus, Hall and colleagues (1994) wrote that the results from this study are consistent with the conclusions that

> *female physicians are more nurturant and expressive and have stronger interpersonal orientations than male physicians. It is perhaps because of differences such as these that male physicians in a recent survey reported a much higher frequency of interpersonal difficulties with patients than did female physicians.* (p. 390)

We should note, furthermore, that the gender of the patient as well as the gender of the physician has a marked impact on the nonverbal communicative interaction of these two parties. Female physicians communicate differently when in the presence of a male patient. When communicating with male patients, female physicians smiled the most, were perceived as more dominant early in the visit (thus becoming more submissive as the interview continued), were less friendly later in the interview, and were more interested and anxious throughout the interaction.

The gender of the physician also affects the communicative responses of patients. Patients made more partnership statements to female as opposed to male doctors and provided more medical information to female MDs. The voices of male patients were rated as more bored when they were interacting with a female doctor and the voices of female patients were rated as more anxious than voice of male patients whether the physician was female or male.

Desired Features of Physician–Patient Nonverbal Communication

Several years ago, two well-known architects from Atlanta came out to inspect my house. As big-city architects, they rarely did work in the suburbs of Atlanta. They might send a summer intern out to check on a small job in outlying areas but these big men themselves made it a practice never to let the dust of anywhere but Fulton County settle on their boots. In fact, I had the sense that they may have stopped at the Fulton County line and changed into jumpsuits that would surely protect them from the inevitable contamination they would encounter in the suburbs in Gwinnett County.

When the big-city architects arrived at my house, they began sniffing around. They implied that they were doing me a big favor by coming out personally to inspect my humble abode. They did not admit of course that they were motivated by the potential of a very large renovation job, even by their standards. They summoned me after a couple of hours to tell me what they would do. They had not bothered to consult with me or check on my preferences; in fact, they told me that the blueprint for the renovation was already clear in their heads. One of the architects said to me "of course we will knock out the north wall of your present house, which will eliminate the fireplace on that side, and the house addition will eliminate your basketball court as well—for starters. That is how we will proceed." He then glanced at me with a look of pride on his face.

I replied, "Wrong. That is not how you will proceed. I believe you forgot one minor detail. My wife and I will be paying for this renovation. Therefore, we will be fully consulted on all aspects of the blueprints. If we should decide to work with you, we will work with you as full partners."

The communication style of these architects is strikingly similar in important respects to the communication style of many physicians in the United States. Although there is some evidence that a number of physicians are seeking to develop a more egalitarian relationship with their patients, the traditional communication style still prevails. Much like the architects from Atlanta, physicians who embrace the traditional communication style assume that they have the right to control communicative interaction with their patients. They assume that their superior knowledge and expertise gives them the right to cultivate an asymmetrical if not downright condescending relationship with the patient in which the physician talks and the patient listens. Physicians grow accustomed to issuing commands in an imperious manner while patients comply without question or complaint.

In this final section of this chapter we turn from a description of the defining features of the nonverbal communication of interacting physicians and patients as it is to a focus on how those features should be changed to make this nonverbal communication more nearly approximate an ideal. We focus on the nonverbal communication of the physician for several reasons even while stressing the interactive nature of communication with the patient. The vast majority of publications on physician–patient communication place the primary focus on the physician. Second, although nonverbal communication training is clearly desirable for both the physician and patient, the training provided in the real world is more apt to focus on and be provided for physicians.

The sad fact is that medical schools in the United States and Great Britain rarely provide formal instruction in communication for physicians. Although medical students may receive some form of communication skills training, it is usually short term and relatively superficial (Frederikson & Bull, 1992). This is a particularly bothersome finding when the benefits of in-depth communication training for medical students and physicians have now been clearly established. In fact, a recent study (Rowland-Morin, Burchard, Garb, & Coe, 1991) found that surgery students who received even rudimentary training in nonverbal communication—that is, they were trained to exhibit direct eye contact and a moderate rate of response—performed significantly better on their oral examinations than surgery students who did not have such training. Interestingly, there is now evidence to suggest that surgical specialists have a greater need for communication training than general practitioners. This may be due in part to the fact that surgeons get so preoccupied with the technical aspects of their work that they become insensitive to the requirements of effective communicative interaction with their patients (Roulidis & Schulman, 1994).

A recent study identifies eight attitudes that should be stressed in medical education. These attitudes are considered pivotal in developing a therapeutic relationship where physicians and patients treat each other as equals when interacting: (a) physicians and patients must exhibit unconditional positive regard for each other in order to foster a helping relationship; (b) the patient must show respect for the physician by visiting the physician only when there is a defensible reason for doing so, such as when the patient is experiencing substantial suffering; (c) the patient's actions and reactions must be reasonable and prudent; (d) the doctor always has the capacity to help the patient in some way; (e) the doctor and patient share the responsibility for "helping"; (f) both patient and physician must recognize that doctors have other agendas beyond patient care; (g) physicians indicate explicitly how far they can go to help patients; (h) patients recognize that physicians are human beings with emotions, feelings, and affectional needs (Wolfe, Ingelfinger, & Schmitz, 1994).

In seeking to modify their existing nonverbal communication style, physicians as well as patients should consider the type of relationship they seek to develop. The new, modified nonverbal communication style should stress the physician's and patient's ability to build rapport with each other, to share control of the medical interview, to be self-disclosing, to provide each other with needed confirmation, and to respond to each other in an empathic manner. Communication training that seeks to modify the nonverbal communicative interaction of physicians and patients can not, of course, seek to do everything. Therefore, we believe that communication training at this moment should focus on the development of the nonverbal skills necessary for the physician and patient to build a rapport and to respond empathically to each other.

Consider first the nonverbal communicative behaviors exhibited by physicians who are effective in building a high level of rapport with their patients. High-rapport physicians sit directly facing the patient with their legs and arms uncrossed and their arms in symmetrical side-by-side positions. High-rapport doctors engage in moderate eye contact with their patients. The fact that high rapport doctors sit with open arms and legs can be interpreted to mean that they are more direct and open and exhibit more concern and interest in the patient. In contrast, low-rapport physicians exhibit asymmetrical arms postures, lean backward in their chairs, show little gestural and postural activity, and sustain eye contact for excessively long periods of time. A major reason why doctors who exhibit these nonverbal communicative behaviors are perceived to have low rapport may be that many of these nonverbal behaviors have been associated with dominance or high status (Harrigan et al., 1985).

Significantly, individuals who are effective in building rapport have consistently been perceived as *warm, enthusiastic,* and *interested.* A study by Heintzman, Leathers, Parrott, and Cairns, (1993) indicated that the five types of nonverbal behaviors that are most effective in building rapport (when they are exhibited at appropriate times and with the proper degree of intensity) are smiling, touching, affirmative head nods, immediacy behaviors, and sustained eye contact.

The study by Heintzman and colleagues compared the effects on communicative interaction of a high- versus a low-rapport supervisor with his subordinates. Although there are differences between this type of relationship and the relationship of the physician and patient, some of the most important findings would seem to apply to the medical context where doctors and patients interact. First, the high-rapport supervisor was perceived by subordinates to be more interpersonally attractive than the low-rapport supervisor. More specifically, the high-rapport supervisor was judged to be higher in both social and task attractiveness than his low-rapport counterpart. Secondly, subordinates reported higher levels of satisfaction when working with the high- as opposed to the low-rapport supervisor. Finally, the rate of compliance by subordinates with requests from the high-rapport supervisor was significantly higher than with requests from the low-rapport supervisor. In short, there is little doubt that the physician who builds rapport with the patient by exhibiting appropriate nonverbal communicative behaviors will be perceived as a more sensitive, caring, and interpersonally attractive individual.

Whereas rapport is a sender-oriented concept, empathy is a receiver-oriented concept. To begin, empathy must be distinguished from pity and sympathy. Pity is negative affect or sadness felt for another's misfortune. Pity connotes in some instances a feeling of sadness combined with perhaps smug superiority in that you are relieved that you have not experienced a similar misfortune. Sympathy in contrast is defined by an active, overt effort to show the person who has experienced the misfortune that you regret it and care for this person. Empathy goes beyond the efforts of the sympathetic person to provide solace and comfort. Empathy is a relational concept that becomes meaningful only at that point where our level of awareness becomes such that we are able to connect with and feel the inner experience of another person. We are able in effect to put ourselves in the place of another in terms of the other person's feeling states (Nadelson, 1994).

Because the positive relationship between a physician's empathy and the patient's satisfaction has clearly been established, additional justification for training physicians to communicate in an empathic manner nonverbally is hardly needed. Significantly, nonverbal communication has been found to be more than twice as important as verbal communication in responding in an empathic manner. Empathic communicators exhibit more sustained eye contact and a more direct bodily orientation than do nonempathic communicators. They also exhibit moderate forward lean and most important of all the nonverbal and verbal components of their messages communicate meanings that are congruent or consistent (Hasse & Tepper, 1972).

Both physicians and patients may use the information provided in this chapter to interact more effectively. To do so, they must attach the highest priority to the development of their nonverbal communicative skills. Physicians who wish to share control of interviews with patients, for example, would be well advised to review Chapter 4 in this book, which details nonverbal indicators of high versus low power and of aggressiveness versus assertiveness versus nonassertiveness. To share control with a patient, a physician must strike a balance between exhibiting those high-power cues that are associated with dominance and those assertiveness cues that signal a respect for the rights of the patient. Surely, both the physician and patient should concentrate on the development of those nonverbal skills that will help them build rapport with and respond empathically to each other. The following guidelines may facilitate more effective physician–patient interaction.

Guideline #1

Physicians and patients should seek to develop their sensitivities to each other's moods, feelings, and emotions by learning to interpret the meanings of each other's facial expressions.

Guideline #2

The patient's strong need for self-concept protection must be met via an explicit discussion by the physician and patient of the specific nature of this need and ways to satisfy it.

Guideline #3

Physicians should seek specialized training in the use of nonverbal communicative behaviors and cues to build rapport with the patient and to respond empathically to the patient.

Guideline #4

Physicians should seek to provide patients with reassurance and positive reinforcement wherever possible in the form of such back-channel cues as head nodding; using expressions such as "ah-ha," "hmmm," "yeah," "okay," or "right"; and lightly touching the patient on the hand.

Guideline #5

Physicians should become thoroughly familiar with nonverbal power and powerless cues as well as nonverbal behaviors that communicate respectively aggressiveness, assertiveness, and unassertiveness so that they understand how to share control when interacting with a patient (see detailed sets of each of these types of nonverbal cues in Chapter 4).

Guideline #6

Both physicians and patients must develop their skill in decoding such nonverbal metacommunicative cues as facial expressions and tone of voice so they may interact with each other in a more sensitive manner.

Guideline #7

Physicians and patients should fill out brief survey forms at frequent intervals on which they evaluate the effectiveness of their communicative interaction with the summarized results being given to both parties.

Guideline #8

A comprehensive course designed to develop the nonverbal communication skills of physicians should be required in the curricula of all medical schools.

Summary

Successful physician–patient interaction requires that both parties be thoroughly familiar with the distinctive problems that they are apt to encounter when interacting with each other. The basic problem may be attributed to the traditional clinical method of education used for decades in medical schools. This method stresses that the physician must dominate and control the interaction with the patient. More specifically, role uncertainty, power differences, and unshared meanings represent serious barriers to effective physician–patient communication.

The most important skills required for effective interaction between physician and patient are nonverbal in nature. In fact, a number of studies support the conclusion that the physician's nonverbal communication is a major determinant of the level of satisfaction experienced by the patient. Not surprisingly, there are multiple reasons why nonverbal communication is functionally important both to the physician and patient. In order to make full use of the functional potential of nonverbal communication with the patient, the physician must be fully aware of the five major communicative functions served by nonverbal communication in the medical context: (a) exchange of emotions, (b) metacommunication, (c) self-concept protection, (d) impression formation and management, and (e) reassurrance.

To enhance the effectiveness of interaction with patients, physicians must first familiarize themselves with the dysfunctional features of their nonverbal communication style. These features are identified in this chapter.

Finally, physicians and patients must give the highest priority to the development of their nonverbal communication skills in order to increase the effectiveness with which they interact. Particular emphasis should be placed on the development of those skills necessary for physicians and patients to develop rapport with each other and to respond to each other empathically. The guidelines presented at the end of this chapter may help patients and physicians to interact more effectively.

References

Beckman, H., Kaplan, S. H., & Frankel, R. (1989). Outcome-based research on doctor–patient communication: A review. In M. Stewart & D. Roter (Eds.), *Communicating with medical patients* (pp. 223–227). Newbury Park, CA: Sage.

DiMatteo, M. R. (1979). Nonverbal skill and the physician–patient relationship. In R. Rosenthal (Ed.), *Skill in nonverbal communication: Individual differences* (pp. 104–134). Cambridge, MA: Oelgeschlager, Gunn, & Hain.

DiMatteo, M. R. (1986). Relationship of physicians' nonverbal communication skill to patient satisfaction, appointment noncompliance, and physicians' workload. *Health Psychology, 51,* 581–584.

DiMatteo, M. R., Linn, L. S., Chang, B. L., & Cope, D. W. (1985). Affect and neutrality in physician behavior: A study of patients' values and satisfaction. *Journal of Behavioral Medicine, 8,* 397–409.

DiMatteo, M. R., & Taranta, A. (1979). Nonverbal communication and physician–patient rapport: An empirical study. *Professional Psychology, 10,* 540–547.

Enelow, A. J., & Swisher, S. N. (1986). *Interviewing and patient care* (3rd ed.). Oxford: Oxford University Press.

Frederikson, I., & Bull, P. (1992). An appraisal of the current status of communication skills training in British medical schools. *Social Science & Medicine, 34,* 515–522.

Hall, J. A., Irish, J. T., Roter, D. L., Ehrlich, C. M., & Miller, L. H. (1994). Medical encounters: An analysis of physician and patient communication in a primary care setting. *Health Psychology, 13,* 384–392.

Hall, J. A., Roter, D. L., & Rand, C. S. (1981). Communication of affect between patient and physician. *Journal of Health and Social Behavior, 22,* 18–30.

Harrigan, J. A., Oxman, T. E., & Rosenthal, R. (1985) Rapport expressed through nonverbal behavior. *Journal of Nonverbal Behavior, 9,* 95–110.

Hasse, R. F., & Tepper, D. T., Jr. (1972). Nonverbal components of empathic communication. *Journal of Counseling Psychology, 19,* 417–424.

Heintzman, M., Leathers, D. G., Parrott, R. L., & Cairns, A. B. III. (1993). Nonverbal rapport-building behavior's effects on perceptions of a supervisor. *Management Communication Quarterly, 7,* 181–208.

Kreps, G. L., & Thornton, B. C. (1992). *Health communication: Theory & practice.* Prospect Heights, IL.: Waveland.

Lane, S. D. (1983). Compliance, satisfaction, and physician–patient communication. In R. Bostrom (Ed.), *Communication Yearbook 7* (pp. 772–799). Beverly Hills: Sage.

McWhinney, I. (1989). The need for a transformed clinical method. In M. Stewart & D. Roter (Eds.), *Communicating with medical patients* (pp. 25–40). Newbury Park, CA.: Sage.

Nadelson, C. C. (1994). Health care: Is society empathic with women? *The empathic practitioner* (189–204). New Brunswick, NJ: Rutgers University Press.

Northouse, P. G., & Northouse, L. L. (1992). *Health Communication: Strategies for Health Professionals* (2nd ed.). Norwalk, CN: Appleton & Lange.

Rosenthal, R. (Ed.). (1979). *Skill in nonverbal communication: Individual differences.* Cambridge, MA: Oelgeschlager, Gunn, & Hain.

Roulidis, Z. D., & Schulman, K. A. (1994). Physician communication in managed care organizations: Opinions of primary care physicians. *Journal of Family Practice, 39,* 446–451.

Rowland-Morin, P. A., Burchard, K. W., Garb, J. L., & Coe, N. P. (1991). Influence of effective communication by surgery students on their oral examination scores. *Academic Medicine, 66,* 169–171.

Stewart, M., & Roter, D. (1989). Introduction. In M. Stewart & D. Roter (Eds.), *Communicating with medical patients* (pp. 17–23). Newbury Park, CA: Sage.

Street, R. L. (1990). Dentist–patient communication: A review and commentary. In D. O'Hair & G. L. Kreps (Eds.), *Applied communication theory and research* (pp. 331–351). Hillsdale, NJ: Lawrence Erlbaum.

Street, R. L. (1991). Information-giving in medical consultations: The influence of patients' communicative styles and personal characteristics. *Social Science & Medicine, 32,* 541–548.

Street, R. L. (1992). Analyzing communication in medical consultations: Do behavioral measures correspond to patient's perceptions. *Medical Care, 30,* 976–988.

Street, R. L., & Buller, D. B. (1987). Nonverbal response patterns in physician–patient interactions: A functional analysis. *Journal of Nonverbal Behavior, 11,* 234–253.

Street, R. L., & Wiemann, J. M. (1988). Differences in how physicians and patients perceive physicians' relational communication. *The Southern Speech Communication Journal, 53,* 420–440.

Wolfe, A. M. D., Ingelfinger, J. A., & Schmitz, S. (1994). Emphasizing attitudes toward the doctor–patient relationship in medical education. *Academic Medicine, 69,* 895–896.

Courtroom Interaction

Millions of Americans now seem fascinated with courtroom dynamics. Surely the nationally televised trials of William Kennedy Smith and O. J. Simpson were fascinating spectacles. Trials such as these turned countless Americans into self-appointed courtroom analysts. Americans now can give microscopic attention to every feature of courtroom interaction that they sense might have communicative significance.

The eye of the television camera has revealed to the general public what has been apparent to attorneys for some time, which is that courtroom interaction is not shaped solely by the words of the participants—the attorneys, the judge, the accuser, the defendant, and the witnesses. The traditional, outmoded view is that court cases are typically won by the side that presents the best evidence. Leading courtroom attorneys have long recognized that the nonverbal communicative interaction that occurs in the courtroom may often be the most important force (Anthony & Vinson, 1987).

The vital importance of nonverbal communication in the courtroom is treated in enlightening detail by trial consultant James Rasicot. The title of his book, *Jury Selection, Body Language & the Visual Trial* (1985), draws attention to the functional importance of nonverbal communication in the courtroom. Rasicot emphasized that law schools have traditionally done a fine job in training courtroom attorneys in the technical aspects of legal work. However, they had done a very poor job of teaching communication skills. The seriousness of this training deficiency becomes apparent when we recognize two things at minimum: Communication is the most important part of the courtroom trial, and nonverbal communication is the most important part of communication because more than over 60 percent of the messages exchanged in the courtroom are transmitted nonverbally (Rasicot, 1985).

Rasicot stresses that attorneys who win the verbal trial but lose the nonverbal trial are ultimately apt to lose court cases:

> *The attorney who wins the verbal trial but loses the nonverbal trial has a diminished chance of winning overall. Communication with jurors increases by insuring that the visual and verbal aspects of the trial compliment and support each other.... [Whereas lawyers and judges are trained to concentrate on the verbal*

content of the trial], a juror is a stranger to the setting and is more accustomed to being visually stimulated. (p. 5)

At the intuitive level, the importance of nonverbal communication in the courtroom is readily apparent. Consider the case of John DeLorean who was charged with setting up a $24 million cocaine deal. His wife, Cristina Ferrare, obviously wanted to help DeLorean claim an image of the greatest utility. Thus, Smith and Malandro (1985) wrote that

A week after her husband was arrested, Cristina Ferrare bought a somber, yet expensive designer wardrobe and cut off her shoulder-length hair. Reports supposedly claimed that she looked more like Joan of Arc in designer sackcloth than a Vogue *fashion model with a well-publicized penchant for sables and jewels. She was dressing for acquittal.* (p. 29)

In this chapter, the term *courtroom* is used in a generic sense. A courtroom is, of course, a room where trials are held, but it is also a room where other legal and quasi-legal proceedings are conducted. Clearly, we do not wish to confine the content of this chapter to the dynamics of nonverbal communication that occur only during a courtroom trial. Many legal and quasi-legal proceedings are held in rooms that are not technically courtrooms. For example, many hearings held by committees and subcommittees of the United States Senate or House of Representative are of great legal consequence. However, they are held not in a courtroom room but in a hearing room.

Four sections make up this chapter. The chapter first focuses on the functional importance of nonverbal communication in the courtroom. The emphasis is on the impact of nonverbal communicative behaviors or cues on interpersonal perception in general and in the management of impressions in particular. The next section identifies and illustrates the functions of specific kinds of nonverbal communication in the courtroom, that is, the functions of dress and artifacts, kinesic behaviors, the use of space, and vocal cues. The third section deals with the logistics of impression formation and management, which involves the use of questionnaires, focus groups, and mock juries to measure and modify the images of participants in the courtroom. Finally, the last section of this chapter focuses on the Anita Hill–Clarence Thomas Senate hearings and the William Kennedy Smith and O. J. Simpson trials. The objective here is to illustrate how the impression management function of nonverbal communication was, or might have been, used to achieve specific objectives in the courtroom.

The Functional Importance of Nonverbal Communication in the Courtroom

Nonverbal communication exerts a pervasive impact on interpersonal perceptions in the courtroom. Smith and Malandro strongly affirm this point by devoting nearly 150 pages of their book to how nonverbal communicative behaviors or cues can be used to control interpersonal perceptions in the courtroom (1985). They give detailed attention to the impact of personal appearance factors on the images of courtroom participants, as determined by clothing, jewelry and artifacts, hair, and makeup. In addition, they identify and illustrate the functions of a wide range of nonverbal communicative behaviors such as touch, use of space, and vocal cues.

The importance of managing impressions in the courtroom has been apparent to attorneys for some time. Three highly detailed books that are particularly rich sources of information on impression management in the courtroom were written by Aron, Fast, and Klein (1986); Bennett and Hirschhorn (1993); and Smith and Malandro (1985). Nonverbal communication in turn frequently assumes the central role in impression management efforts in the courtroom. Famed jury consultant Cathy Bennett wrote in her book with Robert Hirschhorn that

> *It is psychological fact that people's non-verbal language tells us more about them than what they say verbally. Often, when you do not believe what someone is saying it is because [their] non-verbal communication is giving [them] away. Body posture, facial expression, voice intonation, or eye contact are telling you that the person means something different from what [his or her] words are saying. To that end, you must carefully observe jurors at a multitude of levels in order to get a true picture of what they are trying to say.* (Bennett & Hirschhorn, 1993, p. 221)

The legal profession leads the way in the use of image consultants. Not surprisingly, impression management has emerged as an important topic for legal scholars. In the pages of scholarly journals and books in both communication and law, for example, a focus on the applied value and implications of impression management is becoming increasingly prominent (LeVan, 1984; Pryor & Buchanan, 1984; Rieke & Stutman, 1990; Ryan & Syald, 1993; Varinsky & Nomikos, 1990; Wood, 1985). These publications focus directly on how members of legal teams and their clients seek to manage impressions and how jurors and judges form impressions.

Although recent publications on the roles of impression management and formation in the courtroom cover a range of interrelated topics, two areas are receiving particular attention: (a) the functions of nonverbal behaviors and cues as attorneys seek to manage impressions formed by jury members, other members of their legal team, their clients, their witnesses, and themselves (Barge, Schlueter, & Pritchard, 1989; Burke, Ames, Etherington, & Pietsch, 1990; Darby & Jeffers, 1988; deTurck & Goldhaber, 1988; Pettus, 1990; Sigal, Braden-Maguire, Hayden, & Mosley, 1985; Vinson, 1982; Wuensch, Castellow, & Moore, 1991), and (b) the monitoring of judges' nonverbal behaviors and cues to determine if they are revealing either positive or negative biases toward members of a legal team, clients, and witnesses, and, if so, how judicial bias is communicated and what is its nature (Bennett & Hirschhorn, 1993; Blanck, Rosenthal, & Cordell, 1985).

Today jury and trial consultants work directly with attorneys by using the nonverbal profiles exhibited by potential jurors to make inferences about both personal qualities and attitudes. Once a trial begins, jury consultants often are seated in the courtroom a few feet from the jury so that they can study even the most subtle of the jurors' nonverbal behaviors in order to identify their emotional and attitudinal reactions to the given attorneys, witnesses, and clients (Aron, Fast, and Klein, 1986; Bennett & Hirschhorn, 1993).

The Functions of Nonverbal Communication in the Courtroom

Although many different kinds of nonverbal messages are undeniably important in the courtroom, four kinds are particularly important: (a) *personal appearance,* (b) *kinesic behaviors,* (c) *the use of space,* and (d) *vocal cues.*

Personal Appearance

Smith and Malandro (1985) gave illuminating detail to the central role of personal appearance in shaping the impressions that principal players make in the courtroom. In fact, they argued that attorneys must balance their desire to be perceived as credible with their desire to be perceived as approachable or likable.

> *The underlying factor in making this determination is how people perceive you in a neutral state. In other words, are you perceived as a highly powerful or a low power person? Are you perceived as intimidating or friendly, trustworthy or untrustworthy? Understanding these original perceptions will tell us whether or not you already have credibility and if you need to increase approachability. The ultimate blend for an attorney is to have both approachability and credibility.* (p. 32)

Given this perspective, it is not surprising that Smith and Malandro provide two personal checklists for male attorneys. The first checklist features personal appearance decisions that will enhance credibility, and the second checklist focuses on the impact of specific personal appearance items on the male attorney's perceived approachability or friendliness.

Let us first consider personal appearance guidelines. In general, conservative and traditional clothing enhance the credibility of the male attorney. Trendy or poor quality suits as well as sport jackets should be avoided. Wool and wool blends are preferred fabrics for the suits of male attorneys, whereas silk, ultrasuede, and nontraditional fabrics are to be avoided. Male attorneys should wear a white shirt with a gray or navy suit. Eyeglasses are quite acceptable because they have been found to enhance credibility but attorneys should avoid round, wire-rim frames (they make the eyes look small, beady, and untrustworthy), or any type of trendy frame. However, no type of tinted or photosensitive eyeglasses or contact lenses should be worn (anything that makes it difficult to have an unimpeded look at the male attorney's eyes is apt to depress the trustworthiness factor). A beard or mustache is acceptable if well trimmed and conservative (beards may enhance credibility in certain rather formal situations).

The personal appearance guidelines for approachability and friendliness for male attorneys contrast with the guidelines for credibility. Thus, male attorneys who wish to enhance the perception that they are approachable and friendly may decide to wear a sport jacket rather than a suit. If they do wear a suit, they should choose lighter colors such as tan or beige; acceptable fabrics for suits or sport coats in addition to wools include cashmere and wool blends. If eyeglasses are worn, they should be removed periodically to increase the perception of approachability. The approachable male attorney should be clean shaven.

Similarly, a brief look at the personal appearance guidelines developed by Smith and Malandro (1985) for female attorneys is instructive. Female attorneys who wish to maximize their credibility should follow a number of the same guidelines offered for male attorneys with regard to the necessity of wearing high-quality suits that are conservative and traditional. The female attorney may wear bows and pleated blouses; both male-looking ties and ruffles should be avoided because of their negative gender implications, however. The length of the coat sleeves on the female attorney's suit are critically important (for example, sleeves that are too long may suggest that the female attorney is submissive and, hence, lacks authoritativeness and competence); so coat sleeves should be tailored to the appropriate length. A conservative and classic hairstyle is imperative—in particular, female attorneys should avoid wearing hair that is so long that it falls below the shoulders or is so short that it appears to be imitating a male look.

Female attorneys who are dressing to enhance their personal credibility absolutely must avoid designer clothing and accessories—female attorneys who are preoccupied with being fashionable and chic are not apt to inspire confidence in their credibility. In line with this perceptual point, female attorneys may wear limited jewelry but only up to five points, that is, a ring, a pin, earrings, and a necklace.

By contrast, female attorneys who wish to enhance their perceived approachability/likability may wear a contrasting skirt and jacket or even a tailored and conservative dress. She may of course wear a blouse with bow or even with pleats, a slight ruffle, or a soft tie (though she should avoid a male-looking tie). Brighter blouse colors which include pastels such as blue, pink, rose, and green may be worn but she should avoid both bright-colored and white blouses. For cultivating the approachable look, the attorney's hairstyle may be softened so that the hair is brought around the face in soft curls or waves.

In *Jury Selection, Body Language & the Visual Trial* (1985), Rasicot too describes the communicative functions of clothing and artifacts in the courtroom in detail. However, his most original contribution may be his four general conclusions:

1. *Although the visual image is always important throughout the trial, the first few minutes are of critical importance.* First impressions are long lasting and trigger emotions—particularly among members of the jury—that strongly influence subsequent attitudes and perceptions about a given individual.

2. *In criminal cases the defendant should be dressed in such a manner that his or her appearance is inconsistent with the crime.* The objective is to have the jury study the appearance of the defendant and conclude that linking the defendant to the crime is irrational.

3. *In civil cases, the plaintiff should be dressed so that it looks like she or he not only needs the amount of money under consideration but deserves it.* Conversely, the defendant in a civil case should be dressed down to such an extent that it appears that he or she could not afford to pay any court-imposed settlement, no matter how small.

4. *Both the social and professional dimensions of the client's image should be conservative in appearance.*

Each of Rasicot's conclusions could of course be illustrated with examples from actual court cases. Let us consider the third conclusion for purposes of illustration. Not long ago a young baker brought a civil suit for damages against the owner of a bar, which we will call The Strange Cat, and two off-duty police officers. The two off-duty police officers were providing security for the owner of The Strange Cat on the night that the young baker walked up to the bar and ordered a drink. At almost the same time, the baker made a pass at a married woman who was seated next to him. When the case came to court, both the plaintiff and the defendants agreed that the plaintiff was escorted out of the bar at this point by the two security officers. The plaintiff alleged that he was savagely beaten in the parking lot, and he sued the defendants for a six-figure settlement in damages. The owner of The Strange Cat and his two security men denied that excessive force was used.

Presumably, the defense team was familiar with Rasicot's third conclusion. To begin, the defense attorney was nicknamed "Old Gravy Stain," because he was known for having a clearly discernible gravy stain on the lapel of his suit. Clearly, the implication was that anyone who hired Old Gravy Stain as an attorney was a person of modest means. Moreover, both the owner of The Strange Cat and his two off-duty police officers were dressed in such a manner as to suggest that they were just a cut above vagrants. The security officers in particular were dressed in low-quality khaki pants and flimsy shirts that surely would be rejected by the Salvation Army. In short, someone looking at the defendants would most likely conclude that they could not afford to pay, and should not have to pay, anything to the plaintiff.

Kinesic Behaviors

A number of kinesic behaviors or human movements may be communicatively significant in the courtroom. Eye behaviors, gestures, and postures seem particularly important.

The eyes represent a communicative medium of great importance in the courtroom. Jury and trial consultants Bennett and Hirschhorn wrote:

> *You will also want to pay attention to jurors' eye contact during the questioning process. Do they look you in the eye? Do they make eye contact with your client, with opposing counsel, with the opposing client? This will tell you their comfort level in communicating with members of each trial team as well as their comfort level in talking in groups in general. If a juror will not look at you, this indicates he is shy, irritated with you, or thinking. You should follow up to find out what the resistance to making eye contact actually means.* (p. 230)

Surely, in the courtroom as well as anywhere else, the eyes have the potential to serve each of the seven communicative functions identified in Chapter 3. We know, for example, that the eyes indicate the level of attentiveness and interest not only of jury members but also of other principal players in a courtroom drama. Secondly, the eyes of the person on the witness stand are perhaps the central determinant of their perceived trustworthiness or honesty. Finally, the eyes serve a central impression management function in the courtroom.

More particularly, eye behaviors can have other results: the aggressive attorney may stare at witnesses to make them uncomfortable; the more eye contact an attorney maintains with a jury the greater their level of confidence in the attorney; courtroom participants who look up at key points are often perceived to be dominant, whereas those who gaze downward are viewed as submissive; and even the direction of eye contact may have communicative significance. A witness who looks up and to the left while answering a question may be in the "constructing mode" of deciding what answer to give, which may include a deceptive answer. By contrast, a person who looks up and to the right when responding to a question may simply be tapping factual memory (Rasicot, 1985). Similarly, the juror who tries to stare the attorney down is obviously challenging or resisting the attorney, at minimum. Finally, attorneys should pay particular attention to where members of the jury are looking when the attorney is addressing them. If one juror turns and looks at the opposing counsel, that is a bad sign. It probably signals that this juror is more comfortable with the opposing counsel and is seeking her or his approval (Bennett & Hirschhorn, 1985).

Gestures and postures are also important in the courtroom. Adaptor gestures expressed with the hands may communicate valuable implicit messages. For example, jurors and witnesses who exhibit a closed fist are tense at best and angry at worst. All participants in a courtroom should avoid steepling their hands because those who steeple are frequently perceived to be lying or at least withholding part of the truth. Similarly, people who place their chin close to their neck, may communicate either that they are trying to hide something or to cover up something. Finally, a look at the jurors' ankles and feet may be the best indicator of their relative level of comfort or discomfort. As we indicated in Chapter 4, the feet as a medium of communication have very limited potential. On the other hand, the feet are rarely if ever subject to conscious control by a communicator, so the messages they do transmit should be almost completely free from deception.

Courtroom Choreography: The Use of Space

Nonverbal communication plays a central role in the courtroom in the sense that it is used by the attorneys to attain dominance or control. Attorneys have frequently told me that one of their most central objectives in the courtroom is to "gain control." The primary means attorneys use to gain and maintain control in a courtroom is the use of available space.

Attorney and law professor Jeffrey Wolfe treated this subject in an enlightening way in his article entitled "Courtroom Choreography: Systematic Use of the Courtroom" (1985), Wolfe wrote that many factors contribute to the credibility of the case and of each courtroom participant (for example, voice level, order of presentation, questions asked, use of demonstrative evidence, and so on). He stressed that

> *One factor, however, not often considered, is the courtroom itself. To what extent does* use *of courtroom space affect perception and interpretation of one's case? In this writer's view effective* choreography *of the courtroom will enhance the persuasive presentation of the advocate's case.* (p. 29)

Wolfe argued that attorneys gain control in a courtroom, and greatly enhance the persuasive impact of their message, by where they choose to stand. During cross-examination, defense attorneys should stand strategically in a position that makes sustained eye contact between the jury and the person being cross-examined difficult if not impossible. It is particularly important that an attorney's own witness look directly at the jury during direct examination when the attorney is asking the witness whether he or she is telling the truth or asking the accused, for example, whether she or he committed the criminal act for which the person is standing trial. In the latter situation, "the advocate must position himself within the courtroom in such a way as to encourage the witness to look and speak to the jury and the jury to look at the witness. Positioning oneself at the *rear* of the jury box, along the "jury side" diagonal, accomplishes this goal." (p. 31)

Vocal Cues

Finally, the voice is a vitally important medium of communication in the courtroom. Because the voice encodes power (and its opposite—weakness or submissiveness) powerfully, attorneys may wish to speak with a soft voice, perhaps to dissociate themselves from an image of unseemly aggressiveness. Persons accused of aggressive crimes such as murder and rape may be especially concerned with distancing themselves from an image of aggressiveness.

Trial and jury consultants are particularly sensitive to the vocal cues of jurors (during *voir dire*) as sources of perceptual information. Thus, a sudden increase in speaking rate may suggest increased nervousness or aggressiveness. A sudden change in the pitch of a person's voice may also be important. An individual who lowers her or his voice may want to hide something, or at least avoid discussing it. An increase in pitch may suggest an increase in level of the intensity of the emotion being experienced. When a person blurts out something, the content is apt to be truthful. Inappropriate laughter is often a reliable sign of nervousness. Sustained crying raises serious questions about a witnesses' credibility (Bennett & Hirschhorn, 1993).

The Logistics of Measuring Impressions

Before any attempt can be made to manage impressions in the courtroom, the impressions presently being made must actually be measured. Indeed, we will never again see the day where attorneys fly by the seat of their pants. Oh yes, we are amused by stories about Clarence Darrow assuming a "country" dialect while defending a small-town client. We chuckle when I. M. Histrionic, a local attorney, spins out her/his subjective "theory" of manipulating juries by the way she or he dresses.

In point of fact, top trial attorneys in the present day do not rely on their own hunches or subjective opinions to guide the way they communicate nonverbally in the courtroom. They rely on the recommendations of experts. These legal consultants are social scientists who carry around a set of tested, reliable techniques and measuring tools, foremost among them being questionnaires, focus groups, and mock juries. Moreover, these jury and trial consultants use a clear-cut process to obtain and analyze the data on which their recommendations are based.

Gathering, and subjecting to measurement, the information needed to assess the accuracy of impressions being made in the courtroom is hardly a simple matter. Thus, Smith and Malandro (1985) wrote that

> *Our reference to a courtroom image goes far beyond the concept of dressing witnesses and attorneys for court. The projection of an image in the courtroom is manifested and reinforced by all stimuli which enter into the jurors' perception.*

> *This includes behaviors, personal appearance, voice characteristics, word choice,*
> *relationship to others, and so forth. Communication is based on perception. Ev-*
> *erything which comes into the perceptual field of the jurors will affect the image*
> *of a witness, client, or attorney.* (p. 17)

A definite process with a set of steps must be followed to measure the impressions made at a given point in time by one or more of the principal players in a courtroom trial. The logistics for measuring and modifying the impressions made are described in considerable detail in the discussion of impression management in Chapter 10. In essence, a trial consultant must determine to what degree, if any, her or his client's desired image and actual image are discernibly different. To the degree that there is a disparity, consultants must determine what changes can be made in the client's communicative behaviors in order to modify the client's actual image in a way that will bring it in line with the desired image.

In *Courtroom Communication Strategies,* Smith and Malandro (1985) claimed that the most important question to ask before the trial begins is this: What perceptions do I want the jurors and judge to have? The second question is also of central importance: Do all case materials—evidence, arguments, personal appearance factors, and other variables—support this perception?

The authors stressed that to "test for image perception in the courtroom" one or more mock juries should be used and the following five-step process should be followed: (a) identify the image the individual is actually projecting in the courtroom, (b) identify the desired image, (c) determine the nature and the magnitude of the difference between the projected and desired image, (d) identify what modifications in nonverbal communicative behaviors such as vocal cues need to be made, and (e) identify which internal changes in perceptions such as attitudes and beliefs need to be made.

Probably the three most important techniques used to gather information about and to measure the impressions that will be or are being made in the courtroom are questionnaires, focus groups, and mock juries. The use of these techniques is illustrated and described in detail in *Bennett's Guide to Jury Selection and Trial Dynamics in Civil and Criminal Litigation.*

Bennett was the lead jury and trial consultant in the William Kennedy Smith rape trial. In this trial and others where she served as a consultant Bennett made extensive use of these techniques. As we shall see, defense attorney Roy Black used a number of mock juries in the William Kennedy Smith case so that he had precise data that allowed him to predict how impressions might be controlled most precisely in the courtroom.

In Jury Selection (Voir Dire)

Questionnaires administered to members of the jury pool obviously can provide much valuable information about a person's overt attitudes, beliefs, prejudices, and personality traits. The questionnaire is a rather static means of gathering information when compared to focus groups and mock juries, however. Both focus groups and mock juries are frequently used not only before a trial begins but while it is proceeding.

The focus group involves putting together a group that is made up of a cross section of the community with demographics that are as similar as possible to those of the actual jurors. One or more focus groups are used to test part of the prosecution or defense case. Mock trials using mock juries differ from focus groups primarily in length and scope. Mock trials in contrast to focus groups present an entire case (Bennett and Hirschhorn, 1993).

Because the visual and audio components of the trial are now recognized as important, astute attorneys and their image consultants invariably use videotape to present part or all of the trial to a focus group, a mock jury, or both. From this perspective the benefits of running a "mini–mock trial" become clear:

> *To assess the impact of a specific witness, a mini–mock trial is useful. . . . This format can produce honest feedback on the one specific witness, plus other aspects of the case, and assist in witness preparation. You can learn first impressions of the witness and reactions to the witness's dress, non-verbal language and tone of voice, as well as what [the juror] did and did not sense about the witnesses's testimony.* (Bennett & Hirschhorn, 1993, pp. 49–50)

In the Courtroom

The same information-gathering and measurement techniques that are used in jury selection for purposes of image measurement are also used in the courtroom. Consider the example of Jo-Ellan Dimitrius. Jo-Ellan Dimitrius, jury and trial consultant to the defense in the O. J. Simpson case, made maximum use of these tools of the trained social scientist.

Dimitrius's work for the defense was complex. She used four surveys before the O. J. Simpson trial began to assess community attitudes toward Simpson, the prosecution, and potential defense arguments. She also used two groups of mock jurors before the trial began. Finally, Dimitrius picked eight questions from the 85-page jury questionnaire that strongly predicted a juror's vote. By the time the trial began, Dimitrius and her three assistants had created a seven-page synopsis, or "face sheet," for each prospective juror ("The Road to Panama City," 1995).

If you watched more than a few days of the O. J. Simpson trial on television, you probably saw a woman seated only a few feet from the jury who intently studied the nonverbal communication of each juror. The woman was trial consultant Jo-Ellan Dimitrius. If you watched the many talk shows that provided instant analyses of a day or week in the same trial, you may have seen Dimitrius. Before the trial was over, she would not of course talk about her multiple methods for gathering detailed information or how she used that information. Instead she stressed that a defendant who is to receive the strongest defense has a right to jury and trial consultant.

The four focus groups and mock juries that Dimitrius used during the trial were concerned, to a large extent, with image analysis. Thus, the mock jurors rated all attorneys on a variety of personal qualities that ranged from honesty to effectiveness. This information indicated that by the end of the trial, all of the prosecution attorneys ranked lower on impressions made in the courtroom than the defense attorneys. This same data showed that Johnnie Cochran made the most favorable impression among defense attorneys; he was followed by Barry Scheck. Not surprisingly, Cochran and Scheck were chosen to make the closing defense arguments to the jury with Cochran assuming the largest share of this responsibility ("The Road to Panama City," 1995).

The fact that Jo-Ellan Dimitrius became a key member of an O. J. Simpson defense team that was composed of nationally famous lawyers known as the Dream Team should not be surprising. As we shall see, jury and trial consultant "Cat" Bennett was a highly valued member of attorney Roy Black's defense team in the William Kennedy Smith rape trial. Increasingly, top courtroom attorneys are relying on the detailed professional advice of consultants who are experts in the impression function of nonverbal communication in the courtroom.

Nonverbal Impression Formation and Management in the Courtroom

In the final section of this chapter, I will draw on a set of interrelated studies that I and my colleagues have done on impression formation and management in the courtroom or hearing room. The focus of this research is on the functions served by various types of nonverbal communicative behaviors or cues. We will look briefly at relevant parts in the Anita Hill–Clarence Thomas hearings and the William Kennedy Smith and O. J. Simpson trials.

Few prototypes exist for the types of research we are about to present. One example stands out, however. Aron, Fast, and Klein, in the 1987 supplement to their *Trial Communication Skills,* do an in-depth analysis of the communication that occurred when Lt. Col. Oliver North took the stand at a congressional hearing in the summer of 1987. North appeared to defend his role in the Contragate hearings.

Much of analysis by Aron, Fast, and Klein focuses on the multiple functions of nonverbal communication in a congressional hearing room. The researchers gave detailed attention to how North used his own nonverbal communication to dissociate himself from an imposing list of "negative images" that had been claimed for him by parts of the media, political opponents, and concerned citizens. North used nonverbal communication skillfully not only to dissociate himself from these negative images but to associate himself with some contrasting, positive images.

Consider the following example to appreciate North's skillful work as an impression manager. The authors of *Trial Communication Skills* wrote:

> There was one classic exchange when North projected this side of his personality. North said that he thought every penny of the remaining profits from the arms sale should go to the Nicaraguan resistance. When reminded that Albert Hakim was not so willing to turn over the money, North said, "Give me ten minutes with Mr. Hakim." When asked if after 10 minutes he could get Hakim to turn over the money, North responded, "If I can meet with anybody without a bunch of lawyers around, I reckon I could, sir!" and then he broke out into a big grin. (p. 21)

North used this brief exchange to claim four positive images for himself: he was a macho guy, he was a regular guy, he was a nice guy, and he was a truthful person who was up again lawyers who were trying to twist his words. Thus, North used the principle of association discussed in Chapter 10 on impression management. He was able to dissociate himself from a set of highly negative images claimed for him by his opponents while claiming a contrasting, positive set of images for himself via his own communicative behavior on the witness stand.

Finally, the even more central role of nonverbal factors in positively shaping North's image was evident when the authors wrote that "The most obvious image created by North was that of the uniform. Bedecked with medals for valor in battle, wearing the uniform of our country, he contrasted sharply with the politicians and lawyers in their blue suits and red ties" (p. 20).

Thus:

> *The expectation of North was of a devious, sleazy, power-hungry "loose cannon."*
> *Instead, he looked like the all-American boy. His short hair, furrowed brow, and*
> *the gap in his teeth all diffused the image of Dr. Strangelove portrayed by the me-*
> *dia before his testimony began. The short haircut played on the nostalgia of the*
> *1950s. Today, the American People yearn for the old days when things were sim-*
> *pler. North's straight-forward patriotism appealed to this feeling.* (p. 20)

The Anita Hill–Clarence Thomas Senate Hearings

Nonverbal communication does not of course always assume the central role in impression management. Indeed, in the confrontation between Clarence Thomas and Anita Hill before the Senate Judiciary Committee the content of the verbal exchanges was probably of primary importance. Nonetheless, nonverbal communication played a very important role in shaping the impressions that the protagonists made—particularly Judge Clarence Thomas.

In a book chapter titled "Impression Management Mismatch on Capitol Hill: The Anita Hill–Clarence Thomas Confrontation" (Leathers, 1996), I examine the dynamics of impression management in this situation in detail. A careful look at this publication would certainly contribute to a fuller understanding of and appreciation for this section of this chapter.

Clarence Thomas was of course President Bush's nominee to the United States Supreme Court. Anita Hill worked under Thomas's supervision at the U.S. Department of Education's Office for Civil Rights in 1981 and 1982 and at the Equal Employment Opportunity Commission (EEOC) from 1982 to 1983. Thomas had already undergone weeks of interrogation by the Senate Judiciary Committee before the fateful day of October 11, 1991. Witnesses by the score had appeared before the committee, and three volumes of more than 2,200 pages were already devoted to the hearings.

The charges that triggered the confrontation between Hill and Thomas on Capitol Hill were both explicit and sensational in nature. On October 11, 1991, Hill charged that Thomas repeatedly talked to her about sexual acts that he had seen in pornographic films that included women having sex with animals and group sex or rape scenes. Hill asserted that Thomas talked a good deal about pornographic material depicting large penises and breasts. He also commented pointedly about his own sexual prowess with particular emphasis on the pleasure he had given to women with oral sex. Hill asserted that Thomas once picked up a can of Coke while they were meeting together in Thomas's office and said "Who has put pubic hair on my Coke?" (Smolow, 1991, p. 38). Hill alleged furthermore that Thomas alluded to the large penis of a pornographic film actor by referring to the film character's name as Long Dong Silver. Finally, Hill claimed that after embarrassing and humiliating her with such references to sex, Thomas said to her at a dinner celebrating Hill's last day at EEOC that "if I [Hill] ever told anyone of his behavior, that it would ruin his career" (Smolow, 1991, p. 39).

From the moment that Anita Hill made these charges, the Republicans' impression management team moved quickly to try to destroy Anita Hill's credibility. In terms of political pragmatism, it was either destroy or be destroyed. Either Anita Hill's credibility had to be destroyed (or seriously damaged) or Clarence Thomas's own credibility would be destroyed. The latter would have been disastrous for the Republicans because the obvious result would be that Clarence Thomas would join the ranks of such failed Supreme Court nominees as Robert Bork.

In any attempt to destroy Anita Hill's credibility, Republican members of the Senate Judiciary Committee claimed eight major negative images for her. They included the assertion that Anita Hill was a spurned woman; Anita Hill was a prudish woman who experienced "sexual fantasies" as a result of a mental disorder known as erotomania; and Anita Hill was a malevolently motivated, unfair person who was trying to force Clarence Thomas to bear the unbearable burden of the stereotype of the sexually well-endowed, active, and promiscuous black man. The impression management confrontation that took place at the verbal level via a debate about the accuracy of these image claims was important.

The Republican impression managers also used nonverbal communication artfully to communicate implicit messages at the subconscious level. Their basic type of nonverbal persuasion was indirect suggestion. Recognizing that indirect suggestion requires the use of emotional rather than rational appeals, they focused on the controlled display of emotions, particularly by the two central players who proved to be most adept at nonverbal communication: Clarence Thomas and Senator Orrin Hatch.

In some respects Judge Clarence Thomas proved to be very skillful nonverbally. He used his own nonverbal skills to communicate a set of emotions that were consistent with and served to reinforce his contention that he was innocent of the charges. Consider this example of Thomas's reactions to Hatch's statements:

Senator Hatch: I know it outrages you, as it would anybody who is accused of these activities.

[Thomas nods his head up and down as if to signal agreement with Hatch that he is innocent of Anita Hill's charges.]

Senator Hatch: Hill says that he [Thomas] discussed oral sex between men and women.

[Thomas stops nodding his head up and down vertically and begins to shake his head horizontally from side to side as if to communicate denial.]

Senator Hatch: She then said in this statement—and this is the second—after brief discussions about work he would turn the conversation to discussions about sexual interests.

[Thomas continues to shake his head from side to side seemingly to communicate denial and closes his eyes as if to suggest disgust.]

Senator Hatch: And you have denied each and every one of these allegations last night.

[Thomas sighs deeply as one often does when experiencing intense and troubling emotions, displays a discernible expression of facial anger, and shakes his head up and down vigorously as if to affirm his denial of all of these charges.]

Senator Hatch: On several occasions, Thomas told me graphically of his own sexual prowess.

[Thomas begins shaking his head from side to side in denial at the precise moment that Hatch repeats Hill's charges, closes his eyes with an expression that might be described as agony, and finally flashes a facial expression of contempt.]

Senator Hatch: Don't worry, Judge, probably before the weekend's out they will find somebody who will say that.

The primary medium of nonverbal communication Thomas and Hatch used, however, was their voice or vocal cues. We established in Chapter 8 that vocal cues may rival personal appearance in their impact on impressions made. Thomas and Hatch seemed to be acutely aware of the importance of vocalic communication in impression management.

More specifically, both Clarence Thomas and Senator Hatch proved adept at using their voices to communicate a given emotion or to make a desired impression. When Thomas used his face and hands to communicate a given emotion, such as disgust, he also used the pitch, volume, and intensity of his voice to reinforce that emotion.

Thomas probably reached a peak of effectiveness in using his voice to communicate emotions when he said, "Senator I would have preferred an assassin's bullet to this kind of living hell that they have put me and my family through." Thomas delivers each of these words with great vocal emphasis and intensity, and his eyes appear to "tear up" at the end. Thomas pounces on the words "me and my family" through enunciation, increased volume, and vocal intensity and emphasis. Similarly, when Thomas is talking about being unfairly stereotyped as a sexually well-endowed and sexually active black man, Thomas says, "And once you pin it on me, I can't get it off." As he utters these twelve words, Thomas slows his speaking rate way down to emphasize each word, and he thumps the table in front of him with his index finger each time he utters one of these words.

Senator Hatch also proved to be a master at using his voice for emotional effect. One of his most interesting techniques is to increase the pitch of his voice drastically at the end of a strategically important question. The rapid increase in pitch clearly communicates the idea that Hatch is incredulous and suggests that the expected answer to Hatch's question is no. This is one of the techniques that Hatch used to "lead" Thomas through his questioning. Consider the following example:

Senator Hatch: People hearing yesterday's testimony are probably wondering could this quiet, you know, retiring, woman know about something like "Long Dong Silver"? Did you tell her that?

[As Hatch asks Thomas this question, there is a sharp increase in the pitch of Hatch's voice, as if to suggest, "I am incredulous. Surely, a man of your character did not tell her that."]

Senator Hatch: ...if you wanted to seduce her, is this the kind of language you would use? Is this the kind of language a reasonable person would use, is this the kind of language that anybody would use who wanted a relationship?

[As Hatch finishes this series of questions to Thomas, there is once again a sharp rise in the pitch of his voice as if to suggest that he can't believe this and expects Thomas to answer no.]

Although Thomas used nonverbal communication skillfully to communicate a set of intended emotions, he was not successful in making the impression that he was telling the truth. In fact, the results from a systematic study that compared their baseline behaviors with the nonverbal behaviors they exhibited during the Senate hearing suggest that Clarence Thomas, and not Anita Hill, was being deceptive during the televised Senate hearings. Thomas exhibited a shift toward deception on six of seven nonverbal behaviors that have previously been identified as reliable indicators of deception: stutters, illustrators (which decrease for Type I deception but increase for Type II deception), self-adaptors, object adaptors, postural shifts, and speaking rate (Leathers, Vaughn, Sanchez, & Bailey, in press).

Interestingly, a number of nonverbal behaviors that have previously proved to be indicators of deception accelerated markedly when Thomas responded to high-stress questions. Consider, for example, Thomas's response to the question from Senator Biden as to what he did at Anita Hill's apartment:

Thomas: ...and she asked me, ah, to drop in or, ah, to continue discussion and I would have, ah, uh, uh, a Coke or a beer or something and leave, um, that was, ah, again nothing I thought nothing of it, it was, uh, uh, purely innocent on my part and nothing occurred, uh, with respect to that other than those conversations.

During Thomas's answer to the question about the nature of his actions at Anita Hill's apartment, a number of his nonverbal behaviors accelerated markedly. The number of "ahs" exhibited per minute went from 5.56 on the average to 21 per minute at this point in his Senate testimony. Thomas's eye shifts went from an average of 12.29 per minute to 15 per minute during this answer, and his blink rate increased from an average of 8.82 per minute to 12 per minute.

The most striking change in Thomas's nonverbal behavior during his answer to this particular question, however, was his speaking rate. His average speaking rate during his Senate testimony was 136.27 words per minute (in the baseline, Thomas spoke at the rather slow rate of 110 words per minute). While he was speaking about his actions at Anita Hill's apartment, his speaking rate rose to 176 words per minute or 60 percent faster than Thomas spoke in the baseline segments where his veracity was not at issue.

The William Kennedy Smith Rape Trial

William Smith was virtually unknown to the general public in 1991 as he contemplated a trip to Palm Beach, Florida, to be with his close relatives over the Easter weekend. However, his anonymity was suddenly transformed into international celebrity as a result of events that transpired during the late evening of Good Friday and the early morning hours of Holy Saturday.

William Smith met a 29-year-old woman at a local bar. He invited her back to the mansion where he was staying. Subsequently, William Smith's female companion charged that he raped her on the grounds of the mansion. He was indicted, charged with rape, and brought to trial.

William Smith and his multiple advisors instantly recognized that he faced an impression management problem of major proportions. He may have been charged and indicted for rape even if his name were simply William Smith. His name, however, was William *Kennedy* Smith. The fact that William Smith was a Kennedy meant that he would immediately be perceived to have not only an ancestral link with Camelot but to be authenticated by his bloodlines as a member of "America's first dysfunctional family."

In doing an impression management analysis of this trial, it is particularly useful to employ a problem-solution format. William Smith had, of course, multiple problems as his rape trial approached, but certainly one of his most serious problems was the highly negative images claimed for him by an important part of the print media—articles done on William Kennedy Smith and the Kennedy family by respected magazines such as *Esquire, Maclean's, Newsweek,* and *Time.*

As a member of the Kennedy family, Smith lost his personal identity. He became part of a family that had repeatedly been associated with scandal. In the magazines that wrote articles on William Smith, the Kennedy family was referred to as America's first dysfunctional family, a starcrossed dynasty, degenerates, and self-preoccupied hedonists who were "finished."

Newsmagazines claimed even more negative images for William Kennedy Smith because he was a Kennedy man, Sen. Ted Kennedy was his uncle, and Smith was an accused rapist. Over and over the Kennedy men were labeled as sexual aggressors, exploiters of women, philanderers, and insensitive adventurers. Secondly, William Kennedy Smith was repeatedly linked with "Uncle" Ted Kennedy in a highly unflattering way. Ted Kennedy has been the object of some of the most highly negative labeling in terms of image qualities of any public figure in memory: woman chaser, selfish hedonist who is self-absorbed, "Joy Boy," drunk, self-destructive, reckless, and jaded. Finally, William Kennedy Smith's image was damaged by virtue of the fact that not only was he to stand trial for rape but also that unnamed women made additional charges of physical assault against him as he awaited trial. Specifically, William Smith's defense team would have to try to dissociate him from the labels that were repeatedly applied to him: aggressive, dominator, ferocious, animal, and power rapist.

Attorney Roy Black, who was in charge of William Kennedy Smith's defense case, recognized that Smith faced impression management problems of major proportions. In an interview in his law offices in Miami, Florida, on Thursday, May 21, 1992, with the author and Professor Tom Steinfatt, Black made several things clear. Not only was Black fully aware of the value of impression management, but he stressed the importance of dealing effectively with the impression management problems of one's client. In order to predict how the William Kennedy Smith jury would respond to the images claimed for his client, the plaintiff, witness, and members of the defense team, Roy Block stressed that he made extensive use of mock juries.

Recognizing the multidimensional nature of his impression management problem, Black moved skillfully not only to rehabilitate the image of the Kennedy family but also the image of Uncle Ted Kennedy. Nonetheless, Black recognized that his biggest challenge was to reconstruct William Smith's own image. I will draw selectively on the analysis of Leathers, Martin, and Steinfatt (1994) to give the reader a sense of how Roy Black used the principle of association to disassociate William Smith from the highly negative images just described and to associate him with a contrasting set of positive images.

The ultimate test of Black's effort to transform Smith's image would of course involve Smith's performance on the witness stand. Black recognized the importance of gaining and maintaining control in a courtroom by virtue of how the attorney uses available space. Black stressed the importance of "positioning" in the courtroom (referred to previously in this chapter as "courtroom choreography") in his interview with Steinfatt and me. He knew that where he chose to stand could have a controlling effect on William Smith's eye behaviors, for example. Thus, Black positioned himself in front of and at the rear of the jury box so that William Smith was looking directly at members of the jury whenever Black raised questions of Smith's truthfulness during his direct examination. Interestingly, Roy Black told us that he instructed Smith to look directly at the jurors and sustain eye contact with them whenever Black asked Smith directly or indirectly whether he was telling the truth.

The most serious part of the negative image of the print media from which William Smith had to dissociate himself, however, was that of the dominant, aggressive "power rapist" who lost emotional control (he had been described by females who alleged he attacked them as "ferocious" and an "animal"). It was, therefore, imperative that William Smith communicate on the witness stand in such a manner as to be perceived as an unassertive and thoughtful person who was quite unemotional in moments of high stress as his appearance on this witness stand surely was.

Once again, Roy Black began with appearance. William Smith was dressed in such a way as to make himself look "boyish" and "conservative" rather than "aggressive" and "animalistic." His haircut was extremely short and conservative; this was not a power haircut. At the same time, the discernible "wings" of his hair and a slightly unkept appearance seemed to say that Smith was hardly the macho type.

William Smith's visual communication style while on the witness stand was ideal. Smith was visually unassertive almost to the point of immobility. He claimed virtually no personal space with his nonexpansive gestures. Assertive individuals in contrast often claim considerable personal space with expansive gestures that tend to draw attention to their assumed dominance. William Smith exhibited no hand gestures, few postural shifts, and little perceptible bodily movement of any kind. His repeated use of "Sir" as he responded to Black surely reinforced the impression of a polite and considerate young man whose manner was self-effacing.

Careful study of his performance on the stand suggests that William Smith's vocalic communication may have had the greatest impact on the impression he made. Surely Black recognized that vocalic communication is known to serve a central role in the formation and management of impressions. Thus, Zuckerman and Driver (1989) emphasized the importance of vocalic communication in impression management when they wrote that "there is a large literature showing that both voice cues (e.g., pitch, intensity, etc.) and speech cues (e.g., nonfluencies, speech rate, etc.) are rich sources of interpersonal impressions" (p. 68).

We know that the sound of William Smith's voice was potentially very important because vocal cues encode impressions of aggression and power (or their opposites) powerfully (Berry, 1992). Relatedly, vocal characteristics such as pitch range and vocal intensity are central determinants of how emotional or unemotional a person is judged to be.

William Smith spoke with a very soft voice and exhibited a number of qualities of what is known as powerless speech (Hosman, 1989). His soft voice clearly suggested that he is an unassertive if not downright timid person. Relatedly, the fact that Smith often filled his frequent and long pauses with dysfluencies such as "ah" and "um" meant that he was exhibiting a vocal style that has been defined as "powerless." Powerless speech in turn tends to nurture the impression that a person is unassertive, hesitant, and perhaps even weak (Johnson & Vinson, 1990).

Finally, there were two other salient characteristics of William Smith's vocalic communication on the stand that suggested that he was a highly unemotional and deliberative person: (a) he paused for long periods of time before he responded to Roy Black's questions (i.e., he had extended response latency), and (b) his pitch range was very narrow. The fact that Smith characteristically paused for many seconds before responding to Black's questions clearly suggested that he is a disciplined person who keeps himself under emotional control. The fact that Smith talked in a flat voice with almost no variation in his pitch clearly communicated the similar idea that Smith is an unemotional person—the greater the variation in a person's pitch range the more emotional that person is generally perceived to be (Scherer, 1988).

In short, William Smith's vocalic communication on the stand was such as to deny the validity of the print media's image of him: an aggressive, ferocious animal who was known for his lack of emotional control. William Kennedy Smith claimed an image for himself on the stand via his nonverbal communication that contrasted strikingly with the print media's image: *unassertive, unassuming, pleasant, courteous, thoughtful,* and *under emotional control.*

The O. J. Simpson Murder Trial

The O. J. Simpson murder trial surely fascinated millions of Americans. The preliminary hearing alone was watched by 25 to 30 million people. Combined Nielsen ratings for ABC, CBS, and NBC were up 24 percent over normal. CNN's viewership peaked at 7 P.M. with about 1.9 million homes tuned in (Kloer, 1994). The trial itself is widely recognized as the trial of the century.

O. J. Simpson is a national celebrity and has been for some time. In 1968 he led the University of Southern California to a national championship in football and won the Heisman trophy. In 1969 the Buffalo Bills made him the first pick in the pro football draft. In 1973 Simpson became the first person to rush for more than 2,000 yards in one season. He retired from pro football in 1979 and in 1983 he joined ABC-TV as a commentator for Monday Night Football. In 1985 Simpson was inducted into pro football's Hall of Fame. In 1988 Simpson began appearing as Nordberg in the *Naked Gun* movies. On Friday, June 17, 1994, O. J. Simpson was arrested for the double murder of his ex-wife Nicole and her friend Ron Goldman ("O.J.'s Timelines," 1994). The courtroom phase of the Simpson murder did not begin until January 1995. The trial ended on October 3, 1995, with O. J. Simpson's acquittal on both charges of murder.

Many months and years will be required to analyze all of the complex parts of this case. Because the trial ended just before the third edition of this book went to the publisher, a detailed analysis of the role of nonverbal communication in this trial must be presented in future editions. We can, nonetheless, focus attention on the kinds of exciting research that may be done on this trial by nonverbal communication researchers.

Impression management researchers will probably devote more attention to the defense than to the prosecution. This is because the defense made full use of image consultants. They did so from the time the jury was chosen until the final defense arguments were made to the jury. In this regard some of the actions of defense jury and trial consultant Jo-Ellan Dimitrius we have already described in this chapter in the section on the logistics of measuring impressions. For reasons that are not entirely clear, the prosecution decided not to use the advice of a jury consultant during *voir dire*. Moreover, there is no evidence to suggest that the prosecution relied on one or more image analysts throughout all phases of the O. J. Simpson trial.

In its efforts to manage impression in the courtroom, the defense team faced many problems and challenges. The following five seem worthy of attention: (a) How would the defense dissociate O. J. Simpson from the highly negative "private face" image that the prosecution had claimed for him? (b) How would the defense deal with the repeated prosecution claims that O. J. Simpson's guilt would be proved by overwhelming scientific evidence, much of it in the form of DNA test results? (c) How could the lead defense attorney Johnnie Cochran communicate nonverbally in such a manner as to be perceived as more credible than the prosecution attorneys? (d) In what ways could and should the defense control the image O. J. Simpson claimed for himself via his "silent testimony" in the courtroom? and (e) What impression management techniques could the defense team use to help destroy the credibility of key prosecution witnesses while they were on the stand.

The prosecution recognized that O. J. Simpson's highly positive public image would be difficult to attack effectively. They conceded that his public image as a sports hero, a pleasant pitchman for Hertz, a smiling and affable sports commentator, and a good-natured if bumbling foil for Leslie Nielson in the *Naked Gun* movies gave the defense a great advantage.

As soon as O. J. Simpson was charged with double murders, however, his image came under sustained attack by much of the media. *Newsweek* led the attack on Simpson's image with an article titled "The Double Life of O. J." in its August 29, 1994, issue. The negative images claimed for Simpson included a black man who "doggedly worked to fit into the white world," a "carouser" who pursued "white" women, a celebrity golfer who only occasionally visited poor black neighborhoods, a manipulator who practiced his diction so that he would sound more "white" as a corporate spokesperson, a party guy, and a wife batterer. This image attack was followed shortly by a feature article in *Esquire* titled "The Man Behind the Mask." The author, Teresa Carpenter, began by writing that "An accomplished liar fascinates me. So I am frankly in awe of O. J. Simpson" (Carpenter, 1994, p. 84). In this article, O. J. Simpson is described as a thug in a locker room, a phony jock, a world-class womanizer, a man with a drug problem, a narcissist, a brutal wife beater, and a stalker.

The most vitriolic attack on O. J. Simpson's image, however, was mounted by Faye Resnick in her book *Nicole Brown Simpson: The Private Diary of Life Interrupted*. Resnick claimed to be Nicole Brown Simpson's closest friend. The prosecutors relied heavily on claims Resnick made in this book to mount its attack on O. J. Simpson's image during their opening statement.

Resnick graphically describes Simpson as obsessively jealous of Nicole, a bully, a stalker, an animal, a wife beater, and ultimately Nicole Brown Simpson's killer. When Nicole mentioned a former lover of hers while O. J. was present at a public gathering, Resnick wrote that

> *O. J.'s face twitched uncontrollably. His body language was extremely aggressive. Horrified, I watched as sweat poured down his face. The veins in his neck bulged. His cheekbones bunched up, twitching beneath his skin. He ground his teeth in rage and hissed at me, "Why the ... does she do this?"* (p. 9)

In his opening statement to the jury, Christopher Darden too claimed that O. J. Simpson had a Jekyl–Hyde personality. Darden began by saying that "We have been seeing the public face of the actor—the public image. We will expose the other face of O. J. Simpson in this trial." He went on to stress:

> *We will show to you the other face. The one that Nicole Brown encountered almost every day of her adult life. The face she encountered during the best moments of her adult life.... The face you will see and the man you will see is the face of a batterer, a wife beater, an abuser, a controller [long pause]. You will see the face of Ron's and Nicole's murderer.* (CNN, January 24, 1995)

How did the defense team deal with the highly negative images claimed for O. J. Simpson? Cochran's first move was perhaps his most important one. If he did not expose the jury to subliminal perception, he came very close to it. Cochran set a large photograph of O. J. Simpson and his daughter Sydney a few feet from the jury box so that it faced the jurors. He left it there for perhaps an hour during his opening statement. The photograph had been taken at Sydney's dance recital on the afternoon of June 12, 1994; the double murder of Nicole Brown Simpson and Ron Goldman occurred later the night of that same day. As the jurors studied that photograph, they must have been moved to question the credibility of some central prosecution claims, Christopher Darden had claimed in his opening statement that Simpson exhibited the appearance of a bitterly resentful, dazed, and zombie-like killer at daughter Sydney's dance recital. When the jurors looked at the photograph, that is hardly the Simpson they saw. The photograph showed a smiling and seemingly relaxed O. J. Simpson with his arm draped casually around has daughter. Daughter Sydney in turn had a big smile on her face.

Second, Johnnie Cochran knew that the jurors considered the wife-beating charge with its attendant negative images as irrelevant to the charges of murder. This information came to him from the mock juries assembled by trial consultant Jo-Ellan Dimitrius ("The Road to Panama City," 1995). Third, Cochran knew that the positive image that Simpson brought to court would be resistant to change in the minds of these jurors if Simpson's own nonverbal communicative behavior in court was inconsistent with the image of an emotionally undisciplined, obsessive, aggressive animal that the prosecution insisted he was. Finally, Cochran devoted one section of his opening defense statement to claiming a contrasting set of positive images for O. J. Simpson. Among other things Cochran claimed that Simpson was a benevolent man who provided money for the college education of several of Nicole's sisters, set up his father-in-law with a Hertz franchise, was an attentive and supportive father, and was a loving husband.

Cochran attacked the prosecution's "scientific" evidence in a highly original and effective way during his opening statement for the defense, He did it primarily with the use of graphic visual aids. Recognizing the power of visual stimuli, Cochran relied heavily on a set of visual aids that had highly desirable salient characteristics. They were attention gaining, easily comprehensible, and memorable. Whereas the prosecution used visual aids and graphs that seemed to flood the jurors with information overload and deadly dull DNA detail, the visual aids used by Johnnie Cochran made the point concisely and graphically.

Cochran got right to the point when he confronted the prosecution's "overwhelming" evidence. He placed a visual aid that was perhaps 3 ft by 5 ft with a purple background and white letters on an easel near the jury. The white letters spelled out the words *Integrity of Evidence*. Directly beneath these words, within a box with a brown background, were the words *Contaminated, Compromised,* and *Corrupted*. The jury would have probably gotten the point even if Cochran had not uttered a word of explanation (CNN, January 25, 1995).

Shortly thereafter Cochran placed a large photograph before the jurors that showed a woman standing virtually on top of O. J. Simpsons's Ford Bronco and peering into it; the Bronco was attached to a tow truck but obviously had not been towed out of Simpson's estate. There was no police tape or ropes around the Bronco. After noting that two coffee stains were discovered on the hood of the Bronco, Cochran comments that the "Bronco was not secured. It wasn't secured so you cannot count on that evidence."

The Ford Bronco visual was followed by a second visual aid dealing with the integrity of the evidence—the words *Integrity of Evidence* appear in red at the top of another 3-by-5 ft piece of plastic or thick cardboard that was placed near the jury. On the left side of this visual aid below the lettering *Integrity of Evidence* is a drawing of Nicole Brown Simpson's condominium, a drawing of Simpson's Rockingdale estate with the Ford Bronco parked outside, and a drawing of a partially filled blood vial. Large arrows run from the condominium, estate, and blood vial to a large box in the middle with the large letters LAPD in it. From the LAPD box, three arrows point out respectively to an LAPD badge, a police station, and the LAPD laboratory. Each of these arrows has a large question mark running through it. Cochran began by saying "Garbage in, garbage out." A person could be quite dense and still see why it was being suggested that they should dismiss the results from DNA tests. The DNA evidence allegedly had no integrity because is was contaminated, compromised, and corrupted by LAPD officers who were either conspiratorial, bumbling, or both.

To attack DNA evidence more directly, Cochran placed a new visual aid close to the jury. At the top of this diagram were these words in capital letters: **SMALL** AMOUNTS OF DNA FROM SPECKS OF BLOOD. Yes, the word *small* was highlighted on the diagram, which had a blue background. Near the bottom of this diagram was a drawing of a penny. A foot from the penny was a small dot under a box that contained the words *20 nanograms*. Another foot away was another box that contained the words *2 nanograms*. Cochran then commented with a bemused expression on his face that "What we have here is a regular penny on the left. Compare the penny with 20 nanograms of DNA. Twenty nanograms is almost like a pin prick. Much of the evidence you will be asked to make a decision on in this case will be based on a DNA sample of 2 nanograms—an amount so small you cannot see it" (CNN, January 30, 1995). The clear implication was that anything this small is untrustworthy.

Then Cochran placed two diagrams side by side next to the jury. The diagram on the left side illustrated how DNA testing should be used properly under ideal conditions in a medical setting. There were boxes for placing a check mark by clean samples, generous sample size, unmixed samples, single handling, and so on. Next to this diagram was a similar diagram, except the heading for this diagram was FORENSICS rather than MEDICAL. Not surprisingly, the DNA testing done for the LAPD in this case was forensics testing based on samples collected not in an antiseptic operating room but in the field. The boxes available for checking in this second visual aid were dirty samples, minuscule sample size, mixed samples from unknown sources, multiple handling, and so on.

Then to show how the LAPD may have contaminated and corrupted the evidence it collected, Cochran showed a large map of downtown, central, and west Los Angeles. Using a pointer flashlight, he illustrated how the lead LAPD detective took the sample of O. J. Simpson's blood and drove "all the way" out to Simpson's estate in Brentwood—a distance of more than 20 miles. Police regulations require that the police detectives take a blood sample such as this a short distance from headquarters to a lab to have it tested. In this instance, Cochran did not have to spell out the words *police conspiracy* to make members of the jury ponder why the Los Angeles police officer engaged in such an unusual practice.

Finally, Cochran placed another visual aid next to the jury that was labeled DEFENDANT'S SAMPLE OBTAINED VOLUNTARY. This chart showed that 8 ml of blood were drawn from O. J. Simpson at central police headquarters. Subsequently, the prosecution used just over 6 ml of blood to run various tests. The diagram emphasized via the bright red color in the bottom of a test vial, that 1.9 milliliters of Simpson's blood were missing. Cochran hardly had to ask "Why?" when the question had been firmly and effectively planted in the minds of the jurors.

The third question that will surely receive much attention by researchers is how, or whether, lead defense attorney Johnnie Cochran used his nonverbal communication so that he would be perceived as more credible than lead prosecution attorneys Christopher Darden and Marcia Clark. Because the opening statements are frequently considered to be the most important part of the trial, let us consider the performance of Darden, Clark, and Cochran during opening statements.

Darden delivered the first part of the opening statement for the prosecution. In his first direct reference to the jury, Darden said, "And to you ladies and gentlemen of the jury." Darden looked down as he began to make this statement, then paused and looked down again. Darden then said to the jury, "I think it is fair to say I have the toughest job in town today." He looked down as he started to make his opening, substantive statement. As Darden said good morning to the jurors, he gave them a tight, half smile. Then he paused again and looked down into his notes. Darden rarely sustained eye contact with the jury for more than a few seconds. During the first minute that he addressed the jury, Darden broke eye contact and looked down or away 12 times. He spent a maximum of one minute trying to establish common ground with the jury (CNN, January 24, 1995).

Marcia Clark picked up the opening statement by the prosecution at the point where the jury was to preview scientific evidence. Before she uttered a word, she began by coughing.

She then said, "Good morning, ladies and gentlemen." Then she looked down and smiled. She was looking down as she went on so say, "When you hear the amount of evidence we have, you will understand why I need so much help." Her tone of voice at this point seemingly had a condescending tone to it, as if she were addressing a group of young children.

Marcia Clark continued:

> *You've now heard the why. [She paused and looked down into her notes with clasped hands.] Why would Orenthal James Simpson [she paused and looked down into her notes again] commit such heinous crimes? [She paused and looked down at her notes again while her hands were crossed on the podium.] The one simple truth brought to you by Mr. Darden is that Mr. Simpson is a man not a stereotype . . . who can do both good and evil. [She looked down after every phrase in a sentence and clearly read her opening statement from a looseleaf notebook. Like Darden she flipped over a page in her notebook when she was done with it.]*

Darden and Clark clearly both used the lecture mode when they addressed this jury. Perhaps more importantly, they violated guidelines identified in Chapter 11 of this book that one must meet to enhance one's own credibility, They almost always looked down before they began to make a point; this practice has repeatedly been found to depress one's perceived competence. Moreover, they did not sustain eye contact with members of the jury and they frequently looked away from members of the jury.

In contrast, Johnnie Cochran began the defense's opening statement by saying, "Ladies and gentleman, good morning to you." Cochran looked directly at the jury before, during and after uttering these words. Cochran went on to say that "If you have had occasion to go to the movies, you know what this [opening statement] is supposed to be." His eye contact with the jury was sustained and direct. Shortly thereafter, Cochran said, "Here we are now in this search for justice." He not only sustained eye contact with the jury, but his eyes moved slowly from one juror to another as if he were trying to communicate with each juror personally.

Cochran spent at least 15 minutes trying to establish common ground with the jury whereas Darden and Clark together may have spent 2 minutes trying to achieve this objective. Fully aware of the predominantly African American makeup of the jury, Cochran said, "I guess Dr. Martin Luther King said it best when he said injustice anywhere is a threat to justice everywhere. And so we are now embarked on a search for justice—a search for truth." Cochran went on to thank the members of the jury for fulfilling the "highest test of citizenship—jury duty" and stressed that you as jurors are the "conscience of the community."

During the first part of his opening statement, Cochran never looked at his notes. The verbal and nonverbal content of his communication suggested that he was a relaxed storyteller, not a lecturer like Darden and Clark. He frequently leaned toward the jury while resting his right arm on the podium. His slow delivery when combined with effective pauses for effect suggested that the message he brought was a confidential one intended only for members of this jury. Surely, his nonverbal communication style highlights those behaviors that are known to be effective in establishing rapport.

The questions we have addressed here briefly are only a beginning. We have looked at only three members of the defense and prosecution teams and, even there, many questions remain unanswered. For example, why did Marcia Clark undergo a striking change in appearance during the trial? When Marcia Clark gave part of the opening statement for the prosecution, she was dressed in a very dark, navy blue suit; the suit was so dark as to almost appear to be black. The skirt of this expensive, conservative suit was cut several inches above the knee. She wore a white, lace blouse with ruffles with a white bow at the top. Her hair was curly and covered part of her ears.

From the perspective of personal appearance, a very different Marcia Clark gave the final part of the closing argument for the prosecution. Rather than a business suit she wore a light, off-white, two-piece outfit. The skirt was cut to the knee. The top part of the outfit was secured by eight simple, bone-colored buttons. She wore a thin, gold necklace. Her hairstyle had been changed so that her hair was now entirely straight.

Do you believe that Marcia Clark's change in appearance was just a matter of whim? Or do you believe that it was done to modify the impression she was making in the courtroom? If so, what image was Marcia Clark trying to claim by her modified personal appearance? If you refer back to the section on personal appearance in this chapter, you will see that Smith and Malandro have maintained that attorneys must decide whether they wish to make personal appearance choices that will maximize either their credibility or their approachability/likability. Because it is widely conceded that Marcia Clark is a brilliant attorney, certainly she had no need to enhance her credibility.

Perhaps she made a conscious attempt to dissociate herself from an image of being aggressive, abrasive, and cold by softening her personal appearance so that she would be perceived as more approachable and likable. An article in the *San Francisco Chronicle* (Chiang, 1994, p. A1) suggested that that was precisely what Marcia Clark was trying to do. Whereas she was being perceived as "steely" and "hard-edged," Marcia Clark's image consultant worked to "soften" her image by the noted changes in her personal appearance.

What about Judge Lance Ito? At minimum, a judge serves the central role in regulating communicative interaction in the courtroom. Detailed analysis will be necessary to determine whether he fulfilled this function fairly. More important, perhaps, did Judge Ito reveal a bias for either the prosecution or defense by his nonverbal communication?

The fact that both the prosecution and defense thought that Judge Ito was unfair to them at times may suggest that he exhibited a certain balance in his courtroom decorum. Marcia Clark thought that Ito reacted negatively to her unseemly aggressiveness as a woman. Clark "felt she had to pretend to play a deferential submissive female role with him" (Chula-Eoan & Gleick, 1995, p. 54). By contrast, Barry Scheck of the defense team said that "Judge Ito was so outrageous that I had to talk to the jury by using objections. He might as well have taken a seat at the prosecution table" (Franks, 1995, p. 57). Defense attorney Peter Neufeld was also disappointed with Judge Ito because he thought Ito was too concerned with his status as a celebrity. Neufeld was particularly shocked on the day that Ito asked all of the lawyers to come into his chambers to have them watch a clip of the "Dancing Itos" from Jay Leno's *Tonight Show*. The spoof with Ito playing drums with his gavel delighted Ito. He thought it was hilarious (Chula-Eoan & Gleick, 1995).

Finally, there is the important question of what factors shaped the impressions made by key prosecution and defense witnesses as they appeared on the witness stand. Did defense witnesses in general make more favorable impressions than prosecution witnesses because they were carefully rehearsed whereas prosecution witness were not? Did the nonverbal communication of a number of officers of the Los Angeles Police Department on the stand strongly affect the negative impressions they made? In that regard what type of impression did some of the other witnesses—such as LAPD criminalist Dennis Fung, colead LAPD investigator Phillip Vanaetter, and glove expert Richard Rubin—make on you and why?

Summary

This chapter began by stressing the functional importance of nonverbal communication in the courtroom. The legal profession leads the way in the use of image consultants. Research on nonverbal communication in the courtroom has a twofold focus. First emphasis is placed on the functions of nonverbal behaviors and cues as attorneys seek to manage impressions formed by jury members or other members of their legal team, their clients, their witness, and themselves. Second, researchers are monitoring judges' nonverbal behaviors and cues to determine if they are revealing either positive or negative biases toward members of a legal team, clients, and witnesses.

Personal appearance, kinesic behavior, the use of space, and vocal cues serve the most important functions of nonverbal communication in the courtroom. Personal appearance is particularly important in shaping the impressions made by the central players in a courtroom. A basic decision that lawyers and others must make is whether they wish to dress to enhance their credibility or their approachability. Courtroom choreography, or the use of space by attorneys, has recently become a particularly important subject. Attorneys can exercise control of the direction of the eye contact of individuals on the witness stand by where they stand in the courtroom.

In an age where top courtroom attorneys rely heavily on jury and trial consultants the logistics of measuring impressions made in the courtroom is particularly important. This section of the chapter defines and illustrates the three major tools used by social scientists who work as consultants: questionnaires, focus groups, and mock juries. The chapter also describes the process or steps that must be followed to evaluate information obtained by the use of these tools.

Finally, this chapter gives detailed attention to nonverbal impression formation and management in the courtroom by focusing on three recent and highly publicized legal confrontations: the Anita Hill–Clarence Thomas Senate hearings, the William Kennedy Smith rape trial, and the O. J. Simpson murder case. These analyses demonstrate the importance of the impression management function of nonverbal communication in the courtroom.

References

Anthony, P. K., & Vinson, C. E. (1987). Nonverbal communication in the courtroom. You don't say? *Trial Diplomacy, 39,* 35–37.

Aron, R., Fast, J., & Klein, R. B. (1986). *Trial communication skills.* New York: McGraw-Hill.

Aron, R, Fast, J., & Klein, R. B. (1987 Supplement). *Trial Communication Skills.* New York: McGraw-Hill.

Barge, J. K., Schlueter, D. W., & Pritchard, A. (1989). The effects of nonverbal communication and gender on impression formation in opening statements. *The Southern Communication Journal, 54,* 330–349.

Bennett, C. E., & Hirschhorn, R. B. (1993). *Bennett's guide to jury selection and trial dynamics in civil and criminal litigation.* St. Paul, MN: West.

Berry, D. (1992). Vocal types and stereotypes: Joint effect of vocal attractiveness and vocal maturity on person perception. *Journal of Nonverbal Behavior, 16,* 41–54.

Blanck, P. D., Rosenthal, R., & Cordell, L. H. (1985). The appearance of justice: Judges' verbal and nonverbal behavior in criminal jury trials. *Stanford Law Review, 38,* 89–184.

Burke, D. W., Ames, M. A., Etherington, R., & Pietsch, J. (1990). Effects of victim's and defendant's physical attractiveness on the perception of responsibility in an ambiguous domestic violence case. *Journal of Family Violence, 5,* 190–207.

Carpenter, T. (1994, November). The man behind the mask. *Esquire,* 84–100.

Chiang, H. (1994, October 17). Marcia Clark's new look irks female lawyers. *San Francisco Chronicle,* p. A1.

Chula-Eoan, H., & Gleick, E. (1995, October 16). Making the case. *Time* (Special Edition), 48–72.

Darby, B. W., & Jeffers, D. (1988). The effects of defendant and juror attractiveness on simulated courtroom trial decisions. *Social Behavior and Personality, 16,* 39–50.

deTurck, M. A., & Goldhaber, G. M. (1988). Perjury and deceptive judgments: How the timing and modality of witness deception affects jurors' deceptive judgments. *Communication Quarterly , 36,* 276–289.

The double life of O. J. (1994, August 29). *Newsweek,* 43–49.

Franks, L. (1995, October 16). Bitter harvest: Victory in hand, O. J.'s lawyers turn on each other. *People,* 55–58.

Hosman, L. (1989). The evaluative consequences of hedges, hesitations, and intensifiers: Power and powerless speech styles. *Human Communication Research, 15,* 383–406.

Johnson, C., & Vinson, L. (1990). Placement and frequency of powerless talk and impression formation. *Communication Quarterly, 38,* 325–333.

Kloer, P. (1994, July 2). 25 to 30 million watch TV hearing. *The Atlanta Journal/The Atlanta Constitution,* p. A12.

Leathers, D. G. (1996). Impression management mismatch on Capitol Hill: The Anita Hill–Clarence Thomas confrontation. In Sandra Ragan, Christina Beck, Lynda Lee Kaid, and Dianne Bystrom (Eds.), *The lynching of language: gender, politics, and power in the Hill–Thomas hearings* (pp. 84–110). Champaign, IL: University of Illinois Press.

Leathers, D. G., Martin, M., & Steinfatt, T. *The William Kennedy Smith trial as an impression management phenomenon.* Paper presented at the 1994 convention of the Speech Communication Association, New Orleans, LA.

Leathers, D. G., Vaughn, Sanchez, G., & Bailey, J. (in press). Who is lying in the Anita Hill–Clarence Thomas hearings: Nonverbal communication profiles. In Paul Seigel (Ed.), *He said, she said, we listened: A communication perspective on the Hill/Thomas hearings.* Creskill, NJ: Hampton.

Levan, E. A. (1984). Nonverbal communication in the courtroom: Attorney beware. *Law and Psychology Review, 8,* 83–94.

O. J.'s timeline. (1994, June 27). *The Atlanta Constitution,* p. A3.

Pettus, A. B. (1990). The verdict is in: A study of jury decision-making factors, moment of personal decision, and jury deliberations—from the juror's point of view. *Communication Quarterly, 38,* 83–97.

Pryor, B., & Buchanan, R. (1984). The effects of a defendant's demeanor on your perception of credibility and guilt. *Journal of Communication, 34,* 92–99.

Rasicot, J. (1985). *Jury selection, body language & the visual trial.* Minneapolis, MN: AB Publications.

Resnick, F. D. (1994). *Nicole Brown Simpson: The private diary of a life interrupted.* Beverly Hills, CA: Dove.

Rieke, R. D., & Stutman, R. (1990). *Communication in legal advocacy.* Columbia, SC: University of South Carolina Press.

The road to Panama City: How a jury consultant got O. J. back on the first tee. (1995, October 30), *Newsweek.*

Ryan, M. E., & Syald, D. (1993). Women in the courtroom: Increasing credibility through nonverbal behavior change. *Trial Diplomacy Journal, 16,* 253–258.

Scherer, K. R. (1988). On the symbolic functions of vocal affect expression. *Journal of Language & Social Psychology, 7,* 79–100.

Sigal, J. Braden-Maguire, J. Hayden, J., & Mosley, N. (1985). The effects of presentation style and sex of lawyer on jury decision-making behavior. *Psychology, 22,* 13–19.

Smith, L. J., & Malandro, L. A. (1985). *Courtroom communication strategies.* New York: Kluwer.

Smolow, J. (1991, October 21). She said, he said. *Time,* 36–40.

Varinsky, H., & Nomikos, L. (1990). Post-verdict interviews: Understanding jury decision making. *Trial, 26,* 64–66.

Vinson, D. E. (1982). Juries: Perception and the decision-making process. *Trial, 18,* 52–55.

Wolfe, J. S. (1985). Courtroom choreography: Systematic use of the courtroom. *Trial Diplomacy Journal,* 28–36.

Wood, W. R. (1985). Preparation for voir dire. *Trial, 8,* 17–19.

Wuensch, K. L., Castellow, W. A., & Moore, C. H. (1991). Defendant attractiveness and type of crime on juridic judgment. *Journal of Social Behavior and Personality, 6,* 713–724.

Zuckerman, M., & Driver, R. D. (1989). What sounds beautiful is good: The vocal attractiveness stereotype. *Journal of Nonverbal Behavior 13,* 67–82.

Chapter *19*

The Communicative Impact of Microenvironmental Variables

In the latter portion of this book, we have examined the role of nonverbal behaviors in such important contexts as the job interview, the counseling interview, male–female interaction, intercultural communication, physician–patient communication, and the courtroom. This concluding chapter focuses on the impact of microenvironmental variables on communication in important public settings where we frequently interact with others.

Recently, social scientists have become increasingly interested in the impact of environments, and their distinctive physical features, on our perceptions, attitudes, and behaviors (Sommer, 1983). The macroenvironment and microenvironment both function as powerful mediums of communication. Urban planners have established that the affective tone of our perceptions is strongly influenced by such features of our macroenvironment as the physical dimensions of streets, paths, and districts (Lynch, 1960; Leathers, 1976). We now know that such microenvironmental variables affect both land value and crime rate in Tokyo (Hanyu, 1993). Similarly, communication researchers have demonstrated that spatial relationships in the microenvironment may exert a controlling influence on both the quality and the quantity of communicative interaction (Burgoon, 1978; Sundstrom, 1989).

Sommer (1969) emphasized the need to know more about the impact of microenvironments on individuals who engage in face-to-face interaction within their confines when he wrote that

> *Knowledge about man's immediate environment, the hollows within his shelters that he calls offices, classrooms, corridors, and hospital wards, is as important as knowledge about outer space or undersea life. . . . With or without explicit recognition of the fact, designers are shaping people as well as buildings.* (p. vii)

The *environments* within which we interact with others vary widely in scope from entire cities to small groups. The terms *microenvironment* and *proximate environment* are used interchangeably. The proximate environment of a student in a classroom includes the student's desk, the other students, the teacher, the chalkboard, the windows, and the doorway (Sommer, 1966). Frequently included as central, defining features of microenvironments are furniture, lighting, color choice, decorative items, and, most importantly, the amount of space available and the way that it is used (Sommer, 1969; Sommer, 1974; Sommer, 1983).

Designers of microenvironments such as the business office have been concerned almost exclusively with functional questions. Thus, Konar and Sundstrom (1986) wrote that "the symbolic qualities of those workspaces and offices have typically received far less attention in this context" (p. 203). Today that perspective is changing. Designers still are concerned with such practical questions as how many offices they can get in a building with so many square feet and with the most efficient way to light such a building, but they are concerned with more. Designers of corporate microenvironments are also highly concerned with the communicative significance of their decisions in terms of their impact on the corporate image, on customers and clients, and on the behaviors of employees.

Physical features of the office microenvironment can and frequently do serve important communicative functions. They can, for example, define or demarcate the status of the occupant of an office. *Status markers* that serve this communicative function include *furnishings, location, privacy, size,* and *personalization* (Konar & Sundstrom, 1986). Similarly, we also know that the presence or absence of aesthetic and professionally related objects can exert a significant effect on the credibility of the occupant of a faculty office (Miles & Leathers, 1984).

The *design* of the furniture placed in a microenvironment is also an important variable. Considerable research has already been done on the communicative impact of furniture design. Some scholars have concluded that furniture design can communicate specific meanings to users of the furniture (Knachstedt, 1980; Mehrabian & Diamond, 1971; Stacks & Burgoon, 1981); communicate information about an owner's attitude or personality (Argyle & Dean, 1965; Kleeman, 1981; Mehrabian, 1968; 1969; Pile, 1979; Yee & Gustafson, 1983); and contribute to individual differences in affiliative behavior, most notably during user interaction and conversation (Kleeman, 1981; Yee and Gustafson, 1983).

Finally, the *placement* of objects in the microenvironment is very important. For example, companies who own supermarkets know that there is a strong relationship between where a particular type of merchandise is displayed and how much is sold (Sommer, Wynes, & Brinkley, 1992). Even morticians take great care in where they display their caskets. Thus, expensive and inexpensive caskets are rarely displayed next to each other. Emling (1995) stressed that "in principle, a casket showroom is not unlike a new car showroom, or a furniture showroom. Funeral homes place the most expensive caskets near the front of the showroom, the cheap models to the rear" (p. E4). In fact, you may not even be able to find the most inexpensive caskets in some mortuaries if you are not accompanied by a private detective.

Context as Communication

In one sense, it is easy to embrace the old axiom that "Meaning is in people, not in things." The latest thinking and empirical research on the communicative significance of context suggests that this view is both narrow and misleading, however. In fact, Rapoport in his innovative book *The Meaning of the Built Environment: A Nonverbal Communication Approach* (1982) argued that things both elicit and communicate meanings.

Rapoport contended not only that the physical features of the built environment affect communication but also that context is communication. He wrote that

> things do elicit meanings.... *Put differently, the question is how (and, of course whether) meanings can be encoded in things in such a way that they can be decoded by the intended users.... I assume...that physical elements of the environments* do *encode information that people decode.* (p. 19)

Rapoport (1982), Hall (1974), and Sommer (1983) provided impressive support for the thesis that environments, and more particularly the distinctive physical features of given environments, do communicate meaning. The argument is based on the assumption that individuals' communicative behaviors are directly affected by the "meanings" that environments have for them. These individuals, in turn, assume that the placement of furniture or the use of decorative items on a wall in a business office represents a conscious and purposive decision made by a human being. Such features of the microenvironment, therefore, serve a "latent" rather than a "manifest" communicative function. Thus, "by making the selection and placement of elements in a room *purposive* these environmental elements clearly become communicative" (Rapoport, 1982, p. 13).

In short, context, and the defining features of context, *is* a distinctive form of nonverbal communication. "The growing concern about *perceived* crowding, density, crime, or environment quality implies, even if it does not make explicit, the central role of subjective factors, many of which are based on the associations and meanings that particular aspects of environment have for people" (Rapoport, 1982, p. 26).

To the extent that we can exercise conscious control over the physical features of our microenvironments, we may be forced to make a choice between environments that are arousing or pleasant. Mehrabian (1976) maintained that *high-load environments* are emotionally arousing. They are arousing because their physical features force individuals who work there to process much information or cope with many microenvironmental stimuli that are not directly relevant to the work assignment. For example, a business office that features an "open plan" having red wallpaper, no partitions to separate the desks of the occupants, high density, and excessive noise levels, is a high-load environment.

In contrast, a private business office, with walls and a door, subdued wall colors and lighting, and carpeting to control or eliminate disruptive noises, is a *low-load environment*. Although the high-load environment is emotionally arousing and promotes communicative interaction, it can be unpleasant because the collective impact of the microenvironmental stimuli produces fatigue. In contrast, the low-load environment is often perceived as pleasant because its inhabitants do not have to cope with a multitude of arousing microenvironmental stimuli. Nevertheless, low-load environments might not be sufficiently arousing for individuals who work in them, because they do not facilitate either productivity or effective communicative interaction with colleagues.

As we shall see, the physical features of microenvironments such as the places where we work affect not only our own perceptions and behaviors but also the perceptions and behaviors of individuals we encounter in those environments (Sundstrom, 1989). This is particularly true in a workplace such as a private office. The size of the work space and the way that space is used can be major status determinants. To the extent that we can control such variables as the type and placement of furniture we put in our personal office, we can exert a profound influence on the impressions we make. In fact, we now know that the decorative items we choose to put in our offices can markedly affect the defining elements of the image that we project to others. This is particularly true with regard to our personal credibility.

In many applied settings, the communicative impact of microenvironmental variables is now receiving increasing attention. The primary focus of researchers has been on public settings, although some attention is now being given to private contexts such as families (Beeghley & Donnelly, 1989) and homes. In their interesting study of the home environment in a Greek urban community, Hirschon and Gold (1982) made the valid point that the interior of the home is a private setting, whereas the exterior is a public setting:

> *It was recognized that there was a fundamental opposition between interior and exterior space: the former an exclusive realm, restricted to the family and closed to outsiders except under such special circumstances as the granting of formal hospitality to strangers; the latter a shared space, the forum for neighborly contact and social interaction.* (p. 70)

Among the communicatively significant public settings that come to mind are the courtroom (Adelsward, Aronson, Jonsson, & Linell, 1987), the hospital with its various departments, the department store, and the funeral home (Leathers, 1990). Although we interact with other persons in various real-world contexts of importance to us, four kinds of contexts will receive close scrutiny in this text. The classroom, the conference room, the office, and the fast-food restaurant seem particularly important for at least two reasons. Most of us will spend a high proportion of our waking hours in these real-world, public contexts. Moreover, our ability to exercise effective conscious control over selected physical features of such environments is greater than in other real-world contexts such as a factory or a prison. We have the potential to markedly affect the appearance of these four kinds of microenvironments by the decisions we make.

The Classroom Environment

Of the four kinds of public settings considered here, the classroom represents the microenvironment that is least susceptible to change. This is true in large part because of an apparent conflict between the objectives of administrators on the one hand and those of the students and teachers on the other hand. To a considerable degree, administrators are committed to the development of a distraction-free classroom environment, one that minimizes student interaction and affective response while maximizing the potential to regulate and control students' behaviors. In contrast, students and teachers prefer a classroom environment that minimizes the use of control mechanisms while maximizing opportunities for uninhibited communicative interaction.

Administrators who are committed to the traditional classroom environment prefer fixed, straight-row seating; high density; and drab, institutional colors. Experimental seating arrangements and emotionally arousing colors are thought to produce a level of stimulation for the student that is incompatible with effective discipline. Sommer (1974) described this environmental perspective graphically when he wrote:

The assumption is made that learning can take place best in distraction-free, lockable cells. Human contact in the form of casual conversation ("milling around") is a threat to order and a distraction to the assembly line. . . . A humane classroom can represent a refuge in a hard building or a base camp pit from which efforts to humanize the environment can gradually radiate through the austere hallways, asphalt yards, workshops, and locked offices. (p. 83)

Seventeen years after he first examined the impact of his "humane classroom" on student perceptions and behaviors, Sommer and two colleagues returned to their original "soft classroom." The classroom became known as the "soft classroom" because of the texture of the fabric used in the wall decorations, the covered seats, and the carpeted floor. Results showed once again that this humane classroom in contrast to the traditional classroom was viewed by students as more aesthetically pleasing and it enhanced student participation (Wong, Sommer, & Cook, 1992).

The creation of a more humane classroom will not be easily achieved. Administrators typically have almost complete control over such important microenvironmental variables as the size of the classroom, the size of the class, and the type of seating. There are increasing indications, however, that some administrators are beginning to work collaboratively with teachers and students to modify physical features of traditional classrooms that inhibit successful communication and learning. To be successful, such efforts must, at minimum, consider the perceptual and behavioral impact of room size, class size, seating arrangement and choice, teachers' spatial orientations, and the appearance of the classroom.

Classroom size is an important variable. Classroom size clearly determines the actual amount of space available for a given student. Students have well-developed preferences as to the amount of usable space that is designated as theirs. Expressed in square feet of space available to each student, ideal personal space for a lecture hall is 19 to 27 ft; for a study hall, 20 to 29 ft; for a library, 24 to 31 ft; and for a discussion group, 31 to 43 ft (Weldon, Loewy, Winer, & Elkin, 1981).

In a classroom, actual space is less important than perceived space, however. Inadequate space usually results in the feeling of being crowded. The result, frequently, is that students have difficulty in maintaining attention, task performance decreases, and aggressive behavior increases. The feeling of being crowded usually occurs when students feel that their personal space and their privacy are being violated by other students. High school students in particular seem increasingly inclined to exhibit aggressive behavior; it therefore seems important that their expectations regarding the "ideal" amount of space available to them in the classroom not be frustrated.

In fact, a number of low-cost steps may be taken in the high-density classroom to moderate the students' perception that they are being crowded. Such steps include using room partitions, decreasing the number of entrances, choosing rectangular over square classroom designs, promoting acquaintance and mutual cooperation among students, and maintaining a comfortable room temperature (Weldon et al., 1981). Each of these steps is known to contribute to a good classroom environment. The desirability of taking such steps seems obvious in view of the fact that a good classroom environment has been found to be highly correlated with enhanced student performance (Cheng, 1994).

The question of classroom size seems to be far from simple, however. Bigger is not necessarily better. Indeed, an unlimited amount of classroom space may result in low levels of student arousal. *Moderate density seems to represent a desirable compromise between conditions of either low-density or high-density seating.* Moderate density seems to promote student arousal that results in striking improvement in reading speed and comprehension, with only a slight decrease in the ability to acquire and organize new material. High density is another matter. Under conditions of high density, students find it difficult, if not impossible, to assimilate and organize new material, even though their reading speed and comprehension may increase (Weldon et al., 1981).

Class size has a pronounced impact on the amount of student participation. Sommer (1974) found that in a small class of 6 to 20, students participate more than twice as much as they do in a class of medium (21 to 50 students) or large (more than 50 students) size. Even in small classes, however, students participate only 12 percent of the time during a class hour. If student participation and involvement represent desired educational objectives, the peril of ever-increasing class sizes should be carefully considered.

The impact of varying *seating arrangements* on student–teacher interaction is not so well documented. In one experiment, Sommer (1974) actually had a colleague enter 25 classrooms and change chairs from straight-row seating to a circular arrangement. However, the attachment to the straight row was so strong that chairs had to be rearranged to straight-row seating in 20 of the 25 classrooms before the classes began; in many cases the students themselves returned the chairs to a straight-row arrangement.

Although students have come to expect straight-row seats that are bolted to the floor, they have a negative attitudinal response to this type of seating arrangement. For example, Rubin (1972) found that high-IQ students prefer circular and horseshoe seating arrangements, and low-IQ students prefer a flexible seating arrangement that allows the teacher to walk about in their midst. Students almost uniformly report a negative reaction to straight-row seating. They believe that this type of seating arrangement inhibits student participation and interaction with the teacher. Moreover, straight-row seating reinforces the unhealthy perception on the part of the students that this seating arrangement is being used primarily to enhance the teacher's ability to regulate and control their behavior.

Although students can rarely exercise control over such variables as room size, class size, or seating arrangement, *they can usually decide where they will sit.* A number of studies have consistently shown that students who sit closest to the teacher, and who have the greatest opportunity for eye contact with the teacher, participate most and receive the highest grades. The students who choose the most central seating, closest to the front, consistently perform better (Levine, O'Neal, Garwood, & McDonald, 1980; Sommer, 1974; Wulf, 1977).

Students with low grade-point averages (GPAs) will not necessarily perform better if they choose front and center seating, however. Also, we should not assume that students with high GPAs will perform more poorly if they are given seats on the periphery or in the back of the classroom. In fact, students who have been arbitrarily assigned to front and center seating have not received better grades than students assigned to seats in the rear. However, arbitrary assignment to seating in front of the classroom does positively affect participation. Whether front and center seating is voluntary or involuntary, *students participate more in this seating zone* (Levine et al., 1980).

A student who is considering the practical implications of seating choice might feel a little like the person who identified himself as an agnostic Christian. He said he "really did not believe there was a God, but if there was a God he needed some measure of protection." Choosing front and center seating also gives the student some measure of protection. This seating choice may not assure higher grades, but it will ensure greater opportunities to participate and to reinforce the impression of high interest.

Aside from the control they exercise over the seating arrangement, teachers can exert a major impact on the classroom environment by the *spatial orientation* they assume vis-à-vis their students. Hesler (1972) examined the perceptual impact of six types of spatial orientations by teachers: (a) BL—teacher in front of blackboard or front wall of classroom; (b) DK—teacher sitting on, beside, or behind desk; (c) T—teacher in front of desk; (d) S—teacher positioned along the side seats or along side wall; (e) BK—teacher in back of room; and (f) AM—teacher among students.

Teachers who sat on, beside, or in back of their desks were seen as isolated from the students and less warm, friendly, and effective than teachers who stood in front of their desks. So long as their proxemic behavior was deemed appropriate by the students, the teacher was consistently perceived as warmer as they moved closer to them. This research supports the conventional wisdom that *the teacher who wishes to cultivate an image of a warm, caring, and emotionally sensitive individual must seek to interact at the closest possible distance with students but should not violate their personal space or trigger the uncomfortable feeling of being crowded.*

In his provocative essay on an ecological model of classrooms, Doyle (1977) took a position that seems to be counterintuitive. He maintained that the teacher who is to experience "managerial success" must not concentrate on the stimulation of affective responses from a limited number of students but rather seek to exercise prudent control over the activities of all the students while including as many students as possible in every classroom activity. Those objectives led him to the novel recommendation that teachers should actually *increase* the distance between themselves and the student with whom they interact. By increasing interaction distance with the individual student, a greater number of students are supposedly brought within the teacher's conscious level of awareness. Doyle also advised that the teacher not maintain direct eye contact with the interacting student, but scan wider sections of the classroom in order to visually involve the greatest possible number of students.

Whether you accept Doyle's interesting position or not, it highlights a trade-off that teachers must consider. Teachers who give high priority to projecting a favorable image will recognize that the more proximate their interaction with students, the better liked they are apt to be. However, as teachers' proximity to individual students increases, their ability to exercise effective control and discipline over the larger number of students is likely to decrease.

Doyle (1977) highlighted the difficult choice the teacher must make in choosing a proximate or distant spatial orientation vis-à-vis students. He wrote that with "regard to distance and eye contact, at least, the affective and regulatory uses of nonverbal behavior appear incompatible" (p. 186). To literally maintain distance from the students enhances the teacher's ability to control them, but at a considerable sacrifice in terms of the type and intensity of students' emotional responses to the teacher.

The precise effects of *modifying the appearance of classrooms* are not presently known. We have little empirical evidence to bring to bear on this subject because administrators are generally resistant to modifying the appearance of classrooms, which would have to be done if the impact on students' attitudes, their communicative behaviors, and, ultimately, their learning were to be carefully measured. Uniformity in the appearance of classrooms is justified on two bases: It is democratic (pictures or unusual wall colors might offend some students), and a uniform and dull appearance enhances teachers' ability to control the behavior of the students.

Sommer (1974), a pioneer in examining the potentially beneficial effects of making the traditional classroom less drab and sterile, identified the paradoxical nature of the microenvironmental problem when he wrote:

> *The arguments against decorations are the precepts of hard architecture. One familiar refrain is that decoration would distract people from whatever they are doing. The fact that this principle never prevails at the higher echelons of the organization is an interesting paradox.* (p. 96)

Sommer went on to point out that school administrators, such as principals, show no reluctance to decorate the walls of their own offices with pictures and art objects, but they fear the behavioral consequences of similar decorative objects in the classrooms they control.

Sommer actually did modify the appearance of one classroom and found that the impact was highly beneficial. Decorations included three abstract yarn designs on the back wall, two pictures hung on the side wall, and two posters on the front wall. The bulletin board was decorated with flower stickers, a jar of paper flowers was placed on the front table, and a blue fish mobile with three God's-eyes was attached to a wall above the windows.

Reactions of students and faculty to the modified classroom was uniformly positive. Those surveyed viewed the classroom as pleasant, comfortable, cheerful, and relaxing without being distracting. There is reason to believe that students will perform better in such an environment so long as the appearance of the room is not overly arousing and does not reinforce students' perception of being crowded, and so long as the students are not working on a highly complex task.

Mehrabian (1976) also maintained that there is a strong need to modify the appearance of the traditional classroom. Because they appear sterile and drab, classrooms typically represent a microenvironment that is both nonarousing and unpleasant to the student. Aside from cost considerations, Mehrabian contended that school administrators remain committed to the drab classroom because they fear that the introduction of arousing, pleasant stimuli is potentially dangerous. If contrasting wall colors, plants, and paintings were used, they might arouse and stimulate students to such a degree that teachers would no longer be able to exercise the control necessary for effective discipline.

There is little doubt that the classroom environment can be made more arousing and pleasant for the student by the use of innovative seating arrangements, more brightly colored walls and carpets, and decorative items such as those already identified. Because such modifications in classroom appearance are known to positively affect students' attitudes about each other, the teacher, and the school, they would seem well worth experimenting with, in many cases.

Mehrabian (1976) did caution, however, that the appearance of the classroom must be adapted to the type of learning activity being undertaken by the students. He argued that students and teachers who are performing relatively undemanding and unpleasant tasks should be assigned to high-load, arousing classrooms. In contrast, "at times during the day when students and teachers are performing complex, unusual tasks, they should be assigned rooms that are very pleasant but low-load" (p. 158).

The Conference Room Environment

A conference room represents a particularly important type of microenvironment. Many physical features of the conference room can affect the quality and quantity of communicative interaction, the participants' perceptions of each other, and the task performance of a given group. Variables such as room size, room decorations, room color, and even temperature regulation are potentially important and are treated elsewhere in the chapter. The three microenvironmental variables of greatest importance in the conference room are *seating choice, table configuration,* and *communication networks.*

Seating position at a conference table is sometimes determined by status considerations or by habit. When you have freedom of choice in seating position, the communicative implications should be carefully considered, however. The man who sits at the head of a rectangular table significantly increases his chances of being perceived as the leader. As we saw in Chapter 15, males but not females markedly increase the probability that they will be perceived as leaders simply by virtue of sitting at the head of the table. Because women are stereotyped as followers rather than leaders, they are not afforded this same perceptual advantage. Individuals who choose a seat along the sides of a table not only decrease their chances of being perceived as leaders, but also are apt to be perceived as individuals with lower status and less self-confidence.

Seating position affects not only perceptions of leadership potential but also actual leadership emergence in the small group (Sundstrom, 1989). Strodbeck and Hook (1961) found that a person who chose to sit at the end of a rectangular table was elected jury foreman more often than jury members sitting in the other 10 positions. Because the jury foreman is selected before any communicative interaction occurs, the impact of seating choice on leadership emergence is clearly very strong.

Leadership emergence as a result of seating position seems to be jointly determined by the advantages central seating gives a person in controlling communicative interaction and in maintaining direct visual accessibility to the greatest number of discussants. For example, Howells and Becker (1962) conducted an experiment in which five group members sat at a rectangular table, two on one side and three on the other. The leaders who emerged in the five-member groups (by a ratio of more than 2 to 1) were on the two-member side. The greater likelihood that they would emerge as leaders on the two-member side was attributed to the fact that they had visual access to a majority of the group (three), but the people on the three-member side had visual access to only two. Because discussion members seated at the side of rectangular tables have limited visual access to a limited number of group members, it is not surprising that they emerge as leaders much less frequently than discussants seated at the ends of the table.

The *Steinzor effect*, which has received strong empirical support from the results of many studies, is based on the finding that being visible in a group increases interaction, "and since leadership is strongly related to participation, being in a visible position in the small group should increase an individual's chance of becoming the leader" (Baker, 1984, p. 160).

A field study by Heckel (1973) suggested that individuals who wish to emerge as leaders not only select the central seating position in the conference room but also do so at such nontask functions as meals. Persons who do not wish to be chosen as leaders characteristically sit at the side of the table when eating meals. In short, seating choice at a conference table determines to a large degree whether a person will be a dominant figure or a member of the supporting cast in discussions that ensue. *Given the important impression management and control functions of eye behaviors, it is not surprising that individuals who have limited visual access to other group members are in disproportionate numbers relegated to a supporting role.* The converse is also true. Thus,

> *available research evidence points to a clear association between leadership and seating arrangements that allow one person more opportunity than other group members for eye contact with the group. The seat at the head of the table is an example. Leaders tended to emerge in such seats, and people with aspiration to leadership tended to choose them.* (Sundstrom, 1989, p. 325)

Seating position also has a strong impact on how powerful or influential one is judged to be by other group members. Korda (1975) maintained:

> *In meetings where people are seated around a table, whatever its shape, the order of power is almost always clockwise, beginning with what would be the number "12" on a clock face, and with power diminishing as it moves around past positions at three o'clock, six o'clock, nine o'clock, etc.* (p. 101)

If you accept Korda's theory, the most powerful person at a conference table sits at the 12 o'clock position and the least powerful person sits at the 11 o'clock position.

Not everyone agrees that power moves clockwise around a conference table by virtue of seating position. For example, one study (Green, 1975) shows that the amount of the discussants' participation time increases *both* when they choose a seat closer to the leader and when their angle of visual access to the chairperson's line of sight is narrower relative to other discussion members. In Green's study, the important consideration was not whether one sits to the right or left of the centrally seated leader, but how immediate one's visual access is to that leader.

Table configuration or *shape* is also an important variable in the conference room. In 1959, for example, the United States, the Soviet Union, France, and Great Britain were meeting in Geneva to discuss the future of Berlin. Before the talks began, a dispute arose over table shape. The three Western powers wanted a square table, which would have given them a three-to-one advantage in negotiating posture, from a perceptual perspective. Not surprisingly, the Soviet Union proposed a round conference table, in an attempt to neutralize the three-to-one ratio (Sommer, 1969).

Lecuyer (1976) examined the differences between problem-solving groups seated at either round or rectangular tables and their effect on leadership. He found that a *randomly appointed leader was more successful when a rectangular table was used.* The appointed leader at a circular table had more difficulty controlling the flow of the discussion; discussants seated around the circular table more tenaciously supported their own proposed solutions than those seated at the rectangular table. Because the leader at the circular table loses the potential for control and superiority of status which is associated with central seating at a rectangular table, the negative impact of the circular table seems predictable.

Patterson, Kelly, Kondracki, and Wulf (1979) compared the impact of circular versus L-shaped seating arrangements. Both *quality and amount of communicative interaction deteriorated with L-shaped seating arrangements.* Discussants were less involved and less comfortable; they exhibited longer pauses in their conversations, displayed more self-manipulative adaptor gestures, and fidgeted more, by way of postural shifts. The negative impact of L-shaped seating on communicative interaction may be attributed in part to the fact that communication was made more difficult because discussants had much more limited visual access to each other than they had in the circular seating arrangement.

Communication networks consist of the actual paths or channels used by group members to transmit information to one another (see Figure 19.1). In practice, both seating choice and configuration of the conference table are apt to determine the kind of communication network used most frequently. Some discussants may, of course, choose not to participate, with a consequent impact on the types of communication networks that emerge.

Among the more common communication networks that have been experimentally manipulated in group research are the *wheel,* a *Y,* and a *circle.* The Y communication network is used to illustrate a highly centralized type of leadership in which one individual can communicate with other group members who, in turn, are able to communicate only with that individual; the circle is associated with a highly decentralized type of leadership; the wheel combines the advantages and disadvantages of the circle and Y networks.

In his masterful summary of research on seating arrangements in small groups, and the resultant communication networks that emerge from these seating arrangements, Shaw (1981) provided four generalizations of practical importance:

1. A leader is more likely to emerge in a centralized communication network than in a decentralized network.
2. Group members have higher morale in a decentralized than in centralized communication network.
3. Decentralized communication networks are most efficient when groups must solve complex problems, but a centralized network is most efficient when the group must solve simple problems.
4. Centralized communication networks are more likely to result in a work overload for the leader than decentralized communication networks.

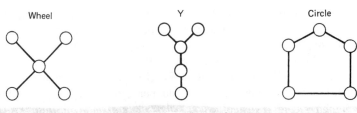

FIGURE 19.1   Communication Networks

Similarly, Sundstrom (1989) provided a useful summary of the effects of small-group communication networks on performance, communication, leadership, decision making, and satisfaction.

From the perspective of communication networks, centralization is desirable for the person who wishes to emerge as leader and retain effective control. Centralization also is desirable when group tasks are relatively simple and when decisions must be made during moments of crisis. Whenever complex tasks are considered and a premium is placed on harmonious interpersonal relationships, the decentralized communication network is preferable.

The Office Environment

With the possible exception of the family home, the office in which a person works is the most important microenvironment. The design and physical features of the office are known to strongly affect attitudes, the quality and quantity of communication with colleagues, and productivity. Entire books are now devoted to the behavioral impact of office design (Wineman, 1986). Many features of our offices are determined not by us but by our superiors and by paid designers who work for them. For example, the size of our office, furniture, carpeting, lighting, and noise control are all important variables that we may not be able to control directly (Cohen & Cohen, 1983; Sundstrom, Town, Rice, & Osborn, 1994).

In the past few years, the open-office plan has received much favorable publicity. *Open offices* contain no floor-to-ceiling walls. Panels that do not extend to the ceiling are used to define the macro-, midi-, and mini-environments in which people interact. Permanent walls and corridors are eliminated.

The open office has become quite controversial, in part because its proponents make broad-based claims about its alleged advantages that are not supported by existing research, while openly attacking the concept of the private office. Thus, proponents of the open office claim that such a spatial arrangement assures the type of visual accessibility of occupants of the office that promotes face-to-face communication, that the sight of busy coworkers in an open office motivates others in the office to be more productive, and that an open office assures that distinctions based on status will be eliminated (Sundstrom, 1989).

The avowed objective of the open-office plan is to facilitate communication and interaction among employees while increasing employee satisfaction and motivation. Because the open-office plan de-emphasizes depersonalized contacts among employees, proponents of this plan maintain that it also promotes cooperation and friendship formation (Becker, 1981).

In practice, the behavioral impact of the open-office plan seems much less desirable than its supporters would have us believe. In part because employees feel that their privacy is being invaded and that they experience an uncomfortable sensation of crowding, open offices have been found to decrease employee satisfaction and motivation. In fact, a number of employees who use open offices have been so affected by perceived increases in noise level, visual distractions, and an accompanying loss of privacy that they report a loss in efficiency (Becker, 1981).

Mehrabian (1976) contended that *a compromise that embodies some of the physical features of the open and closed office is the most desirable, in terms of its attitudinal and behavioral impact on the occupants of the office.* He maintained:

> *Since lower-echelon employees who are assigned offices need privacy and low-load settings for occasions when they perform loaded tasks, such offices should have doors. Doorless cubicles do not afford protection from extraneous environmental stimuli—people walking by, a conversation down the hall, and so on—but do on the other hand tend to isolate workers from one another.* (p. 145)

An employee with a door to his or her office can enjoy privacy when needed by closing it and can have stimulation by leaving the door open.

Occupants of open offices have virtually no control over the variables that affect their perceptions of their own offices nor of the perceptions of persons who interact with them in their offices. Their inability to exercise conscious control over many variables that might give a closed or private office a distinctive ambience may account in large part for employee's negative reactions to the open-office plan. Even those who have their own enclosed offices might encounter frustrations, because they cannot control such factors as office location, size, and configuration. They may not even have the authority to decide on the colors of the walls. This would be an unfortunate restriction because the colors of walls are known to have a considerable impact on the moods of office occupants (Bellizzi, Crowley, & Hasty, 1983).

Many important intraoffice variables are subject to the effective conscious control of the occupant of a private office, however. Those intraoffice variables serve an important role in shaping the image projected by the office occupant and in affecting the nature of the communication that occurs in the private office. Of particular importance are *seating* and *spatial arrangements, furniture arrangement,* and *decorative objects.*

Seating and Spatial Arrangements

Where the occupant of an office chooses to sit will probably determine whether the occupant wishes to dominate a conversation or share control of it with other individuals. It may also indicate whether the office occupant is a superior. You will recall that J. Edgar Hoover sat at a large, elevated desk, and his visitors had to sit well below him at a small table to his right. Nelson Rockefeller went even further to try to assure dominance and perceptions of high power in his office. At times, he ascended a ladder that folded out of a desk drawer and addressed office visitors from the top of his desk.

Korda (1975) maintained that it is much more difficult to do business and communicate effectively with an office occupant who sits behind his or her desk. He advocates a variety of stratagems to lure a person out from behind a desk. He wrote that if you cannot get people to come out from behind their desks, you can

> *put your hat or briefcase on the desk if you want to make them nervous. Note that people with old-fashioned desks that serve as barriers almost always leave them to say "yes," and sit behind them to say "no." Once they have taken refuge behind five-hundredweight of mahogany, you can't argue with them.* (p. 177)

If you wish to stimulate communication with others in your office, and to have them perceive themselves as your status equals, you must take pains to sit as close to them as proxemic norms allow. Two studies by Sommer (1961; 1962) support the conclusion that individuals prefer to sit where they have the greatest visual accessibility to those with whom they interact. Although individuals prefer to be able to face you when interacting with you in a business situation, they will often choose to sit at your side—perhaps on an available sofa—if face-to-face seating would require a separation of more than five feet.

Researchers have also established that where an individual sits has a measurable impact on the amount of communication that occurs and on how individuals perceive someone who selects a certain seat. Sitting around a table, as opposed to sitting in chairs along walls, has been found to increase interaction by almost 100 percent (Sommer & Ross, 1958). Finally, Pelligrini (1971) found that a person who elects to sit at the head of a table, as opposed to other positions, will be perceived as significantly more *talkative, persuasive, dominant, self-confident,* and *intelligent.*

Furniture Arrangement

The business office has been the scene of a number of studies that examine the impact of furniture arrangement on the ways individuals perceive office occupants. Desk placement has been the variable most often manipulated. Results from one study (White, 1953) indicated that patients in a doctor's office were more "at ease" when no desk separated doctor and patient. An extension of this study (Widgery & Stackpole, 1972) found that high-anxiety subjects perceived a counselor to be more credible when there was no desk between them, and low-anxiety subjects perceived the counselor to be more credible when there was a desk between them. Joiner (1971) found people in academic offices have their desks touching a wall significantly more often than people in either business or government and that higher-status office occupants are more likely to place their desks between themselves and the door rather than against a side or back wall.

Whether an office occupant chooses to sit behind a desk or at a table in the office can also have a considerable impact on the impression conveyed. Becker, Gield, and Froggatt (1983) found that professors who sat at tables in their offices, as opposed to sitting behind desks, were perceived as being significantly more fair, friendly, caring, helpful, and open-minded, and were also viewed as better listeners. When seated behind their desks, professors were perceived as more authoritative and aggressive.

Occupants of faculty offices, as opposed to occupants of business offices, are less concerned about their ability to control communicative interaction in their offices than with the impressions they make. Thus, Preston and Quesda (1974) found that occupants of business offices believe that the primary value of furniture arrangement is control of communicative interaction. Occupants of academic offices, in contrast, are relatively unconcerned about the control potential of objects in their office, but they attach considerable importance to the potential impact of such objects on the image they project.

Aesthetic and Professionally Related Objects

We know that the general appearance of an office can affect the perceptions of those who interact within its confines. In a classic study, Maslow and Mintz (1956) devised three "visually aesthetic" settings: a "beautiful," an "average," and an "ugly" room. Subjects were asked to rate a series of 10 pictures on two scales, fatigue–energy and displeasure–well-being. Although the same pictures were used in all three settings, subjects who viewed them in the "beautiful" room rated them significantly higher on energy and well-being than subjects in the other two settings.

Subsequent research has established that interviewees are more self-disclosing in a warm, intimate room as opposed to a cold, nonintimate, room (Kasmar, Griffin, & Mauritzen, 1976). Hasse and Dimattia (1976) reported that counseling interviewees in a large room (13.9 sq m) make significantly more self-reference statements than interviewees in a small room (7.67 sq m). Finally, Bloom, Weigel, and Traut (1977) established that the appearance of an office can affect the credibility of the office occupant. Female counselors were judged to be more credible in a "traditional" office setting, which featured a desk between the counselor and the client, diplomas on the wall, and file cabinets. By contrast, male counselors were judged to be more credible in a "humanistic" setting, which had no desk between the interactants, modern sculpture, and currently popular wall posters.

This study did indicate that aesthetic objects such as wall posters and professionally related objects such as diplomas can affect the credibility of an office occupant when they are present in the office. What this study did not do, however, was determine whether these two types of office decor had a different impact on the perceived credibility of the office occupant. Moreover, this study did not attempt to determine whether the individual dimensions of credibility—competence, trustworthiness, and dynamism—were affected in different ways by the two types of office decor.

Subjects who viewed photographs of the office with and without aesthetic and professionally related objects were asked to use sets of bipolar scales (representing the three dimensions of credibility) to measure the credibility of the office occupant who was not present. Figure 19.2 showed some of the aesthetic objects in the office; Figure 19.3 showed some of the professionally related objects.

Results from this study indicate that aesthetic and professionally related objects had a marked impact on the credibility of the office occupant. The presence of aesthetic objects in the faculty office enhanced the perceived trustworthiness of the occupant. The presence of professionally related objects had a positive impact on both the occupant's perceived authoritativeness *and* trustworthiness.

Professionally related objects seem to be a particularly powerful medium of communication because their presence in a faculty office resulted in a significant increase in both the perceived authoritativeness and the perceived trustworthiness of the occupant of the office. Clearly, faculty members—and perhaps occupants of other types of offices as well—who wish to enhance their credibility should consider the potential benefits of displaying professionally related objects in their offices.

Although both professionally related and aesthetic objects in the faculty office had a significant, positive impact on the perceived trustworthiness of the occupant of the faculty office, *aesthetic objects had the strongest impact on perceived trustworthiness.* The finding is particularly provocative because it contradicts the prevailing view that levels of trust are almost exclusively a function of the overt behaviors of interacting individuals.

The finding that trustworthiness can be strongly affected by contextual variables may have important practical implications. Such a finding may provide particular comfort to the individual who inspires little trust or to one who is widely mistrusted. In one sense, it serves to support the popular belief of image consultants that trustworthiness of a distrusted person may be more effectively enhanced by manipulating certain microenvironmental variables than by modifying the individual's communicative behaviors.

Past research has shown that source credibility may be a function of the source's appearance, reputation, organizational affiliation, and communicative behaviors. This research suggests that source credibility may also be affected by specific decorative objects

FIGURE 19.2

FIGURE 19.3

placed in a person's office. Knowledge such as this should certainly be useful to us as we strive to attain the goal of communicating more successfully in applied settings.

The Fast-Food Restaurant Environment

One distinctive microenvironment of undeniable importance to a large proportion of our population is the fast-food restaurant. Indeed, fast-food restaurants have become one of the most visible and pervasive social phenomena of our time. Nonetheless, the fast-food microenvironment has received little attention from communication scholars, a puzzling oversight for several reasons. First, design directors for the two major fast-food chains in the United States agree that the interior design of their restaurants is the major medium they use to communicate a desired corporate image to the public. Second, the physical features of the fast-food microenvironment are so distinctive that they should have a measurable impact on the communicative behaviors exhibited by customers.

In today's competitive restaurant industry, there is a continuous struggle to be number one in profit and sales. Although many types of restaurants still try to compete for business, the fast-food industry is now dominant in the restaurant business in the United States. The fast-food industry, in turn, is dominated by McDonald's and Burger King.

McDonald's, the undisputed giant of the business, dominates the fast-food industry by sheer size and volume, much as General Motors has dominated the automobile industry. In

1986, McDonald's and Burger King had the highest gross food and beverage sales in the industry; McDonald's grossed about 12.5 billion dollars, and Burger King grossed more than 5 billion dollars. For 1987, McDonald's and Burger King once again finished in first and second place, respectively (*Restaurants and Institutions,* 1988, December 23).

With more than 150,000 employees, McDonald's is the 17th largest company in the world (*Dun's Business Rankings,* 1989). Although its gross sales were slightly less than half of McDonald's for the past year, Burger King has had an average net income of close to 200 million dollars for the past five years.

A colleague and I (Eaves & Leathers, 1991) recently studied five suburban McDonald's and five suburban Burger King restaurants in the Atlanta area. We compared the customers observed in each of these two sets of five restaurants to determine whether there was a difference in their level of *involvement* and *discomfort.* Behavioral indicators of involvement were smiling, amount of talking, head nodding, and leaning. Behavioral indicators of discomfort were fidgeting, extraneous foot movement, postural shifts, and side-to-side movement.

Our theoretical perspective led us to expect that McDonald's customers would be both more involved and more uncomfortable than Burger King customers. Our expectations were confirmed. McDonald's customers exhibited their greater involvement by smiling and talking significantly more than their counterparts at Burger King. Moreover, McDonald's customers exhibited their greater discomfort by fidgeting significantly more and by exhibiting a pattern of more extraneous foot movements, side-to-side movements, and postural shifts than Burger King customers. The obvious question is *why*? Our study indicates that one of the major determinants of the customers' behaviors was the distinctive but contrasting physical features of the microenvironments at McDonald's and at Burger King.

In terms of potential impact on level of customers' involvement and comfort levels, the most important design decisions made seemed to be the size of the tables and chairs. This is so because the size of those furniture items in McDonald's and Burger King proved to be the most important factor influencing the spatial orientations of interacting customers. Certainly, the distance that separates two people can have a major impact on both their involvement and comfort levels.

"Deucer" tables at McDonald's and Burger King are the same size: 21 in. by 24 in. The size and appearance of deucer seats are discernably different, however. Burger King's deucer seat measures 18½ in. wide by 17 in. long, whereas McDonald's deucer seat is 15½ in. wide by 16 in. long. In Burger King's newest restaurants, the deucer seats are mounted to the floor via a steel arm, and they swivel both sideways and back and forth so that forward lean is facilitated. The deucer seats at Burger King sit well back from the table so that customers facing each other and sitting in upright positions will be separated (chest to chest) by a distance of 3 ft 5 in. In contrast, two people seated at a deucer at McDonald's with their feet under the table will be separated by no more than 2 ft 2 in.

The appearance of deucer table and chairs at the two fast-food restaurants is also notably different. Burger King uses wooden tables and chairs; McDonald's uses plastic in both. Because of their size and appearance, Burger King chairs and tables appear to be of higher quality and they appear to be more comfortable. For example, a Burger King deucer chair has 11 supporting wooden spokes in the chair back; McDonald's deucer seats have five plastic spokes or strips for support in the chair back. Both authors experienced noticeable discomfort when seated at McDonald's deucer tables. The discomfort resulted because of the obviously small size of the seats and the inferior back support.

In addition to furniture, three other physical features of the microenvironments at McDonald's and Burger King seem to be particularly important: lighting, color choices, and mirrors and partitions. The contrast in lighting at McDonald's and Burger King is certainly an important feature of the micro-environment. Research on lighting in work spaces has shown that lighting is one of the most important factors contributing to the comfort of individuals who work there. In fact, studies of lighting in professional microenvironments indicate quite clearly that excessive illuminance may cause discomfort. Luminance is the apparent brightness of a surface and is the joint product of illuminance (light falling on the surface) and the surface reflectance (Ellis, 1986).

McDonald's, in contrast to Burger King, is intensely lighted on both the outside and the inside. The high-intensity lighting used at McDonald's is known as "high-intensity discharge" lighting, or HID (Smith & Bertolone, 1986). During the observational phase of this study, a number of customers at McDonald's were observed complaining about the intense light that was attributable to numerous fluorescent lights and large windows, much larger than those at Burger King, which had neither shades nor tinting; Burger King controlled the intensity of lighting within their restaurants with both window shades and window tinting. McDonald's used fluorescent lighting in all the observed restaurants, whereas Burger King frequently used light bulbs with shades. On the outside, also, McDonald's used vertically placed florescent lights. The level of lighting at McDonald's was so intense and high that a McDonald's restaurant can be seen from far away by an approaching motorist.

Color choices made by designers at McDonald's and Burger King are also quite different. McDonald's consistently opts for colors that are known to be stimulating and emotionally arousing (Smith & Malandro, 1985). On approach, a McDonald's restaurant stands out because of the "golden" (actually yellow) arches that show McDonald's name displayed in white letters against a bright red background. In case this color combination is not enough to catch your attention, the American flag is conspicuously displayed in front. On the inside, McDonald's uses the same strong colors with eye-catching wallpaper hues of pure white and yellow. Burger King, in contrast, specializes in more subdued color combinations. Burger King frequently uses rustic colors in an apparent attempt to relax customers or put them at ease.

Both McDonald's and Burger King use mirrors and partitions. Mirrors are presumably used to create the illusion of greater space. McDonald's mirrors are often prominently placed in the main dining room or near the order-taking area. Mirrors are also used at Burger King, but less frequently and not usually in high-traffic areas.

Finally, both McDonald's and Burger King use some partitions. In McDonald's, partitions often seem to serve more of a symbolic than a functional purpose, in the sense that they might provide the customer with increased privacy. McDonald's uses wooden railings to separate one eating area from the other, but the railings are held up by see-through spokes that hardly serve as partitions. Thus, most of the customers in the main dining area have the opportunity to engage in direct visual inspection of most of the other customers. Furthermore, customers in McDonald's, in contrast to those in Burger King, can be directly and easily observed by passing motorists because McDonald's has large windows with no tinting or shades and the level of illumination inside is so high that little is concealed from the prying eye.

Summary

The physical features of the microenvironments in which we work can exert a profound impact on the nature of our communication with others. Our attitudes, perceptions, and behaviors are strongly affected by how arousing and how pleasant those environments prove to be. To the extent that we can consciously control the physical features of our microenvironments, we also have the power to shape the image we project.

Microenvironments of particular importance are the classroom, the conference room, the office, and the fast-food restaurant. Microenvironmental variables that can play a central role in affecting communicative interaction and student performance in the classroom are room size, class size, seating arrangement and choice, the teacher's spatial orientations, and the appearance of the classroom. For successful communication to occur in the classroom, space must be used in such a way as to be stimulating and arousing to the student without being distracting. Students react negatively when they perceive that space is being used primarily to regulate and control their behaviors and also when their personal space and need for privacy are being violated, with the result that they feel crowded. Both students and teachers prefer interacting at the closest possible distances that do not violate proxemic norms.

Microenvironmental variables that have the greatest impact on communication, perceptions, and group performance in the conference room are seating choice, table configuration, and communication networks. Individuals who choose the end seating position are not only more apt to be perceived as leaders but also more apt to emerge as leaders. Leaders function more effectively at a rectangular, as opposed to a circular, conference table. Both quality and quantity of group interaction are impaired by L-shaped seating. Finally, centralized communication networks should be used to facilitate effective leadership, to make decisions at moments of crisis, and to solve relatively simple problems. Decentralized communication networks are preferable if a high priority is given to group morale and the efficient solution of complex problems.

The office is the work environment where most of us spend our working hours. The intraoffice variables that are most susceptible to effective conscious control are seating and spatial arrangement, furniture arrangement, and decorative objects. The impressions we make on office visitors are strongly affected by where we choose to sit and where we place our office furniture. The decorative objects we choose to place in our office can be particularly important determinants of our credibility. We know that aesthetic objects can enhance our perceived trustworthiness, and professionally related objects can enhance our perceived authoritativeness and trustworthiness.

Finally, the distinctive microenvironments represented by McDonald's and Burger King restaurants appear to exert a controlling impact on the customers' behaviors. Customers at McDonald's were both more involved and more uncomfortable than customers at Burger King. The study of the two types of fast-food restaurants demonstrates that microenvironmental variables are far more than a secondary force that may have an inconsequential impact on communication. In fact, context is an important type of nonverbal communication in its own right.

References

Adelsward, V., Aronson, K., Jonsson, L., & Linell, P. (1987). The unequal distribution of interactional space: Dominance and control in courtroom interaction. *Text, 7,* 313–346.

Argyle, M., & Dean, J. (1965). Eye contact, distance, and affiliation. *Sociometry, 28,* 298–304.

Baker, P. M. (1984). Seeing is behaving: Visibility and participation in small groups. *Environment and Behavior, 16,* 159–184.

Becker, F. D. (1981). *Workspace: Creating environments in organizations.* New York: Praeger.

Becker, F. D., Gield, B., & Froggatt, C. C. (1983). Seating position and impression management in an office setting. *Journal of Environmental Psychology, 3,* 253–261.

Beeghley, L., & Donnelly, D. (1989). The consequences of family crowding: A theoretical synthesis. *Lifestyles, 10,* 83–102.

Bellizzi, J. A., Crowley, A. E., & Hasty, R. W. (1983). The effects of color in store design. *Journal of Retailing, 59,* 21–45.

Bloom, L. J., Weigel, R. G., & Traut, G. M. (1977). Therapeugenic factors in psychotherapy: Effects of office decor and subject–therapist sex pairing on perception of credibility. *Journal of Consulting and Clinical Psychology, 25,* 867–873.

Burgoon, J. K. (1978). A communication model of personal space violations: Explication and an initial test. *Human Communication Research, 4,* 129–142.

Cheng, Y. C. (1994). Classroom environment and student affective performance: An effective profile. *Journal of Experimental Education, 62,* 221–239.

Cohen, E., & Cohen, A. (1983). *Planning the electric office.* New York: McGraw-Hill.

Doyle, W. (1977). The uses of nonverbal behavior: Toward an ecological model of classrooms. *Merrill-Palmer Quarterly, 23,* 179–192.

Dun's Business Rankings, 1989.

Eaves, M. H., & Leathers, D. G. (1991). Context as communication: McDonald's vs. Burger King. *Journal of Applied Communication Research, 19,* 263–289.

Ellis, P. (1986). Functional, aesthetic, and symbolic aspects of office lighting. In J. D. Wineman (Ed.), *Behavioral issues in office design.* New York: Von Nostrand Reinhold.

Emling, S. (1995, August 27). Casket markups: 300%. *The Atlanta Journal/The Atlanta Constitution,* p. E4.

Green, C. S. (1975). The ecology of committees. *Environment and Behavior, 7,* 411–425.

Hall, E. T. (1974). *Handbook for Proxemic Research.* Washington, DC: Society for Anthropology of Visual Communication.

Hanyu, K. (1993). The affective meaning of Tokyo: Verbal and non-verbal approaches. *Journal of Environmental Psychology, 13,* 161–172.

Hasse, R. F., & DiMattia, D. J. (1976). Spatial environments and verbal conditioning in quasi-counseling interview. *Journal of Counseling Psychology, 23,* 414–421.

Heckel, R. V. (1973). Leadership and voluntary seating choice. *Psychological Reports, 32,* 141–142.

Hesler, M. W. (1972). An investigation of instructor use of space. (Doctoral dissertation, Purdue University, 1972). *Dissertation Abstracts International, 33,* 3055A.

Hirschon, R. B., & Gold, J. R. (1982). Territoriality and the home environment in a Greek urban community. *Anthropological Quarterly, 55,* 63–73.

Howells, L. T., & Becker, S. W. (1962). Seating arrangement and leadership emergence. *Journal of Abnormal and Social Psychology, 64,* 148–149.

Joiner, D. (1971). Office territory. *New Society, 7,* 660–663.

Kasmar, J. V., Griffin, W. F., & Mauritzen, J. H. (1976). The effects of environmental surroundings on outpatient's mood and perception of psychiatrists. *Journal of Consulting and Clinical Psychology, 32,* 223–226.

Kleeman, W. B. (1981). The politics of office design. *Environment and Behavior, 20,* 537–549.

Knachstedt, M. V. (1980). *Interior design for profit.* New York: Kobro.

Konar, E., & Sundstrom, E. (1986). Status demarcation and office design. In J. D. Wineman (Ed.), *Behavioral issues in office design* (pp. 203–233). New York: Von Nostrand Reinhold.

Korda, M. (1975). *Power! How to get it, how to use it.* New York: Random.

Leathers, D. G. (1976). *Nonverbal communication systems.* Boston: Allyn & Bacon.

Leathers, D. G. (1990). The dynamics of impression management in the sales interview. In D. O'Hair & G. L. Kreps (Eds.), *Applied communication theory and research* (pp. 163–183). Hillsdale, N. J.: Erlbaum.

Lecuyer, R. (1976). Social organization and spatial organization. *Human Relations, 29,* 1045–1060.

Levine, D. W., O'Neal, E. C., Garwood, G. S., & McDonald, P. J. (1980). Classroom ecology: The effects of seating position and grades on participation. *Personality and Social Psychology Bulletin, 6,* 409–412.

Lynch, K. (1960). *The image of the city.* Cambridge, MA: Massachusetts Institute of Technology Press.

Maslow, A. H., & Mintz, N. W. (1956). Effects of aesthetic surroundings: I. Initial effects of three aesthetic conditions upon perceiving energy and well-being in faces. *Journal of Psychology, 41,* 247–254.

Mehrabian, A. (1968). Relationship of attitude to seated posture, orientation, and distance. *Journal of Personality and Social Psychology, 10,* 26–30.

Mehrabian, A. (1969). Some referents and measure of nonverbal behavior. *Behavior Research Methods and Instrumentation, 1,* 203–207.

Mehrabian, A. (1976). *Public places and private spaces.* New York: Basic.

Mehrabian, A., & Diamond, S. G. (1971). Effects of furniture arrangement, props, and personality on social interaction. *Journal of Personality and Social Psychology, 20,* 18–30.

Miles, E. W., & Leathers, D. G. (1984). The impact of aesthetic and professionally related objects on credibility in the office setting. *The Southern Speech Communication Journal, 49,* 361–379.

Patterson, M. L., Kelly, C. W., Kondracki, B. A., & Wulf, L. J. (1979). Effects of seating arrangement on small group behavior. *Social Psychology Quarterly, 42,* 180–185.

Pelligrini, R. J. (1971). Some effects of seating position on social perception. *Psychological Reports, 28,* 887–893.

Pile, J. (1979). *Decorating your office for success.* New York: Harper & Row.

Preston, P., & Quesda, A. (1974). What does your office say about you? *Supervisory Management, 19,* 28–34.

Rapoport, A. (1982). *The meaning of the built environment: A nonverbal communication approach.* Beverly Hills, CA: Sage.

Restaurants and Institutions (1988, December 23), p. 48.

Rubin, G. N. (1972). A naturalistic study in proxemics: Seating arrangement and its effect on interaction, performance, and behavior. (Doctoral dissertation, Bowling Green State University, 1972). *Dissertation Abstracts International, 33,* 3829A.

Shaw, M. E. (1981). *Group dynamics: The psychology of small group behavior* (3rd ed.). New York: McGraw-Hill.

Smith, F. K., & Bertolone, F. J. (1986). In D. C. Hines (Ed.), *Bringing interiors to light: The principles and practices of lighting design.* New York: Whitney Library of Design.

Smith, L. J., & Malandro, L. A. (1985). *Courtroom communication strategies.* New York: Kluwer.

Sommer, R. (1961). Leadership and group geography. *Sociometry, 24,* 99–110.

Sommer, R. (1962). The distance for comfortable conversation. *Sociometry, 25,* 111–116.

Sommer, R. (1966). Man's proximate environment. *Journal of Social Issues, 22,* 59–70.

Sommer, R. (1969) *Personal space: The behavioral basis of design.* Englewood Cliffs, NJ: Prentice-Hall.

Sommer, R. (1974). *Tight spaces: Hard architecture and how to humanize it.* Englewood Cliffs, NJ: Prentice-Hall.

Sommer, R. (1983). *Social design: Creating buildings with people in mind.* Englewood Cliffs, NJ: Prentice-Hall.

Sommer, R., & Ross, H. (1958). Social interaction in a geriatrics ward. *International Journal of Social Psychiatry, 4,* 128–133.

Sommer, R., Wynes, M., & Brinkley, G. (1992). Social facilitation effects in shopping behavior. *Environment & Behavior, 24,* 285–297.

Stacks, E. W., & Burgoon, J. K. (1981). The role of nonverbal behaviors as distractors in resistance to persuasion in interpersonal contexts. *Central States Speech Journal, 32,* 61–73.

Strodbeck, F. L., & Hook, L. H. (1961). The social dimensions of a twelve-man jury table. *Sociometry, 24,* 397–415.

Sundstrom, E. (1989). *Work places: The psychology of the physical environment in offices and factories.* Cambridge: Cambridge UP.

Sundstrom, E., Town, J., Rice, R. W., & Osborn, D. P. (1994). Office noise, satisfaction, and performance. *Environment & Behavior, 26,* 195–222.

Weldon, D. W., Loewy, J. H., Winer, J. I., & Elkin, D. J. (1981). Crowding and classroom learning. *Journal of Experimental Education, 49,* 160–176.

White, A. G. (1953). The patient sits down. *Psychosomatic Medicine, 15,* 256–257.

Widgery, R., & Stackpole, C. (1972). Desk position, interviewee anxiety, and interviewer credibility. *Journal of Counseling Psychology, 19,* 173–177.

Wineman, J. P. (Ed.). (1986). *Behavioral issues in office design.* New York: Van Nostrand Reinhold.

Wong, C. Y., Sommer, R., & Cook, E. J. (1992). The soft classroom 17 years later. *Journal of Environmental Psychology, 12,* 337–343.

Wulf, K. M. (1977). Relationship of assigned classroom seating area to achievement variables. *Educational Research Quarterly, 2,* 56–62.

Yee, R., & Gustafson, K. (1983). *Corporate Design.* New York: Whitney Communications Corporation.

Appendix

Key to the Matching Test in Chapter 7
Part I

A-10

B-12

C-9

D-11

E-15

F-14

G-1

H-13

I-3

J-8

K-6

L-7

M-5

N-4

O-2

Key to the Matching Test in Chapter 7
Part II

   I **Top Five**—Females: F, G, H, J, K   Males: 1, 6, 7, 13, 14
  II **Middle Five**—Females: I, L, M, N, O   Males: 2, 3, 4, 5, 8
III **Bottom Five**—Females: A, B, C, D, E   Males: 9, 10, 11, 12, 15

Index

Abele, A., 58, 62
Abelson, R. P., 29
Adams, G. R., 133, 140, 144, 146, 147, 181, 182
Addington, D. W., 161, 166, 167
Adelsward, V., 398
Aho, L., 93
Ailes, Roger, 215
Akert, R. M., 280
Alagna, F. J., 301
Albright, L., 196
Alexandra, Empress, 59
Alicke, M. D., 25, 196, 205
Allen, T., 278
Allport, G. W., 165, 166
Almaney, A. J., 192, 326, 333, 338, 339, 340
Altman, I., 87, 95, 96, 98, 99, 100, 105, 106
Alwan, A. J., 192, 326, 333, 338, 339, 340
American Sign Language (ASL), 14
Ames, M. A., 370
Ancoli, S., 32
Andersen, J. F., 122
Andersen, P. A., 15, 104, 122, 123, 127, 204, 342, 343
Anderson, N. R., 293
Anderson, R., 145
Andropov, Yuri, 184
Anthony, P. K., 192, 368
Aoyagi, S., 162
April, C., 278
Arat, S., 94
Archer, D., 21, 280, 331
Argyle, M., 54, 70, 123, 126, 127, 159, 161, 163, 178, 279, 396
Arkin, R. M., 188, 189
Aron, A., 140
Aron, R., 370, 378
Aronson, K., 398
Arvey, R. D., 295, 303
Asthana, H. S., 31
Atahan, D., 94
Atkins, C. P., 296
Atkinson, Max, 200, 201, 202, 203
Attorneys. *See* Courtroom nonverbal communication

Auditory communication system, functions of, 13
Axtell, R. E., 344

Bai, D. L., 25
Bailey, J., 382
Baird, J. E., Jr., 227
Baker, P. M., 404
Baldassare, M., 107
Banziger, G., 106
Barak, A., 245
Barbee, A. P., 133, 311
Barge, J. K., 370
Barker, D. A., 57, 138
Barker, L., 57, 138
Barnlund, D. C., 326, 338, 341
Baron, R. A., 297
Barr, W. M., 247
Bauer, R. M., 15
Baxter, J. C., 94, 256
Beaber, R. J., 247
Beavin, J. H., 10, 276
Becker, F. D., 406, 407, 408
Becker, S. W., 403
Beckman, H., 352
Beebe, S. A., 247
Beeghley, L., 398
Begley, P. J., 145
Behling, D. W., 145
Belk, S. S., 336
Bellet, W., 301
Bellizzi, J. A., 407
Benjamin, J. L., 107
Bennett, C. E., 370, 373, 374, 375, 376, 377, 378
Ben-Peretz, M., 344
Berger, D. E., 295
Berry, D. S., 25, 167, 385
Berscheid, E., 131, 145
Bertolone, F. J., 413
Biden, Senator Joseph, 225
Biek, M., 314
Birdwhistell, R. L., 6, 67
Bixler, S., 210